Psychology
of
Adolescence

Books by Luella Cole

A History of Education

Psychology of Adolescence

Psychology of Childhood and Adolescence
(*with John J. B. Morgan*)

Students' Guide to Efficient Study

Psychology
of
Adolescence

sixth edition

Luella Cole, Ph.D.
with *Irma Nelson Hall, M.A.*

HOLT, RINEHART AND WINSTON, INC.

New York   Chicago   San Francisco   Toronto   London

5 6 7 8 9

To the Memory of a Great Teacher

ROBERT H. LOWIE

PREFACE

In this sixth revision the writers have tried to preserve the main qualities and much of the material from the preceding edition, but they have brought the text up to date once more. A few entire chapters and several sections within various other chapters required rewriting, because new points of view or methods of attack upon problems needed to be explained. Also, there are a good many new case studies, and a number of the charts have been redrawn.

As usual, research in some fields has been active, while it has lagged in others. It has, therefore, sometimes been necessary to continue using relatively old studies because nothing more recent has appeared. For example, practically all new material on the age of menarche concerns such groups as Javanese or South Africans; these bits of information enlarge the sum total of human knowledge, but they are not particularly useful for the teacher in an American high school. It is the impression of many doctors that the age of menarche has become lower during the last two decades—one can prove a gradual lowering until about 1940—but the writers were unable to find any reports of the matter for American adolescent girls in recent years. Therefore, the old figures will have to stand. Similarly, the last discoverable investigation of childish and adolescent attitudes toward the telling of small lies for purposes of keeping the social wheels turning without friction was made in about 1925. Whether a thirteen-year-old girl is more or less resistant than her 1925 counterpart to saying, "Oh! What a lovely necklace!" when she thinks it an abomination is therefore not known, and in order to include the matter at all one has to go back to the early and entirely out-of-date study. By contrast, in other fields there are so many reports that not over half of them can even be read and perhaps a tenth of them reported. We have been forced, therefore, to select what seemed to us a fair representation of the most promising studies. The resulting text, we believe, will give a sound, modern view of adolescence, but it is in no sense a compendium. There is inevitably some imbalance, but there seems no way of maintaining an even presentation when the reports are uneven. The writers can report only what has been done.

As in the earlier editions, we have used many case histories, anecdotes, personal reminiscences, figures, pictures, and other illustrative materials, not only to make the text of greater interest to the student but also to clothe the facts with living flesh and blood, so that the reader may see how the various phases discussed in the abstract appear in human development.

We have had some doubts as to how much use is ever made by students of the list of possible projects that has appeared in the last two editions. Since the list, when given *in toto,* may seem forbiddingly long, we have hit upon an alternate plan that seems to us to hold a greater likelihood of use. At the end of each chapter, one, or at the most, two, major topics will be listed, the topics being chosen from those areas in which there is at present inadequate material. It is not our intention that these topics should be assigned to undergraduates; they are in effect suggestions for M.A. or Ph.D. theses. However, the undergraduate who would like to try his or her hand at a little research can find relevant minor problems in Appendix B of the fifth edition. If, however, a student wishes to undertake even a pint-sized investigation, he or she should arrange with the teacher to be excused from a certain amount of outside reading. Otherwise, the course will demand a disproportionate amount of a student's time. The writers hope that these small projects may interest some of the more able students in this field of adolescent development and may lead them, sooner or later, into going on with a similar topic at a higher level. The booklist of fiction and biography has been again revised, as has the list of films (Appendix A).

We trust that the modernizing changes in this edition have produced a text that will be of value to those who deal with adolescent boys and girls.*

Berkeley, California   *Luella Cole*
February 1964   *Irma Nelson Hall*

---

* We shall be glad to answer inquiries about points raised in the book. These should be addressed to Mrs. Robert H. Lowie, in care of Holt, Rinehart and Winston, 383 Madison Avenue, New York 17, N. Y.

CONTENTS

LIST OF ILLUSTRATIONS

LIST OF TABLES

INTRODUCTION

Chapter 1 | The Goals of Adolescence

In a discussion of adolescence as a period in human growth, perhaps the first point to establish is the difference between adolescence and puberty. The latter refers to the relatively brief period of physiological change during which the sexual organs become mature. For girls this period is hardly more than six months in length, but for boys it may last two years, or even longer. Puberty supplies the basis for adolescence but is by no means synonymous with it. The two periods begin at much the same time, but adolescence lasts for about eight years and involves not only the pubertal changes in the body but also developments in intellectual capacities, interests, attitudes, personal adjustments, emotional adaptations, vocational and academic interests, aptitudes, and religious and moral attitudes.

Almost all primitive groups that have been studied have had some kind of puberty rites—sometimes for boys, sometimes for girls, sometimes for both. These ceremonials gave public recognition to the physiological changes that permitted the boy to be ranked from then on as a man and the girl as a woman. Both were ready for marriage, which, being largely a matter of arrangements between families rather than between individuals, did not involve judgment or maturity in either partner. Of adolescence, however, one finds hardly a trace. There was no time in primitive economy for a long period of gradual maturing in interests and attitudes. Nor has there ever been time until the present century. Adolescence as a phenomenon among the young of all social classes is thus a product of modern culture and of a civilization that has enough machines for purposes of production to make the labor of young people unnecessary. It is only recently that education has been prolonged and marriage postponed until a true period of adolescence has become an almost universal phenomenon in the Western world.

In order to trace the manifold changes during adolescence it is sometimes desirable to compare the period with childhood or maturity. It seems, therefore, a good idea to delimit the various levels of growth that will often be referred to later on. The modern psychologist has broken down the stages of growth into relatively small units and has studied each more or less intensively—infancy and early childhood the most and old age the least, although with the present concentration on geriatrics there should soon be more

3

information about the final period of human existence. The entire range from birth to death may be divided as follows:

Infancy	birth–2 years	
Early childhood	2–5 years	
Middle childhood	6–10 years (girls);	6–12 years (boys)
Preadolescence or late childhood	11–12 years (girls);	13–14 years (boys)
Early adolescence	12–14 years (girls);	15–16 years (boys)
Middle adolescence	15–17 years (girls);	17–18 years (boys)
Late adolescence	18–20 years (girls);	19–20 years (boys)
Early adulthood	21–34 years	
Middle adulthood	35–49 years	
Late adulthood	50–64 years	
Early senescence	65–74 years	
Senescence	75 years, onward	

It should be understood clearly that one does not automatically pass from one of these periods to another on a given birthday. One level of development shades gradually into the next; indeed, some stages are so short that each is hardly established before premonitory signs of the following one appear. For the adolescent years the age limits differ for the two sexes because girls mature on an average two years earlier than boys, who do not catch up with them until the last years of adolescence. It will be noticed that the main divisions of the school system correspond roughly to the developmental levels of the years before adulthood.

Each of the periods has its own problems, which must be solved if the individual is to enter the next period without handicap. Adolescence is perhaps no more important a stage of development than any other, but it is the last stage before adulthood, and it therefore offers to both parents and teachers the last opportunity to educate a child for his adult responsibilities.

▶ **Goals of the Adolescent Period**

Near the beginning of the adolescent period the boy or girl achieves sexual maturity and, in some specific capacities, intellectual maturity as well. By the end of adolescence, physical growth is complete and intellectual growth very nearly so. Only severe deprivation can prevent a human organism from reaching adult size, shape, and function, or from growing into its expected mental maturity. In short, nature will provide for these two types of growth, unless some catastrophe intervenes. The real problems of adolescence are therefore emotional, social, moral, and economic.

Most adolescents solve their problems by slow degrees during the ages from twelve to twenty-one. The adolescent with severe conflicts and violent reactions is so much more dramatic than the boy or girl who develops slowly, and without fireworks, that one is likely to overemphasize the storm and stress of the period. In the normal growth of a typical individual, childhood fades, adolescence advances, and adulthood arrives in a gradual, smooth series of small changes and with only temporary and incidental difficulties and disturbances.

The boy or girl enters adolescence with a child's adjustment to the world. No matter how perfect his emotional and social adaptation may be, it is not suitable for adult life. A child is normally dependent upon others, has little or no interest in members of the opposite sex, expects to be supported both emotionally and financially by his family, takes his judgments ready-made from those he admires, and has neither the interest nor the ability to deal with generalized principles. At the end of his adolescence he should be ready to leave his home—emotionally and actually—to maintain himself economically, to manage his own social contacts, to make up his own mind, to establish his own home, and to concern himself with the general principles behind surface phenomena.

In the change from dependent childhood to independent adulthood an individual has to approach many goals, the more important of which are to be presented shortly. These objectives have been grouped for the sake of convenience into nine areas of human interest and activity: emotional maturity, establishment of heterosexual interests, social maturity, emancipation from home, mental maturity, the beginnings of financial independence, proper uses of leisure, the development of a definite point of view about life, and the identification of one's self. These are the same objectives that hold for the years of maturity also; the adolescent can be expected to make only a beginning in leaving his childhood behind him and in preparing to enter adulthood. It is a rare person who achieves adulthood in all phases of existence. The child that one once was keeps popping up from time to time with childish, if not infantile, solutions to the myriad problems of daily life. From that child no one ever fully escapes, but the adolescent should make a beginning in the process of meeting the new requirements of adulthood. In order to emphasize the basic fact of growth, the goals—presented in the next few pages—have been stated in terms of change from a childish toward an adult level.

The first set of problems and goals centers around the attainment of emotional control. Children have little power to inhibit their responses, they have many fears, they are self-centered, and they run away from what is disagreeable. It is, then, one task of adolescence to emerge from childish into adult forms of emotional expression, to substitute intellectual for emotional reactions, at least in recurring situations, and to learn that one cannot escape reality.

Table 1–1: THE GOALS OF THE ADOLESCENT PERIOD

A. *General Emotional Maturity*

From
- 1. Destructive expressions of emotion
- 2. Subjective interpretation of situations
- 3. Childish fears and motives
- 4. Habits of escaping from conflicts

toward

- 1. Harmless or constructive expressions
- 2. Objective interpretations of situations
- 3. Adult stimuli to emotions
- 4. Habits of facing and solving conflicts

B. *Establishment of Heterosexual Interests*

From
- 1. Exclusive interest in members of same sex
- 2. Experience with many possible mates
- 3. Acute awareness of sexual development

toward

- 1. Normal interest in members of opposite sex
- 2. Selection of one mate
- 3. Casual acceptance of sexual maturity

C. *General Social Maturity*

From
- 1. Feelings of uncertainty of acceptance by peers
- 2. Social awkwardness
- 3. Social intolerance
- 4. Slavish imitation of peers

toward

- 1. Feelings of secure acceptance by peers
- 2. Social poise
- 3. Social tolerance
- 4. Freedom from slavish imitation

D. *Emancipation from Home Control*

From
- 1. Close parental control
- 2. Reliance upon parents for security
- 3. Identification with parents as models

toward

- 1. Self-control
- 2. Reliance upon self for security
- 3. Attitude toward parents as friends

E. *Intellectual Maturity*

From
- 1. Blind acceptance of truth on the basis of authority
- 2. Desire for facts
- 3. Many temporary interests

toward

- 1. Demand for evidence before acceptance
- 2. Desire for explanations of facts
- 3. Few, stable interests

F. *Selection of an Occupation*

From
- 1. Interest in glamorous occupations
- 2. Interest in many occupations
- 3. Over- or under-estimation of one's own abilities
- 4. Irrelevance of interests to abilities

toward

- 1. Interest in practicable occupations
- 2. Interest in one occupation
- 3. Reasonably accurate estimate of one's own abilities
- 4. Reconciliation of interest and abilities

G. *Uses of Leisure*

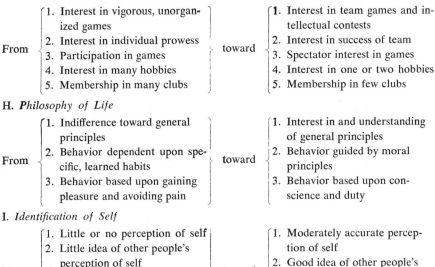

From
1. Interest in vigorous, unorganized games
2. Interest in individual prowess
3. Participation in games
4. Interest in many hobbies
5. Membership in many clubs

toward

1. Interest in team games and intellectual contests
2. Interest in success of team
3. Spectator interest in games
4. Interest in one or two hobbies
5. Membership in few clubs

H. *Philosophy of Life*

From
1. Indifference toward general principles
2. Behavior dependent upon specific, learned habits
3. Behavior based upon gaining pleasure and avoiding pain

toward

1. Interest in and understanding of general principles
2. Behavior guided by moral principles
3. Behavior based upon conscience and duty

I. *Identification of Self*

From
1. Little or no perception of self
2. Little idea of other people's perception of self
3. Identification of self with impossible goals

toward

1. Moderately accurate perception of self
2. Good idea of other people's perception of self
3. Identification of self with possible goals

The second set of problems centers around the attainment of adult attitudes toward sex. The centering of one's emotional attention upon members of one's own sex or upon older people is a typically childish reaction. Neither of these love interests is an adequate cornerstone for an adult adjustment. The pubertal changes usually arouse a great interest in sex, which may find expression in an exaggerated awareness of one's own bodily development or that of other people. During the period both boys and girls do a great deal of experimenting in emotional—not necessarily sexual—relationships. The interest of a boy in *all* girls merely because they are girls, and of a girl in *all* boys merely because they are boys, is strong in early adolescence but should disappear by the end of the period. It should be replaced by a concentration upon a single person as a mate. The adolescent has, then, to develop first an acute interest in possible future mates and then to recover from the incidental effects of this acute interest. During the years when these changes are in progress, a boy or girl gets into more or less serious difficulties, but no trouble can possibly be as serious as the failure of the normal developments to take place.

A third group of problems concerns general social maturity. Until boys and girls establish themselves securely in their social milieu they have little attention for other problems. Adolescent boys and girls tend to show a slavish dependence upon and imitation of their friends. This attitude is definitely helpful during the years it should last, but its continuance makes adult life unduly difficult. Many adolescents are also intolerant—a trait that marks them off from both the child and the adult. The child has the tolerance of igorance and insensitivity to social stimuli, while the true adult has the tolerance of knowledge and understanding.

A fourth set of problems clusters about the establishment of independence from home supervision. Emancipation from home ties is necessary because the adolescent will never become a real adult as long as his parents make his decisions for him, protect him from unpleasantness, and plan his daily life. In most homes the children grow gradually away from the parents, but in some they are pushed out too fast, whereas in others they are kept under restraint too long.

In the intellectual field there are certain objectives to be achieved. Some individuals never develop sufficient mental ability to reach these objectives, but the majority of adolescents could, with training, make more progress toward them than they sometimes do. As people grow older they should become more and more unwilling to accept statements on the basis of authority alone and should want to see the evidence. They want also to know why things are as they are. In early adolescence many interests arise, too many for all of them to continue; later on, there is commonly a narrowing of interests to a few that become permanent. Persistence of intellectual dependence upon authority or of too widely scattered interests is an indication that adolescence has not yet been left behind.

No one is truly an adult until he earns his own living. One set of problems therefore concerns the development of economic adulthood. A child concerns himself only incidentally and quite unrealistically with future occupations; an adolescent tends to overemphasize glamour and to suppose that interest is all one needs for success; an adult has reached a compromise based upon his abilities, his interests, and his opportunities.

In the world of today people have more leisure than they ever had before. It is only recently that educators have realized how necessary it is for an adolescent to learn how to make wise use of his leisure time. One of the important contributions of the high school's extracurricular program to adolescent adjustment lies in its training for the use of leisure. Games and hobbies contribute greatly to the enjoyment of life, but if they demand too much time, energy, or money, the adult has to forsake them. As boys and girls grow older they develop a spectator interest in the more active games, and they begin to substitute the less strenuous amusements of adult life for the rough-and-tumble of childhood.

An adolescent should make a beginning in the development of a point of view concerning the world about him. Sometimes such an integrating attitude toward life has its basis in religion, and sometimes not. Children have neither the intellectual capacity nor the experience in living to make sound abstractions and are therefore unable to develop ideals. The adolescent, however, is almost certain to adopt general principles of conduct, whether or not these principles lead to socially approved behavior. Naturally, it is only the most precocious of adolescents who enter adulthood with a coherent philosophy of life or with a complete set of ideals. A beginning is all one can expect, but as an adolescent nears adulthood he should start to select whatever values he can find to give life a meaning for him.

Finally, during the period of adolescence the boy or girl begins to find out what kind of person he or she is, to see the self with some degree of realism, and to sense what other people think. This process of finding out "who you are" goes on throughout life, but it becomes conscious in the years between childhood and adulthood.

▶ Summary

In modern society a long period of adolescence has replaced the short period of puberty that was recognized as important from early times. Just as primitive peoples utilized the few months of puberty as a period for special preparation of boys and girls for their future participation in the life of the tribe, so modern educators want to utilize the longer period of adolescence for special preparation in meeting the manifold problems of present-day society.

In order to pass from childhood to adulthood the adolescent must solve a number of problems. He must develop heterosexual interests, become free from home supervision, make new emotional and social adjustments to reality, begin to evolve a philosophy of life, achieve economic and intellectual independence, and learn how to use his lesiure time profitably. If he fails in any of these achievements, he fails to gain full maturity. To put the matter in a nutshell, the main business of the adolescent is to stop being one!

▶ References for Further Reading

This text contains five sets of references or other additional materials. There are (1) those in the footnotes, which indicate the source of a table, figure, or statement. At the end of each chapter there is (2) a list of references, divided into two main groups. The first group contains only books—whenever possible, widely used books that should be available even in small libraries. A student would rarely be expected to read more than one of the book references. Some of the assignments cover specific chapters that roughly parallel those of the present text; other references are to books in which some matter treated briefly in the text is presented at greater length. The second group includes titles from monographs, proceedings, reports, yearbooks, and articles in periodicals, each giving results from a definite piece of research. These lists are short and highly selected. They are not to be regarded as adequate bibliographies but only as springboards from which a student may get started.

In addition to the readings for each chapter, there is (3) a list of novels in Appendix A. Each novel exemplifies at least one problem of adolescence. Some books carry a single group of characters from birth through early childhood into the adult years; others describe a cross-section of life during adolescence; still others show how environment may influence growth; some are primarily about adults whose behavior is explained in terms of their personal history; a few deal with abnormal developments. The course will provide a better understanding if each student reads at least three novels, and then writes, instead of a plot summary, a brief statement concerning the problems of adolescence illustrated by each novel. Appendix B (4) consists of a list of motion pictures that deal with different phases of adolescence. The list is not long but has been selected with care so as to contain films that will throw as much light as possible upon typical problems of the period. Even from commercial sources the cost of such materials is not high, and some of the films are distributed *gratis*. At the end of each chapter the student will find (5) a problem or two, sometimes with minor projects under the main heading or headings. These problems are for use as suggestions for term papers, senior theses in the honors' program, or future M.A. theses. Some undergraduates may prefer to substitute a small project for some of the reading.

References for Further Reading

(Please note that publishing information is given only once, when each text or other book first appears. In later references only the author's last name and the title are given. The assignment for each book is in the parenthesis after the citation.)

BOOKS

Other Texts

Ausubel, D. P., *Theory and Problems of Adolescent Development* (New York: Grune and Stratton, Inc., 1954), 585 pp. (Chap. 1 or 2).

Breckenridge, M. E., and E. L. Vincent, *Child Development,* 4th ed. (Philadelphia: W. B. Saunders Company, 1960), 648 pp. (Chap. 1).

Horrocks, J. E., *Behavior and Development* (Boston: Houghton-Mifflin Company, 1962), 711 pp. (pp. 13–28).

Hurlock, E. B., *Adolescent Development,* 2d. ed. (New York: McGraw-Hill Book Company, 1955), 590 pp. (Chap. 1).

Jersild, A. T., *Psychology of Adolescence* (New York: The Macmillan Company, 1957), 438 pp. (Chap. 1).

Jones, H. E., and M. C. Jones, *Growth and Behavior in Adolescence* (Berkeley, Calif.: University of California Press, 1957), 312 pp. (pp. 1–14).

Kuhlen, R. G., *The Psychology of Adolescent Development* (New York: Harper & Row, Publishers, 1952), 675 pp. (Chap. 1).

Wattenberg, W. W., *The Adolescent Years* (New York: Harcourt, Brace & World, Inc., 1955), 510 pp. (Chap. 1).

Other Books

Baller, W. R., *Readings in the Psychology of Human Growth and Development* (New York: Holt, Rinehart and Winston, Inc., 1963), 689 pp. (pp. 329–339).

Seidman, J. M., ed., *The Adolescent: A Book of Readings* (New York: Holt, Rinehart and Winston, Inc., 1960), 870 pp. (No. 5).

ARTICLES

Dales, R. J., "A Method for Measuring Developmental Tasks: Scales for Selected Tasks at the Beginning of Adolescence," *Child Development,* 26:111–122, 1955.

Thresselt, M. E., "The Adolescent Becomes a Social Person," *Journal of Social Hygiene,* 40:130–134, 1954.

Suggested Research Problems [1]

1. Statement of developmental goals that are within the reach of the average adolescent. The present formulations are for adults rather than adolescents.
2. Development of comprehensive criteria for classifying a given pupil as being in a given stage of development.

---

[1] The teacher or student who is interested in small problems for either class discussion or a term paper should look at pp. 702–711 of the *Psychology of Adolescence,* 5th edition, where several per chapter are listed.

PART ONE | Physical Development

Chapter 2 | Growth in Tissue, Muscle, and Bone

ADOLESCENCE is first of all a period of physical and physiological change. This growth furnishes the basis for emotional, social, intellectual, and economic maturity. If a child did not increase his stature, if his muscles did not become strong, if his sex organs did not grow, if his brain did not mature, if his internal organs did not increase in size and efficiency to meet the requirements of an enlarged body, the child could never achieve mature ideas and attitudes, could never support himself, and could never take his place in adult society. Because of these all-pervasive effects of growth, it seems desirable to begin the survey of adolescence with a fairly detailed picture of the physical manifestations of the period, together with some consideration of what these changes mean to adolescents and of typical adolescent responses to them. Teachers need to know the basic facts about growth so that they will not make such an error in judgment as to regard a fast-growing boy as necessarily lazy because he is tired all the time. They need also to remember that their pupils are living, growing, changing, developing organisms and that they have bodies, emotions, and ambitions as well as minds.

This and the next three chapters contain material about general size and proportion, growth in the bones, growth in strength and coordination, and changes in the internal organs. There follows a short chapter on general health during adolescence and a final one for this section on the problems of those children who deviate in some way from the adolescent physical norm.

Naturally, a child grows in every system of the body simultaneously, but his development in all systems cannot be simultaneously described. One has to begin *somewhere* and proceed from the point of departure by logical steps. Otherwise the reader would derive more confusion than clarity from the reading. However, the student should never forget that these serially described developments are all taking place at the same time within each pupil's body. It is therefore essential that a teacher be continually altering and adapting her methods of teaching as the pupils mature.

► **Height and Weight**

General Curves   In the last few decades, growth curves have been based
upon measurement of the same children year after year.
By this technique one gets a more accurate picture of growth in general and
of individual development in particular. This technique is often termed "longitudinal." The curves to be given in this and later chapters are based, when-

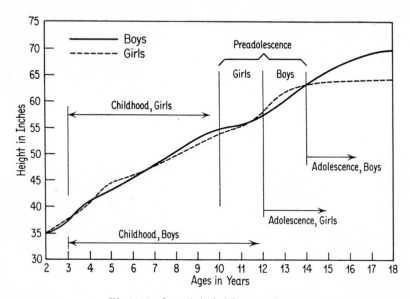

Fig. 2–1. Growth in height, ages 2 to 18

Based on curves found in R. D. Tuddenham and M. M. Snyder, "The Physical Growth
of California Boys and Girls from Birth to Eighteen Years," *University of California
Publications in Child Development*, 1:183–364, 1954, p. 203. (See also J. M. Tanner and
R. H. Whitehouse, "Standards of Height and Weight of British Children from Birth to
Maturity," *Lancet*, 2:1096–1098, 1959.)

ever possible, upon successive measurements of the same children. Results
for boys and girls are given separately in the figures that record growth, because members of the two sexes develop at different rates and in different
ways. Since the facts about adolescence should be related to similar data from
the preceding years, the curves shown in Figures 2–1 and 2–2 show growth
in height and weight extending from age 2 to maturity. The various periods
have been marked off.

   The curve brings out especially the two points that are of importance in
conditioning the attitudes of adolescents. In the first place, it is clear that
growth is rapid just before and during early adolescence. Among boys the

curves for height and weight rise most sharply from ages 12 to 16, with additional smaller gains until 18. The curves are still rising at 18, though slowly. Among girls, growth is rapid in preadolescence but slower during the adolescent period. A second point concerns the relative growth for the two sexes. In childhood, girls average about two inches shorter and a pound lighter than boys of the same age. However, since girls develop in all respects faster than boys, their preadolescent growth begins sooner. Between the ages of 12 and 13 they average a bit taller than boys, and from 11 to 14 they are about seven pounds heavier. By 18 they have reached their adult size, but boys are still growing. At this time girls average six inches shorter and twenty pounds lighter than boys.

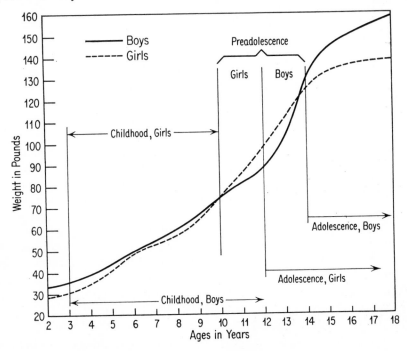

Fig. 2–2. Increases in weight, ages 2 to 18

Based on R. D. Tuddenham and M. M. Snyder, "The Physical Growth of California Boys and Girls from Birth to Eighteen Years," *University of California Publications in Child Development,* 1:183–364, 1954, p. 203.

The curves for weight show parallel developments, but the shapes of the curves are different. The curves in Figure 2–1 are almost straight lines, with a slight tendency to be convex, while those in Figure 2–2 are concave. In extreme form, the difference is between ⌒ and ⌣. This difference in shape comes from the different rates at which final height and final weight are acquired. Whereas a child has half his 18-year-old height by the time he is 3 years old—or she is 2½—he does not gain half his 18-year-old weight until he is 11 or she is 9½. The growth spurt in weight is considerably more marked than that in height. In girls, the onset of puberty has the effect of slowing down the rate of growth. By age 14 most of the girls have begun to menstruate, and there is little further rise to the curve. Among boys, however, sexual maturity has exactly the opposite effect. During pubescence, while boys are acquiring adult sexual characteristics, they grow very rapidly. The differences in the adult height of men and women are in part due to this phenomenon, since the difference during childhood is slight, and members of both sexes enter their puberty at about the same height and weight, although at different ages.

For many boys and girls, the rapid increase in size is quite disconcerting. A boy may gain as much as 6 inches and 25 pounds in a single year. Such a child starts the year at, say, 112 pounds and ends it at 135; he has progressed in 12 months out of the flyweights, through the bantam- and featherweights, and into the lightweights. Since most of his increased height is due to growth in his legs, many a boy finds himself equipped with pedal extremities that get him across a room rather faster than he expected, causing him to overrun his objective; they also tend to get tangled in the furniture. His arms, having grown 4 or 5 inches in length, also contribute to his miscalculations of distance and lead him into a long series of minor tragedies, from knocking over his waterglass because his hand reached it too soon to throwing a forward pass 6 feet over the receiver's head, because his elongated arm automatically produced far greater leverage than he has been accustomed to. In general, girls do not have so prolonged an "awkward age" as boys, partly because they grow less, partly because they grow more slowly, and partly because they grow sooner. However, the tallest and largest of girls have in magnified form the same malcoordination as most boys. It requires time for both boys and girls to get used to being what seems to them altogether too large. This period coincides with the years of junior high school and the first year of the senior high for girls, and for boys with the entire four years of high school. Teachers can therefore expect a few episodes that are minor in themselves but may prove horribly embarrassing to the adolescent.

Growth Rates in Different Groups　　The growth curves shown in Figures 2–1 and 2–2 give a generalized picture that tends to conceal differences among groups or individuals and to combine the effects of many factors rather than to isolate the significance of each. There are a number of factors that have an influence upon both growth rate and final height and weight. Among these appear such background influences as climate, economic status, nutritional level, incidence of disease, family and racial inheritance, size of family, and sex. As already pointed out, girls mature in every respect faster than boys.

It does not seem that climate is a factor of importance in promoting or retarding growth. Both the tallest and the shortest peoples in the world live in the tropics. The popular belief that Swedes, for example, are tall because they live in a cold climate is probably erroneous; at least, the same climate has not added any inches to the height of the Lapps who live in Sweden or to the American Eskimos or to the tribes of Siberia who live in a similar climate. Nor does a hot climate inevitably affect growth. While Italians are shorter than Swedes in general, the desert-dwelling Navajo Indians average a bit taller than Swedes. What influence climate exerts is probably indirect through the nature of the food supply and through the more rapid growth in the higher temperatures of bacteria, with a resulting greater incidence of disease.

Practically all investigators who have studied the matter have found that social and economic status correlates positively with both growth rate and ultimate height and weight.[1] In all cases the differences are small but they are exceedingly consistent from one study to another. The children of professional men and business executives are slightly taller and heavier than those from middle-class homes, who in turn exceed in all aspects of growth the children of day laborers. It is probable that these differences arise from the better diet and better medical care—with resulting freedom from illness —received by children whose parents have a good income.

There are sex differences in the reaction of children and adolescents to malnutrition, illness, and all kinds of environmental stress—with indirect influences upon growth. Girls are less retarded in their growth by inadequate food or illness, and they make up deficiencies in height and weight faster than do boys when the diet again becomes normal. Thus girls in a Belgium orphanage after World War II were nearer than the boys to normal growth for their age, although both sexes had received the same food in the same amounts; and when the diet was enlarged they caught up to their age levels about six months earlier than the boys.[2] The examination of children who survived the Hiroshima and Nagasaki atomic bombings showed the girls to be suffering appreciably less damage.[3] And among the children of Guam, after some years

---

[1] Facts presented in this paragraph come from F. J. W. Miller, S. D. M. Court, W. S. Walton and E. G. Knox, *Growing Up in Newcastle-upon-Tyne: A Continuing Study of Health and Illness in Young Children within Their Families* (London: Oxford University Press, 1960), 369 pp.; J. W. Hopkins, "Height and Weight of Ottawa Elementary School Children of Two Socio-Economic Strata," *Human Biology*, 19:68–82, 1947; H. V. Meredith, "Relation between Socio-Economic Status and Body Size in Boys 7–10 Years of Age," *American Journal of Diseases of Children*, 82:702–709, 1951; J. F. de Wijn and J. H. Haas, "Groeidia-grammen van 1–25 jarigen in Nederland," *Verhandelingen Instituut voor Preventieve Geneeskunde*, 1950, No. 49, 30 pp.

[2] E. M. Widdowson and R. A. McCance, "Studies on the Nutritive Value of Bread and on the Effect of Variation in Extraction Rate on the Growth of Undernourished Children," *Medical Research Council Special Report*, No. 287, 1954, 137 pp.

[3] W. W. Greulich, C. S. Crissman, and M. L. Turner, "The Physical Growth and Development of Children Who Survived the Atomic Bombing of Hiroshima and Nagasaki," *Journal of Pediatrics*, 43:121–145, 1953.

of deprivation, the girls were less retarded than the boys in height, weight, and skeletal growth.[4] It was also noted after the last war that such survivors as there were of Dachau and other concentration camps were predominantly women, although they had received no more food or care than the men. In short, it would appear that the female of the species is relatively hard to kill!

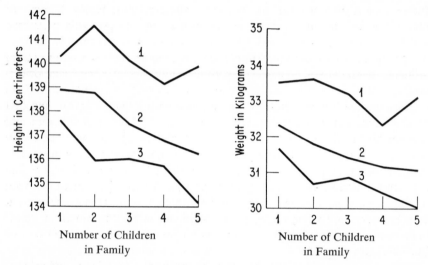

Fig. 2–3. Relation between size of family and (a) height and (b) weight of eleven-year-old children in these families. Socioeconomic status: 1—high, 2—average, 3—low

Based on data from the Scottish Council, *Research in Education,* 1952.

Hereditary factors are probably important in determining final height, type of bodily structure, and adult weight. There are "tall" families and "short" families, in each of which the children tend to resemble their parents, especially in height. However, such normal variations as might appear may be either reduced or intensified by differences in diet or by other environmental factors. The size of the family may also affect the growth of children. Figure 2–3 gives results from an investigation into the relationship between family size, family status, and the height and weight of several hundred 11-year-old children, who had first been grouped according to the number of children in the family —from 1 to 5 or more. The differences in size shown by the children who had no siblings reflect merely the usual differences between social levels. The addition of more children does not at first have an effect upon growth in the three highest social classes; but a third, fourth, or fifth child does influence growth perceptibly, presumably because the family finances will not suffice

---

[4] W. W. Greulich, "The Growth and Developmental Status of Guamanian School Children in 1947," *American Journal of Physical Anthropology,* N.S. 9:55–70, 1951.

to feed so many at the level possible for the first one or two. In middle-class families, the first two children fare well enough, but if the family becomes larger, the growth rate is adversely affected. In the lowest income group of families the presence of even a second child lowers the nutritional level somewhat; and if the family contains three, four, or five children, the situation becomes rapidly worse. These results show how environmental factors may operate to reinforce or offset inheritance. Thus, for instance, the 11-year-old child of two tall parents in the lowest income group will probably be shorter than his parents, if there are several other children in the family.

There are almost certainly basic differences, aside from skin color, among the races of mankind, but the investigations to date have not been able to show just what these differences are or how extensive they may be, mainly because it has not been possible to isolate the effect of race from the influence of family inheritance, nutrition, and environment. That is, it is easy enough to demonstrate differences but extremely difficult to explain them. There are only a few incontrovertible facts, such as: (1) Negro babies grow faster than white babies up until about the age of three and (2) the teeth of Negro children appear earlier and seem more resistant to decay than those of white children. There has not been enough investigation of Oriental, Melanesian, or Polynesian children and adolescents—and especially not enough in recent years—to furnish the data for an adequate comparison of these groups with either whites or Negroes.

There is no doubt that inadequate nutrition has an adverse effect upon growth. In the first half of the twentieth century there were three great upheavals—World War I, the Great Depression of the 1930s, and World War II. All three catastrophes had an effect upon the growth of children and adolescents. World War I certainly slowed growth among European children, and especially among those in Belgium and Austria. There were, however, relatively few statistical studies showing the amount and extent of the damage. After World War II the retardation of growth was probably worldwide but was studied with special care in England, Germany, France, Japan, and Belgium.[5] As an example, the results from the German city of Stuttgart have been selected, mainly because of their completeness.

From 1935 through 1953 the school pupils had been measured in height and weight every year—with the single exception of 1944. The entire study would require a disproportionate amount of space for presentation, so the writers have selected results in weight for boys at the ages of 7, 9, 11, 13,

[5] See, for example, R. W. B. Ellis, "Growth and Health of Belgian Children during the German Occupation, 1940–1944," *Archives of Diseases in Childhood*, 20:97–109, 1945; K. Kimura, S. Hagiya, and E. Kitano, "Effects of War on Stature," *Zinruigaku Zasshi*, 22:23–37, 1959; L. Randoin and J. Maillard, "L'Evolution des Restrictions alimentaires au cours des années 1942, 1943, 1944 pour les catégories des consommateurs," *Bulletin de la Société Scientifique d'Hygiène alimentaire et d'alimentation rationelle de l'homme*, 35:270–325, 1947.

15, and 17. Inclusion of results in height of boys or in the weight and height of girls would only show that the situation here presented applied to all children and adolescents of both sexes and at all ages. Figure 2–4 tells the story adequately. The weight of the children of a given age was fairly stable or showed a slight increase in the years preceding the war; during the first two years of the war there was often an increase in weight, presumably while the nation had more food than usual because of its military victories. In the last four years the average weight declined and remained low for two or three years after peace was made, with a return to the prewar average during the

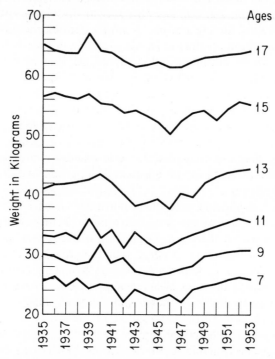

Fig. 2–4. Relation between nutrition and weight for boys, ages 7–17, 1935–1953

Based on P. E. Howe and M. Schiller, "Growth Responses of the School Child to Changes in Diet and Environmental Factors," *Journal of Applied Physiology,* 5:51–61, 1952.

final years covered by the study. It should be understood that these are measures of *different* children and adolescents, not consecutive measures of the same children. The figure is to be read that, whereas the average boy of 15 during the four prewar years weighed about 125 pounds, the average 15-year-old boy in the years 1941–1949 weighed about 116 pounds. The younger children show less loss than the older, probably because what food could be obtained was given mainly to them. It should be noted that the average weight per age had returned to normal by the early 1950s. That is, the general population caught up with itself, but what one does not know is whether or not the particular boys who passed through these ages during and immediately after the war were able to compensate for deprivations and reach normal height and weight.

The Great Depression also had its effect upon growth. The largest measured losses were among the children of middle-class parents, who met the crisis by reducing the nutritional level rather than by applying to public charities for aid. The children of the lowest income groups, however, actually gained more than usual, presumably because the food given them in a public diet kitchen or provided for them by charities was more nourishing than that usually fed them by their impecunious parents.[6]

Statistical studies have demonstrated a general world tendency toward an increase of stature for at least the last century. Measurements of recruits in countries that have had universal military service for decades if not centuries show increases of both height and weight from the earliest to the most recent generations in the same population.[7] In the United States the men who were drafted in World War II were three-fifths of an inch taller and 9½ pounds heavier than their counterparts in World War I. In the middle of the eighteenth century, Frederick the Great had to search all over Europe to find enough men six feet tall to serve as his house guards. At present he could find that many in almost any large California high school.

In this country also the same phenomenon has appeared. Thus, the average 14-year-old boy is 5 inches taller and 24 pounds heavier than his counterpart in 1880. Even in the past 25 years there has been an increase in 12-year-old boys of 3 inches and 15 pounds. Fortunately for posterity, investigators in the state of Iowa and specifically in Iowa City have made surveys in the years 1902, 1919–1920, 1930–1935, and 1952. In order to conserve space only a few sample results will be presented and these will be restricted to the ages covered by all four studies. Table 2–1 shows the average heights for boys in alternate years from age 6 to 16 and the weights for girls from the same decade. The results for the earliest ages are omitted because two of the studies did not measure children below grade 1 and for the upper ages of 18 to 20 because there were too few adolescents of these years still in the high school,

---

[6] C. E. Palmer, "Height and Weight of the Depression Poor," *United States Public Health Reports,* 50:1106–1113, 1935.

[7] See, for example: W. Lenz, "Ursachen des gesteigerten Wachstums der heutigen Jugend," *Wissenschaftliche Veröffentlichungen der deutschen Gesellschaft für Ernährung,* 4:1–33, 1959; E. B. M. Clements, "Changes in the Mean Stature and Weight of British Children over the Past Seventy Years," *British Medical Journal,* 2:897–902, 1953; J. B. de V. Weir, "Assessment of the Growth of School Children with Special Reference to Secular Change," *British Journal of Nutrition,* 6:19–33, 1952.

Table 2–1: INCREASES IN HEIGHT AND WEIGHT FROM 1902 TO 1952

	Boys: Height in Inches					
Year	Age 6	Age 8	Age 10	Age 12	Age 14	Age 16
1902	43.6	47.8	51.0	55.2	59.4	64.4
1919–20	44.4	49.3	53.3	57.2	61.2	65.6
1930–35	45.6	50.4	54.7	58.2	62.8	66.8
1952	46.3	51.6	54.9	58.4	63.3	67.1
Total gain	2.7	3.8	3.9	3.2	3.9	2.7

	Girls: Weight in Pounds					
Year	Age 6	Age 8	Age 10	Age 12	Age 14	Age 16
1902	40.8	48.9	59.9	72.7	94.4	110.8
1919–20	45.3	55.9	66.5	79.4	106.3	119.8
1930–35	45.3	56.4	69.7	91.3	110.9	119.7
1952	46.4	57.9	77.8	100.5	113.1	126.8
Total gain	5.6	9.0	17.9	27.8	19.7	16.0

SOURCE: (1902) W. W. Hastings, *A Manual for Physical Measurements for Use in Normal Schools, Public and Preparatory Schools, Boys' Clubs, Young Men's Christian Associations, with Anthropometric Tables for Each Height at Each Age from 5 to 20 Years and Vital Coefficients* (Springfield, Mass., 1902), 95 pp. (1919–1920) B. T. Baldwin, "The Physical Growth of Children from Birth to Maturity," *Iowa Studies in Child Welfare,* Vol. I, No. 1, 1923, 411 pp. (1930) H. V. Meredith, "The Rhythm of Physical Growth," *Iowa Studies in Child Welfare,* Vol. II, No. 3, 1935, 128 pp. (Boys) and B. Boynton, "The Physical Growth of Girls," *ibid.,* Vol. II, No. 4, 105 pp. (1952) E. S. Eppright and V. D. Sidwell, "Physical Measurements of Iowa School Children," *Journal of Nutrition,* 54:543–556, 1954.

at which level the measurement stopped. The boys show increases in height at successive ages of 2.7, 3.8, 3.9, 3.2, 3.9, and 2.7 inches between 1902 and 1952. The increase in weight for the girls was for the years cited 5.6, 9.0, 17.9, 27.8, 19.7, and 16 pounds. The total increase in weight for the boys (not shown in the table) from 1902 to 1952 varied from 4.6 pounds at 6 years to 25.6 at 14; and the height of girls (also not shown) showed increases varying from 1.8 at 16—after practically all the girls were mature and were growing very slowly if at all—to 5.2 at 12, just before the start of menstruation. These recorded increases in growth are presumably due to the greater availability of food, a better-balanced diet even among the poor, a more equitable distribution of the country's wealth, a decrease in illness, the better medical care of whatever sickness cannot be avoided, the virtual elimination of child labor, and an improved understanding of children and adolescents generally with a resultant prevention of many strains that formerly exerted an adverse effect upon growth.

Individual Differences in Growth Thus far the discussion has concerned groups of children of various ages and types. References to differences between individuals have been only incidental. It seems desirable, therefore, to present a few results for individuals, in order to emphasize the extent of individual differences.

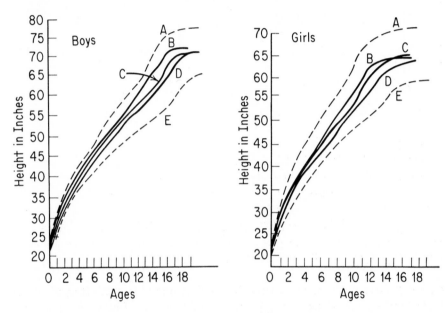

Fig. 2–5. Developmental patterns in height for individual boys and girls. A—an accelerated boy or girl, B, C, D,—three average boys or girls, E—a retarded boy or girl

M. L. Hathaway, *Heights and Weights of Children and Youth in the United States* (Washington, D.C.: U.S. Department of Agriculture, 1957), 131 pp., pp. 92 and 93.

Curves for height and weight for five boys and for five girls appear in Figures 2–5 and 2–6. Curve A is for a boy or girl who shows an accelerated growth pattern. Curves B, C, and D are for those who are growing at an average rate. Curve E demonstrates the growth of a boy or girl who is retarded. A few comparisons should make clear the extent of the differences. For example, Boy A was taller at 13 than Boy E was at 19, and Girl A was taller at 11 than any of the other girls at the end of the measurement. The differences between the tallest and shortest boys at ages 2, 10, and 19 were successively: 4, 10, and 12 inches. The girls at the same ages showed differences of 7, 16, and 12 inches between the tallest and shortest. At these same three ages the heaviest boy outweighed the lightest by 5, 47, and 73 pounds; similar results for the girls were 17, 72, and 85 pounds. Although all the curves in

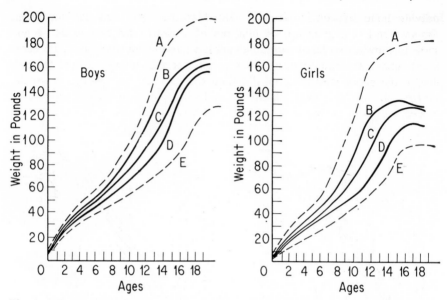

Fig. 2–6. Developmental patterns in weight for individual boys and girls. A—an accelerated boy or girl, B, C, D—three average boys or girls, E—a retarded boy or girl

M. L. Hathaway, *Heights and Weights of Children and Youth in the United States* (Washington, D.C.: U.S. Department of Agriculture, 1957), 131 pp., pp. 94 and 95.

each figure are of the same general shape, no two are identical. It would seem that the prospective teacher might expect to find pupils of all shapes and sizes in her classes.

▶ Bodily Types and Proportions

Of late years, investigators have become increasingly aware of the differences in body build among children and adolescents and of the effect that variations in bodily type have upon individuals. One comprehensive study of men [8] appeared some years ago, and although no study of equal breadth has been made of women, there have been many that were of smaller scope, enough to outline the major types and problems. For both sexes, there seem to be three main types: the ectomorphs, the mesomorphs, and the endomorphs. Most people are mixtures rather than pure types, and it is probable that all individuals have in their physical make-up some elements of all three.

The first type, the ectomorphs, are characterized by having a frail and

[8] W. H. Sheldon, S. S. Stevens, and W. B. Tucker, *The Varieties of Human Physique* (New York: Harper & Row, Publishers, Inc., 1940), 347 pp.

delicate bone structure with long, thin limbs, a small, narrow, flat chest, rounded and sloping shoulders, long but very slender hands and feet, a flat, short abdomen, thin legs, a long, thin neck, a stooping posture, and an S curve in the spine. The musculature is slight, there is little if any fat, and the outline of the bones is often visible through the flesh. Growth of hair is usually profuse all over the body. Outline C in Figure 2–7 is a typical ectomorph. Not all members of this group are tall, but they rather tend to be.

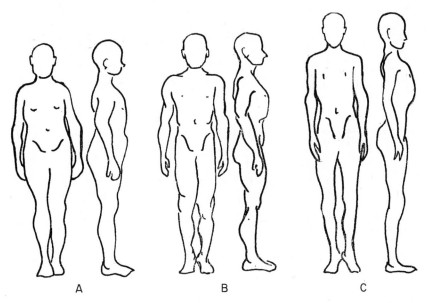

Fig. 2–7. Three types of bodily build among boys, age 18. A—endomorphic type, B—mesomorphic type, C—ectomorphic type

Based on F. K. Shuttleworth, "The Adolescent Period: A Pictorial Atlas," *Monograph of the Society for Research in Child Development,* Vol. 14, No. 1, Serial No. 50, 1949, 69 pp., p. 43.

At the other extreme are the endomorphs. Their bodies are predominantly soft and round and smooth, with a strong tendency to bulge. The trunk is large, round, and very thick; the abdomen is especially large and usually protrudes; the head is round and big, it sits atop a short, thick neck, and it contains a face that suggests a full moon; the upper arms and upper legs are extraordinarily wide and heavy, both arms and legs are short, and the hands and feet are much too small for the rest of the body. The fingers are short and pudgy. Endomorphs in youth have fairly strong muscles, although these are of the smooth feminine type. The bodily weight of endomorphs gives them more power than one would expect. At all ages their skeletons are well covered with a smooth layer of fat which prevents the bony structure from showing through. As they grow older they usually acquire several layers of fat, especially around the abdomen and hips and on the upper arms and upper legs. Their skin is usually quite fine, as is their hair, which is likely to be rather sparse. Silhouette A of Figure 2–7 shows a young endomorph.

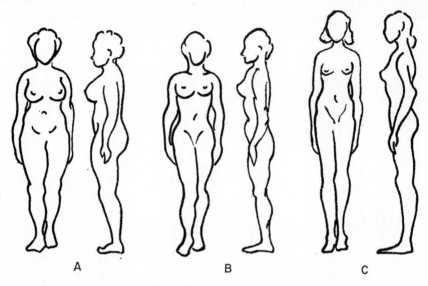

A   B   C

Fig. 2–8. Three types of bodily build among girls, age 18. A—endomorphic type, B—mesomorphic type, C—ectomorphic type

Based on F. K. Shuttleworth, "The Adolescent Period: A Pictorial Atlas," *Monograph of the Society for Research in Child Development,* Vol. 14, No. 1, Serial No. 50, 1949, 69 pp., pp. 38 and 39.

Between these two extremes and having some of the characteristics of both, but fusing them into a distinct physical type, are the mesomorphs. These people have a square, strong, tough, hard, firm body, with a long, straight trunk, heavy ribs, broad shoulders, a fairly large but muscular abdomen, a slender, low waistline, and fairly broad hips. The shoulders are, however, usually so wide that by comparison the hips seem narrow. The neck is long but thickish, and the facial bones are quite prominent. The arms and legs are neither unduly long nor unduly short, but they are powerfully muscled, and the muscles are of the type that form protruding lumps. The forearms, wrists, calves, and ankles are large and thick, with squarish fingers and toes. The skin is thick and the hair coarse. Silhouette B of Figure 2–7 is that of a typical young male mesomorph.

Girls show the same types of body build. Figure 2–8 presents the three "pure" types, when one makes allowances for feminine curves and proportions. Girl C is a slender ectomorph, A is a well-rounded endomorph, and B is a square, sturdy mesomorph. A characteristic of the female mesomorph is that her shoulders are usually wider than her hips.

Indirect Results of Differences in Size and Build Size and shape have a profound influence upon the individual who dwells within the body. In American culture, the boy who is short or weak or lightly muscled is likely to lose status among his age-mates, partly because he does not measure up to popular notions of ideal masculinity. The extreme endomorphs are likely to be the butt of jokes because their layer of fat, though not usually excessive in adolescence, reduces their agility and makes them look feminine. The mesomorphs are generally fairly well satisfied with their build since they have the native equipment for many sports and the proper masculine outlines, but many of them are too short for certain types of competitive games. One investigator [9] studied 256 boys between the ages of 11 and 16, all of whom had inadequate masculine physique. There was no one of them who did not have some problem, large or small, of adjustment, because of his consciousness of his own physical inadequacy. The trials of the tall girl ectomorph are of a different nature. She is as tall as most boys, and since she almost certainly matured much earlier than boys of her own age, she has passed through a period during which she was conspicuously taller than boys in her age group. The female adolescent endomorph usually tries dieting and may exercise diligently, but she continues to be too round and too dumpy looking for her taste. She never has what is regarded as proper adolescent chic because she cannot make herself flat enough and especially because her main protuberances are in the wrong places. The feminine mesomorph is likely to be a tomboy in childhood and a competitor with boys in her adolescence. She may outplay boys until the time when they begin their final growth spurt. Subsequently, their long arms and legs give them such leverage and speed that she can no longer compete. Other girls may look down on the mesomorph because she is not "feminine"; boys often actively dislike her because she is a competitor, not an admirer; and she is almost certain to pass through a period of stress during adolescence because the tomboy habits of her childhood are no longer useful in maintaining prestige and may become actual menaces to her position among either boys or girls.

Adolescents often make quite extreme reactions to compensate for their size. For instance, a tall girl may never go to dances because she is certain to be taller than most of the boys with whom she dances. Or a large girl may go in for athletics, politics, masculine clothes, and a career because she cannot be "cute" and feminine. Or a small-sized boy may become a "grind" largely because he cannot compete on equal terms physically with other boys

[9] W. A. Schonfeld, "Inadequate Masculine Physique as a Factor in Personality Development of Adolescent Boys," *Psychosomatic Medicine*, 12:49–54, 1950.

—and may, if he attempts games, even be beaten by girls. Very tall boys also have difficulties of adjustment. Chairs, desks, beds, driving seats of cars, and even doorways are too small for them. Whenever they are on their feet, they cannot help feeling conspicuous, and they are constantly being reminded of their height by inquiries about the condition of the atmosphere up where they are, and by similar pleasantries. The writer knows one girl of six feet two who was so miserable in American schools that she went to Sweden for her education, where her excessive height would be less conspicuous and where she would not be forced every week into three hours of gymnasium work and four hours of participation in some game—all of which made her acutely miserable.

Proportional Growth   The various parts of the body grow at different rates and reach their maximal development at different times. The head, for example, does the major part of its growing before birth, and most of the rest soon after.[10] At birth it equals one fourth of the baby's total length. At age 6, it is already 90 percent of its adult size and equals one sixth of a child's height. In adulthood, the head is one seventh to one eighth of the body's length. In contrast, the long bones of the arms and legs are extremely short at birth, remain comparatively short during childhood, and then lengthen

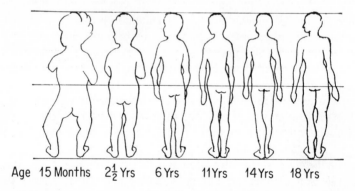

Age   15 Months   2½ Yrs   6 Yrs   11 Yrs   14 Yrs   18 Yrs

Fig. 2–9. Changes in the bodily proportions of one boy from babyhood to maturity

Based on M. Bayer and N. Bayley, *Growth Diagnosis* (Chicago: University of Chicago Press, 1959), 240 pp., p. 22.

quickly just before or during adolescence.[11] At puberty they are four times as long as they were at birth, and at maturity five times as long. The trunk is relatively long at birth but doubles its length by age 6; it grows little from

---

[10] M. Dokladal, "Growth in the Main Head Dimensions from Birth to 20 Years of Age," *Czech Human Biology,* 31:90–109, 1959.
[11] M. M. Maresh, "Linear Growth of Long Bones of Extremities from Infancy through Adolescence," *American Journal of the Diseases of Children,* 89:725–742, 1955.

then until the later years of adolescence. At maturity the trunk is three times as long and wide as it was at birth, and two and one half times as thick. These different rates of growth give the baby, the child, the adolescent, and the adult their characteristic outlines, as illustrated in Figure 2–9. The diagram shows both proportions and size at intervals from birth to maturity. In this figure the outlines have all been reduced to the same height. This arrangement makes it possible to see what the shape of an adult would be, if he maintained throughout life the proportions that he had as a baby and simply grew larger.

The growth of the muscles and the deposit of fat just below the skin have their own pattern and rhythm of development, which is affected only slightly by exercise or by diets unless they are of extremely high or low caloric intake. At birth the muscles make up 27 percent of the total body weight. At age 15 they have become 32 percent and at age 16, 44 percent—or nearly half the weight of the body. During childhood girls often have a slight deposit of fat on their arms, legs, chests, and abdomen—just enough to give them a curved rather than a flat appearance. Boys have much less. Members of both sexes begin to put on larger quantities of fat under the skin at about the period

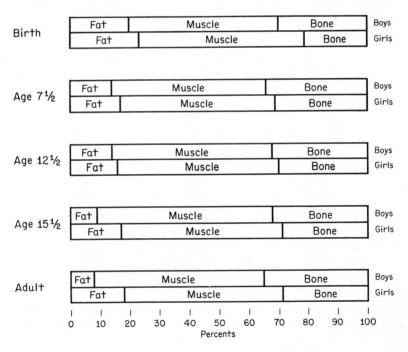

Fig. 2–10. Growth in fat, muscle, and bone

Based on E. L. Reynolds and P. Grote, "Sex Differences in the Distribution of Tissue Components in the Human Leg from Birth to Maturity," *Anatomical Record*, 102:45–53, 1948.

of pubescence. The tendency is especially noticeable in girls, most of whom now have a layer of fatty tissue over almost the entire body. The comparative growth of fat and muscle in the two sexes has been studied in great detail from birth to maturity. The muscles selected for intensive study were those in the calf of the leg. Boys exceeded girls almost from infancy in the breadth of the muscle, while girls exceeded boys in the depth of fatty tissue between muscle and skin. The proportion of fat, muscle, and bone at five different age levels is shown in Figure 2–10. For boys the proportion of fat is never quite as high as for girls. By the time adulthood has been reached, a man's leg contains only 8 percent fat, while a woman's contains 18 percent, but his bones and muscles are both bigger and heavier. These differences became more pronounced with age and continue into adulthood.

It is this characteristic development and the distribution of fat and muscle that prevent a boy from swimming more than a few minutes in cold water in which his twin sister can swim in comfort for an hour. After the beginning of adolescence a boy's increased arm and leg length and strength permit him to swim short distances faster than most girls, but almost any girl can remain in the water as long as she wants to without getting muscle cramps, because her muscles are well insulated by fatty tissue. Moreover, this same tissue allows her to float whenever she gets tired. It is no accident that more women than men finish distance swims, although only a very small proportion of girl swimmers ever attempt them.

▶ Summary

Adolescence is a period of growth. In the course of a few years the individual undergoes changes in both size and proportion—changes that take him from a childish to a mature level. The rapidity, variety, and force of these developments are alike bewildering, even though they are sometimes exciting and satisfactory. Students vary greatly in both size and maturity during the high school years, and the differences precipitate problems. Both the schoolwork and the personalities of junior high and high school pupils are affected by the concurrent processes of growth. It is therefore essential that teachers keep in mind the physical background of adolescence so that they may not attribute to other causes those indirect manifestations that are mainly the result of mere growth.

Growth is affected by various factors, of which the most important are nutrition, sex, and family inheritance. Any prolonged deprivation has its retarding effect upon the rate of development.

During the last century, and especially during the last half-century, boys and girls have been growing taller and heavier than their earlier counterparts were at the same ages. These changes are world-wide and are presumably the result of more food, better living conditions, and better medical care.

References for Further Reading

BOOKS

Other Texts

Ausubel, *Theory and Problems of Adolescent Development* (Chap. 5).

Baller, W. R., and D. C. Charles, *The Psychology of Human Growth and Development* (New York: Holt, Rinehart and Winston, Inc., 1961), 432 pp. (Chap. 9).

Breckenridge and Vincent, *Child Development,* 4th ed. (Chap. 2 or 3).

Horrocks, *Behavior and Development* (Chap. 10).

Jersild, *Psychology of Adolescence* (Chap. 3).

Jones, *Growth and Behavior in Adolescence* (pp. 18–27).

Kuhlen, *The Psychology of Adolescent Development* (pp. 31–64).

McCandless, B. R., *Children and Adolescents* (New York: Holt, Rinehart and Winston, Inc., 1961), 521 pp. (Chap. 9).

Wattenburg, *The Adolescent Years* (Chap. 5 or 7).

Other Books

Pressey, S. L., F. P. Robinson, and J. E. Horrocks, *Psychology in Education* (New York: Harper & Row, Publishers, 1959) (Chap. 2).

Seidman, *The Adolescent: A Book of Readings,* rev. ed. (No. 9 or 11).

Stolz, H. R., and L. H. Meek, *Somatic Development of Adolescent Boys* (New York: The Macmillan Company, 1951), 557 pp. (Chap. 4, 7, or 12).

Tanner, J. M., *Growth at Adolescence,* 2d. ed. (Springfield, Ill.: Charles C Thomas Company, 1962), 325 pp. (pp. 55–77).

ARTICLES

Bayley, N., "Individual Patterns of Development," *Child Development,* 27:45–74, 1956.

Clements, E. B. M., "Changes in the Mean Stature and Weight of British Children over the Past Seventy Years," *British Medical Journal,* 2:897–902, 1953.

Eppright, E. S., and V. D. Sidwell, "Physical Measurements of Iowa School Children," *Journal of Nutrition,* 54:543–556, 1954.

Greulich, W. W., C. S. Crissman, and M. L. Turner, "The Physical Growth and Development of Children Who Survived the Atomic Bombing of Hiroshima and Nagasaki," *Journal of Pediatrics,* 43:121–145, 1953.

Hathaway, M. L., *Heights and Weights of Children and Youth in the United States,* U.S. Department of Agriculture, 1957, 131 pp.

Howe, P. E., and M. Schiller, "Growth Responses of the School Child to Changes in Diet and Environmental Factors," *Journal of Applied Psychology,* 36:51–61, 1952.

Maresh, M. M., "Linear Growth of Long Bones of Extremities from Infancy through Adolescence," *American Journal of the Diseases of Children,* 89:725–742, 1955.

Tuddenham, R. D., and M. M. Snyder, "The Physical Growth of California Boys and Girls from Birth to Eighteen Years," *University of California Publications in Child Development,* 1:183–364, 1954 (any 25 pages).

Suggested Research Problems [12]

1. Study of familial inheritance in height, weight, and body build.
2. Collections of records for individual children, to show growth rates, body build, and reactions to growth. The records are, for the most part, already in existence, and there are many articles about reactions to different growth rates, but the whole thing needs to be pulled together, especially since records and articles are likely to be about different children.

---

[12] See note, p. 1.

Chapter 3 | Skeletal Growth

THE bones of the body change not only in length and size from birth to maturity but also in density and in hardness. In addition, they change their shape. Some of the smaller bones are not present at birth, and some of the larger ones are mostly cartilage. If a baby's bones were not soft, he could never be born, because no rigid body of six to eight pounds could pass down the mother's birth canal.

▶ Bones of Hand and Wrist

The most usual method for determining the growth of the skeleton is to make X-ray photographs of the bones in the hand and wrist, and then to estimate general skeletal age from this sample. The bones that show in such pictures have their own method of growth, which must be understood before the X-ray pictures, shortly to be presented, will be intelligible.

Each finger is composed of three small straight bones which are aligned with a fourth and longer bone in the back of the hand. The thumb has only two short bones instead of three, plus a long one from its base to the wrist. The arm is composed of two long bones, one considerably thicker than the other, the ends of which appear in the pictures. In the wrist there are at maturity no less than 8 small bones marvelously fitted together and shaped to the nearer ends of the long bones which underlie the back of the hand and to the wrist end of the arm bones. There are also two tiny bones that develop during early adolescence on the first joint of the thumb. There is, then, a total of 31 small bones: 3 in each finger = 12; plus 3 long and 2 little round ones in the thumb = 17; plus 2 in the arm = 19; plus 4 in the hand = 23; plus 8 in the wrist = 31. Although there are minor variations from bone to bone, all the long bones of the fingers follow the same general pattern of growth. They become longer and the cartilage slowly changes to bone; that is, the cartilage "ossifies." As a result, the X-ray pictures show a sharper definition, because a hardened bone throws a more clearly outlined shadow than a soft cartilage. In addition to ossifying, the finger bones (called phalanges [1]) and the bones in the back of the hand (called metacarpals) acquire a sort of appendage called an epiphysis, which they subsequently absorb. Each epiph-

---

[1] The singular is phalanx.

ysis grows into a shape that fits the bone to which it becomes attached. Figure 3–1 records the growth in length and shape of five bones and of the epiphyses that eventually fuse with three of them. In column 1 are the outlines, as they appear at birth, of (A) the first phalanx of the middle finger—the phalanx nearest the body—(B) the corresponding metacarpal, (C) one of the bones in the wrist, and (E) the end of the larger of the two bones in the forearm— the radius. It will be noted that there are wide spaces between each two bones in this series.

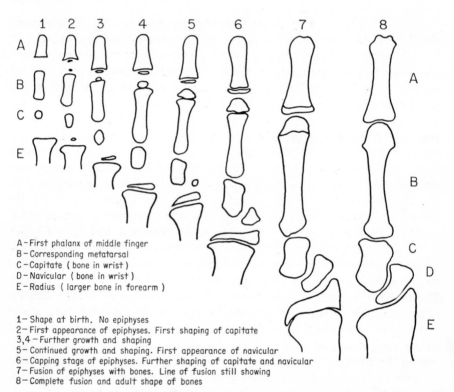

A – First phalanx of middle finger
B – Corresponding metatarsal
C – Capitate (bone in wrist)
D – Navicular (bone in wrist)
E – Radius (larger bone in forearm)

1 – Shape at birth. No epiphyses
2 – First appearance of epiphyses. First shaping of capitate
3,4 – Further growth and shaping
5 – Continued growth and shaping. First appearance of navicular
6 – Capping stage of epiphyses. Further shaping of capitate and navicular
7 – Fusion of epiphyses with bones. Line of fusion still showing
8 – Complete fusion and adult shape of bones

Fig. 3–1. Diagram showing growth of bones and epiphyses

Drawing based on X-ray photographs in T. W. Todd, *Atlas of Skeletal Maturation* (St. Louis: The C. V. Mosby Company, 1937).

The epiphysis of the phalanx first appears as a small dot. Then it flattens out into an oval disc which gradually becomes as wide as the end of the phalanx (column 5) and then develops curved edges that permit it to "cap" the end of the bone (column 6), at the same time fitting itself perfectly over its entire surface. Finally, it grows on to the phalanx. For a little while, a thin line shows along the edge of the union (column 7), but presently phalanx and epiphysis fuse into a single, solid bone (column 8). The epiphysis of the metacarpal also first appears as a dot of cartilage, but it continues to be round, gradually becoming larger (columns 2–5). It then broadens where it will attach itself to the bones, assumes a shape to fit the bone surface (columns 6–7), and finally becomes a knob. It should be noted that the adjoining surfaces of the two epiphyses have also shaped themselves to each other (column 8). The epiphysis of the radius begins as a tiny disc (column 2), becomes an elongated oval (columns 3–4), grows thicker at one extreme than at the other, and becomes shaped on one surface to fit the end of the radius and on another to fit the nearest wristbone (columns 5–8).

The wristbones follow a different pattern of growth. They begin as small round or oval lumps of cartilage and grow, not only by becoming bigger and by ossifying, but by changing their shape. Each bone grows as many distinct "faces" as may be necessary to fit it to other wristbones and to the base of whatever long bones it will move upon. Since each bone in the wrist has a different position and function from those of any other, each has its own pattern of growth. Two samples appear in C and D of Figure 3–1. Bone C begins as a dot of cartilage, becomes round and then oval, elongates, and gradually assumes an irregular shape, with a depression in one face into which a curved end of the second bone (D) fits when both are mature. The nearer end of the metacarpal and the farther face of the bone also develop so as to fit each other. Bone D does not appear until a child is between four and six years old. It goes through the same initial stages as Bone C, then becomes a triangle (column 6), and finally a sort of crescent (columns 7–8), the curves and points of which fit the shapes of adjacent bone structures. When the five bones shown in Figure 3–1 attain adult shape and size—normally at age 17 for girls and age 19 for boys—they articulate upon each other to form a series. At maturity the long bones (A, B, and E) with their fused epiphyses are several times longer than at birth, as indicated by the increasing space they occupy in the diagram.

In the X-ray photographs in Figures 3–2 to 3–9, one can trace the developments already briefly outlined and see what is meant by "skeletal age."

Babies of either sex show similar X-ray results—short, soft bones with wide spaces between them and practically no articulation. By the age of 2 years 3 months the average girl (Fig. 3–2) has developed disc-shaped epiphyses at the base of the phalanges, ball-shaped ones for the metacarpals, and an epiphysis on the radius. Two wrist-bones that were present at birth have reached the oval stage, and two more have appeared. At age 6 years 9 months (Fig. 3–4) the girl has epiphyses that are as wide or almost as wide as the bones they will fuse with, and they have begun to shape themselves to provide a close fit. The wrist now contains seven bones. The increase in ossification is shown by the increased sharpness and clearness of all the shadows. At age 12 years 3 months (Fig. 3–6) the girl's epiphyses are in the capping stage and are ready to fuse with the bones. She has no new bones in the wrist, but

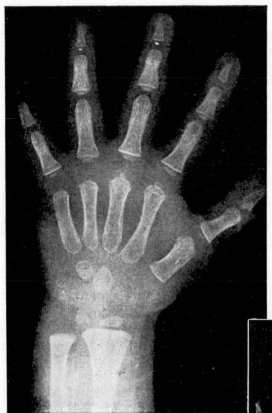

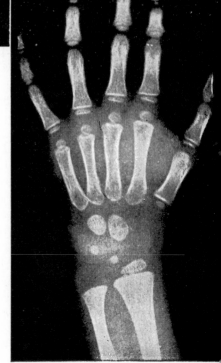

Fig. 3–3. X-ray of a boy's hand, age two years three months

Fig. 3–2. X-ray of a girl's hand, age two years three months

From T. W. Todd, *Atlas of Skeletal Maturation* (St. Louis: The C. V. Mosby Company, 1937), pp. 147, 67. Used with the permission of the publisher.

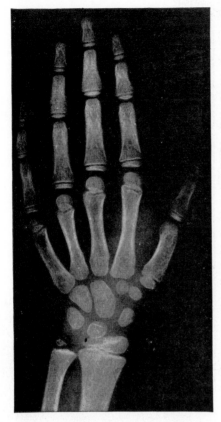 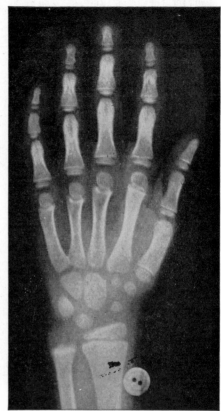

FIG. 3–4   FIG. 3–5

Fig. 3–4. X-ray of a girl's hand, age six years nine months
Fig. 3–5. X-ray of a boy's hand, age six years nine months

From T. W. Todd, *Atlas of Skeletal Maturation* (St. Louis: The C. V. Mosby Company, 1937), pp. 165, 85. Used with the permission of the publisher.

the seven have grown larger and have changed their shapes. By the end of her fourteenth year (Fig. 3–8) much fusion has taken place, although one can still see in many places the thin line between epiphysis and bone.

Figures 3–3, 3–5, 3–7, and 3–9 give a similar series for boys. Figure 3–3 should be compared with Figure 3–2. At least five epiphyses in the boy's hand are lacking and another five are mere dots. The two earliest wristbones are not quite oval, and no others have developed. The bones are appreciably less dense than those of the 2-year-old girl. At age 6 years 9 months (Fig. 3–5) the epiphyses of the phalanges are neither as long nor as shaped as those of the girl (Fig. 3–4) and the metacarpal epiphyses are rounder; there is also more unossified area in the boy's wrist than in the girl's. The boy's bones are,

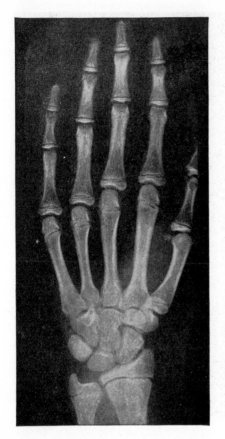 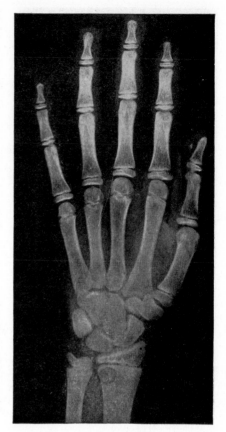

FIG. 3–6   FIG. 3–7

Fig. 3–6. X-ray of a girl's hand, age twelve years nine months
Fig. 3–7. X-ray of a boy's hand, age twelve years nine months

From T. W. Todd, *Atlas of Skeletal Maturation* (St. Louis: The C. V. Mosby Company, 1937), pp. 189, 109. Used with the permission of the publisher.

however, already a bit bigger than the girl's. This difference in size becomes steadily more marked with age. Comparison of Figure 3–7 with Figure 3–6 shows the boy to be still less mature than the girl, since there is less capping, less fusion, and less shaping. The bones of the hand in Figure 3–9 show some fusion of the metacarpals with their epiphyses, but very little elsewhere. The average boy reaches the mature stage, such as appears for the girls in Figure 3–8 about two years later than the average girl. At maturity there is almost no empty space left in the wrist, and the bones have become dense enough to throw a clearly defined shadow on the X-ray plate. At age 14 a boy's hand is appreciably larger than the girl's, and the bones are equally dense, but the fusion is less complete.

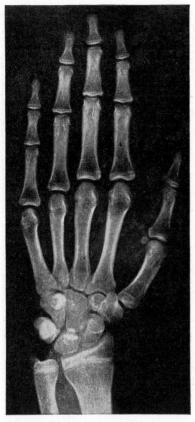 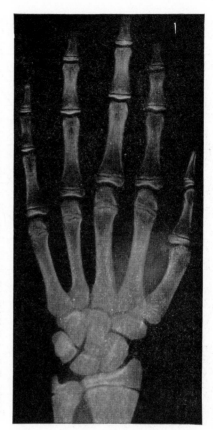

FIG. 3–8   FIG. 3–9

Fig. 3–8. X-ray of a girl's hand, age fourteen years nine months

Fig. 3–9. X-ray of a boy's hand, age fourteen years nine months

From T. W. Todd, *Atlas of Skeletal Maturation* (St. Louis: The C. V. Mosby Company, 1937), pp. 197, 117. Used with the permission of the publisher.

There is a marked relationship between the age of puberty and skeletal age. At age 7 the girls who—as later proved—matured between 11½ and 12½ already had a skeletal age of over 8, and they remained consistently in skeletal age from one and a half to two years ahead of their chronological age. Girls who matured between 12½ and 14½ were with equal consistency from six months to a year retarded in skeletal age after their seventh year. Girls with accelerated, normal, or retarded ages of menarche maintained their relative positions to each other during the entire decade from 7 through 17, and showed still over a year and a half of variation in skeletal age at the last measurement.[2]

[2] F. K. Shuttleworth, "Sexual Maturity and the Skeletal Development of Girls Ages 6 to 19," *Monographs of the Society for Research in Child Development,* Vol. 3, No. 2, Serial No. 5, 1938.

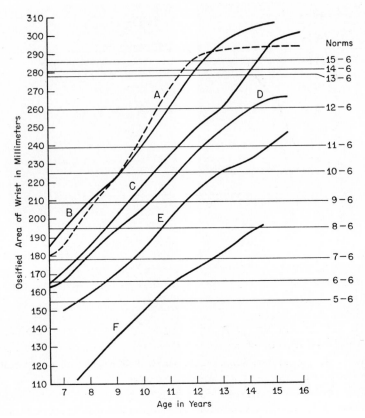

Fig. 3–10. Individual curves of skeletal growth

From P. Cattell, "Preliminary Report on the Measurement of Ossification of the Hand and Wrist," *Human Biology,* 6:461, 1934. Used with the permission of the publisher.

There are large individual variations in skeletal growth. A few individual curves for girls, based upon consecutive measurement of the same individuals, are shown in Figure 3–10. The measures are in terms of the calcified area in the bones of the wrist. The norms for this measurement are indicated by lines drawn across the figure. At age 8, Girl B had a calcified area in her wrist above that of the average girl of age 9½, whereas Girl F's wrist area at the same age was well below that of a normal 5-year-old. At age 14 the corresponding variation for these two girls was from the average of age 8½ to well beyond the average of age 15½. Girl A reached what appears to be her maximum development between ages 12 and 13. Girls E and F were still growing at 16, but Girls C and D showed signs of stopping growth between 14 and 15. Girl F at all ages was extremely retarded. At age 14½, the last measurement made, she had the skeletal age of 8½ years.

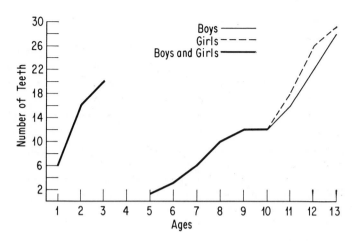

Fig. 3–11. Eruption of teeth

Left—baby teeth   Right—permanent teeth

Based on R. S. Nanda, "Eruption of Human Teeth," *American Journal of Orthodontics,* 46:363–378, 1960.

As may be seen, the comparison of X-rays is a relatively difficult and not too accurate method of measuring skeletal age, because it rests upon personal estimates. Even two experts can differ in the over-all interpretation of a plate. Moreover, the films are heavy and expensive. During the last decade a method has been devised for assigning numbers to the various critical parts of each bone in the hand—or knee or foot, as the case may be—and then totalling the numbers to obtain a single figure, which in turn can be translated into skeletal age. The film is still evaluated but in detail rather than in general, with resultant less chance for disagreement. This technique is still being developed, but it gives promise of great usefulness. The beginning of a comparative growth curve for boys and girls has already appeared,[3] although it does not go beyond age 5½ as yet, because the results are based on successive measurements of the same children, and one has to wait for the children to grow. The more rapid development of the girls was already evident at 6 months and became increasingly clear with each passing year.

▶ **Growth of the Teeth**

The teeth also have characteristic growth rates. The baby teeth begin to appear during the first year of life, and all 20 of them are usually in evidence by the end of the third year. The permanent teeth be-

[3] R. M. Acheson, "A Method of Assessing Skeletal Maturity from Radiographs," *Journal of Anatomy,* 88:498–508, 1954.

gin pushing out the baby teeth when a child is 5 or 6 years old. From that time on until the early years of adolescence a child acquires one or more teeth each year. The 13-year-old has usually 28 of his 32 teeth. The general course of development is reflected in Figure 3–11. Boys and girls show no differences until the girls enter their period of preadolescence, when their curve begins to rise more sharply. If the curves were continued a few years longer, a similar rise for the boys would take place and by age 20 there would again be no significant differences between the sexes. The second molars usually erupt at the beginning of adolescence. Their appearance is one of the surest signs that puberty is close. The third molars, or wisdom teeth, erupt at some time during or after adolescence. The cutting of these molars is often a painful process, and they may cause both dental trouble and emotional distress when they arrive.

There is great variability in the ages for the eruption of any one tooth and in the gradual development of each tooth before it emerges,[4] as determined by X-rays of the jaw. Although averages per age are calculated and are of use as general norms, one should expect the same wide variation in the gradual ossification and eventual eruption of teeth as one finds in any other physical measurements.

▶ **Growth in Facial Bones and Features**

An individual's face also grows, slowly in childhood and then more rapidly in the early years of adolescence. The nose and mouth widen, the nose becomes longer and more prominent, and the jaw juts out farther. The upper part of the face usually grows faster than the lower, the jaw being commonly the last feature to attain its adult size and angle. Although some faces grow in a symmetrical fashion, most do not. Adolescents typically have unbalanced and asymmetrical faces, which are sources of much embarrassment to them. Because the nose generally begins to grow earlier than the rest of the face, the 13- or 14-year-old child seems destined for a while to imitate Cyrano de Bergerac. Matters are not helped by increases in the height of the forehead, since these changes make the upper part of the face too heavy. They also make the eyes seem smaller, although actually these do not change in size at all. In an infant's face, the eyes look enormous; in a child's face, they seem large; in an adolescent's face, they have merely assumed their adult relation to the rest of the face. It is usually a year or two and sometimes longer before the chin develops and nicely balances the already-mature nose, giving the face the underlying bone structure of maturity.

---

[4] S. A. Garn, *et al.,* "The Sex Differences in Tooth Calcification," *Journal of Dental Research,* 37:561–567, 1958, and S. A. Garn, *et al.,* "Variability in Tooth Formation," *Journal of Dental Research,* 38:135–148, 1959.

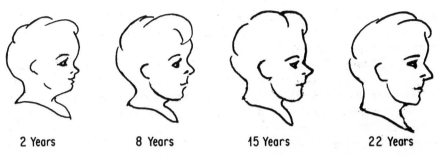

| 2 Years | 8 Years | 15 Years | 22 Years |

Fig. 3–12. Changes in the facial proportions of one boy

Another source of asymmetry of the face during adolescence is its tendency to grow in length before it grows in width.[5]

Figure 3–12 shows a series of profiles for the same boy at four different ages: 2, 8, 15, and 22. The forehead is at first bulging and then flattish, and then again bulges, but in a different way. The nose becomes longer and much thicker. The childish depression just above the nose fills out, and then the jutting forward of the brows produces a concavity of a different shape and type. In the adult profile, the features are larger, more angular, and stand out further than in the childish ones, thus giving the face greater depth. In early childhood the lips are flat, and they do not become full and curved until fairly late in the development of the face. The chin is the last feature to change from youthful to adult size and shape.

▶ **Summary**

The bones of the body grow in length, width, and thickness as children mature. The most characteristic developments during adolescence are the lengthening of all the long bones and the final articulation of all the bones at their respective joints, changes which underlie the increases in height and strength. The teeth show a regular if somewhat variable appearance, the second molar arriving just before the beginning of adolescence and the third molar toward the end of the period. The face changes a great deal, loses its childish contours, and by the end of adolescence has acquired adult proportions.

---

[5] Many of the statements in this paragraph are based upon measurements by A. Bjork, *The Face in Profile* (Lund, Sweden: Berlingska Boktryckerist, 1947), 180 pp., and M. S. Goldstein, "Development of the Head in the Same Individuals," *Human Biology,* 10:197–219, 1939.

References for Further Reading

B O O K S

Other Texts

Horrocks, *Behavior and Development* (Chap. 12).

Other Books

Greulich, W. W., and S. I. Pyle, *Radiographic Atlas of Skeletal Development of Hand and Wrist* (Stanford, Calif.: Stanford University Press, 1950), 190 pp. (pp. 1–29).

Tanner, J. M., R. H. Whitehouse, and M. J. R. Healy, *Standards for Skeletal Maturity Based on a Study of 3,000 British Children, II: The Scoring System for All 28 Bones of the Hand and Wrist* (London: Institute of Child Health, University of London, 1961) (any 25 pages, but preferably the description of the scoring method).

A R T I C L E S

Acheson, R. M., and C. W. Dupertuis, "The Relationship between Physique and Rate of Skeletal Maturation in Boys," *Human Biology,* 29:167–193, 1957.

Dimick, A., and P. Wartmann, "Calcification of the Mandibular Third Molar and Its Relation to Skeletal and Chronological Age in Children," *Child Development,* 27:459–473, 1956.

Falkner, F., "Skeletal Maturation: An Appraisal of Concept and Method," *American Journal of Physical Anthropology,* N.S. 16:381–396, 1958.

Taylor, C. and G. G. Thompson, "Age Trends in the Preferences for Certain Facial Proportions," *Child Development,* 26:97–102, 1955.

Suggested Research Problems [6]

1. Selection from X-rays of children and adolescents with advanced or retarded skeletal age and comparison of the two groups in regard to (a) strength, (b) personality, (c) adjustment, to determine if skeletal age is a factor, and, if so, how important a factor.

---

[6] See note, p. 11.

Chapter 4 | Growth in Strength and in Various Athletic Skills

THE materials of this chapter include measures of co-ordination, agility, strength, and simple athletic abilities such as running and jumping. At the end there is also some discussion of the indirect effects upon personality, social status, and adjustment of having or not having such fundamental motor skills.

Coordination and Agility The development of motor coordination, balance, and general agility during childhood, preadolescence, and adolescence has been shown by several sets of results, each indicative of a different phase of growth. One investigator measured the ability of children to keep their balance when walking on a rail. Each child walked the full length and back three times, and received one point for the completion of each length without falling off. The highest possible score was, therefore, 6 points. The results are shown in Figure 4–1. The girls were slightly superior to the boys in the early ages, probably because they were developing at a

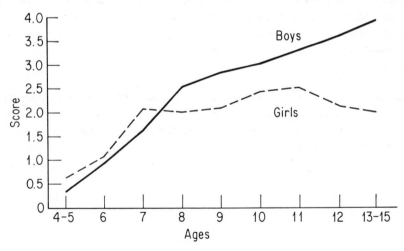

Fig. 4–1. Development of the sense of balance

Based on G. W. Cron and N. H. Pronko, "Development of the Sense of Balance in School Children," *Journal of Educational Research*, 51:33–37, 1957.

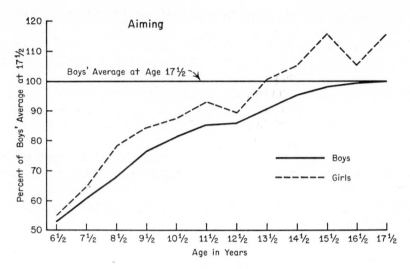

Fig. 4–2. Growth in aiming

From J. E. Anderson, *The Psychology of Development and Personal Adjustment* (New York: Holt, Rinehart and Winston, Inc., 1949), 720 pp., pp. 138, 139. Used with the permission of the publisher.

faster rate than the boys. In late childhood the girls showed a plateau, while the boys continued to improve. In the early adolescent years the scores for the girls decreased until they returned to their own 7-year level. Probably this loss is due primarily to loss of interest. The boys continued to improve at each age level. As a result of masculine improvement and feminine indifference, the distance between the two sexes increased with each year.

Another investigator measured the accuracy in aiming of youngsters between the ages of 6½ and 17½. The average scores on this test appear in Figure 4–2. The score of the 17-year-olds was taken as the standard and other scores were expressed in terms of the percent of each of the male scores at this age. In aiming, the girls exceeded the boys at all ages. They reached the standard at 13½, and from then on scored appreciably above it. Aiming is a skill which requires relatively little strength, but it does take patience, a trait in which many girls excel because they do more things requiring small, accurate eye-hand adjustments than do boys. And they are more mature in all ways, including their eyesight. In their ability to handle a basketball the boys were slightly superior to girls during middle and late childhood, but after the girls entered puberty their rate of improvement became slow while that of the boys increased markedly (Figure 4–3). Since relatively little strength is involved, the difference is due in large measure to a greater familiarity with handling basketballs on the part of the boys, to better leverage, and to greater interest. It is probable that if one compared playing skills among members of basketball teams for boys and for girls the differences would be small.

Although handwriting is not an athletic activity, it certainly consists of several motor skills. Moreover, from a research point of view, it has the great advantage of being a complex of skills acquired more or less adequately by all children and used continually by both children and adolescents. It requires fine hand, arm, and finger coordination rather than strength. In a modern study of the subject, growth in the normal speed of writing was studied at the elementary and secondary school levels. The results by age appear in Figure 4–4. During the childhood years the boys excelled, then they paralleled the girls for three years, but subsequently dropped considerably behind them,

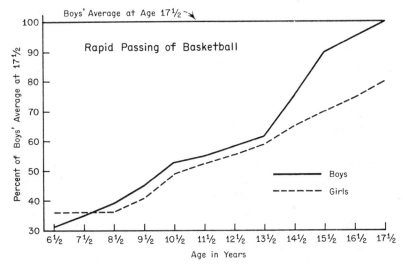

Fig. 4–3. Growth in rapid passing of a basketball

From J. E. Anderson, *The Psychology of Development and Personal Adjustment* (New York: Holt, Rinehart and Winston, Inc., 1949), pp. 138 and 139. Used with the permission of the publisher.

averaging at the end 33 letters per minute slower. The girls showed a much more regular type of development than the boys. In theory, they should have been superior at the early ages as well as later on, since they develop faster; but perhaps their attention to minutiae—whether inherent in feminine nature or handed down by each generation of mothers to their daughters—may have slowed them down in the early ages, when the differences at most would have been small. The differences in the later years probably arise from the much greater physical maturity of girls throughout early and well into middle adolescence, with a resultant better control. It may be, although it has not been proved, that by the time a girl becomes a woman, she has learned to com-

pensate for her inferior muscular equipment by great consistency of performance, by careful avoidance of errors, and by painstaking attention to detail.

Strength Probably the most satisfactory study of strength in adolescence is
one that follows the development, from ages 11 to
17½, of 89 boys and 87 girls. The number of cases is relatively small, but
the same children were measured every six months, with the result that one

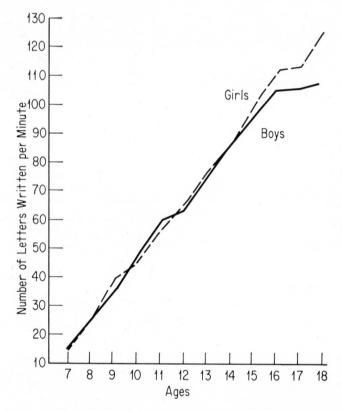

Fig. 4–4. Development of speed in handwriting

Based on Vinh-Bang, *Evolution de l'écriture de l'enfant à l'adulte* (Paris: Delachaux et
Niestlé, 1959), 227 pp., p. 62.

gets a picture of longitudinal growth. Results are given in Figure 4–5 for (1)
strength of grip, for (2) exerting a pull when the arms are held at shoulder
level with the elbows slightly bent and the registering instrument grasped by
both hands at chest level, and for (3) exerting a thrust in the same position.
In strength of grip boys are superior to girls at all ages, but the significant

differences do not appear until the boys begin to mature. The difference between boys and girls at age 11 was 4 pounds of pressure; at 17 it was 20 pounds.

In the pull-and-thrust tests, girls were superior to boys at age 11 by 2 and 7 pounds, respectively. For these tests leverage is especially important, and girls of 11 or 12 have outgrown boys in length of arm, width of shoulder, and weight because they are already preadolescent while boys are not. Their

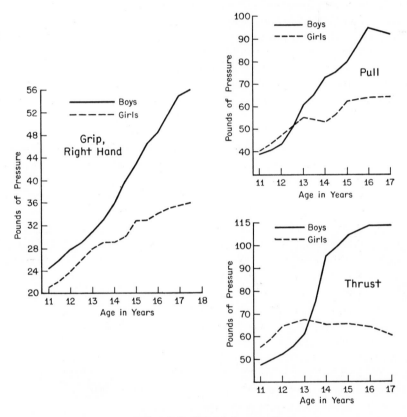

Fig. 4–5. Growth in strength

From H. E. Jones, "Motor Performance and Growth: A Developmental Study of Static Dynamometric Strength," *University of California Publications in Child Development,* 1:35–36, 1949. Used with the permission of the publisher.

ability to thrust is very nearly as good at 11 as it is at 17. Boys, however, make enormous gains in both tests after the age of 13. In all cases the great increase in strength occurs during the years when the largest proportion of boys become mature.

The recorded great differences between the two sexes in strength is due in the main to variations in the size of muscle. One investigator [1] matched girls and boys without respect to age upon the basis of muscle and bone growth in the leg, as shown by X-rays. Between these matched groups there were no differences in any test that involved the leg muscles. In the force of leg thrust and in the height of the vertical jump the two groups were equal, but the boys showed greater hand strength than the girls, presumably because the pairs were matched on the basis of leg, not hand, growth.

Rate of maturity has a great influence especially among boys; at all ages from 11 to 17, the early maturing boys were stronger than boys who matured late. The effect is presumably indirect and operates through the stimulation of growth, as boys are maturing, so that their muscles become stronger and their leverage greater, as their arms and legs increase in length and their hands and feet in size. The same is true of girls, but to a much smaller degree.

Athletic Skills   The development of athletic skill obviously depends upon growth in the length and power of legs and arms, upon increases in muscular strength, upon improvements in coordination, balance, and upon general agility. One investigator, who followed the development of children through the adolescent years from 12 years 9 months to 16 years 9 months, measured each half year the speed with which they could run, the height to which they could jump and reach,[2] the distance to which they could throw a ball, and the width of their broad jump. The results appear in Figure 4–6. In all four forms of exercise the boys made marked improvement, but the girls ran more slowly and could jump a shorter distance as they grew older. Their ability to throw a ball and to jump upward increased a little. The difference between the sexes became greater with the passage of time. At 12 years 9 months the inferiority of the girls was, respectively, on the four tests, a fourth of a second in the dash, half an inch in the upward jump, two inches in the broad jump, and forty feet in the ball throw; four and a half years later it was 1½ seconds, 4½ inches, 2 feet, and nearly 70 feet, respectively. With each passing year after age 13, the girls showed an actual loss in some abilities, presumably because their interests had become social, and they were far more anxious to attract boys than to compete with them.

---

[1] L. Rarick and J. A. J. Thompson, "Roentgenographic Measurement of Leg Muscle Size and Ankle Extensor Strength, in Seven-year-old Children," *Research Quarterly of the American Association of Health and Physical Education*, 27:321–332, 1956. See also E. Asmussen and K. Heebol-Nielson, "Physical Performance and Growth in Children. Influence of Sex, Age, and Intelligence," *Journal of Applied Physiology*, 8:371–380, 1956.

[2] The "jump-and-reach" test was as follows: a child stood facing a wall; with a piece of chalk he made a mark as high up as he could reach with his heels still on the floor; then he jumped and reached, making another mark at the height of his leap. The upward jump was measured by the distance between marks.

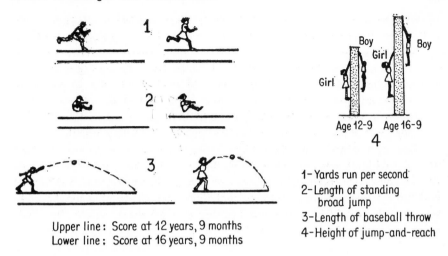

1- Yards run per second
2- Length of standing broad jump
3- Length of baseball throw
4- Height of jump-and-reach

Upper line: Score at 12 years, 9 months
Lower line: Score at 16 years, 9 months

Fig. 4–6. Changes in four athletic skills

Based on A. Espenschade, "Motor Performance in Adolescence, Including Study of Relationships with Measurements of Physical Growth and Maturity," *Monograph of the Society for Research in Child Development*, Vol. V, No. 1, 1940, 126 pp. This reference is old, but the authors were unable to find any more recent study that was as good.

At the upper end of the distribution of athletic abilities, it would seem that each generation of young people is improving upon the previous one. Thus, the last two Olympic teams have included boys and girls from 12 to 15 years of age, and it is not uncommon at the present time for girls to retire at 17 or 18 from amateur competition, and boys 2 or 3 years later. There is not much difference between the records for high school boys and girls and those for college students or even Olympic athletes of previous generations.[3] For example, there was in 1958 just one-tenth of a second between the high school record and the world record for the 100-yard dash. The high school jumpers in 1958 surpassed all Olympic records up until 1956 and the pole-vaulters those up to 1958. It is only in the events that require great strength (the hammer throw, for example) or great endurance (the distance runs) that men of about 25 can consistently surpass adolescent boys by more than the narrowest of margins. The superiority of the present youthful athlete over those of previous generations applies also to the Little Leaguers in baseball. A group of these youngsters at 10 or 11 years of age tested at the average of 16-year-olds in running and some of them could swing a bat at a rate of 100 miles per hour. (The rate for big league players is 115 miles.) The above remarks apply, of course, only to those in the highest one percent of athletic ability. Presumably the speed, agility, and control of boys and girls

[3] J. C. Hale, "Changing Growth Patterns in the American Child," *Education*, 78:467–470, 1958.

in the last years of childhood and the early years of adolescence is one more indication of the greatly increased rate at which the present younger generation is developing.

It is only recently that people have realized the extreme importance of size, strength, and athletic ability, especially for boys, in the determination of social status among children and adolescents. American culture—indeed, Anglo-Saxon culture in general—puts a high premium upon sheer physical superiority. It is not surprising, therefore, that a big, strong, athletic boy feels satisfied with himself and finds himself able to achieve popularity and admiration without any particular effort. The race has been won for him, and he can relax. The path to social success also is therefore smoothed for him and, unless there is some extreme maladjustment either at home or in his schoolwork, he will be a popular member of adolescent society. Boys who score high in tests of strength and agility tend to be rated by their peers as especially fit for leadership.[4] The short, slender, weak-muscled boy of frail build, who cannot meet the competition of his peers, is forced into an uncomfortable position because the clearest road to popularity, through outstanding athletic success, is closed to him. To this situation he may make a number of responses. He may withdraw completely from competition, form perhaps one or two friendships with other noncompetitors, and become a spectator of the life that rushes past him. He may so resent his inferiority that he becomes bitter and as verbally aggressive as he dares to be. Or he may seek a compensation by becoming a buffoon—which gets him attention and sometimes admiration; by gaining academic success—which gets him occasional admiration and very little attention from his age-mates; or by fawning upon the bigger boys, trying to pick up a few pale rays of reflected glory as a hanger-on. He may become sufficiently absorbed and sufficiently successful in the school chorus, on the school newspaper, or in school politics to forget almost that he will never be a football hero.

Sometimes a restricted kind of athletic success can be achieved by a frail, underdeveloped boy, or even by a tubby, fat one, if the school's athletic program is wide enough. Thus, anyone can learn to swim, and both the slender and the overweight lad, or lassie for that matter, have natural buoyancy as compared to the heavily muscled mesomorph who cannot float. The small, slight boy can gain admiration as a diver, especially as the springboard will throw his 100 pounds much higher than it will throw the 180 pounds of a big boy, and will thus give him more chance to do something spectacular and attention-getting. The plunge gives the overweight boy his chance, because the distance an individual can go is directly proportional to weight, once he has mastered the technique of hitting the water at the right angle. If a boy

---

[4] K. R. Bull, "An Investigation into the Relationship between Physique, Motor Capacity, and Certain Temperamental Traits," *British Journal of Education,* 28:149–154, 1958.

is not too small there is a chance that he can play shortstop on the baseball team; to be sure, a long reach is desirable, but at the high school level of performance, its lack can be compensated for by extra agility. If a boy is tall but too slender for the rougher sports, he may succeed either in tennis, in which his extra leverage will offset his lack of strength, or in fencing, because he has an unusually long reach and lunge but presents a narrow target. The one sport in which one small boy in a school is definitely in demand is rowing —and the smaller the coxswain the better. Unless a boy has some crippled condition or a heart deficiency that prevents even mild exercise, he can find something in which he excels, provided the offerings of the school are sufficiently varied. A step in the right direction has been made by organizing separate school teams in basketball, football, and baseball on the basis of weight. A boy can therefore become a star quarterback on the hundred-pound team, have the fun of playing, and achieve a moderate amount of respect. Of course, he would rather be on the A squad with the biggest boys, but success on the E squad provides a not-too-unsatisfying compromise. What has been said of boys may equally well be applied to girls who wish to achieve athletic success. It is no accident that most outstanding feminine divers are small; they cannot race against long-limbed girls, but they have excellent success in diving. However, many small, weak girls need no compensation, because "weakness" is an accepted and even admired feminine characteristic. All a girl has to do is to play up being "helpless" and she can achieve popularity among boys—provided she is a likable person; in short, her lack of strength makes her boy friends feel bigger and stronger than they are and flatters their masculine ego because they have someone to "protect." The small, weak boy has no such comfortable retreat open to him.

One investigator of strength during adolescence compared numerous estimates and measures of emotional adjustment, personality, and social status for the ten strongest boys and the ten weakest.[5] Five of the former occupied positions of popularity and high prestige among their age-mates, four showed a satisfactory status, and only one was unpopular. Six showed excellent emotional adjustment, three were about average, and one had several emotional problems. They were all in good health and all were successful athletes. The ten weakest boys present a marked contrast. All had relatively poor health. No one belonged to any athletic team. Six were so shy and unsure of themselves that they were practically isolated from their fellows and had no social status at all. Four were a bit more assertive but did not succeed in achieving more than a slight degree of prestige, which they were unable to maintain as they grew older. Over the six years of the study, only one showed a consistently good emotional adjustment, three were about average but with evi-

---

[5] H. E. Jones, "Motor Performance and Growth: A Developmental Study of Static Dynamometric Strength," *University of California Publications in Child Development,* Vol. 1, No. 1, 1949, 181 pp., p. 38.

dence of some tension, and the remaining six were markedly maladjusted emotionally.

There is thus evidence that mere size and strength form one important basis for adequate social and emotional adjustment. Naturally, as in any comparative situation, some individuals must occupy positions at the bottom of the series, but if teachers and parents are aware of this possible source of difficulty, they may be able to minimize the effects upon personality and to guide the smaller boys away from destructive expressions of aggression on the one hand, and, on the other, into such compensatory activities as may be open to them, so that they too may find a place in the sun of their age-mates' admiration.

▶ **Summary**

In general, boys and girls tend to be about equally strong and agile during childhood, but with the coming of adolescence, the differences in favor of the boys become increasingly great, while the girls either do not increase or actually lose ground. There is great prestige value in strength and athletic skill for a boy, but very little for a girl in a co-educational high school. Recent generations of both boys and girls who are especially competent in athletics nearly equal the best scores of young men and women of previous generations. If the school's program of sports is sufficiently wide, almost every adolescent who wants to be successful in an athletic endeavor can find something that he can do well.

References for Further Reading

BOOKS

Other Texts

Ausubel, *Theory and Problems of Adolescent Development* (Chap. 5 or 6).
Breckenridge and Vincent, *Child Development,* 4th ed. (Chap. 7 or 8).
Garrison, K. C., *Growth and Development,* 2d. ed. (New York: David McKay Company, Inc., 1959), 559 pp. (pp. 49–76).
Horrocks, *Behavior and Development* (pp. 414–427).
Jersild, *Psychology of Adolescence* (Chap. 4).
Kuhlen, *Psychology of Adolescent Development* (pp. 44–52).

Other Books

Jones, H. E., "Motor Performance and Growth: A Developmental Study of Static Dynamometric Strength," *University of California Publications in Child Development,* Vol. 1, No. 1, 1949, 181 pp. (any two of Chaps. 1, 3, 4 and 7).
Stolz and Meek, *Somatic Development of Adolescent Boys* (Chap. 13).

ARTICLES

Asmussen, E., and K. Heeboll-Nielsen, "Physical Performance and Growth in Children. Influence of Sex, Age, and Intelligence," *Journal of Applied Psychology*, 40:471–480, 1956.

Cron, G. W., and N. H. Pronko, "Development of the Sense of Balance in School Children," *Journal of Educational Research*, 51:33–37, 1957.

Hale, C. J., "Changing Growth Patterns in the American Child," *Education*, 78:467–470, 1958.

Jones, H. E., and N. Bayley, "Physical Maturing among Boys as Related to Behavior," *Journal of Educational Psychology*, 41:120–148, 1950.

McGraw, L. W., and J. W. Tolbert, "Sociometric Status and Athletic Ability of Junior High School Boys," *Research Quarterly of the American Association of Health, Physical Education, and Recreation*, 24:72–80, 1953.

Miller, W. K., "Achievement Levels in Basketball Skills for Women's Physical Education Majors," *Research Quarterly of the American Association of Health, Physical Education, and Recreation*, 25:450–455, 1954.

Rarick, L., and J. A. J. Thompson, "Roentgenographic Measurement of Leg Muscle Size and Ankle Extensor Strength of Seven-year-old Children," *Research Quarterly of the American Association of Health, Physical Education, and Recreation*, 27:321–332, 1956.

Schonfeld, W. A., "Inadequate Masculine Physique as a Factor in Personality Development of Adolescent Boys," *Psychosomatic Medicine*, 12:49–54, 1950.

Suggested Research Problems [6]

1. Further longitudinal studies are needed to trace the development of boys and girls in all kinds of simple games and physical skills. The present "fitness" programs are in need of such scientifically determined standards.

2. Teachers need a list of physical activities that are possible with the usual school equipment and are related to series of simple tests that determine each child's physical capacities at the moment, so that they can use playground games more effectively. There should also be lists of activities appropriate for pupils with different types of handicap.

---

[6] See note, p. 11.

Chapter 5 | Physiological Growth

W<small>HILE</small> the numerous changes already described in bone and muscles are in progress, other developments are taking place in the circulatory, digestive, respiratory, neural, and glandular systems of the body. Many of these changes are of vital importance in conditioning the behavior of the individual boy or girl.

▶ Growth in Circulatory, Respiratory, Digestive, and Neural Systems

Circulatory System   The heart has its own growth rate, as do the other organs of the body. At age 6, it is four to five times as heavy as at birth; at 12, it is seven times as heavy; and at 18, it is twelve times as heavy. During the years of adolescence, the weight of the heart nearly doubles. In childhood, boys' hearts are a little larger than girls'; from age 9 to 13, girls' are larger; from 13 on, boys' hearts grow rapidly, while girls' grow very slowly and not much more. The veins and arteries do not increase in size at the same rate that the heart does. Before adolescence, they have already reached a more nearly adult size than has the heart; and they grow more slowly than it does during the early years of adolescence. Thus, during childhood a small heart pumps blood through relatively large arteries and veins, but during adolescence, a large heart pumps blood through relatively small blood vessels. This condition may impose strain upon the pump for a few years, especially among rapidly growing boys.

Changes in both the size and the tension of the arteries are reflected in measures of blood pressure. From childhood to late adolescence the blood pressure rises steadily from 80 to 85 millimeters at age 6 to age 17, when it levels off at 110–120 for boys and 100–105 for girls, as indicated in Figure 5–1. Sex differences up to age 10 are not significant. From age 10 to 13, girls show a slightly higher average than boys. After age 13, however, the average blood pressure for boys tends to rise above that for girls; and after 16 there is a noticeable difference, because the boys continue to show an increase, while the pressure of the girls decreases until about age 20, when both sexes have reached their normal adult level.

In contrast to blood pressure, the average pulse rate decreases with age for both sexes, but the average for girls is at all ages several beats above that

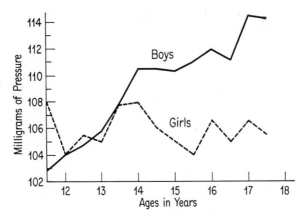

Fig. 5-1. Systolic blood pressure during adolescence

Based on N. W. Shock, "Basal Blood Pressure and Pulse Rate in Adolescents," *American Journal of Diseases of Children,* 68:16–22, 1944.

of boys. This development is shown in Figure 5–2a. The difference between the two sexes becomes even more marked if the pulse rate is taken one minute after a prescribed unit of exercise (Figure 5–2b). In this second comparison, the girls' hearts are consistently about 20 beats above the boys'.

Physiological maturity has a marked effect upon both blood pressure

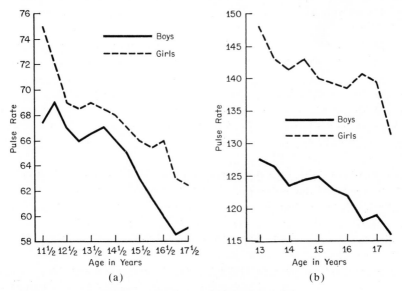

Fig. 5-2. Pulse rate during adolescence

N. W. Shock, "Physiological Changes in Adolescence," *Forty-third Yearbook of the National Society for the Study of Education,* 1:59, 66, 1944. Used with the permission of the publisher.

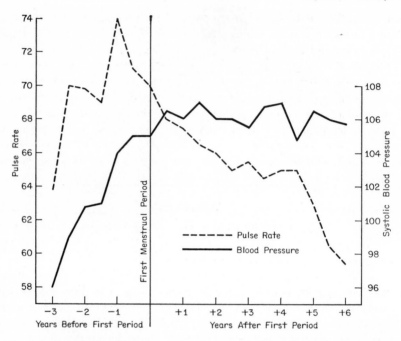

Fig. 5–3. Systolic blood pressure and pulse rate of girls before and after puberty

From N. W. Shock, "Physiological Changes in Adolescence," *Forty-third Yearbook* of the National Society for the Study of Education, 1:59, 66, 1944. Used with the permission of the publisher.

and pulse rate. The changes may be seen most easily in girls, since their first menstrual period affords conclusive evidence of maturity at a particular time, whereas there is no such single criterion for boys. Figure 5–3 shows the results for fifty girls, tested every six months for many years, for both blood pressure and pulse rate. The scale for reading the former curve is at the right of the figure; that for the latter is at the left. When the data are tabulated with reference to each girl's first period and without respect to chronological age, it can be seen at once that blood pressure rose sharply during the three years before puberty and for six months thereafter, and then settled to a new level at about 106. In contrast, the pulse rate, which had been climbing irregularly but rapidly for the years just preceding the first menstrual period, fell off sharply and steadily for the next six years. Physiological maturity thus operated to stabilize the upward trend of blood pressure and to reverse that of pulse rate.

Respiratory System   During childhood the lungs grow slowly, but in early adolescence they increase rapidly in size, especially among boys. Girls have smaller lungs, and most of them do not develop their maximum capacity through constant indulgence in active games. A common measure is called vital capacity and consists of measuring the amount of air that can be exhaled from the lungs after one has drawn in a big breath. Figure 5–4 gives curves for both boys and girls from age 5½ to 17½. The boys exceed the girls slightly in childhood, but during the adolescent years their larger lungs and their greater amount of heavy exercise increase their demands for air over the amount needed by girls, and they therefore have more to exhale.

In general, adolescent lungs are quite capable of handling any burden that is likely to be put upon them. Although they have not yet reached adult volume, they will develop in proportion to the demands of the organism. Except for actual disease (mainly tuberculosis), they are not likely to become abnormal.

Digestive System During adolescence the organs of digestion undergo considerable growth. The stomach becomes longer and increases in capacity. Because of the rapid growth rate in the size of the body, the adolescent needs more nourishment than formerly, and because of the enlarged capacity of his stomach, he craves more food. The net result is usually a tremendous appetite for three or four years. In some adolescents the perpetually hungry condition is so marked that it seems practically impossible for

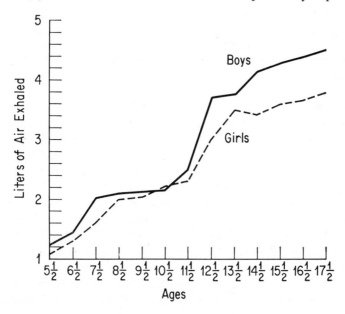

Fig. 5–4. Vital capacity

Based on B. G. Ferris, J. L. Whittenberger, J. R. Gallagher, "Maximum Breathing Capacity and Vital Capacity of Male Children and Adolescents," *Pediatrics,* 9:659–570, 1952; and B. G. Ferris and C. W. Smith, "Maximum Breathing Capacity and Vital Capacity of Female Children and Adolescents," *Pediatrics,* 12:341–353, 1953.

them ever to get enough to eat, although they consume more food in twenty-four hours than adults need in twice that time.

Digestive difficulties during adolescence are doubtless due partly to mere overloading of the stomach, partly to deficiencies of vitamins or calcium, and partly to the marked increase in the secretion of acids by the stomach during adolescence. Furthermore, the boy or girl usually begins to eat meals away from home during this period. Adolescents can be trusted to make a lunch of hot dogs, chili con carne, or hamburgers and French fries, washed down with Coca-Colas or milkshakes, and followed by banana splits or strawberry waffles. It requires the entire period of adolescence for most people to learn to eat a reasonably balanced meal on their own initiative—if they ever do learn. In many adolescent groups, it is considered a social virtue to eat absurd combinations of food at highly unconventional and irregular hours. Such reactions may contribute to emancipation from home control and to status among one's peers, but they also contribute to stomach-aches and other digestive disturbances.

Nervous System   The number of different fibers in the nervous system is practically complete at birth, but not all neural functions are present at that time. So far as gross size is concerned, the nervous system develops very little during adolescence. What growth there is, then, is confined to further development of the fibers, in both length and thickness, and to further contacts among them. It is probable that the complexity of the brain—that is, the total number of contacts between fibers—is greatly increased during the early years of adolescence.

The facts in regard to neural growth are, in any case, not as important to the teacher as the effects. The increased ability to think and, in particular, to generalize is probably the result of the increased complexity of the brain. To be sure, part of the ability to think and reason comes from the individual experiences each person has as he grows older. It is, moreover, not true that children are completely without ability to reason. Their capacities are doubtless underestimated because they sometimes reach erroneous results through their lack of knowledge. For example, the nephew of one of the writers presented the following line of reasoning at about age 6: "Llamas are a kind of camel, but they are very small. Camels are not native to America. Probably camels crossed in prehistoric times from Asia, where they are native, and continued southward till they reached a warm climate. Because the environment was different and perhaps did not contain the foods that made them grow big at home, they became smaller." There is nothing wrong with this reasoning. What the child lacked was sufficient knowledge. The impulse to think in more general terms is perhaps due also to the need for such thinking; the physical, emotional, and social changes during adolescence precipitate problems to which the boy or girl wants an answer. Presumably, the further development of the brain furnishes the physiological basis for the more complex forms of thinking in which the adolescent indulges. Indeed, an outstanding characteristic of adolescent boys and girls is their spontaneous joy in mental activity—even if the topics thought about are not always those presented in the curriculum.

▶ The Glandular System

The Duct Glands   The human body contains both duct and ductless—or endocrine—glands. Although important enough in the total economy of the organism the former are of relatively little importance for the present discussion, since their action has few psychological concomitants. The only points that will be noted in regard to them are the increase at adolescence in the activity of the sweat glands and the frequent failure of the oil glands to drain properly. The oil glands, although sometimes discharging altogether too much oil and producing a greasy appearance, more often fail to drain adequately because for a few years the ducts are too small. The normal discharge therefore hardens, a speck of dirt gets into it during the hardening, and a blackhead appears. The sweat glands also produce distressing symptoms, both directly through perspiration and indirectly through the development of body odors. The boy is upset because his shirt sticks to him at the slightest provocation and is acutely embarrassed when the perspiration on his hands stains the dress of the girl he dances with. With the aid of salves and all manner of deodorants, the adolescent girl carries on a constant fight against perspiration, and especially during her menstrual periods against body odor as well. Neither sex is altogether successful because the glands are both active and sensitive. Not only warmth and exercise produce undesired amounts of perspiration; any emotional disturbance is equally fatal. When a teacher sees a luckless student begin to perspire, she would do well to release him temporarily from whatever academic effort he is involved in. If his attention is being divided between the telltale moisture on his forehead and the intricacies of an imperfect subjunctive, he might as well be excused.

The Ductless Glands   The endocrine, or ductless glands, merit discussion because of their effects, direct or indirect, upon both physical condition and emotional life. First as to their names and locations. They are called the pineal, pituitary, thyroid, parathyroid, thymus, adrenal, pancreas, ovaries, and testes. The pineal and pituitary are located in the base of the brain; the thyroid and parathyroid in the front of the throat; the thymus is in the chest; the adrenals and pancreas are in the abdomen. The ovaries and testes are parts of the sexual organs.

Each gland has its own rhythm of growth. Each has also its specific function in the chemistry of the body. Thus the pituitary controls growth in general, and the increased activity of its anterior lobe is the trigger that sets off the great physical changes of adolescence. It also has some influence in stimulating the appearance of the secondary sexual characteristics. If the pituitary is overactive from birth it will produce a giant; if underactive from birth, a dwarf. When the gland becomes abnormal during childhood or adolescence the person affected develops huge hands, big feet, and coarse features. Puberty is sometimes advanced—that is, it occurs before age 9 in girls or 11 in boys—or retarded until after age 17 in either sex, because the pituitary has become hyperactive sooner or later than usual, although there may be other reasons. There is at least one recorded case of a girl who began to menstruate at 7 months. By the time she was six years old she had a skeletal age of 13½ and the figure of an adolescent girl.[1] Either advanced or retarded puberty presents problems to both parents and teachers. A 9-year-old girl or an 11-year-old boy is not yet ready intellectually, socially, or emotionally to become an adolescent, and the child's associates are not yet ready to understand what has happened to him. Nor can the maturity be kept secret, even if secrecy were wholly desirable, because the girl's breasts will soon develop, as will the boy's genitalia, and their voices will become lower, especially the boy's. These children then become objects of great curiosity and possible ridicule among their peers. A delayed adolescence is almost as bad, although the problems are different. The child fails to keep up with his group in any respect, except intellectually. In his schoolwork he may be successful, but outside the classroom he is like a pygmy among giants, and his social maladjustment is practically inevitable.

The adrenal glands produce two secretions. One affects the development of masculine secondary sexual characteristics, while the other acts in times of emotional stress as a chemical whip on all the nerve centers of the body. The action of this second secretion will be described in more detail in another chapter.

The parathyroids control the absorption of calcium, a chemical necessary for the development of bone, for the nourishment of nerves, and for the clotting of the blood. These glands are tiny but absolutely essential to life. The thymus and pineal glands and the pancreas also contribute to growth, to the assimilation of chemical materials, and to the regulation of various bodily functions, but their work has few if any mental or emotional accompaniments.

The thyroid gland regulates the rate at which metabolism takes place within the body. If the gland is not sufficiently active, an individual is slow, lethargic, and listless because all his bodily processes are retarded. His hair and nails are coarse and brittle, and his skin is thick and leathery. Usually, he is overweight and is likely to suffer from a chronic constipation. An over-

---

[1] W. W. Greulich and S. I. Pyle, *Radiographic Atlas of Skeletal Development of the Hand and Wrist* (Stanford, Calif.: Stanford University Press, 1950), 190 pp., p. 9.

active thyroid causes the bodily functions to proceed too quickly. The heart beats too fast, the digestion is too rapid, and the nerves are overstimulated. The individual is too easily excited, too emotional, too quickly fatigued, too irritable. Usually he is underweight. The thyroid is a chronic troublemaker for adolescent girls, especially in the Middle West.

During infancy and early childhood, the ovaries grow very slowly, reaching about 10 percent of their adult weight by age 8. They then begin to grow a little more rapidly and gain half their adult weight by age 16. Most of the remaining weight is added during the next four years. The boy's testes grow much more slowly. They have only about 3 percent of their adult weight at age 3, and by age 10 they have increased to only 10 percent. After age 10 the rate of growth increases up to age 16. Thereafter it slows down again, and even at age 20 the glands have reached only 60 percent of the adult weight.

The teacher who is alert to the situation will find in her classes many children who need medical attention because of glandular malfunctioning. Sluggishness, sleepiness, overweight, leathery skin, failure to grow, early appearance of secondary sex characteristics, irritability, excitability, jumpiness, inattention, fainting, painful menstruation, fast pulse, and protuberant eyeballs are all danger signals that suggest glandular involvement. Pupils showing such symptoms should be sent at once to the school doctor.

► Sexual Maturity

The maturing of the sex glands is the most important single development of the adolescent years. Indeed, puberty consists essentially in this maturation. The mere physical ability to produce offspring is, however, not nearly as significant at the moment as the added depths and nuances of emotional and social life that develop along with puberty. These emotional developments will be discussed at length in a later chapter. The present discussion will be limited to a description of the physiological changes and the reaction of adolescents to them.

The Sex Organs Before beginning this discussion it seems advisable to make a brief statement concerning normal growth of the organs from birth to maturity. The uterus at birth is over 45 percent of its adult length. Almost at once, however, it shrinks and does not recover its size at birth until a girl is 5 years old. It grows slowly in childhood and then rapidly in preadolescence and adolescence, reaching its adult length and weight by age 20. The penis grows quite rapidly during the first four years of life, increasing from less than a third its adult length to nearly a half. It then grows very slowly during childhood. At age 11 it has reached only half its adult length. Growth then accelerates, especially from age 13 to 17, after which the

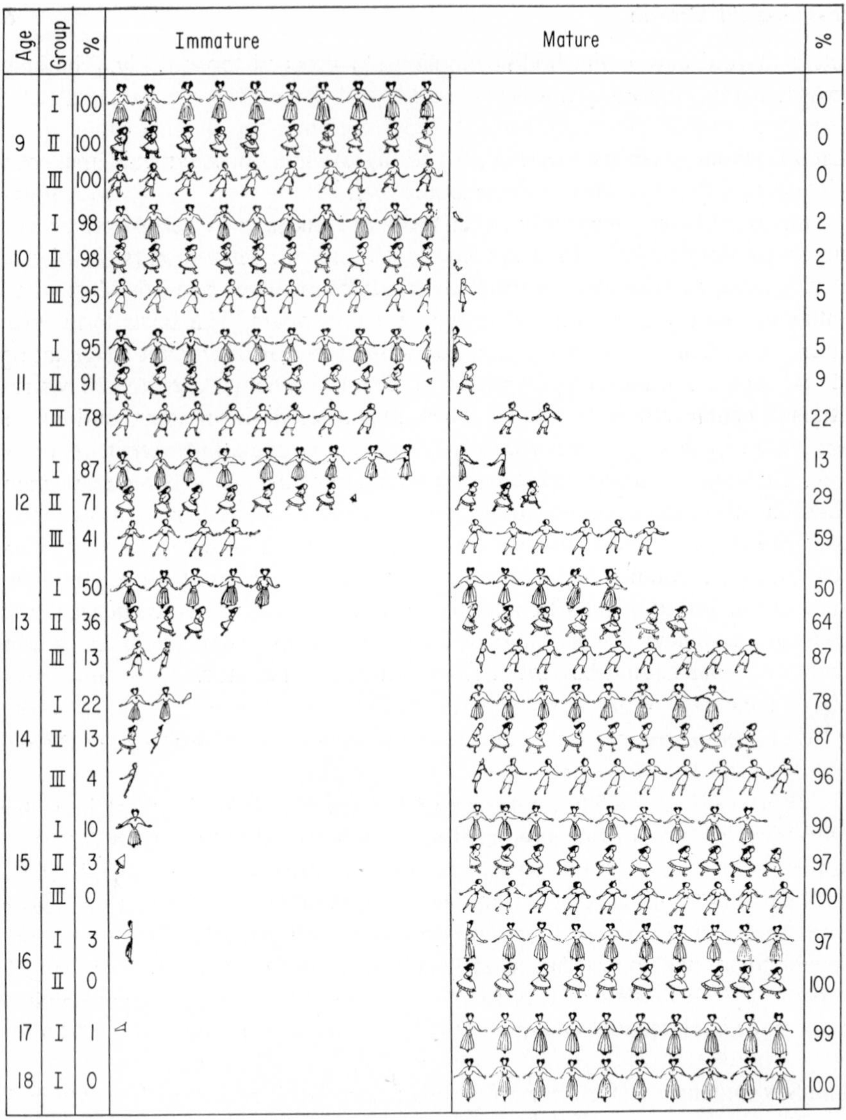

Age	Group	%	Immature	Mature	%
9	I	100			0
	II	100			0
	III	100			0
10	I	98			2
	II	98			2
	III	95			5
11	I	95			5
	II	91			9
	III	78			22
12	I	87			13
	II	71			29
	III	41			59
13	I	50			50
	II	36			64
	III	13			87
14	I	22			78
	II	13			87
	III	4			96
15	I	10			90
	II	3			97
	III	0			100
16	I	3			97
	II	0			100
17	I	1			99
18	I	0			100

Fig. 5-5. Age of sexual maturity in girls

Based on: (For 1904–1925) F. Boas, "Statistics of Growth," *United States Bureau of Education Reports,* 1904, Chap. II, 132 pp.; B. T. Baldwin, "The Physical Growth of Children from Birth to Maturity," *University of Iowa Studies in Child Welfare,* Vol. I, No. 1, 411 pp. 1923; B. K. Atkinson, "A Study of the Athletic Ability of High School Girls, *"American Physical Education Review,* 30:380–398, 1925. (For 1930–1940) R. G. Barker and C. P. Stone, "Physical Development in Relation to Menarcheal Age in College Women," *Human Biology,* 8:198–222, 1936; E. T. Engle and M. C. Schlesnyak, "First Menstruation and Subsequent Menstrual Cycles of Pubertal Girls," *Human Biology,* 6:431–453, 1934; H. N. Gould and M. R. Gould, "Age at First Menstruation in Mothers and Daughters," *Journal of the American Medical Association,* 98:1349–1352, 1932 (material for daughters only was used); M. L. Reymert, "Relationships between Menarcheal Age, Behavior Disorders, and Intelligence," *Character and Personality,* 8:292–300, 1940; (For 1953) A. B. Nicholson and C. Handy, "Indices of Physiological Maturity: Deviation and Interrelationships," *Child Development,* 24:3–38, 1953.

rate becomes slower but continues until a boy has become a young man. Its growth is not complete at age 20.

Age of Sexual Maturity   Girls have shown normally a variation in the age of first menstruation from 10 to 17. Those who mature before age 12 are considered precocious and those who mature at or after age 15 as more or less retarded. Over 75 percent of girls have their first period at 12, 13, or 14. The total distribution of menstrual ages, based upon a combination of many studies, appears in Figure 5–5. Two of them come from before 1925, three from 1930–1940, and one from 1953. Results from these groups (I, II, III) are presented separately, so that one may get an idea of what is called "secular change"—or the change that takes place with time. In all three periods there was less than half of one percent of girls menstruating before age 9; the chart therefore begins with three rows of 10-year-olds, essentially all of whom are immature. The percent remaining so at each successive age appears on the left side of the central line, while the percent of those now mature is shown on the right side. It is clear almost from the first that the 1953 girls matured earlier. All were mature at age 15, whereas the 1930–1940 group was not totally mature until 16, and the below-1925 group until 18. Even over this relatively short period of time, differences have taken place in the rate of growth. If one goes back an entire century, as is possible with European records, one finds an even clearer demonstration of change, as will appear shortly.

The results from boys are less satisfactory than those from girls, because boys have no single moment at which they become physiologically mature. The average boy requires about two years to change from a stage that is clearly prepubescent to one that is clearly postpubescent. Many of the studies classify all boys into only two groups: those who are not yet mature—although they may be somewhere en route to maturity—and those who are. In Figure 5–6 it was necessary to follow this common method of presentation in order to include three groups of studies (I, II, III): two reports come from before 1925, three from the 1940s, and one from 1954. This last one is not entirely satisfactory because it is based on results from boys in a boarding school attended mostly by boys from upper-class families, although some students from lower-class families arrived by the scholarship route; it is therefore probable that the results reflect not only changes with time but also differences from one social class to another. No boys in any of the studies were mature before age 10, and only an occasional boy at age 11. As with the girls, the proportion of immature or maturing boys is shown to the left and the proportion of mature to the right of the central line. The 1954 group was entirely mature at age 15, the 1940 group at 16, and the last of the 1925-and-earlier group not until 18.

It will be noted that boys reach maturity about two years later than girls.

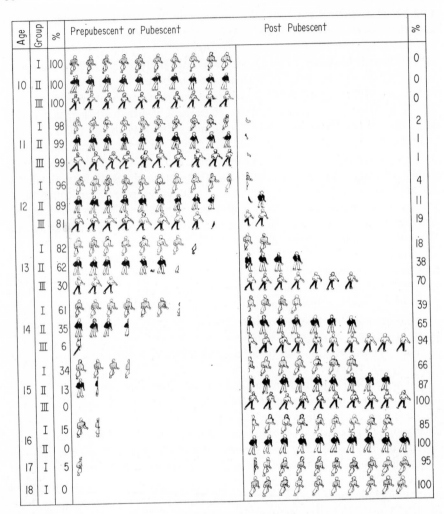

Fig. 5–6. Age of sexual maturity in boys

Based on: (For 1908–1923) C. W. Crampton, "Physiological Growth," *American Physical Education Review*, 13:144–154, 214–227, 268–283, 345–358, 1908; and B. T. Baldwin, "Physical Growth of Children from Birth to Maturity," *University of Iowa Studies in Child Welfare*, Vol. 1, No. 1, 1923. (For 1943–1946) R. W. B. Ellis, "Height and Weight in Relation to Onset of Puberty in Boys," *Archives of Diseases of Childhood*, 21:181–189, 1946, W. H. Schonfeld, "Primary and Secondary Sex Characteristics," *American Journal of Diseases of Childhood*, 65:535–549, 1943, and H. C. Richey, "The Relation of Accelerated, Normal, and Retarded Puberty to the Height and Weight of School Children," *Monographs of the Society for Research in Development*, Vol. II, No. 1, 1937. (For 1954) D. Mulcock, "A Short Study on the Onset of Puberty in Boys," *Medical Officer*, 91:247–249, 1954.

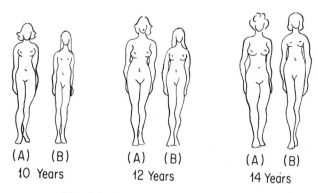

(A) (B) (A) (B) (A) (B)
10 Years   12 Years   14 Years

Fig. 5-7. Early and late maturing girls

F. K. Shuttleworth, "The Adolescent Period: A Pictorial Atlas," *Monographs of the Society for Research in Child Development,* Vol. XIV, No. 1, Serial No. 50, 1949, p. 15. Used by permission of the publisher.

Consequently, there is a period during which the proportion of mature girls is far larger than the proportion of mature boys. As a result, girls are more sex-conscious than boys of their own age. There is some basis for the popular observation that a girl of 13 is already a young lady, while a lad of 13 is still a small boy.

The age of sexual maturity is related to height, weight, and skeletal development. Those who mature earliest are, from age 6, taller, heavier, and more advanced in skeletal development than those who mature later. The outlines in Figures 5-7 and 5-8 present typical comparisons of pairs of girls at ages 10, 12, and 14, and of boys at ages 11½, 13½, and 15½. In each pair, the child to the left matured early and the one to the right considerably later. Differences in height, weight, and closeness to adult proportions may be noted.

The age of maturation may be influenced by climate, race, social status, sex, or family inheritance—in addition to the direct influence from general growth rate and skeletal age. Of these factors, it is already clear that sex plays an important role, since girls mature about two years earlier than boys. It was once thought that girls who grew up in a hot climate had an earlier menarche than those who grew up in a cold one. However, some of the more modern investigations have shown that climate has little or no effect upon the age of maturity. The average age for girls in the tropics was 14.3, while that for Eskimo girls was 14.4.[2] To be sure, Negro girls in the southern states mature

---

[2] R. W. R. Ellis, "Age of Puberty in the Tropics," *British Medicine,* 1:85–89, 1950; V. E. Levine, "Studies in Physiological Anthropology, III, The Age of Onset of Menarche Menstruation of the Alaska Eskimos," *American Journal of Physical Anthropology,* N.S. 11:252, 1953.

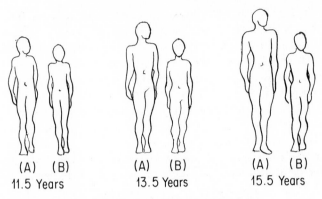

(A) (B)   (A) (B)   (A)   (B)
11.5 Years   13.5 Years   15.5 Years

Fig. 5–8. Early and late maturing boys

F. K. Shuttleworth, "The Adolescent Period: A Pictorial Atlas, *"Monographs of the Society for Research in Child Development,* Vol. XIV, No. 1, Serial No. 50, 1949, p. 24. Used by permission of the publisher.

earlier than those in the North, but probably the differences are due to influences other than climate. It is probable that race has even less effect. In two studies the age of menarche for Negro girls did not vary materially from that of white girls who lived in the same place and came from the same economic level.[3] Between the highest and lowest economic classes there is a small but consistent difference. It was found to be 2 months in Copenhagen, 3 months in Bristol (England), 8 months among Negroes in New York, 6 months among Hindus, 10 months in Durban (South Africa), and 5 months among the South African Bantu.[4] In all probability these differences arise from the better nutrition and the resulting more rapid growth rate among girls from upper-class homes.

One study makes especially clear the influence of nutritional differences between groups.[5] Japanese girls who were born in Japan but reared in California almost from birth, were one and a half years ahead of Japanese girls

        [3] C. L. Henton, "A Comparative Study of the Onset of Menarche among Negro and White Children," *Journal of Psychology,* 46:65–73, 1958; N. Michelson, "Studies in Physical Development of Negroes, IV. Onset of Puberty," *American Journal of Physical Anthropology,* N.S. 2:151–166, 1944.
        [4] K. W. Boylen, G. Rasch, and M. Weis-Bentzon, "The Age Incidence of Menarche in Copenhagen," *Acta Obstetrica et Gynecologia Scandinavica,* 33:405–433, 1954; R. C. Wofenden and A. L. Smallwood, "Annual Report of the Principal Medical Officer to City and County of Bristol Education Committee, 1958; E. Kark, "Puberty of South African Girls, III. Social Class in Relation to the Menarche," *South African Journal of Laboratory and Clinical Medicine,* 2:84–88, 1956; R. J. W. Burrell, M. J. Healy, and J. M. Tanner, "Age at Menarche in South African Bantu Girls Living on the Transkei Reserve," *Human Biology,* 33:181–190, 1961.
        [5] P. K. Ito, "Comparative Biometrical Study of Physiques of Japanese Women Born and Reared under Different Environments," *Human Biology,* 14:279–351, 1942.

born in California but reared in Japan. The race was the same for all of these girls, and the groups were large enough to include members from all social classes. The rather large difference must therefore have come from the better diet and the more adequate medical care given the girls who grew up in California. Another investigator found that Negro girls in the West Indies mature at the average age of 14 years, while in New York the average age is 13.[6]

The immediate family inheritance also contributes something to the determination of the exact time at which a given girl will begin to menstruate. Daughters of early-maturing mothers tend to reach menarche earlier than those of late-maturing mothers.[7] The influence of family heredity is also shown by the relationship of menarchial age to the degree of blood relationship between girls. Whereas unrelated women show a variation of 18½ months in their age of maturity, sisters show a difference of 11 months, nonidentical twins of 10, and identical twins of less than 3 months.[8]

It should be noted that the influences just discussed sometimes reinforce each other and sometimes cancel each other out in individual cases. Thus a German girl whose mother matured at ,11 may, because of the nutritional deficiencies caused by the last war, menstruate late. Or the daughter of a late-maturing mother who came from a poor family may reach menarche earlier than her mother did because the family has moved up in the economic scale and the better diet has had the usual effect. On the other hand, the daughter of a late-maturing mother who has been left a widow and has been forced by circumstances to lower her economic status may reach menarche at an even later age than her mother did.

In many European countries there are records that go back for 100 years or more and show the age at which girls first menstruated. One of the longest records, from Norway (Fig. 5–9), extends from 1840–1950. The average age in 1840 was 17 years 1 month; it decreased steadily during the 110 years covered by the relevant studies until in 1950 it had become 13 years 3 months —a decrease of 3 years 10 months. Similar changes have been found in England, Denmark, Sweden, Finland, Germany, Japan, and the United States. These changes reflect the increasing growth rate which has already been commented upon in Chapter 2.

Secondary Sexual Characteristics The secondary characteristics for both sexes are often of similar type and vary only in the degree of development, as may be seen by comparison of the following lists:

---

[6] Michelson, *loc. cit.*
[7] M. R. Gould, "Age of First Menstruation in Mothers and Daughters," *Journal of the American Medical Association,* 98:1349–1352, 1932.
[8] M. Tisierand-Perrier, "Etude comparative de certains processes de croissance chez les jumeaux," *Journal de Genétique humaine,* 2:87–102, 1953.

Boys	*Girls*
Growth of pubic hair	Growth of pubic hair
Growth of hair under arms	Growth of hair under arms
Heavy growth of hair on face	Light growth of hair on face
Heavy growth of hair on body	Light growth of hair on body
Eruption of second molars	Eruption of second molars
Considerable growth of larynx	Slight growth of larynx
Change of voice by octave	Moderate lowering of voice
Widening of shoulders	Widening of hips
Considerable thickening of muscles	Slight thickening of muscles
Increase in perspiration	Increase in perspiration
Sometimes slight and temporary development around breast nipples	Development of breasts

The growth of pubic hair and of hair under the arms is about the same for both sexes. Facial and body hair are much heavier for boys, but the same

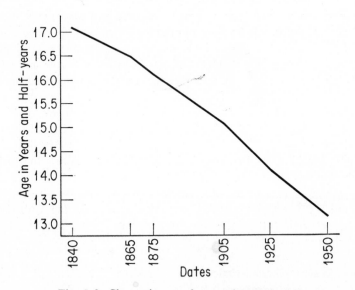

Fig. 5–9. Change in age of menarche, 1840–1950

G. Bachman, "Die beschleunigte Entwicklung des judentlicher verfrühte menarche, verspätete Menopause, verlängerte Lebensdaur," *Acta Anatomica*, 4:421–480, 1948; B. Skerlj, "Menarche und Umwelt nebst einigen anderen Problemen dargestellt an Hand eines norwegischen Materials," *Zeitschrift für menschliche Vererbung und Konstit ut slehre*, 23–299–359, 1939; C. Schiotz, "Menarche Undersokelser ved Oslo kommunale folkeskoler og hoiere Skoler," *Nordisk Medicinsk Tidskrift*, 2:65–69, 1930; V. Kiil, "Menarche-alderen hos skolepeker i Oslo og sammenhengen mellom menarche-older og fysiskutwiklung Statistiche, *Kvartalashelft*, Oslo, 43:84–88, 1954.

developments appear in reduced form among girls as a light down upon the upper lip and on the forearms and lower legs. The voices of children are of much the same pitch, without respect to sex. Thus, in a study [9] of seven- and eight-year-old children, the pitch for both boys and girls averaged close to middle C, about an octave above the average for adult males. A curious fact which emerged from this study was the appearance of "breaks" in the voices of both boys and girls, and of the same average number for members of both sexes. Change of voice among boys usually begins during the fourteenth or fifteenth year with huskiness and lack of control in volume as the first symptoms. The larynx enlarges, and the boy's voice eventually becomes about an octave lower.[10] Many boys experience no marked "breaks." Their voices gradually become lower and heavier without loss of control.[11] One of the writers knew a boy who sang soprano in a church choir until he was 14, then alto for two years, then tenor, and finally bass by the time he was 21, but at no time did he lack the necessary control for singing. Only about half the boys studied have reported "breaks." The girl's voice shows only a moderate degree of lowering, but the childish treble disappears, and the timbre of the voice becomes heavier and richer.

For girls the development of the breasts is the most important of the secondary changes. In one study of the rate of growth of the breasts, semi-annual examinations were made of girls between ages 8 and 15. The breasts developed from a bud to mature size in about three years, between ages 11 and 14. Thirty-eight percent of the girls had small breasts, 28 percent had large ones, and 34 percent had breasts of medium size. In shape, 20 percent were flat, 20 percent were conical, and 60 per cent were round. The various outlines and percentage distributions are represented in Figure 5–10. In 54 percent of the girls, the breasts began to develop before the pubic hair started to grow, in 32 percent the hair appeared first, and in the remaining 14 percent the two secondary characteristics appeared and developed together.

Reactions to Sexual Maturity   The achievement of sexual maturity is of great importance to the boy or girl. It is also the source of some embarrassment. The boy's organs not only grow rapidly in size until he suspects they may show through his clothing, but seem to react without his volition. At night the boy is often distressed by dreams that seem to him highly indecent. He is practically certain to masturbate more or less; even if

[9] G. Fairbanks, J. H. Wiley, and F. M. Lassman, "An Acoustical Study of Vocal Pitch in Seven- and Eight-Year-Old Boys," *Child Development,* 20:63–69, 1949; and G. Fairbanks, E. L. Herbert, and M. Hammond, "An Acoustical Study of Vocal Pitch in Seven- and Eight-Year-Old Girls," *Child Development,* 20:71–78, 1949.

[10] E. T. Curry, "Voice Changes in Male Adolescence," *Laryngoscope,* 56:795–805, 1946.

[11] C. P. Pedrey, "A Study of Voice Changes in Boys between the Ages of Eleven and Sixteen," *Speech Monographs,* 12:30–36, 1945.

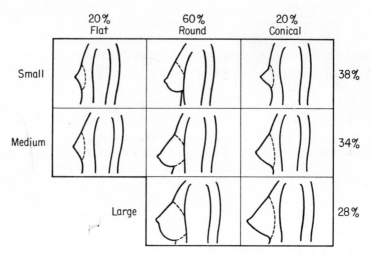

Fig. 5–10. Growth of the breasts

Based on E. L. Reynolds and J. V. Wines, "Individual Differences in Physical Changes Associated with Adolescent Girls," *American Journal of Diseases of Children,* 75:329–350, 1948.

he does not, his nocturnal emissions may embarrass and frighten him. If he does not have frequent discharges, he may become uncomfortable from tension. Most boys require physical relief, which is usually obtained by a combination of masturbation and daydreams of girls.[12] At the beginning of the genital period, the physical stimulation is the more important element, but gradually the intellectual and emotional elements become sufficient for stimulation and fuse with the physical. Girls do not feel nearly as much need for release as boys do.

A boy experiences erections as a reaction to a wide variety of stimuli, some of which are not of obviously sexual character, such as sentimental music, riding in a car or on a train, swinging, or becoming generally excited, as at a football game, or frightened, as when on the way to battle. The commonest stimuli are conversation on sexual matters either with other boys or with girls, pictures of female nudity, pornographic pictures or books, daydreams, love scenes in moving pictures or in books, and dancing. Boys are much more easily stimulated than girls, in part because their organs are external, and in part because their mechanism has a hair-trigger reaction quite missing in girls. An erection, while sometimes disturbing to a boy, is also a source of pride as a sure sign of masculinity.

Single manifestations of masculinity may appear at any age from middle

[12] F. B. Strain, *The Normal Sex Interest of Children* (New York: Appleton-Century-Crofts, Inc., 1948), 210 pp.

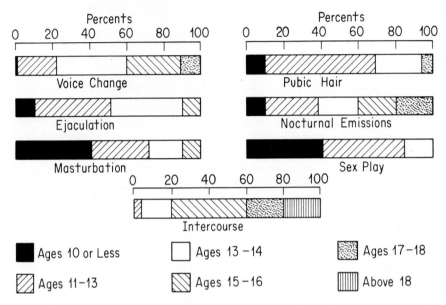

Fig. 5–11. Age distribution for male sexual development

Based on G. V. Ramsey, "The Sex Development of Boys," *American Journal of Psychology*, 56:217–233, 1943, and A. C. Kinsey, W. B. Pomeroy, and C. E. Martin, *Sexual Behavior of the Human Male* (Philadelphia: W. B. Saunders Company, 1953), 804 pp., p. 175.

childhood to late adolescence—that is, from the end of elementary school till toward the end of high school. Evidence accumulated from personal interviews with 291 adolescent boys is summarized in Figure 5–11. The results show that a boy's voice may change, his nocturnal emissions begin, his ability to ejaculate develop, and his pubic hair appear as early as seven, eight, or nine years of age and as late as some age after 16. The percentage of boys having nocturnal emissions increases fairly regularly from ages 13 through 17, but some boys have not experienced emissions until 18 or 19.

Masturbation may begin in infancy and is practiced by a fourth of the boys by the time they are eight years old. By age 12, over three fourths of the boys masturbated, and by age 16, all of them. Since this sexual practice is so widespread, it cannot be called abnormal. So far as is known, the physiological results are either harmless or beneficial; the damage, if any, is emotional. Many boys suffer from feelings of shame and guilt, which often accompany the act, and are frightened half out of their wits by horrible predictions of insanity or impotence in later life. Unless the masturbation is excessive it does no harm provided a boy does not get the idea that he is abnormal. If the boy is neither scolded nor threatened nor made to feel ashamed, he will outgrow the habit. The best single method of either prevention or cure is to keep a boy's life so full of so many interesting things that he has relatively little time for daydreaming and relatively little attention left over from other interests to become absorbed in any form of sexual activity. Sex play is common.[13] It begins as early as four, and the percentage of boys indulging in some form of sex play increases with every year. By 10 years, 45 percent have had such experiences, and by 14 the percent has reached 100. The earliest reported attempts at intercourse were at age 12. By fifteen years of age, 45 percent had at least tried to have intercourse. The percentage increased to 60 at 16 and, in the sample studied, at least one such attempt had been made by 82 percent of the boys before they were 19. Visits to prostitutes were reported as early as 15, and at least one such visit had been made by 40 percent of the boys before their twentieth year. Adults are often shocked by the figures on sex play and sex experience among children and adolescents, but this attitude stems partly from a failure to realize that sexual interests are a normal part of life at all ages and partly from an adult conviction that these interests are "dirty." Each new study of the subject points more and more clearly to the natural spontaneity of such interests and activities and to their widespread occurrence at all ages.

Boys differ from each other as widely in the extent of their knowledge about sexual phenomena as they do in their sexual habits. Results are summarized in Figure 5–12. Some boys know about the origin of babies as early as 5, but others do not learn until 13 of 14. Knowledge of menstruation may be acquired as early as age 8, but as many as half the boys are not aware of it until after age 15. Since most girls are already mature at this age, there would seem to be a need for an earlier imparting of this item of information; otherwise boys are likely to be puzzled and curious about the behavior of girls during their monthly periods. Knowledge of prostitution may be acquired at a very early age; the fact that prostitutes exist is known to all or practically all boys by the time they are 15 years old. Knowledge of venereal disease does not reach half the boys until they are 14, and even at 18 it is not universal. In view of their experiences, this information should surely be provided in early adolescence. Information about contraceptives has been acquired by over half the boys of 12, and by all of them at 18.

The average boy has perhaps a more pronounced emotional reaction to his maturity than the average girl, because he is more acutely and constantly aware of it. His organs are external. They are subject to the incidental pressure of such external objects as wearing apparel or bedclothes. He is forced to touch himself several times a day when he urinates. To himself, his sexual development seems obvious and uncontrollable. If he consults his friends about

---

[13] The facts in the rest of this paragraph are taken from A. C. Kinsey, W. B. Pomeroy, and C. E. Martin, *The Sexual Behavior of the Human Male* (Philadelphia: W. B. Saunders Company, 1953), 804 pp., pp. 137, 141, and 175.

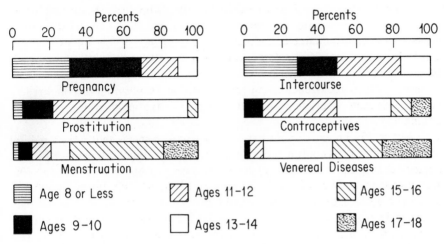

Fig. 5–12. Age distribution for male knowledge of sexual phenomena

Based on G. V. Ramsey, "The Sex Information of Younger Boys," *American Journal of Orthopsychiatry*, 13:347–352, 1943.

his difficulties, he receives chiefly smutty stories and misinformation; if he asks his father, he is often met with embarrassment and evasiveness; if he consults an older man, he is lucky if he is not sent to prostitutes; if, in desperation, he visits some quack, he gets frightened out of his wits. He cannot consult most of his teachers because they are unmarried women. Even his mother can tell him very little; she was never a boy, and by now she has reached a conservative, feminine middle age that is as likely to be horrified as to be helpful.

The attainment of sexual maturity has a profound effect upon an adolescent's status among his age-mates. In many cases the indirect results are more immediately important than the purely physical outcomes. The early-maturing boy is likely to become a leader and to participate widely in school clubs and activities. The late-maturing boy usually suffers from acute feelings of inferiority. He cannot compete with boys of his own age in any athletic activity. Except in purely intellectual pursuits the late-maturer is at a disadvantage.[14] Moreover, his interests and attitudes are different.

A girl's adolescence involves quite different kinds of strain and difficulty from those experienced by boys. A girl may receive a considerable emotional shock from her first menstruation, whether or not she has been warned of its arrival, since there is something understandably terrifying in a hemorrhage that

---

[14] P. H. Mussen and M. C. Jones, "Self-Conceptions, Motivations, and Interpersonal Attitudes of Early and Late Maturing Boys," *Child Development*, 29:61–67, 1958.

cannot be stopped. Bleeding is so associated with unpleasantness that many girls can never dissociate this emotional tone from their menstrual periods, although the total amount of blood lost averages only a few tablespoonfuls. There are a few girls who become so badly disturbed emotionally during their periods that they are quite unlike themselves. Even after the periods are established, their recurrence taken for granted, and any initial discomfort forgotten, girls may experience what boys do not—actual pain from sexual functioning.

About 25 percent of girls have at least some periods that are so painful or difficult that they consult a doctor for relief.[15] Another 21 percent go to a doctor because the bleeding is either so profuse as to be a hemorrhage or so scanty as hardly to be there at all (12 percent belong to the former group and 9 percent in the latter). In addition, 11 percent have severe abdominal pain of a generalized nature during their periods, with nausea, vomiting, and digestive distress. There is undoubtedly some overlapping among these three sets of symptoms, since the same girl may have menstrual cramps, scanty bleeding, and nausea. However, it seems probable that at least a third of the girls maturing in any one year suffer sufficient discomfort to consult a doctor. These figures do not include the many girls who are looked after at home. For the remaining girls—from one-half and two-thirds of the total—the pain is slight, although there may be a general lassitude, some digestive disturbance, and an unusual degree of emotionality and nervousness. Some girls make a practice of spending the first day of each period in bed—and a day's relaxation once a month in comparative isolation from social pressures is not a bad idea. Mothers are likely to be indulgent on this point, so it is probable that a first day in comfortable semi-invalidism will retain its popularity. One can hardly help noticing, however, that when a girl has something she really wants to do, she usually gets up and does it, whether or not she is menstruating. There are, in every school generation, a few girls who never have any sensations at all from their periods.

Almost all girls are more or less embarrassed by or during their periods. They wonder if the pad they are wearing is showing; they wonder if the blood has soaked through their dresses; they wonder if boys can tell if they are menstruating; they wonder if their body odor may have become offensive. They get upset because they have to explain to others why they are not going swimming or why they are not playing hockey. None of these sources of embarrassment form any part of menstrual physiology but are superimposed upon it by adolescent social life. Of all the worries, the concern about a possible stain on her dress is a girl's most constantly recurring dread. Some girls have this fear in such exaggerated form that they will not stand up in class. Since most

[15] L. A. Gray, "Gynecology in Adolescence," in L. T. Menks and M. Green, eds., *Symposium on Adolescence* (Philadelphia: W. B. Saunders Company, 1960), 232 pp., pp. 43–47.

teachers of adolescent youth are women, they should have no difficulty in recognizing and evaluating this behavior.[16]

The girls who mature earliest have a temporary position of prestige among other girls and are often called upon to guide their less mature friends through the first few menstrual periods. A late-maturing girl has the same lack of status experienced by the late-maturing boy, but the situation is not complicated by small stature, partly because there is no general prejudice against short women, partly because success in competitive sports is not so important to her as to a boy, and partly because her growth spurt—being a feature of preadolescence—has already taken place. In fact, if her puberty is delayed long enough, she may do a little extra growing. A girl who tends toward a masculine type of body is also in a somewhat less precarious social position than a boy whose body tends to be feminine. Such a girl may feel that she is altogether too flat and lacking in proper curves, but she will be actually admired by other girls because clothes hang well on her. Also she can gain prominence, if she wishes to do so, in sports and games. In any case, she rarely meets the scorn and ostracism that are often the lot of the too-feminine boy.

When one compares mature and immature girls of the same age, one finds quite marked differences among them in attitudes and interests. A mature girl is interested in boys, in all forms of social life—especially in dances and parties—in personal appearance and adornment, and in sentimental love stories in both books and movies. Her interest in games decreases. She does a good deal of daydreaming and may become quite introspective. The noisy, athletic, objective, energetic young hoyden who does not care how she looks, who still competes with boys, and who regards love stories as silly has not yet reached her maturity.

The three girls described below were all profoundly affected by their menstrual periods, although only one had any marked physical discomfort.

Anna, who did not begin to menstruate until she was sixteen, completely refused to admit she had any periods. After the first three or four she had her hair cut like a man's, wore men's clothes, smoked a pipe, and really appeared to be a man. She was not homosexual, or at least there was never any evidence to that effect. In fact, she appeared to be sexually frigid. She moved to a new place, got a job in an office, passed as a man, and remained there for about three years. Then she decided to change from men's clothes to feminine slacks and

[16] H. H. Davidson and L. S. Gottlieb, "The Emotional Maturity of Pre- and Post-menarcheal Girls," *Journal of Genetic Psychology,* 68:261–266, 1955; M. S. Faust, "Developmental Maturity as a Determinant of Prestige of Adolescent Girls," *Child Development,* 31:173–186, 1960; M. C. Jones and P. H. Mussen, "Self-conceptions, Motivations, and Interpersonal Attitudes of Early and Late Maturing Girls," *Child Development,* 29:491–501, 1958.

to let her hair grow to the length of a normal bob. She had developed a pleasant acquaintanceship with several boys and men in the town where she worked, and many of these friendships continued unbroken for another three years, during which she was really neutral rather than either masculine or feminine. Gradually, she resumed women's clothes, married, and has lived a normal life since. It is probable that Anna would have had some form of maladjustment during her adolescent years, as her home situation was poor and she was not popular in school, but the form her escape from life took was induced by the shock of her first menstrual periods, her conviction that she could not bear a monthly recurrence, and her determination to deny the whole thing by becoming a man.

Louise's first period came when she was fourteen, after she had entered high school and had become quite popular. She had been told by her mother well in advance of the phenomenon and had not seemed at all concerned or worried over the prospect. After the periods were established, however, she began to refuse invitations to parties—not always, but for the days before, during, and after her periods. She gave up swimming and other sports altogether. After about six months of this behavior, she refused to leave the house while she was menstruating, on the grounds that everyone would know her condition and she would be too embarrassed to face people. Her parents tried to talk her out of this attitude, but without success. Louise had gotten the idea firmly fixed in her mind that she was "unclean" during her periods and must stay away from others. This idea is quite common, especially among primitive peoples, many of whom insist that menstruating women occupy a separate hut during their periods lest they contaminate the community. This state of affairs continued throughout Louise's high school career. On the advice of the family doctor, Louise was sent to a girls' college at some distance from home. In this feminine environment, she soon lost her phobia. She is still a bit shy and is easily embarrassed, but she is gradually regaining the social poise that was hers before she began to menstruate.

Madelaine's first periods, at the age of thirteen, were quite painful and she had bouts of nausea during them. After about six months there was no more pain or nausea, only a feeling of heaviness and an occasional cramp or a headache. The physical symptoms were mild, and since Madelaine had perfectly normal organs, her doctor assured her that even these minor discomforts would not continue for long. Actually, they did soon disappear. Madelaine, however, continued to dread her periods and to react emotionally to them. About three days before a period was due she became moody, irritable, and nervous. The symptoms increased as the period came nearer. For about forty-eight hours after the menstrual flow began Madelaine was so bad-tempered, unreasonable, and violent that members of her family learned to leave her alone. After the first two days of the period, she began to regain her usual pleasant disposition and by the end, she was herself again. Madelaine tried to control her outbursts, and as she grew older succeeded to some degree, although she continued to stay alone as much as she could for at least twenty-four hours after each menstrual flow began. To her family, teachers, and friends, Madelaine seemed to be two people: one that was cheerful, lovable, and normal and one that was moody, sullen, suspicious, irritable, and explosive. This Jekyll and Hyde transformation continued until after Madelaine was married and had had her first child. The long absence of menstrual periods during her pregnancy, plus the complete absence of discomfort after they reappeared, seemed to have broken the cycle, and the sunny, happy Madelaine has been the only one in evidence since.

The first girl described above had had little security in her childhood, had always been a tomboy, and had not been given any proper information about sex before her first period. It is probable that menstruation influenced the form of her maladjustment but was only an additional and final cause of it. The second girl made in exaggerated form the withdrawing reaction that is common and normal. Most girls fear that some odor or the appearance of a blood stain will betray their condition, but the vast majority manage to overcome this fear. The notion that a menstruating woman is unclean is widespread and common among primitive peoples and is the basis of many taboos. The second girl showed no abnormal behavior but rather a too extreme form of a normal attitude. The third girl's condition is not easily explained and was probably due to glandular involvement. She had been a remarkably stable child, and she is now a remarkably stable woman. Had there been a history of a moody disposition, and especially of sudden swings from one extreme to another, one would assume that the menstrual period merely acted as a trigger to precipitate a mood that would have appeared sooner or later anyway. As it was, the black mood was linked definitely with menstruation and never occurred at any other time. There may have been a deep-seated, unresolved conflict at the bottom of the phenomenon, but it seems more probable that the causes were mainly physical and that they operated through the effect of ovarian secretions upon other glands.

Adolescent girls have other worries that are based upon physical characteristics. Girls who are unusually tall or fat become extremely self-conscious. So also do girls with unusually large hands or feet or legs. They are even more upset than boys by any irregularities in facial growth. A skin blemish is a source of profound concern, and hair that for some reason cannot be persuaded to lie properly in the accepted mode of the moment is almost as bad. Girls are worried if their breasts are too small and even more upset if they are too large. Many a girl is deterred from games in which she would love to participate because her breasts obviously move when she runs or jumps. Even though the development of the breasts gives prestige value to a girl, she is not altogether easy in her mind about their conspicuousness. The widening of the hips is likely to inspire an attack of rigid dieting, on the assumption that fat rather than bone is the cause. Most adolescents are much too hungry to continue their dieting for long, but an occasional strong-minded damsel needs a sane explanation of the change which has suddenly precipitated her from a size 14 to a size 18 dress. Most modern girls are annoyed but not unduly alarmed by the appearance of hair on the arms or face, because the ubiquitous beauty parlor will attend to the matter, but there are still a few girls who are made miserable by facial hair and do not know what to do about it. Of the secondary changes, however, the breasts give rise to the most frequent embarrassment. Like the boy's sex organs, they are external, they move, and they show through the clothing. In one study, over 40 percent of the girls complained of discomfiture over such manifestations as have just been enumerated.[17]

The School and Adjustment to Sexual Development   The changes discussed in the preceding section occur mainly during the time that boys and girls are in junior high and high school. The problem is particularly acute in the former, because of the difference in the rate of development between boys and girls. The mixture of physically mature and immature boys and girls is sure to create problems in evoking interest and in directing the activities of the group.

In one respect in American schools adolescence is made relatively easy for girls and relatively hard for boys. When a girl has a problem she can go to her favorite teacher and ask questions without much if any embarrassment and with good prospects of getting a sensible answer. Thus a girl can, in emergencies, find an adult woman of whom she is fond, in whom she has confidence, and to whom she is not related. A boy has no such wide choice of personalities, since so few of his teachers are men. He cannot, without deep and perhaps lasting embarrassment on both sides, talk of sexual problems with his women teachers. There remain the coaches of various sports, and to them he goes in times of stress. Much of his schooltime adolescence is inevitably spent in a predominantly feminine atmosphere, which intensifies his problems and offers little aid in their solution. To offset his difficulties in school, the average boy has more ready access to information about sex outside school; unfortunately, however, some of the information he thus picks up is not true.

Because American boys and girls go through school together and because promotion is based more upon age than upon scholastic achievement, children of both sexes and similar ages reach junior high school at just about the time when girls begin to mature in large numbers. The period from ages 12 or 13 to ages 14 or 15 is the worst possible time for boys and girls to be educated together, because they are too dissimilar in their size, physiological age, in-

---

[17] H. Angelino and E. V. Mech, "Some First Sources of Sex Information as Reported by 67 College Women," *Journal of Psychology*, 39:321–324, 1955.

terests, and attitudes. The number of problems in the average classroom would be appreciably reduced if in junior high school the boys were taught by men and the girls by women, if the sexes were kept separate in classes and in games, and if only at social events were there more than casual, voluntary contacts between them. The first steps toward maturity are easier for the individual if the situation is not complicated by the presence of girls among boys or boys among girls. Once functions and attitudes are established, members of the two sexes are probably better off together. Separation from late childhood onward raises more problems than it solves, but separation from 12 to 15 has proved beneficial where it has been tried.

▶ Summary

Adolescence is a period of internal change and development as well as of skeletal and muscular growth. Every system of the body is altered to some degree. The outstanding change is the establishment of sexual maturity, which is evidenced by both primary and secondary changes. The process takes some time in both boys and girls. The former need about two years for the development from childhood to early maturity. Girls begin to develop two years earlier than boys and reach their adult stage more quickly. The age at which sexual maturity develops has become steadily lower during the last century or even half-century in every country in which it has been studied. Members of both sexes display a variety of attitudes toward the changes in their bodily functions and these attitudes influence their personalities, their schoolwork, and their general adjustment to life. Of all the developments that take place during adolescence, the coming of sexual maturity is the most profound and the most significant in its influence upon the behavior and interests of boys and girls.

References for Further Reading

BOOKS

Other Texts

Ausubel, *Theory and Problems of Adolescent Development* (Chap. 3 or 4).
Garrison, *Growth and Development,* 2d ed. (pp. 23–49).
Horrocks, *Behavior and Development* (pp. 356–376).
Hurlock, *Adolescent Development,* 2d ed. (Chap. 2 or 3).
Jersild, *Psychology of Adolescence* (Chap. 3).
Jones, *Growth and Behavior in Adolescence* (pp. 41–58).

Other Books

Baller, *Readings in the Psychology of Human Growth and Development* (pp. 377–392).

Seidman, *The Adolescent: A Book of Readings,* rev. ed. (No. 10).
Stolz and Meek, *Somatic Development of Adolescent Boys* (Chap. 4, 5, or 14).

ARTICLES

Burrell, R. J. W., M. J. Healy, and J. M. Tanner, "Age at Menarche in South
  African Bantu Girls Living on the Transkei Reserve," *Human Biology,*
  33:181–190, 1961.
Davidson, H. H., and L. S. Gottlieb, "The Emotional Maturity of Pre- and Post-
  menarcheal Girls," *Journal of Genetic Psychology,* 68:261–266, 1955.
Faust, M. S., "Developmental Maturity as a Determinant in the Prestige of Ado-
  lescent Girls," *Child Development,* 31:173–186, 1960.
Ferris, B. G. *et al.,* "Maximum Breathing Capacity and Vital Capacity of Male
  Children and Adolescents," *Pediatrics,* 9:659–670, 1952.
Ferris, B. G., and C. W. Smith, "Maximum Breathing Capacity and Vital Capacity
  of Female Children and Adolescents," *Pediatrics,* 12:341–352, 1953.
Henton, C. L., "A Comparative Study of the Onset of Menarche among Negro
  and White Children," *Journal of Psychology,* 46:65–73, 1958.
Jones, M. C., and P. H. Mussen, "Self-Conceptions, Motivations, and Interper-
  sonal Attitudes of Early and Late Maturing Girls," *Child Development,*
  29:491–501, 1958.
Levin, V. E., "Studies in Physiological Anthropology, III. The Age of Onset of
  Menstruation of the Alaska Eskimos," *American Journal of Physical Anthro-
  pology,* N.S., 11:252, 1953.
Mussen, P. H., and M. C. Jones, "Self-Conceptions, Motivations, and Interpersonal
  Attitudes of Early and Late Maturing Boys," *Child Development,* 29:61–67,
  1958.

Suggested Research Problems [18]

A modern study of the age of physical maturity among both boys and girls is
  badly needed.
A modern study of the amount of information about sexual phenomena at different ages is also needed, since present-day children have more such information than children of even a decade ago.
A collection of case-studies showing reactions to sexual maturity would be most
  useful.

---

[18] See note, p. 11.

Chapter 6 | Health during the Adolescent Period

THE present and growing emphasis on health as a positive, dynamic characteristic of the total person is particularly applicable to the concepts of health during adolescence. It is increasingly true that the advances of medicine and public health practice are contributing to the current happy fact that adolescence is the period of life which is freer of disease than ever. However, there exists a less happy situation with regard to those causes of mortality and morbidity which are grounded in the sociological and psychological factors of this span of life. The present chapter will attempt to show the over-all picture of health during adolescence.

The world in general is a healthier place than it used to be, and adolescents share in the relative freedom from disease that has greatly reduced infant mortality and appreciably increased the average life span. Today's children are born into a safer world. They are prevented from developing many diseases which would shorten or limit their lives, and have a good chance of passing through childhood and into maturity in a state of vigorous physical and mental health. In any given year, about two-thirds of the adolescents in a community are not sick enough at any time to see a doctor.

One specific example of the reduction in frequency of disease appears in Figure 6–1, which shows deaths from infectious and noninfectious diseases in the general population of the United States from 1900 to 1960. This chart gives dramatic evidence of the extent to which modern drugs and hygienic practices have enormously reduced fatalities from an entire category of diseases. The reader should note the sharp rise caused by the world-wide epidemic of influenza in 1918 and the accelerated decline in the same line with the intensified development of antibiotics and other medical controls after World War II. There has, unfortunately, been no such decrease in death from noninfectious diseases.

▶ Mortality and Morbidity in Adolescence

On the whole, adolescence is a healthy period of life for a majority of the young people in the United States, even though there are wide differences, from social and economic causes, in the degree to which this tendency is supported. Still further advances in medical management, scien-

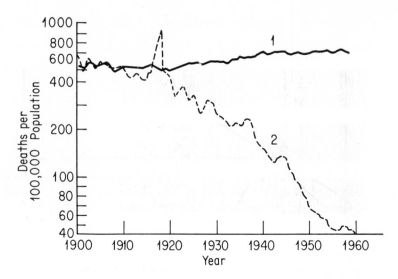

Fig. 6–1. Deaths per 100,000 of the general population, from chronic noninfectious diseases and from acute infectious diseases, 1900–1960. 1—chronic noninfectious diseases, 2—acute infectious diseases

Annual Report for 1961 (Washington, D.C.: U.S. Department of Health, Education and Welfare, 1962), p. 135.

tific research, and social development may be expected to continue the present reduction of many handicapping diseases and many psychosocial problems which now undermine the great potential for health that furnishes adolescents with their abounding and abiding vitality.

Figure 6–2 shows a typical distribution of disease rates for adolescents during the year 1957. In this particular year, two-thirds of all the acute conditions reported were respiratory; probably the high frequency was related to the influenza epidemic in the fall of 1957. Transient changes of this kind will occur in any year, but they tend to even out when sufficient figures are available to indicate trends. The "infectious and parasitic" category includes the common childhood diseases such as measles, mumps, and chickenpox, and these of course are less frequent in the adolescent period, although they may be rather more serious for the individual when they occur at any age beyond childhood. The large number of injuries is consonant with the rates which will be noted in the mortality figures below.

Mortality rates show a great deal of difference between the adolescent and the general population. Figure 6–3, while it is limited to the reports of one large state, shows these differences in terms of the percentages of deaths from major causes; the rates for the age group from 15 to 19 appear in the

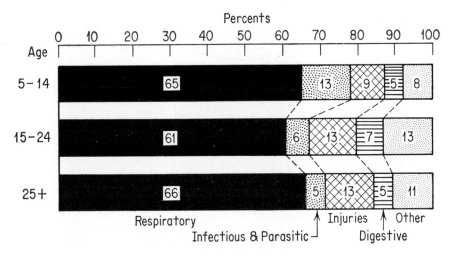

Fig. 6–2. Disease rates from different conditions

"Health Statistics: Children and Youth: Selected Health Characteristics," Public Health Service Publication, No. 584–C1 (Washington, D.C.: U.S. Department of Health, Education and Welfare, 1959), 43 pp., p. 6.

inner circle, and those for the general population in the outer circle. It is clear at once that the chief cause of death in adolescence is accident rather than any disease or any combination of diseases. Most of the accidents occur in connection with motor vehicles. If the death rate from this source, plus that of other accidents, suicide, and homicide are added together, the total comes to 67 percent, leaving only one death in every three due to natural causes. Theoretically, two out of every three adolescent deaths could be prevented by the improvement of the social and psychological conditions under which young people are growing up, by better training in the handling of automobiles and by improved mental hygiene.

In most states every adolescent over 16 can be and usually is licensed to drive. Therefore, there are many more adolescents on the road than there have been in the past, and the toll in death is enormous. Yet the over-all rate of traffic accidents is in fact decreasing in the general population. In 1937, there were 105,205 deaths with a population of 100 million and 30 million cars on the road, whereas in 1961 [1] there were 91,500 deaths, with 183 million population and 76 million cars on the road. There are of course great geographical and local variations in the number of traffic deaths and accidents, but in all areas the group of young males from 16 to 24 contributes far more than its share to the total. Clearly, there are social and psychological reasons far beyond the mere increase in the volume of traffic.

---

[1] *Traffic Safety,* 61:6 and 33, 1962.

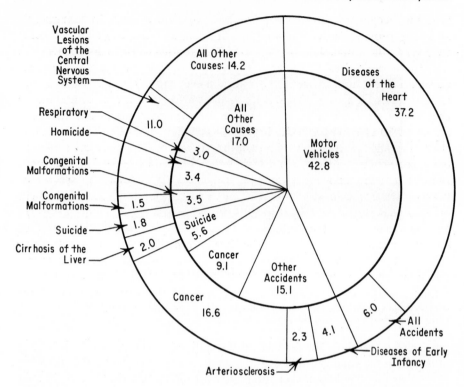

Fig. 6–3. Percentage causes of death in the adult population as compared to those in the adolescent period, in California. Outer circle—causes of death among adults, inner circle—causes of death among adolescents.

Based on *Statistical Report,* California Public Health Department, 1959, 84 pp., p. 43 (15–19 group); *California State Abstracts,* State of California, 1961, 218 pp., p. 108 (General population) (figures from 1959 statistics).

Many schools currently have very active driver-training programs, the effectiveness of which is recognized by some auto insurance companies by a 10 percent reduction in rates for trained drivers below the usual high insurance cost for this age. The training, however, is only a part of the answer to the problems involved in adolescent management of a car. Most young people have, by the time they undertake to drive alone, an adequate amount of physical development and, in most cases, of muscular coordination to control a car, and they are endowed with the fastest reaction-time they are ever likely to attain. They are, however, at a period when the maximum influence of the cultural pressures on the symbolism of the car is operative. Furthermore, a car is an instrument of extraordinary responsiveness to the inner pressures of personality, and it too often becomes the means of expressing latent hostility, need for recognition, fearfulness, or social uncertainty which are common to all young people. The combination of these cultural and psychological pressures make the automobile the greatest killer and maimer of adolescents.

In the sample results shown in Figure 6–3, suicide was the fifth most frequent cause of death in adolescence in a single state. Over the whole of the United States, at ages 10–14, suicide is the thirteenth cause of death, and at ages 15–19, the sixth cause. Furthermore, a recent study [2] indicates that there are about 50 attempted suicides for every one which terminates fatally. In this study, the highest frequency was found at age 18, in 299 individuals seen in one poison-control clinic over a period of three and a half years. The attempted suicides gave the following reasons for their attempts: despair, 37 cases; emotional upset, 35; jealousy, 11; school problems, 14; family problems, 5; birth of illegitimate child, 9; drug addiction, 5; no reason, 183. These categories are too vague to be of much solid use without further study, of course, but they do indicate the range and the relative frequency of problems. It is probable, however, that many if not most of these reasons are only rationalizations that followed the suicidal attempt rather than causes that precipitated it.

► Contribution of the School to Adolescent Health

The areas of health which involve psychological pressures, both in their origin and in their resolution, are those in which the nonmedical members of the school staff can take the most constructive action. Similar pressures are operative in influencing the acceptance or nonacceptance by adolescents of differences in growth rates, in facial idiosyncrasies, or in sexual development. They affect the adolescent's handling of personal difficulties, whether these are transitory reactions to the problems of maturing or are lingering and unsolved maladjustments from childhood that have erupted anew under the special pressures of the adolescent period. There are also some matters of health about which a teacher needs to be informed, even though she can directly do little about them in the course of her daily procedures. But she can be aware of them and can be alert to their effect upon her pupils.

The teacher has four primary responsibilities with regard to the health of the student: first, alert observation and awareness of the possible implications in classroom behavior; second, knowledge of the medical resources in both the school and the community, especially of those agencies to which pupils may be sent for diagnosis, help, or advice; third, sensitivity to the possibilities in the school program for information and guidance which will promote a sound and creative program oriented toward the prevention of common adolescent problems; and fourth, willingness to help compile statistics that will

---

[2] H. J. Jacobziner, "Attempted Suicides in Children," *Journal of Pediatrics,* 65:519–525, 1960.

give an accurate picture of health during the school years.[3] This last activity is important because the teacher is the one responsible but not related adult who has the opportunity to see adolescent behavior from day to day over long periods of time.

The remaining sections of this chapter will serve to bring to the teacher's attention some of the fields that are of highest importance to her in her efforts to educate modern youth to its full possibilities. The discusson will be centered around six main topics: the development of healthy attitudes toward sex; the pressing need for greater concern with dental care; the problems of diet; the pressures arising from sheer overfatigue; the understanding and acceptance by adolescents of variations in developmental rate, physique, and so on; and the general problem of mental hygiene. These topics will be discussed in order.

1. Healthy Attitudes toward Sex   A quite obvious area of stress centers about problems of sex. Good sexual hygiene is extremely necessary to keep normal boys and girls comfortable, contented, and well-adjusted. Adolescents cannot be expected to understand the changes that have taken place in their bodies or to acquire sensible attitudes toward them without help from adults. Presumably the relevant information and training are best given by parents, but since many parents do not seem able sufficiently to overcome their own somewhat guilty attitudes toward sexual matters to discuss the situation with their children, it becomes necessary for the school to provide both the information and the training in attitudes.

A glance at usual sources of information about sex as reported in a number of studies should convince one that the school would do well to include instruction in sexual matters in some required course (Fig. 6–4). Parents were the main source of information for about a third of the girls and a fourth of the boys, and about 10 percent of the adolescents had obtained their instruction from some adult other than the parents—a doctor, teacher, or older relative, for example. Nearly a third had read books dealing with the subject. Friends of the same or the opposite sex were a source of information for a third of the boys and nearly as many of the girls. There were a few who stated that they had never received instruction from anyone. In general adults, books, and school courses contribute too little and age-mates contribute too much—of which some items are almost certainly misinformation.

In addition to the presentation of facts about sex, a school should do everything it can to build up a healthy attitude toward all matters pertaining to sex. The many problems faced by adolescents can perhaps best be discussed in the mental hygiene class, if there is one and if all pupils take it. Otherwise these questions also become material for the hygiene course. Sex is so important to adolescents that they need, in self-defense, to develop a sane attitude

---

[3] G. M. Wheatly and G. T. Hallock, *Health Observation of School Children*, 2d ed. (New York: McGraw-Hill Book Company, 1956), 488 pp., p. 4.

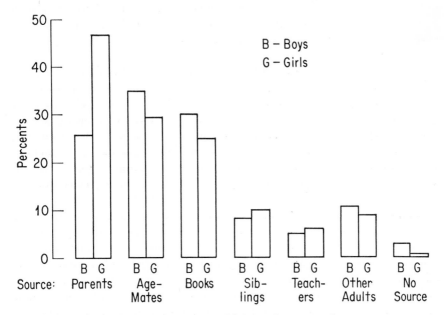

Fig. 6–4. Reported sources of information concerning sex

Based on C. S. Deschin, *Teen-Agers and Venereal Disease* (Washington, D.C.: U.S. Department of Health, Education and Welfare, 1961), 167 pp.; H. Angelino, E. R. and E. V. Mech, "Self-Expressed First Sources of Sex Information," *Psychology Newsletter,* 9:234–237, 1958; H. Angelino and E. V. Mech, "Some First Sources of Sex Information as Reported by 67 College Women," *Journal of Psychology,* 39:321–334, 1955; and "Youth's Attitudes toward Courtship and Marriage," *Report of Poll, No. 62* (Lafayette, Ind.: Division of Educational Reference, Purdue University, 1961), 16 pp., p. 3a.

about it. The discussion of sexual problems should not be postponed too long. A realistic hygiene program, from the junior high school on, should take into account also the needs of those boys and girls who must leave school early. These young people are going out into the community to develop as personalities and as citizens with a potential for good that is frequently as high as that of those who remain longer in the student status, but the very situations which lead to their early departure from school often indicate a greater-than-usual need for early and intensive help from school and community. Every social worker, clinic worker, personnel manager, and juvenile court official is in daily contact with the innumerable health problems which arise from information that is "too little and too late."

Adolescents will almost certainly obtain the facts they need from some other and less desirable source, in case both parents and school fail them, but the sources are likely to impart a feeling of shame and secrecy along with the information. These feelings may color the entire subsequent life of adolescents, especially their early heterosexual adjustments, and may make it difficult for them in turn to educate their children. The story below is a tragic record of what is likely to happen if no instruction is given.

Mark was the bright, early-maturing son of a wealthy but quite disturbed woman whose own problems with sexual adjustments had led her into four socially prominent but personally disastrous marriages, and Mark into complete confusion concerning who his current "father" was. By the time he reached an age at which information about sex might reasonably have come from either of his parents, he was too aware of some vague misery in his mother's condition and too much at odds with his current stepfather either to seek or to have much likelihood of receiving a balanced discussion of the problems he felt pressing in on him from all directions. Possibly the most outstanding impression which he gained from his mother, without actual verbal communication, was that somehow sex was connected with love and security, and of these comforts he was feeling much in need. He found the customary back-fence advice from his friends moderately sickening to him, especially as his informants did not have the vocabulary of proper words to put a "polite" aspect on relationships; but at least such information was available, and was in fact eagerly offered. By twelve, Mark was quite fully developed sexually from a physical point of view, and this maturity gave him rather a special status in the locker-room and resulted in prodding by his less squeamish peers toward "taking advantage" of his gifts. A senior in his high school made the quite-readily-available arrangements for him with a prostitute little older than he, and Mark, fortunately not traumatized as he might have been, found that this game was one that he could play with considerable satisfaction. He had the money and the means. He had very "proper" school associations with girls, but was never far from losing his control with them, and as soon as he had a "steady," he talked her into bed with little difficulty. By this time, at fifteen, he had another and a belligerently unfriendly stepfather, so for the summer he left home to work on the ranch of a friend. During this time he contracted a venereal disease from a local farm girl, and carried it back to his girl friend when he returned home. A county program for the location and treatment of people with venereal disease swept into its net the country girl and, through her, traced Mark. Full of horror and misinformation, he at first refused to damage—as he saw it— the "nice girl" he was going with by giving her name to the investigators. The public health nurse had three counseling sessions with him in the course of his treatment, and finally persuaded him to let them help the girl, who by this time had a rampant infection, although she had not the dimmest appreciation of her danger. This boy was neither delinquent in the usual sense, nor impoverished economically—he was ignorant, insecure, and more in need of love than he could possibly admit. It is almost fortunate that he was, however inadvertently, stopped in his pattern by a disease at a curable stage, and was given a chance at re-education concerning sex. If that re-education is further reinforced, he may be able to give his children a better chance than he had to learn without so much distress.

Venereal disease is a real threat to the health of many adolescents in the United States. Despite several intensive programs of identification and the widespread use of chemotherapy to control known cases, the number of infections occurring per 100,000 of the population in 1956 and 1960 was as shown in Table 6–1. These are only *known* cases, and they probably represent

Table 6–1: EXTENT OF VENEREAL INFECTION IN TWO ADOLESCENT
AGE-GROUPS IN 1956 AND 1960

		Occurrences per 100,000 of the General Population			
Type of Infection	*Year*	*Ages 10–14*		*Ages 15–19*	
		Males	*Females*	*Males*	*Females*
Gonorrhea	1956	7	29	455	364
	1960	14	25	484	349
Syphilis	1956		1	9	11
	1960		1	21	19

SOURCE: *Venereal Disease Sheet of the Communicable Disease Center, Atlanta, Georgia* (Washington, D.C.: U.S. Department of Health, Education and Welfare, 1961), 30 pp., p. 15.

many untraced contacts. The absolute size and relative increase of the problem is apparent and appalling.[4]

2. Dental Defects One of the most common, least observable, and least treated of all adolescent health problems is the presence of dental defect. Neglect of dental care may have serious health, cosmetic, and social-psychological effects throughout adolescent and adult life. The American Dental Association surveys estimated that in 1958 the average 16-year-old youth had 7 decayed, missing, or filled teeth. In fact, less than 4 percent of the high school population was considered free of dental problems![5] Of the whole nation, nearly 30 percent get no dental care at all, about 30 percent get "bare minimum" care, and only 40 percent get yearly examinations. Since the obtaining of dental care is a major economic problem, and

[4] C. S. Deschin, *Teen-agers and Venereal Disease: A Sociological Study of 600 Teen-agers in New York City Social Hygiene Clinics* (Washington, D.C.: U.S. Department of Health, Education and Welfare, 1962), 167 pp.
[5] *Dentistry in the United States: Needs and Recommendations* (American Council on Education, 1961), 68 pp. Facts stated later in this paragraph also come from this reference.

since there is very little social planning for treatment at either private or governmental levels at present, there is a gross amount of social inequality in the care received by young people from different economic backgrounds. There are only a few communities using fluoridation, despite its demonstrated ability to reduce by about 50 percent the dental caries of children who drink fluoridated water from birth. The available dentists are too few and too ill-distributed to cope with the number of those needing help. The profession sees as acute needs—aside from the problem of cost—the development of preventative programs, extended care for children, increased availability of orthodontic care, fluoridation of water systems, increased school programs, and dental research.

While the teacher can do little about the acute problems of the youth with dental needs, there is a real opportunity in this field for the classroom influence of attitudes, and for education of both the adolescents themselves and their parents toward meeting this need.

3. Dietary Problems   Another area of stress arises from the often peculiar and inadequate diet of adolescents.[6] A recent symposium on growth and health during the period has pointed out that the high school group was, irrespective of economic level, the least well nourished in the entire population. Although in a few cases the economic situation accounts for the deficiencies in adolescent nutrition, most of the problems that underlie the inadequate diet are evoked by the peer pressures and cultural confusions to which boys and girls are subjected. Unfortunately, these pressures become intense at the time when pupils are just beginning to eat away from home and to select at least some of their own food.

During adolescence the actual need for food is great. An average boy from ages 13 to 16 needs more calories than the average man does: 3200–3300 as compared with 3000 a day. From 16 to 20 his requirements are still higher, 3600 calories. Girls from 13 to 15 need more than the average woman: 2400–2600 calories as compared with 2300, but from 16 to 20 the needs decrease and 2400 calories are enough.[7]

The failure in nutrition is not, except in rare pathological cases, due to any physiological failure in appetite. The fairly vigorous adolescent can and will consume almost incredible amounts of food. Even a lass who announces with a tragedienne's accent that she is "pining away" for a lost boy friend

---

[6] The facts in this paragraph come from E. J. Dvorak, "School and College Health Services," *Review of Educational Research,* 26:522–541, 1956; P. B. Mach and A. deP. Bowes, "The Nutrition of Older Girls and Boys," *N. C. Stark Laboratory for Human Nutrition Research Bulletin,* No. 1, 1955, Denton, Texas, 107 pp.; and L. J. Bogert, *Nutrition and Physical Fitness* (Philadelphia: W. B. Saunders and Company, 1960), 650 pp.

[7] L. J. Bogert, *Nutrition and Physical Fitness* (Philadelphia: W. B. Saunders and Company, 1960), p. 497.

may polish off three glasses of milk, a steak, assorted vegetables, four slices of bread, and two desserts. One candidate for malnutrition is the homely girl who cannot unload her problems on a sympathetic family and seeks to solve them by systematic starvation in order to obtain a "glamorous" figure. Another is the boy who is so absorbed in a round of campus activities that his nourishment consists of a cup of coffee swallowed before a pregame morning band practice, a quick hot dog with assorted condiments at a corner stand while he discusses a fraternity crisis with a committee, a bag of candy during the afternoon, and a dinner of cold creamed tuna and canned peas washed down by more coffee—with disregard for the accompanying salad—during a dinner meeting of the campus newspaper staff.

Peer-culture pressures on diet are more severe for girls than for boys. Fashions and the elements of chic, as shown by film-star models and women's magazines and society pages, vary from decade to decade, but almost always present an "ideal" which is highly specific—one year bosoms are the symbol of the desirable woman of screen and fashion, the next year the wasp waist may be the rage—and usually quite unobtainable by any substantial portion of the female population. Since in the current, cultural pattern some area of the body is supposed to have an extremely slender contour, the adolescent girl often tries hard to establish a sort of "basic figure" of slimness—but she may be undernourished as a result. For the girl whose body build and appetite tend to be generous, there is a constant pressure to diet—and usually some pretty weird practices come under her notion of dieting. Cycles of starving when her desire for slimness is uppermost and of stuffing when her appetite reasserts itself leave her figure about where it was originally, but her body and personality—not to mention her schoolwork and her friendships—may be suffering from the abuse. Most boys and girls are too healthy and too hungry to carry on this fashionable foolishness for long, but if maintained, it can become a serious health hazard.

Sound nutritional patterns should certainly be explained to adolescents, but a teacher can as effectively talk to a blank wall unless she liberally laces her information concerning vitamins and proteins with the motivations of achieving a clear skin, building more athletic endurance, and so on; or she can attach the discussion of nutrition to relevant materials from the World Health Organization, using the weight of international concern to reinforce the immediate nutritional needs of her students; this approach appeals to those who reach first for the service-to-others frame of reference.

One also has to realize that food patterns are deeply ingrained in cultural, socioeconomic, and familial practices, and are extremely resistant to change. For instance, one Negro boy with whom one of the writers talked was greatly concerned about the eruptions on his face; upon questioning, it appeared that all three of his meals consisted of identical food—low quality, half-cooked bacon, fried corn pone, and coffee. When he was asked if he thought the diet could be supplemented by other food, he answered that as far as he knew, there was nothing else in the house and he doubted if his mother knew how to cook any other food. For the boy himself, the Gordian knot could be cut by getting him a job in a cafeteria and helping him select his first few meals from an array of foods of which he had never even dreamed. But changing the family food pattern would not be easy. In less extreme cases, there are usually elements of good nutrition in the family diet, and by emphasizing the positive approach of praising what one can and refraining from derogatory remarks, one can often make a real contribution through the adolescents to the well-being of the entire family. It is certain that if the teaching is to be incorporated into behavior in an enduring and useful way, it has to be adequately motivated from the adolescent's point of view.

4. Overfatigue   Another area of strain is the overfatigue that many high school pupils show. To be sure, they are all full of an abounding vitality, of which the teacher is only too aware. The average high school boy or girl uses up more calories in one day than a teacher does in three. They are forever on the go; if their attention is caught, they will work endlessly at a given chore; they rush about at top speed; they burn up energy in vigorous games; they violate most of the rules of hygiene, but at the time they seem none the worse for it. They are often restless in class for no other reason than the mere strain of sitting quietly when all their urges are to get up and "do something." Probably this period of high energy would not last for long, even with the best of hygiene, but it might endure a bit longer than it usually does if adolescents could be persuaded to take a little better care of themselves. But it is uphill work to convince a healthy 16-year-old that he should slow down; his activity gives him so much satisfaction—both physical and social—that he has no motive for restricting himself and every motive for urging himself on to even greater outlays of vital force.

The situation becomes increasingly serious in the case of the adolescent who is out to prove that he can "take" anything. Possibly he can. But probably the drive of his personality needs will push him beyond his physical limits. The most obvious place to look for overfatigue is in the area of competitive sports, although there are other places, as will presently be noted. While high physiological and bodily efficiency is typical of this age group, adolescents can be motivated by the tremendous peer pressures and emotional overload of competitive situations into exhausting themselves and pushing a normally adequate body past its critical level of endurance, with subsequent lifelong damage. One of the writers recalls an awkward, lumbering lad who was too poorly coordinated to play football successfully, and because the boy was eager to do what he could "for the team," the coach made him an animated tackling dummy. When the first team was working on defense patterns, this lad carried the ball. He was slow enough that the technique of the defense pattern could be demonstrated. He spent entire afternoons being dumped from all conceivable angles. The coach and his teammates praised him for his willingness to perform this relatively menial chore, and admired him for his stamina; although he never played more than a few minutes at the end of a game that the first team had already won, he felt he was an integral part of the scene—and he was—until he nearly died from a strangulated hernia.

5. Recognition and Acceptance of Growth Patterns Some general information and discussion of individual differences in physique, growth rate, stamina, coordination, and so on would do much to help adolescents, especially those who are too shy or self-conscious to ask for aid. Most adolescents are dissatisfied with something about their particular size or shape: they are too tall, too short, too fat, too thin, too underdeveloped, too clumsy, too asymmetrical, or too uneven in their physical capacities.

Some of these conditions are mere by-products of growth, but the pupils may regard them as being lifelong tragedies. The boy with the adult nose and the childish jaw does not know that time will bring balance to his face, nor does the late-maturing boy know that his present slight stature will change and that he may develop, just as other boys have done earlier. Even when the matter is permanent—as it is for an extremely tall girl—the school can contribute something by helping the adolescent to accept his or her build and to capitalize upon whatever advantages it may have. Above all, the teacher must never forget that a barely discernible cast in a sensitive girl's eye may be as disastrous to the girl's over-all living efficiency and happiness as the loss of a leg is to a longshoreman.

It seems useful to present the story of a student who thought she had a permanent, unchangeable defect, to which she was adjusting only by withdrawing from human contacts as much as she could and by concentrating her entire life upon book learning. The escape came from a fellow-pupil after two years of misery; it should have come from the school within the first semester of the girl's attendance.

Nancy was the youngest daughter of a wealthy family. Her two older sisters were pretty children and grew up to be attractive adolescents. Both attended a socially excellent boarding school, where they did mediocre work but were popular and had a good time. Both girls had expensive debuts, and both are now married. Nancy was a homely and awkward child. By the time she was four or five years old, her socialite mother had completely rejected her. Her father, a successful trial lawyer, was sorry for his ugly duckling and was kind enough to her when he remembered her existence, but he also neglected her, largely because he spent relatively little time with his family and left the upbringing of the three girls to his wife.

When Nancy became old enough to enter school, her father wanted her to be sent to public school, but the mother was unwilling to agree and equally un-willing to enter the child in the fashionable day school attended by the children of her friends. She therefore hired a combination teacher, companion, house-keeper, and watchdog to act as governess to Nancy, sent the two away to the country, and circulated the rumor that her youngest daughter had a tendency to tuberculosis and could not attend school. Nancy and her governess lived in almost complete seclusion until the girl was fourteen. The father saw her about once a month, but the mother not more than two or three times a year. At this point, the governess died, and some new disposition had to be made of a homely, awk-ward, isolated, sensitive girl. After much discussion, some of which Nancy over-heard, the mother entered the girl in a small, obscure, distant boarding school, using the girl's middle name as a last name.

By this time Nancy knew very well that she was a disgrace to the family, that her mother was bitterly ashamed of her, and that her sisters did not wish her to speak to them if she should meet them in any public place. She was also con-vinced that their estimate of her was quite correct. At fourteen, Nancy was a tall, thin, awkward, homely girl who shuffled along the school corridors looking at her own feet and avoiding as many contacts as possible. At mealtime she sat where she was told to sit, passed the bread or the butter as requested, kept her eyes on her plate, spoke to no one, and answered only in monosyllables if spoken to. In class her work was brilliant, but she recited with her eyes on the floor and she often stammered when called upon. Because of her superior work in school she was often asked by her teachers to help girls who were having difficulties, and these tutoring sessions brought her in contact with a number of girls who eventually not only admired but liked her.

Although Nancy came from an excellent family, she had been given little or no help in those skills that her mother could most readily have taught her. She did not know how to select clothes, to use make-up, to maintain a conversation, or even to be gracious. During her first two years in boarding school Nancy had to acquire the simple, basic, social skills that she badly needed. Her schoolwork remained excellent, she had reasonable success in school athletics, and she had many acquaintances although no close friends. She continued to wear any clothes that were bought for her by her mother and to throw them on without effort to make herself attractive, although she was always clean and neat. During her third year she was called upon to tutor the most popular girl in the school. The school idol was not long in seeing Nancy's true worth and in becoming her loyal friend. Since Nancy had plenty of money, her new friend simply sent Nancy's clothes to the Salvation Army, spent over $400 in buying new ones, turned Nancy over for a day to an expert beautician, and convinced Nancy that attention to appearances was really necessary.

What emerged from the weekend spree of buying and self-improvement was an extraordinarily handsome girl, who was not conventionally pretty but was cer-tainly striking. Never again could Nancy be overlooked. With the handicap of her ugliness removed both publicly and in her own mind, Nancy became happy and moderately popular. Because of her abilities she was encouraged to go on to college. There, in a new environment among people who did not know she had ever been homely, she attained outstanding success. She is now happily married to a man of excellent background. In her leisure time she continues to tutor high school youngsters and works voluntarily with a social agency, taking neglected and rejected children into her own home, where she gives them such understanding and affection that many of them recover. An ironical conclusion to this history is the fact that Nancy's social status is appreciably higher than that of either sister and she is, at forty, the best looking one of the three.

This study is also relevant to the immediately following paragraphs on mental hygiene, since the solving of the basic problem might have been useless without an alteration in the girl's attitude toward herself.

6. Mental Hygiene   There is a great deal of casual public concern about the subject of mental health, and an almost equal amount of confusion about it. The adolescent needs to learn, as do his elders, that mental health is a highly individual matter, and is not to be equated with conformity, with an absolute standard, or with a static condition. Mental health is the attribute of a living organism, and is related to the individual's setting, his inner and outer experiences as well as to the bases upon which he has organized them, and to his psychobiological condition at any given time. The school can be of great assistance in helping the adolescent to feel that his own personality has great value, that the difficulties he has with himself are not necessarily abnormal although they may appear monumental to him, and that there is help available for him in solving these problems. He need not stand alone.

Certainly the problems of mental health are suitable for discussion in any consideration of the health of the adolescent, but because they present great complexities, they will be taken up in more detail in subsequent chapters concerning the social and emotional developments of the adolescent period. It will suffice here to point out that this area is of major concern and includes such critical problems as mental illness, addiction to narcotics, psychopathic delinquency, suicide, and the vast fringe of disturbed young persons who need help in coping with their feelings.

An idea concerning the size of the problem can be gained from a survey made in one large metropolitan area, in which teachers were asked to report the number of pupils in their classes who they felt needed either extra help from the school because of minor emotional problems or referral to skilled psychiatric consultation because of deep emotional disturbance. In the ninth through the twelfth grades, the teachers reported that 6.6, 6.9, 4.4, and 2.0 percents respectively of their pupils needed the extra help, and that 2.4, 2.1,

2.8, and 0.8 percent were in acute need of psychiatric assistance.[8] It is tragic to add that very few of these young people have much chance of receiving the help they require, because the schools are lacking in adequately trained consultants, and even in a sufficient staffing of school counselors. Nor do most communities have a sufficient number of centers to which children or adolescents can be sent for help with serious maladjustments.

The observant teacher can do much to notice, to report, to inform, and to prevent unnecessary complications that arise from the classroom management of these young people. Furthermore, while the teacher neither can nor should assume the position of diagnostician or therapist to the disturbed adolescent, she is often able to alleviate much of the unhappiness of a boy or girl who is not profoundly disturbed but has some transient problem with which he or she needs assistance and counsel.

Finally, the writers would like to emphasize the need for giving young people information about sources of help for various problems. There would be fewer victims of inadequate care if the young people involved knew where to go for help; that is, if they knew about clinics, hospital out-patient service, and so on. Probably the best way to get rid of the numerous quacks is not by legislating—although that attack also has its place—but by telling people where they can get better treatment. An amazing proportion of adolescents are reduced to back-fence methods because no responsible person has ever told them what facilities in their community may be available. The number of adolescents who cannot find a solution of any kind is reflected by the suicide rates in this age group; one of the first ten killers is the adolescent's own despair.

▶ Summary

The recent rapid development of public health programs, with their emphasis on community participation in the prevention of disease, the prolongation of life and the active promotion of health makes a strong contribution to the positive approach to the subject. Further, the rather acute national concern with the fitness of the youth population and the drive for increasing programs for better physical development in the secondary schools has re-evoked as a major educational goal the long underplayed ideal of "a sound mind in a sound body."

During adolescence, when boys and girls are developing their own abilities to care for themselves but are powerfully influenced by family and peer pressures, adequate information and guidance in matters of health are major responsibilities of the school. Alert, understanding handling of both expressed and unexpressed needs and problems is essential to the individual welfare of adolescents and ultimately to the welfare of the community. To

---

[8] *Mental Health Survey of Los Angeles County, 1957–1959* (California Department of Mental Hygiene, 1960), 566 pp., p. 513.

make instruction in health and hygiene a functioning part of the adolescent's life, it must bear a relation that *he* can recognize to his own needs and to the patterns of the world in which he lives.

References for Further Reading

BOOKS

Other Texts

Ausubel, *Theory and Problems of Adolescent Development* (Chap. 6 or 17).
Breckenridge and Vincent, *Child Development*, 4th ed. (Chap. 4).
Garrison, *Growth and Development*, 2d ed. (pp. 269–293).
Hurlock, *Adolescent Development*, 2d ed. (Chap. 3).
Kuhlen, *The Psychology of Adolescent Development* (pp. 71–85).
Wattenberg, *The Adolescent Years* (Chap. 7).

Other Books

Barker, R. G. *et al., Adjustment to Physical Handicap and Illness* (Social Science Research Council, 1953), 430 pp. (Chap. 1 or 2).
Harnett, A. L., and J. H. Shaw, *Effective School Health Education* (New York: Appleton-Century-Crofts, 1959), 421 pp. (Chap. 3 or 6).
Turner, C. E., *School Health and Health Education*, 4th ed. (St. Louis, Mo.: C. V. Mosby Company, 1961), 471 pp. (any 25–30 pp.).
Wheatley, G. M., and G. T. Hallock, *Health Observations of School Children*, 2d ed. (New York: McGraw-Hill Book Company, 1956), 488 pp. (pp. 1–30).

ARTICLES

Angelino, H., and E. V. Mech, "Fears and Worries Concerning Physical Changes: A Preliminary Study of 32 Females," *Journal of Psychology,* 39:195–198, 1955.
Bayer, L. M., and M. M. Snyder, "Illness Experience of a Group of Normal Children," *Child Development,* 21:95–120, 1950.
Eichorn, D. H., and J. P. McKee, "Physiological Instability during Adolescence," *Child Development,* 29:255–268, 1958.
Fryer, D. G., and M. P. Rich, "Denial of Illness in Relation to Intellectual Functioning," *Journal of Nervous and Mental Diseases,* 131:523–527, 1960.
Staton, W. M., "The Adolescent: His Physical Growth and Health," *Review of Educational Research,* 24:19–29, 1954.

Suggested Research Problems [9]

1. A study over a number of years of those adolescents who attempt suicide, especially an examination of their previous school record, behavior, and expressed attitudes, with the purpose of identifying any premonitory symptoms

---

[9] See note, p. 11.

that might be of value in preventing such emotional trauma in the future.
2. Study of a large number of adolescent boys who have had traffic accidents, to
determine, if possible, the attitudes that have contributed to the unwise
handling of their cars. For each boy the investigation should take place as
soon as possible after the accident. It would be best to work in cooperation
with the juvenile court in this problem.

Chapter 7 | Physical Deviation

ALMOST every individual has some slight deviation from the norm, but most such variations serve only to enhance the sense of identity. One person has a middle toe that is as long as the second, another has a mole between the shoulder blades, and a third has a pair of eyebrows that do not quite match. But these deviations are accepted, or something fairly simple is done about them. Or, the condition may be somewhat more serious but still something one can live with, such as an unusual susceptibility to colds or a tendency toward constipation; these conditions are a little harder to deal with because they present problems of health, which those mentioned above do not. The adolescents to be described in the following chapter show deviations of a more extreme nature and of many types. A teacher is almost certain to meet some, if not all, of these types in the course of her work. She therefore needs some comprehension of the handicapping conditions, a sympathetic understanding of adolescent reactions to them, and an adequate knowledge of what assistance both she and the pupil can obtain, inside the school and out.

This chapter begins with a presentation of the frequency with which different handicaps occur within the general population—and specifically among those of school age—and goes on to a discussion of typical adolescent reactions. Then there is a section describing typical cases of physical deviation, plus a final section on the provisions that are commonly made for the best handling of these boys and girls in the school.

▶ General Frequency of Physical Deviation in the Adolescent Population

All material on frequency will be presented in this section. The teacher needs to have some notion of how many pupils she can expect to be handicapped in each of the several ways about to be described. This section should serve as a general and necessary background for the whole problem of physical deviation.

Practically all results are based upon samples that are taken at random from an entire population. The results are influenced not only by the size of the sample and the methods used in selecting it, but also by the attitudes and interests of those making the survey. Thus, if a survey were made by a teacher, by a social worker, by a school doctor, and by a specialist in any medical field of the defects shown among the same hundred children, the resulting lists would be different, both in number and type of the conditions reported. The investigations to be presented in this section are to be regarded as representative samples, not as gospel truth. They were all based upon an adequate number of cases, and they were all done with care, but they do not always agree and at best the results are only approximations. They should, however, be sufficient to give a teacher an orientation for the later sections of the chapter.

1. General Surveys   A National Health survey of the school population involving over 50,000 children and adolescents has provided information about handicaps at two age levels, 0–14 and 15–24 years. Figure 7–1 shows the degree of physical impairment for the two age ranges. In both groups, the orthopedic defects form the largest single class; in the

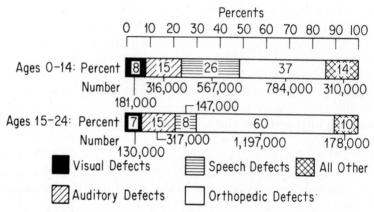

Fig. 7–1. Distribution of impairment in two age groups

Based on "Health Statistics: Children and Youth, Selected Health Characteristics, July 1957—June 1958," *Public Health Service Reports* (Washington, D.C.: U.S. Department of Health, Education, and Welfare, 1959), 43 pp., p. 15.

latter they more than outweigh all the others put together. The main difference between the two age levels lies in the reduction of speech defects from 26 percent of the total to 8 percent. In the entire group 83 percent showed no defects; the remaining 17 percent showed one or more, but of these defects 82 percent imposed no restriction upon activity and 98 percent no restriction upon mobility.[1]

[1] *Health Statistics: Children and Youth, Selected Health Characteristics, July 1957—June 1958* (Washington, D.C.: U.S. Department of Health, Education, and Welfare, 1957), 43 pp., p. 17.

2. Defects in Vision, Hearing and Speech   In order to show the number of visual defects with which children arrive at school age, a few results will be given from a survey of a single county. The testing included all children entering the kindergarten or first grade, all new entrants in any grade up through the sixth, and all children referred by teachers. It might be mentioned in passing that less than 2 percent of the teachers' referrals turned out to be unnecessary. The results of the survey are presented in Table 7–1. Just over 85 percent of the entrants had no visual defect. The

Table 7–1: FREQUENCY OF VISUAL DEFECTS IN A SCHOOL POPULATION

Types of Defect	Numbers	Percent of Those Having Any Defect At All
One defect, only	1419	70
Decreased visual acuity	86	4
Refractive error	1034	51
Inadequate coordination	242	12
Organic defect	57	3
Two defects, in varying combinations of those listed above	552	27
Three defects, in varying combinations of those listed above	59	3
Total	2030	100

SOURCE: H. R. Weatherbe, "Modified Clinical Technique Vision Screening," *Journal of Health, Physical Education, and Recreation,* 32:23–24, 1961. Used by permission of The American Association for Health-Physical Education-Recreation.

testers classified the defects they found as concerned with visual acuity, refractive error, coordination (muscular balance), and organic conditions. Of those children who had any defect at all, 70 percent had only one, 27 percent had two, and 3 percent had three.

The incidence of visual impairment is not evenly distributed over the school-age range, and tends strongly to increase during the later part of adolescence. The constant use of the eyes in modern life—both in school and out—imposes enough strain to overtax vision. Two studies throw light on the increase of visual defect with age. In one case,[2] mass vision tests were given to 6000 children between the ages of 5 and 18. In the first two grades, less than 5 percent failed the tests, but in the twelfth grade 30 percent failed. A second study [3] concerned the change in vision in the same individuals over

[2] H. M. Leverett, "Vision Test Performance of School Children," *American Journal of Ophthalmology,* 44(4):508–518, Part I, 1957.
[3] M. W. Morgan, "Changes in Refraction over a Period of Twenty Years in a Non-visually Selected Sample," *American Journal of Optometry and Archives of the American Academy of Optometry,* 35:281–299, 1958.

a period of twenty years. In 1934, a group of 150 children was selected for study of general growth patterns. Among other tests they were given tests of vision. At this time the average age was 13 years. In 1954, when the average age was 33, the investigator retested 95 of the original group. At both age levels the girls showed nearly twice as many eye defects as the boys. At the second examination 25 percent of the men and 47 percent of the women had defective eyesight. It was estimated that by the time these young adults reached the age of 50 all the women and at least half of the men would have defective vision.

In addition to those pupils who have moderate and easily corrected visual defects, there are about 70,000 children and adolescents of school age who have visual impairments so serious that they are classed as having only partial vision.[4] Many of these are in public school, either in special or in regular classes. They are there either because there are no facilities for their special care or because there are programs in the classrooms to integrate them into the school activities of their age group and to give them a more normal life than they can have in an institution. It is well to point out that these pupils share the problems of any adolescent,[5] with certain practical and qualitative differences, and that they have special problems of social and emotional adjustment because of their handicap. Completely blind pupils also sometimes attend the public schools.

There is an unusual lack of coherence in both standards and methods of testing and reporting deafness. The estimates have ranged from 2 to 21 percent for impairment of hearing among school children and from 1 in 700 to 1 in 2500 for actual deafness.[6] In a careful study of an entire school population, by means of audiometric tests, some interesting and probably typical results were obtained.[7] Of the 1726 pupils, aged 5 through 14, nearly 7 percent failed the tests at least once. The retests were given every two years—making a longitudinal series of four complete surveys. At age 8, there was an increase of approximately 2 percent over the incidence of defect among the same children at age 6; similar increases of 1 percent occurred at age 10 and again at age 12. These results suggest that a high school teacher can expect 7 out of every 100 pupils in her classes to have some degree of impairment in hearing.

The number of pupils with speech defects has been estimated from sam-

---

[4] *Social Work Yearbook, 1960* (National Association of Social Workers, Boyd, 1960), 800 pp., pp. 433–434.

[5] B. Lowenfeld, "The Blind Adolescent in a Seeing World," *Exceptional Children,* 25:310–315, 1959; and G. L. Able, "The Blind Adolescent and His Needs," *Exceptional Children,* 26:309–334, 1960.

[6] L. E. Connor, "Determining the Prevalence of Hearing-Impaired Children," *Exceptional Children,* 27:337–344, 1961.

[7] S. H. Wishik, E. R. Kramm, and E. M. Kock, "Audiometric Testing in School Children," *Public Health Reports,* Vol. 73, No. 3, 1958, pp. 265–278.

ples, as in the case of both hearing and vision. Although the total number found in a given survey depends in some measure upon what minor defects the investigator includes, the percentages for stammering alone are remarkably stable. Three studies all arrived at almost the same figure for the occurrence of stammerers in the general population: 0.5 percent, 0.6 percent, and 0.55 percent.[8] The relation of boys to girls varied from 7 to 1 to 3 to 1.

It is estimated that there are 1,300,000 stutterers in the United States, of whom half are of school age. The condition can begin at any age but usually does appear between 2 and 4, when children are learning to talk. Particularly vulnerable is the only child and the boy who has two or three older sisters. Boys are slower in their physical development than girls, and in their linguistic development very much slower. Therefore a boy is less well able to withstand the adult pressure exerted upon the only child or the female-based expectation of parents whose standards for linguistic progress have been formed by two or three daughters.

3. Frequency of Orthopedic Disabilities   About 5 children in every 1000 in the general population under 21 years of age can be expected to require special help because of orthopedic defects. As shown in Figure 7–1, difficulties of this type more than equal the total of all other defects among adolescents. The mere size of the problem has led to the development of both private and governmental agencies for providing services to handicapped youth. In 1958–1959 the federal, state, and local contributions to the Crippled Children's Services totaled over $52,660,000.[9] Even this large sum did not meet the need. The federal appropriation for 1961 was 20 million.

In the past there were many adolescents who were crippled by poliomyelitis. In 1954 doctors reported 38,483 cases, of which 18,308 were of the paralytic type. By 1959 the total had decreased to 8415, of which 6289 were paralytic.[10] The decreases have continued and may be expected to do so at an even greater rate. In fact, the disease can be eliminated by systematic immunization. For some years, however, there will continue to be a few adolescents who are more or less crippled by the disease.

---

[8] P. Henderson, "The Incidence of Stammering and Speech Defects in School Children," *Bulletin of the Minnesota Public Health Laboratory Service*, 6:102–105, 1947; W. Johnson, "To Help the Child with a Speech Handicap," *Child*, 15:12–14, 1950; M. D. Schindler, "A Study of the Educational Adjustment of Stuttering and Non-stuttering Children," pp. 348–357 in W. Johnson and R. R. Leutenegger, *Stuttering in Children and Adults* (Minneapolis, Minn.: University of Minnesota Press, 1955), 472 pp.

[9] *Social Work Yearbook, 1960* (National Society of Social Workers, 1961), 760 pp., pp. 433–437.

[10] "Health and Vital Statistics for the United States," *Public Health Service Bulletin No. 584-B35* (Washington, D.C.: U.S. Department of Health, Education and Welfare, 1960), 50 pp., p. 22.

4. Chronic Illness Allergies of various types are common. They may be reactions to certain foods, to medicines, to pollens, to skin or hair of either people or animals, to dust, to feathers or kapok, or to practically anything. If a child is allergic to any ordinary element in his environment he shows his trouble early—usually by the end of his second year. Allergies tend to remain dormant during middle and late childhood but to show an upswing in both frequency and severity during preadolescence and adolescence. The types of allergy also vary somewhat with age. Hives and eczema predominate in early childhood, hay fever and asthma during adolescence.[11]

The mortality from tuberculosis has been greatly reduced in the last decade. The rate in 1960 was 6 deaths per 100,000 in the United States as compared with 20 per 100,000 in 1951. However, the incidence remains a good deal too high. According to the National Tuberculosis Society, in 1962 in the United States one new case of the disease was reported every seven minutes.[12] The total number of cases given for 1958 was 1,200,000. It is probable that almost every high school teacher will have in her classes from time to time an adolescent who is developing the disease or has returned to school after it has been arrested.

About diabetes there seem to be only estimates by various authorities. In one report the total given for the entire country was 3,000,000, of whom 15 percent—or 450,000—were children or adolescents.[13]

From the above brief presentation one can see that, despite the general high level of health during adolescence, there are some young people who are handicapped or ill. Their presence in the school population poses problems for the classroom teacher.

▶ **The Adolescent's Reactions to Physical Handicaps**

In general, it is the adolescent's *reaction* to handicap that is important, because he feels himself to be "different." It is this sense of difference that is in many instances the real limitation.[14] A physical handi-

---

[11] L. M. Bayer and M. M. Snyder, "Illness Experience in a Group of Normal Children," *Child Development,* 21:105, 1950.

[12] Figures supplied by the screening committee of the National Tuberculosis Society.

[13] H. Sparks, *Easing a Life Sentence,* 1958. From a radio address, based on materials furnished by Doctors Solomon and Brown of the Medical School of the University of California at Los Angeles.

[14] B. A. Wright, *Physical Disability—A Psychological Approach* (New York: Harper & Row, Publishers, 1960), 408 pp., pp. 179–208; L. Levine, "The Impact of Disability," *Journal of Rehabilitation,* 25:10–12, 1959; P. H. Mussen and D. K. Newman, "Acceptance of Handicap: Motivation and Adjustment in Physically Disabled Children," *Exceptional Children,* 24:255–260, 1958; and C. Smock and M. Cruickshank, "Responses of Handicapped and Normal Children to the Rosenzweig Picture-Frustration Study," *Quarterly Journal of Child Behavior,* 4:156–164, 1952.

cap does not need to be of a serious nature, medically speaking, for it to be a problem to the adolescent, because the condition may affect profoundly his concept of himself and through his self-concept his relationships to his peers. The strain for the boy or girl arises from either of two sources—from the obvious nature of the handicap or from its failure to show at all. The boy with three fingers missing on his throwing hand cannot play baseball for reasons that are clear enough but may make him feel as if he were some kind of a monstrosity, whereas the boy with a cardiac insufficiency is equally unable to play but for reasons that cannot be seen, much less explained to other adolescents. Both youngsters tend to underrate themselves, and both suffer from chronic frustration.

A skillful teacher can be most helpful to a handicapped pupil, provided she understands his problems and accepts him as he is. Her acceptance is influential in the establishment of a similarly receptive attitude from the adolescent's age-mates. If a teacher can provide circumstances in which the handicapped adolescent can find success among his peers, she can make a major contribution to his welfare.

In handling children with chronic physical handicaps the teacher should try to avoid frustrating situations as much as possible, because such children tend to react strongly and to become deeply disturbed. It is therefore essential that the teacher avoid situations in which a pupil's disability puts him in a markedly inferior position or in a potentially frustrating one.

▶ Defects and Handicaps in the Schoolroom

The various defects and handicaps to be discussed in this section have been grouped under the headings: (1) defects of vision, (2) defects of hearing, (3) defects of speech, (4) orthopedic disabilities, (5) chronic illnesses, (6) skin conditions, (7) glandular and nutritional problems. Any teacher can expect to have in her room pupils who are handicapped in one way or another, and she should have some understanding of the conditions and a deep appreciation of the widespread effects of such conditions upon both personality and social relationships.

1. Defects of Vision Inadequate vision is so obvious a handicap and so common as to merit first place in the discussion of defects. In the lower grades children can learn much by ear and thus avoid eyestrain, but each successive year demands more and more reading, both in school and out. In high school the demands upon vision increase rapidly, and defects become even more important in influencing school work.

Teachers do not always recognize the symptoms: holding the book too close to the eyes, going to the board to read what is on it, going to stand under the clock in order to read the time, squinting, rubbing the eyes, shading them from light, complaining of pain after reading, becoming irritable after or clearly uncomfortable while reading or doing other close work, and so on. If a pupil with defective vision really wants to study he will strain his eyes, complain of discomfort, and be treated. Many pupils, however, do not have a passionate desire for learning, so they build up the defensive habit of neglecting their work as a way of saving their eyesight. They do not complain of eyestrain because they rarely do enough reading to feel any. Their main symptom is not pain, but abstinence from study. The fundamental defect is often so covered by emotional attitudes about schoolwork that they themselves do not know why they hate studying or become restless after a few minutes of reading. A teacher should suspect inadequate eyesight whenever apparently intelligent pupils do not study. The story below describes a common reaction of the pupil with astigmatism, farsightedness, or muscular disbalance.

Neil entered high school with a record of good work in the primary grades, average work at the intermediate level, and poor work in junior high school. It had been assumed that he was a dull pupil who was making heavy weather of his schooling because he was approaching the limits of his ability. Neil had had four tests of intelligence before leaving junior high school. On the first—a group test for use with primary grade children before they could read—and on the Binet he had earned IQs of 121 and 113. On the last two—both group tests involving reading—his IQs were 87 and 84. The high school counselor read the record and was struck both by the loss of IQ and by the progressively poorer schoolwork. She wondered if the boy were deteriorating and therefore sent for him to come to her office.

During the subsequent interview Neil showed little insight into his difficulties. His chief complaint was that the teachers gave too long assignments. Upon further questioning he admitted that he had never liked to read. He enjoyed school but was afraid he would not be able to finish the twelfth grade. He regarded failure as a disgrace and seemed unduly preoccupied with thoughts of failure. He had recently begun to fancy that other pupils were calling him stupid behind his back. In spite of his evident discouragement, the counselor felt that the earlier IQs were more accurate than the later ones, but if they were correct then there must be some block, defect, frustration, or handicap that was interfering with normal progress. Neil's dislike of reading was especially curious, assuming that he was fundamentally bright rather than dull. The counselor decided to watch the boy read and see what she could deduce from his procedure, so she pretended to be busy with finishing a report and asked him to read his history assignment until she was free again to continue the interview. As she shifted papers about on her desk, she covertly watched him. Neil read about three minutes and then began to wiggle and twist. At the end of five minutes he was glancing out the window, closing his eyes for several seconds at a time, and becoming more and more restless. Presently he went out to get a drink, then to go to the toilet, then to look at something on the bulletin board, and then to make a telephone call. At the end of thirty-five minutes he had completed barely five pages of reading. His behavior had impressed the counselor as being much like that shown by small children who see just well enough to read a little but not well enough to read comfortably. She therefore asked Neil about his eyesight; as far as he knew, it was normal. He was clearly not nearsighted, and he said he had never been troubled with headaches. Nevertheless, the counselor sent him to an oculist, who found a slight astigmatism and a slight muscular imbalance. Both conditions were mild, but together they made reading an uncomfortable procedure. In the first three grades Neil had learned to recognize the commonest words but had followed the stories by guesswork and had learned other subjects largely by ear. He was able to read for only two or three minutes without discomfort, and he simply stopped reading before the discomfort developed into pain. Being a bright child he got along well enough at first, but in the intermediate grades the reading load became heavier and not everything in his books was discussed in class. However, he picked up enough by listening carefully and by reading in short snatches to keep up with the class average. In junior high school his failure to read became too great a handicap, even for a bright mind. Two of his teachers had evidently suspected a reading deficiency and had independently given him tests, but Neil could always pull himself together for the few minutes that were necessary for a test, so he made good scores on both occasions, although he was a little slow. The boy's defect was hidden even from himself, but it had influenced both his progress in school and his emotional attitudes.

The wearing of glasses made consecutive reading possible for Neil, and he no longer had to protect himself by neglecting his work. For a semester Neil attended a class in study methods, since he had to learn how to work efficiently. By the end of his freshman year Neil was doing good work. During the following summer he read from morning till night. The world of books suddenly burst upon him, and he was fascinated with the ideas he found. His parents had to chase him out of the house to play for a while each day. Neil is now a successful and well-adjusted college sophomore.

2. Defects of Hearing The young person with a hearing defect has a very difficult social situation with which to deal. His handicap is either not obvious at all, in which case he has constant difficulty—but for no perceptible reason—in communicating with his peers, or else he is wearing a hearing aid and suffers from the sense of "differentness" which is painful to him. In either case, the teacher who is aware of the condition and of its effects can do a great deal to reduce or avoid the pressures which make the hearing-handicapped student prone to isolation and vulnerable to any of the many problems which grow out of inadequate communication. The young person who is completely deaf has the same difficulties in intensified form.[15]

---

[15] For a good discussion of this point see E. Levine, *The Psychology of Deafness* (New York: Columbia University Press, 1960), 383 pp.

Inability to hear clearly affects all learning experiences in school and can have permanent effects upon the individual's total personality.

The symptoms of hearing defect are usually quite obvious: frequent requests to have questions repeated, indifference to noise or the whispering of other children, failure to look up from work at some sound that is sufficient to attract others, cocking the head sideways to listen, failing to catch directions given orally, speaking in a "flat" voice, and putting the fingers into the ears to rub the canal. Such items of behavior are sometimes regarded as mere personal idiosyncrasies and are therefore disregarded. The indirect results of inadequate hearing are illustrated by the following history:

Edward is a young man of twenty-five and, at the present time, a graduate student in a large university. He happens to be majoring in an overcrowded field, and even the graduate classes are large. Edward began to lose his hearing when he was about sixteen years old and was not accepted in the army at eighteen because he could not pass the hearing tests. Edward comes of a French family and did not learn to speak English until his family came to this country when he was about fifteen. At first he attended a French day school and did not therefore make serious efforts to learn English until after his hearing had begun to deteriorate. His English is now fluent, and he has an unusually large vocabulary, but he cannot hear well enough to correct his mispronunciations, which are numerous.

Edward had increasing difficulty with his work as he progressed through high school and college. He has a quick mind and is a good enough student, insofar as what he can read is concerned; but he does not hear with sufficient accuracy what the teacher says in class, even though he sits in the front row. A class discussion is practically lost as far as he is concerned. He has wanted to get a hearing aid, but he has never been able to get enough money ahead to acquire one. Although Edward's undergraduate record was good, his graduate marks are always on the edge of eliminating him. He can get a "B" in most of his courses, but once in a while, when a professor has a light voice or if there is an unusual amount of class discussion, he gets a "C." Since he has to maintain a "B" average, every "C" has to be balanced by an "A," and in a group of any size it is almost impossible for him to get the highest grade. His major field is so popular that even the seminars enroll fifteen to twenty students. Since Edward does not know which student will be called upon to talk on any given day, he cannot be sure of sitting near enough to hear the student's report. His only "A's" in graduate work have come from his thesis work, in which the contacts were entirely individual.

Edward has relatively few friends, although he is a pleasant lad for the most part. In recent years he has developed a suspiciousness about people that is probably based upon his incomplete hearing. Edward has been strongly advised to take a semester off from his university work, earn enough money to get whatever hearing aid is best for him, and return to school with as little handicap as may be possible. Otherwise, he will certainly never get the degree he wants. And his social contacts and chances for employment will remain on a level far inferior to that consonant with his superior abilities.

3. Defects of Speech Many investigators of speech difficulties do not distinguish between stuttering and stammering. Actually, both are often called stuttering, and in some instances the same child shows the two defects simultaneously or at different times. It seems, however, worth while to describe both types of defect. Stuttering consists of a repetition of a sound, as in the song: "K-k-k-k-k-Katy, B-b-beautiful K-k-Katy . . ." Stammering is quite different. The stammerer does not repeat sounds; he is unable to make any coherent noise at all. His mouth opens, his jaws move, and he tries hard—but nothing happens. The accompanying facial contortions are painful to watch. Sometimes the stammerer finally breaks through a "block," and sometimes he does not.

Stammering betrays its emotional origins most clearly by it capricious appearances and disappearances. There are, for instance, concert singers who stammer when they talk; ministers who preach fluently but stammer in talking with parishioners; students who stammer in their native English but speak acquired French or German or Spanish without defect; businessmen who conduct as much business as possible on the telephone because they stammer only when face to face with another person; children who recite aloud to themselves in their rooms without hesitation but cannot say the same words in class; actors who are tense and hesitant in speech off the stage but relaxed and fluent on it (even when they have to invent a few lines to cover an unexpected pause); teachers who often stammer in one class and never in another; and so on. One of the writers knows a young man who teaches his college classes with not more than two or three attacks of stammering in a year, but he is as likely as not to come to grief in asking his best friend for a match.

Explanations have been sought by many investigators, but most of the obvious lines of research have proved to be blind alleys. They have, however, served to prove what stuttering is *not* due to. For instance, there is no difference in the structure of the speech organs between the stuttering and normal child. There is no convincing evidence that the condition is caused by forcing a lefthanded child to use his right hand in school. There is no difference in either the range or the average of mental ability; stammerers vary in IQ from 80 to 130, with an average at 100—just like any other group. While it is true that speech defects tend to run in families, they do not seem to be hereditary. What is far more probable is that the emotional conditioning that produced defects in the parents is handed on by them to their children, since most parents tend to perpetuate in their own homes the home in which they grew up. The most tenable theory at present is that stuttering is only one possible manifestation of children who are emotionally maladjusted. It is not an entity in itself but just a symptom. However, the spasmodic disturbance of speech so distresses the parents that they concentrate all their efforts upon trying to remove the symptom without ever discovering the underlying cause. They may be likened to a doctor who tries to reduce a temperature without knowing what produced it. The stutterer himself has even less idea of what is the matter with him. The only trait that seems to distinguish him from other emotionally disturbed and neurotic children is his intense fear of speaking—and this phobia is probably a result, not a cause. He does not stutter because he is afraid to speak; he is afraid to speak because he stutters.

There is actually one outstanding difference between stuttering and normal children—a general slowness of motor development. Out of 50 stuttering children, all but 3 were retarded in motor development for their age, and 23–46 percent—were retarded by 5 years or more.[16] This motor disorganization does not cause stuttering, but it presumably does act as a predisposing condition upon the basis of which the speech defect may develop. There are a good many people whose motor control is equally poor, but they do not stutter.

The earliest step toward the development of a speech defect has nothing to do with speech. Because of the parental treatment he has received the prestammerer is already insecure, anxious, emotionally immature, self-conscious, self-centered, excitable, and morbidly afraid of such things as frighten most small children. These are the traits of any neurotic child, and they predate the development of overt symptoms that call attention to difficulty. The fears and anxieties are at first diffuse and unidentified, but if the child is not carefully handled he becomes confused, he feels incompetent and guilty, and often ends by becoming extremely hostile.[17]

As in the case with other defects, the response of the sufferer is more important than the condition. It is not long before a stammerer discovers that his inability to speak is a ruinous handicap in his efforts to attain status among his age-mates or to make progress in school. Times without number he experiences the frustration of knowing the answer but being totally unable to give it after his teacher has noticed his wildly waving hand and called upon him. He suffers also from a fear of ridicule or of pity, from acute self-consciousness and embarrassment, and from a hopeless sense of permanent inferiority. As one adolescent sufferer gave witness, "One day another stutterer and I were called on to speak in English class. When he spoke first, they all pitied him. I walked right out of the room and straight to a movie house. I

---

[16] P. Ozeretsky, "Psychosomatic Studies of 50 Stuttering Children," *Journal of Orthopsychiatry*, 16:114–133, 1946.
[17] The above discussion is based largely upon A. I. Murphy, and R. M. Fitzsimmons, *Stuttering and Personality Dynamics* (New York: Ronald Press Company, 1960), 519 pp.; and A. B. Dominic, *Stuttering: A Psychodynamic Approach to its Understanding and Treatment* (New York: The Julian Press, 1954), 304 pp.

can't stand it when people pity me." [18] At the onset of adolescence, with its powerful social and emotional drives, the stammerer has fresh troubles. He cannot have dates, or go to dances, or even talk to girls in the school corridors. He is usually too self-conscious to play games well, he cannot take a normal part in group discussions, he is rarely asked to join clubs. If he has a bosom friend, it is likely to be another outcast like himself. As the years roll by, the act of talking becomes more and more closely associated with struggle, tension, frustration, failure, disappointment, discomfort, displeasure, and perhaps punishment.

Any constructive treatment for stammering requires a long time and usually involves a change in a child's entire life. So far as direct treatment of the defect is concerned, there is nothing that a teacher can do or should attempt to do. She can, however, make some indirect contributions that may be of vital importance. She can begin by bringing about a change in the attitude of the other children toward the stutterer—making her explanations when he is out of the room. She can also give him the little extra attentions that children all love, can make him feel accepted and wanted, can assign to him small chores that do not require speech, and can provide an atmosphere in which he can relax and feel safe. She can protect him from the ridicule or bullying of other children and from her own impatience. She can realize that the defect is going to influence progress in all fields of endeavor and can avoid making too many demands or setting unreachable standards. In a practical way, she can inform herself about the nature of speech defects, she can find out where the sufferer can be referred and make sure that both the child and his parents go where they can obtain the expert help that she cannot give.[19] Teachers as a group can also contribute to the entire problem of stuttering by getting before all parents, through the Parent-Teacher Association, the main facts about the genesis of speech defects. This procedure will not cure any pupil who already stammers, but it should prevent a number of well-intentioned parents and teachers from making stammerers out of normal children.

The history given below describes one type of home background that produces both stammerers and other types of neurotic children.

Jimmie's mother is a self-willed, self-assertive, aggressive woman, who rules her husband and children. She is rigid in her thinking, conventional in her behavior, unable to relax her hold on anything or anyone she regards

---

[18] O. Bloodstein, "The Development of Stuttering: I. Changes in Nine Basic Patterns," *Journal of Speech and Hearing Defects,* 25:219–237, 1960.

[19] V. A. Anderson, "The Speech Handicapped Children in the Classroom," *Education,* 77:103–107, 1956; and E. Konigsberg, "How the Teacher Can Help the Child with a Speech Defect," *New York State Education,* 44:320–324, 1957.

as hers, meticulous about her housekeeping, and obsessively perfectionistic toward her children. Both children have been rigidly trained to be neat, to keep their possessions in order, to hang up their clothes, to be unobtrusive, and to do as they are told. In her own way, the mother is intensely proud of them. The father is an overanxious, well-meaning, childish, and futile individual. He overprotects both his children and tries to compensate for their mother's stern handling by coddling them as much as he dares to. The daughter has worked out her own compromise. She conforms on the surface to her mother's requirements, but she dislikes her mother and adores her father. She is sly, deceitful, self-centered, and—aside from her affection for her father—as cold as her mother. Young Jimmie is a confused, dependent, shy, anxious, fearful, frustrated child. Both his parents demand more of him than he can give. He strains himself to the utmost to meet their expectations, but he knows that he will never succeed. As a result, he feels inferior and insecure. The family housekeeper is a naturally sympathetic woman, but she has refused to become involved emotionally in the situation. She sees better than anyone else what is happening, and when Jimmie has one of his screaming nightmares she is the only one who can quiet him. At such times he violently rejects his mother.

Jimmie's difficulties with speech began as soon as he tried to talk. Both parents were so eager to have him reach perfection that they pushed him. Jimmie has a normal degree of general intelligence, but his linguistic ability is definitely low and his vocabulary small. His first reaction to being high-pressured into speech was to become mute for hours on end. These periods drove his father frantic with worry and his mother frantic with frustration. Since his first solution met with so bad a reception, Jimmie took refuge in a stammer. Even his mother reluctantly admits that discipline and punishment are of no avail in controlling the stammer, but she does not know any other method of approach. The father tried rewarding his son for each perfectly spoken sentence, but this method backfired, because Jimmie worked so hard to get the reward and his father's approval that he stammered worse than ever. His sister adds to his troubles by furnishing a contrast in fluency and by giving him many a sly dig that passes unnoticed by his parents. She regards him as a competitor for the father's love and has no intention of letting him trespass on her preserves.

Jimmie has recently shown a tendency to remain in the kitchen with the housekeeper, playing quietly and wordlessly in a corner. It is probable that he feels secure there, since she asks him no questions and makes no demands upon him. The woman has a friendly attitude toward Jimmie, but she also has a genius for minding her own business. It seems that the boy's one hope for recovery is to go away from home, preferably with the housekeeper, for a trial period of at least a year, as a means of finding out what mere relief from pressure will do for him. During the trial year he should not see his parents. It remains to be seen what action will be taken. The father is deeply concerned about his son and is willing to sacrifice his own pleasure in seeing the boy every day to the lad's present and future development. The mother, however, cannot admit failure; like other dictators, she has to be right all the time. If she can think out a rationalization that absolves her from blame, she may agree to a separation. If Jimmie remains within his present family group he is not likely to stop stammering.

4. Orthopedic Disabilities   The term "orthopedic" refers to those types of disability that arise from the paralysis, malformation, or limited use of some part of the body. Although it is true that the adolescent with a shrunken arm or a missing hand faces some special problems of "differentness," he has certain advantages over the less obviously handicapped youth because his reasons for limitation are clear to everyone: if he succeeds in making a good effort to use what abilities he has, he is given a role of honor in his group. Moreover, he is generally in good health. One of the writers knew a boy with one badly damaged hand who became his school football team's expert place-kicker; someone else held the ball for him, and there was nothing wrong with his feet.

Sometimes the teacher can be instrumental in assisting the orthopedically handicapped adolescent to achieve a fuller adjustment by being aware of both his emotional and physical needs and resources, and by helping him to make the most of the inner strengths and the support of the community which can be made available to him. In the case below, the boy would quite probably have continued on his way throughout school with a moderate amount of capability, but the resourcefulness of the teacher made it possible for him to extend his potential in several directions.

Alan R. came to the eleventh grade of a large suburban high school with the advantages of a sturdy spirit of endurance, a high although not brilliant intelligence, and a well-developed set of social skills which he had acquired in the accepting atmosphere of the rural school he had attended until his family moved to a large western state for the economic advantages it offered his father. His most obvious disadvantage was the almost complete loss of the use of his right arm, following an accident on the family farm. He had been given adequate immediate medical care at the time, but the crushing of the arm was too extensive to allow him to use it normally, and there was no continuing therapy accessible to the rather isolated family. With his excellent health and the support of his warm, cooperative family, he did not feel the loss as a desperate one, especially as there was little pressure on him in the rural setting. When, however, he entered the eleventh grade in the new high school, he found that the pace was considerably greater than he could cope with as a "stranger" who was also "different," and these tensions began to show in his school work, and in emotional depression. Among the contributing factors was his increasing awareness of the vocational problems his disability might present, since through testing and experience he was becoming aware that his interests were definitely not academic, even though he did quite well in his school subjects most of the time. The teacher took advantage of one of the testing sessions to arrange for Alan some counseling interviews with the guidance department of the school, at which time he was also given information on the programs available to him through state and local agencies for special training after he left school, and for continued medical care if a review of the problem indicated that ongoing therapy would be of assistance. Through the school nurse, information about the state medical services for children with orthopedic disabilities was given to the boy's family, and they undertook to set up a consultation for the re-evaluation of his possible use of therapy under more extensive services than had been available in the rural community. With the more positive, rather than merely accepting, attitudes of parents and school apparent to Alan, he began to gain a better sense of being able to do something active about his situation himself. Furthermore, the counseling sessions gave him an opportunity to express many of his feelings around his disability, beside the directly vocational and academic planning it opened to him. The teacher concommitantly planned activities for the classroom in which Alan could take a more active part, thus helping him to move from the position of a resigned bystander and into one of affirmative satisfaction in his school and peer activities. He will still have a long way to go in meeting the challenge to make the most of his abilities, but he is, thanks to the active interest of the teacher, well along the way to a fuller participation in his world than he had thought possible.

5. Chronic Illnesses   The general heading of this section covers such deviations from normal health as tuberculosis, anemia, diabetes, allergies, heart conditions, and nervous diseases. Of course, the pupil who is acutely ill with any of these conditions is not in school, but the teacher often has in her room at least one pupil whose activities are limited by a chronic condition which is due to one of these diseases.

A pupil's reaction to many such illnesses is conditioned by the fact that his ailment does not "show." He is under the strain of having a physically limiting disease that is not at all obvious to his age-mates but which makes the vigorous life of the typical adolescent rather difficult. The easily-fatigued, the diabetic, the allergic, the nervous adolescent cannot even explain the nature of his difficulty to his age-mates, because the causes are too special and too technical. Pupils with these handicaps often react violently against their bondage to disease. They need help in meeting their own feelings of defeat and in working out a program that will bring them the respect of their peers without further endangering their own health. Teachers can be of much service in helping pupils to maintain the activity level recommended by the physician. These pupils cannot safely be stimulated or pushed; they often have to be guarded against themselves. It is also essential that the best possible vocational guidance be given, since the young person with a chronic and perhaps permanent condition faces a lifelong handicap and must be directed toward a vocational goal that is within his physical capacities.

Illness is usually accompanied by changes in personality. In the case of the chronically ill pupil, the changes may become permanent. One interesting study, covering 16 months of research with 58 diabetic children,[20] concerned the personalities of the pupils while they were under care for their physical condition. A significant pattern that emerged from the study was the tendency for diabetic children to give a deceptive appearance of unusual maturity and control. Because of their condition, these children must begin very early to take an active part in both medication and diet; they therefore learn the outward forms of control and restraint before they are able adequately to meet the imposed emotional strain. This combination of outer maturity and inner immaturity is frequent among chronically ill pupils. Another common modification of personality is a return to dependent infantilism, with constant demands for help or for exemption from requirements or for special treatment. Teachers should be very cautious in pushing these children and adolescents and should give support to help them meet their problems.

An illustrative case from the clinical experience of one of the writers is typical in both its course and the interweaving of physical and emotional problems.

Jenny was seen in an allergy clinic at the age of 12. She was in good physical condition except for a mild degree of malnutrition and scars on her forearms that indicated previous skin problems. The child sat on the edge of her chair and listened while her mother expatiated upon her "difficulties with Jenny," alternately weeping and being quite apathetic about the whole thing. It soon appeared that the mother was unhappy about her separation from her husband; she found it difficult to face the day alone after Jenny had left for school. Previously, the child had had rashes on her arms from eating eggs. As she grew older she could tolerate a small amount of egg in such food as puddings or cakes, but from time to time she still had a rash. Even more significant was her violent scratching of her arms whenever the emotional tension in the home became unbearable. At such times her arms had to be bandaged to prevent infection. Jenny had been miserable at school because of her conspicuously bandaged arms, for which she could give no rational explanation, and had developed a hearty dislike for the classes she had previously enjoyed. The mother was too wrapped up with her own troubles to do much more than give Jenny a reasonably adequate diet, and she had a tendency to cling to her daughter whenever her own difficulties with her husband became acute.

During the junior high school years Jenny had had a respite from her allergies, but, shortly before the beginning of her freshman year in high school, her father abruptly deserted the family. Jenny's mother, totally unable to manage a job and her child simultaneously, applied for assistance, and at this time the

---

[20] E. M. Bennett and D. E. Johannsen, "Psychodynamics of the Diabetic Child," *Psychological Monographs,* No. 382, 68:23–25, 1955.

family came to the attention of the clinic. At the same time, the school truant officer talked with the clinic, because Jenny's mother had requested a home teacher for her daughter on account of her "physical handicap." Actually, Jenny's teachers were finding it almost impossible to keep the girl in school in spite of her good work. About the middle of the morning on the average of three days a week, she had violent attacks of asthma although she arrived at school apparently well.

After medical, school, and other reports were coordinated at a staff meeting, it was agreed that a home teacher should be requested for Jenny, with the understanding that the mother would work toward the goal of letting Jenny attend a six-week session of summer school. It was necessary to recognize the mother's need for the girl's presence at home, even while initiating counseling to help her accept her daughter's maturing independence. It was also necessary to relieve Jenny of her sense of guilt in leaving her mother, a feeling that seemed to be the trigger for her genuine allergy reaction. Success in reaching the long-range goal of a normal school life for Jenny will depend upon the ability of the family to solve its emotional and medical problems, together. Jenny must have a chance to establish normal peer relations, as well as to clarify her attitudes toward her mother. She also needs rest. Therefore, the home teacher is a part of the process of rehabilitation, not a permanent solution.

The adolescent with a "cardiac limitation" is not uncommon in the classroom. Thus, a survey of college students showed 4 in 1000 students to have a heart disease.[21] In the earlier years of adolescence the incidence is likely to be higher. In this age group many of the conditions are functional and will improve with a few years of proper care. This type of physical deviate has an especially hard problem because he has to go slowly among peers who are going full-speed ahead. Also, he does not usually either feel sick or look sick. He is truly disabled, and without assistance in adjustment he is likely to become crippled—not by his physical condition, but by his emotional reactions of resentment, fear, or dependency.[22] What such a child needs above all is guidance into such activities as are possible for him, through which he can gain a respected place among his age-mates. He cannot be a football hero, and he cannot be editor in chief of the school magazine, but there are other less strenuous and quite satisfying activities in which he can be successful and through which he can make his contribution to the life of the school.[23] The central problem is to keep his necessary limitation from turning into frustration and despair.

---

[21] A. Goggio, "Heart Disease in University Students," *Annals of Internal Medicine,* 37:155–163, 1952.

[22] J. Newman, "Psychological Problems of Children and Youth with Chronic Medical Disorders," in W. M. Cruickshank, ed., *Psychology of Exceptional Children and Youth* (Englewood Cliffs, N.J.: Prentice-Hall, Inc., 1956), pp. 391–440.

[23] L. Bellak and F. Haselkorn, "Psychological Aspects of Cardiac Illness and Rehabilitation," *Social Casework,* 34:483–489, 1956.

Teachers are also sometimes the people who recognize the meaning of premonitory symptoms and send a student to the school physician, with a resulting diagnosis of heart disease, long before the matter has become critical.[24] The most obvious symptom is a failure of breathing to return to normal after a recess or noontime period, during which the boy or girl has been running about. All the pupils come back into the classroom in a more or less breathless state, but the one with an inadequate heart goes on panting much longer than anyone else.

Nervous diseases are particularly baffling to those who do not have them —and even to those who do. Only two will be mentioned here—epilepsy [25] and chorea (St. Vitus's dance). As modern treatment of epilepsy improves, more and more of these children are able to attend the regular schools, especially at the secondary level. Few illnesses present as dramatic and difficult a problem for class, teacher, and victim as does a *grand mal* seizure of epilepsy, which is terrifying to the other pupils, embarrassing for the victim, and profoundly disorganizing to whatever work is in progress. Aside from the problem of seizures, the teacher can help both the pupil and his family to accept his handicap. Often parents themselves cannot regard the matter with calmness, and their emotional state brings about insecurity and rejection, which in turn may increase the frequency of the seizures. A teacher can sometimes arrange a referral of not only the pupil but the entire family to a suitable counseling service. In a study at the Massachusetts Memorial Hospital it was found that the views of parents concerning the illness and proper handling of their epileptic children were not only actual misconceptions but were also a reflection of their own emotional problems and especially of their feelings of guilt in their conscious or unconscious rejection of the afflicted children. Teachers also need to be aware of their own feelings and to be careful not to add another rejection to those of parents and classmates. The condition itself is a medical problem, but the attitudes toward it are often more distressing than the disease.[26]

Chorea is also an easily recognizable disease in its acute form, but milder types may remain undiagnosed. The most noticeable symptoms are the tics —that is, involuntary twitching of the face, arms, or shoulders—and a general malcoordination of the entire body. A pupil showing such symptoms, which sometimes appear only under stress, should be sent at once to the school physician. The milder forms, with an occasional, more serious episode, may run on for years, as shown in the second history given below.

---

[24] S. J. Robinson, A. Potter, and D. M. Aggelek, "Undetected Heart Disease under the Teacher-Observation Method," *Journal of School Health,* 25:172–174, 1955.

[25] P. H. Hoch and R. Knight, *Epilepsy: Psychotherapeutic Aspects of Convulsive Disorders* (New York: Grune & Stratton, Inc., 1947), 214 pp.

[26] L. A. Hartman, "Responses of Parents to Patients with Seizures," *Smith College Studies in Social Work,* 25:81–84, 1951.

These two case studies give brief descriptions of the kind of symptoms and reactions that may well lead a teacher to suspect a nervous disease. It should be noted that both the epileptic and the choreic child had difficulties of social adjustment that were secondary results from the illness. The general public probably has less understanding of this type of handicap than of any other; some people even go so far as to confuse nervous diseases with mental derangement.

It was the observation and concern of a seventh-grade teacher that led Nora to medical treatment before her problem became a major handicap. She had always been a quiet, rather reserved child who did not discharge her emotions easily; and the various disturbances of her early years had piled up inside her, long before there was any outward manifestation of them.

Nora's father had deserted the family when she was three years old and a younger sister was two. Her tense, overprotective mother suddenly found herself unable to provide for two small children and was forced to place them in the care of an elderly relative so that she could take a full-time job as a housemaid. The relative was fairly willing to have the two little girls with her, but she was physically not able to endure the noise they made; so she repressed them to a level of quiet that she could stand. One day Nora rebelled against the pressure and ran away from home. Presently she fell into a drainage ditch, was rescued by police, and sent to a hospital for treatment and observation. At this point the mother quit her job, went on relief, and took her two children home with her.

For the next few years Nora's life proceeded fairly normally. She did moderately well in school and presented no serious problems. But she was always overdevoted to her mother and not successful in her contacts with her age-mates. When she entered the junior high school she had reached the ugly duckling stage of development, and she began to feel ashamed of her faded but neatly mended clothes and of her residence in a run-down section of the town. Her schoolwork began to get poorer and her social contacts poorer still. At first, her mother was mainly irritated at what seemed to her a criticism of her best efforts under trying circumstances, and she was too occupied with her own troubles to notice how sick Nora was. The girl's teachers, however, not being personally concerned, did not fail to notice that Nora sometimes "fell asleep" for a few minutes, that she occasionally wandered into the wrong room, that she complained of being sick to her stomach but seemed more confused than nauseated. Finally, Nora wandered into the boys' toilet in one of her moments of mental fog and was sent to the principal for "discipline" by a teacher who did not know her. Eventually, she reached the school nurse, who also felt that something was wrong, but was not sure what.

Through the efforts of the local PTA, the school had obtained funds to give each child a two-week vacation in the mountains. When Nora's turn came, she went with a group of boisterously happy adolescents to a camp, where, in the noisy, enthusiastic company of fifteen age-mates she felt herself rather isolated.

One day she went on a long, hot hike that exhausted her. Shortly after her return to camp a counselor found her standing in the blazing sun by the lake, with her clothes wet and wrinkled and blood on her mouth. Two hours later she was in an emergency room of a children's hospital.

The emergency doctor could find nothing obviously wrong, and by the time Nora and her mother had talked the matter over, Nora had made up a story about falling off the dock. She was afraid to tell anyone that she could remember nothing of what had happened. This episode would have come to little had the school counselor not happened to drive mother and daughter home from the hospital. This friendly adult soon observed the emotional barrier between her two passengers and decided something should be done before matters got worse. So she called upon the help of the hospital's social worker, and together they gathered all possible information about Nora. When the teacher, the nurse, the social worker, the camp counselor, the school counselor, and the doctor had the materials before them, the picture that emerged looked very much like epilepsy. The group recommended that Nora should have a complete physical examination, but it was a month before the mother could be persuaded to take her daughter, who seemed to her "perfectly well," to the clinic. The electroencephalogram confirmed the diagnosis of epilepsy, probably caused by brain concussion—perhaps when she fell into the drainage ditch. Subsequent medical treatment proved effective in controlling the seizures. Both the school psychologist and the medical social worker helped mother and daughter to an understanding and acceptance of the situation. Under this improved care, Nora is returning to school. She will probably always need medication, but she can expect to have a reasonably normal life.

The following history was selected because it covers an entire life span. The individual described is now a woman well over sixty, and the long history of a life of nervousness, without emotional involvement, should be instructive. This woman came from a family in which rheumatism in various forms was common; she herself has had inflammatory rheumatism, sundry attacks of shingles, and has not been able to sit at a desk since her college years because of ever-present neuritis in her shoulders.

Cecile Marie was from birth a somewhat overactive child, but she was normally healthy until she was 4 years old. At this time her mother was slowly dying. The child was so active and talkative that she was too much of a problem to her ailing mother, so Cecile Marie was sent during the day to a nearby private school. The teacher usually accepted only children in the kindergarten or first and second grades, but she thought Cecile Marie, being intellectually advanced for her age, would be able to do kindergarten work without trouble. The child adored the school and could not get there early enough or remain long enough. She worked unremittingly at such chores as paper weaving, sewing designs on cards, coloring pictures, or stringing beads. Her work was excellently done, but the teacher evidently did not notice the intense effort needed for a child of barely four to complete assignments designed for six-year-olds— and by modern standards too hard for them—nor was she otherwise than pleased that Cecile Marie listened to whatever the older children were doing, learned to read, and memorized everything she heard, whether she understood it or not. Her father, upon whom her care had devolved, was a little disturbed by his small daughter's insistence upon going over and over her new acquisitions each evening after she went to bed—reciting poems or multiplication tables, spelling words to herself, and so on; by her difficulty in getting to sleep; by her nightmares; and by her obvious feelings of compulsion about her schoolwork. During the five months that she attended the school, Cecile Marie lost weight steadily, her facial muscles began to twitch, her hands could no longer do the fine work they had done earlier, her vision was often foggy, and she was unable to remain still for more than a few seconds. The climax came one evening when her temperature soared and she began to have convulsive spasms. The doctor had no difficulty in diagnosing chorea (St. Vitus's dance). The acute symptoms lasted only a few days, but it was a year before Cecile Marie could live a fairly normal life, and she still had many tics and mannerisms, which became worse if she were subjected to strain. Her face then contorted every few seconds, her arm and shoulder muscles twitched, and she never knew what results her shaking hands would produce.

When Cecile Marie was 6, she entered the first grade, but by the end of the second week she had another attack of chorea. Thereafter, each autumn, when the other children went back to school, she accompanied them for only a day or two, by which time she was so tired that she willingly remained at home, where she followed a quiet routine: breakfast in bed and study in bed until about noon; lunch with the Chinese cook, who spoke little English and believed that small children should be silent at mealtimes; an hour's rest after lunch, and then more reading until 3:15, at which time she set out to meet the neighborhood children on their way home from school. With them she played until 5:00 and then returned home to take a prolonged hot bath to quiet her twitching muscles. Then back to bed for supper and some quieting occupation, such as a puzzle or a game of solitaire, until "lights out" at seven-thirty. It was midnight or later before she got to sleep.

From time to time, Cecile Marie had a tutor who came to the house three times a week, but even this small stimulation was found to be just the extra load that she could not carry; hence most of the time she was given assignments by her father or grandfather. At about the age of twelve, at her constant urging, she was allowed to register for one course at a nearby private school, where she received individual teaching three times a week for an hour. This work she loved dearly, but it precipitated a third attack of chorea. After that, there was no more formal schooling until, as an almost full-grown woman, she had sufficient vitality to attend classes with reasonable regularity. Her progress was made even more difficult by persistent recurrences of rheumatism of an inflammatory character, from which she is rarely free.

At no time was this child an emotional problem. She found plenty to do at home, she was comfortable, happy, loved by her family, reasonably popular among her age-mates, and completely unconcerned about the differences between her daily life and that of her friends. Her schoolwork at home was interesting, she had time to read in her father's extensive library, and she always had a period of playtime with her age-mates. Cecile Marie was not maladjusted, unstable, or unhappy; she was merely sick and nervous.

Throughout her life this woman has had to follow a somewhat restricted routine in that she could not constantly be with people. She has twice resigned jobs that she liked because the continuous presence of other people made her irritable and tense. She must still spend some hours of the day alone. She is a stable, well-adjusted person who takes life as it comes and rarely fusses about anything. As long as the pressure is kept low, she shows only a slight superficial nervousness, but tension soon brings back the tics. It is characteristic of her lack of general emotionality that she was a tournament golf player for some time and was never afflicted with the kind of emotional stage fright that bothers many people. Cecile Marie is an excellent example of a person who is merely nervous, without emotional complications.

6. Skin Conditions Pimples and boils are not merely infections; they are emotional hazards. Probably nothing so embarrasses an adolescent as a rash, an outbreak of pimples, or some other distressing skin condition. The mere lack of ordinary physical attractiveness can also be damaging to an adolescent, as indicated in the case study on p. 97. Sometimes disfigurement is of a more enduring type. The adolescent who is marked by scars, by any of several congenital malformations of the features, by birthmarks, by large and badly placed moles, and so on, is in a most difficult position in his or her social life. The young are not noted for their diplomacy, and compassion develops only with maturity; the peers of a disfigured child are likely to be less than helpful unless they are themselves helped by an understanding adult. Such conditions may make a pupil feel that he is not normal and never will be, that his appearance is offensive to others, that he will be rejected if he makes advances, that he is an outcast. He develops these ideas because of the reaction of others to him. The teacher can be of great assistance to the disfigured pupil, and as an influential adult leader she can do much to bring about his acceptance by others, provided she herself accepts him.

Disfigurement as a social and vocational problem is becoming more and more recognized. A recent study made with voluntary patients at three New

York clinics [27] showed 47 percent of the applicants for surgical correction of facial defects stated that their disability "first became a problem at adolescence." Of the group, 73 percent considered themselves to be severely disfigured, whereas the doctors rated only 22 percent in this category. The patient's perception of himself was given serious consideration in determining the procedures to be undertaken.

The following history of one girl's misery and of its effect upon her entire life is more enlightening than any discussion is likely to be.

As a little child Louisa was spontaneously gay and happy, with a great feeling of security in her mother's devotion. She was in kindergarten before her age-mates began to tell her that her face was "funny" or "dirty" or "all purple." Louisa's house contained no mirror, and she had therefore not known that she had a large, dark birthmark across her nose, half her forehead, one cheek, one ear, and her upper lip. Her mother had concealed the condition as long as she could and had almost smothered the child with love to compensate for the defect. The affection had in it an element of compulsion, which made one feel that the mother had been originally repulsed by the birthmark and was now overcompensating as a means of escape from what she considered an abnormal attitude of rejection. During her childhood Louisa often forgot for hours or even days at a time that she had a birthmark. Once in a while some age-mate made fun of her, but most children accepted her without more than an initial period of inspection prompted mostly by curiosity. With the approach of adolescence, however, and with the development of a quicker perception on Louisa's part, the social situation underwent a marked change for the worse. Louisa discovered that people did not want to look at her because her appearance made them feel ill, and she realized that her childhood chums, now become highly sensitive to social pressures, found her a handicap to their prestige. After a few rebuffs Louisa withdrew from more than casual contacts with age-mates. Louisa went to high school, with the intention of becoming eventually a cataloguer in some library, not because the work attracted her but because it involved working behind the scenes where social contacts would be few. Rebuffed, isolated, and withdrawn, Louisa had reached the stage of asking only for peace and shelter. Then the miracle happened. One day she read a newspaper article about a new make-up cream that hid scars or birthmarks. Secretly and without more than a faint hope of relief, she bought some, and on an afternoon when her mother was caring for a sick friend she tremblingly followed the directions and was completely stunned by the face that looked back at her from the mirror. It was not only free of blemish, it was pretty—except for its petulant expression. Louisa and her mother

---

[27] M. I. Stewart, "Surgery: Only the First Step," *Rehabilitation Record,* U.S. Department of Health, Education and Welfare, 23:27–30, 1962.

experimented with the compound for some days, and then, convinced of its effectiveness, the girl changed her plans. She and her mother moved to another city and Louisa went to college, where she eventually became a teacher. Her social success was beyond her wildest dreams, and her personality developed along what were probably its normal lines. She had as many friends and dates as any other girl, and even filled a few minor roles of leadership. Louisa is now a happy young teacher who is understandably successful with "problem" children. She has almost forgotten that she has a birthmark.

7. Glandular and Nutritional Problems   More than a few adolescents suffer from malfunctioning of the endocrine glands, although often the condition is only temporary. One type is almost certain not to be overlooked, although the nature of his trouble is not always recognized: the pupil who is nervous, jumpy, excitable, and precocious physically. The pupil at the other extreme is likely to be regarded as merely dull because he is apathetic, underactive, uninterested in school, and sluggish in his reactions. Usually he or she is sexually retarded as well. Boys of this type become the butt of none-too-subtle adolescent humor, and girls meet with avoidance and rejection. These pupils are sick, even though they may not seem so to a layman, and should be under a doctor's care. They can usually remain in school, but some adaptation to their condition is necessary. Many of them are first identified by teachers.

Adolescents tend to be slender, even those who will later put on weight. The routine medical examination will identify the undernourished, and the school nurse will presumably take steps to arrange for a better diet at home, if she can, and will in any case order milk at recess. The school doctor may order rest periods during the day and will almost certainly prohibit any but the lightest of exercise or of extracurricular participation, in order to prevent an unnecessary squandering of energy. The problem is mainly medical. The teacher's contribution consists partly in realizing that a seriously underweight student has as little energy for learning as for anything else, partly in refusing to push him beyond the limits of his vitality, and partly in helping him to achieve a greater maturity. One of the writers once knew a young teacher who had in her class a boy who was 25 pounds underweight. The school system was small, and the only official aid she could get was the allotment of a quart of milk a day. On her own initiative she arranged for him to drop two classes and to spend the time out on the playground sitting in the sun. He usually took a book with him, but he rarely read much. He watched the classes play games but took no part in them, except sometimes to help the first- or second-grade teachers arrange the children properly for a game. At the end of three months he had gained 15 pounds and was well enough to finish successfully the work involved in his reduced schedule. It often taxes a teacher's skill to aid such pupils in attaining a more mature personality without involving them in situations that are beyond their physical limitations.

The extremely fat adolescent girl is a very unhappy creature. She is commonly rejected by her age-mates, who are at a stage of development during which they set great store by appearances, and she makes little appeal to boys. Some overweight girls become motherly in their effort to find some possible relationship with boys, and others become frankly immoral, thus obtaining attention of a kind even though it is only a substitute for what they really want. The fat girl needs help from her family, her doctor, and her teachers if she is to find happiness and a normal adjustment. Medical treatment is not the teacher's business, but she can give the fat pupil a good deal of aid and comfort, without which the best of medication may prove of little avail.

The fat boy is not much better off, although he can sometimes find a kind of acceptance in becoming a clown. His extra poundage make him too awkward for participation in games—the surest road to admiration among male adolescents. His deposits of fat under the nipples and on the buttocks give rise to all manner of unseemly comments in the dressing rooms or showers. If he has money he may try to buy his way into acceptance or at least tolerance by paying for everyone's cokes and sandwiches. And sometimes he becomes the purveyor of pornography, partly because girls reject him entirely and partly because in this way he can gain attention from some of his male peers.

Most people think of overweight as being a direct result of mere overeating. Sometimes it is, but there are other elements in the causation. These boys and girls usually have a glandular insufficiency, they are usually underactive, and they are almost sure to be emotionally disturbed. Many of them do not overeat. A study [28] of adolescent boys showed that the nonobese lads actually ate more than the obese, but that the latter even in a summer camp were less active than the former. At camp the obese boys ate only 3430 calories a day against the slimmer lads' 4628 calories, and at home the chubbies were down to 3011—under the average for their age group—while the slim ones consumed 3476, near the theoretical optimum.

The original tendency to obesity may sometimes come from glandular dysfunction, but as soon as an adolescent puts on enough weight to feel himself to be "different," his emotional reaction further complicates the situation. He may reduce his intake—but usually without increasing his activity—or he may begin to use food as a defense against his tension and anxiety. Or, an already-overweight girl who finds herself rejected may comfort herself with sodas and sundaes, cakes and cookies, hot dogs or doughnuts and coffee. Un-

---

[28] P. S. Stefanik, F. P. Heald, and J. Mayer, "Caloric Intake in Relation to Energy Output of Obese and Non-obese Adolescent Boys," *American Journal of Clinical Nutrition*, 7:55–62, 1959.

fortunately, the more she comforts herself, the more she has to comfort herself about! Obesity is a disease that arises from many causes, which are commonly pyramided on top of each other.

▶ Participation of the School in the Management of Disabilities

In working in the classroom with adolescents affected by the various physical handicaps just described, the teacher is not alone. She is likely to have the services of a school health program with medical and nursing personnel, and quite possibly some service in mental health. Almost all high schools now have a school nurse or a school doctor, or both, and some schools have also arrangements for dealing with problems of emotional maladjustment. The appropriate person may be in the medical service, or in the psychological or counseling service. In specific cases, the school doctor or the nurse will call in whatever help may be needed. The proportions of schools having trained psychiatric or clinical consultants is quite small, but assistance can usually be obtained from outside the school when it is really needed.

In many schools, special classes are available for those pupils who have health problems or conditions which will affect their total adjustment to the learning process. Such classes are at present, unfortunately, insufficient; however, their number is increasing in many areas. Large urban school districts commonly provide classes which are taught by specially trained teachers and furnished with whatever physical equipment is appropriate to the handicaps of the pupils. The frequency of such provisions is shown in Table 7–2. There are not enough such classes of any type, but the most conspicuous lack is

Table 7–2: PROVISION FOR SPECIAL CLASSES FOR THE HANDICAPPED
IN URBAN CENTERS
(Percentages of schools having various degrees of coverage)

Condition	Full Coverage	Limited Provision	No Provision
Physical handicaps	23.3	15.5	61.2
Visual defects	11.0	8.2	80.8
Hearing defects	11.7	7.3	81.0
Mental retardation	41.1	28.3	30.6
Slowness in learning	15.2	42.9	41.9
Emotional disturbances	2.9	11.8	87.3

SOURCE: *National Education Research Bulletin,* Vol. 39, No. 2:42–46, 1961.

in the provision for emotionally disturbed pupils and for those with defects of vision or hearing. Classes for the physically and mentally handicapped are more numerous, probably because these children are burdens in the ordinary classroom. Many school districts, however, make no provision for any of these conditions. The regular classroom teacher, therefore, has to play a major role in the handicapped pupil's adjustment to school life.

► **Summary**

In dealing with handicapped children the teacher has four important, immediate functions. First, she should carry out whatever treatment is recommended by the school or private physician in the interests of a child's best development. Second, she should maintain an even, accepting emotional atmosphere in her room, so that the disabled, restricted, or disfigured pupil can find a safe haven there. Third, since the teacher is the person who sees the day-to-day behavior of each child, she should feel responsible for identifying pupils who are in need of help. These three functions are fairly clear and obvious.

Her fourth function is to make outside contacts in the interests of her pupils' welfare. Often, even when parents know that they should consult "someone," they do not know to whom they should go, nor are they able to take the initiative because they feel that such action would brand them as parental failures. But the same parents will usually react positively to a teacher's suggestions and will go to a clinic or counselor for help, if she makes the initial contact for them. She should be better informed than the average citizen about special agencies both in the school and in the community.

The pupil with a physical handicap is always under strain, probably in inverse proportion to the obviousness of the handicap. He needs help in growing into a normal individual, and the other pupils need help in developing a sympathetic understanding of his problem. The teacher is in the best position to give the aid these children need, for not the least of their requirements is an appropriate adaptation of schoolwork and alert but sympathetic supervision to keep them from overtaxing themselves. A teacher may also be the only person who can interpose a block in the vicious circle that develops when a pupil's overreaction to a handicap makes his condition worse and thus produces a greater handicap which in turn disturbs him still more, and so on. The pupil's parents may so overemotionalize the situation that their efforts to help him impose additional strain, or they may transfer to him their own tension, even though their intentions are of the best. Sometimes mere acceptance is enough to break the circle, and acceptance plus referral plus treatment stands a good chance of being successful.

In handling children with chronic physical handicaps the teacher should try to avoid potentially frustrating situations as much as possible but without overprotecting the pupil so much that he fails to recognize the social and physical limitations that are common to everyone. A teacher can develop attitudes and techniques to help a handicapped pupil become an active member of an understanding and harmonious classroom group; she can make sure he is aware of the medical and social resources of his community so that he may avail himself of them to further his rehabilitation and growth; and, most significantly, she can evoke his perception of himself as a whole person with capabilities and potential strengths which can make him a contributing member of his society.

References for Further Reading

BOOKS

Other Texts

Kuhlen, *Psychology of Adolescent Development* (pp. 68–91).

Other Books

Anderson, C. L., *School Health Practice*, 2d ed. (St. Louis: The C. V. Mosby Company, 1960), 530 pp. (pp. 81–98).

Crane, M. M., *et al.,* "Screening School Children for Visual Defects," U.S. Department of Health, Education and Welfare, *Children's Bureau Publication No. 345,* 1954, 92 pp. (pp. 1–4, 47–56).

Cruickshank, W. M., ed., *Psychology of Exceptional Children and Youth* (Englewood Cliffs, N.J.: Prentice-Hall Inc., 1955), 576 pp. (Chap. 1, and any one of 6, 7, or 8).

Dominick, A. B., *Stuttering: A Psychodynamic Approach to its Understanding and Treatment* (New York: Julian Press, Inc., 1954), 304 pp. (Chap. 1 or 5).

Frampton, M. E., and E. D. Gall, eds., *Special Education for the Exceptional* (Boston: Porter Sargent, 1956), Vol. III, 653 pp. (Chaps. 1–2 and Section 7).

Levine, E. S., *The Psychology of Deafness* (New York: Columbia University Press, 1960), 383 pp. (Part I, Chap. 2).

Murphy, A. T., and R. M. Fitzsimmons, *Stuttering and Personality Dynamics* (New York: The Ronald Press Company, 1960), 519 pp. (Chap. 1 or 9 or any 25 pp. from Chap. 3, 4, 5, or 6).

Seidman, *The Adolescent: A Book of Readings,* rev. Ed. (No. 12).

Stuart, H. C., and D. C. Prugh, eds., *The Healthy Child* (Cambridge, Mass.: Harvard University Press, 1960), 507 pp. (pp. 460–472).

ARTICLES

Anderson, V. A., "The Speech Handicapped Child in the Classroom," *Education,* 77:103–107, 1956.

Bellak, L., and F. Haselkorn, "Psychological Aspects of Cardiac Illness and Rehabilitation," *Social Casework,* 34:483–489, 1956.

Bennett, E. M., and D. E. Johannsen, "Psychodynamics of the Diabetic Child," *Psychological Monographs,* Vol. 68, No. 382, pp. 23–35, 1955.

Koegler, R. R., "Chronic Illness and the Adolescent," *Mental Hygiene,* 44:111–114, 1960.

Martin, M., "The Hard-of-Hearing Child at Home and in School," *Understanding the Child,* 18:111–113, 1949.

Stainbrook, E., "Health and Disease and the Changing Social and Cultural Environment of Man," *American Journal of Public Health,* 51:1005–1012, 1961.

Suggested Research Problems [29]

1. An investigation of the school, community, and state resources for the assistance of adolescents with physical handicaps. Also a study of counseling and health services within the school, to which the teacher can have recourse in dealing with handicapped adolescents. The work should eventuate in a brief manual to help teachers understand the nature of such difficulties and to deal effectively and constructively with them.

2. A follow-up study of children's eyesight from the time they enter the first grade until they graduate from high school—or leave school. This type of longitudinal study is especially needed, starting with an appraisal of eyesight during the first semester of school and following the same children as long as possible, preferrably into adulthood.

---

[29] See note, p. 11.

PART TWO | Intellectual
Development

Chapter 8 | Mental Growth

SINCE the very earliest studies of adolescence, stress has been placed upon the characteristic intellectual development of the period. There is such an increase of mental power that subject matter too difficult for freshmen in high school or in college is easily learned by the same pupils when they become seniors. A high school teacher notes also marked increases in judgment, reasoning, comprehension, and memory. Some of the observed development in mental power comes from neural growth, but part of it is doubtless due to the piling up of experience and knowledge. By the end of the eighth grade a child has accumulated a considerable store of basic information and has reduced many simple skills to such an automatic level that he can use them in his thinking. He has, for instance, acquired meanings for about ten thousand words, and therefore has a vocabulary with which to think. Several mathematical skills are now habitual, many elementary scientific facts have been thoroughly absorbed, and there has been considerable experience with cause and effect relationships. The childhood years may thus represent a gradual development of sufficient experience to serve as a basis for more complicated thinking. In many curves of learning one finds long plateaus covering the periods during which basic skills are being acquired. At the end of such plateaus there is usually a sudden and marked rise in learning rate, presumably because of the coordination of simple skills without any known neurological development in the learner. This integration of experience, with childhood serving as a plateau, is perhaps one cause of the relatively rapid intellectual development during adolescence.

The present chapter begins with a brief discussion of the nature of intelligence tests and the ways in which the scores from them are generally expressed. Almost all work in the development of intelligence is based on test results, so it seems desirable to give a background for understanding the values and shortcomings of these measures. There is also a discussion of the various ways in which results from tests of intelligence may be expressed. There follows a consideration of the variability in the IQ and of the effects of environment upon the development of intelligence, as measured by tests. The last section includes data on the growth in intelligence for groups and for individuals.

Obviously, the two most important questions about a test of intelligence are: "What does it measure?" and "How accurately does it measure?" The first query refers to the test's validity, the second to its reliability. In order to estimate whether or not a test is valid—that is, whether or not it really measures what it is designed to measure—one has first to come to some conclusion regarding the nature of intelligence. At least three points of view are possible, as summarized below:

1. Intelligence is a separate entity consisting of inborn elements only, and is independent of emotional, educational, and environmental factors.
2. Intelligence is a separate entity consisting of inborn elements, but it can be influenced by emotion, education, and environment.
3. Intelligence is an integral part of the total dynamic functioning unit called personality and is interdependent with emotion, education, and environment.[1]

The first assumption is the oldest one. If one believes it to be true, then one supposes that intelligence is determined entirely by heredity and is unaffected by anything that happens after birth. Thus, if one child is very bright and another is very dull, the distance between them could not be reduced by emotional upsets, lack of schooling, or withholding of adequate nourishment in the case of the bright child or by complete emotional security, excellent schooling, and adequate nutrition in the case of the dull child. A starving genius would, by this definition, be just as superior to a well-fed moron as a well-fed genius would be superior to a starving moron. Also, as a corollary, one must assume that an adequate measure of intelligence will yield a statement of intellectual status that does not change throughout life. Unfortunately for those who hold this view, the accumulated evidence of four or five decades does not give the proper support. When a child at age 8 gets an IQ of 119 and, after a prolonged session in a sanitarium for tuberculosis, has an IQ of 94, it becomes doubtful if intelligence is something that is fixed and immutable. Similarly, this definition does not agree with the findings that adopted children sometimes come nearer in their IQ to their adopted than to their natural parents, especially when the former are very intelligent and the latter rather inferior in mental capacity. Relatively few people at the present time believe this statement to be true, in its extreme form, at least.

Perhaps the commonest assumption at present is expressed in the second statement above: that is, that intelligence is a separate entity—presumably inherited—but that its growth can be either retarded or accelerated by environmental factors. Thus, inadequate nourishment, disease, inadequate stimulation, or preoccupation with emotional problems dulls it, whereas good health, a wide variety of stimulation, and good personal adjustment allow it

[1] E. Fromm and L. D. Hartman, *Intelligence: A Dynamic Approach* (New York: Doubleday & Company, Inc., 1955), 52 pp., p. 2.

to increase to whatever level is permitted by the original inheritance. This point of view is supported by facts and gives one possible explanation of them. It explains why Johnny, who had an IQ of 105 before his parents were divorced and before he became a sort of emotional football between them, now has an IQ of only 88. It explains also many differences brought about by environment.

In recent decades as the result of intensive research into factors affecting the intellectual development of the same children over a period of years, many educators have come to feel that intelligence is just one phase of an entire individuality and is intimately bound up with all other phases. In short, there is nothing fixed about it. It goes up and down with circumstances. A bright child can become actually duller and a dull child actually brighter, depending upon what happens to other phases of the complete personality. By this theory, each individual inherits a complex of completely interdependent traits, and any change in one is automatically accompanied by changes in the others. This may be the view that all psychologists will eventually hold regarding the nature of intelligence.

It might as well be admitted at once that, unless a test is given orally, it is dependent in some measure upon schoolwork, because the pupil at least has to read the test, and he may have to read the directions as well. However, since the results of group tests are likely to be used for purposes of classifying pupils into grade levels, the inclusion of simple bits of school-learned material raises no great difficulty, although they prevent a test from measuring "pure" intelligence—provided this could ever be done. For example, one might present a child with such series of numbers as those shown below and ask him to write the next number in the series on the line at the end.

$$9 \quad 8 \quad 7 \quad 6 \quad 5 \quad \_\_\_$$
$$12 \quad 14 \quad 16 \quad 18 \quad 20 \quad \_\_\_$$
$$1 \quad 3 \quad 2 \quad 4 \quad 5 \quad \_\_\_$$

So far as puzzling out the sequence is concerned, one might be measuring "pure" intelligence, but the pupil has presumably been taught to count in school; so one is automatically measuring a small learned skill at the same time. It is best therefore to admit at once that a test constructor can rarely follow Binet's original principle to select items that a child has had a chance to learn but that no one has taught him.

The testing of adolescent or adult intelligence is even more difficult than the testing of childish abilities, because with increasing experience the members of an age group become more and more differentiated, and the constructor of tests finds it harder and harder to find material for test items that will be hard enough to test the higher age groups but will not be so specialized that some portions of the population will be utterly unfamiliar with the concepts. In the last three decades several investigators [2] have tried to develop tests that are appropriate for adolescents and adults, but no one has been wholly successful to date. In most earlier studies, in which tests developed on children were used, adults showed a steady loss of intellectual power after the age of about 20. No thoughtful person really believes that such losses begin until a much later age, and the tests constructed more recently seem to indicate that there is a plateau of some length during the years of maturity before any decrease appears. As tests that are more and more appropriate to the measurement of mature intelligence are constructed, it may be that native ability will be shown to grow steadily up until senescence. More data on this point will be presented later.

The most widely used individual test is the Binet, first published by Binet in 1910, revised for use with American children in 1912, again revised and extended by Terman (known as the Stanford Revision of the Binet Scale) and once more revised, with additional tests to be used in the repeated examination of the same children, as the Terman-Merrill Revision. It is now, after a third revision, called the Stanford Binet Intelligence Scale. Since this test has provided several basic concepts, it seems worthwhile to describe it briefly. This famous test is always given individually. It runs from age 2 to "superior adult." [3] The method of scoring consists in first finding the year at which a child can pass all the tests; this year is then used as a base. The examiner next gives the tests for the following two or three years, until he feels certain that the child has reached his limit. The values for the tests passed above the base are then added, in the fashion illustrated below:

Basal Age—7	No. of Tests Passed	Months' Credit per Test	Total Credit
Age 8	5	2	10 months
Age 9	3	2	6 months
Age 10	0		0
			16 months

Mental Age is 7 years plus 16 months, or 8 years, 4 months

The Binet Scale introduced the idea of mental age. To this concept was later added the IQ, which is an abbreviation for intelligence quotient: the mental age, abbreviated usually to MA, is determined by what tests a child passes— as explained above. The IQ is the ratio between a child's chronological age

---

[2] D. Wechsler, *The Measurement of Adult Intelligence,* 3d ed. (Baltimore, Md.: The Williams and Wilkins Company, 1955), 110 pp.; L. M. Terman and M. A. Merrill, *Measuring Intelligence* (Boston: Houghton Mifflin Company, 1937), 481 pp.

[3] See the *Stanford Binet Intelligence Scale Manual* (Stanford, Calif.: Stanford University Press, 1960), 363 pp.

and his mental age. If his mental capacity is exactly what it should be for his age, his IQ is 100; if he is more advanced mentally than others of his age, it is more than 100; if he is developing more slowly than others in his age group, it is less than 100. Thus, a child with a chronological age (abbreviated to CA) of 5 and an MA of 10 would have an IQ of 200; that is, he has much more ability than an average child of his years. A child with a CA of 10 and an MA of 5 would have an IQ of 50; that is, his mental growth is far below the expected level for his age. To get the IQ one simply divides the MA—reduced to months—by the CA—similarly reduced—as shown below.

$$CA—10 \text{ years } 11 \text{ months} = 131 \text{ months}$$
$$MA—13 \text{ years } 4 \text{ months} = 160 \text{ months}$$
$$131) \ 160 \ (1.22 = IQ$$
$$\underline{131}$$
$$290$$
$$\underline{262}$$
$$280$$

This child has 22 percent more mental ability than one expects from a child of his age. In actual practice the IQ is multiplied by 100 to get rid of the decimal point. The 1.22 above would therefore be read as 122.

The total range of recorded IQs is from about 20 to 200. These arrange themselves in a normal curve, as shown in Figure 8–1. Below the figure is given the classification of IQs. These range from idiot to genius. It should be noted that 79.5 percent lie in the low normal, normal, and high normal groups.

Since 1916 there has been development of the group tests of intelligence. The motive for this trend was largely practical. The Binet examination takes at least forty minutes to give and may take well over an hour. Only one child can be tested at once. The time needed for testing all the children in the first grade of a school was prohibitive, and any subsequent testing, to check on the

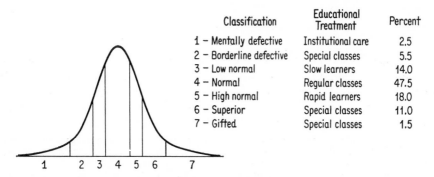

Classification	Educational Treatment	Percent
1 – Mentally defective	Institutional care	2.5
2 – Borderline defective	Special classes	5.5
3 – Low normal	Slow learners	14.0
4 – Normal	Regular classes	47.5
5 – High normal	Rapid learners	18.0
6 – Superior	Special classes	11.0
7 – Gifted	Special classes	1.5

Fig. 8–1. A normal curve

accuracy of the first IQ or to study growth, was out of the question. The group test of intelligence seemed the answer to these purely practical difficulties, but it has certain drawbacks along with its undoubted advantages.

In the first place, it has to be "objective"; that is, the pupil must record his answers in such a way that his paper can be scored by anyone, even a clerk. Unless scorers make clerical errors, all of them will get the same score for the same paper. The objectivity is necessary for a further reason. In giving the Binet, the tester can clear up doubtful or irrelevant answers by further questioning, but with a whole class such a procedure is impossible. So the answer to each question has to be either right or wrong. Moreover, the objective form eliminates not only excess scoring time but also minimizes the effects of schooling. It is true that the pupil has to read the test, at least beyond the third grade, but he does not have to write, to compose, or to spell. If these educational skills were added, the results would be even less a reflection of ability than they are when only reading is involved.

It is interesting and enlightening to trace the variations of mental development in individual pupils, as in Figure 8–2. Children A, B, and C, who were tested yearly from age 2 to age 18, all show relatively little variation in

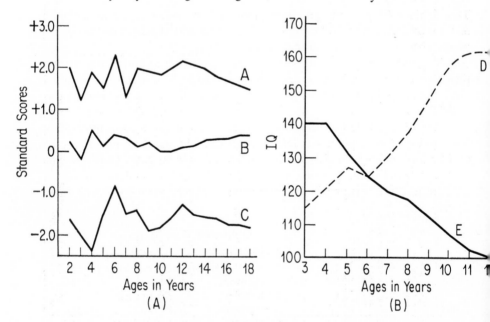

Fig. 8–2. IQ variations in the same individuals

(a) Based on MP Honzik, J. W. Macfarlane, and L. Allen, "The Stability of Mental Test Performance between Two and Eighteen Years," *Journal of Experimental Education,* 17:317–318, 1948.
(b) Based on L. W. Sontag, C. T. Baker, and V. Nelson, "Personality as a Determinant of Performance," *American Journal of Orthopsychiatry,* 25:555–562, 1955.

the IQ results. Any one test would have classed these children as superior, bright, or normal. Between the ages of 3 and 12 Child E decreased from 140 to 100 in IQ. During the same years Child D showed an increase from 115 to 165. The performance of these last two children was highly variable and demonstrated a marked trend in one direction or the other.

Further light is thrown upon the causes of variability in the IQ by following the case history of a single child and relating the IQ variations to nonintellectual factors in his life. The boy whose record appears in Figure 8–3 varied from 106 at 1½ years, to 123 at 6 years, to 163 at ten, to 122 at 18. This lad seems to have had a manic-depressive type of personality and was

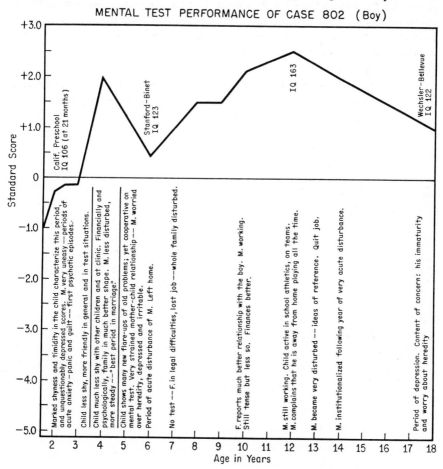

Fig. 8–3. Variations in IQ as related to background factors

M. P. Honzik, J. W. Macfarlane, and I. Allen, "The Stability of Mental Test Performance between Two and Eighteen Years," *Journal of Experimental Education,* 17:309–324, 1948, p. 320. Used by permission of the publisher.

sometimes abnormally listless and shy, sometimes highly overactive. The examiners who gave him the tests at the earliest years reported that the scores were too low because the boy had no interest in the test and was unwilling to exert himself. He was also at times in poor physical condition. At age 4 he made a conspicuously high score. At age 6, he had been in bed twelve weeks with episodic asthma (of possibly psychosomatic origin), his father was in a sanatorium with tuberculosis, and his mother had a full-time job. His highest IQ coincided with the return of his father to normal life, the recovery of his mother from an operation, and his own first reasonably healthy years and first favorable reports from school. The examiners who gave the tests at ages 9 and 14 reported that the boy could not be stimulated into really trying. The last score, at age 18, was preceded by a period of great excitement, over-activity, emotional preoccupation, and compulsive stealing. The personal disorganization shows in the lower IQ level. This boy's personality is of a type that interferes considerably with his mental functioning. Moreover, his home situation and pressures often combined to operate upon the already unstable child and depress his scores. Apparently, the date of the yearly test coincided just twice with an optimal personal and social situation.

Influence of Environment   It is not difficult to demonstrate that test scores are influenced by the culture in which the individuals tested have lived and the experiences they have had up until the time of the testing. Thus, an investigator of Polynesian children reports complete uselessness of the test in the Binet scale that requires children to choose the prettier of two faces, one of which is very ugly. The Polynesian children refused point-blank to make any selection until they were told the social caste of each pictured individual, and then they unerringly chose the one belonging to the higher caste. It made no difference whether the higher ranking were assigned to the prettier or the uglier of the two faces. If the children were told that both faces were of people from the same caste, both were adjudged equal in pulchritude. Since prettiness in the abstract is unknown in this culture, a test based on Anglo-Saxon concepts was completely useless. Those who have done research with Indians are unanimous in testifying that an intelligence test with a strict time limit cannot properly be used with Indian subjects. Native life puts no premium whatever upon time; indeed, one rarely succeeds in hurrying Indians for any reason and certainly not for purposes of making a good score on a test. However, if they are allowed to complete a test at their own rate, Indian adolescents make scores closely approximating those of white children of the same age. Indian children score as inferior to whites on a test that requires them to "draw a man," but as superior to them if the test directions are changed to "draw a horse." [4] Country children usually score

<hr/>

[4] P. H. Du Bois, "A Test Standardized on Pueblo Indian Children," *Psychological Bulletin,* 36:523, 1939.

below real capacity on tests of intelligence. They, too, are in no particular hurry. Moreover, many items of the average intelligence test are based on experiences one has in a city but does not have in the country. Thus the answer to the question on the Binet scale, "What would you do if you were going some place and missed your train?" depends upon whether the trains run once an hour or twice a week. Country children also do poorly on the Binet test about finding a ball in a round field, probably because they are not willing to accept the idea that a field *could* be round. They want to know how it could be plowed, how it could be fenced, and so on; it is often almost impossible to bring their attention to the problem of finding a ball in a field that to them seems an impossible phenomenon. Norms for widely used intelligence tests are based almost exclusively on urban children. These tests automatically handicap pupils from any other type of background. Moreover, the city child sees more tests than rural or foreign children do; he develops a sophistication about them and does not waste time in examining them as novelties.

There are two contradictory types of evidence concerning the effect that adoption into a superior home has upon the intelligence of children whose mothers, at least, were of inferior ability. Two contrasting studies have been selected for presentation. In one case 129 adopted children were first classified into three groups: those whose mothers had an IQ of 70 or less (87 cases); those whose fathers were casual laborers or unemployed (11 cases); and those who belonged in both these classifications (31 cases). The IQs of the children, adopted at the age of about 6 months and tested at 5 years of age, were found to be as presented in Table 8–1. These children had IQs far above what one would expect, in view of their heredity.

Table 8–1: CHANGES IN IQ

Group	IQ Average	Above 120	Below 80
A	105.5	15	4
B	110.3	28	2
C	104.1	—	—

SOURCE: H. M. Skeels and I. Harms, "Children with Inferior Social History: Their Mental Development in Adoptive Homes," *Journal of Genetic Psychology,* 72:283–294, 1948.

A more recent study, however, contradicts these findings. As shown in Figure 8–4, which gives the correlation—for children of different ages at the time of the testing—between (1) the IQ of "own" children and the educational level of their parents, (2) the IQ of adopted children and that of their natural mothers, and (3) the IQ of adopted children and the educational level of their adopted parents. In both the two former cases, the children became more and more like their natural parents as they grew older. The relation with adopted parents was at all ages not far from zero.

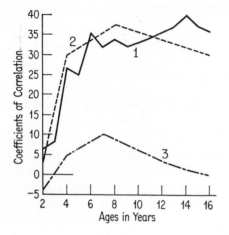

1 – IQ of "own" children and parents' educational level

2 – IQ's of adopted children and their real mothers'

3 – IQ of adopted children and the adopted parents' educational level

Fig. 8–4. Heredity vs. environment

Based on M. P. Honzik, "Developmental Studies of Parent-Child Resemblance in Intelligence," *Child Development,* 28:215–228, 1957.

Intelligence and Race   There is a vast literature on this subject, but much of it is unreliable because the tests used were developed upon white, urban children and therefore include many "culturally loaded" items. On the early applications of tests to Negroes they made relatively low scores as a group—although individual members made excellent scores—but more recent work has indicated that the differences are largely due to inappropriateness of the tests.[5] Although Negro children as a group usually score quite a bit lower than white children from the same town or city, Negro adolescents are much closer to white adolescents. Moreover, when one analyzes an examination by test, one often finds that the Negroes exceed whites on certain of the subtests that made up the examination.[6] Or, if one studies specific answers by whites and Negroes, one finds that the Negroes get a lower score primarily because they do more poorly on items that reflect "white culture." This fact would explain why Negro children score lower in relation to whites than Negro adolescents do; that is, the children had not yet had a chance to absorb white culture, whereas the adolescents had.

One rather old but still significant study [7] shows the relationship between the test scores made by Negro children and the length of time they had been

[5] M. M. Curti, "Intelligence Tests of White and Colored School Children in Grand Cayman," *Journal of Psychology,* 49:13–27, 1960.

[6] W. A. Woods and R. Teal, "Subtest Disparity of Negro and White Groups Matched for IQ's on the Revised Beta Test," *Journal of Consulting Psychology,* 21:136–138, 1957.

[7] O. Klineberg, *Negro Intelligence and Selective Migration* (New York: Columbia University Press, 1935), 66 pp.

resident in a southern city. All those included in the study had spent their earliest years upon more or less remote farms and had mingled little with whites until the family moved to the city. Children who had been in the city one year scored far below white children of the same age, but with each added year of urban residence, their scores came closer to those of their white age-mates. If intelligence were fixed by heredity, this result would be nonsense. After five years of city life and exposure to white culture, the Negro children were only a little below the white level.

This section on racial differences is short because the writers feel sure that most differences found between races are due to the nature of the tests, which are firmly rooted in white, urban culture, that the scores made by other groups reflect only the degree of exposure to that culture, and that any differences which may exist between races are too buried under irrelevancies to be valid. It seems probable that all races are about even in natural abilities.

It has long been the conviction of psychologists that one had only such intelligence as one inherited and that all environment could do was to provide or withhold stimulation. That is, the heredity factor far outweighed the environmental. Perhaps, however, this view needs to be modified. It is possible that during the earliest years of life a superior environment might add a few cubits to a child's inherited mental stature. The point is far from proved, and the weight of evidence is still in favor of the predominant importance of heredity in determining the limits of intelligence, although no one denies that environment may operate to prevent a child from reaching as high a level as he could.

▶ Growth in Intelligence

General Intelligence   As in the case of physical growth, it is best to measure intelligence by means of longitudinal studies; that is, by repeated measurements of the same children. One such study reports the growth of boys and girls from birth until age 21. The curve for both sexes combined is presented in Figure 8–5. It will be noted that growth was rapid up until about age 12, after which the rate—at least as measured by the tests used—decreases a little. Mental growth is still going on at the last age reported; indeed, there is little indication that it is even slowing down.

From the early days of testing there has been argument as to the point at which mental growth stopped and that at which deterioration set in. It was at first supposed that a person had developed by the age of 18 all the mental power he was ever going to have, and that from then on any apparent increase was due merely to experience in using what ability he had. Recent research [8]

---

[8] N. Bayley, "On the Growth of Intelligence," *American Psychologist*, 10:805–181, 1955; E. E. Ghiselli, "The Relation between Intelligence and Age among Superior Adults," *Journal of Genetic Psychology*, 90:131–142, 1957.

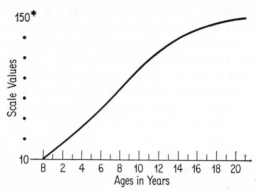

Fig. 8–5. Growth curve in general intelligence

* The scale values are arbitrary units of uniform size. It is the shape of the curve that is important.

Based on N. Bayley, "Individual Patterns of Development," *Child Development,* 27:45–74, 1956.

has cast doubt upon this assumption. It now seems probable that growth continues up to at least 50, and even later among those whose initial ability was superior. A curve from 25 years ago, a recent curve, and one of the writers' own guess as to the ultimate shape of the growth curve, are presented in Figure 8–6. Such loss as takes place in the later decades of life is by no means

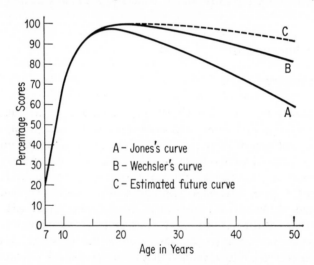

Fig. 8–6. Adult intelligence

(A) Based on H. E. Jones and H. S. Conrad, "The Growth and Decline of Intelligence," *Genetic Psychology Monographs* (No. 3), 13:223–298, 1933.
(B) Based on D. Wechsler, *The Measurement of Adult Intelligence* (Baltimore: The Williams & Wilkins Company, 1944), p. 118. Used by permission of The Williams & Wilkins Company.

uniform. The scores on the verbal tests either remained essentially the same or improved from adolescence on, but the performance tests showed a decline. This result may be due in large measure to decrease in manual dexterity with age and is not a true reflection of intellectual decline. One investigator gave the Army Alpha Examination to 127 men who had first taken it as soldiers 30 years earlier; there was a slight increase in total score, and on no test was there any decrease.[9] Thus, it begins to look as if the decades of adulthood did not show any such losses as were at first supposed to occur.

Children develop intellectually at a rate that is directly proportional to their initial capacity. This growth, which seems hardly fair, is one more instance of "to him that hath shall be given." If one follows over a decade the development of several groups of children who showed markedly different degrees of intellectual ability to start with, each group will retain its relative position from one age to another, although an occasional child will accelerate or decelerate in his growth rate. But for the groups as wholes the original relationship continues consistently, becoming if anything more rather than less marked with the passage of time.

In mental as in physical growth there are wide variations among individuals. Figure 8–7 shows curves of growth for four boys and four girls. Boy A grew rapidly and remained at all ages superior to any of the others. Boy B represents an average development. Boys C and D both grew slowly, but the former picked up a little speed in his adolescent years, whereas the latter did not. Girls A and B are both superior, but the development of Girl A is rather irregular; there are three regressions in her curve. Girl C is in the average group, but she also shows regressions. Girl D grew slowly but quite regularly. The growth of individual children usually shows these variations. It should be noted that the difference between the brightest and the dullest boy or girl becomes greater with age.

Relation of Intelligence to Social Level and Occupation   There have been a great many studies concerning the relationship of intelligence to social and economic variations. It seems sufficient to present two that are typical. The first gives results from the testing of draftees in World War II. It will be seen at once that the three highest groups in Figure 8–8 are composed of men who deal with words and mathematical symbols as part of their regular business. Either they were verbal types to begin with and therefore chose a kind of work in which their specific abilities would make them successful, or else their work had given them unusual experience in dealing with verbal symbols, or very likely both. The test was, of course, verbal; it therefore gave these men a chance to make high scores. The groups at the bottom of the distribution are those who work with their hands. Their regular work

---

[9] R. B. McHugh and W. A. Owens, "Age Changes in Mental Organization: A Longitudinal Study," *Journal of Gerontology,* 9:296–302, 1954.

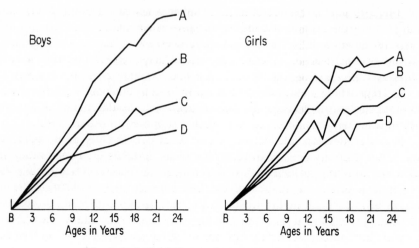

Fig. 8–7. Individual growth curves in intelligence

Based on N. Bayley, "Individual Patterns of Development," *Child Development,* 27:67, 1956.

does not therefore give them constant experience in the manipulation of verbal symbols. It is difficult to tell whether the results reflect anything more than differences in the reinforcement of native abilities by one's customary activities. One has also to consider that the tests are of a type developed on urban residents. Those from other environments might be expected to make scores below their real ability.

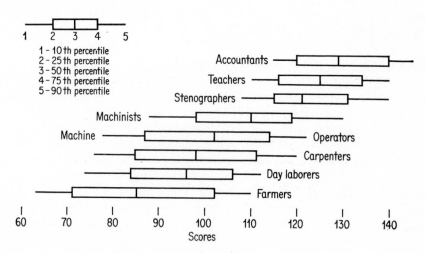

Fig. 8–8. Relation of intelligence test scores to employment

Based on N. Stewart, "AGCT Scores of Army Personnel Groups by Occupation," *Occupations,* 26:5–41, 1947.

Investigations in the relationship of intelligence to social status are also open to a certain amount of criticism because those adults from the "upper" classes of society usually become members of that class through having more than average intelligence to start with. Conversely, adults from the "lower" classes may be there because they do not have enough ability to rise higher. In the United States classes are sufficiently mobile that they are, to a considerable measure, reflections of basic abilities; this would not be so in a society in which class standing was inherited. There are, of course, certain families in any community who receive a high ranking on the basis of inherited wealth, but these are in the minority. The particular study selected for presentation concerns the relationship of scores made on two tests by 14-year-old boys from families that were rated as having social status at all levels from high to low. The results appear in Figure 8–9. For the reasoning test, the relationship is very consistent. The higher the class of the family from which the boys came, the higher score they made. The relationship of the spatial test is not quite as close and is somewhat variable. This second test measures a particular type of ability that may occur in anyone, but even in this case the general relationship is clear. There is, however, the "source of error" referred to above: that intelligence is one of the determiners of social class. If the boys from the higher groups may be assumed to resemble their parents, they presumably have a superior inheritance.

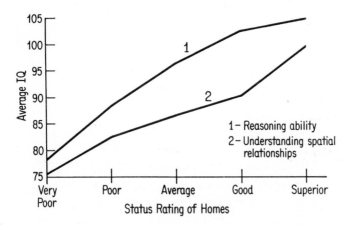

Fig. 8–9. Relation of intelligence test scores to social classes

Based on K. W. Eels, *Intelligence and Cultural Differences* (Chicago: The University of Chicago Press, 1951), 388 pp., p. 148.

▶ **Summary**

Throughout the modern school system tests of intelligence are in frequent use. A teacher therefore needs to develop an understanding of them so that she can know what they will and what they will not do, and can give meanings to the customary scores. A pupil's intellectual level is an important factor in conditioning his schoolwork, although it is by no means the only factor.

A single measure of intelligence is only an approximation at best. It may be a child's best performance, his worst, or anything in between. It is not until one has enough repeated measures to establish a *pattern of growth* that one is safe in making predictions.

During the high school years there is a marked growth in mental power. A teacher should therefore change the nature of her assignment as the pupils mature. The power is there, waiting only for the right stimulus.

In the past the school has emphasized intellectual progress to the detriment of social and emotional development. The modern school has sometimes swung rather too far in the opposite direction and has tended to neglect intellectual development in order to concentrate more heavily upon social and emotional adjustment. In such schools the classroom has become ancillary to the playing field and to the committee room. Educating the "whole" adolescent includes giving his newly developed mental powers something to grow on. A teacher can do much through her daily assignments and her classwork to stimulate eager interest and to promote intellectual growth.

References for Further Reading

B O O K S

Other Texts

Ausubel, *Theory and Problems of Adolescent Development* (Chap. 10).
Baller and Charles, *The Psychology of Human Growth and Development* (Chap. 10).
Garrison, *Growth and Development,* 2d. ed. (pp. 77–96).
Horrocks, *Behavior and Development* (pp. 453–468).
Jersild, *Psychology of Adolescence* (Chap. 5).
Jones, *Growth and Behavior in Adolescence* (pp. 63–78).
Kuhlen, *Psychology of Adolescent Development* (Chap. 3).

Other Books and Monographs

Anastasi, A., *Psychological Testing,* 2d. ed. (New York: The Macmillan Company, 1961), 659 pp. (Chaps. 2, 3, 8, or 9).
Lehman, H. C., *Age and Achievement* (Princeton, N.J.: Princeton University Press, 1953), 359 pp. (Chaps. 18–19).
Owens, W. A., "Age and Mental Ability," *Genetic Psychology Monographs,* 48:3–54, 1953.
Seidman, *The Adolescent: A Book of Readings,* rev. ed. (No. 15).
Sontag, L. W., *et al.,* "Mental Growth and Personality Development: A Longi-

tudinal Study," *Monographs of the Society for Research in Child Development,* Vol. 23, No. 2, Serial No. 68, 1958, 85 pp.

ARTICLES

Bayley, N., "Individual Patterns of Development," *Child Development,* 27:45–74, 1956.

Bayley, N., "On the Growth of Intelligence," *American Psychologist,* 10:805–808, 1955.

Curti, M. W., "Intelligence Tests of White and Colored Children in Grand Cayman," *Journal of Psychology,* 49:13–27, 1960.

Ghiselli, E. E., "The Relation between Intelligence and Age among Superior Adults," *Journal of Genetic Psychology,* 90:131–142, 1957.

Honzik, M. P., *et al.,* "The Stability of Mental Test Performance between Two and Eighteen Years," *Journal of Experimental Education,* 17:309–324, 1948.

McHugh, A. B., and W. A. Owens, "Age Changes in Mental Organization: A Longitudinal Study," *Journal of Gerontology,* 9:296–302, 1954.

Woods, W. A., and R. Teal, "Subtest Disparity of Negro and White Groups Matched for IQ's on the Revised Beta Test," *Journal of Consulting Psychology,* 21:136–138, 1957.

Suggested Research Problems [10]

1. The development of more appropriate tests for measuring intellectual growth during the adult years.

2. There is need for a brief manual giving hints as to the evaluation of results from tests of intelligence and pointing out various factors that must be taken into account in interpreting test results.

3. Comparison of races or social groups are all unduly influenced by the nature of the tests, which are based primarily upon white, urban, middle-class children and adolescents. New tests will have to be devised before such comparisons are valid.

---

[10] See note, p. 11.

Chapter 9 | Special Intellectual Abilities

THE present chapter will deal with such special facets of intelligence as are usually referred to as memory, imagination, suggestibility, humor, and reasoning. In earlier days the popular misconception was of a "mind" divided off into areas, each with an underlying area in the brain. These mental "functions" were assumed to operate independently and to be educable, one by one. Although this time-honored view has been abandoned in the light of modern research, such mental facets as imagination and reasoning still remain. These capacities are not, however, separate "functions." What differentiates reasoning from memory, for example, is the purpose toward which the integrated effort of the *entire intelligence* is directed. Presumably all these abilities involve use of one's total capacity, rather than any isolated portion of it, but the end in view varies from one "function" to another, as does a person's relative proficiency. It is thus possible, in spite of certain destructive criticism, to employ these terms with this somewhat changed meaning. The presentation is inevitably somewhat uneven because the amount of work done in different areas is uneven. Some of it is admittedly old, but it is still of value in shedding light upon adolescent growth, and it has not yet been replaced by more modern investigations.

▶ Memory

According to popular misconception, children have better memories than have adolescents or adults. What is true is that they are much more willing to memorize; most adults do not like monotony and therefore prefer logical to rote learning. The typical adolescent distaste for memorizing is even more intense. Although children do not resent memorizing, they are not especially efficient at it. They tend to substitute memorizing for reasoning, probably because they get more rewards from adults for a well-memorized answer than they do for one based upon childish and often fallacious reasoning.

The Binet examination gives evidence of growth in memory. A child of $2\frac{1}{2}$ can repeat two digits after hearing them read aloud once; at 3, he can repeat three digits; at $4\frac{1}{2}$, four digits; at 7 years, five; at 10 years, six. A superior adult can repeat eight.

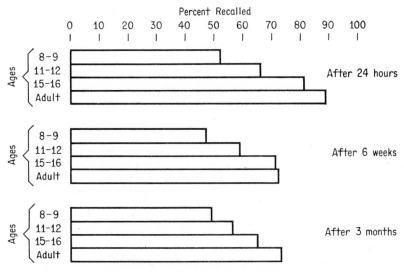

Fig. 9–1. Memory for a motion picture

Based on data in P. W. Holaday and G. D. Stoddard, *Getting Ideas from the Movies* (New York: The Macmillan Company, 1933), Table XIII.

One investigator measured recall of a moving picture seen once. Memory was tested three times—immediately after the movie, a month later, and three months later. The results appear in Figure 9–1. On all three occasions, the children remembered least. The adolescents recalled more than the children but were in turn inferior to the adults at all times. Most studies of memory were made before 1925.[1] One that is slightly more recent is reported in Figure 9–2. It involves the number of lines of poetry that school pupils of different ages could learn under the same conditions. The 7-year-olds averaged 9.8 lines; there is a steady gain at each successive age, the 18-year-olds averaging 22.4 lines. Other results confirm the above conclusions.[2] For example, grade school children could recall only 26 percent of the ideas presented in a film, whereas college students recalled 61 percent. Each successive grade in between these two extremes showed a gain over the previous one. In all these studies there is clear evidence that ability to memorize and recall increases with age. There is some fairly recent evidence that the amount remembered is influenced by the degree of success and satisfaction that the learner derives from the results of his efforts.[3] It is probable that a pleasant

[1] For a good study of the older type, see W. H. Pyle, *Nature and Development of Learning Capacity* (Baltimore, Md.: Warwick and York, Inc., 1925), 119 pp.

[2] M. A. May and A. A. Lumsdane, *Learning from Films* (New Haven, Conn.: Yale University Press), 1958, 357 pp.

[3] A. O. Jager, "Einige Emotionale, Conative, und Zeitliche Bedingungen des Erinnerns," *Zeitschrift für Experimentelle und Angewandte Psychologie*, 6:737–765, 1959.

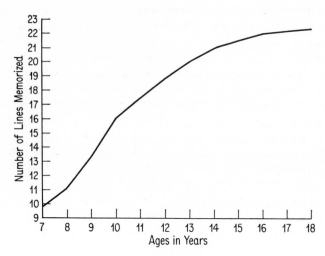

Fig. 9–2. Memory for poetry

Based on J. B. Stroud and R. Maul, "The Influence of Age on Learning and Retention of Poetry," *Journal of Genetic Psychology,* 42:242–250, 1933.

emotional tone can increase the amount recalled, whereas an unpleasant tone can contribute to a greater and faster forgetting.

It is not difficult to see why interest in memorizing has lagged. In former times memory was so overemphasized that the reaction against its use has been violent. The entire spirit of the progressive movement has been against rote learning. The essence of the reform has been to make school material so interesting and so meaningful to children that they will not need to memorize. After some years of going to an extreme in the matter, educators have realized that for some kinds of material, memorization is a great timesaver. It should not be forced upon pupils, naturally, and they should learn when to select rote memory as an efficient means of learning and when to select some other method. Memorization does not insure understanding, and an adequate understanding sometimes makes memorizing unnecessary, but neither statement leads to the conclusion that learning "by heart" should always be avoided.

▶ Imagination

Imagination is obviously difficult to measure, and reports on it are few. Good reports are even fewer. Yet any high school teacher senses the development of imagination during the adolescent years. Adolescence is a period during which youngsters produce poems, stories, songs, and drawings in profusion, but no test has yet been devised to measure adequately the growth of imagination behind these developments. It is therefore necessary to resort to less objective forms of measurement.

One rather general investigation consisted in showing pictures to pre-adolescent and adolescent girls and asking them to write an imaginative story, of the fairy-tale type, about one of them.[4] Nearly half the pupils (ages 10 to 14) produced brief and banal stories, merely described the picture, or included only bits of narrative imbedded in descriptive details; 44 percent of the "stories" thus showed essentially no imagination. The remaining 56 per cent of the children wrote real stories that showed some degree of imagination, and the highest 9 percent showed a great deal. It may very likely be that imagination is quite as much a function of personality structure as of age and that the trait develops with age only among those to whom the gods have given it in the first place.

One old but still interesting investigation [5] is based on an analysis of compositions written by 2642 boys and 2138 girls between ages 9 and 18. The problem set them was to finish a story, the beginning of which was provided; given, also, were hints as to the nature of their compositions.

This is the beginning of a story about the moon.

"On a recent night," narrated the moon, "I was sliding through heavy clouds of snow. My beams tried to pierce them in order to see what was happening on earth. Finally, the clouds parted before me and . . ."

You are to finish the story. You may choose any one of the five themes suggested below:

1. The moon sees a shipwreck.
2. The moon has a conversation with the giant, Roland, at the town hall of Bremen.
3. The moon comforts a sick man who is lying in bed.
4. The moon tells about a camp of hikers in the neighborhood of Bremen.
5. The moon talks with a pupil who cannot prepare his lessons.

By these directions, every pupil was led into a situation in which he had to use his imagination. He could, however, choose the topic around which his fancy played most readily; and he was free to introduce whatever embellishments and minor incidents might occur to him.

There were three outstanding differences between the themes of child and adolescent. The children represented the moon primarily as an acting being, while the adolescents described the moon's thoughts and emotions. The older pupils enlivened their stories with various minor episodes, droll happenings, and artistic touches, while the children clung to their central theme. The children's style was bald, but that of the adolescents showed numerous embellishments. The girls showed evidences of maturity earlier than the boys. The differences specifically in imagination are revealed in the

---

[4] M. D. Vernon, "The Development of Imaginative Construction in Children," *British Journal of Psychology*, 39:102–111, 1948.

[5] Th. Valentiner, "Die Phantsie im freien Aufsatze der Kinder und Jugendlichen," *Beiefte zur Zeitschrift für Angewandte Psychologie*, 1916, 168 pp.

two excerpts below, which are typical, respectively, of good childish and good adolescent imaginative power.

Child's Entire Story I [the moon] watched a boy for a while through the window, then I knocked on the windowpane. The boy opened the window and peered out, looking around curiously. Then I laughed at him and asked him how his schoolwork was going. I climbed in through the window and sat down near him. I was very willing to help him, just as I am always willing to help, and so I seated myself at his desk, took up the pen, and did some arithmetic for him. . . . Then I told him he shouldn't lose courage so easily. After that I took up a book and read aloud to him. (Boy, age 10)

One Section of Adolescent's Story Finally, the clouds beneath me separated and I could see the earth, that lay in nighttime darkness. Now I had the task of assigning jobs to my children, my dear little moonbeams. Then I had to watch each one to see that he carried out his task accurately. At first I watched my youngest moonbeam-child, for this one was greatly given to playing tricks and required my observation. With a merry glance he slid off my lap and went giggling down to earth. On the market place of the city there stood a large house, where the old burgomeister lived. At the back his great windows stood open in the room where he lay asleep. My little moonbeam slipped laughing inside and—Oh Dear!—the rascal tweaked the worthy old gentleman's nose. That I really hadn't expected. Quickly I called my child back to me and forbade him strictly to go down again to earth tonight.

Then I looked to see what another moonbeam was doing. I saw a wanderer who had lost his way through a dark forest. There appeared my moonbeam right before his feet, just as he, without realizing it, was about to fall into a deep ditch. Now he could see his way and again find his path, and he thanked my dear child heartily for his friendly showing of the way. Then I saw another moonbeam whose friendly light fell into a room where a sick child was passing a sleepless night. He had been tossing in the dark room, but when the moonbeam lightened the gloom, he became quiet and dropped off to sleep.

Suddenly I noticed to my consternation that my little rascal had slipped off my lap. I ran my glance over the entire half of the earth that I am able to light up at once, but he was not to be seen. Then one of his brothers told me where he was. There he sat on a white cloud, whispering and giggling. . . . Quickly I called him back to me and boxed his ears and told him that as punishment he must remain up here with me for a week. (Boy, age 16)

The child's story is, on the whole, prosaic; the tale would not have varied materially if he had been helped by his uncle. The adolescent not only puts in many imaginative touches, but he uses more space explaining how people reacted and felt than in telling what they actually did.

One interesting investigation [6] that has been reported on this complex subject of imagination was concerned with adults who were creative in their own fields and had already achieved a reputation for imagination in ratings by their peers. As controls, the investigator used his current crop of Ph.D. candidates, who were adult, intelligent, well-adjusted, but not especially creative as far as known. The tests used to compare these two groups were of many types: development of patterns from square bits of colored tile, elaboration of simple line designs, interpretation of random ink-blots into a meaningful whole, statements of picture preferences, the creation of poetic phrases to express a given idea, the designing of stage sets, the planning and executing of diagrams to present the basic ideas in a set of data, and so on. The known creators differed from the controls in a number of traits. They showed great independence of judgment, accuracy, breadth and depth of observation, and exceptional vigor. They were able to synthesize impressions into wholes, they were willing to accept the truth without distorting it, they were sure of their own ability to be flexible, and they had a rich fantasy life. In the expression of their designs and ideas they tended to complexity, novelty, and asymmetry. Of course, adolescents in high school are not old enough to have reached a mature level in respect to imagination, but a teacher who keeps the above description in mind can find the beginnings of these traits in the more imaginative 10 percent of her students. These trends should be fostered whenever and wherever they do appear, because they are of great potential value to society.

The development of one girl's imagination from preadolescence into the earliest years of adulthood is well illustrated by the samples below. Although only one individual is involved, the study has at least the merit of being "longitudinal." This particular individual wrote much better poetry than the average, but its excellence does not prevent adolescent traits from appearing and disappearing with age. It is pleasant that the poems are of high intrinsic merit,[7] but their quality is irrelevant to the present discussion. The first poem is a description of a scene, presumably based upon pictures but involving some degree of imagination; it has a standard form, it displays no emotion, and it gives practically no interpretation. In its objectivity it is quite characteristic of late childhood. The second poem shows in its details the same descriptive tendencies as the first; it also expresses fancy and imagination in abundance but not much emotion, although it certainly does create a mood. The poem shows a breaking away from traditional form, a highly characteristic trait of adolescent work, and it makes repeated use of a word arrangement until it becomes almost a mannerism; that is, the author uses a noun, and

---

[6] F. Barron, "The Psychology of Imagination," *Scientific American,* 199:150–170, 1958.
[7] The writers are indebted to Ursula Kroeber for permission to quote these few samples of her many interesting poems.

immediately repeats it with an added adjective. This discovery of a new technique and its overuse are extremely adolescent. The theme of the third poem centers around love for an ideal mate, a typically adolescent topic. In thought, it is the most conventionalized of the series, it is rather sentimental, and it does not have the restraint of later productions, but its relative lack of clichés and its imaginative detail make it far better than most adolescent love poems. The fourth poem is again a lyric outpouring about youth and love, but on an appreciably more adult level. There is much emotion, the elation in the first two verses being in contrast to the desolation of the third. The feeling is so intense that it tends to swamp the meaning. The second, third, and fourth are all untraditional in form. They represent experiments and—in all probability —revolt against convention. A period having these characteristics is likely to appear in the adolescent writings of those who accepted traditional forms as children and at least sometimes returned to them voluntarily in adulthood. Revolt and experiment are an integral part of adolescence. The last example is a sonnet, a typically adult form of poetry. The theme shows a continuance of adolescent revolt against the idea of death, but there is the beginning of resignation. The poem is deeply emotional but shows great restraint.

Rite Primeval (age 12)

Throb and thrum of native drum
Through the jungle booming,
Silhouettes seen through the nets
Of lianas, in the glooming.

Leap and dance, plunge and prance
From eve till break of day,
Through the night an age-old rite
Beats on its rhythmic way.

The Unicorns (age 14)

Hush, oh hush, be silent now, be silent, hush, be silent, be still,
Hush, be still, and you shall hear, if you listen,
The slow low gallop of the unicorn herd,
Cantering slow, cantering soft, down to the silver stream
That sings as it flows and flows as it sings:
Hush, be still, you may hear the song.
Close your eyes in the dark, the dark, the sweet soft dark of the night or a dream,
And white in the dark you shall see the flanks, the sides and the necks,
The white arched necks of the unicorn herd,
Cantering down to the silver stream, the singing stream,
Arching their hoofs, their silver hoofs, flashing their horns, their spiral horns;
Be still in the dark, the gentle dark, you may hear the stream and the galloping hoofs.

Krasnovsky [8] (age 16)

Here it is, here it is, it is like a hand on your eyelids, it is like a little bell in the rain,
It is like the little stem of a flower. . . .

Awaken, oh my soul: put forth your hands,
Take up the hills and the waters of day-break, breathe on the wide slopes and the mist
  on the sea,
Take up these things, that are love; find out your love's street and his hills, find out his
  sleep,
Sit at his table, bow your head with his, and find out all his dreams.
Take up these things, that are love, are forever love, but for you only an hour:
Arise, awake, awake to your love, that calls to you with the tender voice of the dawn,
With the tender voice of a dream. . . .

The Hunter (age 19)

O your youngness is like a deer
stiff-legged: like the wind
now bright, now bleak.

Rose and fire is love, fire in the wind,
the flute's voice of silence,
and the highness of the moon.

Skull-white, the moon: and the wind
dying: ash the rose, the fire,
fallen the flute's voice,
and the hunter is on the hills of Spring.

Sonnet (age 22)

I am expert in youngness: all the days
Of verdure and of April have been mine.
And I have learnt the land where springs the vine
Splendid to summer; have I to change these ways?
Apprentice of mortality, to praise
The windless autumn, the regretful wine
That sucks its crimson from the year's decline,
And I learn November's land, who am of May's?
Immortal make the Spring those fortunate
Who gallantly the green-strown ways ascend
In youngness to their death, nor hesitate.
While I, though knowing where all seasons tend,
Yet cling to their obscure descent, and wait
As if for more than death, at seasons' end.

---

[8] *Krasniy* means "beautiful" in Russian. Krasnovsky was an imaginary man, an ideal figure.

The entire series of poems shows a high degree of imagination and a strong tendency to word pictures. In childhood the latter tended to be so profuse as to obscure the meaning rather than illuminate it. In the last two poems it is well controlled and kept subordinate to the meaning. Emotion is at first lacking, then there is a deluge of it, but finally it is put under sufficient restraint to be highly effective.

In the course of years, objective tests of imagination will doubtless appear. In the meantime, one must be content with the indications of increased imaginative power as revealed by such evidence as that shown above.

▶ Suggestibility

There has not been much research in recent decades into the degree of suggestibility at different ages, but two investigations seem worth reporting.[9] The results in the first were expressed in two ways: the percent of pupils at each age from 5 to 18 who were suggestible and the percent of responses of a suggestible character shown at each age. Small children scored as very suggestible. During late childhood and adolescence the curves began to fall steadily. At the age of 18, only 18 percent of the students and 4 percent of the answers were classified as suggestible. Teachers soon learn that adolescents cannot be guided by suggestion as easily as children can be. The common form, "Wouldn't you like to read another chapter?" has to be abandoned and something more mature substituted.

The second investigator reports that suggestibility seems to be a form of dependency behavior that is related to personality rather than to age. To be sure, individuals usually become less suggestible as they grow older, but that result occurs because they have pursued the normal course of becoming independent in their reactions and judgments as they grew older. Children who are unusually dependent accept suggestion, especially when it is given by any adult and more especially if given by an adult upon whom they are dependent.[10]

▶ Reasoning, Thinking, Judging, Obtaining Insights

It is probable that the above words all refer to the same kind of ability to deal constructively with facts, to rearrange them, to draw conclusions, or to "see through" them. Investigations in this field are numerous, but only a few samples can be presented. The discussion will begin with a listing of some "comprehension" questions of the Stanford-Binet scale; will

---

[9] M. L. Reymert and H. A. Kohn, "An Objective Investigation of Suggestibility," *Character and Personality,* 9:44–48, 1940.

[10] L. F. Jakubczak and R. H. Walters, "Suggestibility as Dependency Behavior," *Journal of Abnormal and Social Psychology,* 59:102–107, 1959.

continue with a summary of an experiment with junior high school children testing their ability to see through a poem; will go on to four studies of the ability of adolescents to give explanations, to reason about conclusions, or to "see through" a parable or joke to its inner meaning; and will conclude with an analysis of the methods that college students use in solving problems.

1. There is, first of all, the Binet examination, with its series of "comprehension" questions. Growth is reflected by successive steps, as follows:

Age 4: Why do we have houses?

Age 7: What is one thing to do when you have broken something that belongs to someone else?

Age 8: What makes a sailboat move?

Age 10: Give two reasons why most people would rather have an automobile than a bicycle.

Age 11: Donald went walking in the woods. He saw a pretty little animal that he tried to take home for a pet. It got away from him, but when he got home his family burned his clothes. Why?

Average Adult: What does this saying mean: If you would eat the kernel you must crack the nut?

Superior Adult: Give three reasons why people use typewriters that cost so much when they can get pen and ink for a few cents.[11]

These tests require an ability to judge and draw inferences. Many years ago Binet and Terman realized the value of such tests in measuring basic intelligence.

2. Three decades ago, an investigator studied a different type of insight by asking grade and junior high school pupils to "see through" a short "poem" to its meaning. Although the investigation is old, there is no reason to think that the results would be different, had it been made yesterday.

I ate a small green apple;	Why does he wish he had never met the apple?
It tasted good, and yet—	Because the apple made him sick.
I wish that small green apple	Because the apple was sour.
And I had never met.	Because the apple had worms.
	Because he was not hungry.
	Because green apples are not good for children.[12]

Figure 9–3 gives the curve for growth in insight as measured by a total of five poems, also the curve for the poem quoted above. This form of thinking shows a steady gain throughout the grades.

3. Investigations of how children and adolescents explain phenomena give evidence concerning the ability to generalize and reason. In one study, pupils between the ages of 8 and 16 were asked such questions as: why

---

[11] L. M. Terman and M. A. Merrill, *Measuring Intelligence* (Boston: Houghton Mifflin Company, 1937), 412 pp., Form L, described on pp. 75–132.

[12] From W. H. Pyle, *Nature and Development of Learning Capacity* (Baltimore, Md.: Warwick and York, Inc., 1925), p. 544.

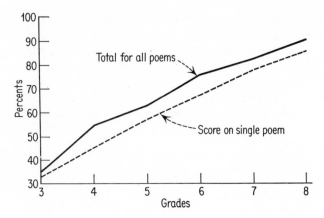

Fig. 9–3. Growth in the ability to understand the meaning of poems

From W. H. Pyle, "An Experimental Study in the Development of Certain Aspects of Reasoning," *Journal of Educational Psychology*, 26:546, 1935. Used by permission of the publisher.

pebbles sink when thrown into water, why a windmill turns, why water runs up into a tube that is small enough, what makes a bicycle go, and the like. The answers from which the students were to choose were of three general types, which were called phenomenistic (A), logical (B), and mechanical (C). The first type of explanation includes such answers as "The pebble sinks in water because it is white"; the child has put together two phenomena that have no connection beyond mere contiguity in time or space. The logical type of answer gives an explanation of sorts, but it is incomplete. The pupil choosing such an answer uses such concepts as weight, density, or gravity, and his explanation is sensible as far as it goes, but it is given in static terms. The third type of answer includes such explanations as: "A bicycle goes because, as the pedals are pushed, the chain makes the wheels turn." This explanation is made in terms of movement. The incidence of these three types of explanation, as given in the first part of Figure 9–4, shows a decrease in the phenomenistic and an increase in the other two during the years of preadolescence and the early years of adolescence.

The second part of Figure 9–4 shows results from a single question about what should be done to balance an uneven seesaw. The explanations supplied were of five types, of which the following examples may be given:

To balance a seesaw, a bigger block is needed at one end than the other because:

1. One end is lower than the other, and the other end is higher.
2. The board is not even on its two ends.
3. The two sides do not balance.

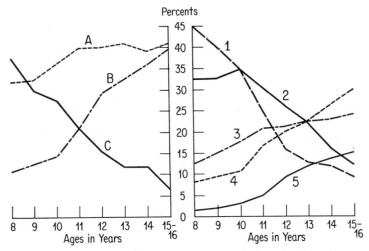

Fig. 9–4. Growth in the understanding of mechanical phenomena

Based on J. M. Deutsche, "The Development of Children's Concepts of Casual Relations," *University of Minnesota Monographs in Child Welfare,* no. 13, 1937, pp. 139, 141.

4. One side is a good deal heavier than the other.
5. One side is longer and heavier, and needs a weight to balance it.[13]

At age 8, answers of type 1 are commonest, and those of type 5 are practically nonexistent; the types occur in frequency in order from 1 to 5. At ages 15 and 16, the order is almost exactly reversed. It seems curious that only 15 per cent of the oldest group marked the fifth type of answer.

4. Adolescent ability to obtain insights, to judge, or to think is well measured by an old but distinctive and interesting experiment in the comprehension by children and adolescents of the sayings and parables of Jesus.[14]

---

[13] The first explanation lacks mechanical facts, general principle, and cause and effect relationships; the second contains a mechanical fact but is incomplete and gives no principle; the third mentions a principle but does not tie it in with the mechanical facts; the fourth gives the facts but lacks a principle; the last contains a fairly complete mechanical explanation, with the principle.

[14] For the younger generation that does not know its Bible, these two parables are quoted below:

Matthew 13:3. "Behold, a sower went forth to sow, and as he sowed some seeds fell by the wayside and the fowls came and devoured them up. Some fell upon stony places where they had not much earth and forthwith they sprung up because they had no deepness of earth; but when the sun was up they were scorched and because they had no root they withered away. And some fell among thorns and the thorns sprung up and choked them. But others fell on good soil and brought forth fruit, some a hundredfold, some sixtyfold, and some thirtyfold."

Matthew 7:24. "Therefore whosoever heareth these sayings of mine and doeth them, I will liken him unto a wise man which built his house upon a rock; and the

In this investigation a series of intelligence tests was first given to 637 children and adolescents, who were then classified on the basis of mental age. The study reports the percentage of children at each mental age who were able to understand each saying or parable. As illustrations, results of two parables will be shown: (A) "The Sower" and "The Two Foundations." In the same figure are the results in the development of comprehension for three sayings of Jesus: (1) "What shall it profit a man, if he shall gain the whole world, but lose his own soul?" (2) "Men love darkness rather than light, because their deeds are evil," and (3) "Judge not, that ye be not judged." The results are presented in Figure 9–5. The gains between the mental ages of 8 and 11 are gradual. Then there are large increases up to about 14; after

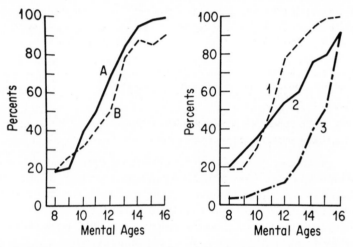

Fig. 9–5. Growth in the comprehension of the parables and sayings of Jesus

Based on S. P. Franklin, "Comprehension of the Sayings of Jesus," *University of Iowa Studies in Character,* 2:1–65, 1928.

14 the gain sometimes continues and sometimes not, depending largely upon the height reached by the curve at that point. In this investigation one finds a reflection of an increase in the ability to understand allegories and double

---

rain descended, and the floods came, and the winds blew and beat upon that house, and it fell not, for it was founded upon a rock. And everyone that heareth these sayings of mine and doeth them not shall be likened unto a foolish man which built his house upon the sand; and the rain descended, and the floods came, and the wind blew and beat upon that house; and it fell; and great was the fall thereof."

The student might also note the familiar phrases that have entered English speech from just these two parables: "to fall by the wayside," "to found one's house upon a rock," "and the rain descended and the floods came," "and great was the fall thereof." In miniature, these excerpts show the effect of Bible reading in previous generations upon everyday speech.

meanings. Teachers often sense this development, but proof of it is not always found in investigations using objective tests.

5. In another and quite recent experiment, 600 boys and 500 girls from 10 to 16 years of age were asked either to read a poem called "The Ne'er-do-well" or to see a silent film called "The Contest between the Hedgehog and the Hare." They then wrote an account of what they had seen or read. Both the poem and the film provided ample opportunity for characterization and insights. The "score" on these themes consisted of the number of statements that showed awareness of emotional responses, motives, or insight into traits of personality. The results appear in Figure 9–6. One such comment was made by over half the boys and girls at 10 years of age; few made as many as two, and none made three or more. The amount increases slowly at first and then shoots up after the years of pubescence. At 15 or 16 years, 96 percent of the boys and 100 percent of the girls made at least one comment; half to three-fourths made two; and 15 and 30 percent respectively made three or more.

6. It is probable that an age scale could be made by using different kinds of jokes that seemed amusing to children of different ages. The Binet scale has one item of this sort in the "absurdities": "The police found the body of a man cut into 27 pieces, and they think he killed himself." Those children who "see through" this gruesome statement are greatly amused! Children who are

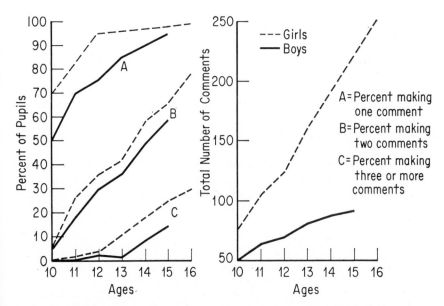

Fig. 9–6. Relation of age to awareness of emotions, traits of personality, and motives

Based on U. Undeutsch, "Neuere Untersuchungen zur Altersgestalt der Pubeszens," *Zeitschrift zur Experimentale und Angewandte Psychologie*, 6:578–588, 1959.

too immature mentally do not see any contradiction in the two halves of the sentence. To see the point of any joke, the hearer must know whatever facts are needed for the interpretation, must have enough mental power to make associations among several elements all held in his mind at once, and must have had some experiences that are relevant to the situation portrayed in the joke. Nothing is more frustrating than trying to understand the jokes in the "funny" magazines of another country—even when they are in one's own language. Thus, the Englishman may find no humor in the *New Yorker,* and some Americans cannot imagine why the English think the cartoons in *Punch* are amusing. Similarly, if one does not know that Dedham is about five miles from Boston or that a main artery south goes through it, and if one has never known any proper Bostonians, one fails to understand the joke about the Boston lady who traveled from her home to California; when asked by what route she had crossed the country, she replied, "Via Dedham." But without the proper background, this joke falls completely flat.

Children do not, in general, care much for verbal jokes and witty remarks. They do not understand them, they are still not quite sure what is real and what is nonsense, and the whole situation makes them feel insecure. Slapstick and mimicry they can grasp and appreciate, but jokes are likely to make them uncomfortable. At some time between twelve and fourteen most children begin to "see through" jokes and therefore to enjoy them.[15]

One well-known authority on the psychology of childhood and adolescence summarizes the development of humor from 10 to 14 years of age in the list that follows.

Age 10: Humor is of obvious type and not funny to adults. Some of it is slapstick, but much of it is reaction to anything unexpected.

Age 11: Humor is "corny" and often smutty. Much laughing at misbehavior and minor accidents. Child can understand a little adult humor, but his own humor is still of a different type.

Age 12: Many practical jokes of an obvious kind. Teasing. Some exchange of banter with adults.

Age 13: Rather less humor than at earlier or later ages, but the beginnings of sarcasm as a form of humor.

Age 14: Humor used against parents or others in authority, smutty jokes among members of one's own sex, dislike for display of humor on the part of parents.

Age 15: Beginnings of ability to see something funny when one is oneself teased or "kidded." Beginnings of irony as a form of humor.

Age 16: Ability to understand cartoons and other more subtle forms of humor. Participation in adult jokes and beginnings of spontaneous production of humor on an adult level.[16]

[15] M. Wolfenstein, "Children's Understanding of Jokes," *Psychoanalytical Studies of Children,* 8:162–176, 1954.

[16] A. Gessell, F. L. Ilg, and L. B. Ames, *Youth: The Years from Ten to Sixteen* (New York: Harper & Row, Publishers, 1956), 542 pp., pp. 243–346.

One German investigator has described various types of jokes—and jokers. There is the direct, obvious, uncomplicated, jolly, practical joker and teller of anecdotes, to whom everything is funny.[17] He does not plan his humor, and he is not really witty; he just bubbles over, laughing merrily at his own jokes, many of which are rather indecent. A second type is the solemn-faced, subtle individual whose jokes are polished, intentional, highly verbal, and witty, with hidden meanings that are sometimes so well hidden that the listener is not quite sure whether or not the remark is intended to be funny. A third type delivers his somewhat gruesome jokes with a sledge hammer and almost invariably at the wrong time and to the wrong person. Professional humorists and satirists are of the second type. Everyone knows at least one person who fits well into each of the above descriptions.

It has also been suggested that humor is a product of background factors quite as much as of maturity.[18] A joke that is funny to one group of people is not funny to another, because of the differences in the previous conditioning of the two groups by their life experiences to date. This statement is especially true if the jokes are at the expense of one of the groups. In this particular case jokes about Negroes were funny to white college students but not to Negro students, and vice versa. Humor thus derives from culture as soon as an individual has developed enough mental power to "see through" jokes at all.

7. A detailed and interesting study in the ability of college students to solve problems has been carried on by means of personal interviews, during which, after an initial period of getting acquainted, the student talked out loud as he thought through his answers.[19] The object of the investigation was to trace the thought process and to note where and why it went astray—not to determine how many problems a student could solve. As a student thought aloud, the observer made a record of his errors and miscues, using the following list, of which only a portion of the details are reproduced:

I. Understanding the nature of the problem

   A. Ability to start the problem (comprehension of directions)

      1. Rereads directions aimlessly—does not concentrate sufficiently to understand directions on first reading.

      2. Lacks understanding of the terms and phrases in the directions.

      3. Depends on the questions rather than the directions for an understanding of the nature of the problem.

---

[17] M. Koch, "Konstitutionelle Varianten des Sinnes für Komik," *Zeitschrift für Psychotherapie, Medicin, und Psychologie,* 5:203–214, 1955.

[18] R. Middleton and J. Moland, "Humor in Negro and White Subcultures: A Study of Jokes among University Students," *American Sociological Review,* 24:61–69, 1959.

[19] B. Bloom and L. J. Broder, "Problem-solving Processes of College Students," *Supplementary Educational Monographs,* No. 73 (Chicago: University of Chicago Press, 1950), 109 pp.

B. Ability to understand the specific problem . . . .
  1. Has difficulty as a result of improper reading of directions . . . .
    a. Makes no attempt to read the directions . . . .
  2. Forgets or loses sight of the directions.

II. Understanding of the ideas contained in the problem

A. Ability to bring relevant knowledge to bear on the problem
  1. Possesses little or no knowledge about the ideas contained in the problem.
  2. Is unable to use whatever relevant knowledge is possessed bcause of the presence of unfamiliar terms and ideas.
B. Ability to comprehend the ideas in the form presented in the problem
  1. Is unable to translate the difficult and abstract terms of the problem into simple and more concrete terms or into more familiar terms . . . .

III. General approach to the solution of problems

A. Extent of thought about the problem
  1. Makes little or no use of hypotheses as to the correct solution.
  2. Makes little or no attempt to set up and use criteria which the solution must meet . . . .
B. Care and system in thinking about the problem
  1. Makes little or no attempt to reorganize the problem in order to gain an understanding of the material.
  2. Makes little or no attempt to delimit the possible answers or choices . . . .
C. Ability to follow through on a process of reasoning
  1. Carries reasoning part way through completion, then gives up . . . .

IV. Attitude toward the solution of problems

A. Attitude toward reasoning
  1. Takes the attitude that reasoning is of little value—one either knows the answer or does not . . . .
B. Confidence in ability to solve problems
  1. Makes little attempt to attack the problems which appear to be complex and abstract.
  2. Makes only a superficial attempt to reason through a problem, then gives up and guesses . . . .
C. Introduction of personal considerations into problem solving
  1. Has difficulty in maintaining an objective attitude in certain problems because personal opinions play an important part . . . .[20]

This analysis breaks down the process of problem solving into four steps: understanding what is to be done, understanding the ideas contained in the problem, approaching the problem, and attitude toward the solution obtained. It also lists the most frequent of the errors made by students attempting to

---

[20] B. Bloom and L. J. Broder, "Problem-solving processes of College Students," *Supplementary Monographs*, No. 73 (Chicago: University of Chicago Press, 1950), 109 pp. Copyright 1950 by The University of Chicago.

reason. Some of these would appear to arise from the personality of the reasoner, some from the nature of his methods, and some from the type of problem he is attempting to solve.

Two recent investigations throw a little more light upon the processes of reasoning, and especially upon its consistency from one problem to another. In general, there is a high correlation between ability to solve two problems if the two are alike in structure, but not if they are different. This result suggests that reasoning does not exist as a separate entity that can be applied to anything but is a reaction made to a given problem. Individuals also transfer both attitudes and methods of attack. If a person is rigid in his thinking about one problem, he is likely to be rigid in his approach to others, especially if they are of similar structure; and a method that is successful in one problem tends to be used in others, without respect to its appropriateness. It was found extremely disturbing to most people if they were asked to verbalize their processes aloud or if they were required to meet a time limit. Probably either requirement altered the situation enough to affect the thinking responses. Reasoning appears to be such a fragile process that it is especially vulnerable to even small alterations in the nature of the problem.[21]

▶ **Summary**

With the oncoming of adolescence many special facets of intelligence develop at a rapid pace. The child does not memorize, or see humor in many of its forms, or reason as well as an adolescent, although he is far more suggestible. One outstanding development of the adolescent period is the ability to "see through" situations of all kinds to their inner meaning. High school boys and girls still make many errors in reasoning—as who does not?—but they show great progress over their capacity in this respect during their childhood years. A wise teacher will make assignments or set problems that call forth the full use of these newly developed special abilities.

References for Further Reading

B O O K S

Other Texts

Breckenridge and Vincent, *Child Development,* 4th ed. (Chap. 10 or 11).
Kuhlen, *Psychology of Adolescent Development* (pp. 106–139).

---

[21] R. H. Goldner, "The Individual Differences in Whole-Part Approach and Flexibility-Rigidity in Problem-solving," *Psychological Monographs,* 1957, Vol. 71, No. 21 (Whole Number 450), 18 pp.; and L. Brunk, E. G. Collister, C. Swift, and S. Staton, "A Correlational Study of Reasoning Problems," *Journal of Experimental Psychology,* 55:236–241, 1958.

Other Books and Monographs

Bloom, B., and L. J. Broder, "Problem-Solving Processes of College Students," *Supplementary Educational Monographs*, No. 73 (Chicago: University of Chicago Press, 1950), 109 pp. (Chap. 2 or 3).

Stein, M. I., and S. J. Heinze, *Creativity and the Individual* (New York: Free Press, 1960), 428 pp. (Chap. 2 or 12).

ARTICLES

Barron, F., "The Psychology of Imagination," *Scientific American*, 199:150–170, 1958.

Buswell, G. T., "Patterns of Thinking in Solving Problems," *University of California Publications in Education*, 12:63–148, 1956.

Gomulicki, B. R., "Individual Differences in Recall," *Journal of Personality*, 24:387–400, 1956.

Jakubczak, L. F., and R. H. Walters, "Suggestibility as Dependency Behavior," *Journal of Abnormal and Social Psychology*, 59:102–107, 1959.

Middleton, R., and J. Moland, "Humor in Negro and White Subcultures: A Study of Jokes among University Students," *American Sociological Review*, 24:61–69, 1959.

Morgan, H. B., "Differences in Logical Reasoning Associated with Age and Higher Education," *Psychological Reports*, 2:235–240, 1956.

Williams, D. C., *et al.*, "Mass Media Learning and Retention," *Canadian Journal of Psychology*, 11:157–163, 1957.

Wolfenstein, M., "Children's Understanding of Jokes," *Psychoanalytical Studies of Children*, 8:162–176, 1954.

Suggested Research Problems [22]

1. Longitudinal studies of memory, imagination, or reasoning.
2. Complete re-evaluation of memory as a tool in learning.

---

[22] See note, p. 11.

Chapter 10 | Intellectual-Cultural Interests

THE adolescent boy or girl has many interests. Some of them are continuations of childhood pursuits, but many are new. High school pupils show their interests by their preferences for games or other diversions; by their choice of books, magazines, radio or television programs, and motion pictures; by their ambitions; by the type of things they collect; by the kinds of books they read. The exact form that these interests take depends upon the environment. Because of the interrelation between adolescent drives and the environmental possibilities for their expression, the term "intellectual-cultural" has been used in describing these interests. The materials on this subject are diverse and numerous. If all relevant data were summarized, one would have a whole book. The writers have tried, therefore, to select a relatively few studies that illustrate the main trends. There will be an introductory section on the manner in which adolescents spend their time. The next section deals with interest in the three main methods of mass communication and entertainment at present—television, radio, and motion pictures. There is a brief section on collecting, a longer one on play, and a closing section on interest in various types of reading—books, newspapers, magazines, and comics.

► Adolescent Activities

A study of 2000 boys and girls in grades 9 through 12 produced a long list of things that the adolescents did during their leisure hours. The students replied to a series of some 60 questions about their activities by marking one of three statements: that they rarely or never had indulged in this activity, that they had sometimes indulged but less than once a week, that they had indulged once a week or oftener. By taking the activities carried on by 10 percent or more of the students at a rate of once a week or more, one derives the list presented in Table 10–1. The activities are many and varied. As might be expected, those appealing to the largest proportions of the student population are social in nature. In addition to those listed there were many others that were carried on less than once a week, such as: refinishing things in a home shop, building electronic equipment, making clothes from patterns, writing poetry or plays or stories, riding on a motor-

Table 10–1: ACTIVITIES OF ADOLESCENTS

	Percent	
	Boys	*Girls*
1. Social Activities		
Attended meeting of club outside of school	32	39
Rode around in car with friends in evening	53	41
Snacked with friends in soda fountain or restaurant	46	40
Hung around, just loafing or talking	43	36
Attended dances not sponsored by school	16	14
Attended movies (with friends)	21	25
Attended church social meetings during week	13	23
Went on dates	27	40
2. Games and Sports		
Played individual games, such as bowling or swimming	44	30
Played on organized teams (football, etc.)	27	10
Hunted, fished, hiked, or camped	34	7
Played outdoor games	23	9
Ridden on bicycle	25	16
Played indoor games (table tennis, etc.)	19	14
3. Use of Mass Media		
Listened to records with friends	27	34
Listened to radio	85	91
Watched television	97	95
4. Miscellaneous		
Repaired mechanical things	27	2
Shopping and window shopping	14	43
Attended church services	48	58
Written letters to friends	15	44
Talked on telephone between 15 minutes and 2 hours a day	19	46

SOURCE: Figures taken from the Purdue Public Opinion Panel, *Report of Poll No. 64* (Lafayette, Ind.: Division of Educational Reference, Purdue University, 1962), 20 pp.

cycle, working on collections of stamps, going to plays or concerts, roller skating, attending athletic events not sponsored by school, painting or sculpturing, acting in plays outside of school, carrying out scientific experiments at home, experimenting with plants, attending parties, caring for animals, designing clothes, making speeches, developing new recipes, and writing articles for publication—presumably in a student paper. All of this activity is in addition to television viewing. The picture one gets from such results is of days that are overcrowded to bursting point.

Young adolescents in grades 7 and 8 reported, aside from television and radio, such spontaneous activities as hobbies, reading, games, caring for animals, cooking, doing chores at home, riding bicycles, and gardening, plus eating and sleeping. Except for the last two, these interests require more or less initiative on the part of the adolescents.[1]

In spite of much complaint to the effect that television has supplanted all other activities, children and adolescents still do homework and home chores, and they still play. According to one study [2] homework occupies 6 percent of a child's time in grades 5–8, 12 percent in grades 9–10, and 16 per cent in grades 11–12. Children in the first group reported 52 percent of their leisure time as spent in play; those in the second group average 42 percent; and those in the third, 33 percent. Home chores are also reported in some detail in a 1960 investigation, as shown in Table 10–2. So far as the writers can recall their own youth, the type of chore has not changed much,

Table 10–2: HOME CHORES OF ADOLESCENTS

	Boys	Girls	Both Sexes
Mark the household chores you do regularly			
Clean own room	50	89	70
Make own bed	39	81	61
Run errands	54	62	58
Wash or dry dinner dishes	29	83	56
Mow lawn	69	29	49
Clean and dust	17	79	49
Wash the car	59	34	46
General care of garden or yard	52	28	40
Small repairs around house	53	15	34
Baby-sit with younger siblings	19	33	26
None	6	1	4

SOURCE: Purdue Opinion Panel, "Youth Looks at Politics, College Education, Jobs, and Family," *Report of Poll No. 60* (Lafayette, Ind.: Division of Education Reference, Purdue University, 1960), 22A.

although modern gadgets doubtless reduce the time needed. It may seem as if the girls carried a disproportionate load, but for them the work is vocational training. Only 6 percent of boys and 1 percent of girls reported no chores.

[1] S. M. Amatora, "Home Interests in Early Adolescence," *Genetic Psychology Monographs,* 65:157–174, 1962.
[2] Unless otherwise indicated, the materials of this section come from W. Schramm, J. Lyle, and E. B. Parker, *Television in the Lives of Our Children* (Stanford, Calif.: Stanford University Press, 1961), 324 pp.

▶ **Interest in Television, Radio, and Motion Pictures**

Aside from newspapers, which have been a means of disseminating information and culture for a long time, there are four important mass media: the movies, the radio, the record player, and television. All of these have important roles in the lives of boys and girls. Of these media, the movies have the longest history and television the shortest. Radio and television have become almost universal American phenomena.

Television Television is not yet 20 years old, but it already occupies an important place in the lives of children and adolescents. Its growth has been phenomenal. In 1950 there was a television set in only one home in every 15; in 1960, 7 out of every 8 homes contained a television set. In 1948, only 100,000 sets had been produced by manufacturers; by the end of 1959, the production line had turned out over 50,000,000. Whatever one may think of it, television has arrived as a factor in American life—and it is here to stay. The immediate impact of television has been felt most keenly by the radio and moving picture industries. The former has to some extent recovered, as will be pointed out later on, but the movies have not, at least not as yet. As compared with other media, television occupies a predominant place, as shown in Table 10–3, which summarizes the use of different media at three grade levels—grades 2, 6, and 12. Children and adolescents still read, although not as much as they did. The relatively high reading of the

Table 10–3: USE OF VARIOUS MEDIA BY CHILDREN AND ADOLESCENTS

Media	Grade 2	Grade 6	Grade 12
TV (hours per day)	2.2	2.9	2.3
Radio (hours per day)	1.1	1.2	1.9
Number of movies per month	1.0	1.6	1.1
Books (number read in past month)	1.1	2.1	1.0
Magazines (number read in past month)	0.8	2.6	2.8
Comics (books read in past month)	0.6	2.3	0.7
Percent reading daily paper	3.0	57.0	66.0

SOURCE: W. Schramm, J. Lyle, and E. B. Parker, *Television in the Lives of Our Children* (Stanford, Calif.: Stanford University Press, 1961), p. 36. Reprinted with the permission of the publishers, Stanford University Press. © 1961 by the Board of Trustees of the Leland Stanford Junior University.

daily paper probably comes from the use of papers in the social studies class as source material for the present trends in social and political life. It should also be mentioned that television has greatly decreased the sales of both comics and pulp magazines. In fact, it has been more effective than any "citizens' committee" has ever been.

One of the first questions to be answered about television concerns the number of hours spent watching it by children at different age levels. The average amount for 2196 school pupils in grades 1 through 12 in a single city was about 2.4 a day on weekdays, plus 2.8 on Sundays. The total time per week appears in Figure 10–1. In general, the girls tend to watch slightly less than the boys; they are also somewhat more variable. The amount of watch-

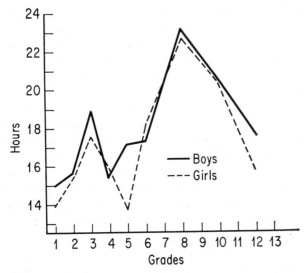

Fig. 10–1. Hours per week spent in watching television

Based on W. Schramm, J. Lyle, E. B. Parker, and L. Z. Freedman, *Television in the Lives of Our Children* (Stanford, Calif.: Stanford University Press, 1961), pp. 216–218.

ing reported by this study increased up until grade 8 (average age, 13). Possibly the two peaks at grades 3 and 8 may come from use of television in the schools in these grades. In any case, one-sixth of a child's waking time from the age of 3 on is given over to television; and up until grade 10 more time is spent watching television at home than is spent in school.

The use of television in the schools is extensive and becoming more so. In a report published in 1957, for example, in the St. Louis area, in 415 schools out of 696, the 135,000 pupils in 3467 classrooms watched in-school programs each week. In Washington City, Maryland, there was a closed network linking 48 schools with an operating staff (in 1958) of 14 television teachers, and 60 lessons were broadcast each week, after a preparation by the classroom teachers. Another school system showed an average of 21 hours per we.k in 1959 for elementary school children and 12 for high school students. Presumably the exact amount varies from one city to another. In order to get more recent figures, the writers visited two school superintendents in nearby cities in California and asked for an estimate of what use was made of television in their schools. The answer was that individual teachers varied greatly, some using it two or three times a week and some almost never. There was no current use of closed circuit television in these schools, perhaps because of the local educational station. Television was especially popular among language teachers, because the pupils can hear different natives talk. In some states one can obtain a high school diploma through television classes.[3]

The use of television is not distributed evenly among all children or adolescents. The children of fathers who graduated from college begin use of television four to six months earlier than the children of fathers who did not finish high school.[4] If the parents are themselves heavy users of television, the children tend to be also.[5] Among the children of "white collar" workers, 36 percent were found to be heavy users and 64 percent light users; for the children of "blue collar" workers, the percents are almost exactly reversed: 66 percent heavy and 34 percent light users.[6] Children with a high IQ watch far less than the average—7.3 hours for the six weekdays, plus 0.8 of an hour more on Sunday.[7]

The type of programs favored by children and adolescents is about what one would expect. In grade 1, children report viewing children's programs 60 percent of the time and adult programs the remaining 40 percent. By grade 6, the viewing of children's programs had dwindled to 21 percent, with 79 percent of the programs being those intended for adults. In adolescence, the viewing is almost exclusively of adult programs. At all ages the boys preferred westerns and crime stories, while the girls showed a preference for situation comedies and popular music, although they also watched both crime stories and westerns sometimes. The percent of children watching and liking different types of program changes from one age level to another. Children between the ages of 6 and 10 are fascinated by puppet shows and animal stories. But they have little interest in situation comedies and even less in popular music. By age 16, the positions are exactly reversed. The two childish types of program have no appeal whatever for adolescents, but the interest in comedies and popular music grows steadily with every passing year.

When asked which medium (books, magazines, newspapers, comics, television, radio, or movies) they would miss most if they did not have it,

[3] E. Exton, "Television at Work in the Schools," *American School Board Journal,* 134 (6):49–50, 70, 1957.

[4] Schramm, *et al., loc. cit.,* p. 226.

[5] *ibid.,* p. 227.

[6] *ibid.*

[7] *ibid.,* p. 225.

the children of all ages and levels of intelligence voted preponderantly for television. The other choices were related to the level of intelligence. The results from grade 10 are typical, as shown in Table 10–4. Of the students with high IQs no one voted for magazines, comics, or movies as their favorite medium; 13 percent said they would most miss books, 6 percent chose the newspaper as their least dispensable medium, and 25 percent voted for radio.

Table 10–4: SELECTION AND IQ

Intellectual Level	Books	Maga- zines	News- papers	Comics	Tele- vision	Radio	Movies	No Answer	Total
High IQ	13	0	6	0	53	25	0	4	100 [a]
Low IQ	0	2	10	2	51	27	10	2	100

[a] Totals do not add to 100 because some children marked two.
SOURCE: W. Schramm, J. Lyle, and E. B. Parker, *Television in the Lives of Our Children* (Stanford, Calif.: Stanford University Press, 1961), p. 235. Reprinted with the permission of the publishers, Stanford University Press. © 1961 by the Board of Trustees of the Leland Stanford Junior University.

Among tenth-graders of low IQ no one chose books as indispensable, 2 percent chose magazines, 2 percent comics, 10 percent each voted for radio and movies, and 27 percent voted for radio.[8] The two groups are much alike as regards their preference for television and radio, but some bright children chose books as indispensable.

The proportion of children and adolescents who like what they see on television varies with both age and intelligence.[9] School pupils in grades 6 through 12 were asked to react to the statement "I generally like anything I see on TV" by telling to what degree this statement was true of their own viewing. Between grades 6 and 12 there was a good deal of change, as shown in Figure 10–2. In grade 6 a total of 61 percent indicated that the statement applied in some degree to them (total of first three columns), while 36 percent said it did not apply to them (total of last two). In grade 12 the corresponding percents were 28 and 68. That is, the pupils became less acceptant of content as they grew older.

A similar relationship appeared between liking television offerings and level of intelligence.[10] The results from grade 12 may be taken as typical. In this grade 20 percent of the high IQ students found the programs of some interest (none marked them as always interesting), while 80 percent either often or always found them uninteresting. For the students with low IQs the corresponding percents were 37 (6 percent still accepted wholly what they saw) and 63.

---

[8] Schramm, *et al., loc. cit.*, p. 235.
[9] Schramm, *et al., loc. cit.*, p. 237.
[10] *ibid.*, p. 241.

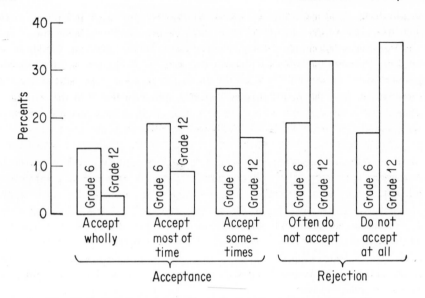

Fig. 10–2. Relation of maturity to degree of acceptance or rejection

Based on W. Schramm, J. Lyle, E. B. Parker, and L. Z. Freedman, *Television in the Lives of Our Children* (Stanford, Calif.: Stanford University Press, 1961), pp. 216–218.

There are a number of reasons why children and adolescents like television. In the first place, they enjoy it, just as children of all generations and ages have always enjoyed looking at pictures. One of the writers can remember bringing home box after box of stereoscope pictures and looking at them by the hour—and being punished for "wasting too much time." Second, they obtain a good deal of information—even though some of it one might wish they did not acquire. Third, they find it conducive to their social development, because they can watch television together with others, whether family or friends, boys or girls, and the presentations give them something to talk about after the picture is over. Fourth, the viewers derive certain benefits from their devotion to the electronic Pied Piper.[11] They find relief from their frustrations, deferment of their problems, wish fulfillment, and escape from boredom. Moreover, they find personalities with whom they can identify themselves. These are the same values that in previous years and centuries have been derived from folk tales, sagas, books, movies, and radio. All of them have value, although they have different value for different people.

It seems fairly certain that television produces some undesirable results. On the average, children get a half-hour less sleep than they did in pretele-

---

[11] E. B. Parker, "The Functions of Television for Children," Ph.D. Thesis, Stanford University, 1960.

vision days,[12] and some heavy viewers may average as much as an hour or two less sleep. There do not seem to be any deleterious effects upon the eyes of children and adolescents who are heavy users of the medium. Children and adolescents who use television above the average study less at home and do poorer work in school.[13] These results may, however, be related only indirectly, because the heavier users are often either duller than the average or come from homes in which there is little interest in school progress; therefore they would not be stimulated to study much either at home or at school, with or without television. There are other, more subtle results of television. It tends to reduce the socializing and active play of children and to reduce the frequency with which they show initiative; it may produce a good deal of tension, it may increase rather than decrease aggression, and it may frighten children and cause adolescents to become anxious.[14] It leads to a good deal of confusion among small children—as when the man who was killed on Monday is back in business on Tuesday, thus proving that death is not permanent. And it sometimes produces callousness, presumably in those who were frightened earlier and have become uncommonly detached and unfeeling as a means of self-protection.[15]

To the above, some people would add the contribution of television to delinquency. While it is true that the use of television has paralleled the increase in the rate of delinquency, it is unlikely that there is a direct relation between the two. The relationship is much the same as that previously thought to exist between the movies and delinquency. For example, a young criminal might say he stole because he saw people stealing in the movies and imitated them. If this statement is taken on its face value, one might say that the movies contributed to delinquency, but one has to remember that for this one boy who stole there were several thousand boys of the same age who saw the same picture and did not steal as a result. Also, that other boys of the same age learned to steal in many other ways than from the movies. The same arguments apply to television. The boy who becomes delinquent has been a predelinquent for a long time, and he is already looking for ideas that will enable him to perform some criminal act. He may find them in a

---

[12] E. E. Maccoby, "Television: Its Impact on School Children," *Public Opinion Quarterly,* 15:421–444, 1951.

[13] L. F. Scott, "Relationship between Elementary School Children and Television," *Journal of Educational Research,* 52:132–137, 1958.

[14] W. A. Belson, "Measuring the Effect of Television: A Description of Method," *Public Opinion Quarterly,* 22:11–18, 1958; E. D. Glynn, "Television and the American Character" in W. Y. Elliott, *Television: Impact on American Culture* (East Lansing, Mich.: Michigan State University Press, 1956), 382 pp.; E. E. Maccoby, "Role-Taking in Childhood and the Consequences for Social Learning," *Child Development,* 30:239–252, 1959.

[15] R. Zajonc, "Some Effects of 'Space' Serials," *Public Opinion Quarterly,* Vol. 18, No. 4, pp. 367–374, 1954–1955.

newspaper, in a magazine, in a book, in a movie, or on the television screen. And wherever he makes his discovery, it will be because he is looking for it. Like every other child the delinquent finds in television whatever will satisfy his needs.

Radio   There are at present some 170,000,000 radio sets in the United States.[16] No one knows what proportion of them are being carried around by adolescents—thanks to the transistor—but the total must come to a goodly number. Radio is still popular among adolescents for a number of reasons. One important reason is that listening to the radio can be combined with almost anything, and the major part of listening is so combined. Adolescents listen while they drive a car, while they mow the lawn or wash dishes, while they study, while they prepare snacks, while they eat, while they take a bath, while they play solitaire, while they wash their hair, and so on. Any activity that does not of itself make too much competing noise may be combined with radio listening. Television cannot so easily be combined with other activities in a similar way.

One habit of most adolescents is to keep the radio going while they study. Many parents have been greatly distressed, and some have forbidden radio playing during study hours; but as soon as the adolescents were old enough to follow their own preferences, they promptly turned it on again. There has been some research into the effects of this habit upon studying. To the surprise of the investigators, those students who always studied with the radio on did better schoolwork than those who never played it while studying. The pupils themselves report only beneficial results. The writers have quizzed several adolescents to find out why they could study better with a distraction than without one and have found reasonably good explanations. To begin with, many youngsters love noise and companionship and abhor silence and solitude. They would prefer to study together, but since this arrangement is often impracticable, they compromise by turning on the radio. The nub of the matter is that they have been educated in the midst of social stimuli and find solitude to be unbearable, distracting, and frightening. Silence is to them not a blessed relief from noise but an absence of all supporting human presence and is correlated in their minds with rejection and unpopularity. Adolescent testimony is to the effect that they do not actually listen to the radio, but as long as it is going, they are not alone. Since they cannot have their peers with them every minute, they substitute the radio, which produces enough background commotion to let them relax. This unique point of view— unique to an older generation, certainly—is a possible result of the present intense socialization from the cradle to the grave, and those adults who grew up without such pressure will have to accept this curious by-product and let

---

[16] *Statistical Yearbook,* 1961 (United Nations' Publishing Service, 1961), 679 pp., p. 646.

the radio run on and on. Some adolescents, especially in the 15–19 group, turn their radios to the disc jockeys for a wide variety of music, which helps them to "unwind" after a day of intense stimulation. Still others use the sound as an intermittent resting place for their thoughts, a sort of aural coffee break. Carefully calculated use of these last two approaches was first made extensively during World War II in industrial plants, and industries financed research on the optimum sound level and sound quality because it was well worthwhile to them in terms of worker effectiveness.

There seem to be two schools of thought about the effect of listening to radio or watching television upon the health and emotional adjustment of children and adolescents. Most of the earlier articles about radio listening reported undesirable emotional effects upon children.[17] Their blood pressure went up, and their pulses beat more rapidly, especially during exciting episodes. Attendance at horror films or addiction to crime stories over the radio or—more recently—watching similar presentations on television was reliably reported to produce nervousness, fear of being kidnaped, difficulty in sleeping, nightmares, and nervous habits, such as nail biting. These effects were especially noticeable if the children listened or watched during the evening. Studies of this type appeared with fair frequency before 1950. Two more recent studies contradict these earlier ones. What is not at all clear is whether the nature of the programs has improved, with the elimination of those elements that were precipitating the observed symptoms, or whether modern culture has bred a race of children who have been exposed from the cradle to mass communication and are therefore not as naive about it as those of earlier decades. Both these more recent studies compare children who are chronic and excessive listeners to the radio with those of the same age who do not listen at all or only on rare occasions.[18] Neither investigator found any fundamental difference between the two groups as regards nervous habits, interrupted sleep, fears, or dreams by either day or night. Either the earlier reports concentrated upon children who were already nervous, in which case the listening might well have a bad effect, or else children have acquired sophistication and do not become emotional, as they did earlier. This latter interpretation may be the correct one.

---

[17] See, for example, J. J. DeBoer, "Radio and Children's Emotions," *School and Society,* 50:369–373, 1939; F. Frank, "Chills and Thrills in Radio, Movies, and Comics: A Psychiatric Opinion," *Childhood Education Monographs,* Vol. XXV, No. 2, 1948, 42 pp.; and M. I. Preston, "Children's Reactions to Movie Horror and Radio Crime," *Journal of Pediatrics,* 19:147–168, 1941.

[18] F. Heisler, "Comparison between Those Elementary School Children Who Attend Moving Pictures, Read Comics, and Listen to Serial Radio Programs to Excess and Those Who Indulge in These Activities Seldom or Not at All," *Journal of Educational Research,* 42:182–190, 1948; R. A. Riccioti, "Children and Radio: A Study of Listeners and Non-Listeners to Various Types of Radio Programs, in Terms of Selection, Ability, Attitudes, and Behavior Measurement," *Genetic Psychology Monographs,* 44:149–159, 1951.

Motion Pictures   The decline of the motion picture industry is clearly reflected in the number of films produced. In 1948, 894
new films were made in the United States; in 1961 the total had shrunk to
211.[19] Almost all studies on the attendance of children and adolescents at
movies and on the effects movies have upon them were made at least a decade
ago. At the present time, the attendance is certainly much lower than it was.
According to one report, the average attendance at movies in a sample population dropped from 2.8 times a week to 0.7 times a week from pretelevision to
posttelevision days.[20] If this is a representative sample, the motion picture is
not now the force that it once was in the lives of adolescents. In 1944 no less
than 75 percent of a large adolescent group attended movies at least once
a week, and 30 percent attended three to five times a week.[21] Such figures are
no longer true. One may, however, assume that such films as are seen produce effects similar to those formerly produced, except that a less frequent
attendance might affect the intensity—either by enhancing the effect of the
occasional movie or by diminishing the cumulative effect of overattendance.
A study made in 1950–1951 showed movie attendance from age 15 to age 25
to average once a week.[22]

One reason that children and adolescents do not go to the movies as they
once did is simply that there is not enough time in their day for a consecutive
three-hour period for any one activity, aside from school. Moreover, they
are deriving their ideas of the nature of movies from oldish films shown with
a generous sprinkling of commercials on television, and they feel no great
urge to explore the matter further. In adolescence there is somewhat more
interest in movies than there is earlier, largely because boys and girls can
go to movies together and enjoy each other's company away from home
supervision. The nature of the film does not seem to be as alluring as the
social values involved. Thus far, the movies have not been able to compete
against television, mainly for reasons that have little if any relation to merit.

When two thousand English adolescents 13 to 16 years of age were asked
in 1949 to answer questions concerning the films they had seen during the
previous week they showed preferences both as to the type of film and as to
the outstanding characteristics they liked.[23] Boys as usual preferred films dealing with war, drama, and adventure stories, while girls liked drama, stories of

---

[19] Statistical Yearbook, 1961, *loc. cit.*, p. 641.
[20] J. R. McGeehan and R. L. Maranville, "Television: Impact and Reaction in
Lexington, Kentucky," *University of Kentucky Bulletin*, 1953.
[21] U. H. Fleege, *Self-Revelation of the Adolescent Boy* (Milwaukee, Wisc.: The
Bruce Publishing Company), 1944, 384 pp.
[22] R. Fendler and R. Leicht, "Community Behavior: Changes with Maturity," in
M. S. Allwood, ed., *Studies in Mass Communication* (Geneva, N.Y.: Hobart and William Smith Colleges), pp. 60–61, 1950–1951.
[23] W. D. Wall and E. M. Smith, "Film Choices of Adolescents," and "Effects of
Cinema Attendance on the Behavior of Adolescents as Seen by Their Contemporaries,"
British Journal of Educational Psychology, 19:121–136 and 53–61, 1949.

home life, and comedy, and rated adventure films very low. The boys rated love stories and fantasies so low that these were not included among their first ten choices. When the results were tabulated by school grade, there were changes during the four years of secondary school; interest in westerns, gangster stories, and mysteries declined, while that in musical comedies rose somewhat for both sexes. The characteristics that appealed to adolescents were excitement, realism, and humor for members of both sexes, violence for the boys and both "star appeal" and sentiment for the girls. In fact, girls seemed to choose their films more for the star than for the plot. The effects of the movies, as seen by age-mates, were principally in the imitation of superficial matters: ways of doing the hair, of walking, of talking, or of using make-up.

Recently, a German investigator divided a considerable number of adults into three groups: the occasional viewer, the habitual movie-goer, and the addict.[24] Some adolescents also showed addiction, but with them it was usually a passing phase. The addict differs from the person who goes often to the movies because the former is driven to the theater by his needs whereas the latter is either killing time or just amusing himself. The true addict is a neurotic person with defective relationships toward others, who has turned to the hypnosis of pictures and the dreams that they create for him. The artistic or informational value of the pictures plays no role. He is as dependent upon his own method of escaping the world as any user of narcotics. Once in a while a teacher may find a child or adolescent who is becoming an addict. She would do well to report what she has noted to the school psychologist.

Several investigations of the effect of a single motion picture upon attitudes have been made at one time or another, beginning three decades ago with the measurement of anti-Negro prejudice before and after seeing "The Birth of a Nation." It seems worthwhile to present briefly one sample study which measured the effect of "Tomorrow the World"—the story of a Nazi youth (Emil) in America—upon such attitudes as the treatment of Jews, value of "youth" organizations, use of fear and force as bases of discipline, free expression of opinion in newspapers, radio, or books, treatment of a conquered enemy, and so on.[25] About fifteen hundred pupils in grades 7 through 12 took part in the experiment. A few sample results appear below.

The largest group of pupils recognized the basic problems of adjustment faced by a Nazi boy in America, and recommended severe discipline and re-education as means of solving his problems and improving his adjustment. The larger proportion expressing this view tended to be in the upper grades rather than in the lower. The next largest group did not see the problems clearly, felt the situation to be without a solution, and simply rejected Emil

[24] C. Fervers, "Zur Psychologie des Filmerlehens," *Zeitschrift für Experimentelle und Angewandte Psychologie,* 6:800–807, 1959.
[25] M. J. Wiese and S. G. Cole, "A Study of Children's Attitudes and the Influence of a Commercial Motion Picture," *Journal of Psychology,* 21:151–171, 1946.

as an undesirable alien. The remaining students recommended kindness and re-education as the means of helping Emil, were quite sure he could become a good American, but did not clearly grasp the basic problems. That is, those who best understood the situation favored a firm treatment of Emil, while the advocates of kindness were inadequate in their thinking. The investigators purposely selected some schools enrolling children who belonged to minority groups—Jews, Mexicans, or Negroes—or to groups with points of view different from those of the general population—Mormon children and adolescents, for example. In general, the Jewish and Negro pupils showed greater condemnation and less mercy than others of the same age, while the Mormons tended to a greater degree of kindness and sympathy. As a result of seeing the film, the pupils in general showed an increased faith in American ideals —even though members of minorities were aware that these ideals are not always carried into practice—an increased condemnation for the use of force or fear, a greater sympathy toward the Jews, and a stronger tendency toward a merciful treatment of enemies.

It remains to say a few words about the discriminatory effect of all mass media upon children, adolescents, or adults. Each person sees in a film or a production of any kind what he is looking for. A boy with his mind on dates sees ways of love-making; a girl with her mind on clothes sees fashions; a youthful delinquent sees methods of prying open a locked window; a puzzled mother sees a way of influencing her recalcitrant daughter; a grown man catches a reminiscent whiff of his boyhood—and all from the same picture, television presentation, or radio program. Each person sees selectively. One cannot therefore rate any method of mass communication as either bad or good. Whatever moral value is derived from them is put there by the observer rather than by the maker.

▶ Interest in Collecting

The modern boy and girl make collections, but not to the extent that former generations did. The writers have an idea, not vouched for by anyone else, that the efficiency engineer has so eliminated the "wasted" space in the modern house, and has so compressed the "functional" space, that there is no room for a small child to put a collection. For example, a brother of one of the writers gathered together perhaps a quarter of a ton of rocks, which were labeled and displayed on long shelves in his attic room, the walls of which he had decorated with a collection of wildlife scenes, perhaps a hundred of them tacked up, edge to edge. There was still plenty of room left for the necessary furniture, clothes, books, albums, skates, tennis rackets, and other impedimenta. But where in the small apartment of recent times—or even in the small home, for that matter—could a child store a collection of rocks, or of anything bigger than a postage stamp? Every inch is "planned," and rarely is there a space for the storage of children's "junk."

Modern youngsters collect such things as model airplanes, phonograph records, or miniature figures, but the expense prohibits large collections. Children still try to collect things that are within their financial resources—picture postcards, snapshots, coupons, stamps, and the like, but their efforts are somewhat hampered.

To study the impulse to collect and to trace its development and expression, one has to go back about two decades in order to find relevant investigations. The things collected vary not only with age and sex, but also with the times, the environment, and the opportunities for storage. A group of 808 boys between the ages of 9 and 16 reported a total of 5685 collections, or 7 per boy; 868 girls of the same age reported 7161 collections or 8.2 per girl.[26] The percentage of children at each age who made collections varied from nearly 90 percent at age 9 to 60 percent at age 16. The number of collections per age began with 1 for most 6-year-olds, increased to 2 at 7 years, and to 4 or 5 by 8. Between 9 and 13 the number of collections rose to some figure between 8 and 10; these are the ages when the collecting mania is normally in full force. At 15 and 16 the boys had from 4 to 5 and the girls from 4 to 6 collections, and at 17 and 18 about 4. At all ages girls made more collections than boys. Rural children far exceeded urban children in collecting, although in adolescence the difference was not marked.

The things that are collected at different age levels are more interesting than the mere numbers. In general, boys collect stamps, coupons, and small figures of animals. As they grow older, they collect less and less. There is, of course, an occasional exception to this statement, and if a man is a collector, he is likely to be intense about it. But the usual effect of age upon the male psyche is to stop collections altogether rather than to change their nature. Girls collect coupons, picture postals, and snapshots; as they grow older, they collect dance programs, letters, theater programs, photographs, and all small accessories—such as handbags, earrings, lipsticks, scarves, and so on. In fact, many women remain inveterate collectors most of their lives. During childhood the things collected are valued primarily for their own sake; in adolescence, the collections are likely to have a sentimental value; in adulthood, the main motive is the acquisition of greater prestige or the profitable use of leisure time. Phonograph records are collected at all ages.

▶ **Interest in Play**

Even maiden aunts and bachelor uncles know that children play different games at different ages. They give the little boy a rubber

---

[26] P. A. Witty and H. C. Lehman, "Further Studies of Children's Interests in Collecting," *Journal of Educational Psychology*, 21:112–117, 1930, and "Collecting Interests of Town and Country Children," *Journal of Educational Psychology*, 24:170–184, 1933; and W. N. Durost, *Children's Collecting Activities in Relation to Social Factors* (New York: Bureau of Publications, Teachers College, Columbia University, 1932), 115 pp.

ball for Christmas, the older boy a baseball bat, the early adolescent a tennis racket, and the older adolescent a deck of cards. Their nieces are favored successively with rag dolls, roller skates, skis, and a book of crossword puzzles. Such normal developments with age have been traced in detail by a number of investigators. The needs that are satisfied through play vary from one age level to another. Even when the same sports persist, the reasons for indulging in them are not the same at successive ages. A girl of 8 skates because of the pleasure in bodily movement; at 10 she likes to race against other skaters; at 13 she plays ice hockey and belongs to a girls' skating club; at 15, she does figure skating—to show off before boys; at 18, she skates largely because boys do and because the sport offers one more chance to attract them. Thus, a single sport may be popular for many years but for vastly different reasons.

Figure 10–3 shows one characteristic game or diversion for boys and for girls at ages 3, 5, 9, 12, 15, 17, and 19. It is clear at once that there are marked changes. The 3-year-old plays mostly alone and amuses himself with simple objects. The 5-year-old plays in groups of two or three and runs about in active but unorganized games. The older boy plays marbles or flies a kite. There are also a number of popular group games that are usually called by the same names as those of the later years, but they are not played in the same way. For example, what a small boy calls "baseball" is usually a game played by perhaps four boys against five others. His form of football involves an indeterminate number of urchins; after they have chosen sides, everyone runs and jumps on everyone else, without much regard to teamwork or to the progress of the game. By the time a boy is 12 years old he prefers hiking, camping, skating, and swimming. In early and middle adolescence, the favorite activities are highly organized group games, played with established rules. In late adolescence interest in games has become more passive than active; already the average boy has begun to develop the attitude of the average man, who derives pleasure from watching sports rather than from participating actively in them.

Among girls there are parallel developments. The little girl begins, as her brother does, by playing alone at such simple amusements as banging a pan with a spoon. By five, however, differences in interest between the sexes have begun to show. The 5-year-old plays with her doll and also likes such group games as London Bridge, farmer in the dell, or drop the handkerchief. The 9-year-old likes to serve "afternoon tea," or to "dress up"; she also plays many active games such as run sheep run, or hare and hounds. At 12 her amusements are more like a boy's than they were earlier. Swimming, roller skating, and hiking are especially popular. So also is reading. By the age of 15 practically all athletics are popular, and the average girl is more active in her amusements than she ever is again. Movies, dances, and parties vie with athletics, however, and are equally popular. The 17-year-old is strongly

Ages

Fig. 10–3. Typical play activities at different ages

187

social in her interests—dates, parties, and dances engage most of her attention. She still like sports—swimming or skating, for example—but organized games do not interest her much any longer. She reads, sews, looks in the shop windows, and talks interminably over the telephone. At 21 she is even less active, although she develops some degree of spectator interest in active games, but her real diversions are social gatherings of various kinds, reading, and above all the movies, radio, and television.

Play is by no means the aimless activity that it sometimes seems to adults. It serves definite purposes, and it has definite motives: it leads to prestige among one's peers; it is a means of social participation—and hence a means of learning elementary social skills, such as taking one's turn; it is a form of creative self-expression; it often leads to future work. Moreover, it provides a child with an outlet for his emotions and tensions, it gives him exercise, and it may serve as an escape into adventure. Play provides a continual form of self-testing and helps supply a child with knowledge of his own limitations. Sometimes the competitive element in personal prowess becomes overemphasized and needs to be checked, in the interests of both the group and the individual. In adolescence play takes on a social value that is of great help to boys and girls. Often the voluntary submission of one's own drives to the good of the group first appears when a student wants to become a member of a team and realizes that the success of the team is the important thing. Diversions of various types also provide a framework within which heterosexual contacts are easily made. The hours spent in dancing, skating, or playing tennis with members of the opposite sex give an adolescent experience and background in intersex relationships. From both a physical and a social point of view, play is of vital importance to both children and adolescents. Toward the end of adolescence most boys and girls have become spectators rather than participants; and when they do play games they are motivated by a desire for exercise, diversion, or social intercourse rather than by the competitive drive.

The games children play and the intensity of their interest in games or exercise are thus indicative of their developmental age. It will be noted that girls mature earlier than boys in that their social interests appear sooner and their concentration upon organized group games disappears earlier. There is more or less overlapping in interests at all ages, and the fundamental drives are much the same for both sexes, but the forms of expression are somewhat different, partly at least because of environmental pressures. Thus boys are given carpentry sets and encouraged to build things, while a girl has to beg, borrow, or steal a hammer and saw if she wants to use them. On the other hand, girls are given dishes to play house with; any boy who uses them is likely to be called a sissy. The interests are not therefore purely spontaneous but are conditioned by social attitudes transmitted to children from previous generations.

Play among boys at least has a definite relation to size, health, and strength. An investigator who selected the highest and the lowest 10 percent in strength and physical fitness among a group of young adolescent boys found that the high group greatly exceeded the low in all forms of active games, in their spectator interest, and in their social activities.[27] The 10 percent with the lowest vitality exceeded the high group in reading and in making things —activities that demand relatively less strength and effort. There is no information as to whether the members of this latter group preferred such activities or indulged in them only because they were barred from successful competition with more vigorous age-mates.

► **Interest in Reading**

It would be possible to list the books that were found most interesting last year to boys and girls of different ages, but because the turnover in new books is so rapid, the lists would be of little value by the time this book was printed. Except for a few old favorites, like *Little Women* and *Treasure Island,* most of the titles on a current list would be unfamiliar to the average student reading this book, since his or her earlier favorites are already supplanted. It seems best, therefore, to limit the present discussion to types of books rather than to give specific titles. The types that appeal at different age levels are indicated by the sketches in Figures 10–4 through 10–8, which show jackets of books for boys and girls from late childhood through late adolescence. Since the jacket of a book is supposed to indicate its nature, a series of jackets reflects interests at various ages.

The child of either sex who can just barely read likes a small-sized book with many pictures and a simple plot about animals or other children. Little girls like fairy stories better than small boys do, but it is not till middle childhood that the main sex differences appear. At the elementary school level most boys like stories that deal with war, Boy Scouts, athletics, or strenuous adventure. In the preadolescent years many boys develop a craze for reading an entire series of books. The themes center mainly upon adventures and athletics. The plot is rather stereotyped; for example, the poor but honest boy meets undeserved failure but triumphs in the end over his wicked enemies. The characters also tend to be types rather than individuals. It is not until the later years of adolescence that romantic novels make an appeal to the average boy, and some boys never care for them. Girls show a somewhat different development. During elementary school their interest is chiefly in fairy stories and tales of home or school life. They also read entire sets of books about the same main character. There is a short period during preadolescence when they like adventure stories, preferably of a romantic nature. With the

---

[27] D. B. Van Dalen, "Differential Analysis of the Play of Adolescent Boys," *Journal of Educational Research,* 41:204–213, 1947.

Girls   Boys

Fig. 10–4. Reading interests in childhood

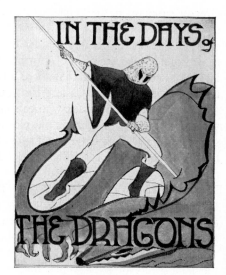

Girls   Boys

Fig. 10–5. Reading interests in preadolescence

Girls   Boys

Fig. 10–6. Reading interests in early adolescence

Girls   Boys

Fig. 10–7. Reading interests in middle adolescence

Fig. 10–8. Reading interests in late adolescence

beginning of adolescence, they become almost immediately interested in romantic literature; most girls of 13 are already reading love stories. They also
show great devotion to the continued story in popular magazines and a more
pronounced liking than boys have for detective stories, and they read more
accounts of travel. Once the liking for adult fiction is established, it pushes
out the juvenile forms.

The figures from one typical investigation [28] of the reading interests of
14,324 pupils in grades 7 through 12 are summarized in Table 10–5. The
results are based upon the withdrawal of books from the school library and
therefore do not show all the reading the pupils did, but presumably they do
show a fair cross section. Boys concentrated upon stories of adventure, romances, and tales of animals—in the earlier grades—while girls put romance
first, with adventure stories, mysteries, and animal tales considerably lower.
For both sexes interest in adventure and animal stories decreased with age,
while that in romances increased. Boys tended to spread their interests over
more kinds of reading than did girls, who concentrated upon romance.

Another investigator found that adventure stories which told of physical
hardships and dangers were far more popular among boys than among girls,
while those that did not stress the physically grim showed much less difference in appeal to the sexes.[29] That is, girls did not object to adventure per
se, but they preferred to be spared the details of suffering. Boys showed a

---

[28] P. S. McCarty, "Reading Interests as Shown by Choices of Books in School Libraries," *School Review*, 58:90–96, 1950.

[29] G. W. Norvell, *Reading Interests of Young People* (Boston: D. C. Heath and
Company, 1950), 262 pp., pp. 52, 56–57.

differential interest also in stories about wild animals and sports of all kinds. Girls had an excessive liking for biographies of women, mysteries, stories of home life, love stories, and tales that were sentimental though not involving a love theme. They liked essays better than boys did but readings in science less. In all studies girls read more than boys did. At all ages, for both sexes, fiction was from two to three times as popular as nonfiction.[30]

Table 10–5: TYPES OF BOOKS WITHDRAWN FROM LIBRARIES
BY ADOLESCENTS
(Figures are in percents, which total 100 for each grade.)

Boys and Grade							Girls and Grade					
7	8	9	10	11	12	Types of book	7	8	9	10	11	12
29	33	29	28	20	17	1. Adventure	12	10	11	8	6	4
23	20	24	25	34	36	2. Romances	47	51	53	54	58	57
14	13	13	10	5	3	3. Animal stories	11	9	6	4	2	2
6	6	8	8	9	7	4. Biographies	5	5	7	7	9	6
6	8	8	7	5	5	5. Sports	1	1	1	1	1	1
5	6	7	6	5	7	6. War stories	1	1	1	2	1	2
8	6	4	4	3	2	7. Detective stories	11	7	6	4	1	1
2	2	2	2	3	3	8. Science	1	2	1	2	1	1
1	1		2	5	7	9. Arts	1	1	1	3	7	12
1	1	1	1	2	2	10. History	1	1	1	1	2	1
1	1					11. Mythology (fairy tales)	1	1		1		1
	1	1	1	2	1	12. Humorous stories	1		1	1	1	1
		1	1	1	1	13. Occupations				1	1	1
4	2	2	5	6	9	14. Miscellaneous	2	3	4	6	7	8
						15. Career stories (about women)	5	8	7	5	3	2
Average per year: 8.7 books							Average per year: 10.5 books					

SOURCE: P. S. McCarty, "Reading Interests as Shown by Choices of Books in School Libraries," *School Review*, 58:93–94, 1950. © 1950 by the University of Chicago Press.

The Purdue investigations [31] show similar results. The main voluntary reading consisted of adventure stories, romances, and mysteries; 54 percent of the boys and 43 percent of the girls read such materials. Reading of biography and nonfiction was reported 11 and 12 percent respectively for boys and girls; of science, mechanics, social problems, and history by 10 and 16 percent. Religious reading was very low (5 and 4 percent) with the perusal of classic novels and dramas at the bottom (only 3 percent for each sex).

[30] McCarty, "Reading Interests as Shown by Choices of Books in School Libraries," *loc. cit.*
[31] Purdue Opinion Panel, *Report of Poll No. 54, loc. cit.*, p. 25a.

A librarian who is head of the young people's collection in a public library has given the writers verbal testimony as to the present reading habits of preadolescents and adolescents. To begin with, three-fourths of the school pupils in the junior high, and an even larger proportion in the senior high school, have and use public library cards. Within the last five years she states that there has been a visible change in the reading habits of adolescents. They are reading more adult books than formerly, and a greater number of serious books; they have a lively interest in science fiction, but the story must be based upon actual findings and theories in science in the real world; they condemn the merely sensational and impossible. They are greatly attracted to historical novels and biographies. The boys read more of the former and the girls more of the latter. Both read stories of adventure or romance, but they also read a good deal of nonfiction. In the fall of 1962 a list of the ten best-sellers among adolescents was published; six of the ten were nonfiction and dealt with some serious problem of modern life.[32] Among preadolescents there is often a devotion to a series of stories that center around a given character or locale, but by the years of adolescence this interest has largely disappeared. Within the last decade there has been a reduction in the reading of condensed, oversimplified versions of literary masterpieces—once very popular—because today's young people want to read these classics in their full-length form. Dramas of all types are so popular that the library cannot keep on hand enough copies to meet the demand. Although the hours spent in watching television and in going to the movies decrease the available time for reading, both media stimulate the desire to read. It is a daily experience to have adolescents ask for a standard literary classic because they have seen a half-hour presentation of some kind on television or have seen a movie version of the book and now wish to read the whole thing.

Reading has great value for adolescents because of its possible contribution to their development. It can provide relief from tension, opportunity for working out aggressive drives harmlessly, information for the resolution of conflicts, and characters for easy identification. Reading can also result in security and self-realization for an adolescent's inner life, better interpersonal relations with his family and peers, changes in behavior, new ideas, and increased appreciation of many life activities. The crucial problem would seem to lie in getting the right books to the right adolescents. The values of reading are there, but boys and girls need help in finding them. In recent years, books have been used as a constructive form of treatment with delinquents because of their value in providing new identifications, new ideologies, new satisfactions, and new patterns of living.

According to one report,[33] college students spend from two to eight

---

[32] C. Fadiman, "Teenagers' Top Ten for Fall," *This Week Magazine,* September 23, 1962, p. 28.
[33] W. Abraham, "The Reading Choices of College Students," *Journal of Educational Research,* 45:459–465, 1952.

hours a week upon free reading of their own choice. Seniors reported less such reading than freshmen. There were great differences from one college to another, though no explanation was given for this phenomenon. There did not seem to be any recognizable trends in the type of book read. The selections covered an extremely wide range, however.

Most adolescent boys read magazines that deal with mechanics, sports, athletics, and heroics, while girls of the same age tend to concentrate upon magazines that contain "true life" stories, material about women's arts, stories of movie stars, and adult fiction of a sentimental character. During high school, boys and girls read an average of four magazines regularly, three others often, and another six sometimes. At all ages the girls incline more than boys to love stories, while the boys read more than do girls about current events. The most widely read magazines are *Life, Reader's Digest, Time, Newsweek, Look,* and *Saturday Evening Post.* Since high school girls are far more avid readers than boys of the same age, the fiction magazines that rate high in frequency have a mainly feminine appeal: *McCall's, Redbook,* and *Ladies Home Journal,* and the like. Most girls read *Seventeen, Glamour, Chic, Mademoiselle,* and *Ingenue.* As adolescents grow older many of them pass through a stage of reading pulps. Science fiction rates high among the boys and detective stories among the girls, although some girls read the former and some boys the latter. In one study of eleventh-grade students, the girls read a total of 37 different magazines and the boys a total of 31.[34]

The comics in the newspapers are read to some extent by children, adolescents, and adults, but peak of the interest in them comes between 10 and 12 years of age; thereafter, there is a decrease, although most people of all ages glance at a comic strip once in a while. It is a type of reading frowned upon by adults. Disapproval of parents and teachers has had little effect upon this type of reading, although the advent of television has diminished interest in comics considerably. Books of comics are still favorites among children, even among those who also read good literature. The popularity of this type of reading matter may be inferred from Table 10–6. Comics are at all ages a little more popular among boys and men than among girls and women. It

Table 10–6: PERCENTS OF INDIVIDUALS READING COMICS AT DIFFERENT AGES

	6–11	*12–17*	*18–30*	*30*
Boys	95	87	41	16
Girls	91	81	28	12

SOURCE: Based on O. A. Witty and R. A. Sizemore, "Reading the Comics: A Summary of Studies and an Evaluation: I," *Elementary English Journal,* 31:501–506, 1954.

is curious that so much interest persists into the adult years. Among children such reading is virtually universal and among adolescents it is extremely pop-

[34] A. Shatter, "Survey of Student Reading," *English Journal,* 40:271–273, 1951.

ular. The IQ of students in grades 11 and 12 who read books of comics was found in one study to be 94 and 88, respectively, as compared with an average of 108 and 110 for all students in these grades.[35] For girls, comics give many helpful hints upon how to be feminine and popular, they show successful romance and dating, they provide some humor but usually not as an end in itself, and they center around adolescent characters. They probably also act as a vicarious means of wish-fulfillment.[36] To a considerable extent each child finds in the comic books what he is looking for—just as he does in the movies. If he is already aggressive and rebellious, the books are likely to increase these tendencies; but the well-adjusted child does not seem to be greatly affected. For all children the books may act as means of working off aggressions at the level of fantasy. Comics certainly have some features that are bad, but perhaps not so much on moral as on literary grounds. They are unrefined and full of bad English—one of the writers found "irregardless" twice in one book; the characters are often bad mannered and coarse. They sometimes depict types of violence that the movies' moral code would exclude. The cruelty often makes an adult shudder, but aside from its unrefined setting, it is no worse than the cruelty described in horrendous detail in *Quo Vadis?* It is not desirable that children read *Quo Vadis?* either, because they become upset and frightened. The comics merely portray the same type of scenes and in infinitely worse style.

All the early investigators of the comics were as one in condemning them, on the grounds that they frightened children and upset their metabolism.[37] Also, there have been a few tragedies because children patterned their imitative play after the models they found in the comic books. More recent investigations do not go quite so far in condemnation. One investigator found no effect at all upon either schoolwork or personality. Possibly the efforts of the publishers to make the books less offensive in taste are having results.[38] Another not only found no adverse effect but thought the comics exerted a small but beneficial influence upon mental health.[39]

The comics seem to be here to stay, at least for the foreseeable future. They do have some virtues, aside from their almost universal appeal. They have a simple vocabulary, for example. Each book contains about 10,000

---

[35] L. Bender and R. Lowrie, "The Effect of Comic Books on the Ideology of Children," *American Journal of Orthopsychiatry,* 11:540–550, 1941.

[36] F. C. Kinneman, "The Comics and Their Appeal to Youth of Today," *English Journal,* 32:331–335, 1943; and L. Bender, "The Psychology of Children's Reading and the Comics," *Journal of Educational Sociology,* 18:223–231, 1944.

[37] See F. Wertham, "The Comics—Very Funny," *Saturday Review of Literature,* May 29, 1948; G. L. McIntyre, "Not So Funny Funnies," *Progressive Education,* 22:28–30, 1945; and Frank, "Comics, Radio, Movies, and Children," *loc. cit.*

[38] F. Wertham, "Are They Cleaning Up the Comics?" *New York State Education,* 43:176–180, 1955.

[39] A. M. Rose, "Mental Health Attitudes of Youth as Influenced by a Comic Strip," *Journalism Quarterly,* 35:333–343, 1958.

words, of which 9000 are among the commonest in the language. There is some slang, but such words do not exceed 5 percent of the total.[40] They are often read by children who would otherwise do no out-of-school reading at all. Since the cartoon form cannot be eliminated, perhaps it can be used more constructively than it is—as has been done in a series that depicts stories from the Bible. With better drawing and better stories, and with the elimination of the cruelty, bad manners, slang phrases, and coarseness, the comic book may take its place as a positive contribution to children's literature.

American children begin to read the newspapers as early as the fourth grade, usually in school. Daily reading begins in about the eighth grade, an activity encouraged by most parents and all teachers, many of whom make assignments that call for such reading. In high school the newspaper is much read and much valued, especially by the brighter students.[41]

The replies of 2000 high school students about their reading of newspapers are revealing;[42] 85 percent felt that the reading of current news was an important part of their education. The average time spent per day was 10 minutes, and 36 percent read the editorials at least sometimes while 39 percent read them regularly. These figures compare favorably with similar reports from adults.

One American phenomenon is the mushrooming of the sports page in the newspapers. Even as sober a paper as the *New York Times* has increased its sporting news to 7.5 percent of its total. Most local papers run a great deal higher, usually between 20 and 25 percent of the space being devoted to sports. This development—from 5 to 15 percent in 1900—is a reflection of the great spectator interest that the American public of all ages and both sexes have in sports. It is of a piece with the crammed stadiums for football games and the great arenas packed for basketball contests. Adolescents share in this general enthusiasm and are, indeed, among the most ardent readers of the sports pages.[43]

There is little doubt that the radio and, more recently, television have reduced the amount of reading done by children and adolescents. Radio listening begins long before children can read, and many of them develop the "radio habit" by the time they are able to read easily and therefore do not read as much outside school as they otherwise might. In any case, if a child listens to the radio or watches television for two or three hours a day, he

---

[40] See G. E. Hill, "The Vocabulary of Comic Strips," *Journal of Educational Psychology*, 34:77–87, 1943.

[41] W. Schramm, *et al.*, "Patterns in Children's Reading of Newspapers," *Journalism Quarterly*, 37:35–40, 1960.

[42] Purdue Opinion Panel, "Youth Looks at Education," *Report of Poll No. 54* (Lafayette, Ind.: Division of Educational Reference, Purdue University, 1959), 28 pp. (pp. 25a, 27a).

[43] S. L. Pressey and W. E. Crates, "Sports and the Public Mind," *School and Society*, 72:373–374, 1950.

has no time for reading. In fact, with the aid of the movies, radio, and television, a child *can* almost avoid the printed page altogether, except when he is in school. However, children and adolescents from good homes do still read a good deal and for those who do, there is a large array of beautiful books from which to make a choice.

► **Summary**

Adolescents have a plethora of interests—more than they have time to pursue. In former decades they were influenced mainly by what they read, in books or in newspapers. Then moving pictures became all-powerful. About four decades ago, the radio became a source of ideas and experiences. In the last decade television has been added. Adolescents are thus subject to immense pressures from sources over which the school has no control at all. The teacher of today must at least live with these various forms of stimulation, and if possible she should use them constructively in her teaching. The mass media are well established and are much too powerful to be ignored. The best that a teacher can hope for is to guide students to the most profitable forms of presentation and to encourage them to bring into the classroom what they learn through these various outside media of communication. This procedure at least gives the teacher a chance to discuss ideas with the pupils and to guide their thinking and reactions.

The desire to make collections still exists, but the modern environment does not give it the scope that it needs for a full flowering. Although children do not spend as much time playing as they did in earlier generations, they continue to show the same stages of development in their play activities, which are of value to them in providing both opportunities for social contacts and for expression of the emotions. Reading is by no means a lost art. It may be that because the modern child learns to read rapidly he actually covers almost as many pages during his school years as his father did—and almost certainly more than his grandfather did. His choices for voluntary reading reflect much the same developmental trends that children and adolescents have always shown.

References for Further Reading

BOOKS

Other Texts

Garrison, *Growth and Development* (pp. 129–158).
Horrocks, *Behavior and Development* (pp. 533–541 and 575–587).
Hurlock, *Adolescent Development*, 2d ed. (Chap. 7 or 9).
Jones, *Growth and Behavior in Adolescence* (pp. 108–129).
Kuhlen, *Psychology of Adolescent Development* (Chap. 5).

Other Books and Monographs

Amatora, Sr. M., "Home Interests of Early Adolescents," *Genetic Psychology Monographs,* Vol. 65, pp. 137–174, 1962.

Bogart, L., *The Age of Television* (New York: Frederick Ungar Publishing Company, 1956), 348 pp. (Chap. 2 or 12).

Books for the Teen Age, New York Public Library, 1962, 50 pp.

Hartley, R. E., *et al., Understand Children's Play* (New York: Columbia University Press, 1952), 372 pp. (Chap. 1, 2, or 3).

Riccioti, P. A., "Children and Radio," *Genetic Psychology Monographs,* Vol. 44, pp. 149–159, 1951.

Roos, J. C., *Patterns in Reading,* 2d ed. (American Library Association, 1961), 172 pp. (any 20 pages).

Schramm, W., *et al., Television in the Lives of Our Children* (Stanford, Calif.: Stanford University Press), 1961, 324 pp. (pp. 211–243).

Seidman, *The Adolescent: A Book of Readings,* rev. ed. (No. 45).

ARTICLES

Albert, R. S., and H. G. Meline, "The Influence of Social Status on the Uses of Television," *Public Opinion Quarterly,* 22:145–151, 1958.

Belson, W. A., "Measuring the Effects of Television: A Description of Method," *Public Opinion Quarterly,* 22:11–18, 1958.

Burns, D. G., "Newspaper Reading in the Secondary Modern School," *British Journal of Educational Psychology,* 25:1–9, 1955.

Coffin, T. E., "Television's Impact upon Society," *American Psychologist,* 10:630–641, 1955.

Holton, S. M., "The Pursuit of Happiness," *High School Journal,* 37:165–168, 1954.

Lewin, H. S., "Facts and Fears about the Comics," *Nation's Schools,* 52:46–48, 1953.

Neubert, R., "Recreation and the Teen-Ager," *National Association of Secondary School Principals' Journal,* 39:145–150, 1955.

Rose, A. M., "Mental Health Attitudes of Youth as Influenced by the Comic Strip," *Journalism Quarterly,* 35:333–342, 1958.

Schramm, W., *et al.,* "Patterns in Children's Reading of Newspapers," *Journalism Quarterly,* 37:35–40, 1960.

Wertham, F., "Are They Cleaning up the Comics?" *New York State Education,* 43:176–180, 1955.

Zajonc, R., "Some Effects of 'Space' Serials," *Public Opinion Quarterly,* 18, 367–374, 1954–1955.

Suggested Research Problems [44]

1. Study of collections made at the present time by children and adults.
2. Analysis of a typical community to determine (a) what recreation is available for children and adolescents and (b) what individuals of what ages use which facilities and to what extent.

---

[44] See note, p. 11.

Chapter 11 | Intellectual Deviation

ONE of the most significant outcomes of the testing movement is the objective proof that children differ from each other in almost every intellectual trait. The total range of IQs thus far determined varies from 20 to 200—that is, from an idiot to a genius. This entire range of IQs forms an unbroken series from the lowest to the highest, but for purposes of convenience it is generally divided into a number of levels. It is usually assumed that children with an IQ between 90 and 110 are of normal ability for their age; this group makes up about two thirds of the entire population. Those with IQs from 80 to 90 are classed as dull normal and those from 111 to 130 as bright. The ability of these two groups is slightly below or slightly above the average. Below the dull normal group, with IQs from 70 to 79, come the borderline defectives. At the two ends of the distribution are the gifted and the true defectives. The bright and dull children learn respectively a little faster or a little more slowly than those in the central group, but both master the material of the elementary school, the former perhaps in a semester less time than the average pupil and the latter in somewhat more time than the normal child. That is, the time has to vary, unless the standard of performance in strictly academic work is lowered. Modern promotion policies tend to advance pupils without respect to their basic achievement, thus varying the accomplishment rather than the time.

The present chapter is concerned only with those at the top or at the bottom of the high school distribution—not with those who are slightly above or below the normal mental development for their age. Both groups have recognizable characteristics, both have special problems, and both require an education that is adjusted to their needs. It is also probable that they should have specially trained and specially selected teachers.

The intellectual deviates in any school population are those who score in the extremes of intelligence *for their group,* not for the entire world. Since the distribution changes as pupils proceed through the grades, the same children are not deviates at all levels. In high school the pupils in the "brilliant" group have IQs from about 140 up to 190. At the other end of the distribution, the pupils in the "dull" group have IQs that range from 85 downward. The differences between these approximate limits and those just given for the general school population are due to the elimination that has taken place during the first eight years of school. Because the lowest IQs have already been weeded out, the extremes of the remaining distribution fall in a different place. The line of demarcation between these small, extreme groups and the rest of the high school population cannot, of course, be drawn in a hard-and-fast manner, and the limits suggested above are only approximate. The main thing to remember is that even these relative limits shift from one level of education to another, in terms of each fresh distribution.[1]

Table 11-1: SOCIAL STATUS AND SUBSEQUENT EDUCATIONAL LEVEL OF THOSE STUDENTS IN THE HIGHEST FOURTH INTELLECTUALLY OF A HIGH SCHOOL CLASS

Socioeconomic Status	Percent of Group	*Subsequent Educational Level*			
		Did Not Finish High School	*Graduated from High School but Did Not Enter College*	*Entered College but Did Not Graduate from College*	*Graduated from College*
Upper and Upper-Middle Class	18	0	2	2	14
Lower Middle Class	41	2	15	5	19
Upper Lower-Class	32	3	14	5	10
Lower Lower-Class	9	2	6	1	0
Total Percents	100	7	37	13	43

SOURCE: R. F. de Haan and R. T. Havighurst, *Educating Gifted Children* (Chicago: University of Chicago Press, 1957), 276 pp., p. 34. © 1957 by The University of Chicago Press.

The remaining sections of the chapter will discuss the highest and the lowest groups at the high school level. What is said about them applies in reduced measure to those who are classified as a little above or a little below the average for their grade or age.

▶ The Brilliant Adolescent

Talented students come from all levels of society, although not in equal numbers. One investigator classified the families of brilliant students in one small city into four socioeconomic levels. As may be

---

[1] For example, the failing graduate student is typically a person who is well above the average of the general population in intelligence, but he is definitely inferior to the highest 5 percent in verbal intelligence, from whom most graduate students are drawn. There is always a bottom to a distribution, no matter where it is cut off.

seen in Table 11–1, the majority of these students came from the middle classes, but nearly 10 percent of them from the group that was lowest socially and had the smallest income. The last four columns of the table indicate what education these students received, after their entrance to high school. Seven percent did not finish high school, another 37 percent graduated from high school but did not enter college, 13 percent entered college but did not graduate, leaving only 43 percent who graduated, or less than half this group at entrance to high school. It is clear that social norms and economic resources play their part in the persistence of high school pupils into higher educational levels. Whereas no one in the highest socioeconomic class failed to finish high school, no one in the lowest succeeded in finishing college, and only 1 percent of the latter even entered. This loss of over half the country's richest asset— the brilliance of its next generation—is a tragedy.

Characteristics   There are two popular misconceptions about the very bright child: that he is small for his age and that he is queer. Both assumptions are wrong, as will presently be shown. The first probably comes from the fact that gifted children are usually accelerated in school and are therefore in classes with others who are about two years older; they therefore may seem to be small, but this error would be corrected if they were compared with children of their own age. Actually, brilliant children average taller and heavier than normal children of their chronological group; they also mature earlier. The typical situation is shown in Table 11–2. These gifted children were taller and heavier than the average, and there was nothing in the least sickly about them. In general, brilliant children and adolescents are as superior physically as they are mentally.[2] The social and emotional maturity reported in Table 11–2 will be discussed later on.

Superiority in size continues into adult life. In Terman's study of one thousand brilliant boys and girls, whom he had at that time followed for 25 years, the men averaged five feet eleven inches as compared with the national average of five feet seven and a half inches and the general average for college men of five feet eight and a half inches.[3] Twenty-eight percent were six feet tall or over; not even the California sunshine can be held entirely responsible, since it did not shine exclusively upon them. The young women average five feet five and a half inches as against parallel averages of five feet three and a half inches and five feet four inches. At the time of the last investigation (1955), when the brilliant children of the 1920s had become middle-aged men and women, the robust health they had shown in childhood was still with them: only 2 percent of the men and 3 percent of the women reported ill-health, and the death rate among them was approximately two-

---

[2] See, for instance, W. B. Barbe, "Characteristics of Gifted Children," *Educational Administration and Supervision,* 41:207–217, 1955.

[3] L. M. Terman and M. H. Oden, "The Gifted Group at Mid-Life," *Genetic Studies of Genius;* Vol. V (Stanford, Calif.: Stanford University Press, 1959), 187 pp., p. 34.

thirds that of the general population.[4] Evidence from two other sources supports the above facts: the men who made the highest scores on the Army intelligence tests were taller and heavier than those who made low scores,[5] and

Table 11-2: CHARACTERISTICS OF GIFTED STUDENTS

Characteristics Spontaneously Reported as Best Describing Personally- known Gifted Pupils	Number among 340 Students
A. Health	
1. Vigorous	100
2. Average	231
3. Poor	1
B. Physical Development	
1. Well-developed	108
2. Average development	225
3. Immature development	3
C. Grade Placement	
1. Young for grade	154
2. Average for grade	166
3. Old for grade	6
D. Behavior	
1. Better than average	218
2. Average in conduct	133
3. Poor in conduct	6
E. Emotional Maturity	
1. Poised and balanced	168
2. Average maturity	144
3. Emotionally immature	18

SOURCE: G. E. Hill, R. J. Lauff, and J. E. Young, "Identifying and Educating Our Gifted Children" (Athens, O.: The Center for Educational Service, Ohio University, 1957), *Pupil Services Series, No. 1*, 45 pp., p. 20.

winners in a national search for talent were heavier and taller than the average for their ages.[6]

Intellectually, the brilliant pupil stands out clearly and has done so from early childhood. He learns with unusual rapidity and retains what he learns.

[4] Terman and Oden, *loc. cit.*, pp. 29 and 33.

[5] W. D. Altus, "The Height and Weight of Soldiers as Associated with Scores on the Army General Classification Tests," *Journal of Social Psychology*, 29:201–210, 1949.

[6] H. A. Edgerton, S. H. Britt, and R. D. Norman, "Physical Differences between Ranking and Nonranking Contestants in the First Annual Science Talent Search," *American Journal of Physical Anthropology*, 5:435–452, 1949.

Usually he concentrates without effort and spontaneously uses economical methods of study. An outstanding mental characteristic is his ability to see relationships, to generalize, to distinguish the essential from the nonessential, and to see through facts to their logical conclusions. For the brilliant pupil ideas have a real fascination. He is vitally interested in both facts and theories. He wants to learn. From his earliest years he shows a liking for playing with ideas and for rearranging them in new combinations. This sort of mental exercise develops by the years of adolescence into real originality and resourcefulness. Indeed, the essence of brilliance is probably a combination of the ability to make generalizations and this spontaneous originality in handling ideas. The merely bright child with a splendid memory and a quick reaction time has neither of these qualities in larger measure than the average person.

Table 11–3: MEDIAN SCORES ON THE CONCEPT MASTERY TEST FOR VARIOUS GROUPS

Group	Number	Median Score
1. Subjects of Gifted Study	1004	141
2. Electronic Engineers and Scientists	95	92
3. Graduate Students (A)	161	120
4. Graduate Students (B)	125	121
5. Applicants for Ford Foundation Fellowships	83	116
6. Undergraduates	309	92

SOURCE: L. H. Terman and M. H. Oden, "The Gifted Group at Mid-Life," *Genetic Studies of Genius* (Stanford, Calif.: Stanford University Press, 1959), Vol. V, p. 60.

There have been three follow-up studies of Terman's 1000 gifted children, who are by now about 50 years of age. The first, second, and third follow-ups all showed that the gifted individuals were still very superior.[7] The gifted group had originally made high scores on the Binet—from an IQ of 135 up to 190. In 1939–1940 they again scored high on another test of intelligence, and in 1950–1952 surpassed their previous score on a duplicate form of the same test. On this second form, taken when the gifted children were 40 to 45 years old, their median score was at the 96th percentile for the general population, and 90 percent of them scored above the 75th percentile. All but two out of the 961 tested scored above the median. Their continued superiority is indicated also by a comparison of their latest test scores with those of other groups, as shown in Table 11–3. This table shows the brilliant children to be as superior in adult life as they were in childhood.

[7] R. L. Thorndike, "An Evaluation of the Adult Intellectual Status of Terman's Gifted Children," *Journal of Genetic Psychology,* 72:17–27, 1948. See also: B. S. Burks, D. W. Jensen, "The Promise of Youth," *Genetic Studies of Genius* (Stanford, Calif.: Stanford University Press, 1930), Vol. III, 482 pp.; L. M. Terman and M. H. Oden, "The Gifted Child Grows Up," *Genetic Studies of Genius,* 1947, Vol. IV, 448 pp., *ibid.,* Vol. V, *loc. cit.,* pp. 60ff.

The brilliant student has almost always been an academic success; and when he is not, the reasons are personal rather than intellectual. He is commonly accelerated one or two years. His school marks are high, especially in subjects demanding judgment, generalization, and logical thought. If a gifted child does not do superior work, there is something radically wrong with the child, the family, or the school. Sometimes the fault lies with the school because the work gives too little opportunity for the exercise of independent thinking or because the teachers have failed to recognize brilliancy. Some superior students in high school are still unawakened from mere lack of adequate intellectual stimulation. Society cannot possibly afford to let highly endowed students become mediocrities. There are altogether too few superior individuals born; none of them can be wasted.

Socially, the brilliant adolescent is—like everyone else—what his environment has made him. If he has been treated as a prodigy and has been a center of interest, he may have an unpleasant personality. If he has been allowed to concentrate upon academic work to the exclusion of social activities he may be markedly introverted. If he has had excessive parental protection because of his intellectual success, he may be spoiled and babyish. Unless environmental factors have been unfavorable, however, the brilliant adolescent is usually a cooperative and responsible person.[8] He is willing to be guided in his work and personal development. He gets along with others at least as well as the average pupil, and often better. He makes friends easily. His participation in extracurricular affairs is higher than that of his classmates. He has somewhat more chance than others of being a leader among his age-mates. He has more interests, participates in more activities, and has more hobbies than the average pupil. He especially likes activities that demand thinking and collections that require classification. In general, gifted pupils are superior also in character traits; and the more superior they are, the more likely are they to score high on tests of personality.[9] They are conspicuously more courageous, sympathetic, self-confident, and honest than the average. They show an early development of self-criticism and sense of responsibility, and although they are independent they are also cooperative.

When Terman's gifted children were in elementary and high school, they showed much the same range of social adjustment as other children of their age, but their average was higher and fewer of them suffered from extreme maladjustment. That is, they were a mentally healthy group when first identified. In 1940, 80 percent of the young men and 82 percent of the young women were still in good mental health, while 16 and 14 percent, respectively, had

---

[8] B. M. Horrall, "Academic Performance and Personality Adjustment of Highly Intelligent College Students," *Genetic Psychology Monographs,* 55:3–8, 1957; V. H. Jensen, "Influence of Personality Traits on Academic Success," *Personnel Guidance Journal,* 36:497–500, 1958.

[9] G. Lightfoot, *Characteristics of Bright and Dull Children* (New York: Bureau of Publications, Teachers College, Columbia University, 1951), 136 pp.

some slight, but not serious, unsolved problems, and 4 percent from each sex were seriously maladjusted. In 1947, the parallel figures for this group were 78 and 80 percent, 17 and 15 percent, and 5 percent.[10] In 1955, the figures were 69 and 66 percent, 22 and 25 percent, and 6 percent for each sex.[11] The actual numbers of insane people among the living men and women who could be located were 11 in 1940, 18 in 1945, and 21 in 1955, or 0.8 percent, 1.3 percent, and 3 percent. Common figures given for the national averages indicate that from 8 to 10 percent of the general population will at some time be in a mental hospital. The figures for mental disease among the brilliant children in their adult years were far below the normal expectation. In other words, insanity is less common among the brilliant than among those of average ability; and the rate for the gifted is even further below the rates for dull people and defectives.

The students in high school who may be regarded as brilliant have a number of characteristics that mark them off from other students. Because of the independence of local school systems in this country, each school tends to set up its own criteria for the identification of the talented. One list of necessary traits for a single system [12] is listed below. Some of these indications have to do with school work. Since the entering high school student already has an academic history, one should use this accumulated record, with the addition of present evaluation as to other indices.

1. IQ of at least 120
2. An advancement over 9th grade standing of 2 or more years in reading
3. An advancement over 9th grade standing of 1 or more years in arithmetic
4. An outstanding achievement record in previous grades
5. High ratings by present or recent teachers in the following traits:
    a. Curiosity or habit of questioning
    b. Persistence
    c. Interest in academic material
    d. Responsibility
    e. Physical drive and vigor
    f. Ability to think creatively
    g. Ability to work independently
    h. Ability to face failures without emotional disturbance
    i. Ability to get along with others

As may be noted, the concept of talent that emerges from this list is not that of the solitary, unhealthy, "genius" but that of a well-rounded individual for whom ideas have a fascination, an individual whose emotional, physical, and social development have kept pace with the intellectual.

---

[10] Terman and Oden, "The Gifted Child Grows Up," *loc. cit.,* p. 105.
[11] Terman and Oden, "The Gifted Group at Mid-Life," *loc. cit.,* p. 37.
[12] J. West, "Teaching the Talented," *Education,* 78:434–438, 1958.

Treatment   There are basically three adjustments that can be made to the presence of superior pupils in a school population: they can be left where they are and allowed to proceed with their classmates without any change of curriculum; they can be accelerated at the rate of a half grade or a grade each year until they get into a class where the work is a challenge to their minds; or they can be "kept back" with their age-mates and given a greatly enriched curriculum, which may consist either of the same sort of thing studied by the others only more of it, or of new subject matter that they alone pursue. If either the first or the third method is selected, the brilliant child may remain in the same room as his age-mates, or he may be placed in a special room with other brilliant children. All these possible procedures have their advantages; what the proponents of each do not always realize is that all of them also have their disadvantages. The typical arguments are summarized in Table 11–4. The basic contrast is between academic adjustment and personal adjustment. The reader of articles on how brilliant children should be taught is likely to emerge with the conviction that the gifted can develop their minds only at the expense of their personalities, or vice versa, but that one or the other has to be at least partially sacrificed. The writers are not in agreement with this conclusion. There seems to be plenty of evidence that acceleration has a beneficial effect upon schoolwork and some evidence that it does not interfere with personal adjustment. Thus, in several recent studies of accelerated college students, the accelerated did better work than those of average age, more of them graduated, and more of them participated in student activities.

The question whether or not to advance pupils must be answered by studying the effects of acceleration or nonacceleration on both schoolwork and personal adjustment.[13] Already there are several studies of the effect of allowing secondary school students to condense their high school and college education into seven years instead of eight. Such a program has been followed at the University of Chicago, Ohio State University, Columbia, Harvard, Yale, and Princeton—and on a smaller scale elsewhere. In all cases, no harm seems to have been done. Results from one excellent study may be briefly summarized. The students concerned were accelerated during the war years.[14] They compare favorably with a control group made up of students of the same intellectual level. They got higher marks, they participated in more student activities, they were elected to more offices, and they scored higher on tests of intelligence. In every way they were as good as, or superior to, those who took four years instead of three. Detailed comparison of the accelerated and control groups gives the following information, which is based

---

[13] C. Elwell, "Acceleration of the Gifted," *Gifted Child Quarterly*, 2:21–23, 1958. A. B. Morgan, "Critical Factors in the Academic Acceleration of Gifted Children: A follow-up Study," *Psychological Reports*, 5:649–653, 1959.

[14] M. A. Flesher and S. L. Pressey, "War-Time Accelerates Ten Years Later," *Journal of Educational Psychology*, 46:228–238, 1955.

Table 11–4: METHODS OF DEALING WITH SUPERIOR CHILDREN

Method	Advantages	Disadvantages
1. Leaving child in regular room: a. Same curriculum as for other children.	Child remains with his age-mates. Competes in games with those smaller than himself.	Child wastes his time, becomes bored, learns to loaf, often becomes a problem from idleness, does not acquire love of learning.
b. Enriched curriculum: more of same subjects.	Same as above.	Child finds work somewhat more interesting, but much of what he learns is still too easy.
c. Enriched curriculum: new subjects.	Same as above. Subjects are more likely to be challenging and to follow child's interests.	Child is aware that he gets special treatment. Administration is difficult for teacher.
2. Puttting child in special class with other brilliant children: a. Enrichment but no acceleration.	Child learns more and competes with his peers. He also learns to work efficiently. He usually loves school. He gets better teaching.	Child is separated from his out-of-school friends. He may become conceited. His class group is probably of several chronological ages.
b. Enrichment plus acceleration.	Same as above.	Same as above but more so. Child may become quite isolated. New interests also erect a barrier. He gets little training in democracy or in adjusting to his mental inferiors.
3. Accelerating child by either special class or double promotions, into a room with pupils from 2 to 3 years older than he.	Same as for 2a and 2b. Years of productiveness increased.	Child cannot compete socially or in games with children who are more mature and bigger. He is likely to become a social outcast and to overconcentrate on books.
For high schools 4. Allowing elastic schedules that permit student to take as much as he can pass.	Pupil is interested in his work, he has enough to keep him busy, he is laying the foundation for college work.	Pupil may be overtrained or may take so much work that he has no time for social activities.

SOURCE: Based on Education Policies Commission, *Education of the Gifted Child* (Washington, D.C.: National Educational Association, 1950), 88 pp.

upon personal testimony.[15] The accelerated students reported less strain, less feeling of limitation in social activities, less interference in the production of their best work, more challenge in their courses, and a great satisfaction in the saving of time. More of them continued with education after college and more were employed; they married about a year sooner than the members of the control group and are taking an equal part in community activities as adults. A slightly smaller proportion (2 percent) were married, and 7 percent fewer had children.

Table 11–5: COMPARISON OF OCCUPATIONAL CLASSIFICATION IN 1940, 1950, AND 1955 (MEN)

Occupational Group	*Percent of Employed Men* *		
	1940 (N-724)	*1950* (N-762)	*1955* (N-757)
I. Professional	45.4	45.6	45.6
II. Managerial, official, and semiprofessional	25.7	39.4	40.7
III. Retail business, clerical, skilled crafts, and kindred	20.7	12.0	10.9
IV. Agriculture and related occupations	1.2	1.8	1.6
V. Semiskilled occupations	6.2	1.2	1.2
VI. Slightly skilled trades	0.7	—	—

* The slight variations in the number employed at each period are caused, in part, by the student status of some subjects at the earlier dates; in part, by deaths during the fifteen-year span; and, in a very few instances, by incapacitation at one time or another.

SOURCE: L. M. Terman and M. H. Oden, "The Gifted Group at Mid-Life," *Genetic Studies of Genius,* Vol. V (Stanford, Calif.: Stanford University Press, 1959), p. 81.

If any permanent damage had been done by acceleration, it ought to appear in the Terman follow-up studies. In their school days, over 4 percent of these children were accelerated from three to four and a half years; 24 percent were accelerated from two to two and a half years; 50 percent were accelerated from one to one and a half years; and 12 percent, one semester. All but 10 percent finished high school before they were 18. Ninety percent were, therefore, accelerated more or less. The boys of the group have made a more than satisfactory adult occupational record, as indicated by Table

[15] See R. Strang, "A Symposium on the Gifted Child," *Journal of Teacher Education,* 5:210–232, 1954; N. Kogan, "Studies of College Students," *Journal of Counseling Psychology,* 2:129–136, 1955; S. L. Pressey, "Age of College Graduation and Success in Adult Life," *Journal of Applied Psychology,* 30:226–233, 1946; I. A. Berg and R. P. Larson, "A Comparative Study of Students Entering College One or More Semesters before Graduation from High School," *Journal of Educational Research,* 39:33–41, 1945.

11–5, which shows the classification of their work in 1940, 1950, and 1955—from 20 to 35 years after their selection as brilliant children—at the latest date, 86 percent of the men were in the two highest classes, and less than 3 percent were below Class III. It is harder to evaluate the occupational success of the women, since half of them are housewives and mothers. The unmarried women—64 out of 629—are for the most part—92 percent—employed full time, and the others part time, aside from two or three who do not work at all. Of the 72 widows, 78 percent were working full time. Nearly half of the married women also had full-time jobs (in 1955), and 10 percent more worked part-time. Of the 253 women who were employed full-time, 165—or 66 percent—were in the professions. Both the men and the women who were selected as brilliant in their childhood have, therefore, made unusually high records in their occupational status.

Those who favor enrichment rather than acceleration offer the following kind of argument: When superior children are allowed to move rapidly through the grades they lose the normal, close, daily contact with their age-mates and enter a group of children who are so big that the young accelerates cannot play with them and so mature in their interests that the younger children cannot fit into their social groupings in or out of class. With the coming of puberty the differences between the young brilliant child and his older classmates are intensified. Even though superior children mature earlier than children of average ability, their acceleration in school may be so great as to offset their maturity. Some of them enter high school before puberty. Consequently, the discrepancy in emotional reactions and social interests is brought into high relief. They do not fit readily into extracurricular activities at the high school level. They cannot get excited about dances and parties, they have little interest in members of the opposite sex, and they are not big enough to be successful in athletic competition. Their nonacademic problems are therefore likely to be acute. It is undoubtedly true that a brilliant child can be accelerated too much, as has been repeatedly demonstrated by case histories. The above argument applies in such instances, but it does not necessarily apply to any advancement at all for any pupil.

Schoolwork for the Gifted   The greatest single need of the brilliant student in high school is a course of study that will stimulate him into putting forth his best efforts and will prepare him for subsequent academic work. The curriculum for superior students in high school should certainly lead to a real mastery of the tools of learning as well as to the establishment of efficient habits of study. The brilliant adolescent should learn one modern language, at least; he should read until he has made a start at getting acquainted with his heritage of culture; he should develop a large general vocabulary and the beginning of several technical vocabularies; he should obtain a mastery of elementary facts in biological and nonbiological science; he should reduce elementary algebra to a technique he can use; he should know the outstanding facts in the history of the world and have some grasp of social and economic developments; he should be able to express himself correctly and easily in writing. These are the tools of the brilliant mind; without them, thinking on the higher levels cannot be done. The ordinary high school course often fails to supply the superior student with those essentials which must act as a basis for his future development if he is to take the place in social evolution reserved for the talented. A fine social adjustment and agreeable personality will not atone for the lack of these elements of thought essential to the academic levels beyond high school.

It is not necessary to alter the essential nature of the curriculum, although minor adaptations to each group of gifted freshmen are desirable. There is nothing the matter with the traditional subjects, except that the students who would enjoy them are not given large enough amounts of such intellectual food to satisfy their hunger. The study of Greek grammar, for example, even in the traditional manner, can be an exciting experience for a group of linguistically talented young people who already have the necessary background and training for the work. In fact, many of them will like it better than they like a highly "modernized" curriculum because it is more exacting and demands a more satisfying use of superior talents.

A second characteristic of high school education for the brilliant pupil is that it must give him training in self-discipline and hard work. Genius may not be an infinite capacity for taking pains, but it cannot grow without an infinite capacity for concentrated effort. The really superior student learns so rapidly and forgets so little that ordinary classwork calls for barely more than a casual glancing at assignments. The superior mind derives no training and little profit of any kind from work that is too easy. Most certainly a superior mind will not be of much use to the world unless its possessor learns how to harness and drive it.

Third, the material to be learned should be presented in a stimulating manner and the student encouraged to use his initiative and originality to the greatest possible degree. Nothing is more fascinating to a person of alert mind than the process of thinking. The teacher of superior students should give them continual opportunity to demonstrate insights, to reason out problems, to make conclusions, to sense interrelationships, to handle ideas, to discuss theories, to see unity behind multiplicity. To provide for maximal stimulation, brilliant students should come into contact with the finest minds on the teaching staff. A successful teacher of brilliant students once gave one of the writers the following recipe for the proper instruction of superior students: "First, you demand the impossible, and then you keep out of the way while the youngsters deliver it." This capsule of methodology is useful for those who work with superior young minds.

Fourth, a brilliant student's studies should be arranged so that he sometimes works with groups and so that some of his work is directed toward service to the school. A superior student's first jobs are to master basic ideas, to learn how to work, and to develop his native talents, because by becoming himself he can best serve the world. That is, his immediate aim is self-development, but his ultimate aim is service. At the secondary school level, as at any other, he sometimes needs to work alone. However, there are always in progress several joint projects and some of immediate social usefulness, and in these he should do his share, like any other student. For instance, a few bright youngsters who are interested in botany can prepare a properly collected and labeled exhibit of local flora; if the project is well planned, they will learn a good many facts about botany, and they will develop social skills and ideals of service without which their talents cannot be put to the best use. Gifted adolescents need an ideal of service, and they need experience in joint undertakings, but not all their work should be "socialized." The solitary burning of the midnight oil is the natural way of genius.

Finally, the adequate handling of talented students involves not only (1) the identification of the students and (2) an enrichment of their work, but also (3) a careful counseling of them to plan their education, to develop their personalities, and to help them select their vocation, and (4) an encouragement of intellectual, emotional and social growth through generous participation in extracurricular activities. In short, it is necessary to find the talented, guide them, and provide for maximum growth along all lines.[16]

The basic instructional needs of brilliant adolescents are fairly obvious. They need to be taught in small classes of the seminar type, they should do extensive reading, they should work often on projects—with a minimum of direction—and they should be stimulated into developing their talents. No one quarrels with these basic principles. The difficulty lies in adapting them to the school situation.[17]

In three respects, then, the treatment of brilliant students should differ from that given their classmates, and in one respect it should be parallel. In the nature of the material studied, in the amount studied, and in the manner of presentation their work should be different; but in its training for social participation and social responsibility, it should be the same. If such a program were adhered to, the awakening of the superior pupil would more frequently take place in high school, instead of being delayed till the last years of college and sometimes even later. The curriculum as taught in many present-day high school classes involves a tragic waste of the best intellects in each generation of students.

[16] L. W. Gilfoy, "Educating the Most Able High School Students in Indianapolis," *Education,* 79:25–29, 1958.

[17] C. A. Bish, "Special Programs for the Academically Talented," *New York State Education,* 46:339–386, 1959. See also, J. Small, "Developing Superior Talent," *School and Society,* 86:219–222, 1958, and G. Hildreth, "School-wide Planning for the Gifted," *Educational Administration and Supervision,* 41:1–10, 1955.

Any proper teacher is vitally interested in the discovery and encouragement of talent. A few points in respect to the nature of genius might be in order. In the first place, genius is not synonymous with a high IQ. Intelligence is only one element in the composite of traits that characterize the talented. In a special class for bright children there are often one or two with very high IQs who are extremely quick learners, unusually efficient workers, industrious, and quick of perception, but they show little creativity, even when encouraged to do so. They have great intellectual ability, and they can become immensely useful adults, but they are not geniuses. Some teachers are not as efficient as they could be in recognizing unusual ability, because they are blocked by their own prejudices and misconceptions. They have not yet learned that genius occurs where one finds it, and is not the property of any social class, race, creed, system of education, or nationality. A Noguchi, a Carver, a Steinmetz, or an Edison simply happens. If a teacher wants to encourage unusual talent, she must first recognize it, and she will not do so if her own prejudices get in the way.

Characteristic Problems of Brilliant Pupils   The superior adolescent has problems of various kinds—intellectual, vocational, social, and emotional. His chief intellectual problem is to find something on which to sharpen his wits. A second problem in the same field is the delimitation of his interests. The brilliant adolescent is typically the person who sets out to master the entire universe. His intellectual interests need to be focused, not diffused. He often requires guidance into an extra-heavy load of those courses that will furnish a sound preparation for later work.

The main problems of a brilliant adolescent are undoubtedly personal. He has the same problems that any other boy or girl of the same age has, but in addition he generates some of his own. It is hard for him to learn tolerance of those who are not as quick as he is. Since he is bright, he cannot help noticing that he learns faster and does better schoolwork than other children. He therefore tends to become domineering and altogether too sure of himself; because he knows more than his age-mates, he thinks he knows it all. He is almost sure to be verbally clever, and this tendency, if unrestrained, easily makes him a "smart aleck." One of his outstanding characteristics is his ability to concentrate upon what he is doing, but this ability can also lead him astray in case he thinks too much about his own affairs and too little about the concerns of others. A superior adolescent has already developed certain abilities beyond the normal for his age, and along these lines he is especially successful. Because he is successful, he is likely, if left to himself, to concentrate more and more upon his special interests. The things he likes best to do are precisely those that will further widen the gap between him and his own age group. Genius carries within itself the seeds of its own destruction, and one job of the school is to keep this vicious circle from developing. There is usually nothing wrong with the fundamental social ability of brilliant pupils, but sometimes, through sheer neglect, they do not develop these abilities.

The relatively few brilliant students who are seriously maladjusted show their condition clearly enough. Outside class they either stay by themselves or fling out caustic remarks about the utter futility of all nonacademic pursuits, or publicly refuse to attend football games, dances, or other such activities for which social rather than intellectual maturity is necessary. They tend to play with younger children or to hang around adults. In short, according to their degree of vitality and combativeness, they show either a humiliating acceptance of their social ineptitude or else a derisive attitude toward others—an overcompensation for their maladjustment. These attitudes are not typical of genius but they do exist, and quite unnecessarily.

One investigator studied the home backgrounds of a small group of students, all with IQs of more than 120. Half the students were high achievers, while the other half were not.[18] The two subgroups were carefully paired as to intelligence and socioeconomic level. Only a few differences were found in the family backgrounds. The parents of the high achievers shared more in their children's activities, ideas, confidences, and standards; they imposed fewer restrictions and used less severe disciplinary measures. These attitudes evidently gave the adolescents enough support to encourage them in their work. It was also noted that these parents did not appear overprotective, and they did not exert pressure for high marks—two attitudes that are likely to produce underachievement in school.

The case studies below illustrate some of the problems of brilliancy and some of the possible solutions. The reader can doubtless add more from personal observation.

Leopold was the oldest son of a rather wealthy family.[19] His IQ on several tests varied from 155 to 165. As soon as he entered the first grade of school it was at once evident that the work was far too easy. Leopold had been reading since he was four years old and hardly needed the word drills of the first grade. His facility with numbers was also extraordinary, and he was entirely fascinated by music.

His parents' first adjustment to the problem of educating Leopold consisted in advancing him to the second grade at once and then sending him to school only for the morning session, during which he took part in all group activities and spent the rest of the time in helping slow readers or giving extra drill to children who did not know their number combinations. He also helped the teacher make and put up decorations. His penmanship and spelling were relatively poor, and he took a normal part in the classwork devoted to these subjects. During the after-

---

[18] W. R. Morrow and R. C. Wilson, "Family Relations of Bright High-Achieving and Under-Achieving High School Boys," *Child Development*, 32:501–510, 1961.

[19] This case should be compared with that of Oscar on pp. 263–265.

noon he practiced the piano and flute, took music lessons, studied catalogues of phonograph records, selected what he wanted, rearranged his collection, listened to his records in various sequences, and generally amused himself until his age-mates were out of school. He would have remained absorbed in his music for hours if his mother had not interrupted him every day at three thirty and sent him out to play until dinnertime. On Saturdays he was not allowed to spend any time in musical pursuits, but on Sunday he sang in the church choir and spent most of the afternoon listening to records. This general routine continued through-out elementary school. Aside from his first advancement of one year, he was never accelerated. He did a great deal of outside reading, upon which he reported to the class, he helped slow pupils, and he generally made himself useful. Leopold early acquired the attitude that because he could learn faster than others he had more time in which to be of some use in the world.

At the end of elementary school Leopold's parents felt that he was not learn-ing as much as he easily could and that he was therefore wasting time. On the other hand, they did not wish to interfere with his excellent social adjustment. During the year that Leopold was in the eighth grade they began to talk about spending some time in Europe. They brought home a number of travel books, many of which Leopold read. Gradually, they broached the idea of a year's schooling in France or Germany, where he could learn another language. Leopold himself proposed a school in Switzerland where he could learn two or three lan-guages. He and his parents therefore spent a couple of months in Switzerland where he visited several schools and enrolled in the one he liked best. His par-ents remained near him for another six weeks, by which time he was so engrossed in learning French, German, and Italian, in going to concerts, in taking piano lessons, in practicing, and in participating in all sorts of school activities that he hardly knew when they left. The other boys at the school were of many national-ities, and Leopold learned to adjust to them. He remained there for three years, during which he completed enough courses for entrance to an American college. Each summer he came home and renewed his friendships. The first summer he went off to a camp, but the last two he spent at home, playing tennis, going to parties and picnics, swimming, and dancing. He was the first boy in his group to own a radio, and as a result his home became the rendezvous for the "crowd."

It will be noticed that Leopold gained another year in academic standing during secondary school, but he hardly realized it because he was in small, un-graded classes most of the time. Even though he learned three languages to the level of fluent use, added violin playing to his other accomplishments, took sing-ing lessons, learned to ski and skate, and read three books for every one read by other pupils, he finished the work of an American twelfth-grade class and entered college before his seventeenth birthday.

At this time he was average in height and above average in weight for his college group. He played ice hockey, basketball, and soccer, he made the fresh-man swimming team, he joined the band, the choir, the orchestra, the composers' club, the Deutscher Verein, the French club, and the Christian Association (this last mainly to play the organ for the hymns). His first year he carried a normal sixteen hours of work; the next year he was permitted to take twenty, and the last two years twenty-five and twenty-six respectively. In most classes he received A's and had no mark below a B. During his junior year he was elected as one of the judges of the student court and as a senior he was president of student government and of his own fraternity. He made Phi Beta Kappa but never wore his key until he was middle-aged. He was much prouder of the letter he won in basketball.

Leopold chose to complete his education by becoming a musicologist. He also studied composition and has done quite a little composing as an avocation. He is also a volunteer member of a well-known orchestra. Since taking his Ph.D. in musicology he has fitted out a yacht with the necessary recording instruments and spends part of his time doing valuable research at the ends of the earth. He specializes in such investigations as are too expensive for the average scholar to undertake, even with a moderate backing from national research funds. Leopold's work is first class, his reputation is excellent, and he is a normal and delightful individual. There is nothing of the long-haired genius about him, and unless he is among other specialists he does not talk in an erudite manner.

During the war Leopold wanted active service, but he was assigned to Intelligence and spent most of his time listening to and translating foreign broadcasts. This man's parents were, of course, aided in their treatment of him by the fact that they were wealthy, but more important were their sanity and their understanding of his needs and problems. Leopold is now a normal, useful adult whose actions are governed by a strong sense of social responsibility.

Ruth T. is at present a successful writer of fiction. She is as well known as any woman writer in the United States. Ruth's history is of special interest, partly because it covers the years of fulfillment as well as those of promise and partly because she had the kind of difficulties that beset the brilliant child and adolescent.

Even as a baby Ruth was extraordinarily active. From her earliest days she showed a remarkable motor control and high verbal ability. She began to read before she was 4 years old; no one taught her, but she pestered her parents and older siblings until they told her what this or that word meant. In fact, she learned in spite of parental desire to have her wait until she was older. As soon as she entered the first grade Ruth began to have difficulties chiefly because the work was ridiculously easy. To keep this child under control her teachers gave her one double-promotion after another. By the time she was 8 years old Ruth had completed the first six grades of school. Her teachers wanted to slow down her rate of progress since she would otherwise be ready for high school before she was twelve. Ruth's own choice was to begin Latin. This subject was hard enough to prevent her from advancing more than one grade each year for the next three years. By then, however, she was again going too fast, so she learned first French and then German. With three languages acting as dragging anchors against too much speed she did not reach high school until she was a normal 14, but she had already mastered a sizable piece of secondary schoolwork.

Ruth entered the public high school, where she found herself a year behind most of her friends, since they were chronologically older than she and she had purposely been held back. With characteristic independence she went to the principal, arranged to take examinations in her languages, and to elect enough extra work to let her catch up with her friends. The heavy load kept her moderately busy for a year, but soon after her sophomore year began she again became bored from having nothing to do and started to get into mischief, to talk back to her teachers, to be a "smart aleck" in class, and to do all manner of bizarre things. Punishment merely brought out her aggressiveness—often giving her a chance to be verbally cleverer than her teachers—and she was soon in conflict with the school. Again her parents withdrew her from public school and sent her to a private academy, where she found what she most needed—a heavy schedule, an active social life, a great many competitive games, and an stimulating faculty. She was given extra work in practically every class and especially in those in which she showed the slightest tendency to become troublesome, since her teachers realized that this superior student simply must be kept busy or her active and independent mind would soon lead her into defiance of authority. In the course of three years Ruth took almost every class offered in the school and carried out a number of extra reading and writing projects. She was in great demand as a writer of skits and songs and even entire plays. In her senior year she voluntarily read epics in Latin, Greek, French, German, and Old English—which she had studied by herself one summer—located what she regarded as roughly parallel passages, translated them into corresponding meters in English, and wrote a commentary of some thirty typewritten pages. This labor of love kept her busy for weeks but did not prevent her from winning the school's scholarship prize or from taking first place in the Regents' examinations. In both secondary school and college Ruth was a member of many school athletic teams and belonged to a normal number of clubs. She was moderately popular and had many friends. After her first year in college she acquired a reputation of being something of a genius and was therefore permitted to show slight eccentricities.

By the end of her college career Ruth knew that she wanted to be a writer, but she also knew that she had nothing yet to say that the public might want to hear. After graduating she first got a small job on a newspaper, then a minor position with a publisher. In her free time she constantly wrote, but threw almost everything away. Then for two or three years she did library research for other writers, eventually becoming a steadily employed ghost writer because of her facility in imitating styles. At thirty she married a surgeon somewhat older than herself and had two children. She was over thirty-five when she wrote her first novel, which was immediately successful. Since that time she has kept the home fires burning, brought up her children, been active in the political life of her city, and written a great many short stories and novels.

Ruth did not have a completely easy and comfortable childhood or adolescence. She had to learn to work with others who were slower than herself and to keep out of trouble. Her quickness often betrayed her into hurting the feelings of those she loved, and her independence of mind stimulated her into one revolt after another until she was mature enough to harness it. Her love of winning drove her into a good deal of senseless competition until she got it through her head that winning was not important. In short, she had many of the typical difficulties of the superior student.

▶ The Adolescent with Inferior Mental Capacity

When the extent of individual differences was first realized it was tacitly assumed that mentally inferior individuals furnished the criminals, the paupers, the unemployed, and the unemployable. More has since been learned as to the nature of mental inferiority, and of late years much has been done in the way of adjusting dull people to their environment—and vice versa. It now appears that while delinquency and other forms of asocial behavior are more frequent in a group of dull adolescents than among average or bright youngsters, they are by no means necessary accompaniments of mental inferiority.

The individuals whose mental capacity is below average for the general population may be grouped roughly into four divisions. Lowest are the idiots, whose adult mental age does not exceed 2 years; they never go to school. Next come the imbeciles, often called "trainable" defectives,[20] with a mental age from 3 to 7 or 8 years; by the time they are adults they can complete about the first three grades of school, provided the methods of teaching are appropriate. Then come the morons, often referred to as "educable" defectives, with an adult mental age from 8 to 11 or 12; few of them can finish elementary school with understanding and mastery of the material, but some of them do get into junior high school in these days of generous promotion policies. Finally come the dull children, with adult mental ages between 11 and 13 and IQs from 70 to 85. These pupils are the intellectual deviates at the lower end of the high school distribution. In considering high school pupils, the first three groups may be eliminated from consideration, except as results from them may illustrate what can be done even more effectively with the fourth group. As to the number of retarded children, it has been estimated that in each 1000 school children there is one that will have to be trained in an insti-

---

[20] R. Gibson, "Changing Concepts of Mental Deficiency," *Mental Hygiene*, 43: 80–82, 1959.

tution and may have to remain there all his life, plus one or two that are trainable in the community and may be expected ultimately to support themselves.[21]

It is necessary also to differentiate between feeblemindedness and mental retardation, between absolute and apparent feeblemindedness, and between true defect and social or educational impairment.[22] If a child is truly feebleminded, he is also socially incompetent; by the definition of former days, he is one who "cannot handle the ordinary affairs of life with prudence." The mentally retarded child may have no higher intelligence, but he is socially competent. That is, he cannot learn what is in books, but he can learn to lay bricks, to play an oboe, to mix sodas, or to work on a farm; and because he gets along well with other people, he can probably, after being properly trained, hold a job and stay out of trouble. It is easy for an inexperienced person to mistake such conditions as deafness, withdrawal from reality, chronic illness, or emotional conflict for mental defect. Neurotic children are often so confused by their environment as to present a picture of stupidity. The "problem" child's true ability may well be concealed behind his misdeeds and his constant hostility. The pupil with undiagnosed deafness is almost sure to be considered stupid. And teachers are especially prone to mistake educational impairment for defective intelligence.

In the last few decades there has been marked interest in following up the careers of defective or dull pupils who have been trained in special classes of the public schools or in institutions for the feebleminded. In one instance, 50 men and 24 women who had been discharged from a state training school for defectives were investigated. All were working, and two-thirds of them had held the same job for at least a year.[23] To be sure, most of them were doing simple chores in either a hospital or an orphanage, where they were to some extent supervised, but they were able to maintain themselves economically, although they were undoubtedly of defective intelligence. In a second study, the careers of 15 girls and 30 boys with an average IQ of 65 were followed by means of personal interviews, which covered their work experience, their home life, and their general social conduct.[24] About half the group were at the moment of interview unemployed, but had been working and expected

---

[21] M. A. Wirtz and R. Guenther, "The Incidence of Trainable Mentally Handicapped Children," *Exceptional Child*, 23:171–172, 1957.

[22] E. A. Doll, "Mental Disease and Neurophrenia," *American Journal of Mental Deficiency*, 57:477–488, 1953; W. H. Guertin, "Differential Characteristics of the Pseudo-Feebleminded," *American Journal of Mental Deficiency*, 54:394–398, 1950; E. M. Bower and J. H. Rothstein, *Diagnostic Problems in Mental Retardation* (San Francisco: San Francisco State College, 1957), 64 pp.; R. Gibson, *loc. cit.*

[23] E. C. Howard, "Employment of Patients Discharged from the St. Louis State Training School," *American Journal of Mental Deficiency*, 60:397–402, 1955.

[24] L. Peterson and L. L. Smith, "The Post-School Adjustment of Educable Mentally Retarded Adults in Comparison of that of Adults of Normal Intelligence," *Exceptional Children*, 26:404–408, 1960.

to continue presently. The women who were working had kept the same job for an average of three years, and the men for a year and a half; their employers were almost uniform in commenting favorably upon their work. The great majority of them lived in the poorer districts of the city—85 percent— and an even larger proportion—98 percent—in substandard housing. Half of both sexes were unmarried. As a group these men and women did not utilize the city's recreational facilities, and only 9 out of the 45 even registered for voting. They had many more conflicts with the law than the average adult, but mostly for minor offenses. Although the majority of the men had been called up for military service, few were accepted, because of their obvious mental defect. The picture is not wholly rosy, but it is undoubtedly much better than it would have been, had these adults not been trained in special classes during their school years. All members of the group had been self-supporting at least part of their adult lives, and some of them regularly so.

One more report is of interest. It covers the careers of 1000 dull boys who had been for at least six months in a trade school. The highest IQ was 107; nearly 90 percent had IQs below 90, and 65 percent had quotients from 80 down to 66. Most of these boys were dull rather than defective, but the great majority of them did not have the capacity for high school work. At the time of the follow-up 23 had died, 270 were in the armed services, and 22 were unemployable. Of the remaining 685 graduates of the school, 38 percent were making at least $30 a week and 20 percent were earning as much as or more than the average industrial worker. Only 11 men (1.1 percent) were in penal institutions.[25]

From these studies it can be seen that dull adolescents, high-grade morons, and even some imbeciles can be trained so that the majority of them make good social and vocational adjustments in the community.

Characteristics of the Dull Adolescent   Defective children are, to start with, of inferior physical development. At 20 years of age an average defective is about as tall and as heavy as a schoolboy of 15; but his head is smaller, and his brain is lighter. In addition, defectives have more defects of eye, ear, nose, and teeth than normal children, and they are much more likely to have speech defects. A teacher often gets the impression that dull pupils are unusually large, but this effect is produced by their customary retardation, which places them in classes with pupils two to three years younger than themselves. If compared with their age-mates instead of their school-mates, they would appear small.

The defective shows his most severe defects, as one would expect, in the intellectual field. The dull pupil has especial difficulty with abstractions.

---

[25] W. J. MacIntosh, "Follow-up Study of 1000 Nonacademic Boys," *Journal of Exceptional Children,* 15:166–170, 1949.

He has little interest in ideas. He is typically a nonverbal, nonacademic person. He has difficulty in learning to read at all and rarely succeeds in achieving sixth-grade competency before he leaves school.[26] Quite often a dull pupil's inferiority does not become marked until the years of junior high school. He can learn the definite, factual material presented in the elementary grades, although perhaps a little more slowly than other pupils. It is not until the subject matter becomes too extensive and too theoretical for him that his defects stand out clearly.

Socially and emotionally, dull adolescents are no different from other people. They can usually make and keep friends of their own or even superior ability. They can fit into the social milieu from which they come. Indeed, these dull children often get along well in nonacademic pursuits; they are willing to be led, they are delighted with any attention shown them, and they are devoted to their friends. There is no reason to suppose that social incompetence is inevitable in dull and low-normal individuals, although many of them have developed a deep-seated hostility to the world even before they enter school because they have already experienced rejection, aversion, and discrimination.

One investigator [27] studied a group of institutionalized defective children between the ages of 7 and 14, with an average IQ of 55 and a range of IQs from 43 to 72. Their social "quotients" varied from 38 to 94, with a median of 70. They were still, as a group, less effective socially than the average, but their social competence was far ahead of their intellectual level. Such studies suggest that with training, even an adolescent with defective intelligence can acquire at least a low-normal personal adjustment.

Naturally, however, many dull adolescents develop undesirable personal traits because too much is asked of them. They become discouraged, disillusioned, unhappy, truculent, and sometimes delinquent. Because good adjustment is made out of successes, not failures, such traits appear at any level of intelligence among those who believe themselves to be chronic misfits. If dull children show unfavorable traits more frequently than do those of average ability, it is because they have more reason for despair. In school they occupy an unenviable position at the bottom of the class. They soon learn that no matter how hard they try, their efforts will rarely be successful. Chronic academic failure arouses either profound feelings of inferiority, self-distrust, and physical timidity, or a defiant attitude toward the school. Outside school, an environment of urban civilization may be too complex for them. More often than not, they are rejected by their parents, who feel as frustrated,

---

[26] R. H. Hungerford, C. J. De Prospo, and L. E. Rosenzweig, "The Non-Academic Pupil," *American Journal of Mental Deficiency*, 53:547–557, 1949.

[27] A. C. Mitchell, "A Study of Social Competence of a Group of Institutionalized Retarded Children," *American Journal of Mental Deficiency*, 60:354–364, 1955.

tense, and unhappy as the child. In addition, many parents have a sense of shame and guilt. Such attitudes are soon sensed by the child, who then finds himself unable to obtain normal emotional satisfaction and security in his home.

One of the problems of the retarded child is his rejection, more or less openly, by his parents. He usually does not receive the family support that a physically sick child is likely to be given. His reaction to rejection may take any of several forms, of which withdrawal or aggression are the commonest. Both extremes are about equally bad, and either adds greatly to the burden of maladjustment, which may become far too heavy for a person of limited intelligence. The only way to make a dent upon this problem is to work through the parents, who are frequently resistant and on the defensive. Actually, many of them feel guilty and think they are somehow to blame because their child is subnormal. They sometimes project their own feelings of guilt by punishing their retarded child severely and adding a fear of them to his already overloaded emotional life. However, if one is patient, one can often persuade the parents to rid themselves of their guilty feelings, to accept their child as he is, to substitute encouragement for blows, and to salvage what can be saved—instead of simply regarding the child as a manifestation of the "will of God," about which nothing can be done. In short, although the parents admittedly have a problem, they can learn to live with it.[28]

On the moral side, the dull pupil's inability to think in abstract terms is especially noticeable. The word "amoral" has been coined to describe the condition of a person who behaves contrary to accepted moral standards, not intentionally but because he is unable to grasp the underlying concepts. According to the Binet scale, a child must have a mental age of 12 before he develops even elementary concepts—such as an understanding of "pity," "sympathy," or other single virtues—and a considerably higher mentality seems needed for an adequate understanding of generalized principles of behavior. Since the dull adolescent often does not have this degree of mental ability, he cannot do such thinking as is involved in solving moral problems.

The dull adolescent is, then, a nonintellectual person who has difficulty with any kind of abstract thinking. His school standing is usually average or a little below average in elementary school, but becomes steadily lower thereafter. His social adjustment depends upon his particular experiences, but is more likely to be poor than not—unless he receives special training—because both in school and out his environment makes demands that cannot be met successfully by a person with his intellectual equipment.

---

[28] M. Murray, "Needs of Parents of Mentally Retarded Children," *American Journal of Mental Disease and Deficiency,* 63:1078–1088, 1959; and A. Blatt, "Group Therapy with Parents of Severely Retarded Children," *Group Psychotherapy,* 10:133–140, 1957.

Treatment   From the first days of compulsory education, schools have had
                 to deal with the problem of what to do with the back-
ward child. For many decades the routine treatment for dull boys was to beat
them; dull girls also received punishment but of a less severe nature. The
futility of this treatment eventually became evident, and teachers substituted
the retardation of slow learners, holding them back for as many years as
necessary until they met the academic requirements of each grade. As a result
of this policy, a typical third-grade class would contain not only normal 8-
year-olds but also dull and defective pupils ranging in age from 10 to 16.
The high school teacher was, however, not called upon to find a solution to
the problem: the grade school teachers had retarded the dull pupils until these
were over the compulsory age, after which they left school of their own accord.

    For the last twenty years investigators have been proving that retarda-
tion is not the answer. The proof is of two sorts. The earlier type, in point of
time, showed clearly that pupils who repeated grades knew no more at the
end of the second or third time through than at the end of the first. That is,
retardation had failed in its primary purpose—the better mastery of material
that had not been learned earlier. Naturally, there are always a few cases in
which an individual pupil does make progress, usually because he is a normal
child who was for some reason absent a great deal, or because some inhibiting
cause such as inadequate eyesight has been eliminated, or because he had
been in violent conflict with his first teacher but liked the second one, and
so on. In general, however, the causes which prevented pupils from learning
the subject matter the first time were still operative, and the second try was
just so much wasted time so far as educational achievement is concerned.
The third and fourth attempts were even less productive.

    The second objection comes from the mental hygienist and concerns the
effect of failure and retardation upon the pupil. Nonpromoted pupils have
fewer friends, and they are definitely unpopular with their classmates, who
are, of course, not their age-mates. Retarded children are rated low by their
teachers on most traits of personality. At least a fourth of them are behavior
problems. Not all retarded pupils are mental defectives, although many are.
For instance, the distribution of IQs for 89 pupils who were one year retarded,
42 who were two years retarded, and 8 who had failed of promotion three
times was found to be, in comparison with the normal distribution, as indicated in Figure 11–1. Even in the slowest group there are some children of
normal intelligence, and among those having only one retardation, over half
had IQs above 90. The net result of retardation for most children is, thus, a
failure to profit academically and a more serious personal maladjustment
than existed earlier.[29]

    During the last decade or more, these facts about the futility of non-

    [29] A. R. Mangus, "Effect of Mental and Educational Retardation on Personality
Development of Children," *American Journal of Mental Deficiency,* 55:208–212, 1950.

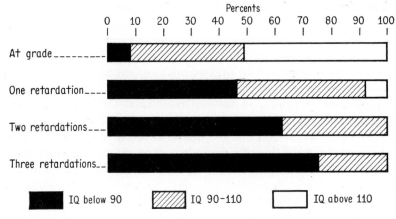

Fig. 11–1. School retardation and intelligence

Based on figures in A. A. Sandin, *Social and Emotional Adjustment of Regularly Promoted and Nonpromoted Children* (New York: Bureau of Publications, Teachers College, Columbia University, 1944), p. 21.

promotion have found their way into school policies. In many schools every pupil is promoted every year, regardless of achievement. As a result, the high school teacher now finds in her classes those dull and nonacademic students who would never have reached high school in any earlier period. The situation has precipitated a profound reorganization of work and a change in educational objectives at the high school level in order to make possible a profitable use of time for either average or dull students. Teachers may regret the changes, but American education is dedicated to teaching all the children of all the people, to developing each pupil in any way that is of profit to him, and to preparing the members of each generation for a contented and adequate adulthood.

A constructive program for dull adolescents in high school would start by abandoning the traditional curriculum, which is not only too hard but largely irrelevant. A program having several different elements should be substituted with the triple goals of giving training for eventual occupational adequacy, of developing social competence, and of bringing about a comfortable and adequate personal adjustment.[30] This new curriculum would include five types of work. First, a review of the essential skills from elementary work, with application to common adult problems. Second, there should be immediate preparation for earning one's living. For girls, this phase of training would include such courses as typing, office work, sewing, cooking, domestic service, buying, child care, and so on. For boys, the vocational training

---

[30] G. O. Johnson, "Providing the Mentally Retarded with Realistic Self-Understanding," *Vocational Guidance Quarterly*, 3:67–69, 1955.

would require courses leading to the skilled and semi-skilled trades—bricklaying, carpentry, cement work, tile setting, printing, shoe repairing, upholstering, and the like. A third element in the high school program would give direct preparation for daily life; this training would consist mainly of courses dealing with problems of mental hygiene, social adjustment, and homemaking. Fourth, there would be an adequate amount of training in good uses of leisure time: experience in games, in various avocational forms of handwork, in reading whatever books or magazines will be read at all, and so on. Finally there would be what, for lack of a better term, might be called "moral training." Perhaps the main thing to remember about planning a curriculum for dull pupils is that it should be *different,* not merely a diluted form of what already exists.

The dull adolescent needs careful vocational guidance. If left to himself he is likely either to have no objective at all or to select an inappropriate one. Many occupations are closed to him, but he may not realize it. If he makes no vocational plans he is practically certain to drift into dead-end jobs, at best, because he is unprepared for anything else and is not bright enough to pick up skills on the job. He may join the ranks of the unemployed, since his untrained abilities are of too low an order to be easily marketable, or he may enter the criminal ranks because he has little success in earning a living otherwise. If a dull adolescent fixes his imagination upon a vocation that is quite beyond his abilities, he meets with discouragement, failure, disillusionment, and frustration. Early and frequent help in selecting a vocation is therefore essential.

Educational Programs   The scope of the programs now in use varies from small but sometimes effective efforts by a few teachers and parents to systematic state-wide plans. The department of education in each state usually has a proposed plan for the teaching of dull children. In general, the pupils are to be sorted out by the end of their first school year and put into special classes, in which they will remain. They progress through school somewhat more slowly than other pupils, but since the classes are ungraded, there is no moment of nonpromotion. Often the same teacher moves through the grades with them. In the course of their elementary school days these pupils master sufficient skills in academic subjects to place them in perhaps the fourth grade, but the emphasis upon such work is never strong. Those who are bright enough to reach high school at all may have as high as sixth-grade ability in reading or arithmetic, but almost never anything higher. The main emphasis from the beginning is upon the acquisition of good personal habits and of adequate muscular skills. In their younger years these pupils have to be given tasks that will develop their powers of coordination sufficiently to permit later vocational training. As they progress through school, they spend more and more time in various forms of handwork. At the high school level they usually receive vocational training and further help in adjustment to their homes and community. Insofar as they are able to profit by the work, they learn something of elementary social science, this latter being the core of their academic work at this level. Any further work of this kind would do little to improve their academic proficiency and might do much to mar their personalities.

The methods of teaching retarded pupils are much the same at all levels. One sticks to essentials, one demonstrates each step slowly, one avoids theorizing, and one assumes that practically nothing is already known. It takes a special kind of person to teach such children: a really "dedicated" teacher. Also, one who *can* give a simple explanation in terms of everyday experience, as many otherwise capable teachers cannot do. Many a dull child can learn that a half of four ears of corn is two ears of corn, that a half of four inches is two inches, that a half of four slices of bread is two slices, but he cannot take the normal generalizing step that a half of four is two, no matter what objects are being considered. The teacher cannot, therefore, afford to get away from the specific.

Since the present generous promotion policies deliver more and more dull adolescents every year to the high school, there has been much interest in the development of suitable work for them. Some of the programs and classes are planned for retarded youth in the community, after they leave school, and some for inclusion in the high school offerings.[31] These plans, whether for use in school or community, emphasize four main topics: physical and mental health, homemaking, social relationships, and occupational training. A typical program appears in Table 11–6. The authors of such plans have evidently as their objective the education of dull students to be useful, normal individuals, and they make not the slightest effort to turn these dull pupils into scholars.

Outstanding Problems of Dull Adolescents The first problem of the dull boy or girl is the same as the first problem of anyone else—to be loved, to be accepted, to feel secure.[32] It is an especially difficult matter for him because he has probably already been rejected many times. He is probably the un-favorite child of the family and the un-favorite child in the schoolroom. In an effort to find acceptance he often plays with children who are somewhat younger, from whom he can obtain a bit of respect and with whom he can compete with some measure of success. When groups of subnormal adolescents were asked what they worried about or would like to have

---

[31] E. M. Kelly, "Are We Providing Opportunities for the Older Mentally Retarded?" *Exceptional Child,* 21:297–299, 1955; R. W. Purcell, "Community Classes for Retarded Youth," *Motive,* 1:4–13, 29–30, 1954.

[32] A. F. Alford, "Mental Health Despite Mental Retardation," *Lancet,* 268:1233–1235, 1955.

changed, 80 percent mentioned items having to do with home and family adjustment. Matters of personal or social inadequacy were given by 68 percent, fear of punishment by 26 percent, and concern about health by 39 percent.[33] These worries are not different from those of other adolescents; these dull boys and girls merely have more of them and have them in intensified form. The first thing they need from their school is acceptance.

Table 11–6: A PROPOSED PROGRAM FOR SLOW PUPILS IN HIGH SCHOOL

Period	Monday	Tuesday	Wednesday	Thursday	Friday
1	Physical and mental health; societal interrelationships: boys and girls				
2	Woodworking: boys Homemaking: girls	Physical education: boys and girls	Woodworking: boys Homemaking: girls	Physical education: boys and girls	Woodworking: boys Homemaking: girls
3 (In home-room)	Group guidance: boys and girls	Clubs	Group guidance: boys and girls	Clubs	Group guidance: boys and girls
4	Remedial reading: boys and girls	Physical education: boys and girls	Remedial reading: boys and girls	Physical education: boys and girls	Guidance in reading: boys and girls
5	Occupational guidance and training. Individual guidance and training in tool subjects				
6	Home mechanics: girls Home mechanics: boys				
7	Language development; socialization; free activities for boys and girls			Attendance at Youth Center	

SOURCE: S. A. Kirk, *et al.,* "Educating the Mentally Handicapped in the Secondary Schools," *Illinois Circular,* Series A, No. 51, Bulletin no. 12, 1951, 53 pp.

A dull adolescent also needs to be guided into work in which he is successful. A solution of this problem consists of more than just telling him that he is destined to be a digger of ditches. The main thing is for him to develop a pleasant emotional tone toward those things that he can do best. If this can be achieved, he can be more easily guided. The school can make a start on this problem by providing a large and pleasant room, in which the dull adolescent can find both security and success—no matter in what. He will undoubtedly work with his hands, but this is no disgrace. He should have a chance to try out a number of possible activities and gradually narrow his

[33] C. L. Stacey, "Worries of Subnormal Adolescent Girls," *Exceptional Children,* 21:184–186, 1955.

interest to the one or two things that most appeal to him. If a dull pupil can feel pride in work well done, no matter what it is, and can derive emotional satisfaction from doing work that he can do, half his troubles are over.

The dull adolescent's third personal problem is the acquisition of acceptable social and moral behavior. For his own safety, he must have achieved the necessary habits before he leaves school. Before him lie the usual stresses and strains incident to adult life. He will be called upon to make decisions, and he will not have the mental capacity to reason out for himself what decision he should make. Only habits so ingrained as to be an integral part of himself will bring him safety through danger. If he leaves high school as a thoroughly happy individual, well adjusted to his social group, equipped with what vocational and academic skills he will need to earn a living, enthusiastic about his work, and well grounded in fundamental habits of honesty, responsibility, and decency, the dull adolescent is hardly more likely to err than the rest of mankind.

Illustrative Case Studies   The three histories below have been selected because they show successful treatment of dull junior high and high school pupils.

Natalie was nearly 16 when she reached high school. She had twice been retarded in the lower grades and still felt unhappy over her failures to be promoted. Since she was a small girl she could pass for 14 and usually did so. Although her retardations had given her an emotional scar, they had at least deposited her on the high school's doorstep with more maturity of mind than would otherwise have been the case.

Upon entrance to high school Natalie elected a college preparatory course, although she was advised not to because her recorded IQs on three tests of intelligence were 82, 87, and 91. When the "warning" lists reached the counselor's office in November, Natalie's name appeared on four of them. The counselor sent for the girl to talk over the situation with her and found the child frightened out of what wits she possessed by her own conviction of prospective failure and by her inability to make sense out of her assignments. She was passing her social studies course, and such work as she had handed in in English was good enough but she was badly behind in it. It was arranged that for immediate relief Natalie should drop three of her five courses, should make up her back work in English, and should come to the counselor again before she made out her schedule for the next semester. Natalie received Cs in both courses. When she visited the counselor she stated that she wanted to go on with both history and English, but she did not know what else to take. Her out-of-school interests were chiefly confined to sewing, embroidery, crocheting, knitting, and simple forms of painting—coloring, putting geometrical designs onto glass, block-printing cloth, copying Christmas cards, and the like. She showed some of her work to the counselor. It was evident that Natalie was a painstaking, accurate, unimaginative, neat copyist in whatever she did. The counselor enrolled her in a class in design and one in leatherwork. At the end of the second semester Natalie received a B, two Cs, and a D. She has continued in high school, taking one or two academic and two or three vocational courses each semester. She gets mostly Cs and Ds and an occasional B, but she has never failed anything. She is proceeding so slowly that she will need five years to graduate, at which time she will be nearly 21. Her parents are glad to have her keep on in school, and Natalie herself is as young in spirit as she is in mind. In earlier generations Natalie would certainly have been eliminated. Under present conditions she will probably graduate. Her presence in school has harmed no one, and her continued success in such work as she can master at all has given her a sense of adequacy and confidence in her ability to earn her own living. She will probably be a useful citizen in some humble task, and she will be the happier for having the satisfaction of graduating from the local high school—"just like everyone else."

R. was an adolescent Negro boy who had been arrested for carrying a switch-blade knife, although there was no evidence that he had ever used it for anything more lethal than sharpening a pencil. He was at once put on probation and his case turned over to a social worker for guidance. The boy's school history was very poor, because he had never learned to read. Repeated tests produced IQs ranging from 64 to 117, depending upon how much reading was involved. When R. was 13, he had disliked school so much that he began to play truant and had been arrested and sent to a state institution. Upon release, he had become friends with some undesirable boys and was picked up in a raid, although he did not seem to have been more than a spectator.

R.'s mother was a domestic, a hard-working but not very bright woman. His father was an itinerant preacher—a rigid, cold, domineering man, who leaned heavily upon physical discipline in handling his son. Even before the boy entered school, the father began to "prepare" him for learning to read. What the preparation did was to connect in R.'s mind the act of reading and the harsh discipline of his father. In school the child made no trouble, but he could not learn to read. The others boys called him "Big Stupe" and picked on him. After his effort to escape schooling by truancy, he made no better progress in the reading classes of the state institution, although he was by that time 17 and had been given all kinds of remedial treatment. At that point the family broke up completely: a brother drowned, a sister went into a tuberculosis sanitarium, another sister moved into a brothel, and the mother returned to her own family in another state. The father hired a succession of housekeepers, but he was unable to keep R. at home and the boy was getting completely out of his control.

Since the home was so unsuitable, the social worker had R. returned to the state reformatory, where he became a model inmate. A program of therapy was at once instituted to help R. see that he was using his refusal to learn to read as a weapon against his father and that he would not learn to read until he could find some way of reducing his resentment. The father proved unexpectedly co-operative, and a sort of truce between the two was effected. R. is now learning to read with relatively little difficulty.

It is probable that this boy is not feebleminded, but his intellectual level is certainly not higher than low normal. As long as maladjustment was piled on top of his inferior ability, he seemed much duller than he was. He still needs help, but there is now hope that he will eventually be able to make an adequate and normal adjustment to society, although he is likely to need guidance and counseling from time to time throughout his life.[34]

Gordon was a neighborhood friend of one of the writers. He was a nice, extremely well-mannered boy, but quite dull. In school he was always liked, he was cooperative, he did his best—and at age 15 he had progressed to the sixth grade, where he finally gave up his efforts to graduate from elementary school. (At the present time, this boy would doubtless have been able to achieve his child-hood ambition of graduating.) His real ability and interest lay in the field of music. He sang in a choir, he played the piano by ear, and he was slowly learn-ing to play a violin. The difficulty was that he could not learn to read the score. A piano score was completely beyond him, and his slowness with the violin was not due to lack of technical skill but to slowness of comprehension. One day a music teacher in the neighborhood—a kindly woman to whom he had spontane-ously turned for guidance and advice—listened to his violin playing and told him frankly that, although his execution was excellent, he would never be able to compete with the thousands of other violin players in the world, and she advised him to study the oboe. This instrument has a relatively small range of notes, the score is simple, and the technique is not difficult to master; but, since it is not a solo instrument, the most ambitious and talented members of each generation of musicians are inclined to avoid it. But it has a great advantage in that every orchestra has to have at least one oboe player, because the whole orchestra tunes to the oboe. The competition is not severe, and the need is great. So Gordon turned to the oboe. His subsequent life has been commonplace and happy. He lives surrounded by the music he loves, he is a respected and trusted member of a good orchestra, he is happily married, he has never been out of a job—and he remains a dull man whose IQ was probably never above 75.

▶ Summary

The high school contains a small number of extreme deviates at each end of the distribution of intelligence and a considerably larger group of those who vary slightly from the average. The extremely bright

---

[34] H. M. Newburger, "A Case of Reading Disability," *National Probation and Parole Association Journal,* 1:15–19, 1955.

and the dull both have their characteristic traits and are distinguishable from the average by their physical, social, and emotional development quite as much as by their intellectual deviation. For neither extreme group is the usual high school curriculum appropriate. The brilliant need more and harder work that is presented in the most stimulating manner possible. The dull need less that is academic and more that is immediately applicable to life. Similar but less extensive changes are needed if work is to be adjusted to the needs of those who vary to a lesser degree above or below the average.

References for Further Reading
BOOKS

Other Texts

Horrocks, *Behavior and Development* (pp. 468–475).
McCandless, *Children and Adolescents* (Chap. 8).

Other Books and Monographs

Baller, *Readings in the Psychology of Human Growth and Development* (pp. 440–446).

Bower, E. M., and J. H. Rothstein, *Diagnostic Problems in Mental Retardation* (San Francisco: San Francisco State College, 1957), 64 pp. (pp. 3–14).

DeHaan, R. F., and R. T. Havighurst, *Educating Gifted Children,* 2d. ed. (Chicago: University of Chicago Press, 1961), 362 pp. (Chap. 4, 7, 8, 9, or 10).

Educational Policies Association, *Education of the Gifted Child* (Washington, D.C.: National Education Association, 1959), 88 pp. (any 20 pages).

Frampton, M. E., and E. D. Gall, *Special Education for the Exceptional Child* (Porter Sargent, 1955), Vol. III, 699 pp. (pp. 478–487).

French, J. L., ed., *Educating the Gifted; A Book of Readings* (New York: Holt, Rinehart and Winston, Inc., 1959), 555 pp. (pp. 57–81).

Hill, G. E., *et al., Identifying and Educating Our Gifted Children* (Columbus, O.: Ohio University Press, 1957), 43 pp.

Horrall, B. M., "Academic Performance and Personality Adjustment of Highly Intelligent College Students," *Genetic Psychology Monographs,* Vol. 55, pp. 3–83, 1957.

Hutt, M. L., and R. G. Gibby, *The Mentally Retarded Child* (Boston: Allyn and Bacon, Inc., 1958), 334 pp. (pp. 264–287).

Keough, J., *Practical Programs for the Gifted* (Chicago: Science Research Associates, 1960), 192 pp. (Chaps. 3 and 5).

Saenger, G., *The Adjustment of Severely Retarded Adults in the Community* (New York State Interdepartmental Health Resources Board, 1957), 176 pp. (any 10 cases).

Terman, L. M., and M. H. Oden, "The Gifted Child in Mid-Life," *Genetic Studies of Genius,* Vol. V (Stanford, Calif.: Stanford University Press, 1959), 187 pp. (Chap. 5, 6, or 11).

Wallin, J. E. W., *Education of Mentally Handicapped Children* (New York: Harper & Row, Publishers, 1955), 485 pp. (Chap. 3, 7, or 11).

A R T I C L E S

Barbe, W. B., "Characteristics of Gifted Children," *Educational Administration and Supervision,* 41:207–217, 1955.

Bobroff, A., "Economic Adjustment of 121 Adults Formerly Students in Classes for Mental Retardates," *American Journal of Mental Deficiency,* 60:525–535, 1956.

Cowan, L., and M. Golman, "The Selection of the Mentally Deficient for Vocational Training and the Effects of this Training on Vocational Success," *Journal of Counseling Psychology,* 23:78–84, 1959.

Flesher, M., and S. L. Pressey, "War-time Accelerates Ten Years Later," *Journal of Educational Psychology,* 46:228–238, 1955.

Foale, M., "The Special Difficulties of the High-Grade Mental Defective Adolescent," *American Journal of Mental Deficiency,* 60:868–877, 1956.

Gibson, R., "Changing Concepts of Mental Deficiency," *Mental Hygiene,* 43:80–86, 1959.

Jensen, V. H., "Influence of Personality Traits on Academic Success," *Personnel Guidance,* 36:497–500, 1958.

Johnson, G. O., "Providing the Mentally Retarded with Realistic Self-Understanding," *Vocational Guidance Quarterly,* 3:67–69, 1955.

Morgan, A. B., "Critical Factors in the Academic Acceleration of Gifted Children: A Follow-Up Study," *Psychological Reports,* 5:649–653, 1959.

Morrow, W. R., and R. C. Wilson, "Family Relations of Bright High-Achieving and Underachieving High School Boys," *Child Development,* 32:501–510, 1961.

Murray, M., "Needs of Parents of Mentally Retarded Children," *American Journal of Mental Deficiency,* 63:1078–1088, 1959.

Paterson, D. G., "The Conservation of Human Talent," *American Psychologist,* 12:134–144, 1957.

Peterson, L., and L. L. Smith, "The Post-School Adjustment of Educable Mentally Retarded Adults in Comparison with that of Adults of Normal Intelligence," *Exceptional Children,* 26:404–408, 1960.

Small, J. J., "Developing Superior Talent," *School and Society,* 86:219–222, 1958.

Stacey, C. L., "Worries of Subnormal Children," *Exceptional Children,* 21:184–186, 1955.

Strang, R., "Gifted Adolescents," *Exceptional Children,* 23:10–15, 1956.

Stubblebine, J. N., and R. D. Roadruck, "Mental Program for Mentally Defective Adolescents," *American Journal of Mental Deficiency,* 60:552–556, 1956.

West, J., "Teaching the Talented," *Education,* 78:434–438, 1958.

Suggested Research Problems [35]

1. Follow-up study at five-year intervals of 1000 "dull" children from time of diagnosis—probably in grades 1, 2, or 3—until each person has been followed for fifty years.

2. Intensive study of at least 500 brilliant adolescents who are underachievers in school and intend to drop out of school as soon as they can, to determine factors that contribute to the loss of superior minds and methods for preventing such losses.

---

[35] See note, p. 11.

PART THREE | # Emotional
Development

Chapter **12** | **Emotional Growth**

T<small>HERE</small> is a wealth of information on emotional development, both normal and abnormal, from infancy to old age. Obviously, not all of this material is of value to the secondary school teacher. It is the authors' intention to summarize in the present section those points which are relevant to everyday association with adolescents. With this object in view, theoretical discussion may be almost entirely omitted. The present section will contain chapters on the general nature of emotions and their normal growth; the nature of conflicts and their possible solutions; the development and measurement of personality; and the description of abnormal emotional states with which a teacher sometimes has to deal.

Human Needs Various psychologists and others have made lists of the basic human needs, basic human urges, or basic human drives. All three phrases refer to the same phenomena, and many people use them interchangeably. A useful definition of a drive is as follows: "The impulse toward self-preservation, ego maximation, and group conformance, the development of which is deeply rooted in biological constitution and markedly influenced by the social nature of man's existence." [1] It is important to remember that each individual carries within himself, from birth to death, certain inner springs of feeling that may be aroused by any of a number of stimuli, and certain desires that are of such fundamental importance to him that he constantly seeks gratification for them.

The list presented in Table 12–1 is a combination of several lists by a number of writers. One can see at once that the fundamental needs are of several sorts. Some are clearly physical, others have a less obvious physical basis, if any. Urges of this latter type are often called "drives for ego satisfaction," such as the desires for approval, for self-expression, for love, or for security. Still others arise because man is a social animal and must therefore maintain some kind of personal relationship with his neighbors. He desires friends, praise, loyalty, prestige, and leadership. Drives of this kind are especially strong in the adolescent years, during which more or less re-forma-

---

[1] *Psychiatric Dictionary*, Part II, Supplement (New York: Oxford Medical Publications, 1953), p. 626.

Table 12–1: THE BASIC HUMAN NEEDS

A. *Striving for Physical Security*
   1. Need to stay alive
   2. Need to avoid danger
   3. Need to relax
   4. Need to recover when ill or injured

B. *Striving for Sexual Satisfaction*
   5. Need for heterosexual attention and affection
   6. Need for release of tension

C. *Striving for Love and Acceptance*
   7. Need to be loved
   8. Need to feel secure
   9. Need to have friends
   10. Need to be popular
   11. Need to belong to groups
   12. Need to please others
   13. Need to be praised

D. *Striving for Status and Recognition*
   14. Need to have and keep possessions
   15. Need to be a leader
   16. Need to follow a leader
   17. Need to control others
   18. Need to protect others
   19. Need to imitate others
   20. Need to have prestige
   21. Need to be accepted
   22. Need to escape blame

E. *Striving for Intellectual Life and Creativity*
   23. Need to conform
   24. Need to express oneself
   25. Need to seek stimulation
   26. Need to think
   27. Need to acquire facts
   28. Need to relate and interpret facts
   29. Need to organize
   30. Need to find explanations

F. *Striving for Realization and Improvement of the Self*
   31. Need to grow
   32. Need to be normal
   33. Need to overcome handicaps

34. Need to work toward a goal
35. Need to be independent
36. Need to oppose others
37. Need to resent coercion
38. Need to find oneself

SOURCE: Modified and rearranged: A. H. Leighton, "Psychiatric Disorder and Social Environment," *Psychiatry,* 18:267–283, 1955; L. Raths and L. Metcalf, "An Instrument for Identifying Some Needs of Children," *Educational Research Bulletin,* 24:169–185, 1945; R. N. Sanford, *et al., Physique, Personality and Scholarship* (National Research Council, 1943); H. Schacter, *How Personalities Grow* (Bloomington, Ill.: McKnight and McKnight Publishing Company, 1949), Chap. 2; C. M. Lucas and J. E. Harrocks, "An Experimental Approach to the Analysis of Adolescent Needs," *Child Development,* 31:479–487, 1960; C. Buhler, *Values in Psychotherapy* (New York: Free Press, 1962), 246 pp., p. 110. The exact arrangement is the writers' own.

tion of the ego generally takes place, as the boy or girl seeks an acceptable place among his or her peers. Man also has intellectual needs. He wants to know, to understand, to organize, and to interpret. Above all, he likes to think, even though the subject of his thoughts may not always be socially approved.

Even a casual inspection of the list in Table 12–1 should convince a reader that different people, while sharing to some extent in all these needs, differ enormously among themselves as to the relative strength of the various drives. To one person the mere need to go on living is so strong, and the social drives so weak, that he arranges his life to satisfy this one need and eventually becomes a recluse and a hypochondriac. In another the need to be admired is the most powerful of the lot, while a third is ruled by his need for self-expression. The miser and the millionaire have a strong need to get and keep material possessions; the nun has a profound need to believe in some power outside herself, to follow where others lead, and to protect those weaker than herself; the demagogue's deepest desire is to control others, to lead them, to be worshipped by them; and so on for everyone in the world. Some needs tend to go together harmoniously, but a given person may show a most inharmonious combination of simultaneous desires. Thus, a desire for a hero's prestige may exist beside an intense desire to avoid danger. Most of one's reactions between being born and dying are made because they contribute directly or indirectly to the satisfaction of some need or to a restoration of equilibrium after a need has had no adequate outlet for some time, or a drive has long been frustrated.

Although any drive may operate at any age, under circumstances that precipitate it, the needs are not normally of equal importance at all ages. Thus, the need for care and protection is intense in the earliest years and again at the end of life, but—barring emergencies and profound shocks—it is in abeyance during the years of adolescence and adulthood. The desire to learn about things is strong in the early years, but often decreases in proportion as more and more is learned, although the desire to understand phenomena, which starts rather low, increases with age. Perhaps nothing so separates the true scholar from the average man as the continuation throughout the scholar's life of an intense "desire to know." The need to avoid blame increases, probably because children soon learn of the punishment that may be meted out to those who admit their faults. The desire to work toward a goal is almost nonexistent in early childhood, but acquires increasing force with the passage of time. The need to attack others is at first rather high—as any nursery school teacher knows—but children soon learn to substitute other forms of expression mostly verbal, as they become more and more sensitive to social pressures.

As these drives develop, they produce more or less tension, which mounts until it becomes so uncomfortable that it has to be discharged in some kind of reaction. Thus when a child who is accustomed to being the focus of parental affection sees his parents pay attention to his newly born brother or sister, he begins to feel uncomfortable because his own ego drives are frustrated, and he pushes himself forward in some way in an effort to recapture his former position. If his behavior brings about the desired results, the tension disappears. Similarly, a young man who has fallen in love generates a good deal of inner tension, which finds normal expression if the object of his affection falls in love with him.

However, life is not so arranged that drives can always be satisfied, either within a short time, or, in some cases, at all. Therefore the tension, instead of being discharged, becomes greater. As long as it continues, the individual is in an emotional state. His ego desires a satisfaction that his environment prevents him from obtaining. Eventually the urge will find some form of expression that satisfies him more or less and gives relief from strain. For instance, a high school boy who has the normal desire for socal recognition from his age-mates may find his urge blocked by the poverty and low social standing of his parents, by the inferior school records of older siblings, and by his own small, undernourished body. As day after day goes by without satisfaction of his drive for recognition, his frustration increases. He may get relief by becoming a member of a delinquent group, in which his misdeeds bring him satisfaction for the fundamental urge that is in itself perfectly normal.

The whole matter of conflict and the possible solutions and escapes from the resulting discomfort will be discussed more fully in a later chapter and will not, therefore, receive further attention here.

Nature of an Emotional Experience An emotion may be defined for the specialist in many technical words, but for the layman the familiar, simple definition of an emotion as a "stirred-up state of the entire organism" is probably more understandable. Or, if further definitions make the matter any clearer, an emotion may be called "a response of the entire human being to a stimulus" or an "integrated reaction of the total organism." It should be remembered that an emotion, however defined, is not the same thing as a basic drive or a basic need; it is the reaction that accompanies either the satisfaction or the frustration of a basic need. Thus, an individual has a need to be accepted by his age-mates, to be loved by his intimates, or to express himself in some way. If these drives are fulfilled, he is happy, joyful, contented, or in love. If the drives are frustrated, he is angry, frightened, worried, jealous, anxious, or full of sorrow. The emotions are thus related to the basic drives but are not identical with them.

All emotions involve some temporary physiological adjustment in the individual, and the curious thing about this physical reaction is that it is nearly the same for all emotions, although some small physiological indications have been found between the internal patterns of response for fear and anger.[2] The main differences, however, are in intensity. That is, one can be annoyed, irritated, angered, or infuriated; or one can be apprehensive, worried, frightened, or terrified. The changes become more profound, more extensive, and more exhausting with each increase in intensity, but they are basically the same for the same level of disturbance for all emotions. The following description will therefore serve for all.

The entire body participates in the reactions that are components of an emotional experience. These physical changes are produced through the action of the autonomic nervous system. This is *not* the central nervous system. The two systems exist alongside each other, with little interrelation between them. The nerves of the central nervous system run from the sense organs—eyes, ears, nose, tongue, and skin—to the spinal cord, cerebellum, or brain, whence other nerves run to the skeletal muscles. This system is under voluntary control. It is the system by means of which, for instance, one eats a bowl of cereal, or hits a tennis ball, or pounds a nail, or puts on lipstick. The nerves of the autonomic system run mostly to and from the internal organs and are not under voluntary control. Indeed, so long as this system functions normally, the individual does not even know he has it inside himself. It is the autonomic system that keeps the heart going, the lungs breathing, the stomach and intestines digesting, the kidneys excreting, and the glands of the body manufacturing and delivering their chemicals. Its main distributions are to the following organs, taking them in order from the head downward: the eyes (not to open or close them, but to dilate the pupil), the tear glands, the mucous membrane of the nose and mouth, the salivary glands in the mouth, the parotid glands, the larynx, the heart, the lungs, the stomach, the liver, the pancreas, the intestines, the kidneys, the adrenal glands, the bladder, the

---

[2] A. F. Az, "The Physiological Differentiation between Fear and Anger in Humans," *Psychosomatic Medicine,* 15:433–442, 1953.

colon, and the genitals; there are connections also with the main blood vessels and with the sweat glands in the skin.

A diagram of these connections appears in Figure 12–1. As indicated, the system has three main divisions, the cranial (shown in the figure by the nerves at the left and top), the sympathetic (shown at the right), and the sacral (shown at the left and bottom). The first and the last work together in direct opposition to the sympathetic branch and are therefore usually called, collectively, the parasympathetic branch. Nerves from both sympathetic and parasympathetic branches run to all the vital organs enumerated above. The function of the sympathetic branch of the autonomic system is to inhibit digestion, to constrict the blood vessels, to dilate the pupil of the eye and the bronchioles of the lungs, to make the hair stand erect, to release blood sugar from the liver, to stimulate the secretion of sweat, to release adrenalin from the adrenal glands, to increase the blood pressure and pulse, and to check the flow of saliva. The action of the parasympathetic branch is exactly the opposite. These nerves make the heart beat more slowly, constrict the pupil of the eye, increase salivation, increase stomach and intestinal action, dilate the blood vessels, reduce the blood pressure, and stop the secretions from the adrenal and sweat glands. During normal periods the two divisions are evenly balanced, but when an emotion develops, the sympathetic branch is in the ascendancy; then, as the emotion subsides, the parasympathetic branch becomes stronger until the normal balance is restored.

This arrangement of nerves that operate during an emotion explains some of the characteristics of an emotional experience. For example, when one is insulted, he cannot help *feeling* angry, because the emotion is served by nerves not under his control, although he can refrain from answering or from fighting, because the nerves that run to his speech mechanism and the muscles in his arms and legs are under his control. It is a fertile source of maladjustment that people can thus refuse an emotion its normal outlet; the feeling is so powerful that, if one outlet is blocked, it will find another and perhaps even less desirable one. A strong emotion often precipitates incidental physical symptoms, such as the nausea and diarrhea that many athletes experience for hours before a competition, or the dead faint of a person who is terribly frightened, or the breathlessness, blushing, and perspiration of a young man trying to propose. After an emotion has passed, the individual is suddenly exhausted because of the upheaval within his fundamental processes and is likely to drop off to sleep wherever he is, as is dramatically shown in the pictures of soldiers released from duty who go instantly to sleep before they have time enough to move themselves out of danger.

As soon as one begins to experience an emotion, the physiological changes start. An almost immediate effect is the secretion of adrenalin by the adrenal glands. The adrenalin is discharged by the glands into the blood stream, by which it is carried over the entire body within a few seconds. Its

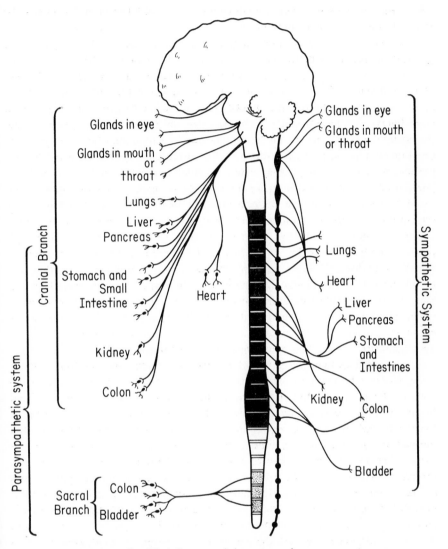

Fig. 12–1. Simplified diagram of the autonomic nervous system

Based on C. H. Best and N. B. Taylor, *The Physiological Basis of Medical Practice* (Baltimore: The Williams and Wilkins Company, 1961), 1554 pp., p. 1295.

action upon different bodily structures is varied. It acts upon the stomach to retard the normal digestive processes. In extreme cases the peristalsis of the stomach and intestines completely ceases. During an emotion only about 15 percent of the normal amount of gastric juice is secreted by the stomach. The salivary glands cease functioning almost entirely. The emotion acts upon the liver, causing this organ to discharge into the blood stream the sugar that is normally stored in it.[3] This sugar is carried by the blood stream to the muscles. It is the "food" which the muscles require for their contractions. The adrenalin further acts upon the small muscles controlling the amount of air that can be taken into the lungs. These muscles become relaxed so that the person who is angry breathes in more oxygen and discharges more carbon dioxide than he normally does. The breathing of the person becomes more rapid and somewhat irregular. The adrenalin also acts upon the blood vessels which supply the abdominal organs, driving the blood from the abdomen into the muscles, nervous system, and lungs. Another effect is a change in the composition of the blood: those chemicals that make it coagulate more quickly increase. The adrenalin directly affects the heart muscles, and causes the heart to beat more rapidly and with more power. As a result of this change, the blood pressure rises for the duration of the emotion. It is the driving of the blood from the viscera into the muscles and to the surface of the body generally that produces the redness of the angry person's face and the general feeling of warmth that he experiences. The adrenalin also causes the sweat glands in the skin to function, thus producing dampness in the palms of the hands and on the face. Tears, sometimes quite inappropriate to the emotion, often flow because of the stimulation of the lachrymal glands. There may be loss of bladder or colon control, and, in the case of men and boys, sudden erections that have no sensible relation to the emotion being felt. The muscles which control the skeleton, because they are supplied with an extra allowance of blood sugar, often contract until they quiver with sheer tenseness. During an emotion the individual has actually a greater strength and a greater endurance than during his usual calm state, but he does not have the control over his muscles that he has when he is not emotionally disturbed. Thus is an actual fight between two people of normally equal muscular development, one of whom is extremely angry and the other of whom is quite calm, the angry fighter has the greater strength and is likely to damage the other seriously if he ever succeeds in landing a blow, but his muscular control is often so poor that he cannot hit his opponent at all, while the unemotional opponent continues to land much lighter blows whenever he wishes to do so.

It should be clear that the internal changes are preparation for some kind of violent action, such as running away or fighting. If the excess adrenalin and sugar are not used, if the generated readiness to act is not discharged in some way, pathological developments may follow. It is not necessary that the "natural" form of discharge be used. Any activity that uses up the excess glucose in the muscles is as good as any other. The discharge may also take the form of words or even thoughts. If the individual's emotional steam is

---

[3] See S. Cobb, *Emotions and Clinical Medicine* (New York: W. W. Norton & Company, 1950), Chap. 5.

not released, however, it will perpetuate the seething inside him, will precipitate conflicts, and will eventually discharge itself through abnormal channels.

▶ The Life History of Three Major Emotions

Emotions appear early in life. From birth, babies show a general state of excitement when they are stimulated. Their main response is an undifferentiated howling and thrashing about. Presently, however, the onlooker can tell whether the baby finds a given stimulation pleasant or unpleasant. Further differentiation soon occurs, and the emotions of fear, rage, excitement, and joy become recognizable. The child of two has added jealousy, love, and hate to his repertoire. By the time he enters school, he has a full emotional equipment. The differentiation of the generalized excitement seen in infancy into a number of emotional states thus takes place long before adolescence.

At different ages, individuals are susceptible to different stimuli. At any one age they fail to notice some to which they have previously reacted, and they become aware of others to which they have heretofore been indifferent. It may, for instance, suddenly strike a third-grade child that schoolwork is competitive, and this new idea may generate in him a feeling of shame because he has thus far puttered happily about at the bottom of the class. Other stimuli, once powerful, may lose their meaning or may arouse a different emotion. Thus the 10-year-old boy thinks it is funny to pull out someone's chair just as that person is about to sit down in it, the adolescent scorns such behavior as a "kid trick," and the adult is fearful of possible injuries to the coccyx. The expression of the emotion also varies with age, the change being mostly away from direct, obvious, violent behavior and toward subtlety. The jealous 4-year-old openly pushes his rival out of the way and seizes the center of the stage, but the jealous woman of forty leaves the spotlight on her rival while she indirectly and with seeming innocence makes her appear ridiculous.

The type of presentation in the following section brings into relief the effect of age and experience upon emotional behavior. The general background against which emotions develop has already been discussed, but the particular situations that thwart the drives and thus produce frustration differ from one age level to another. In most recent work on the emotions the tendency has been toward synthesis rather than toward analysis. However, it seems to the writers that the study of single emotions has certain values in helping a student to see the underlying mechanisms and to understand why the frustration of a basic drive should be disrupting. Naturally, one should not become so intent upon specific stimuli and reactions that he loses sight of the total individual or the total environment. For purposes of clarity and emphasis, therefore, the analytical approach has been preserved, with the expectation that the insertion of many case studies and the later discussions of frustrations, conflicts, and problems will afford the material necessary for an adequate synthesis and application of the treatment to life situations.

To the person who becomes angry or frightened, the whole experience comes in one piece, but for purposes of clarity and understanding, one can divide such an episode into three parts: the exciting stimulus that precipitated the anger or fear; the period of emotional disturbance; and the response made, by means of which the pressure built up during the emotion is discharged. The second of these somewhat artificial divisions consists of the internal adjustments described above, which vary mainly with the body's ability to react. A teacher needs to understand the nature of these internal changes, but there is nothing that she or anyone else can do about them. There are, however, great changes from birth to death in the stimuli that precipitate emotional episodes and in the reactions that are made. A biography of an emotion must, therefore, concern itself primarily with the causes and effects of emotional upheaval.

A "life history" of each possible emotion would result in far too long a discussion, even if there were adequate data for such a treatment. Moreover, there is no accepted list of emotions. Some psychologists list three, four, or five emotions; others admit about a dozen, and there are a few who enumerate even more. The exact number of emotions need not be determined so far as the forthcoming treatment is concerned. The writers would be inclined to group the emotions into three types, depending upon the kind of behavior they lead to, and to list the emotions as follows: anger, jealousy, hatred, and hostility as emotional states of an aggressive character; fear, worry, dread, sorrow, embarrassment, regret, and disgust as inhibitory states; and love, affection, happiness, excitement, and pleasure as joyous ones. A single emotion from each group has been selected for discussion in some detail. The treatment given could, however, be extended to any other emotion concerning which sufficient evidence was available. The main thing for teachers to realize is that, although internal changes during an emotion vary only in intensity, the stimuli for and reactions to emotional stimulation have typical stages of development that can be traced just as surely as the stages of intellectual growth. Illustrative material from three emotions should make this point sufficiently clear.

Emotional States Leading to Aggressive Behavior   In this group of emotions, anger is the one selected for discussion, partly because it is more frequently and easily aroused than the others and partly because there is a considerable body of literature about it. The situations that produce anger will first be considered.

The baby becomes angry if he is not fed when hungry, if his soiled clothes are not replaced by clean, dry ones, or if his freedom of movement is restricted. Small children become angry if someone takes a toy away from them. And they become annoyed if some occupation is interrupted, especially if they must now do something that holds no interest for them. There are also many outbursts over the establishment of toilet routines.

For adolescents the causes of anger are quite different. They have been studied by means of "anger diaries"—records kept over a period of time concerning the causes of anger, the reactions made, and sometimes the duration of the emotion.

A few typical stimuli that aroused anger in adolescents are listed, in their own words, below:

1. My mother makes me get home before midnight.
2. My boy friend ran his fingers through my hair and made me look a mess.
3. My father's fraternity turned me down after giving me a big rush.
4. My girl said she'd go to the movies with me, but when I called for her she'd already gone with someone else.
5. My math teacher calls on me by saying, "Now let's hear from our football hero." She knows I can't answer her silly questions.
6. I postponed a date to oblige a girl friend who had two men coming on the same evening, and she hung onto the really nice guy all the time and left me with a poor stick.
7. I paid $70 for my dress and the shop assured me it was an exclusive model, but when I got to the dance, there was another girl with a dress just like mine.
8. I tripped over the last hurdle and everyone in the stands just laughed.
9. My French teacher makes me try to pronounce words with nasals in them and when I do the kids laugh, and when I won't he bawls me out.
10. My brother took the new sweater I was going to wear to the school picnic, and I had to go in my old one.

One investigator asked a group of college women to keep both anger and fear diaries for a week, writing down emotional episodes as soon as possible after their occurrence. The students also indicated in each instance whether the precipitating situations were actually present or were something recalled from the past or anticipated for the future. The average number of anger reactions a week per student was 16, with a range from a completely pacific 0 to a bellicose 42. The fears—to be discussed further in the next section—averaged 12, with a range from 2 to 36. The number of episodes of each type correlated with each other with a coefficient of 0.72, suggesting that there is an underlying degree of emotionality that affects all reactions; that is, those who were most often angry or afraid were also most frequently excited, happy, in love, jealous, or melancholy, while those who lacked fear or anger also lacked strong expressions of other emotions. The situations precipitating fear or anger differed in one important respect from each other: feared situations were mostly in the future, a few in the present, and almost none in the past—70, 27, and 3 percent, respectively. Almost all situations precipitating anger were in the present—94 percent of them—with 3 percent in the past and 3 percent in anticipated situations.

The thwarting of plans and a threatened or actual loss of status contributed nearly three fourths of the situations that led to anger. When plans were frustrated, the agent was a person in 46 percent of the episodes; an institutional factor—such as rules and regulations, red tape, or "schedules" in 23 percent; personal inadequacy in 16 percent; and the perversity of things, accident, or chance in 15 percent.[4]

Causes of adult anger have hardly been investigated, but what evidence there is suggests some continuance of childish irritation at objects that refuse to function and adolescent sensitivity to social slights, real or imagined. A new type of stimulus is, however, fairly frequent. Adults become angry over such matters as the failure of an able man to be promoted or the interference of government agencies in their business enterprises.

The three levels of development may be summarized as follows: In early childhood, anger comes most frequently from conflicts over playthings or daily routine. In adolescence, the causes of anger are primarily social. The individual gets into a situation in which he feels himself embarrassed, ridiculous, offended, or annoyed. The adult also becomes angry if his work or leisure is too much interfered with, and he is inclined to feel concerned over abstract justice or social conditions. It is small wonder that the child, the adolescent, and the adult sometimes fail to understand one another's reaction to the same situation.

The reactions made when one is angry also show a development. The small baby becomes quite rigid; he screams and beats the air with his arms and legs. This is his only reaction, probably because his mental and muscular development is so slight that other reactions are not possible. The preschool child also cries, screams, and becomes stiff; in addition, he kicks, strikes, bites, scratches, stamps his feet, jumps up and down or throws himself on the floor. Elementary school children, especially boys, made a direct, physical attack upon whoever has angered them. By adolescence the responses of either leaving the scene or substituting a verbal for a physical attack have become predominant.[5] There is little actual violence, although there is frequent reference to the deliberate suppression of such behavior. Instead, the boy or girl tends to substitute the reactions of pacing the room, being generally restless, going out for a walk, or indulging in some violent exercise as a means of working off emotion. Some slight degree of subtlety is shown by those who refuse to speak to the people who have made them angry or hurt their feelings. Finally, there is a persistence of infantile behavior in the form

---

[4] A. Anastasi, N. Cohen, and D. Spatz, "A Study of Fear and Anger in College Students through the Controlled Diary Method," *Journal of Genetic Psychology,* 73, 243–249, 1948.

[5] A. Gesell, F. L. Ilg, and L. B. Ames, *Youth: The Years from Ten to Sixteen* (New York: Harper & Row, Publishers, Inc., 1956), 542 pp., pp. 338–341.

of stamping the feet, or kicking things, on the part of the boys, and of crying, on the part of the girls. Among adults, the verbal responses have almost completely taken the place of all other forms, although women still cry and men still kick things. It should also be noted that the younger the individual, the more immediate is the release of emotional tension. Direct release is perhaps best physiologically for the person who is under tension, indirect release the next best, and suppression—with its storing up of tensions—quite undesirable at any age.

The duration of the anger also varies somewhat with the age of the individual. Among preschool children, the outbursts last less than five minutes. For college students the average period is fifteen minutes, and the total range from one minute to forty-eight hours. The number of anger experiences a week does not seem to vary greatly with age; the main differences are to be found in the situations causing anger, in the responses made, and in the duration of the responses.

Emotions Leading to Inhibitory or Defensive Behavior The second of the three most powerful emotions is fear, which seems to be present from birth. The typical reactions are paling, trembling, perspiring, becoming rigid, panting, and—subsequently or coincidentally—running away. These reactions may become attached to practically any stimulus and are not necessarily attached to more than a few. Most of the things a human being fears he has learned to be afraid of.

In recent decades various efforts have been made, through the use of questionnaires and tests, to obtain information as to the fears and other emotional attitudes of normal children and adolescents. Below is a list of the worries mentioned most frequently by fifth- and sixth-grade children, whose ages would be roughly from 10 to 13.[6] They were afraid of or worried about such things as these:

Failing a test in school	Being hurt by knives, guns, poison, fire, floods
Father or mother being sick	
Father or mother working too hard	Being in an accident, holdup, burglary or fight
Getting a bad report card	
Father losing his job	Being sick, suffering, choking, dying
Being late to school	Losing money while doing an errand
Being left in the dark	Losing one's fountain pen
Being hurt by animals	Losing one's friends

Most high school pupils continue to show a number of typical childish fears, but new sources of worry appear because they are subject to many new pressures and drives. Adolescents concentrate upon such anxieties as the following: fear of school examinations, automobile accidents, and dis-

---

[6] See, for example, J. B. Winker, "Age Trends and Sex Differences in the Wishes, Identifications, Activities, and Fears of Children," *Child Development,* 20:191–200, 1949.

ease; worry over inadequate funds, lack of ability, getting a job, loss of work by parents, or appearance of the home; fear of being sinful, of being led astray by bad companions; worry over being unpopular or unsuccessful, over hurting other people's feelings, over being shy, self-conscious, dull, or lonely, over being tempted to cheat, over losing one's religious beliefs, over making a bad impression upon others, over being unable to concentrate; fear of growing up, of blushing, of being socially incompetent, of having sexual experiences, of masturbating, of daydreaming, of having crushes, of disappointing one's parents; concern over having pretty clothes and lots of friends; anxiety about being different from others, being teased or scolded, being treated unfairly, being too closely watched, being laughed at, or being a failure. These myriad anxieties may be grouped under six main heads: worries related to the problem of emancipation from home, those related to maintenance of social status, those concerned with educational adjustment, those concerned with vocational selection, those related to problems of sex, and those that offer a threat to existence.[7]

In the "fear diaries" kept by college students, the situation that precipitated the reaction in 40 percent of the cases was the likelihood of failure (or of a low mark) in schoolwork, the prospect of a loss of status in 31 percent, the possibility of illness or accident in 17 percent, and the probability of conflict with the family in 6 percent. Some worry about schoolwork seems to be inevitable. It turns up in one study after another as a chronic condition. For instance, among 1100 pupils who varied in age from 12 to 18, worry about school was very common,[8] especially among boys—perhaps because they usually do poorer school work and therefore have more to worry about. Some typical results appear in Figure 12–2. At most age levels boys from homes in the upper socioeconomic groups worried more about school than those from lower-class families, probably because the pressure was greater. For the girls the reverse was true; girls from lower-class homes may not be thirsty for knowledge, but the school offers them their best means of escape from poverty, either through adequate vocational training or marriage with boys from higher-class homes whom they met in school. These girls may worry more because they have more at stake.

In the adult years, new worries arise. Concern about money and job security lead all the others; then come health and appearance. Somewhat below these, but still frequent, come failure in business, political convictions, religious convictions, family and marital adjustments, lack of confidence, sur-

---

[7] See, for example, H. Angelino and C. L. Shedd, "Shifts in the Content of Fears and Worries Relative to Chronological Age," *Proceedings of the Oklahoma Academy of Sciences,* 34:180–186, 1953; R. L. Brown, "These High School Fears and Satisfactions," *Understanding the Child,* 23:74–76, 1954; Gesell, Ilg, and Ames, *op. cit.,* pp. 341–343.

[8] H. Angelino, *et al.,* "Trends in the Fears and Worries of School Children as Related to Socio-Economic Status and Age," *Journal of Genetic Psychology,* 89:263–270, 1956. See also, R. L. Brown, "These High School Fears and Satisfactions," *Understanding the Child,* 23:71–76, 1954; and Gesell, Ilg, and Ames, *loc. cit.,* pp. 341–343.

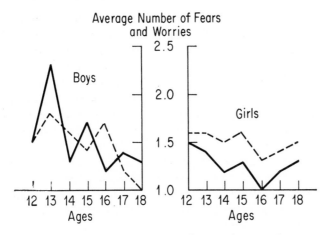

Average Number of Fears
and Worries

—High socioeconomic status   —Low socioeconomic status

Fig. 12–2. Worries and fears of school children as related to age and status

H. Angelino, J. Dollins, and E. V. Mech, "Trends in the Fears and Worries of School Children as Related to Socioeconomic Status and Age," *Journal of Genetic Psychology*, 89:263–271, 1956. Used by permission of the publisher.

render of cherished ambitions, and sexual morality.[9] These are fears of a different type from those in childhood, but some of them are quite like worries that appear during adolescence.

Fears are created by the physical and social world as it exists. Certain typical adult worries could be greatly reduced if not eliminated by a different organization of society that would provide for more even distribution of wealth, a lessening of class consciousness, an elimination of prejudice, a better guarantee of steady work, and a greater security against a destitute old age. The universality of such fears is shown by the readiness with which people accept any government that they hope will relieve them of these anxieties. Man is well on his way to conquering the physical forces in the world, but it remains to be seen whether or not he can control those that are social or emotional.

The reactions to fear are not varied. The main behavior is a rigidity of the entire body and an intense pallor. The running-away behavior is usually secondary to the immobility. The reactions shown by persons of all ages are in large measure variations, more or less subtle, upon these two central patterns. The baby grows rigid and pale; he is helpless to do anything else. Small children often run away, preferably toward a protector. As children grow older and their intellectual abilities mature, they discover that the mores do not approve of cowardice, so they learn to do their running away before

[9] R. A. Dykman, E. K. Heimann, and W. A. Kerr, "Lifetime Worry Patterns of Three Diverse Adult Culture Groups," *Journal of Social Psychology*, 35:91–100, 1952.

the stimulus appears; that is, they learn to avoid situations that may cause anxiety. Thus the pupil who is afraid to address the class in his oral English work develops a spurious toothache on the day he expects his turn to come. He is running away just as clearly as if he had fled from the classroom, only in a less conspicuous manner. The adult who is afraid has usually better control than the child or adolescent, but a protracted strain will break him down to the childish levels of rigidity, crying, and running away. Thus many a man collapses from anxiety while his young wife is enduring a twenty-four-hour labor at the birth of their first child. Fear reactions are rarely converted into secondary forms, as anger responses are. They are controlled better as a person grows older, and they are avoided whenever possible; but they are always lurking behind the individual's defenses, presumably because of their close relation to the most fundamental of all needs—the need to stay alive.

Recent wars have demonstrated the universality of fear. Even young, healthy, vigorous men who in civilian life would have been ashamed to admit their fright spoke simply and honestly to one another of their panic. Modern warfare is so frightful that the human spirit cannot find in it enough uplift to cover the agonizing fear that gripped every man sometimes and some men frequently. In order to keep normal men as free as possible from panic, the Army during World War II emphasized the treatment of fear as one topic in its indoctrination. The principles set forth boiled down to a number of simple rules that are as useful in peace as in war:

1. Learn to recognize the early symptoms of fear, so that you know when you are becoming frightened.

2. Don't be ashamed of your fear. Better men than you have known it.

3. Think objectively about the situations in which you may become frightened and plan in advance what you can do. If you have work to do, keep your mind on it; if the time must be spent in waiting, decide what you will do or think about to fill the time.

4. Talk to your friends sometimes about your anxieties. Don't try to keep your fears a secret.

5. Remember always that other men are depending on you. If you blow up, they're sunk.

6. Have all the fun you can, as long as you can, up to the last split second. Nothing keeps panic away from you and your buddies as successfully as a sense of humor.

7. Although you admit your fear to your intimates, try not to show it publicly, because it is so contagious.[10]

These rules may well be applied to situations in ordinary civilian life.

Fears have a tendency to entrench themselves firmly and to spread over an individual's entire life, distorting and circumscribing it, as in the story below:

[10] Condensed and adapted from J. Dollard, *Victory over Fear* (New Haven, Conn.: Yale University Press, 1944), 64 pp.

Dorcus was a girl of 18 who had been sick during much of her childhood. She had not been able to go to school although she sometimes played quiet games with other children after school hours or on rainy Saturdays. In the course of her first 15 years of life Dorcus had to have several operations, for all of which she was given ether. With each successive operation it became harder and harder for her to take the anesthetic, and on the last occasion she had to be held down on the table by main force. As long as Dorcus continued to live quietly at home there seemed to be no aftereffects of the trauma she suffered at each operation. Soon after her entrance to high school, however, she began to show some odd reactions. She would not take the subway from her home to the school—the quickest means of transportation; she would not ride in the school elevators; she would not use the locker assigned to her; and she fought frantically against any hand put upon her either during her physical examination or in games. Her fear of being forced into a situation in which she might be hurt was so intense that she shook off, in obvious terror, even such slight contacts as a guiding touch on her arm, and her claustrophobia was so compelling that she could not bear to put even inanimate objects such as books and papers into a locker where they would be unable to get out. Elevators and subways raised the claustrophobia to an unbearable pitch. After a short time in high school, Dorcus was sent to the school psychologist, who was not long in discovering the connection between the girl's history of operations and her fear. Dorcus explained readily that when she went under ether she had always dreamed that she was in a coffin and buried alive. She had always awakened in panic which presently transferred itself to the moment at which the dream began as she went under ether, and caused her to fight madly from the first whiff until she was completely unconscious. Her revolt against physical restraint was, of course, a reaction to a stimulus that recurred, although in greatly attenuated form, whenever the slightest force was used to push her into a course of action, or whenever she found herself in a small, enclosed space. This girl's fear was hard to cure because it had a basis in a series of severe and repeated emotional shocks. Dorcus eventually made a fair recovery, largely because she was a very intelligent girl and was able to develop a good understanding of the situation. She has learned to ride in subway trains and elevators without more than an occasional qualm, and she can even go through tunnels under rivers, although she still has to grit her teeth to remain quiet. Two or three rather torrid love affairs have taught her to like being touched. Once in a while, in the office of a dentist or a doctor, she still shows a tendency to hysteria if the nurse tries to hold her hands or to restain her in any way while the doctor is giving her a treatment, but the outbursts are relatively rare and are not nearly as severe as they were earlier. This girl's history is instructive in showing how a fear can condition an individual's entire adjustment to society. Dorcus was rapidly becoming an outcast among her age-mates because of her peculiarities, which seemed to them to be merely silly. If she had not been helped she could easily have become the most unpopular girl in the school.

Fear is destructive. Its only value is to prevent one from doing something that is dangerous or unwise. It is therefore useful for survival in moments of actual physical danger under primitive conditions. In a modern environment, however, the reactions may lead to unnecessary injury or death, as in a theater fire when the running-away response may be the only cause of fatalities. In general, worry only interferes with accomplishment and leads to maladjustment. The conquest of unnecessary fear has become an important problem of mental hygiene.

Emotions Leading to Joyous Behavior   The third of the fundamental emotions is love. As in the case of both fear and anger, there is a definite development from infancy to adulthood in the stimuli which cause this emotion. It is probable that the bodily background also changes with age, since children are undeveloped sexually and since individuals beyond middle age have more or less lost their sexual vigor. Because of the physiological changes at puberty, the bodily turmoil into which love precipitates the adolescent is both profound and unexpected. He has already experienced the emotion which in childhood passes for love, but he has not had the same internal adjustment. Whereas a small child may be just as angry as an adolescent, he is not normally in love in just the same way.

In the Freudian literature one finds much concerning the development of erotic interest, with special emphasis upon the importance of the earliest stages of growth. Five more or less distinct stages are recognized: the oral, the anal, the Oedipal, the latent, and the genital. The earliest period continues from birth till the time the child stops nursing. It is a period of dependence, during which the satisfaction of all the baby's needs comes from his mother. When she nurses or fondles him, he reacts by laughing and crowing. Since hunger is his chief driving force, nursing is his chief joy, and his mouth is the chief area through which pleasure comes—hence the name of this stage. During the second and third years of life, the child is being trained to use the toilet, and his erotic interests become attached to these activities. Most children get pleasure from their eliminative processes and show a desire to play with the products. This anal stage is of relatively short duration. During both of the two earliest periods the child's interest is focused on himself. Between, roughly, the ages of 4 and 6, he passes through the Oedipal state. The name is derived from a Greek myth of a boy who unknowingly killed his father and married his mother. During this period the little girl "falls in love" with her father and becomes hostile toward her mother, and the little boy "falls in love" with his mother and becomes jealous of his father. The resulting Oedipus complex is normally resolved before or soon after the entrance to school, partly by the interest in age-mates and partly by association with a greater number of adults. The child who has emerged from these three lowest levels now enters a period of latency during which his love life is quiescent and he is concerned chiefly with working out a satisfactory relationship with his peers and with gaining control over his immediate environment and over himself. With adolescence the genital stage begins.

It should be pointed out that thus far there is relatively little objective proof of the above theory of development. For instance, breast-fed babies, who should derive more satisfaction than bottle-fed babies, do not seem to be any better adjusted in later life than the latter.[11] Premature or delayed toilet training has not been shown to have a measurable effect upon subsequent personality. All one can say at the present time is that the existence of these levels, as based upon observations, may be taken for granted, but that their significance cannot be; nor can one assume that they form a *proven* series of the expression taken by an underlying sexual drive. The concept has, however, been of value in clinical work and in understanding certain intergroup relationships. It has also permeated modern thought and speech. To date, however, no one can offer objective proof of its accuracy, and perhaps such proof will never be possible, even though the theory be entirely correct. In any case, one should know what the Freudian ideas in this respect are and should use the concepts whenever they seem to shed light upon human problems.

In psychological literature the person or thing that inspires the emotion of love has been termed the "love-object." The love-objects that are most powerful in arousing the emotion vary with age, just as the situations arousing either fear or anger also vary. The first love-object for babies of either sex is undoubtedly the mother, or the person who looks after them. The mother usually remains the exclusive love-object during the first year of life. Later on, she may be displaced by the father or she and the father may be about equally potent in arousing the child's affections. A mother is not usually displaced in the affection of her sons although she is quite often superseded by the father in the affection of her daughters. The reason for this situation appears to be partly that many women are actually more attached to their sons than to their daughters and partly that many men are unwilling to display their affection toward their sons for fear the boys will become sissies. By the time a son is perhaps 2 years old the average father is unwilling to fondle or kiss him or otherwise display a love which may be quite as deep as that which he feels toward his daughter. However, there are no social inhibitions operating against his caressing his little daughter as much as he wants to. Consequently, girls in the second or third years of life often transfer their deepest love to their fathers, whereas boys are less likely to do so. In any case, throughout the child's early years of life, the parents, or older persons functioning as parents, remain the chief objects able to bring about

---

[11] H. Ozlansky, "Infant Care and Personality," *Psychological Bulletin*, 46:1–48, 1949.

the emotion of love. As soon as the child goes to school, a particular teacher may displace one or both of the parents, but the teacher belongs in the same category as an adult and is not therefore a new type of love-object—though she may arouse the jealousy and antagonism of the parents.

A person of approximately the same age as one's parents is thus an infantile type of love-object. Some children, however, are allowed or even encouraged to continue fixations on parents, older friends, or teachers. If this situation persists into the years of adolescence the child is far too dependent upon older people for his emotional satisfaction, and he is usually abnormally attached to his own home. If the situation goes on into adult life, it becomes truly serious, because the individual falls in love with people much too old. A young man of 25 is rarely happy for long with a woman of 45; nor is a young woman likely to remain in love with a man who is a great many years her senior. Middle age and youth are appropriately adjusted as parent and child or as teacher and pupil, but not as husband and wife. Dependence for emotional satisfaction upon older generations is a symptom of persistent infantilism.

This fixation upon adults, often adults of the opposite sex, continues normally through the early years of childhood—that is, till about the sixth or seventh year. From this time, for a few years, children are usually more deeply attached to some other child of their own age and sex than to anyone else. Parents sometimes resent this situation and try to discourage the attachments. This second period of development, in which the love-object is another person of the same sex and approximately the same age (sometimes a little older) has been referred to as the "homosexual" stage. It is the same as the Freudian "latent" stage. These childish attachments are perfectly normal and are a necessary step in the gradual emancipation of a child from the emotional ties which bind him to his home. The period of devotion of boys to boys and girls to girls continues, usually becoming more intense, up to the years of adolescence. The attachments are so strong that boys and girls 11 or 12 years of age will have nothing more to do with each other than is absolutely necessary. As one lad remarked, "I like people—almost all kinds except girls." And girls refer to boys as "horrible," "just pests," or "disgusting." [12]

There is evidence that interest in members of the same sex continues for some girls for a long time. The attitude may be shown only by excessive affection for girl friends, but often it appears as a "crush"—that is, an intense devotion to an older woman. Most women teachers in high school have to contend, at one time or another, with a crush. The type of girl who develops a crush is usually a somewhat isolated individual who has had only superficial ties with her feminine age-mates and very little contact with boys. She may

[12] Gesell, Ilg, and Ames, *op. cit.,* p. 345.

be afraid of boys, or quite indifferent to them, or friendly with them in an objective way, but for one reason or another they have never aroused her affections. Or it may be that she has never aroused theirs. Such a girl has to fixate her affections upon someone, and since her normal development is temporarily blocked, she reverts to a childish pattern and attaches herself to an adult of the same sex. A number of situations tend to condition a girl in such a way as to make an attachment to an older woman seem to her a natural reaction. If, for example, she is away from home for the first time, and especially if the mother is a central figure in her home, she may turn to a teacher primarily as a mother-substitute. Or, if she has grown up in a home in which the mother was absent, she may have developed an intense desire for affection from an older woman and so attaches herself to the first such person who is kind to her. The crush used to be greatly in evidence in girls' schools and women's colleges, but Henry Ford and his followers have undermined the crush by delivering to the feminine campus a fair crop of young men on weekday afternoons and all day Saturday and Sunday. Most crushes die from competition, but a teacher still sees one occasionally.

The homosexual type of love-object, regardless of comparative ages, is obviously not desirable as a permanent stimulus. In some instances, however, an individual remains in this stage of development and becomes permanently attached to other members of his or her own sex. Usually such adults are considered definitely beyond the pale and may be quite ostracized. If the public would stop regarding childish attachments as "abnormal" and would look upon them rather as a sign of immaturity, a great deal of despair could be eliminated.

During adolescence a third stage usually emerges, in which the love-object is another individual of approximately the same age but of the opposite sex. For the majority of individuals this adult and socially approved type of love-object completely takes the place of the two previous types as far as the deepest emotions are concerned. Naturally, girls still love their mothers and fathers, and they still love their girl friends and teachers, but their deepest emotions are centered upon boys as love-objects rather than upon either parents or friends. Usually the transfer from friends of one's own sex to members of the opposite sex is easy and natural: all that seems to be needed for normally adjusted youngsters is the presence in the environment of a large number of possible love-objects. If a girl goes to a high school in which five hundred boys are enrolled, she is presented with five hundred potential love-objects, among which she will discover at least a dozen suited to her particular personality. All she needs is enough boys to choose from. Similarly, all a boy normally needs to distract his emotion from friends of his own sex is a sufficient assortment of girls.

As the transfer is being made, boys and girls present types of behavior that are rather baffling to adults. The boys hector and tease the girls, hide their books, catcall to them, and hang about on street corners waiting for them to pass. One has to remember that throughout childhood boys who are chums constantly pummel and shout names at each other; physical or verbal attack is a boy's commonest expression of affection. It takes some lads quite a while to discover that this familiar mode of behavior, even in its mildest forms, will not do for expressing their interest in girls. On occasion the boys, being young and having little judgment, may go too far, but as long as their behavior is within bounds it should not be punished, and, if reproved, only on the basis of bad manners, not bad intentions. Girls are quite capable of preventing most excesses themselves, and they are well aware that they have often deliberately precipitated a boy's reactions. The girl whose books are snatched, whose hair is pulled, or whose appearance is greeted by catcalls is convinced of her popularity. These early heterosexual manifestations are very trying to adults, but they seem satisfactory to the participants.

Toward the end of adolescence or early in adult life there should be a narrowing of the field to one person of the opposite sex and of approximately the same age. Out of possible love-stimuli the young man or woman should select one as a permanent mate. The man about town and the career girl who continue for years to "play the field" have not taken this last step. Their frequent change of love-object classes them not as sophisticates but as 16-year-olds.

The normal development shown by stimuli giving rise to the emotion of love may be summarized as follows: The first love-objects are adults of the same or opposite sex; the second love-objects are normally persons of about the same age and the same sex; and the third are persons of about the same age and the opposite sex. During the years of infancy and early childhood, when the child's chief need is for care and security, he loves most those who give him these elements. When he begins to strike out for himself, he loves most those people who best recognize him as an individual—his friends, who incidentally serve to break his early bonds with his home. Finally, he reacts to a type of love-object which, sooner or later, will lead to marriage and will permanently end his infantile attachment to his parents.

As a sort of summary of the emotional developments of the period the writers are including a series of quotations from the diaries of adolescents. Of course, those who write diaries at all are highly verbal and are probably more given to introspection than their age-mates. However, because they can and do record how they feel, their entries may be regarded as expressing such feelings as most adolescents have but are not so free in expressing, at least not in writing. The student who reads these excerpts is almost certain to find one or two that accord well with his or her own remembered feelings at a particular time or over a particular period.

Age 19, 9: I love this house and all the lovely rooms with their precious things. I love the brown walnut desk and bookshelves with their riches. I love the armchairs in which so many beloved people have sat and the little smoking table with Mother's flowers on it. Our house is my dearest home. Without those loved rooms I could never have had the strength to live.[13]

Age 19, 8: How much joy is in me, as mere youthfulness. I am happy in the morning when I get up. I am happy about the morning coffee that can taste so wonderful. To tear the page off the calendar in the morning can be a joyful experience. What more could I want from life than that which I have every day—or isn't that too much?

Age 17, 4: My soul is troubled; that is, if I even have one. How will it live? In school one is stuffed with facts that can be understood by the mind, but the soul dwindles more and more. Everything is a mad race. . . . I read, but not for my soul, only to keep my mind occupied and to have something to do. I lack every capacity to be inspired, every strength of youth. I live my life without really living at all.

Age 19, 6: I am never free from a steady pressure of discontent in my heart that becomes stronger when I think what I wanted to do during this vacation and how little I actually accomplished. What you write about my inferiority complex is all very well, but it is even worse than you think. I know that to know only a little can be cured— that isn't it. It is much worse that I have no interests at all, that fundamentally everything is all the same to me. You know it does not come from my deepest heart or from actual need, except perhaps for reading. But reading is for me only a method of killing time, a flight from my empty mind, where there is nothing. Be so good as to name any good points in my nature. I know of none. But absolutely none. Basically I am unfriendly, egotistical, jealous, and suspicious. And good characteristics? Upon thinking it over, I don't find any. Earlier I thought I was to a certain extent clever, but I have buried this notion as a fantastic bit of imagination. . . . I am unfortunately and to my great anger very clear that I am empty. I am average or even less than average. Sad, but true. . . . I have always thought that I would remedy my faults, but now that I have time to apply a remedy, I am no better, and I have grave doubts about myself. . . . I am too lacking in energy to pull myself together. Oh, how I despise myself because I amount to nothing!

Age 19, 4: Fear! How well I know you: fear of making mistakes, fear of people, fear that God will cease His goodness and leave me to die.

Age 19, 7: I believe it will be better now. I can again laugh and sing and hope. No one believes me how wonderful it is. To me it is almost a miracle, after those horrible days. Can one go through such a year, through such chaos of sadness and sense of being lost? Is it possible that at nineteen years of age life seems . . . to be a black hole full of pain? Did I really live through these days without hope, with only trifles to comfort me? Must it be that we stumble through this desert, in order to make the vegetation really acceptable?

Age 16, 5: In the evening we danced. I was crazily, madly in love, and he also. Do you know that we could no longer bear it among all those people? We danced a lot together, our hands almost cramped themselves together, and we both felt a shy passion when a tremor went through our bodies, until finally all those silly people with their morals became all one to us and we went out and kissed each other, and I know it was no sin, for we found each other frightfully desirable. . . . I am today just as

---

[13] W. Abegg, *Aus Tagebuchern und Briefen junger Menschen* (Basel: Ernst Reinhart, 1954), 172 pp. These excerpts are respectively from pages 85, 40, 92, 166, 45, 39, 39–40, 57, 44, 67, 66, 38.

crazy. This morning I got the first letter from him. He writes completely enchanted; he holds me so dear! I noted that in the letter, although he did not say so. He is named Karl Heinz. I could shout it for joy in the air: KARL HEINZ, KARL HEINZ, KARL HEINZ! The summer afternoon was also beautiful. We were on the boat and danced. In the evening he took me to the railroad station and we sorrowfully took leave of each other. Do you know, it is always remarkable that when I am with him I am not gay but serious and almost sad. I don't know how this happens.

Age 16, 11: If with this summer my life comes to an end I would wish that the minister should read in this book of my love [for him] and that he should say the last words over my bier. . . . It would be a last, glowing sweet summer; a summer that made life rich—or rather richer, for all the years were good. The last was the hardest and the best.

Age 18, 2: I feel only that unpleasantness that always meets me when love is extinguished. In the beginning I felt only a hot desire for Nell. Now everything is dead in my soul. And there is left only a wish for a great, encircling love. . . . What my kind of love means only nauseates me, and I feel regret for having lived through it. Faithfulness is no empty madness. It is only love that lasts forever. And it is a curse that I believed love to be only a diversion.

Age 19, 4: With Nanette's help I have made good progress in French. . . . She also helps me often to regain my spiritual balance and acts upon my nervousness as a pacifying drug. Naturally, being with a woman brings a certain danger with it. And my hot blood often rises in waves, but at its highest point I have never lost control of myself. What prevents me from taking the last step is not fear of consequences or the lack of agreement on Nanette's part but the moral responsibility. If I were a realist I would say: Why should I do it on account of this one short moment of happiness, or why should I not do it? What holds me back? But I am no realist. I feel too deeply and can therefore picture to myself how it is for a woman if it later came to a break, and then my sense of responsibility prevents me. If I were entirely sure that I would later marry Nanette I wouldn't hesitate for a moment, and my religion wouldn't hold me back.

Age 15, 11: Do you know, I am so crazy, so endlessly twisted, especially today once again. What is wrong I don't know. . . . I get surer and surer every day how difficult life is. It isn't meant to be laughed at. I'd like just once to cease raving, but I don't know how to. . . . What is life for anyway? At the moment I don't know. . . . When I think of life, this is the question: What have I created? Actually, nothing. I go to school, work, read, come home, but to what purpose? Last week I read the *Kreuzer Sonata* by Tolstoi. It drove me nearly mad. If that is the way things are, one might as well let himself be buried now as to endure.

▶ Objective Measures of Emotional Maturity

Within the past three decades, investigators have been working on tests for measuring emotional attitudes and emotional maturity. The results are expressed in terms of "emotional age," a concept roughly paralleling that of "mental age." Thus a 15-year-old girl with an emotional age of 12 shows the emotional reactions expected of 12-year-olds; she has a retardation of three years, and an "emotional quotient" of 80.

The tests used to determine emotional age consist actually of the measurement of attitudes, opinions, and interests. One such scale contains four subtests which investigate what a pupil thinks is wrong, what he worries about, what he is interested in, and what traits he admires. Children think many actions to be wrong, they are afraid of many things, they have wide interests, and they admire a large assortment of traits. Adults are far more lenient in their judgment of right and wrong, they have lost many of their fears, they have fewer interests, and they admire only a limited number of human characteristics. The scores for this test are therefore high for children and low for adults. It will be noticed that the scale of values at the left of the figure runs from a high score at the bottom to a zero score at the top; by reversing the usual series—low to high—the resulting curves rise in the conventional manner. Results from this test appear in Figure 12–3. At all ages the girls show a greater degree of maturity than the boys. Their curve begins to rise sharply between 13 and 15; the steepest part of the boys' curve occurs later.

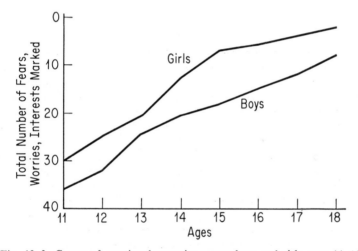

Fig. 12–3. Curves of emotional maturity among boys and girls, ages 11–18

Based on data from S. L. Pressey and L. C. Pressey, "Development of the Interest-Attitude Tests," *Journal of Applied Psychology,* 17:1–16, 1933, and C. P. Stone and R. G. Barber, "The Attitudes and Interests of Pre- and Post-Menarcheal Girls," *Journal of Genetic Psychology,* 54:27–71, 1939.

It is possible to measure emotional age by studying either the wishes or the specific interests of children and adolescents. Children of both sexes wish mainly for material things, while adolescents want mostly intangibles: to be more popular, to be successful in sports, to be better looking, to have a professional career. In late adolescence wishes for a good job or a happy marriage become predominant. Presumably as a reaction to World War II, the commonest wish in a 1954 study was for permanent peace.[14] A somewhat older investigation traced the changes in wishes from the first through the twelfth grade. Small children wanted roller skates or sleds. The desires of the high school population centered upon self-improvement ("I wish I could do better schoolwork") and upon social relationships ("I wish I had a girl friend," or "I wish I could help my mother more"). The trends were much the same for boys and girls, but the latter showed increases or decreases in specific wishes a little earlier than the former; only on wishes concerned with sports were there large sex differences. Two samples are shown in Figure 12–4. The lines numbered (1) show the percentages of boys and girls at different ages who wanted specific things; these lines contrast with those numbered (2) that give similar results for those who wanted self-improvement or better social adjustment.

Figure 12–4 also shows the development of four specific interests between grade 6 and the end of college—a range of 10 years from an average age of 12 to 22. The items shown are from a test in which the students first

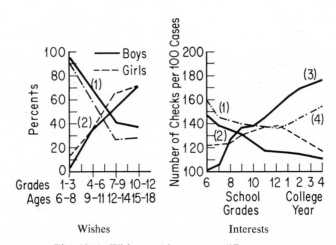

Fig. 12–4. Wishes and interests at different ages

Based on A. T. Jersild and R. J. Tasch, *Children's Interests and What They Suggest for Education* (New York: Columbia University Press, 1949), pp. 108, 116 (Wishes); and S. L. Pressey and A. W. Jones, "1925–1953 and 20–60 Age Changes in Moral Codes, Anxieties, and Interests, as Shown by the X–O Tests," *Journal of Psychology,* 39:485–502, 1955.

marked all those things in which they felt any interest—and then double-marked the one thing in each set of five in which they had the most interest. The score on each item consists of the total number of marks thus assigned.

[14] H. V. Cobb, "Role Wishes and General Wishes of Children and Adolescents," *Child Development,* 25:161–171, 1954.

Two items—roller skating (1) and horseback riding (2)—show a decrease with age; in contrast, dancing (3) and shopping for clothes (4) showed an increase. These detailed results show the relationship between interests and age and explain why tests based on interests and wishes are used to estimate emotional maturity.

The measurement of emotional maturity gives a clue to the behavior of sundry social misfits. Certain delinquents, for instance, are found to have relatively high mental ages, but low emotional ages. The intractable children in school, who precipitate a goodly proportion of the situations requiring discipline, are also characterized by retarded emotional development. The "problem" employee in industry and the "problem" professor in college have also been shown to have the interests, drives, attitudes, and reactions of children or adolescents, and therefore to be unemployable in work demanding adult behavior. The Army and Navy were not long in discovering that measurements of emotional age were useful in indicating men who would have difficulty in adjusting themselves to military life. Of all the conditions that prevented men from becoming soldiers, mere childishness, in one form or another, was the commonest. Some of the men could be educated into maturity quickly but others could not.

Emotional immaturity shows itself in a number of easily recognizable symptoms. The immature adult is extremely self-centered. He likes to show off any little skills that he has—doing card tricks, for instance. When he is in the wrong, he finds excuses for himself so that he can avoid feeling guilty. He dodges away from reality, especially if the situation is unpleasant. He resents authority. He avoids difficult tasks. His conduct is inconsistent and unpredictable. He wants the center of the stage. He easily becomes jealous, and when he likes people at all, he tends to have crushes or to worship them.[15] In short, he is a child in an adult's body.

Measures of emotional age are now used to supplement results from tests of intelligence. Forty years ago bright children were often accelerated in school as fast as their ability permitted, without respect to their social or emotional competence. The results of such rapid advancement on the basis of ability alone are shown in the following study.

Oscar was a boy of 9 and already in the eighth grade at the time when one of the writers first became acquainted with him. The following year the high school principal refused to accept Oscar as a freshman because of his youth, although he did not question the boy's capacity to do the work. Oscar's social adjustment was none too good at best, and it would not have been helped by admission to high school, where he would have been six or seven inches shorter and about forty pounds lighter than the other boys. Oscar's father therefore with-

---

[15] Based upon L. P. Thorpe, *Child Psychology and Development* (New York: The Ronald Press Company, 1955), pp. 474–475.

drew his son from school altogether and sent him to a private tutor. This move put an end to what little social contact Oscar had with his age-mates, and he became a complete isolate. Even when he did his best to play with other boys, he was unceremoniously rejected, except by those well below his own chronological age, among whom he functioned as a kind and resourceful adult mind in a child's body. Oscar spent 90 percent of his waking hours in studying Latin, Greek, geometry, and algebra, and the remaining 10 percent in being a supernursemaid to a group of 5- to 7-year-old children.

Oscar was ready to enter college when he was 12 years old, but he was not accepted for another three years, during which he acquired a reading knowledge of French and German, a fair mastery of world history, and a working knowledge of archaeology. In due course he entered college, completed the requirements in two and a half years, and graduated at 18. Again he had to wait before he could continue his education, because the graduate school would not accept him until he was 20. He spent the two years in Egypt as an unpaid young assistant of an archaeological party. He had collected the material for his Ph.D. thesis and had finished a first draft of his thesis before he was allowed to enter the graduate school. He received his Ph.D. when he was 22. Since then he has become an outstanding classical archaeologist, but he has never been popular with either his co-workers or his students. Oscar retained his childishness well into middle age, but he has finally shown signs of social and emotional maturity in recent years. When he was nearing 50, he had a sort of "nervous breakdown" accompanied by a profound melancholia. He voluntarily entered a rest home for the summer. While there, he was looked after by a pleasant, even-tempered, competent woman of about his own age. She made him so comfortable and gave him such a sense of security that he married her. She had been an orphan and had had such a hard time in life that the prospect of looking after only one wealthy and pliable man instead of a succession of complaining patients seemed like heaven to her. She is an uneducated but basically intelligent woman, who is glad to care for Oscar in return for security, present and future. She has no idea what his erudite monologues are about, but she listens pleasantly, says "Yes" or "No" or "Well, now!" at intervals, and darns socks or hems towels "so as not to waste the evening." For Oscar she is ideal. Her commonplaceness has provided just the rock he needed for emotional security.

Oscar is not yet and probably never will be a normal individual, but he is gradually mastering the simple social skills that he should have acquired as an adolescent. He is beginning to see dimly what other people are like. His more advanced students and he are meeting together in class with understanding and even a mild feeling of affection. Among his colleagues Oscar has lost most of his earlier habits of alternately pushing himself into and dominating conversation or of retiring into a silent isolation. His overcompensatory behavior was both aggressive and unpleasant and it had often brought him ridicule and overt rejection, but at least it resulted in human contacts, whereas his alternate behavior gave him safety at the cost of loneliness. This brilliant mind is gradually emerging from the maladjustment of an improper education.

If this boy's emotional age had been measured and taken into consideration, he would presumably not have been so drastically accelerated. At present the approved procedure is to measure a child physically, mentally, socially, and emotionally, and then to consider all these factors in determining his grade placement.

▶ **Summary**

An emotion is an experience that affects an individual's vital processes, stimulating him to greater activity than is normal. The central changes that accompany emotions may be mild or intense, but their nature does not alter as one grows older. There is, however, an observable evolution in the types of stimulus that arouse emotional states and the types of response that are made. A child's causes of anger are relatively simple and personal; his reactions are direct and explosive. An adolescent reacts primarily to fear situations that are social in character, in which he feels his status to be involved; his reactions show some degree of subtlety, but he is quickly broken down to childish levels if he is exposed to pressure. A child's affection is usually centered first upon his mother, and then upon his father or other adults; in the case of a girl, fixation upon the mother is often supplanted at an early age by a possessive love for the father. During childhood, members of both sexes are deeply attached to other children of the same sex and age. In adolescence an interest in heterosexual love-objects arises; at first the interest is transitory and somewhat promiscuous, but soon it becomes centered on only two or three companions of the opposite sex, and eventually upon only one. Interests and attitudes change as a result of these developments. It is therefore possible to measure the level a given individual has reached by obtaining from him a statement of his interests, attitudes, hopes, fears, and identifications. From such measurement one derives an emotional age which should be used—along with mental, physical, social, and educational ages—in the handling of children and especially in their placement in the school grades. Emotional life furnishes the basic drives that impel an individual to action. These drives vary in strength not only from person to person but from age to age. When they cannot be satisfied, they lead to frustration and conflict, which may be resolved in a number of ways, some of which are more healthy than others. Emotions inevitably find some outlet; if one is blocked, another is substituted.

References for Further Reading

B O O K S

Other Texts

Baller and Charles, *The Psychology of Human Growth and Development* (Chap. 6 or 7).

Garrison, *Growth and Development,* 2d. ed. (pp. 98–127).

Horrocks, *Behavior and Development* (pp. 554–564).

Hurlock, *Adolescent Development,* 2d. ed. (Chap. 4).

Jersild, *Psychology of Adolescence* (Chap. 7, 8, 9, or 10).

Jones, *Growth and Behavior in Adolescence* (Chap. 7).

Kuhlen, *The Psychology of Adolescent Development* (Chap. 6).

Other Books and Monographs

Baller, *Readings in the Psychology of Human Growth and Development* (pp. 243–276).

Frank, L. N., *Feelings and Emotions* (New York: Doubleday & Company, Inc., 1954), 38 pp.

A R T I C L E S

Angelino, H., *et al.,* "Trends in the Fears and Worries of School Children as Related to Socio-Economic Status and Age," *Journal of Genetic Psychology,* 89:263–270, 1956.

Barshak, E., "A Study of Happiness and Unhappiness in Childhood and Adolescence, of Girls in Different Countries," *Journal of Psychology,* 32:173–215, 1951.

Brown, R. L., "These High School Fears and Satisfactions," *Understanding the Child,* 23:74–76, 1954.

Cobb, H. V., "Role Wishes and General Wishes of Children and Adolescents," *Child Development,* 25:161–171, 1954.

Suggested Research Problems [16]

1. It would be of value to make a survey of the various forms of emotional expression in adolescence, with the aim of determining those that are acceptable in the culture of today and are possible within the framework of the school setting. Various possible outlets through creative work should also be considered. The ultimate objective would be the presentation to teachers of acceptable forms in sufficient variety that she would have a wide choice of suggestions in individual cases.

---

[16] See note, p. 11.

Chapter 13 | The Emerging Self

THE identification by each individual of his own fluid but unique organization is a lifelong process. However, this development seems to reach intensification during adolescence, when the constellation of life experiences, of expanding horizons, of deepening emotions, and of widening social contacts evokes a central need in the adolescent to recognize himself as a whole person, and to relate himself to other individuals and to the social patterns in which he lives.

Although this process is actually a complex and virtually indivisible function of the total organism, certain characteristics of it can be observed by examining ways in which the individual's perception of himself depends on the responses he makes in exploring the relationships between what he wishes and what is possible to him as a member of the human group. In the simplest terms, this process constitutes a constantly changing balance between his needs and the demands, frustrations, and rewards of his milieu. For the purposes of this discussion, the difficulties typically encountered by adolescents in their normal growth will be considered in terms of the needs and drives, goals and values involved in the development of a self-concept.

There are almost as many definitions of "self" as there are writers on the subject. A definition of "self" should give recognition to the presence of unconscious elements in the motivations and needs of an individual, but should also recognize the conscious, goal-seeking effort to make adjustments within the everyday world and to evolve an identity which has continuity, some consistency, and some adaptability. This effort becomes inextricably associated with the value system of the adolescent, particularly in a complex society in which he meets many expectations, not all of which are compatible. It is his sense of self, his evaluation of where he wants to go, and what he wants to be, which enables him to integrate the kaleidoscope of experiences into a coherent style of life and into a consistent core of basic resources. Identity is developed slowly and not without difficulty for each individual. These difficulties are in most cases situational and developmental and are seldom the product of profound disturbance. A teacher can often be most helpful in guiding the adolescent toward understanding that his struggles to establish his identity are a normal part of human development.

►The Continuity of the Developing Self

Even a small child soon learns that certain things are *his*—his parents, his home, his toys; perhaps even sooner he discovers that *he* has desires—things that he wants, feelings that he enjoys, supports that he needs, urges that he must follow. Certain events, things, and people give him satisfaction; others merely get in his way. As he grows older, his needs and attitudes change. Some investigators have felt that there are no inherited elements in the personality; others, and these are more numerous, seem to feel that certain traits either are inherited or are acquired at an extremely early age. In any case, no one denies that attitudes, drives, and satisfactions change. That is, the self is thought of as being extremely flexible and as constantly altering, usually in response to environmental pressures that lead the self into setting up goals, with resulting integration into patterns. Conflicts may also rise, but only when the goals of the different patterns are themselves incompatible. Social motivations are directed toward objectives that either will enhance the self—allowing it to develop further—or will defend it from a situation that is sensed as dangerous to its stability or growth. Throughout life, an individual keeps on striving toward one goal after another and trying to integrate experiences and attitudes into a coherent whole. But the integration is constantly being torn down by changes in internal development—such as those already described for the period of adolescence—or by changes originating in the environment, especially in interpersonal contacts. These interferences may or may not be real; their indispensable characteristic is that the individual *thinks* they are real.

During adolescence much reorganization and reorientation take place. The considerable alterations are, however, not discontinuous with those of childhood or those of adulthood, but rather reveal an emergent personality which has historical background, and is moving into the future with an increased awareness of the present, if the developmental process flows forward without major distortions. These distortions will be discussed later on. For the present it is useful to consider only the usual effects upon the self of meeting the demands of normal physiological, intellectual, and social changes. Recognition of areas in which stress usually occurs should help both the teacher and the student to evaluate the problems involved, to develop resources for meeting them, and to avoid damaging ways of managing those frustrations which are almost certain to arise.

It should also be appreciated that the more definite the social norms of the adult group around him, the easier it is for an adolescent to adjust himself, because he at least knows what his objectives are. Rigidity is not a desideratum, but clearness is. In a rapidly changing society he does not always even know where he is supposed to be going. The resulting disorganization may take several forms, of which a common one is the rejection of the adult world *in toto,* plus an attempt to obtain a firm anchoring in peer groups. The adolescent boy who is at home just long enough to sleep and to gulp down breakfast has probably already made this transfer. It will serve him for a while, but presently he must either grow up or remain a perennial adolescent.

Certain elements of the self-concept can be measured. A common technique consists in giving a large number of statements or adjectives—often 100—already typed upon separate cards and asking the individual to sort the cards into seven piles. He puts the cards containing statements that he considers "most like him" into pile 1, those with slightly less resemblance into pile 2, and so on down to pile 7, which contains those cards with statements that are "most unlike him." There is usually a limit to the number he may put into any one pile, so he has to evaluate the statements or adjectives and distribute them in terms of his own self-concept. Such a procedure gives a fair picture of what a person thinks of himself. If other people are asked to rate the same individual by sorting the same cards to show what they think he is like, one can get some idea of the accuracy of the subject's self-concept. In general, those adolescents with a fairly accurate picture of themselves have a better adjustment and are less defensive than those whose self-concept is distorted and inaccurate.[1]

Most adolescents recognize not only a real self but also an ideal self— the person they would like to be. There is almost always some discrepancy between the two perceptions. In general, the larger the discrepancy, the greater the tension and the more serious the emotional maladjustment. The degree of self-satisfaction—that is, the closeness between the perception of the real and ideal selves—correlated in one study [2] 0.70 with total adjustment, 0.59 with social adjustment, 0.56 with freedom from symptoms of withdrawal, 0.55 with feelings of belonging, and 0.50 with sense of personal worth and community relations. The adolescents who rejected themselves—that is, showed a high discrepancy between the real and ideal selves—were anxious, oversensitive, unhappy, restless, distractible, and tense.[3] They felt themselves unable to meet the expectations of their parents. Both the self-accepting and the self-rejecting students did equally good work in school and were of equal intelligence. The acceptance of one's self is also related positively to tolerance and willingness to accept others.[4]

---

[1] B. Chodorkoff, "Self-Perception, Perceptual Defense, and Adjustment," *Journal of Abnormal and Social Psychology,* 49:508–512, 1954.

[2] T. E. Hanlon, P. R. Hofstetter, and J. P. O'Connor, "Congruence of Self and Ideal Self in Relation to Personality Adjustment," *Journal of Consulting Psychology,* 18:215–218, 1954.

[3] J. V. Mitchell, Jr., "Goal-setting Behavior as a Function of Self-Acceptance, Over- and Underachievement, and Related Personality Variables," *Journal of Educational Psychology,* 50:93–104, 1959.

[4] See, for instance, K. T. Onwake, "The Relation between Acceptance of Self and

One's self-concept changes with age and experience in a number of ways. It normally becomes broader and more complex, more accurate, clearer, and more consistent. True adults learn to accept themselves as they are—faults included—and to face the inescapable conclusion that they are not perfect. They thus avoid the constant tension of those who never accept themselves as they are.

The normal growth of self-perception and values is reflected by any number of commonplace happenings and interests. For example, a boy wants in turn to become an Indian fighter, a pirate, a forester, a structural steel worker, an aviator, a race-track driver, a precision mechanic, a naval designer, and a bridge engineer. Or a girl progresses in her reading interests from fairy tales to stories of home life to adventure yarns to love stories to biographies of famous women—and probably to books on baby care and nutrition. The developing ego and its idea of itself are also reflected simply but pertinently in the names by which an individual wishes to be called at different stages of development. A child of two is probably called by a nonsensical nickname, based upon his first effort to pronounce his own name. If his name is "Jonathan" he may emerge from babyhood as "Yo-Yo." This tag is acceptable enough to his two-year ego, but his four- or five-year ego finds the babyish tag definitely insulting, and he announces that his name is "Jonnie." By the time he is nine or ten, his ego rejects the diminutive ending, and he wishes to be known as "Jon." If at this point he can pick up some meaningless nickname, such as "Kip" or "Wuz," so much the better; he feels more secure among his age-mates. As he approaches adolescence and feels the paramount need to be as much like his peers as he can and as conspicuously masculine as he can, he may reject "Jonathan" altogether as lacking in the desired masculinity and write his name as "John"—an undeniably male name of high anonymity. But in his young manhood, when he wants to establish himself as an individual, he takes back the "Jonathan" because it better satisfies his changed ego attitudes. By the time he is a middle-aged banker he may be happier with "J. Addison Jones" as a name that fits his own picture of his status better than "Jonathan A. Jones."

► **Patterns of Adjustment to Frustration**

Everyone has to live through longer or shorter periods of time during which he is unable to proceed toward his goals. At all ages it is one of the commonest experiences in life to be frustrated by circumstances or by one's own nature. If an experience is damaging to an individual's con-

Acceptance of Others Shown by Three Personality Inventories," *Journal of Consulting Psychology,* 18:443–446, 1954; and W. F. Fey, "Acceptance by Others and its Relation to Acceptance of Self and Others, a Revaluation," *Journal of Abnormal and Social Psychology,* 50:274–276, 1955.

cept of himself or to his capacity for further growth, this result is usually due to the individual's reactions to the situation rather than to the nature of the experience itself. Adolescents sometimes try to resolve their difficulties by methods that are a good deal more damaging than the original situation was. They can be guided into less extreme and less bizarre patterns of response, but they can no more avoid frustration and conflict than, as small children, they could have avoided skinning their knees or cutting their fingers.

Frustration is the feeling of helplessness, disappointment, inadequacy, and anxiety that is produced by interference with an ego drive. This complex feeling, plus the consciousness of uncertainty as to what should be done next, produces a general tightening and defensiveness of the whole organism. Thus interference with a drive leads to frustration, which leads to tension, which leads to response, which leads to readjustment—good or bad. The trigger that sets off the series is the interference with a drive which has its roots in a human ego. The blocking may be due to any number of causes, external or internal. For example, an adolescent boy who feels a need of friendship with girls may be blocked because he is in a boys' boarding school where he has few chances to meet girls, or he may be checked at home by the presence of a possessive mother who effectively keeps girls away from him and him away from them. Such conditions act as external privations over which he has little control. Or his desire may be blocked by internal difficulties, such as the fear of appearing ridiculous, by shyness, or by a conviction that he would be unable to talk to a girl. In still other instances, a drive does not come to normal fruition because it is not as strong as some competing drive. The boy who wants more girl friends may also want to become a famous surgeon; he has to spend so many hours in the laboratory and in studying that he has no time for social life. His urge is blocked therefore, by his own competing desire for prestige. As can readily be appreciated, any given ego attitude has a moderately good chance of being either partly or wholly frustrated before it can be satisfied. People differ greatly in their tolerance of frustration. They differ also in the readiness with which they can find and enjoy substitute means of satisfaction when the more direct ones are blocked. And they differ in the type of escape from conflict that they select. What they share is the necessity to reconcile their own needs with the demands of society.

In theory the pattern of escape should lead to a better relationship with other people, should be conducive to mental health, should make future adjustments easier, should benefit society, and should not divert one from one's goals in life. Unfortunately, there are no perfect patterns. All of them are forms of compromise between what the individual ego wants and what it can get. However, it is often helpful to check against these criteria any given compromise in order to estimate its values and to recognize its defects.

Some forms of escape occur more frequently than others, and many of them—if used in moderation—are relatively harmless. They are also highly useful because they permit the self to develop, to reconcile its conflicting drives, and to shed its feelings of guilt. It is when one pattern of escape is established as a fixed method for dealing with all reality that it becomes dangerous.

The patterns of evasion are classified, mainly in the interests of clearness, into five groups in Table 13–1. Two sets of terminology are given because both phrases appear in the literature.

1. Most people at some time try simple repression as a pattern of response, and a few persist in its use. Repression is an almost complete block to a drive that is for some reason considered inadmissible by the underlying ego structure. At best it brings only partial escape. It consists essentially of convincing oneself that a given impulse is wrong and of thenceforth denying its existence. It is the sort of reaction made, for instance, by an honorable man who finds himself in love with his brother's wife. The main difficulty in its use is that emotions do not stay repressed; they merely submerge and then pop up somewhere else in more or less disguised form, often being even more destructive than fulfillment of the original drive would have been. The individual who tries simply and directly to repress an emotion does not usually distort the situation that has produced it; he denies its reality altogether. Other patterns of response involve more or less distortion.

2. An individual is distorting reality if his conception of it—or of some phase of it—differs markedly from that of other people. Distortion is not a deliberate act of misperception; it is an interpretation that for some reason relieves the ego of strain, but it is entirely unconscious. The first escape on the list of distortions is rationalization. An individual is rationalizing when he gives a minor or faked motive for conduct that arises from some other motive that is too painful for him to accept. Thus, a dull freshman girl in high school may want to go to college but at the same time may be aware at least dimly that she has too little ability to do so. To admit openly that she is stupid would undermine her ideal of herself, so she rationalizes her conflict of desires by saying that she prefers the commercial to the college preparatory course because all her friends are taking it, because it leads to quicker financial returns, or because she had rather take "modern" subjects like shorthand than dull, stuffy, "impractical" courses. She has distorted reality because she has not given a true picture of it—but the distortion is more palatable than the truth. Since these patterns are usually unconscious, the user is not aware of the distortion. In such a case as that given above the ego has avoided damage by a relatively slight distortion.

Projection is a less desirable pattern of response than rationalization, partly because it involves a greater distortion of reality and partly because it is more crippling to one's attitudes. Since, however, the average human being has great difficulty in saying such simple words as "I was wrong," or "I

Table 13–1: ESCAPES AND ADJUSTMENTS

1. Escape by denying reality (adjustment by repression)

2. Escape by distorting reality (adjustment by deception)
   a. Rationalization
   b. Projection
   c. Segregation
   d. Sour grapes
   e. Displacement

3. Escape by retreating from reality (adjustment through surrender)
   a. Regression
   b. Fantasy
   c. Conversion

4. Escape by attacking reality (adjustment through attack)
   a. Physical aggression (delinquency)
   b. Verbal aggression

5. Escape by compromising with reality (adjustment through compromise)
   a. Compensation
   b. Sublimation
   c. Identification

SOURCE: Adapted and modified from N. Cameron, *The Psychology of Behavior Disorders* (Boston: Houghton Mifflin Company, 1947), pp. 142–186; J. M. Josselyn, *Psychosocial Development of School Children* (Family Service Association of America, 1948), 134 pp.; P. M. Symonds, *The Dynamics of Human Adjustment* (New York: Appleton-Century-Crofts, 1946), Chaps. 8–20; H. Schacter, *How Personalities Grow* (Bloomington, Ill.: McKnight & McKnight Publishing Company, 1949), Chaps. 12–15; and L. P. Thorpe, *The Psychology of Mental Health* (New York: The Ronald Press Company), 1950, pp. 133ff.

wasn't able to do it," this pattern is popular. Suppose, for instance, that a pupil who has tried very hard to pass a course in English composition finds he is failing. Failure is most uncomfortable, so he is likely to resort to a convenient "projection" [5] of the blame. He may say that his father is a foreigner and speaks little English at home, that his mother was always a poor speller and never liked to write compositions when she was in school, and that his older sister also had trouble with English. In this way he can explain his own failure in terms of heredity and home environment, thus projecting the blame onto somebody else and relieving himself of guilt. By an obvious distortion of reality he has escaped from the emotional situation altogether.

"Segregation" is a name given to the practice of keeping different sets of motives and practices from interfering with each other and precipitating

---

[5] At other places in this book the term "projection" is used in another sense—that is, in the meaning of displacing one's own attitudes or drives onto another person, attributing to that person what is not acceptable to the ego. It has also the above meaning, however.

crises. The classic example of this pattern is the factory owner whose drives for personal welfare and dominance lead him to underpay and overwork his laborers, overcharge his customers, and generally make money out of other people's misery. But on Sundays he is dominated by another set of objectives —a desire for prestige in belonging to and helping to support a religious group, a desire to bask in approval, and a desire to save his own soul. He is therefore on Sundays a devout worshiper. The common interpretation of his conduct is that he is a hypocrite, but this appellation is often erroneous. The man is actually sincere in accepting two contradictory sets of beliefs. He defends his ego from conflict and strain by keeping each set of goals in its own compartment. He honestly believes in Christianity, but his life would be thrown into confusion if he allowed such a percept as "Do unto others as you would have them do unto you" to get mixed up with his business. He distorts reality because he accepts as true in one frame of reference what he rejects as false in another. Such a man may be comfortable enough at the moment, but he is walking a tightrope. If he falls off, the damage to his ego may well be irreparable.

A fourth type of evasion in this group is called "sour grapes," the name being derived from the Aesop fable about the fox who could not reach the grapes he wanted and so comforted himself with the conviction that they were too sour anyway. When an adolescent states loudly that all fraternities and other secret organizations are worthless, he is probably displaying exactly the same pattern of response. At an earlier time he was very likely driven by the usual social urges of adolescence to set up as his immediate goal an election to a fraternity. His failure to be chosen was so crippling, the threat to his status so powerful, and the need to change his objective quickly so pressing that his self-concept would have collapsed under the strain had he not found an escape that preserved his ego structure intact but permitted a change of goal. What would have been a crushing defeat has therefore been turned into a defiant attack, and that particular emotional problem has disappeared. This pattern is definitely bad because it precipitates more problems than it solves.

The last of the escape patterns involving distortion is called "displacement." It is a response by which a destructive emotion that is generated by one person or set of circumstances may be transferred to another. Suppose, for example, that a pupil has been punished unfairly by his school principal and that he feels intense resentment. His first impulse may be to injure the principal, but he is restrained by a fear of consequences. The principal has a status that he dare not attack. As long as his hostility continues to boil inside him, he is in a state of profound disorganization. On the way home from school he happens to meet a small, shy, inoffensive Negro boy against whom he has no complaint, but he nevertheless attacks him and inflicts upon him at least some of the damage he would like to have done to the principal. His emotional response was displaced from the real but untouchable object of his wrath to an object that he could assault with far less danger of punishment and no likelihood of damage to himself. This transfer of emotion is not conscious; the matter would be much less serious if the boy were intentionally "working off" his anger. Unfortunately, he transfers his emotion so completely that he really hates the Negro boy instead of the principal, and may presently begin to hate all Negroes. This pattern is at the base of much race and intergroup prejudice. The distortion of reality is extreme, and the actual damage to the ego is also extreme, but it brings momentary relief. It is the process by which the thoroughly maladjusted person finds a scapegoat for the wrath that would otherwise destroy him quicky—instead of gradually!

3. The escapes in the next group are brought about by ignoring reality and erecting a neurotic bulwark against it. The commonest pattern of this type is evasion by regression or surrender. Thus, the shy daughter of a domineering mother finds her first efforts at life on a mature level quite unsatisfying because she comes into frequent, sharp, painful conflict with her mother, by whom she is always defeated. If the daughter has already developed a secure image of herself and if she is supported by her age-mates, she will revolt and leave her mother—actually or emotionally—but if her ego structure is insecure and she is isolated from her peers, her most probable escape is by surrender and regression to a childish level, at which her mother's domination seems natural and her own chief urge is to please her mother. The mother–little girl relationship has at least the merit of being peaceful—but it is peace bought at the price of surrender of the ego and reversion to childish goals.

Undoubtedly the commonest of all escape patterns is the substitution of daydreaming for action as a means of draining off painful emotions. Fantasy is fairly common at all ages and practically universal in adolescence. For the most part it is beneficial and does no apparent harm, as long as the daydreamer is perfectly sure which is the dream and which is the reality. For instance, a girl may want desperately to be popular but is not, or she may have to stay home from a dance, to which all her urges are driving her, because she has no appropriate clothes, or she may simply be too sick to go. Her unpopularity, her poverty—which may consist only of having no *new* dress to wear—or her illness is a reality. Of these she can probably face illness with no more than temporary strain. It is "respectable." Her poverty, real or imagined, is harder to accept, and she may be completely unable to face her negative social status. One possible way of defending her ego is to indulge in a daydream of being the belle of the ball. It is when the isolated daydreamer begins to think she *is* the belle of the ball that the pattern becomes dangerous. When and if the substitution of fantasy for reality becomes habitual, the dreamer is mentally ill, and the ego may be damaged beyond repair.

Finally, in this third group, there is escape from harsh reality into illness or physical handicap. This response permits the individual to escape the immediate situation that he cannot face, although it does nothing to resolve the underlying conflicts, but merely changes their mode of expresson. It often does not altogether rid the user of guilt, but the feeling is attached to something else rather than to the original cause. This method of avoidance always looks spurious to the outsider, who has difficulty in believing that the illness or seizures of whatever type are real and not mere alibis. For instance, one of the writers had a secondary school student who was under doctor's orders to cut all of her examinations because of the serious arm cramps that she developed. These were not mere imagination. The muscles in her arm stood out from the tissue and contracted so violently that on one occasion they dislocated a bone in her wrist and on another they pulled a tendon loose; her hand was drawn backward until it was almost against her forearm. The pain was excruciating. To imagine that anyone would undergo such agony on purpose is ridiculous. It is true that this student had a pronounced fear of examinations, which she began to dread in elementary school. On the day of an examination, she was in a state of profound disorganization, in which many conversion symptoms, such as diarrhea and dizziness, were already observable. She never succeeded in writing more than a few words before the cramps developed. Although it introduced a new kind of suffering, it removed her from her emotional conflict by making the writing of a test impossible and at the same time it absolved her from the normal feeling of guilt. On the oral examinations that were substituted for the written—or, rather, unwritten—ones, this girl did poorly, and her marks in all subjects were barely passing. For reasons not entirely clear, this girl had very early set up an objective of academic success as her main ego goal, an attitude which led her to elect the hardest possible courses, and she was completely caught in an emotionally loaded situation which was so threatening that anything was preferable to the destructive power of reality.

It may already have been noted that these evasions by surrender and retreat, if they become fixed methods of avoiding interference with basic satisfactions, will lead to neurotic or even psychotic behavior. In other words, neurotic reactions may be thought of as constituting a defense thrown up by the self against conditions that are intolerable, against drives that seem shameful, or against feelings of guilt.

4. Some individuals are too vigorous to retreat or compromise and too clearheaded to deceive themselves by distorting reality, on major issues at least. They therefore attack the situations or symbols of those situations that are inhibiting the full expression of their desires and try to demolish the reality that is interfering with their satisfactions and goals. For instance, a vigorous boy from a poor family is likely to wish he had more money. He does not, however, sit down and daydream about the money he would like to have, nor does he tell people that all great men were once poor boys or that wealth is all

delusion anyway and not worth fighting for. His pattern of response consists of going out and stealing some money, or an object that he can turn into money. He may also let off some of his emotional steam by scratching the paint off handsome new cars, by shouting scurrilous comments at well-dressed children, or by throwing a rock at a shiny top hat as its wearer is making his way to church on Easter Sunday. The less important modes of defiance are usually classed as rowdyism; if the reactions are serious, they are delinquencies. The delinquent is thus a person who is protecting himself from a damaging reality by attacking it. The attack may be either physical or verbal. In the latter case, it takes such forms as excessive criticism, scurrilous remarks, rumors, cruel jokes, unpleasant nicknames, catcalling, and the like. The damage to the underlying ego structure is extreme, as will be pointed out in greater detail in the chapter on delinquency.

5. The last group of possible escapes contains those that are probably best for mental health. The individual does not distort reality to escape from his own guilt or inadequacies, he does not pretend that reality is not there, and he does not try to demolish it. He does, however, divert its impact and works out a compromise which, while not giving complete satisfaction, at least gives enough to provide relief from tension, to channel urges into harmless and sometimes useful modes of expression, to permit continuation in his pattern toward his goals, and to protect his ego from serious crippling. The first of these patterns is called "compensation." This term means simply that an individual compensates for a poor showing in one aspect of his life by a good showing in another. A common example of this response is seen in the pupil who is too small for athletic competition and too shy to be a social success, and who therefore compensates by getting the best grades in class and by being regarded as an academic prodigy. Actually, success in his studies may be only his third choice, but it gives at least some satisfaction to his drives for recognition among his peers. Unfortunately, his concentration upon academic work may serve to alienate him still further from the social intercourse and physical exercise that he badly needs. Actually, his ego is already suffering a good deal, and his pattern of response is leading him to reject several phases of life in which he needs competency to become a normal, well-balanced individual. Compensation is good as far as it goes, but it needs supplementation.

If it were necessary to pick out one pattern as the best of the lot, most people would choose sublimation. One sees this process at work when the school bully is appointed as the school policeman. His urge to dominate has been diverted from twisting the arms of little children to seeing them safely across the street. His urge to inflict pain is being controlled by his urge to be admired. His exhibitionistic tendencies are satisfied by his uniform or armband, which sets him off from the others. His behavior now leads to satisfaction, whereas before it was not only undesirable in itself, but led to further punishment, further ostracism, further tension, and further damage to his ego structure. The boy's fundamental drives have not changed; their mode of expression is, however, constructive instead of destructive.

At the end of this long list of possible reaction patterns comes a most convenient pattern of adjustment known as "identification." It is particularly useful to those who for some reason are inferior. For instance, a girl of average ability with brilliant parents and one or two older and equally brilliant siblings is in no position to reach the family standard of superiority. Although she might be admired as bright in some families, she is headed for strain, despair, failure, and tension in her own. Through hero-worshiping identification she can escape some of her troubles because one does not expect to compete with one's heroes. One sees the same pattern in the humble bookkeeper who says with pride, "My firm did a half-million dollars' worth of business last year." He has escaped from his own insignificance by his identification with something bigger and more important. This pattern is relatively harmless, but one sometimes sees an extreme use of it that has led to disaster. One of the writers knew a pair of nonidentical twins, a brilliant boy and a girl of only average intelligence. The difference was further widened by parental attitudes, which allowed the boy freedom and put shackles upon the girl. She lived mainly in her brother, was always his best listener, had only such friends as he had, became his chief assistant in his work, and accepted his triumphs as her own. When he died, she emerged from the expected physical collapse as nobody: she had no independent self, she had no goals, she had no drives, she did not have even a home or a job. She still exists, but, in any real sense, she died when her brother did.

The last three patterns are especially useful because they meet at least some of the criteria set up at the beginning of this discussion: they are relatively healthy for the individual, they often lead to a better relationship with others, and in moderation they do not interfere too much with the usual goals of life.

All the patterns discussed above have an immediate value because they permit an individual to defend his image of himself against attack. When they are used occasionally, their effect upon the user is beneficial rather than otherwise. But as habitual responses they are unsatisfactory because they warp the personality and they lead to ever more damaging situations that the weakened ego is even less able to meet. A teacher should therefore realize that persistent projection, rationalization, compensation, daydreaming, regression, conversion to physical handicap, and hostility are all danger signals. They indicate the existence of chronic frustration, tension, and maladjustment. Early recognition is essential if a pupil is to be prevented from developing a warped ego and an abnormal personality. A teacher is not supposed to be a psychiatrist, nor should she embark upon treatment, but she should be able to recognize common escape patterns.[6]

▶ **Patterns toward Integration**

The goal of the teaching-guidance program has been stated in a very positive manner by a recent study [7] as: "helping the adolescent to a healthy personality that actively masters the environment, possesses unity, integration, and identity, and is able to perceive both self and world correctly." One of the positive ways in which the adolescent determines his identity is through reflections from significant figures around him. More and more of the responsible adults working with adolescents subscribe to the necessity of establishing examples of conduct and self-management which will at least offer solid standards against which a developing young person can test his own value systems, even though he may not accept the adult values *in toto* for himself. This method of determining a pattern of values shows the positive, constructive, rather than the escapist, use of identification. More will be said on this topic in a later chapter. When the person or group with whom the adolescent identifies himself can offer him models of integrated, realistic, sensitive and responsible behavior, the adolescent's concept of "what is an adult" is advanced.

The integration of a self-concept is the function of the living, healthy organism. The pressures of the environment are, however, so close that it is frequently necessary to help the adolescent to see that there is a long-run as well as a short-run goal and solution to any situation, and that the problem he finds so frustrating today may be something of which he will, himself, make constructive use at a later time. Characteristic of the positive development of the self is the ability to sustain a difficult situation for the sake of a potential goal—an ability that develops during adolescence toward its mature capacity. A teacher can help adolescents to see the forest, and not break their hearts over the trees. The boy who despairs wildly of his ambition to become a chemist because for some reason he simply cannot understand the whole subject of valence can be led to see that he is not really a "bad chemist" because of this failure to understand a segment of work and that he is suffering from a temporary block, the nature of which can be determined. The teacher can thus help him to see through his present inadequacy to his potential ability and can prevent a deterioration in his image of himself. If he can see himself as a "striver," not as a "failure," and if he can simultaneously understand that

---

[6] See L. C. Miller, "Short Term Therapy with Adolescents," *American Journal of Orthopsychiatry*, 29:772–779, 1959.

[7] E. Landy and E. Scanlan, "The Relation Between School Guidance and Psychiatry for Adolescents," *American Journal of Orthopsychiatry*, 32:682–690, 1962.

he must work through his immediate difficulties to a solution before his more remote goals can be reached, his self-concept will be reinforced in a constructive manner. Even though he may in the end have to recognize that his remote goal is actually beyond him, the experience will have been useful in demonstrating methods of dealing with frustrations.

Another positive resource lies in opening up the possibilities for the adolescent to act creatively in a wide variety of situations in which he can attain immediate satisfactions and realizations of needs within socially constructive and allowable patterns. Given the opportunity to meet its progressively more complex needs to at least a minimal degree, the emerging self will usually evolve toward more creative goals. In terms of the emergence of the self, the adolescent is most emphatically growing, but in the direction of increased self-command, flexibility, expansibility, and creativity. The apathy with which the adolescent is often charged is quite likely to be replaced by activity toward self-realization, if the opportunity is presented. Some recent studies have developed interesting evidence that progress in the ability to deal with fluid, evocative situations and concepts is an attribute not only of the highly creative person, but of almost any person who is adequately stimulated.[8] It then becomes a reasonable responsibility of the adult world, including the teacher, to provide the adolescent with as rich a range of experiences and creative solutions as may be possible, in order that he may grow in realization of his self and may progress toward ever higher goals.

▶ **Summary**

The sense of identity grows, develops, changes as an individual passes from one age level to another. It responds to basic needs, and in turn may itself supply both motivations and goals. It integrates drives and responses into patterns that are satisfactory for its growth. When it is threatened, it protects itself from danger by patterns of escape that will at least "hold the line" until something better can be substituted. There are many possible escape patterns, but they vary a good deal in their nature, their usefulness, and their capacity to eventuate in normal adjustments. Almost everyone uses nearly every possible pattern at one time or another, but most people settle upon two or three that are relatively undamaging to the ego, acceptable to society, and consonant with their own goals. Those who do not find a healthy form of escape find an unhealthy one and may destroy themselves in consequence. A teacher is in a position to note the escape patterns used by her pupils. If she can learn to recognize them, her understanding of adolescent problems will grow and her instructional procedures will profit

---

[8] S. Kasper, "Measurement of Adjustment in Adolescence," *Psychological Monographs,* Vol. 76, No. 6, Whole Number 525, 1962.

accordingly. The argument for strong standards of personal responsibility and social constructiveness is in no way contradictory to the encouragement of exploration and imagination; given these, the adolescent can frequently make remarkable and usually satisfactory adjustments of his needs to the demands of his society and can attain a sense of identity within that society without the excessive use of escape mechanisms.

References for Further Reading

BOOKS

Other Texts

Baller and Charles, *The Psychology of Human Growth and Development* (pp. 382–400).

Horrocks, *Behavior and Development* (pp. 488–496).

McCandless, *Children and Adolescents* (Chap. 6 or 10).

Wattenberg, *The Adolescent Years* (Chap. 17 or 18).

Other Books and Monographs

Baller, *Readings in the Psychology of Human Growth and Development* (pp. 622–631).

Hoch, P. H., and J. Zubin, *Psychopathology of Childhood* (New York: Grune and Stratton, 1955), 303 pp. (pp. 207–284).

Moustakas, C. E., *Self-Exploration in Personal Growth* (New York: Harper & Row, Publishers, 1956), 284 pp. (Chap. 2 or 3).

Opler, M. K., ed., *Culture and Mental Health* (New York: The Macmillan Company, 1959), 563 pp. (pp. 1–20 or 501–516).

Seidman, *The Adolescent: A Book of Readings,* rev. ed. (Nos. 33, 53, or 59).

Stacey, C. L., and M. F. DeMartino, eds., *Understanding Human Motivation* (Howard Allen, 1958), 507 pp. (any 20 pages in Chap. 3 or 5).

ARTICLES

Block, J., and B. Martin, "Predicting the Behavior of Children under Frustration," *Journal of Abnormal and Social Psychology,* 51:281–285, 1955.

Chodorkoff, B., "Self-Perception, Perceptual Defense, and Adjustment," *Journal of Abnormal and Social Psychology,* 49:508–512, 1954.

Engel, M., "The Stability of the Self-Concept in Adolescence," *Journal of Abnormal and Social Psychology,* 58:211–215, 1959.

Hanlon, T. E., P. R. Hofstaetter, and J. P. O'Connor, "Congruence of Self and Ideal Self in Relation to Personality Adjustment," *Journal of Consulting Psychology,* 18:215–218, 1954.

Kris, E., "Neutralization and Sublimation," *Psychoanalytic Study of the Child,* 10:30–46, 1955.

Leighton, A. H., "Psychiatric Disorder and Social Environment," *Psychiatry*, 18:367–383, 1955.

Nixon, R. E., "An Approach to the Dynamics of Growth in Adolescence," *Psychiatry*, 24:18–31, 1961.

Rube, P., "The Inner World of Adolescence," *American Journal of Psychotherapy*, 9:673–691, 1955.

Washburn, W. C., "Patterns of Self-Conceptualization in High School and College Students," *Journal of Educational Psychology*, 52:123–131, 1961.

Zimmer, H., "The Roles of Conflict and Internalized Demands in Projection," *Journal of Abnormal and Social Psychology*, 50:188–192, 1955.

Suggested Research Problems [9]

1. A longitudinal study of pupils' self-concepts, beginning in grade 7 and continuing through grade 12, by means of periodic assignments in whatever class seems most suitable. With perhaps two such assignments each year, it should be possible to trace developmental change in the entire group and in individual students.

2. One might select the self-estimates of 50 or 60 boys who have dropped out of school and pair them with the expressed self-concepts of boys who remained. After two years or more, there should be a follow-up study, to see what changes had taken place in the two groups.

3. Teachers would find helpful a well-chosen set of illustrations describing typical incidents in school, in which typical adolescents sought typical escapes from their problems.

---

[9] See note, p. 11.

Chapter 14 | **Personality**

Since a teacher is in some measure responsible for the development of her pupils as individuals, she should have an understanding of typical explorations in the field of personality. In order to develop an integrated and informed viewpoint of her own, she needs an introduction to at least a few theories of personality and an acquaintance with some of the commoner measuring instruments. Since one task of the modern teacher is to help her pupils to work toward their fullest self-realization, a brief consideration of theories of personality may contribute to building a frame of reference for her own observations and for her conduct of classroom activities. She may be called upon to administer tests of personality, or she may desire to use such measures for her own guidance. In any case, she cannot read today's educational literature without some background in both the theories and the measurement of personality. The present chapter is intended to provide such an orientation.

For the purposes of this book, personality will be regarded as a fairly stable configuration of tendencies—acquired or inherited—around which the individual attempts to integrate his experiences and from which his behavior emerges. It seems probable that there is a very early establishment of the central core of traits in each individual. It is, however, clear that personality changes more or less throughout the life span as a result of the environmental pressures to which it is subjected. External expressions at least, and quite possibly the central traits also, are affected by the total life experience of the individual. These external expressions, or behavior, are the only directly observable facts; the theories of the over-all structure of personality are always based upon inferences, and even these are inevitably interpreted through the personality of the observer. It is, however, possible to recognize that each individual is a consistent and unique person, not quite like anyone else, whatever problems of cause, origin, or modification may still remain for exploration.

All members of a society constantly exert pressures upon each other and constantly adapt themselves to such pressures. The extent to which these everyday stresses can cause personality to alter, or the stage in development at which alteration becomes difficult if not impossible, or the exact circumstances under which modification takes place are all questions that have not yet been answered. There is certainly some evidence that not even the central core becomes established as early as was once thought. For example, during and after World War II when many thousands of children lived in concentration camps, there was a remarkable alteration in personality in a great many cases. The deprivation of stimuli in these camps appears to have been damaging to the development of adequate personalities, especially among the younger children who had little memory of any other kind of life. Recent experimental attempts to explore the effects of drastically reduced stimuli on the functioning of the "normal" individual have taken place under such artificial conditions that it is difficult to draw any firm conclusions from them, but there seems to be support for the hypothesis, long indicated by studies on babies in low-stimuli environments, that stimuli, and even some stress, are necessary to human personality at almost any developmental stage. The ongoing, emergent nature of personality would appear to be more consistent with the findings and theoretical bases of recent study than are the more rigid concepts of many earlier theories.

▶ Theories of Personality

In order to evaluate the various problems involving human personality that are met by every teacher, it is desirable that the student should become aware of at least some of the many viewpoints from which material relating to the nature, structure, and development of personality may be considered. All the approaches, as summarized by a later table, share one characteristic: each reflects the background, particular studies in the field, and personality of the theorist who organized each interpretation. The resulting diversity provides a wide variety of ideas and provocative glimpses into both methods and assumptions. Many of the theories are quite complex. The presentation in this chapter will err on the side of simplicity: its purpose is to present to the student a few brief sketches, on the basis of which he can select further reading along any line that seems exciting to him.[1] No effort will be made to present every theory that has appeared; the sketches are restricted to a few that are representative of certain distinctive contributions to the present body of thought.

Since a good deal of the material that one reads has been influenced by the psychoanalytic point of view, it seems reasonable to start with its originator, Freud, and the students of Freud who modified, expanded, and developed the fundamental concepts.

Freud's theory has three basic concepts. First, that the important elements of personality, which form the core, are fixed during the first two or three years of a person's life. The experiences themselves are "forgotten," but

---

[1] See especially, M. I. Stein, *Contemporary Psychotherapies* (New York: Free Press, 1961), 386 pp.; and C. Buhler, *Values in Psychotherapy* (New York: Free Press, 1962), 251 pp.

the reactions made to them remain and become the fundamental elements in the developing personality. His earlier work stressed the importance of the libidinal, or sexual aspect of the personality, but in his later work he shifted his emphasis to aggression as a main determinant of personality. It is flatly impossible to present a reasonably accurate explanation of the enormously complex implications of his classic formulation of the id, the ego, and the superego as the basic components of the personality without doing violence to the subtle and fruitful developments which have flowed from these hypotheses in subsequent work. While there is little objective evidence for this structure, and while much objection is quite reasonably made to the oversimplification of these concepts into a rigid division of the self into warring parts, it should be pointed out that Freud himself came to modify these into a continuous and flexible system. The basic problems of the instinctual, impulsive id, of the emergent ego as an adaptive pattern with which reality is first met, and of the superego as the conscious, socially-absorbent and culturally-influenced controller of the personality, remain essentially controversial constructs. Naturally, the theory rests upon a host of observations by Freud himself in the course of his extensive experience with neurotic and psychotic patients; but he was an observer, not an experimentalist. His theory may be, therefore, either the enlightening insight that comes to the expert or a mistaken concept. At the present time, no one can state definitely which it is. However, his work is so fundamental to subsequent theoretical developments, that the student would do well to read some of Freud's original works and some of the interpretations which discuss implications of his work.[2]

Jung was a student of Freud's but he soon began to differ on many points from his teacher. He insisted especially upon the importance of purpose and aim in modifying and channelizing personality. He believed that each person, with psychic energy—often called the libido—as a driving force, moves constantly toward a more "complete" form of development, by stages that are expressed in terms of goals, from mere survival in infancy through the dominance of sexual expression in adolescence to the level of cultural, philosophical, and spiritual goals in maturity. The predetermined pattern is assumed to unfold in regular stages, but with individual variations in the steadiness and intensity with which each phase is developed. When an individual has achieved his own development, he integrates all the elements by sublimating the discharge of psychic energy from the more primitive toward the more differentiated and culturally useful expressions, usually in a pattern either introverted—that is, inwardly focused—or extroverted—that is, socially focused. Jung also contributed the idea of the "complex," the existence of certain constellations of attitude and reaction. This term has come into everyday usage. His word-association tests, designed to measure a

---

[2] For example, C. Thompson, *Psychoanalysis: Evolution and Development* (New York: Grove Press, 1957), 251 pp.

person's emotional reactions to key words and ideas, have become standard procedure, especially in the investigation of aberrant attitudes. He has also made extensive use of anthropological materials in explaining all phases in the development of personality.

Another follower of Freud is H. A. Murray.[3] His emphasis has been upon the biological components of personality and on the enormous complexity of the individual as a functioning organism. Unfortunately for the reader, he has seen fit to invent a vocabulary that is even more complex than his theories. It is difficult to condense the almost symphonic sweep of his theoretical position into the layman's vocabulary, and the following account necessarily omits many of the finer points. The interested student would do well to read some of his original work for the special poetic quality of his writing.

In contrast to those who have studied specific fragments of behavior or special traits, by "personality," Murray means the *total person*. He considers that "every person is an emergent entity of and in a certain physical, social, and cultural milieu." Personality is a coordinating force in man's life. It endures throughout life, and it both transforms and is transformed by the developmental process. It exists as a day-to-day function of the individual but is seen by others only in its specific expressions. The resulting abstraction on the part of the observer as to the nature of the underlying personality may or may not conform to the pattern that actually exists in the individual being observed. Thus, to put the matter in capsule form, a man who listens politely to what everyone has to say but contributes little is often considered a pliable person with no mind of his own—a deduction based on observation—when to himself he is merely being well mannered and knows exactly what he thinks about the topics under discussion.

Murray uses the same concepts—the id, the ego, and the superego—in much the same meaning as Freud had used them, except that he credits the id with an additional function of organization and retention of the culturally acceptable as well as the primitive impulses. Since the individual's basic needs and emotions are expressed in both negative and positive terms, the ego is enabled to act as a scheduler of the positive elements of the id and a suppressor of the inacceptable ones. The superego then assumes the character of a culturally implanted but highly internalized control system which acts to interpret and impose the standards that the individual gradually learns from outside authority—parents, teachers, peers, and so on. To these three entities Murray adds an ego-ideal to which he gives great importance, as the individual's picture of the role he wishes to fill both in his internal life and in his relationship to his environment. This role may be allied with or opposed to

---

[3] H. A. Murray and C. Kluckhohn, *Personality in Nature and Culture* (New York: Alfred A. Knopf, Inc., 1953), p. 6.

the superego. Since it obviously undergoes many changes as the individual grows from babyhood to adulthood, its inclusion serves to strengthen Murray's emphasis upon the capacity, indeed the necessity, of change and development in the personality well past the childhood freezing point proposed by more orthodox psychoanalysts.

As the personality develops in response to environmental pressures, it advances toward its goals, it reduces conflict, and it coordinates motivations with goals, thus leading to a unique directionality in each individual. From this concept Murray develops detailed lists of the determinants of goal seeking, breaking them down into twenty specific needs. Some needs find their expression mainly in the inner satisfaction of the individual, but most of them involve interaction with the environment. Throughout his work Murray makes the relationship of need to goal paramount. Although he follows the general Freudian pattern of putting much weight upon the satisfactions or deprivations of infancy and early childhood, he elaborates considerably upon them, particularly in classifying the recognizable effects of factors in later life.

The factor-theorists—Cattell especially—have developed a psychometric approach to the problems of personality. They feel that test scores which measure specific abilities or interests can yield comprehensive information about human personality, provided one applies the tests to a large enough range of human beings. According to this approach, the structural elements of personality are traits, which are often divided into "source" and "surface" traits, the former being constitutional and the latter being produced by environment. These traits are derived from tests rather than from theoretical considerations and are arrived at by consideration of life records, self-ratings, and test results, plus statistical analysis. Certain traits appear to be reliably present in all individuals and tend to occur more often than not in clusters. This purely empirical approach has its advantages in that it does not rest wholly upon anyone's preconception of what personality consists of, but it also has its limitations. It probably measures chiefly surface traits, although tests might be constructed that would measure source traits as well, and it is inevitably limited in scope to its own findings. If the tests actually measure *all* possible human traits, the statistical handling of the results might be expected to make a real contribution to the theory of personality, but to date the tests probably do not measure more than a few possible components—and no amount of jumping through statistical hoops will make a trait appear unless it was measured by the test in the first place. Moreover, this approach suffers from the difficulty that is inherent in all analyses: it is often easier to take something to pieces than to put it back together again. It remains to be seen to what extent test results can be synthesized to give a coherent picture of the totality of human personality.

One of the strongest voices raised at present for consideration of the uniqueness of the individual personality is that of Gordon Allport. He is suspicious of any values to be obtained by transferring the statistical and objective techniques from other scientific fields directly to investigation of human complexity, especially at present, since the factors are too dimly understood to be suitable for rigid analysis. He swings to the other extreme of possible approaches and insists upon the special, richly-proliferating, and essentially inseparable characteristics of each individual personality. He is interested primarily in function and change,[4] and he does not believe that there is a constant self or ego that endures from birth to death. He is a strong champion of the normal human personality as a consciously developing, goal-oriented, insightful individuality which passes through a number of recognizable but not rigidly fixed stages. This point of view provides a good balance for other types of approach that are focused either upon abnormal personalities or upon interpretation of statistical results.

In order to complete this brief survey of current theories, three other writers on personality have been selected. These writers differ widely among themselves in many facets of their basic concepts, in their method of approach, and in their interpretations. They are Kurt Goldstein, Eric Fromm, and A. H. Maslow. Each contrasts markedly with the other two.

Goldstein, a neuropsychiatrist, inclines strongly to emphasize bodily structure and physical maturing as the basic elements in personality. According to his organismic theory, the normal organism realizes itself as an interrelated, initially organized combination of physical and psychological forces working together to produce personality. In the process, the personality is involved with the environment, since it steadily tends to adapt itself to its surroundings or to control the outside world to meet its own inner needs. To study the nature of this development, the organismic theorist concentrates intensively upon the individual. The figure-ground relationship is a basic concept, which proposes that there are "natural" figures embedded in the personality but flexible and adaptable to the ground in which they grow. As the whole personality develops, the inherent qualities of its personal pattern will emerge through a maturation process which is concomitant with the biological maturation taking place. However, if the environment presents problems too great for the natural pattern to overcome, other patterns of response may develop in defense. These are highly inconsistent with self-realization and may therefore prevent full, natural maturation. Such a theory does not seem to make sufficient provision for environmental effect or for the influence of cultural differences from one background to another, and it pays little attention to the learning processes.

At the other end of the scale is a group of psychologists and sociologists who are highly concerned with the effects of environment upon human per-

---

[4] G. W. Allport, *Becoming* (New Haven, Conn.: Yale University Press, reissue 1960), 105 pp.

sonality. Most of these theorists accept a basically psychoanalytic viewpoint as to the construction and dynamics of personality, but each one has added or modified the central theme in terms of his own view of the interrelationship of heredity and environment.

The environmentalist studies personality by tracing the development of individuals throughout their entire life span, to observe the growth of the given biological potentials into the mature personality. The personality is presumed to start with a few inherited elements but to grow mainly through its environmental contacts. Eric Fromm is a good representative of this school of thought. He assumes that *only* through social contacts can a human being satisfy his basic needs. He sees the creative possibilities of the individual as inseparable from those of his fellow men, and relatedness as the essential quality of human needs, because men do exist in societies and cannot realize their possibilities or their identities except as their culture permits these developments. Variations in culture therefore automatically produce variations in personality and also condition the acceptance of personality.

The interest in motivational psychology has also produced a theory of personality. An example of this approach [5] is that of A. H. Maslow, who sees the structure of human personality as evolving from the following pattern of needs:

> Need for physiological continuance of life
> Need for safety
> Need for belongingness and love
> Need for esteem
> Need for self-actualization
> Need for knowledge and understanding
> Need to experience aesthetic pleasure

Maslow feels that these needs emerge as the individual develops in response to life situations, and that any one of them may serve as a channel for another. These needs emerge roughly in succession, as prior needs are basically satisfied. From individual to individual and from time to time there is great variation in the relative importance of the needs and in the degree to which the person is able to fulfill them, or to reach self-realization. Also, the culture may place more or less emphasis on certain needs, and the individual may not even be aware of some of them, as such, although he may unconsciously act because of them.

There are, thus, many theories and many approaches, all differing at least in some respects from each other. Probably no theorist denies the presence of some inherited features in the pattern of personality, and presumably

---

[5] A. H. Maslow, *Motivation and Personality* (New York: Harper & Row, Publishers, 1954), 409 pp.

none disregards environmental forces altogether. The differences consist partly in the relative weight given the various possible components, partly in the extent to which the patterns are considered as resulting mainly from internal growth or from external pressures, and partly in the degree of purposefulness assumed to be inherent in the developing personality.

The main purpose of the above presentation has been to provide a background for a better understanding of the widely used tests of personality that will shortly be described. Table 14–1 is included as a summary of the foregoing discussion. In it the various theorists are rated as to a number of points

Table 14–1: COMPONENTS OF VARIOUS THEORIES OF PERSONALITY

	Heredity	Early Developmental Experiences	Organismic Emphasis	Unconscious Determinants	Psychological Environment	Field Emphasis	Learning Process	Group Membership Determinants	Continuity of Development	Purpose	Personality Structure	Self Concept	Uniqueness
Freud	H	H		H	H	L	L	L	H	H	H		
Jung	H		H	H		L	L	L	L	H	H		
Murray		H	H	H	H	H	L		H	H	H		
Lewin	L	L	L	L	H	H		H	L	H			H
Cattell	H		L		L	L	H				H	H	
Allport		L	H	L		L		L	L	H	H	H	H
Goldstein		L	H	L	H			L	L	H	L	H	L
Fromm								H		H			
Maslow *	L	H	H		H			H	H	H	L		

H—high (emphasized)   L—low (unemphasized)

* The ratings on Maslow are the writers' own.

SOURCE: Reprinted with permission from C. S. Hall and G. Lindzey, *Theories of Personality* (New York: John Wiley and Sons, Inc., 1957), 572 pp., p. 546.

about their theories of personality. It may be seen that there is great variation. What one stresses, another may ignore. This great diversity arises to some extent from the differences in the personalities and life experiences of the theorists. A clinician does not see the same things in human conduct that a neurologist sees, nor the same things that are obvious to a statistician; a social scientist has a still different approach. Only with the continuing development of techniques, attitudes of scientific approach, and the most scrupulous care in validation with various nonrestricted groups will clearer theoretical structures emerge. Meanwhile, from the ferment of multiple viewpoints and explorations comes the stimulation for further hypotheses. The individual teacher may study these current theories with a view to a consistent but flexible approach to the day-to-day problems presented in the classroom, and the enrichment of a personal focus on the nature of the human personality.[6]

▶ **Tests of Personality**

Various people have constructed tests of one kind and another for the purpose of measuring at least a few facets of personality. Some theorists have made tests in order to get further light on their assumptions; in other cases, a psychologist who was more or less influenced by a given school of thought has constructed a test that in his opinion might eventuate in something interesting. Since tests of personality are new, comparatively speaking, none of them is as yet too well authenticated, although all are of interest and all give some kind of information about personality.[7] The main difficulty in their use is that the score has to be interpreted; as it stands, it often means nothing. A copy of a given pupil's tests may be sent to five "experts" for interpretation, with the resulting assembly of five more or less divergent opinions. The source of the variation is the indirectness of the measurement. One cannot measure personality directly, as a doctor determines blood pressure or bodily temperature, but indirectly, as a doctor observes symptoms and diagnoses disease. Any two doctors will agree, within the narrow limits of error in making the measurement, on what a patient's blood pressure is on a given day because the measurement is direct and objective, but they may not agree in the least upon what disease he has, because a diagnosis is a subjective inference. So also is a diagnosis of personality.

Two warnings about tests of personality should perhaps be given. First, some of them were devised for the express purpose of identifying those individuals who are suffering from disturbances of personality. The items were therefore selected as covering the common neurotic or psychotic symptoms. As a result, one cannot make a "normal" score on these tests because the items were not selected to reflect normality. By no means all tests are of this type, but the user should be forewarned against uncritical use of any test without reference to the basis upon which its items were selected. Second, the teacher should never attempt to interpret by herself the scores on tests of personality. It cannot be overemphasized that the administration of such tests as will shortly be described, and most particularly their application to the problems

---

[6] The student who is interested in reading further might find it valuable to look into the works of Alfred Adler, Gardiner Murphy, W. H. Sheldeon, Harry S. Sullivan, Karen Horney, Carl Rogers, H. Eyesenck, or D. O. Hebb.

[7] A comprehensive discussion of the bases, technical and administrational problems, and availability of psychological tests (including addresses of test publishers) may be found in O. K. Buros, *Tests in Print* (Gryphon Press, 1961), 479 pp. The Introduction, pp. v–xx, should be of particular value to the teacher. Current developments in the testing field may be followed in the latest edition available of *Mental Measurement Yearbook* (Gryphon Press) (The 5th Edition was published in 1959), and in the periodical *Educational and Psychological Measurements.*

of individuals, is the task of a highly qualified and trained person. It is very easy to misinterpret test scores as giving more solid evidence than they do. If no experienced person is to be found, the teacher would do better to approach problems by some means other than testing.

1. Tests Involving Self-report   Attempts to measure specific aspects of personality began about fifty years ago. The tests are of numerous types, each of which has its merits and its shortcomings. The earliest forms consisted of questionnaires, inventories, and life histories. In all three of these the individual gives what information he can spontaneously produce about himself, usually in answer to specific questions. The most obvious shortcoming of this approach is that it rests upon the test-taker's unsupported, subjective report.

For example, a young man says—either orally or in answer to a written question—that he has never had a girl friend. There is no easy way of checking this statement. He may have different standards from other people's as to when a feminine acquaintance should be classified as a girl friend, he may have forgotten some experiences, or he may be lying, intentionally or unintentionally. Moreover, a person obviously cannot tell what he does not know. In many instances his own explanations of his motives may not be correct because his true motives are unconscious. If he has a serious area of conflict, for example, he probably cannot consciously report it without therapeutic assistance. In short, any form of direct verbal or written report has all the disadvantages of any subjective mode of inquiry. It does, nevertheless, often contribute to an understanding of an individual's self-concept—that is, his own idea of what kind of person he is.

The sample items shown below were taken from the Minnesota Multiphasic Personality Inventory or the Allport Ascendancy-Submission Scale: [8]

      2. Is it hard for you to be calm when things go wrong?
     22. Are people often unfair to you?
     34. Do you feel that you are punished for too many little things?
     54. Are you usually invited to school and neighborhood parties?
     67. Have you often felt that older people had it in for you?
     88. Do you usually find it hard to go to sleep?
    116. Do you find it easy to make new friends?
    141. Do your folks seem to feel that you are interested in the wrong things?
    156. Are some of your teachers so strict that it makes schoolwork too hard?
    179. Do you like most of the boys and girls in your neighborhood?

As may be seen, the test covers a wide range of topics. The Minnesota Test is so arranged that its scores fall into patterns which reflect presumed basic

---

[8] Any teacher who is interested in the use of questionnaires should examine also the High School Personality Questionnaire, a copy of which may be obtained from the Institute for Personality and Ability Testing, Champaign, Illinois.

groupings of personal traits. It is used primarily to indicate those students who deviate from the normal. The patterns are therefore patterns of abnormal personalities—the paranoid, the schizophrenic, the depressed, or the hysteric. Like all inventories, it is intended for use in surveying and sifting entire groups. That it has some diagnostic quality as well is an added attraction.[9]

Questionnaires and inventories are not substitutes for personal interviews but are of value as preparatory steps toward interviews. They serve also to call attention to those pupils who are most in need of help.

2. Rating Scales A second type of personality test consists of measures that are somewhat more objective than the inventory or questionnaire. The earliest form, the rating scale, supplements an individual's opinion of himself by the ratings made by other people about him. The rating scale is, however, a somewhat unreliable instrument, even under the best of circumstances, perhaps because one person's opinion of another is not notably accurate.

In order to demonstrate the use of such scales, one of the writers has rated a young acquaintance whom she has known for several years and has had adequate chances to observe. The ratings appear in Figure 14–1. This girl has a number of problems. She is shy, impatient, and careless, quick tempered and a little thoughtless. She also does not seem to have the usual gaiety of youth. One infers that sometimes she has outbursts of boastfulness, which may be merely overcompensations for her shyness. She has many positive qualities and is intelligent enough to control her faults, if she understands what they are. Probably a counselor could do a great deal to improve this girl's social adjustment.

3. Projective Techniques Some of the more recent tests are of the so-called projective type.[10] They merit this name because the individual taking the test unconsciously reads into the materials his own life experiences and attitudes. That is, he projects himself. The theory underlying such tests is that the ego habitually thrusts onto the external world its own unconscious wishes; if these were ever to become conscious, they might be most painful, so they are attached to something or someone outside the self. If, then, a pupil is presented with a set of materials that give him a chance to project his attitudes, he will follow his customary pattern of response and do

---

[9] See, for example, R. J. Hampton, "The MMPI as a Psychometric Tool for Diagnosis of Personality Disorders among College Students," *Journal of Social Psychology,* 26:99–108, 1947; M. S. Gould, "Teacher Prognosis Scale for the MMPI," *Journal of Educational Research,* 49:1–12, 1955.

[10] For a comprehensive survey of this type of testing, and details of many more tests than can be illustrated in this text, the student is referred to the latest edition of H. M. Anderson and G. L. Anderson, *An Introduction to Projective Techniques* (Englewood Cliffs, N.J.: Prentice Hall, Inc., 1954), 720 pp.

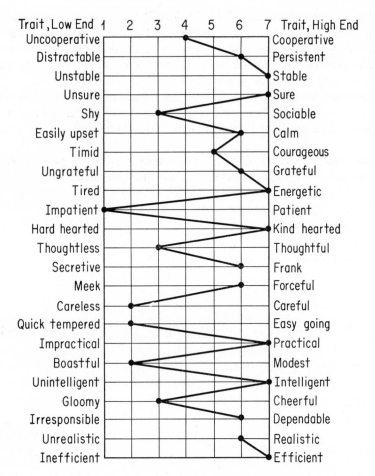

Fig. 14–1. Rating scale, showing one girl's profile

F. E. Fiedler, *Leader Attitudes and Group Effectiveness* (Urbana, Ill.: University of Illinois Press, 1958), 69 pp., p. 65. Used with the permission of the publisher.

so. For instance, if the examiner shows a child a picture of a woman crying— but with no clue in the scene as to why she is crying—and asks what the picture is about, the child has to project into his narrative his own reasons for crying or his own idea of other people's reasons. Whatever he says, he is going to reveal something about himself. Or, he may be presented with a series of puppets and asked to select a family from them. His selections and his rejections, the reasons he gives for either, and his arrangement of his puppets are all significant because he is almost certain to project into his selection his feelings toward his own family. If, for example, a child selects a family of puppets without any mother, especially if he has one himself, this rejection of the motherlike puppet indubitably means something. It might, for example, indicate an unconscious conflict of so disturbing a nature that even the idea of a mother has been repressed. Further play may give some clue as to the underlying attitudes, but the significance must be interpreted with care by an expert in the use of the test concerned.

There are so many projective tests that only a few of the most widely used can be discussed. Those selected for the main consideration are the Sentence-Completion Test,[11] the Thematic-Apperception Test, and the Rorschach.

The sentence-completion form of projective test is by far the simplest to understand. It consists merely of such sentences as these:

1. I feel hurt when _____
2. I object strenuously to _____
3. I often make believe that _____
4. My father used to _____
5. I liked one teacher in high school because she _____
6. The people I dislike most are those who _____

Each introductory clause presents the student with a situation for which he must supply a conclusion, presumably by telling what he would do, or customarily does, in similar circumstances. No two people are likely to complete the sentences in the same way. Incomplete sentences of the types listed above require an individual to project his own personality into the finishing of the sentence.

Of all the projective techniques, the Thematic Apperception Test [12] and the Rorschach are the best known and most widely used. Both have been discussed in hundreds of articles in professional journals. The TAT—as the Thematic Apperception Test is usually called—consists of a series of pictures, each of which shows a scene that might have a number of explanations. The individual who takes the test is asked to explain the picture and to give an imaginary reconstruction of what went before and what followed. Although a good deal of emotion is portrayed in each picture, it is not clear just what the excitement is all about. The subject must therefore read into the pictures some fantasies or interpretations of his own. The raw material for a pupil's story comes from his own experiences and is colored by his own needs. The stories are scored for many factors in the dynamics of personality, the empha-

---

[11] For a good report of such a test, see J. B. Rotter, J. E. Rafferty, and E. Schachtitz, "Validation of the Rotter Incomplete Sentences Blank for College Screening," *Journal of Consulting Psychology,* 13:348–356, 1949.

[12] For a description of this test and the methods of scoring it, see the following articles: B. Aron, *A Manual for the Analysis of the TAT: A Method and Technique for Personality Research* (Berkeley, Calif.: Willis E. Berg, 1949), 163 pp.; L. J. Lindzay and S. H. Hennemann, "Thematic Apperception Test: Individual and Group Administration," *Journal of Personality,* 24: 34–44, 1955.

sis being largely dependent upon the purpose for which the test is given, and the interpretation varying with both the context and the orientation of the interpreter. Its intent is not to establish "norms," or "good" solutions but to evoke responses which may give indications of the personal problems and thought processes of an individual in a specific context. The nature of the outcome is also examined, since it is a product of needs and pressures, and is rated as a successful or an unsuccessful solution.[13]

One of the most interesting and valuable studies using the TAT involved the administration of 42 cards to 20 adolescent boys and 20 adolescent girls.[14] One picture from this series is reproduced in Figure 14–2. These adolescents told a total of 1680 stories. The investigator collected a complete life history of each pupil, plus an autobiography written by the pupil himself, ratings from teachers, results from questionnaires concerning such matters as likes and dislikes, or relations to family and age-mates, a record of each pupil's dreams, and several observational samples of behavior. The investigator thus had a great deal of information about each adolescent, to which he could relate the stories stimulated by the pictures.

The first point about the results has to do with the themes of the stories. These are of two types, environmental and psychological. Usually, a story had more than one theme; the 1680 stories produced a grand total of 4804 environmental and 5499 psychological themes. Both numbers include repetitions. The themes that made up 88 and 87 percent, respectively, of the two types are listed in Table 14–2. The first three environmental themes equaled 59 percent of the total. By far the commonest psychological theme was aggression. There was no adolescent among the 40 studied who did not have some aggressive themes in his or her stories. The chief differences between the rank order of environmental themes for boys and girls was that the former told relatively more stories about punishment, accidents, and strangeness, while the latter told relatively more about separation or rejection, school, and appearance. In psychological themes, the boys show more motifs reflecting eroticism, excitement, repentance, ambition, and escape than the girls, but fewer motifs concerning altruism, depression, anxiety, thinking, joy, and concealment. The escape theme occurs so rarely among girls that it is not among the first thirteen; its place is taken by the theme of guilt over real or imagined acts of disobedience, deceit, or other wrongdoing.

The individual stories told by the boys and girls are interesting and revealing. The two quoted below illustrate different themes and show what the raw material as produced by adolescents looks like.

---

[13] For case histories and discussion of the Thematic Apperception Test, see W. E. Henry, *The Analysis of Fantasy* (New York: John Wiley and Sons, Inc., 1956), 305 pp. A history of particular interest to the student might be chosen for further class discussion.

[14] P. M. Symonds, *Adolescent Fantasy: An Investigation of the Picture-study Method of Personality Study* (New York: Columbia University Press, 1949), 397 pp.

Fig. 14–2. Picture for the thematic apperception test

From P. M. Symonds, *Adolescent Fantasy: An Investigation of the Picture-Study Method of Personality Study* (New York: Columbia University Press, 1949), No. 17. Used with the permission of the publisher.

Table 14–2: THEMES

| *Environmental* | | | | | *Psychological* | | | | |
| | *Number* | *Per- cent* | *Rank Order* | | | *Number* | *Per- cent* | *Rank Order* | |
			Boys	Girls				Boys	Girls
Family relation- ships	1595	33	1	1	Aggression	1562	28	1	1
Economic condi- tions	632	13	3	2	Eroticism	459	8	2	4
					Altruism	401	7	5	2
Punishment	614	13	2	5	Depression	349	6	6	5
Separation or rejection	397	8	5	3	Excitement	312	6	3	10
Accident or illness	297	6	4	6	Anxiety	310	6	8	3
School	251	5	6	4	Repentance	305	6	4	9
Peer social life	130	3	8	7	Ambition	268	5	7	8
Strangeness	125	3	7	10	Thinking, decision	248	5	9	6
Place of residence	98	2	9	9	Joy, happiness	193	4	11	7
Appearance	75	2	—	8	Escape	136	2	10	—
					Concealment	119	2	13	11
					Goodness	112	2	12	12
Total	4214	88	—	—	Total	4774	87	—	—
All Others	590	12	—	—	All Others	725	13	—	—
Grand Total	4804	100	—	—	Grand Total	5499	100	—	—

SOURCE: P. M. Symonds, *Adolescent Fantasy* (New York: Columbia University Press, 1949), pp. 80–81.

Story A (Aggression) [15] This boy's father had died twenty years ago, when he was one. The boy is now 21. Father left insurance. Boy got a car. Decided to show it to mother. Drove it 80 miles per hour. Sped along. Saw old woman coming out on street. Hit her. Drove home. Screamed "Mother, Mother." Realized it was his own mother. Rushed back to street of accident. She was dying and said she hoped he wouldn't be so mean after this. She died. He went to jail and got life imprisonment.   (Harold, age 13; story 22)

Story B (Depression) Appears as if woman receiving letter is expecting bad news. Look in face doesn't seem to indicate any enthusiasm in receiving letter. Seems as if she's in a different world, the look in her eyes. Seems her taking letter was just a mechanical motion. Woman is very ordinary looking and looks more like secretary than housewife. Perhaps her boy friend has written her that due to financial conditions and the tie-up in work they cannot be married for at least a year. She had an inkling this would happen because of his actions in recent weeks. She feels, perhaps, he doesn't love her any more and is merely using that as an excuse to break off. I don't feel they ever will get married (I am awfully pessimistic). Girl will never forget him. (Albert, age 17; story 1)

[15] These excerpts are from P. M. Symonds, *Adolescent Fantasy* (New York: Columbia University Press, 1949), pp. 85 and 84.

It will probably have been noted that these stories indicate the existence of conflicts, almost inevitably conflicts that are unsolved. In general, if an individual works out a conflict in reality its nature is revealed by his behavior. Thus a delinquent boy often acts out his conflicts, and the observer can deduce a good deal about them from the boy's symptoms. If, however, an individual inhibits the outward expression of his conflicts, he works them out in fantasy, either openly or in disguised forms. If the underlying drives are acceptable to both the child and society, the expression is usually open; but if they are unacceptable, they will be expressed through symbols and through displacement.

Some recent work has been done with the TAT to modify it for use with cultures other than that of the United States, upon which its interpretation has been mostly based. Obviously the interpretation which an individual puts upon a pictured scene involves expectations that have been developed by his cultural context. Thus the physical size and position of the woman in Figure 14–3, from the regular TAT series, would probably be interpreted very differently by a young person with the social expectations of an oriental society than by one of a Western society, without the interpretation giving much information concerning the individual himself. Therefore, the pictures should be focused on the particular milieu in which they are to be used. An example of the kind of adjustments suitable to a particular culture is given in Figure 14–3. Bringing the pictures into the pattern of cultural expectations for specific groups extends their usefulness, although it does complicate even further the problems of interpretation. This expectation-awareness, however, is an important development in the designing of personality tests.

No other projective technique is as well known or as widely used as the Rorschach.[16] A mere list of the existing references dealing with it would fill an entire book. It consists of a series of cards on each of which there is an irregularly shaped blotch of ink. Five are in gray and black only, two have some red spots, and the last three have many colors. The person taking the tests is merely asked, "What might this be?" He then reads his own interpretation into the blot by telling what he thinks it is. The scorer notes not only the total responses, but also the number of associations given, their quality, type, and originality, the lack or the profusion of detail, reaction to the appearance of color, and so on. The person taking the test perceives in the meaningless ink blots only what his experiences have conditioned him to see, just as he

---

[16] For good and not too technical discussions, see S. J. Beck, *Rorschach's Test,* Vol. I, *Basic Processes,* 2d ed., rev., 1949, 227 pp., and Vol. II, *A Variety of Personality Pictures,* 1945 (New York: Grune & Stratton, Inc.), 402 pp.; M. R. Harrower-Erikson and M. E. Steiner, *Large Scale Rorschach Technique,* 2d ed. (Springfield, Ill.: Charles C Thomas, Publisher, 1951), 353 pp.; H. E. Esenbach and E. F. Borghaia, "Testing Behavior Hypotheses with the Rorschach," *Journal of Consulting Psychology,* 19:267–273, 1955; E. Crumpton, "The Influence of Color on the Rorschach," *Journal of Projective Techniques,* 20:150–158, 1956.

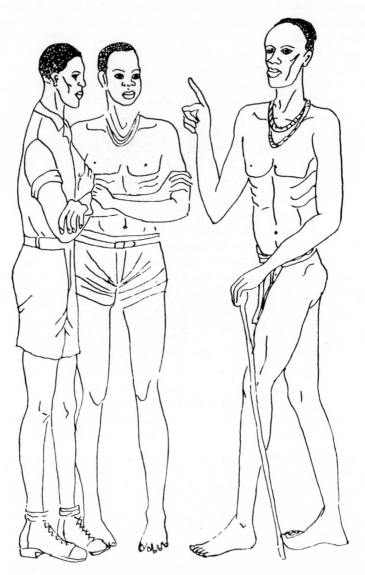

Fig. 14–3. Picture for thematic apperception test for Southwest African natives
Used by permission of Boris Iflund and Ella Marie K. Loeb.

bases the story he invents for each picture in the TAT test upon his personal experiences, emotions, and reactions. In the latter case, however, he has some hint of meaning from the picture, whereas in the former he must supply all the meaning himself.

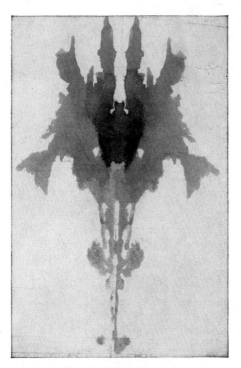

Fig. 14–4. Ink blot test

The ink blot in Figure 14–4 was not taken from any test but does show some of the features typical of the Rorschach, such as symmetry, differences in shading, and lack of any deliberately imposed content. This blot was shown to an 11-year-old boy and a 40-year-old woman; although the "test" was not given with the carefully controlled procedure of actual testing, the answers illustrate what sort of responses one gets from this type of measurement.

Boy, age 11: It's a dog's head with a dark nose in the middle, or a whole bunch of flowers; [turning paper around] there's an oil well spouting, in the top part, or it could be a giraffe in the jungle; [side turn] there are two little birds, each in a nest, or, if you think you're looking down on it from the top, it could be two geese in flight. Just that very dark place in the middle looks like the silhouette of a kitten's head and shoulders.

Woman, age 40; I don't know, it's sort of messy. I guess an animal of some sort. Maybe a real fancy hat with a long ribbon. Looks silly to me.

In spite of the casual administration of this item, the general pattern of production varies in somewhat the same way as in the real Rorschach, with great differences in the number of responses. The boy responded freely to both large and small areas, turned the card about a good deal, and showed a rather special spatial sense in his reference to the geese in flight—an idea possibly derived from children's moving pictures of nature. The woman showed much constraint and some resistance; probably she saw more than she said. Her production is small in amount and lacking in detail, possibly a reflection of her limited education and background as well as of her personality. The scoring of a properly administered Rorschach is far too complex to be explained here, and the interpretation—although there is some standardization—remains more of an art than a science. In the hands of a skillful tester, however, the Rorschach can give fairly consistent and valuable information as to the structure of personality, especially in its unconscious elements.

There are, thus, as many different approaches to the measurement of personality as there are theories.[17] Presumably each type of test measures something about the complex of traits usually thought of as personality, but thus far no single test gives a comprehensive picture. Several of them do result in profiles that suggest certain neurotic or psychotic structuring of personality. It will be noted that each kind of test contributes some element that the others do not. A comprehensive series of questions honestly answered may indicate what the test-taker thinks of himself; any form of rating scale may add pertinent information as to what other people think of him; a projective technique will give him a chance to reveal the things that are disturbing him and to some extent the structure of his personality. All three kinds thus have their uses.

Tests of all kinds but those of personality in particular are subject to influence by the cultural setting in which they are developed and administered, by the orientation and attitudes of the person giving the test, and by the already-made adaptations to his social milieu of the person taking the test. More attention has been given of late to this aspect of measurement than was the case in earlier work in the field of personality. The attitudes of the man who devised the theory upon which the test is based and those of

---

[17] For other methods of measurement see S. Rosenzweig, *Psychodiagnosis: An Introduction to Tests in Clinical Practice of Psychodiagnosis* (New York: Grune & Stratton, Inc., 1949), 380 pp.; R. P. Falls and R. R. Blake, "A Quantitative Analysis of the Picture Frustration Study," *Journal of Personality*, 16:320–325, 1948; J. Bernard, "The Rosenzweig Picture-Frustration Study: I and II," *Journal of Psychology*, 28:326–332, 333–344, 1949; M. Lowenfeld, "The Mosaic Test," *American Journal of Orthopsychiatry*, 19:537–550, 1949; and H. Doerken, "The Mosaic Test—A Second Review," *Journal of Projective Techniques*, 20:164–171, 1956; J. Krout, "Symbol Elaboration Test," *Psychological Monographs*, No. 310, 5–11, 1950; K. Machover, *Personality Projection in the Drawings of the Human Figure* (Springfield, Ill.: Charles C Thomas, Publisher, 1949), 181 pp.; D. R. Stone, "Recorded Auditory Apperception Tests: A New Projective Technique," *Journal of Psychology*, 29:349–353, 1950.

the man who devised the test which reflected the theory are inherent in the test itself and exert an influence in determining what is measured and what the measurements mean.

► Types of Personality

There have been many efforts to classify people into "types." The trouble has always been that after an investigator has selected from the population those who, upon any basis, may properly be grouped together, he still has a great many individuals left over who do not fit into any category. Indeed, these "mixed" types are so numerous as to arouse some doubts as to the practical value of typing. It is the writers' opinion that each individual is a type all by himself, although he may show a resemblance to other people. Even in such an objective matter as physical types, one finds a continuum from one extreme to the other rather than a classification of everyone into a given number of different, discreet types. It seems probable that the subjectivity of measurement, whether of single traits or of total personality, will make classification into types even more difficult. Perhaps, however, the prospective teacher should have some idea of what efforts have been made to date.

One approach lies through the statistical handling of ratings on separate traits. The interrelations produce certain constellations or clusters. Each cluster is assumed to represent a group of characteristics that coalesce to form a type of personality. The number of such clusters, as well as the particular selection of characteristics, varies with the nature and extent of the data used by an investigator, and with his method of handling them. To demonstrate the nature of the results, two clusters are shown below:

Cluster 1   arrogant, exhibitionistic, talkative, boastful, argumentative, conceited, stubborn, pugnacious, tactless, rigid, hostile, ruthless, acquisitive.

Cluster 2   naive, modest, submissive, grateful, tolerant, peaceable, childlike, gentle, self-effacing, self-distrustful, self-dissatisfied, quiet, dependent.[18]

In common speech, persons showing the first cluster of traits are dubbed braggarts, while those showing the second are called wallflowers.

A second approach, although also using ratings of traits to some extent, includes the intensive observation of each individual's actual behavior, measures of his acceptance by age-mates, scores in aptitudes and general intelligence, ratings of emotional stability and reactions, plus other data, in the determination of types. From one classification based upon this broader foundation five types of personality emerged—the self-directive, the adaptive, the submissive, the defiant, and the unadjusted. However, of the 114 sixteen-

---

[18] R. B. Cattell, "The Principal Trait Clusters for Describing Personality," *Psychological Bulletin*, 42:129–161, 1945.

year-old boys and girls, the total population of that age in the small city that was studied intensively, only 66, or 58 percent, fitted into these five categories.[19]

The fundamental trouble with the classification of personalities has always been that the human animal is a highly complex and sensitive organism that continues to modify itself as long as it exists. Even if an individual starts with a basic type of personality, life soon pokes in a dent here and puffs up a bulge there. Moreover, any human being has many contradictory drives, such as the desire to be dominating and the desire to be submissive, but these competing tendencies are stimulated by different circumstances. For example, one of the writers has a lifelong friend who is, as a general thing, argumentative, intolerant, aggressive, and outspoken, but in the presence of her crippled sister she is a model of charm, politeness, consideration, thoughtfulness, tact, and submissiveness. Both patterns of behavior are real, coexistent, and spontaneously natural. Such contradictions make the path of the classifier hard.

▶ **Summary**

The last two decades have seen a great development of tests and other measures designed to investigate personality, or at least some of the traits that make up the complex of personality. Almost anything a person does and almost any attitude he expresses shows his personality to a greater or lesser extent. The inventories of traits and attitudes were the first type of measurement to appear. More prominent at present are the various kinds of projective techniques, among them the Rorschach and the Thematic Apperception Test. In using tests of personality a teacher must be extremely cautious in her interpretation and evaluation of the results; if possible she should consult experts. The classifying of personalities into types has not progressed as far as one might wish, and it is possible that such groupings would be too general for usefulness in individual cases, even if made.

References for Further Reading

BOOKS

Other Texts

Ausubel, *The Theory and Problems of Adolescent Development* (Chap. 7).
Baller and Charles, *The Psychology of Human Growth and Development* (pp. 369–382).
Breckenridge and Vincent, *Child Development,* 4th ed. (Chap. 12).
Garrison, *Growth and Development* (pp. 216–238).
Hurlock, *Adolescent Development,* 2d. ed. (Chap. 15).

---

[19] R. J. Havighurst and H. Taba, *Adolescent Character and Personality* (New York: John Wiley and Sons, Inc., 1949), 315 pp.

Jersild, *Psychology of Adolescence* (Chap. 6 or 17).
Jones, *Growth and Behavior in Adolescence* (pp. 289–308).
Kuhlen, *Psychology of Adolescent Development* (Chap. 4).
Wattenberg, *The Adolescent Years* (Chap. 20).

Other Books and Monographs

Anastasi, A., *Psychological Testing,* 2d. ed. (New York: The Macmillan Company, 1961), 657 pp. (Chap. 18, 19, 20, or 21).

Cronbach, L. J., *Essentials of Psychological Testing,* 2d. ed. (New York: Harper & Row, Publishers, 1960), 515 pp. (Chap. 2 or 15).

Grinker, R. R., and H. M. Hughes, eds., *Toward a Unified Theory of Human Behavior* (New York: Basic Books, Inc., 1956), 375 pp. (pp. 325–340).

Lindzey, G., ed., *Assessment of Human Motives* (New York: Holt, Rinehart and Winston, Inc., 1958), 485 pp. (pp. 3–32).

ARTICLES

Allport, G. W., "The Open System in Personality Theory," *Journal of Abnormal and Social Psychology,* 61:301–310, 1960.

Bernard, J., "The Rosenzweig Picture Frustration Study: I and II," *Journal of Psychology,* 28:326–332, or 333–344, 1949.

Cattell, R. B., *et al.,* "A Re-examination of Personality Structure in Late Childhood and Development of the High School Personality Questionnaire," *Journal of Experimental Education,* 27:73–88, 1958.

Csank, J. Z., and H. E. Lehman, "Developmental Norms on Four Psychophysiological Measures for Use in the Evaluation of Psychotic Disorders," *Canadian Journal of Psychology,* 12:127–133, 1958.

Kelly, L. E., "A Consistency in the Adult Personality," *American Psychologist,* 10:654–681, 1955.

Kuder, G. F., "Expected Developments in Interest and Personality Inventories," *Educational and Psychological Measurement,* 14:265–271, 1954.

Motto, J., "The TAT in the Counseling Process," *Vocational Guidance Quarterly,* 8:29–36, 1960.

Schafer, R., "Psychological Test Evaluations of Personality Change during Intensive Psychotherapy," *Psychiatry,* 18:175–192, 1955.

Stevenson, I., "Is the Human Personality More Plastic in Infancy than in Childhood?" *American Journal of Psychiatry,* 114: 153–161, 1957.

Suggested Research Problems [20]

1. Through school, counseling, or clinic records locate a group of at least 50 young adults who were given projective tests when they were in high school.

---

[20] See note, p. 11.

They should then be retested with the same instruments and comparison made with the earlier records, with the purpose of determining the predictive value of the tests, not only through the correlation of the two scores but also and more importantly the relation of the earlier test to such objective criteria of adjustment as work, permanency of jobs, marital happiness, divorce, arrests, and so on.

Chapter 15 | **Emotional Deviation**

I<small>N</small> order to discuss emotional deviation clearly, it is necessary to understand some of the factors which contribute to any definition of what constitutes either normality or abnormality. Although it is not possible to clarify in a single chapter—or perhaps in a single lifetime—the many stated and implied assumptions that are being made when the term "abnormal" is used, the essential point can be stated briefly: that is abnormal which does not conform to the standards of the observer. Thus, inevitably, what one person considers abnormal another does not. Within some primitive societies, for example, behavior patterns that would be sufficiently handicapping to warrant hospitalization in a modern urban context are cause for high status and are of value to the community. Both the individual under consideration and his observers exist within an enormously complex cultural pattern, which includes their assumptions, their personalities, their life histories, and the intellectual and emotional responses that they share as members of a particular society. Interpretation as to the meaning of behavior reflects also the school of thought and theoretical assumptions of the observer, who may see deviation as a result of suppressed unresolved conflict, or of physiological imbalance, or of distorted interpersonal relationships, or of maladjustment to the social norms. However, it is generally acceptable to define a serious deviation in personality as one which handicaps the individual in his relationships within his usual social context, either because of the disturbance that his behavior causes or because of the suffering he undergoes in attempting to fulfill his needs.

In reading through the literature on emotional disturbances in adolescence, the teacher is almost certain to encounter frequent use of the terms "neurotic" and "psychotic." [1] From the theoretical viewpoint, there are, of course, many shades of meaning associated with these terms, and they may shade into each other in any specific instance. However, for the beginning student a generally accepted simplification seems advisable. If an individual has an emotional problem of some inconvenience in his daily life, a problem

---

[1] For technical definitions of terms the teacher should check a standard psychiatric dictionary, such as L. E. Hinse and R. J. Campbell, *Psychiatric Dictionary* (New York: Oxford University Press, 1960), but she should remain alert to shadings of these standard meanings from author to author.

with which he cannot deal on the basis of common-sense, of which he is usuall aware, and for which he will generally seek treatment of his own accord, h is said to be "neurotic." The "psychotic" person, on the other hand, has prob lems which are deeply built into his total personality and are often of suc early origin that he is unconscious of the degree to which they handicap him He rarely seeks help voluntarily when he is in the depths of his problem, anc the usual estimate in the past has been that in most cases his cooperatior could not be elicited for some forms of psychotherapy, which involve extensiv conscious discussion of difficulties. However, there have been many advance in the treatment of even serious involvements of the personality, some of then based on the use of drugs to make the patient accessible, if only briefly, tc human contacts.

However, the teacher needs to know little of origins or therapies except as these topics may interest her,[2] since she is unlikely to have deeply disturbec adolescents in her classes for any length of time. A teacher is neither a diag nostician nor a therapist; she is an observer. She needs, therefore, a genera knowledge of deviation as a background, an ability to recognize common symptoms of common maladjustments, an understanding of the ways in which emotional disturbances affect all aspects of a pupil's life, and a willingness to establish supportive relationships with students who need her help. For the teacher, the main setting is the classroom. In this little world she has an ex cellent opportunity for the observation of emotional disturbance, because she sees the pupils almost every day against a familiar background. If pupils are in her class for a year, there is time enough to note some developmental trends as well. Moreover, by management of her classroom she can do much to pre vent further emotional problems and to create an atmosphere in which she can be helpful.[3]

It is usually conceded that adolescence may be a time of peculiar vul nerability to conflict and maladjustment, since this period in human growth combines the maximum sexual and social pressures with the maximum degree of physical instability. The adolescent, therefore, who has been driven by too many pressures in childhood may develop acute difficulties when his ability to resist new pressures is being taxed to the utmost by the adjustments he must make in the course of his adolescence. There is little evidence that adoles cence is of necessity a period of emotional distress differing substantially from the earlier or later periods of life, but both the frequency with which past

---

[2] For an extended discussion, see M. I. Stein, *Contemporary Psychotherapies* (New York: Free Press, 1961), 386 pp.

[3] For a discussion of this point see I. Tallman and S. Levine, "The Emotionally Disturbed Child in the Classroom Situation," *Exceptional Children*, 26:114–126, 1960; W. Allinsmith and G. W. Goethals, *The Role of the Schools in Mental Health* (New York: Basic Books, 1962), 337 pp. See pp. 38–133 for an extended discussion concern ing the prevention of emotional deviation.

problems are evoked and the range of possible disturbances that emerge from his present life are excessive during this period.

► Frequency of Emotional Deviation

It is extremely difficult to estimate how many individuals per 1000 of any given age have emotional problems of sufficient severity to require treatment. Wholly aside from the inevitable differences from place to place in the keeping of records and reporting of cases, there is the further complication that the whole matter rests upon the opinions of the observer, and his opinions in turn rest upon his idea of what constitutes an emotional problem.[4] It is quite possible for one team of investigators to study a given population and find many deviations from normal, while another team, studying the same population, finds fewer. The best one can do is to quote results from an assortment of typical studies and hope that the truth lies somewhere among them.

In 1959 there were in the United States 1430 outpatient clinics for the care of the emotionally disturbed.[5] Nearly one-third of the states had community mental health acts to develop their facilities for outpatient care, and there was a notable and rapid increase in the provision of hospitals which would take patients for day only or night only care, thus enabling the patients to remain in contact with their communities while under treatment. The number of mentally disturbed patients admitted to state hospitals has therefore declined slightly in many states. Outpatient care has made possible also the shortening of hospitalization for many patients; at present 60 to 90 percent of new state hospital admissions are discharged within a year, most often to sustaining outpatient care.

Of all the patients handled by the mental hygiene program in one state a fourth were put under clinical care in their own communities, 18 percent were sent to institutions for the mentally retarded, and the remaining 57 percent were sent to resident hospitals for the mentally ill.[6] These figures represent a slight decrease from two years earlier in the last group—although the figure still remains high—and a large increase in the first group. More disturbed patients could be kept in their own community, where they can get emotional support from family and friends, if they would come to the clinic sooner. In the same state's neuropsychiatric clinics, 12 percent of new patients

---

[4] For a concise discussion of some possible criteria for evaluating mental health, see M. Jahoda, *Current Concepts of Positive Mental Health* (New York: Basic Books, 1958), 136 pp., pp. 22–53.

[5] Information on this paragraph is taken from *Book of the States* (Council of State Governments, 1962), 616 pp., p. 361.

[6] *Statistical Report Year Ending June 30, 1960* (California Department of Mental Hygiene, 1961), 98 pp., pp. 68–73.

in the last year were between 12 and 17 years of age, as were 13 percent of those seen in the mental hygiene outpatient clinics. Even though these figures show that many adolescents are being given care, there is still a serious gap between this response and the magnitude of the need. A recent [7] survey made in this same state indicated that the need for psychological and psychiatric services in the school group from the 9th to the 12th grades was not being met. Even when a student had been referred for treatment, there was a wait-ing period of from three to four weeks before an initial interview with psy-chologists and social workers in private practice, of from 28 to 104 weeks at some community psychiatric clinics, and from 5 to 28 weeks in such non-psychiatric community agencies as school guidance clinics, family welfare agencies, and others giving supportive treatment which might assist the dis-turbed adolescent. The total distress to the youngster and the family which these waiting periods represent is far beyond statistical presentation. In actual numbers, a total school population of 532,567 yielded 12,701 who were con-sidered to be seriously disturbed and 39,155 who were moderately disturbed and could have benefited from treatment. Very few of these young people will, until more facilities are available, have that prompt supportive care which might prevent the intensification of their disturbance into a major ill-ness.

In one university of 7000 students, 600 cases were under some form of psychotherapy.[8] About 40 students withdrew each year because of serious maladjustment. Of those under therapy, approximately half were on long-term treatment because of the seriousness of their maladjustment. The refer-rals to the clinic were increasing rapidly at this university in 1955, and other studies elsewhere have confirmed this trend. It is not, however, clear whether there is actually greater need for treatment with each passing year or greater willingness on the part of the students to come spontaneously to the clinic or greater sensitivity on the part of teachers in sending them there.

▶ **Classification of Deviates**

In the past a number of more or less elaborate schemes for diagnosis and classification have been in vogue. Of late there has been a movement away from the naming or labeling of mental illness, partly be-cause experts could not agree among themselves as to just what they meant by their labels and partly because the mere act of putting a name to a con-

---

[7] The figures in this paragraph are taken from the *Mental Health Survey of Los Angeles County, 1957–1959* (California Department of Mental Hygiene, 1960), 566 pp., pp. 513, 308, and 528.

[8] H. B. Carlson, "Psychiatric Casualties in College," *Educational Administration and Supervision*, 41:270–276, 1955. For a somewhat different approach, see J. S. Davie and R. M. Rust, "Personal Problems of College Students," *Mental Hygiene*, 45:247–257, 1961.

dition may give a false impression of certainty about it. In any case, it has been felt that the systems were too rigid to reflect properly the great variation of human reactions. The more modern approach is to define emotional disturbances along a continuum of some basic concept—either in terms of the degree of disturbance to the fundamental ego structure or in terms of the problems presented overtly. Since the secondary school teacher is concerned only with observing and reporting behavior, it seems best to present emotional disturbances in terms of symptoms. Therefore, no attempt will be made to present any medical system of classification, although a student who reads material in abnormal psychology will be sure to encounter various systems.

For the purpose of this book, a nontechnical presentation of maladjustments seemed desirable. The authors have therefore used a simple classification that is largely in terms of behavior, since that is what the teacher sees. There are four groups. The first group includes those adolescents who show relatively minor disturbances of behavior, without apparent deep involvement of the personality. The underlying condition may be potentially serious, but the present behavior is not far outside the normal range. The second group is made up of those who have severe behavior problems but may not impress the observer as being emotionally ill. In their case, the personality has been previously damaged, but they have made adjustments that, while of low social acceptability, are satisfactory to them; consequently, they do not at first acquaintance impress one as being "abnormal." In the third group are those who express their maladjustments through physical illness. Here again there is great involvement of the personality, but the form of expression is most effective in concealing the damage. Finally, there is a group of those who have suffered severe changes of personality and are expressing their difficulties either through a withdrawal from a life that they cannot adjust to or through a distortion of the life around them in an effort to make it more bearable. These adolescents are the ones who impress even the most casual observer as "queer." The members of this group most frequently show too little overt behavior, not too much.

The varied disturbances in personality and the emotional maladjustments of various kinds often stem from precisely the same external deprivations or situations. Thus, the failure to obtain comforting and supporting aid from one's parents, especially in the early years when they constitute the growing child's entire world, causes more or less damage to the developing personality, but the behavioral expressions of the damage may vary greatly. Just which visible form the fundamental, underlying emotional maladjustment may take depends apparently more upon how the individual reacts to the damage done than upon the damage itself. Thus, for example, parental overdomination appears in the history of many adolescents with emotional deviations; one may become an uncontrollable delinquent, another a withdrawn neurotic, a third an invalid, and a fourth a constant dabbler in esoteric religions. What one sees are the forms through which a person expresses his difficulties, and these forms are many. Furthermore, the overt behavior may spring from many causes. It is a frequent, serious error for the less sophisticated observer to lump all instances of a particular kind of behavior as "typical" of a single type of deviation. In actuality, any seven pupils who show,[9] for example, the symptoms of running away from home, may do so for many different reasons. Each youngster may have several motivations, but the inexperienced person may ascribe the running away to a single cause and may therefore consider all seven pupils as having the same underlying emotional problem.

The descriptions of emotional deviations in the remainder of this chapter are purposely expressed, insofar as possible, in nonmedical terms. The many histories of individuals are written as they might have been written by any observant layman. Neither descriptions nor histories are intended for reading by a specialist; they are for a teacher who has only a layman's knowledge of medical matters. It is very desirable that the reader should look up a few of the references given at the end of the chapter in order to become aware of the complexity of causation, the extensive study, the infinite variations, and the delicate handling that constitute the medical approach to the matter of mental and emotional abnormality. The oversimplified presentation in this chapter will serve as a basis, but the reader would do well to add to it. In general, the writers have restricted the illustrative material to case studies of adolescents, although there is an occasional record of an adult, in order to show the long-term effects of maladjustment, if the basic problems are never solved.

▶ Patterns of Emotional Deviation

The first sections will describe four types of individual: the adolescent with feelings of inferiority, the pupil with anxiety, the boy or girl with moods, and the adolescent with a specific fear or compulsion who seems otherwise normal.

Patterns of Reaction, without Major Changes of Personality   Perhaps the easiest deviation to understand is the feeling of inferiority, since everyone has such a feeling at one time or another. The adolescents in this group merely show an overreaction or else they make this response to a totally inadequate stimulus. Presumably the development of the feelings depends upon how strong and how secure a personality the pupil had before he discovered his area of inferiority. The conviction that one is personally or socially inferior is very real to many adolescents, and some of

---

[9] For case histories illustrative of this point, see B. West and F. T. Rafferty, "Initiating Therapy with Adolescents," *American Journal of Orthopsychiatry,* 28:627–639, 1958.

them are unable to bear the resulting stress. The background factor that elicits such feelings may be an actual one—severe crippling, marked social handicaps, genuine ugliness, or slowness of comprehension, for example—but the important aspect is the adolescent's emotional conviction that he is inferior. In many instances there is either no actual basis or only what might be called a comparative basis, as when, for example, a girl who is lovely to look at feels herself inferior because she is only the second loveliest girl in the class.

Feelings of inferiority manifest themselves at all ages but are perhaps more common in adolescence than at other times. It is during these years that the boy or girl first begins seriously to evaluate himself. He studies himself in the mirror and gets upset because his face is out of proportion. He examines his clothes and is distressed if they are not up to the standard he observes around him. He evaluates his friends and often makes efforts to get into social groups that he feels to be more successful than his own. He begins to consider his ability and personality. He wants to understand his place in the world, and he all too often fixes upon a vocational or social ideal that is almost impossible of attainment by a person of his personality and intelligence. For the first time differences in wealth and material possession become important. Social relationships between boys and girls precipitate adolescents into situations in which they feel awkward and incapable. It is not surprising, then, to find feelings of inferiority especially common in early adolescence, because boys and girls are facing many new situations and have not yet had time to evaluate adequately either themselves or the new needs in their lives.

There are two typical but quite different forms of behavior that may be shown by adolescents who are suffering from chronic feelings of inferiority. The first type is simple and obvious because the inner frustration shows on the surface. The pupil is unwilling to attempt any activity in which his real or imagined inability might become evident. He therefore withdraws from competitive activities, even from those in which he could succeed. He is generally diffident, self-conscious, and unsure of himself. He complains of anxiety, fear of failure, inability to get his work done—perhaps of such physical conditions as insomnia, excessive sweating, and palpitations. If the situation continues long enough, the galling sense of inferiority spreads to other fields and the character of the boy or girl becomes permeated with a sense of futility.

Some pupils, however, are not content to stay in the background and admit their insufficiencies. Instead, they make every effort to cover them up so that others will not suspect the existence of an inferiority. Usually an individual with this type of reaction tries so hard to conceal his handicap that he overdoes the matter; his resulting "overcompensation" displays his true feelings quite as blatantly as a withdrawal, but less obviously to the uninitiated. Thus the pupil who is afraid of physical combat and ashamed of his fear boasts loudly of his prowess, secretly hoping no one will call his bluff. The pupil who knows he is stupid persists in volunteering several times a day.

The pupil who has no social graces makes repeated attempts to be the life of the party. The student who has had an uneventful life invents thrilling experiences. All such behavior, directed toward the covering up of inferiority, even from the pupil himself, is of a compensatory nature. The teacher should learn to see through the ordinary forms of overcompensation and to recognize them for what they are—the drives of an ego that is frustrated but will not be suppressed.

There are two case histories in this section. The first is of a boy who had an actual, but seemingly not important, inferiority, upon which he had piled a considerable degree of maladjustment. This lad made no effort to deceive himself as to his rather peculiar shortcoming. The second story is of another boy who could not face himself as he was and therefore used all manner of overcompensatory reactions to defend his ego.

Beryl A., already an accomplished commercial artist at 16, was earning a prosperous living by doing illustrations for the local utility company while he was still in high school. Bright, economically secure, talented, he seemed to be set for a sunny future. This was not the way it worked out. Beryl's talented hands were, by a trick of congenital misfortune, so small that their fantastic appearance at the end of his long bony adolescent arms was often the occasion for uproarious laughter from his peers. In the social context of his parents and their friends he was wholly accepted, but he derived little comfort from the sympathetic understanding of these adults. To the distress of all, he spent more and more time over his drawing board until every moment away from school was occupied with paint, never with people. Finally, urged by his parents to seek counseling, Beryl came to the office of the college's counselor in mental health. He could discuss his problem with the counselor, but he could not face his peers with comfort. Then one day he went to the infirmary with a nasty infection on his thumb, and was dumbfounded when the nurse not only gave no sign that anything was remarkable about his hands but said, "Oh—I hadn't noticed" when he bluntly asked her about how she felt concerning his hands. No miracles of quick recovery occurred, but it was vividly impressed on him by this experience that his physical inferiority was really neither remarkable nor hideous. Gradually, in the company of college peers with more maturity than those he encountered in high school, and with the growing sense of his own complex individuality, he began to accept and be accepted in social situations. He will always have a problem, but it is assuming proportions he will find manageable and compatible with a normal adjustment to life.

Tony was an Italian lad of 17 who would have been handsome if it were not for his petulant expression. When someone began to talk with him his face underwent a change and a flashing smile appeared, but the radiance vanished the moment the other person's attention moved away from Tony to someone else

Tony's teacher characterized him as being insolent, hyperactive, vain, peculiar, and unpredictable. He frequently caused minor disturbances in class, chiefly because he could not bear to be out of the limelight and would draw down punishment upon himself by making a scene rather than remain ignored. His insolence often took the form of "wisecracks" at which the class would laugh.

Upon examination this boy turned out to have an IQ of only 94, a level that is low for success in high school unless a pupil is willing to compensate for his mental inadequacy by extra effort. Tony was doing either failing or barely passing work in every class. He believed that his teachers discriminated against him and gave his work poorer grades than it should receive. He showed the examiner one of his notebooks which was quite neat and legibly written, but upon closer examination it appeared that Tony had merely copied what his teachers had put upon the blackboard without any evidence of comprehension and without organization. He had no notes on reading because, as he freely admitted, he never read his assignments on the ground that "the stuff is all too silly to waste time on." On a reading test he scored at the sixth-grade level. It is probable that his abstinence from reading had resulted from his failure to comprehend what he read and from his dislike of any occupation that offered no chance for showing off. On the playground he liked to break into a game that was proceeding nicely by grabbing the ball and refusing to give it back, and he liked to sit on the sidelines making loud and generally abusive comments upon the activities of the players. He was fairly adept at a number of sports but no one wanted him on his team because Tony monopolized the game, even when his team was losing, by trying to play all positions himself. His natural talents in athletics were good enough to have won him prominence on school teams, but he would not submit to the grind of practice and therefore missed the opportunity to shine as an athlete.

Tony lived with his mother and stepfather. His two sisters were ten years older than he and already married. During his childhood he received much attention from his mother and even more from his sisters, who greatly enjoyed having a live doll to play with. Tony's father had been an Italian immigrant. During his lifetime the family lived in a poor section of the city among other Italian immigrants, but after the mother's remarriage they moved to a better part of town, where they still do not feel entirely comfortable. The mother's second marriage was a severe shock to Tony, and he was clearly jealous of his stepfather. Gradually, however, he accepted the situation with fairly good grace, probably because his stepfather, who is a traveling salesman, was away from home during the week and sometimes for longer periods. Tony was thus able to retain his position as the chief attraction in the family most of the time. Tony's mother has overprotected him. She has the same rather empty good looks as her son, and one suspects that she has the same rather empty mind. She has many explanations for her son's failure to be popular. Mostly she bases her excuses upon the supposed envy of other boys because Tony is so handsome. His stepfather is aware that the mother is too indulgent with Tony, but he does not feel he can interfere because of his own rather precarious position as an outsider who has only recently joined the family circle.

It seems probable that Tony is overcompensating for both an intellectual and a social inferiority. In his franker moments he admits that he is not a success, either in school or out. At home he has always been the center of admiration and affection, and he does not know how to get along in any other kind of relationship. If he is disregarded for a few hours his basic feelings of inferiority overtake him and so threaten his ego that he is stimulated into any kind of action that will center attention upon him again. It is possible that if Tony drops out of school, where the competition is too severe for him, and goes into some kind of work within his capacities he could learn to relax. When Tony is older, and if he could qualify for it, he would make an excellent maître d'hôtel, a position in which his natural charm and good looks would be an advantage, in which he would feel himself important. With careful handling he may yet be a success, but without it he is likely to become more and more of a problem because he cannot let down his defenses without more damage to his ego.

Anxiety Probably everyone suffers from anxiety in greater or lesser degree from time to time as the result of specific situations for which anxiety is a reasonable response. This emotional condition becomes a problem when it persists over a long period of time or recurs with such intensity as to incapacitate an individual for daily living. It may range from a slight, vague apprehensiveness about even minor problems to an all-pervading fear so intense as to affect concentration and memory and to lead to emotional and physical exhaustion.

The anxiety itself may best be thought of as a form of adjustment which, while unpleasant, is by no means as devastating to the ego as an attempt to face the underlying conflicts would be. Of course, it is not a good form of escape from an unsolved problem because it promptly produces so much maladjustment that the sufferer has to use further forms in order to escape from the escape!

The state of anxiety as observed in a particular individual at a given time may be either situational or chronic. In the former case it is sometimes intense, but it is sooner or later resolved, because the situation changes, although the feeling of anxiety may persist beyond the crisis that produced it and may set a pattern for responses in the future. It is probable that a person with a chronic anxiety developed the condition originally in response to some situation that threatened his security, but either the threat never quite materialized or it is a continuing threat that never disappears. Therefore, the feeling tone that was once appropriate persists and is usually attached to a variety of new stimuli that may be unrelated to the precipitating situation.

The uncertainty of self-concept which often characterizes the adolescent period is a fertile source of anxiety. The conflicts between the expectations held for an adolescent by his family,[10] between his own past patterns of reaction and his emerging ones,[11] between his long-range goals and the fluctuations of his daily performance, between his desire to achieve and his fear of failure,[12] all may engender severe anxiety.

Both parents and teachers may induce feelings of insecurity in children or adolescents by too great a pressure for achievement in school. The son or daughter of upwardly-mobile, middle-class families are especially susceptible targets for pressure of this sort, because the progress in school of the younger generation is an essential part of the over-all plan for increased social prestige for the entire family.[13] As a result, even such a comparative failure as getting average instead of superior marks in school may load an adolescent with feelings of anxiety and guilt. The story below describes such an overburdened and anxious high school student, whose best is not good enough for her aspirations, which are based upon the academic success of parents and siblings.

Mildred M. is a high school girl with an anxiety that centers around the marks she receives on assignments, reports, and examinations. She bores her age-mates by her constant chatter about marks—what percent she received, her general up-or-down trend in each course, her apprehensions about examinations, and so on. Twice, when she knew that a teacher was correcting papers, she has sneaked into the teacher's homeroom at recess and has been discovered as she searched through the papers to see if hers had been scored. She has also been caught changing the marks on her papers before she took them home. She has saved every returned paper since her entry into high school (except a few that she threw away during the first month, an action she now regrets), and every Sunday afternoon she spends two or three hours leafing through them and pondering her progress or lack of it. She is often greatly upset by the weekly review. As the day of an examination approaches, she becomes more and more apprehensive. After it is over, she gives her family and friends a play-by-play account of what she wrote and why. Unlike pupils who become hysterical about examinations and are unable to take them because their heads ache violently or because they are suffering from nausea, Mildred remains apprehensive without discharging her

---

[10] H. Platt, G. Jurgensen, and S. Chorost, "Comparisons of Child-rearing Attitudes of Mothers and Fathers of Emotionally Disturbed Adolescents," *Child Development*, 33:117–122, 1962.

[11] See, for example, G. W. Bronson, "Identity Diffusion in Late Adolescence," *Journal of Abnormal and Social Psychology*, 59:414–417, 1959.

[12] J. W. Atkinson and G. H. Litwin, "Achievement Motive and Test Anxiety Conceived as Motive to Approach Success and Motive to Avoid Failure," *Journal of Abnormal and Social Psychology*, 60:52–63, 1960.

[13] E. Douvan and J. Adelson, "The Psychodynamics of Social Mobility in Adolescent Boys," *Journal of Abnormal and Social Psychology*, 56:31–44, 1958, and A. N. Hieronymus, "A Study of Social-class Motivation: Relationships between Anxiety for Education and Certain Socio-economic and Intellectual Variables," *Journal of Educational Psychology*, 42:193–205, 1951.

emotional load by means of any projective technique. What little relief she gets comes through the normal channel of answering questions correctly or from preparing assignments well. Unfortunately, however, Mildred's successes do not occur often enough to discharge more than a fraction of the pressure.

The reasons for this girl's condition are not far to seek. She is the one person of average ability in a family of superior verbal intelligence. Both parents and two older siblings made Phi Beta Kappa, and an older sister, now in college, almost certainly will do so. The parents became acquainted with each other when they were members of a high school honor society. After they graduated from college, the father went into business, and the mother concentrated on raising a family. Neither has had contact with professional people—who might have influenced them to evaluate marks more temperately—and both have sought refuge from their present boredom by reliving their own academic success in their children. Ever since she can remember, Mildred has heard high marks praised and admired as the *ne plus ultra* of life. Thus Mildred continues to be afraid of examinations, anxious about assignments, fearful of an unsuccessful college career, and apprehensive of eventual failure in a life that is rigidly evaluated in tenths of a percent!

Moodiness   In a recent study of two thousand pupils in grades 7 through 12, one girl expressed feelings that are common to many adolescents:

> One of the difficulties of teen-agers is these moods. Sometimes they get up in the morning feeling wonderful. Instead of talking they feel like singing. Other days they feel wretched and depressed. They can hardly drag themselves around. These moods come and go in a mysterious way, for just no reason at all.[14]

This statement reveals both the moodiness and the baffled feeling about it, a feeling that often causes more disturbance than the mood itself.

An acceptance of these normal swings of mood among adolescents by their parents and teachers serves to help young people through this period by de-emphasizing the importance of incidental and short-range changes. The skillful teacher can even make constructive use of these fluctuating patterns by providing creative or sedative activities, so that the adolescent can learn to make constructive use of his upswings and to check his downswings. He may remain a moody individual, but he is no longer at the mercy of whatever feeling happens to seize him, and he is less likely to be overwhelmed by extreme fluctuations than is a person who has never had such training. If there is no serious, pervasive, continuing problem underlying these elations and depressions, most boys and girls will reach an individual equilibrium that

---

[14] R. Strang, "Adolescent Views on One Aspect of Their Development," *Journal of Educational Psychology,* 46:42, 1957.

is maintained by internal checks, which permit mild emotional swings but prevent the adolescents from going off the deep end at either extreme of their own emotional range.

High school teachers soon become familiar with the normal moodiness of adolescence. It differs from abnormality in three quite recognizable ways. First, it has a discernible and sensible cause, although at times the reason seems inadequate. Thus a boy may become deeply despondent because he did not make the second track team or a girl may be all agog because she received a good mark on her weekly theme. In contrast, the abnormal moods often seem unrelated to environmental stimuli. Second, the moodiness is too extreme and too intense to be mistaken for an ordinary variation of attitude. Third, the abnormally moody adolescent is driven by his moods. He does not possess them; they possess him. A teacher should be able to recognize the difference between the ordinary ups and downs of adolescent emotion and the extreme driving moodiness that is not normal. The study below describes a typical state of abnormally intense depression, with a typical trigger of physical illness, which predisposed the patient to low resistance toward long-latent conflicts. Psychiatrists point out that an illness need not be severe to act as a trigger; it need only occur at a vulnerable point in the patient's life.

Long John was a tall, stringbean of a lad in the junior year of high school. He was still awkward and apparently not yet accustomed to being his adult height. Even before he began his adolescent growth, however, he had acquired a reputation as a buffoon, and he had continued in this vein, presumably because it gave him an easy escape from the predicaments into which his new size often precipitated him. To his teachers he was a half-curse and a half-blessing, since his ebullient spirits could save awkward moments from becoming more awkward but could bring on fits of hysterics in other pupils at inopportune times. Long John's grandfather, father, two uncles, and one brother were all doctors, and the family owned the local hospital and composed its resident staff. It had always been assumed that the boy would join in the family profession and in his turn become the "young doctor" of the group. Long John never told anyone that the constant discussions of illness and symptoms at the dinner table turned his stomach or that he would much rather draw cartoons than study medicine. His drawings were original and clever, although the humor in them needed control and refinement, but the talent was there. When the school nurse, a little concerned about the boy's extreme thinness, asked him to tell her just what he had had to eat the day before, he replied, "We had diseased kidneys for breakfast, a stomach cancer for lunch, and a particularly gory tonsillectomy for dinner. It's what we always have in our house." To Long John humor was a refuge; it served to hide, perhaps from himself, his fear of his own failure as a doctor.

The boy indubitably had moods, as all his teachers had noted, but the first time the seriousness of his variations was appreciated was during a "stunt show" that the junior class staged for the rest of the school. Everyone was excited and merry, and there was great applause when Long John appeared on the stage and began some of his customary clowning. He kept on and on. After a while, although the other pupils still laughed, members of the faculty began to be worried. In the end, the school doctor—with considerable presence of mind—joined the act and managed to get the boy off the stage. The doctor at once drove Long John home and delivered him, still talking nonsense at the top of his voice, to the bevy of local medical talent that constituted John's family. The boy talked for several hours longer before drugs finally put him to sleep. The next day John lay in bed, silent and motionless, but on the following day he was back at school and in his customary frame of mind. The school doctor presently made an occasion to talk with John, but he was unable to get past the façade of fluent speech and humorous comment.

The next semester John began a course in zoology, as a first step toward his proposed medical career. From the first, he had great trouble with the laboratory work. Somehow, he never succeeded in dissecting anything, not even an angleworm. His first month's report showed a failing mark in his laboratory work. His father was greatly disturbed and scolded John for frittering away his time in drawings and social life instead of getting his schoolwork done. John's teachers noticed that his moods were even more pronounced and unpredictable than ever. When he was not the life of the party he was glum and silent. All his schoolwork deteriorated, and he began to stay away from the zoology laboratory altogether. One night he did not come home for dinner and was picked up about 2 A.M. by the police and returned to his family; he seemed confused and very tired, and could give no coherent explanation of where he had been or why he had not come home as usual.

The following morning John had a high temperature and was clearly suffering from influenza. With the usual vitality of adolescence, he soon recovered and was back at school in about ten days. He was in one of his excited moods and was quite objectionable in class because he wanted to talk all the time. One of his teachers made an appointment for him to see the school doctor after the last class, but John did not keep the appointment. Nor was he home at dinnertime. The family was about half through dinner when a low humming sound suddenly attracted the attention of John's mother, who could not identify it. She said it sounded like a vacuum cleaner, but none was being used at the time. The men looked at each other and ran for the garage. There they found John, nearly dead from carbon monoxide. Since he had attached a piece of hose to the exhaust and led the other end into the car, there was no question as to his intent. His father and uncles worked over him all night and finally saved his life. In the following days of weakness John finally admitted his problem—that everything connected with medicine made him acutely ill and he could never fulfill the plans of his family. The experience had taught John's father something. He discovered that he had pushed his much-loved son almost into a suicide's grave. From then on, there was no more talk of John's being a doctor. Moreover, his father made arrangements for John to talk over his difficulties of temperament with a psychiatrist. There is now every hope that Long John will some day be a successful and happy commercial artist, whose moods will stay within normal limits.

This history shows outstanding features of depression with suicidal attempts, hostility toward the father, great sense of guilt and inadequacy, and a disguised fear of punishment. Some authorities feel that the overwhelming of the ego by pubertal sexual drives is the most frequent cause of depressive suicides in adolescents, but often the salient, observable feature is the rejection—actual or perceived as such—of the boy or girl by the father-figure. In the above instance the father seems to have wanted his son to be a continuation of himself rather than an independent individual, and the boy's efforts to fulfill this wish led him into constant conflict with his own interests, his own abilities, and his own needs—but his feelings of guilt kept him trying until his problems became more than he could bear.

Obsessions and Phobias   To the casual observer, a phobia does not look much like an obsession, but they have their origin in the same motivation and they share an inner compulsion that is generally not understood by the sufferer himself. Usually there has been a severe, long-since-forgotten, traumatic, emotional episode, to which the reactions of fear and anxiety were quite natural but were accompanied by equally strong feelings of guilt or shame and were therefore repressed. At some subsequent date an object, situation, or person reminiscent of the original experience appears and precipitates a reaction that was once sensible but now seems ridiculous. The sufferer from this condition cannot give an explanation because he has forgotten the missing links in his story, either through passage of time or through repression. A similar type of explanation may be offered for obsessions. Presumably, while the traumatic experience was only partly repressed, it kept popping back into consciousness. Since sheer repression was not burying the objectionable memory fast enough, the individual tried prevention. At the first hint of returning recollection he diverted his attention by such distractions as walking three steps backward and blinking the eyes twice with each step. As a result of his distracted attention, the painful memory never became fully conscious. It should be noted that in all probability the defensive behavior really did work the first few times it was tried. The now-unconscious memories keep trying to thrust themselves up and succeed sufficiently to make the individual feel tense and apprehensive. When the pressure gets high enough he performs his ritual and gets relief for a while, although he has long since forgotten what he is defending himself from. He has lost the connecting link between stimulus and response, but he has not forgotten that his mannerism, whatever its nature, has in the past brought him relief.

There is no sense in trying to "educate" such a person out of his obsession, because he will succeed only in adding to his other troubles a new feeling of guilt and distress at his lack of self-control.

Although a person may develop a phobia about anything, certain types of stimuli are more common than others: fear of small, closed spaces—claustrophobia; fear of open spaces; fear of looking down from a high place; fear of being alone, of falling down; and fear of death, knives, tunnels, storms, wind, or lightning. Generally, the stimuli are such as might normally cause a feeling of disquiet. Most people do not like to be shut in a closet or to look down from the top of a tower, but such experiences are only unpleasant, not terrifying. Similarly, most persons have more or less fear of the water, but they can inhibit it long enough to learn how to swim; a person with a phobia about water cannot be persuaded even to take a bath. The abnormal thing about most phobias is, therefore, their terrifying intensity rather than their nature.

The history below is that of a young man who had been beset by obsessions and phobias all his life.

Benjamin is now a young man of 24, who has recently come voluntarily to a psychiatrist for help with his problems. An investigation revealed the following significant points in his development.

The boy's parents seemed normal enough, although his father was regarded as a "difficult" person, both at home and at work, because of his extreme fussiness and desire for exactitude. He was a small, insecure person who overcompensated for his inherent inferiorities by being pompous and pedantic; probably, his urge for exactitude was developed as a defense mechanism. The mother was a tolerant person who was efficient and in general kindly, but she did not give the feeling of emotional warmth. The boy was an only child. His early childhood was normal enough, in a superficial way, except that he had temper tantrums if anyone touched his belongings, especially if these were rearranged.

In the course of the years from 5 to 18, Benjamin showed a number of compulsions and phobias. At one time he touched the top of every picket in every fence, and went back to touch any that he had missed. At another time he made sure to step over every crack in the paving with his left foot. Throughout these years he believed in magic numbers, although he changed the number from time to time. For two or three years he arranged everything in groups of four, then he had a period during which he arranged objects strictly by size, from large to small. If his groupings were altered by someone else, he became depressed and feared the worst. He also made collections of many kinds, mostly of worthless trash, such as bottle tops, thrown-away cigarette butts, or oval pebbles. He needed an hour to reach school from his home, although he had to travel only five blocks, because he was constantly turning aside to hunt for such trifles. He was desperately afraid of all small animals and would not enter a friend's house if there were a dog or cat there. He also felt that only by going home, taking a bath, and putting on fresh clothes could he rid himself of the bad luck that would follow whenever a girl with red hair walked across the path in front of him. These elaborate precautionary measures were rarely needed, however, since he took elaborate care to avoid redheads!

In school his work was average or above. His only low grades were in arithmetic, and in this case his low mark came primarily from his refusal to solve any problem that contained the numbers 7, 13, or 19. He rejected some of the reading assignments on grounds equally fanciful. During his high school years he insisted in occupying the last seat in the back of the classroom, because he could not bear to have anyone behind him. The only time he ever rode on an escalator he had to be controlled by a policeman who happened to be standing behind him, because he went into a complete panic and started to climb over people. He could study only after everything on his desk was arranged in a particular way.

In short, this boy had been showing serious maladjustment from his earliest years, but his parents had done nothing about it. His mother said the behavior was just "Benjamin's way," and his father was rather glad to see his son being properly careful and neat. His teachers were often distressed and had sent him to the school doctor, but without cooperation from the parents little was accomplished. So Benjamin jogged along through school, usually friendless and isolated and—by his standards—grossly misunderstood. In general, people found it easier to disregard the boy's oddities than to do something constructive about them. Benjamin lived in the days before counselors and school psychologists; perhaps today he would receive the help he needed. It was not until he had a job he liked and a future with promise that he finally took matters into his own hands and consulted a psychiatrist. The precipitating cause was his inability to cross the street in front of his apartment. He could catch a bus at the corner in the morning, but on the return trip he had to ride to the end of the line, pay another fare and ride back, so as to dismount on the right side of the street. This performance not only took a great deal of time and doubled his return fare, but it was a source of much merriment among other members of the office force.

The real sources of Benjamin's fears and compulsions were never clear. It was, however, evident that he had an absorbing fear of death or injury and an abiding trust in magic and witchcraft as means of preventing damage to himself. It is true that he was badly maladjusted, but most of his troubles were the results of his phobias and compulsions rather than the causes of them. He had suffered much ridicule, and he had made real efforts to eliminate his peculiarities, but in the end he had found the ridicule easier to bear than the feelings of uncertainty and the conviction of tragedy that filled his mind if he omitted any of his preventive measures. Benjamin's history shows both how a form of escape perpetuates itself until the individual is virtually helpless to free himself and how a fundamental maladjustment can color a person's entire life by its driving force.

Both the phobia and the obsession are probably survivals of an early adjustment to an actual emotional trauma, and they persist because the emergency still exists. The original shock has never been discharged, only hidden, and it is still trying to force its way into consciousness. Against this intrusion the obsessions and phobias stand guard, either to prevent the emergence or to convert the inner panic into fear of some external object. The usual method of treatment has been, therefore, to try to discover of what the trauma consisted, to drag the hidden episode out into the light of day, to solve the conflict, and to discharge the fear once and for all.

Disorders of Conduct, with Compensatory Personality Adjustment   The conduct disorders are sometimes easy to recognize; the fact that their source is often obscure and their treatment extremely difficult is of no immediate concern to the teacher. She can hardly help noticing when an "acting out," [15] aggressive pupil enters her group and proceeds to make chaos and disorder out of her peaceful room. The aggressive, explosive pupil cannot be either overlooked or ignored, but a teacher can make his condition either better or worse by her treatment of him. It is a little more difficult to recognize the so-called psychopathic personality, which may be more destructive to the individual in the long run than mere explosiveness. The youngster whose destructiveness takes the form of overt delinquency is discussed elsewhere in this text and will therefore not be described here. The present section will be confined, then, to two types: the aggressive personality and the psychopathic personality. Both types are hard for a teacher to deal with, especially in a group.

The young people who may be so classified are not out of touch with reality, so they cannot be regarded as psychotic; that is, they are not—in the parlance of the street—crazy. Their perceptions and interpretations of the people and events around them are distorted by their own needs and experiences to a degree that makes them deviate from normal behavior. There has been much work on the aggressive child, from which a teacher could derive some hints as to treatment, but the psychopath is still a problem to everyone.

Whatever the reasons are that lead to overtly hostile reactions to adults, there seems no question that these boys and girls who lump all grown-ups as enemies have suffered severe emotional deprivations from an early age. A child or adolescent who has a reasonably normal personality can manage to control his behavior even under adverse circumstances, provided he is given some ego support, but the hostile or psychopathic child cannot do so, partly because he cannot use such ego support as he might receive. These

---

[15] F. Redl and D. Wineman, *Children Who Hate* (New York: Free Press, 1951), 253 pp.; and B. Bettelheim, *Love Is Not Enough* (New York: Free Press, 1951), 386 pp.

children not only do not ask for help, they do not even want help, and will not accept it except to exploit it. Nothing dents their convictions that adults are to be hated.[16] A teacher cannot, therefore, hope to assist such a pupil by giving him encouragement and support, and she has to be watchful of exploitation; that is, a special consideration or permission that would rejoice the heart of most pupils is likely to be used by the hostile child for his own purposes. There is often no "good" answer to the problems of these pupils, or at least none that the classroom teacher can supply.

Edward R., at twelve, had somehow survived the first six grades of school—or perhaps it would be fairer to say that the school had survived six years of him!—because he had flashes of such good intelligence that his despairing teachers were inclined to give him one more chance. Moreover, the principal of the school had come from the same background which had produced Ed and was not only sure that the boy would eventually emerge from it—as he had—but was able to interpret to his teachers the effects of the despair and rejection that Ed was enduring. The boy seemed to be dimly aware of his own capabilities, but was nevertheless unable to use them consistently, even when it would be to his advantage to do so, because the most minute frustration plunged him into an inkwell-throwing fury. He would then marshal a hundred reasons why, with the world of adults conspiring against him, he could never complete the assigned task. He wanted desperately to escape from his squalid home, his screeching sisters, his cringing, unemployed father, and his hate-ridden mother, who used him primarily to vent her wrath upon. He did not have in his home an example of a man's dignity or of a mother's love, but rather than seek them elsewhere, he simply denied their existence. Time after time the school counselor tried to talk with Ed about his problems, but the boy met every advance with coldness and contempt. He might have continued his precarious course barely within the tolerance of school had not his transfer to junior high school precipitated a series of events that eventually landed him in the state hospital for the mentally ill, because there was absolutely no other place that could contain his wrath. The first precipitating factor was the death of his father just as Ed was entering his own period of puberty with its customary problems and strains. The father's death led to the family's moving to a suburban community, to which Ed's mother wanted to return after fifteen years of resentful absence. Here she expected to resume her former respectability and social life, but she soon found that she and her children were unacceptable. Against Ed the community was especially incensed; he was a disgrace and an outrage, and they were critical of him, a feeling that he returned with interest. Confronted with a set of socially alien standards and sensing the

---

[16] A. C. Rosen, "Treatment of the Disturbed Personality," *California Youth Authority Quarterly,* 10:24–29, 1957; and F. Redl and D. Wineman, *Controls from Within* (New York: Free Press, 1952), 327 pp.

frustration of his angry mother, Ed's thin and inadequate control gave way completely. The young teacher who got whipped across the face with a ruler when she remonstrated with Ed about drawing red lines across his reading book was in no mood for enlightened tolerance and the new principal was a gently reared man who knew violence only by hearsay; when Ed's mother was asked to come to the school for a conference, she answered with a string of invectives and then lashed Ed with a belt. In a cold white rage, Ed broke each and every window in the house while his frightened sisters watched in terror, and then strode off into the city to lose himself among companions who at least understood him. The police who eventually picked him up did not have a quiet night. Ed was too violent to be put with the other delinquent boys and too young to be put among adult criminals, so in the end he was sent to the mental hospital. There he was placed on a ward with fifty-eight other boys, many of whom had serious mental illnesses. There was not enough personnel to give him the tolerance and support that he needed, and there was no way for him to achieve the little successes from which control may be built. The hospital psychiatrist did help him some by allowing him to express freely his fury and his total dissatisfaction with the world, but some of the benefits were more than offset by the imposition of the ward routine necessary for the survival of the other inmates.

At no time was this boy troubled by delusions or hallucinations; he had no seizures, no illness. He was always clear in his mind and completely in touch with his miserable world. By the time he was 14 he was sufficiently adjusted to leave the hospital, but then the question arose as to where he should go. There was no place. To return him to his home, which had been a potent factor in shaping his personality, would have been fatal. To keep him longer on a ward with mentally ill and sometimes deteriorated boys would be almost as much of a tragedy. No foster home would take him. The complete absence of any proper residential setting with adequate orientation toward rehabilitation is one of the greatest lacks in the treatment of these disturbed adolescents.

Some decades ago the term "psychopathic personality" was coined to describe certain types of disorders in behavior.[17] In order to prevent common misunderstandings of the condition, it might be well first to state what it is not. It is not a neurosis nor a psychosis. There is a complete absence of delusions. There is usually no indication of nervousness. There is no obvious distortion of personality and in many cases no serious defect in theoretical reasoning. The individual shows no depression and no anxiety—not even when he should. His intelligence is generally within the normal range, and is sometimes superior.

---

[17] Many psychiatrists do not consider the psychopathic personality to be an entity. However, this uncertainty as to the adequacy of the diagnosis does not need to confuse the teacher. No one denies that the behavior patterns exist and are recognizable. Just

The possessor of a psychopathic personality may have great superficial charm. To the casual observer he gives an appearance of complete sanity,[18] and he shows in everyday situations an outer layer of acceptable functioning. This mask of sound mental health is, however, only a façade. Upon further acquaintance the psychopath shows his true personality. His condition reveals itself in four main types of reaction.

First, psychopaths are basically unreliable, irresponsible, untruthful, and deceitful, even when they have nothing to gain thereby. They can lie without the slightest indication of discomfort. It is generally not difficult to convince them that some particular thing they have done is wrong. They admit their guilt cheerfully and often promise to do better, but then they continue to do exactly as they please.

A second characteristic is their emotional shallowness. They may, for instance, go through the motions of making a fluent apology for some misdeed, but the apology is fluent because there is no feeling behind it. They have little affection to offer, and they often remain throughout life unattached to other people. They show neither remorse nor shame for even their most glaring misdeeds. Because they are barren emotionally, they are conspicuously callous and unfeeling in their treatment of others, not appreciating at all the emotional impact of their acts upon other people.

Third, psychopaths are essentially solitary people, unresponsive to interpersonal relationships. Their behavior is in general asocial rather than antisocial, although under slight stress they become antisocial as well. They are extraordinarily unresponsive to kindness from other people. While they have affairs with members of the opposite sex, these affairs do not seem to have any real emotional significance for them. Their sexual relationships are casual, intense, and often of short duration. They seem to have no capacity to see themselves as others see them, or to realize how other people feel about them. Their reactions are made to gain pleasure and to avoid pain, without the intervention of such inconveniences as a conscience or an awareness of social pressure.

Finally, since psychopaths do what pleases them at the moment, they live disordered and purposeless lives. Even a consistent revolt is beyond their powers of organization. To be sure, they are sometimes defiant and explosive, but these manifestations are reactions to incidental blocking of some momentary desire. These people do not commit major offenses, although they are likely to be constantly in difficulty for minor infractions of the law, their most

how these patterns should be grouped and what they should be called are matters best left to the specialist.
[18] H. Cleckly, *The Mask of Sanity: An Attempt to Clarify Some Issues about the So-Called Psychopathic Personality* (St. Louis: The C. V. Mosby Company, 1950), 560 pp.; and S. B. Maughs, "Current Concepts of Psychopathy," *Archives of Criminal Psychodynamics*, 4:550–557, 1961.

frequent clashes occurring because they are drunk and disorderly. They do not usually devote themselves to organized crime because crime requires planning, and psychopaths do not plan ahead.

Presumably the psychopath's asocial, purposeless, and often self-defeating behavior is an expression of drives, disturbances, and conflicts that lie deep in his unconscious and urge him to self-destruction. For he does destroy himself as far as deriving either pleasure or value from life is concerned. He does not even seem to get pleasure or relief out of his sins and misdeeds. He does not, for example, drink to escape an intolerable strain or insoluble emotional conflict. Alcohol promptly disorganizes him still further and urges him on into even greater uselessness. What a normal person cannot usually grasp is that the psychopath enjoys being disorganized and has no interest in improving himself. He is not ashamed of his life; it is his normal relatives who feel the shame for him. The psychopath does not act like a normal human being basically because he cannot seem to express or feel normal human emotions in more than a superficial and fleeting way.

The man described below shows the egocentricity, the resistance to modification, and the callous insensitivity that characterize the psychopathic personality.

George V. is probably the least worried man in his office and certainly no one who saw him striding confidently down the street on his way home to his latest wife would note anything obviously abnormal about this attractive man of thirty-five. Of course, no one in town knows him very well, because he arrived about a month ago, talked his way rapidly into an insurance office as an "experienced salesman" and in a whirlwind courtship married a young schoolteacher who found his dashing air and bright chatter irresistible. The men in the office are sometimes uncomfortably aware that he seems to know very little about insurance, but there is no denying that he charms the customers—often right from under the noses of salesmen who had been working up a careful program with them—and gets their signatures on his credit lists. Currently he is top man in sales of policies, but the boss has a queasy feeling that many of those policies will not be sustained long. The young wife is feeling some misgivings, too, since a letter which was forwarded from another state proved to be a demand for support of two children George had neglected to tell her about. However, if George's usual pattern holds good again, it should be several months before things begin to fall apart so obviously that he will quietly leave some night for destinations unspecified.

This is a very well-established pattern now, and George is quite comfortable with it. Except for one close scrape with the reformatory when he was twelve, George has never been in trouble with the law and probably will not be in the future. He is moderately intelligent, attractive, healthy, undisturbed by doubts about himself or others, and utterly unable to understand why an occasional victim of his way of life is terribly upset, particularly if it is a woman who protests that she took their marriage vows seriously. If he does come up against legal trouble, it may well be because he has lost track of the proper succession of divorce-marriage-divorce-marriage and has neglected to include one or the other step. He has been in and out of four marriages so far, and the end is not in view. As an adolescent he found his charms were enough in demand to exact sexual surrender as part of his "price" with the attractive but loose-moraled lassies he dated from the age of eleven, when he left school. Then it became more advantageous to him to establish a reliable source of meals and attention, and he married a very young barmaid who saw in him an arrogant hero. After their daughter was born, and took some attention away from George, he decided things were getting dull and joined the Army without bothering to tell his wife. He did not get in any serious trouble in the Army, but as soon as his enlistment was over he left for the southern state where he was born and fast-talked himself into a job far beyond his educational capacity. Some of the town oldsters remembered George with sympathy as the lad whose father died in an asylum and who as a tiny baby was placed in a seemingly endless succession of foster homes while his mother sought to support him. Others remembered him a bit harshly as the "little devil" who manipulated every susceptible kid in town into trouble but seemed to keep clear himself. Finally, someone recalled that he had walked away from an accident that killed his "best friend," and that while he had been cleared of responsibility so far as the crash was concerned, he talked a lot about how sorry he was for the friend but he had not, in fact, stayed with him while he was pinioned under his car and had never once visited the bereaved parents. On the whole, the town was glad to see George leave when he became bored with the job just before his employers decided his social talents could not compensate for his neglected tasks and they agreed to accept his resignation—with relief.

How long this sort of thing can go on may be doubtful. In any event, it is of no serious concern to George. He expects to "get by." It is probable that he will succeed altogether too well for the comfort of others.

The Disturbed Adolescent with Somatic Problems   It is becoming increasingly evident that physical and mental health are interrelated and affect each other.[19] Already there is an enormous literature in this vital and comprehensive field. Although it is now considered probable that particular physical conditions neither cause nor arise from particular emotional traits, as was at first supposed, almost any physical condition can be triggered by almost any emotional disturbance and almost any emotional disturbance can be made more acute by almost any abnormal physical condition. The patterns in which

---

[19] See, for example, F. Dunbar, *Emotions and Bodily Changes*, 4th ed. (New York: Columbia University Press, 1954), 1192 pp., especially pp. 79, 323–325, and 754; F. Alexander, *Psychosomatic Medicine: Its Principles and Application* (New York: W. W. Norton Company, 1950), 300 pp.

disease of the body is related to the emotional make-up of the individual, therefore, are seldom conceived of by theorists of this decade as rigidly determined
by any given set of characteristics. The trend [20] is strongly toward the ac-
knowledgment of the close interrelationship of the mind-body whole; it is
probable that psychological, chemical, hereditary, and environmental factors
and pressures coexist in an individual and that a disturbance in one set of
components produces a disturbance in others. It is as yet not altogether clear
by what process the underlying emotional problems of a person become transmuted into physical symptoms, but it is inescapably clear that this transformation does take place.

Prominent among the situations that are likely to cause maladjustment,
which in turn may be converted into physical disease, is that complex of
stresses and strains that are lumped together under the term "maternal rejection." Since the need to be loved is extremely strong, the rejection has a
profound effect, although it may take an indirect form of expression. One
physician who studied sixty-three children that showed clinical symptoms of
asthma, hay fever, or eczema, and compared them with thirty-seven nonallergic children, found maternal rejection to be of overwhelming importance.[21]
Of the sixty-three allergic children, 98 percent were rejected; of the thirty-
seven nonallergic, who were also patients but with other complaints, the figure was 24 percent. In a more or less comparable group of unselected school
children, it has been reported to be 13 percent. A quotation from the report
is, however, more convincing than any figures:

> Some of the mothers stated that the children were "accidents" and that they had
> not wanted them. Said one, "He was an accident. I hated having him. I didn't want
> him and I wouldn't look at him for at least three days." . . . Said another, who had
> never cuddled or played with her six-year-old child, "When she was a baby I could at
> least put her in bed and out of sight and forget I had her. . . ." Still another said of her
> eight-year-old, "I didn't really want her. I was scared to have her. I've just existed since
> she was born. If anybody mentions having a baby I think they're crazy." Incidentally, this
> mother had from the child's birth turned over her entire care to a relative.
>
> Resentment in a good many women was unmasked. The mother of a small, blonde
> three-year-old gritted her teeth and muttered, "I actually felt I could kill her. I wanted
> to throw her against the wall and bash her brains out." . . . The mother of a boy
> almost seven exploded, "I've no other children, thank God! He almost killed me when
> he was born. I should never have had him. I'm a nervous wreck. He makes me ill.

---

[20] For a detailed discussion of the background models for much of the current
theory, see R. R. Grinker, *Psychosomatic Research* (New York: Grove Press, 1961), 215
pp., pp. 29–52.

[21] H. Miller and D. W. Baruch, "Psychosomatic Studies of Children with Allergic
Manifestations: I, Maternal Rejection: A Study of Sixty-Three Cases," *Psychosomatic
Medicine,* 10:275–278, 1948.

Physically ill. I spank him till he gets nervous and I get nervous. I threaten to send him away. He's driven me to distraction. Just mad." [22]

It does not take much imagination to realize that a child who is exposed for years to such maternal attitudes is likely to develop abnormalities and distortions of personality, which may be expressed by psychosomatic disorders, perhaps because small children cannot fight directly against such parental attitudes as those just indicated.

Stephen, at 13, would have been the handsomest boy in his ninth-grade class if he had not been disfigured by the constant oozing of skin eruptions that turned his olive skin into a pulpy, sore, itching mess. Several other boys in his class frequently had pimples and one or two had acne, but Stephen's case was so much worse than theirs that he was the butt of all the jokes from those slightly less miserable than he, and he was anathema to the girls. The school nurse had made repeated efforts to interest Stephen's mother in medical attention for the boy, but was met by a rather frightened insistence that the situation "was all Stephen's fault because he won't stop clawing at his face." Also, she insisted that the boy's father would never pay out good money for "a lot of medical nonsense."

One day the teacher noticed blood running down onto Stephen's collar and sent him to the school nurse, who bandaged the skin break and then arranged for him to talk with the school psychologist. Among other things, the psychologist asked Stephen to draw a picture of his family, with results shown in Figure 15-1. He drew his mother as a meek and gentle person, her hair being made black presumably to emphasize her Italian darkness with which her husband was forever taunting her. His stepfather was drawn as a big bruiser, although he was in fact a small sturdy man. Stephen drew himself as falling—and possibly giving a covert kick as he fell—and blotted out his face. Subsequent conferences brought out much hatred of the brutal stepfather and an ambivalent attitude toward his mother. He adored her and bitterly resented his stepfather's treatment of her, but he was also annoyed with her for putting him into such a difficult situation. He had always had an oily and easily infected skin. As he entered puberty, he had tried to scrub his face extra clean, but had been mocked by his stepfather as "trying to be a Latin lover." Stephen could not fight back directly at his stepfather, because the latter was too menacing. His rebelliousness and confusion acted as triggers to his skin condition.

This lad did not recover a normal skin until some time after he ran away from home, and not immediately then, since he presumably met new problems; but eventually, as his unhappy home receded into the background of his conscious-

---

[22] Miller and Baruch, "Psychosomatic Studies of Children with Allergic Manifestations," *loc. cit.*, pp. 276–279. Used by permission of the publisher, Paul B. Hoeber, Inc.

Fig. 15–1. Drawing of a family

ness, his skin did clear, although there will always be scars from the infections. There will also probably always be emotional scars, and it is likely that any later difficulties will follow the pattern already established.

Every teacher has pupils or friends who react to strain by having physical ailments. In mild forms this type of manifestation is common. Some pupils have stomach upsets, some have skin eruptions, some have difficulties of breathing, some have violent headaches, some cannot eat. The particular connection is partly accident and partly predisposition. To the outsiders the symptoms often look spurious, but they are not. The vomiting is real, the skin condition is real, the asthma is real, the headache is real. But the fundamental cause is emotional.

The Adolescent with Deep Involvement of the Personality Many adolescents, confronted with a world that seems to them too difficult to understand or adjust to, retreat into a dream world for refuge or comfort. In fact, practically everyone does so in a modest way from time to time. However, the degree of the retreat, its frequency, and the extent to which it involves the whole personality vary enormously. The need to flee back to an infantile state of dissociation from life probably depends not only upon the nature of the "trigger" situation but also upon the degree to which the person had followed a normal pattern of development until the stress became too great to bear. The consistent tendency to meet problems by withdrawing from them is very dangerous, because it produces an ever-increasing inability to meet the next problem and sets up a pattern that will lead to worse trouble as time goes on. When a child has unpleasant and unsupporting experiences at an early age, he may develop no reliable patterns for meeting everyday difficulties; since he has few resources, and since life keeps presenting him with more and more complex problems as he grows older, he becomes overwhelmed and tries to retreat further and further into childhood and infancy in order to reach a level at which he can find security. This habit of retreat from an impinging environment, which is seen as painful and confusing, takes a great part of the victim's energy and attention, so that he becomes socially isolated; moreover, he has never developed the necessary basic social skills, because he has been retreating all his life. The withdrawal itself walls him off more and more from the possibility of having normal human contacts, emotions, and satisfactions. The terribly quiet child in the classroom who wants dreadfully not to participate is exactly the one to whom the teacher needs to pay attention because he may be retreating to an unreachable level.

Sometimes the withdrawal is relatively mild. While destroying some of the individual's potential usefulness to society, it may nevertheless serve as a basis for existence of a sort, and never go further. Even in mild instances, however, it is clear that the personality is deeply involved. The social isolate in the schoolroom who grows up into a reticent, retiring, unobtrusive adult and lives a solitary life, working at some task well behind the scenes where adjustment to people is not too essential, is a good example. He or she is emotionally sick and could be helped by therapy, but the case is too mild to come to official notice for years, if ever. Those pupils who are developing such a withdrawn personality are no trouble to a teacher, except that sometimes she cannot get their attention.

Although there are certainly many notable exceptions, there is some indication in recent studies that there are shared patterns in the backgrounds of these withdrawing students. One such study,[23] now proceeding on a longitudinal basis to follow a group of children born in 1942 in a middle-sized Midwestern town, has found that the withdrawn children of the group, as determined by extensive testing and casework, had the following characteristics: they were more often girls than boys; they were likely to be over-age for their grade; they were below the group average in all of their verbal, spatial, and reasoning abilities; they tended to come from relatively large families, not broken by death or divorce; they were retarded in social development and had inadequate relationships with individuals of their own sex, and neither chose nor were chosen as friends by the opposite sex. They were less likely than other deviate groups to come from the lower classes. While many of these characteristics could be either causes or effects, the effort to study the problem over a long period of time and with wide community resources represents a solid advance in the methods of studying this problem before it becomes a full-blown, and often irreversible, withdrawal of the total person from all normal human contacts.

The history below tells briefly the story of a girl who is moderately withdrawn from life. She is still in some contact with reality, but the pattern of her reaction is already apparent.

Since Jean Rheibel's teachers are aware that she has normal intelligence, they are stimulated into all sorts of ingenious schemes to help Jean in bringing her grade average up to where she may pass into the 9th

---

[23] P. H. Bowman, R. F. DeHaan, J. K. Kough and G. P. Liddle, "Mobilizing Community Resources for Youth," *Supplementary Educational Monographs No. 85* (Chicago: University of Chicago Press, 1956), 134 pp., p. 35.

grade with her classmates. The only unstimulated one seems to be Jean, who just cannot pay enough attention to what goes on in class to grasp much of the material. She seems hardly to hear the voices of her eager teachers. She is not so much disobedient as just absent from the discussion in any meaningful way, and her assent to tasks is almost as empty as her passive indifference to class activities. The schoolroom and the social life of lunchtime flow around her unnoted, unresisted, and meaningless. At home, Jean "moves in a dream," as her nagging mother asserts. She never resists orders from her mother by anything more energetic than standing behind her father's chair, and she soon complies when he makes no effort to discuss the issue with either Jean or her mother. She showed considerable animation and interest when a baby brother was born, but her mother, never very warm with Jean, turned completely away from her to care for the sickly infant, and the girl felt briefly resentful. Actually Jean had to take over much of the baby's physical care during its illness because her mother "just couldn't handle that filth." Jean did the best she could for the baby without much appreciation. The early death of the baby left Jean feeling vaguely guilty; probably she had a secret fear that maybe her resentment of the affection given the fragile child had had something to do with its death. She knew she had not intentionally neglected the baby, but had she really done so because of her own feelings? When she tried to discuss this problem with her father, he turned his back and, typically, smoked his pipe in silence. Discussion with the mother was out of the question. So now Jean drifts through her days, hearing as little as possible and doing only enough to keep a precarious peace in the family, seeing less of the world around her each day and finding more reality in her own fantasy. A warm, sensitive, and patient adult in her life, or a special set of experiences and circumstances which bring her rewards in the real world around her may yet stop the course of her withdrawal. On the other hand, it would take little more in the way of unresolvable problems and frustrations to send her further into the dream, from which she may never emerge.

In recent decades there has been a good deal of research into the home background of those young people who have withdrawn so far that they are no longer in contact with reality. There seems to be moderately high agreement among investigators as to the character of the parents and the nature of the parent-child relations in the homes from which this type of mentally ill person comes. To put the matter briefly, the father is a nonentity, the mother is either overtly or covertly rejective, and the child is not wanted. Most of the research has concerned the mothers, partly because they were the dominant parent in the homes studied and partly because mothers are the central figures in a child's environment during the early years of his life, when his basic traits are developing. Upon adequate study, the mothers divide themselves into three distinct types which have in common a basic rejection of the child, although the forms of rejection are different.

The first is the openly hostile, domineering, aggressive mother who does not want to be bothered with her child and simply neglects him. These women are severe in their discipline, they constantly emphasize their child's short-comings, they compare him unfavorably with others, they are emotionally cold, and by nagging, threatening, and ridiculing him they openly express their attitude by showing scorn or disgust at behavior that is entirely normal for their child's age. Quite often behind this attitude there is a burning resentment because the child's birth thwarted some ambition of the mother's, or a profound disgust on her part toward sexual relationships, or a fierce resentment toward the pains of childbirth. In short, the child has, in his mother's view, wrecked her life or caused her unnecessary shock and pain, and she never forgives him for it. The second type shows quite different reactions. These mothers are overanxious, overprotective, and oversolicitous. They baby their child, fuss over him, protect him from the ordinary hazards of childhood, keep him away from age-mates, prevent him from growing up emotionally, and generally surround him with what is often referred to as "smother love." This behavior looks like the exact opposite of rejection, but there is reason to believe that it often arises from the same sources as openly rejective behavior and is, indeed, mainly a guilt reaction. Such a mother can never do enough for her child because she can never escape the feelings of guilt that come from an unconscious hostility and rejection. Her maternal overprotection is therefore a defense against herself, and she cannot relax it lest her shameful guilt of not wanting the child overcome her. Other overprotective mothers have different motivation, although their treatment of their children shows no significant differences from that just described. They are not compensating for an underlying hostility. They have identified their children with themselves, concentrated their whole lives upon them, and they protect them as they would protect themselves. An overprotective mother smothers her child just as completely, whether her behavior is "pure" or "compensatory." A third type of mother, whose behavior may push a child along the path toward schizophrenia, is the perfectionistic type. She is very ambitious for her child, she demands perfection from him, and her standards of behavior are higher than any small child can reach. She puts her faith in a rigid schedule and rigid training. She loads her child with cultural "extras"—music lessons, dancing lessons, singing lessons, riding lessons—she insists fanatically upon good manners, and she pushes her child into superior social groups if she can. She is prim, proper, and prissy. She regards sexual interests as disgusting and sinful. She is oppressively righteous. She is concerned with the externals of life and with fitting her child to take his place in her social world, but she is stingy with expressions of affection. Thus she wants her child to achieve the impossible, she constantly urges him on to greater efforts, criticizes even his best performances, and she denies him any real reward by denying him love. These three types—the hostile, the overprotective, and the perfectionistic—

may exist either separately or in several combinations. Perhaps the worst complex of traits is shown by the mother who is both rejective and perfectionistic. She is cold, hard, critical, severe, domineering, restrictive, rigid, righteous, and ambitious. In her defense, it should be said that she is usually the product of a childhood quite as unhappy as that of her children.[24]

Once the withdrawal pattern is well established, the withdrawn adolescent has little hope of emerging with a normal adjustment to life, even after treatment. Since the deviate of this type has never made an adequate adjustment to the outside world except for his own primitive needs, he does not have the resources to make use of further experiences, because all situations come to him already distorted by his faulty contact with reality. Two investigators [25] cite the case of a young man who had been admitted to a mental hospital at the age of 11 and had been given all kinds of treatment. After about two years he was able to return home and to maintain himself after a fashion. But when seen again some ten years later he had remained anxious and apprehensive, he showed only infantile emotions—such as his desire to marry some older woman who would look after him (that is, to find a mother-substitute)—and he still felt both himself and the world to be unreal. His recovery is about as good as can be expected under the present treatments, although new chemical approaches may be more rewarding. It is therefore necessary to identify the withdrawn child as soon as possible, before his retreat has become so extensive that he cannot any longer profit by contacts. The teacher is in the best position to recognize the withdrawn adolescent; his parents are too accustomed to his reactions to notice them, and in any case, they do not have daily experience with normal adolescents with whom to compare him.

The Pattern of Suspicion and Projection   The adolescent who shows this type of maladjustment is, above all, suspicious, and strongly inclined to blame his failures upon circumstances or upon other people. He is likely to be rigid and inflexible in his attitudes, he often misinterprets the best-intended acts by his classmates or teachers, he resists directions —usually distorting them. He complains steadily of unfairness; he blames everyone except himself. He gets furious because another pupil has "stolen" his idea for a theme, he regards being given a slightly critical look as a personal insult, he accuses the teacher of having favorites, and so on. If this pattern develops far enough the individual is said to be paranoid. The full-blown paranoid rarely appears during adolescence; it takes time and experience to develop the thoroughly distorted outlook on life that characterizes

[24] S. Reichard and C. Tilliman, "Patterns of Parent-Child Relationships in Schizophrenia," *Psychiatry,* 13:247–258, 1950.

[25] A. M. Freedman and L. Bender, "When the Childhood Schizophrenic Grows Up," *American Journal of Orthopsychiatry,* 27:553–566, 1957.

this form of deviation. However, the temperament from which it evolves appears at least by adolescence and often earlier. The tendencies are there and will build up into a most serious deviation if they are not somehow modified. One should not confuse these manifestations with the rebellious behavior of the adolescent who believes that all adults were invented just to be a nuisance to him. Both types are hostile and negative, but the merely rebellious can be reached by kindness; the adolescent with paranoid tendencies usually regards kindness as a trap and looks for the catch in it. Although it is difficult to win such an adolescent's confidence, a teacher can sometimes do so. The story below illustrates typical paranoid reactions and suggests the damage done if the tendencies remain unchecked. It is worthwhile to take some pains with this type of deviate because the damage, if not at least halted, is likely to be severe.

Edward is a 16-year-old boy with a chronic grouch. He believes himself to be a promising young inventor, but somehow things go wrong with each of his inventions. He has already had correspondence half a dozen times with the Patent Office because his applications have been turned down. Actually, his inventions, while often excellent, are not new. On one occasion, for instance, he invented an egg-beater with a double set of bearings so that one rotation of the wheel would produce two rotations in the lower part of the instrument. The chief difficulty with this invention is that it has already been invented, although as an original effort of a 16-year-old boy it shows real promise.

Edward's schoolwork has been good in mechanics and average along other lines. Two years ago he had a series of infections in his ears, developed a mastoid, and was in bed for six months. Upon the advice of his doctor, he remained out of school during the second semester, although by then he was able to be up and working at a bench he had built in the back of the garage. This year of illness had a most unfortunate effect, aside from its undermining of his vitality. He lost his former contacts with school friends, he had a disproportionate amount of time during which to work on his inventions, and when he returned to school he was a year behind those with whom he had been since his kindergarten days. He now feels annoyed with the school because he is in classes with pupils he looks down upon as being too young for him, he is chronically annoyed with the Patent Office for refusing his applications, and he is constantly in hot water at home because of his increasing indifference toward school.

About a month ago Edward left school and went to work in a garage. He held his job only two weeks and was fired because he insisted upon trying to sell the customers various little gadgets he had invented. He was surly when reprimanded and on several occasions refused to carry out orders. The boss mechanic reported him as having excellent mechanical ability and even admitted the value of some of Edward's inventions but stated that the boy could not tell a good gadget from a poor one. Criticism, however, was taken in such bad humor that Edward rarely received any assistance from anyone else in estimating the value of his ideas. Within a few days Edward got another job which he held less than a week, and from which he was discharged for very similar reasons. He is now at home spending practically his full time puttering around and trying to work out an invention for which he has neither the equipment nor the scientific preparation; moreover, it has already been invented.

Edward is definitely the paranoid type. Everyone else is always wrong, everyone is jealous of him, everyone treats him unfairly. He is always able to defend his side of a discussion with a mixture of arguments half true and half false. He still does not see why the Patent Office refuses to give him patents and ascribes their behavior primarily to jealousy of his youth. Nobody can tell Edward anything, and he is so completely isolated from his friends that there is no one in whom he has any real confidence.

Special Problems   Somewhat different from the usual problems of emotional deviation in adolescence, but intimately bound up with emotional difficulties, are those of drug addiction and alcoholism. The latter is increasingly a problem, but it is difficult to get any solid statistics on frequency. The young alcoholic rarely comes to the attention of the school, and if he is apprehended by the police it is usually in connection with some other offense as, for instance, driving while intoxicated. The case is then recorded as a traffic violation and gets lost in the traffic figures. For the adolescent age range there are only a few isolated reports, one of which states the following facts: [26] in 1959 about 45 percent of the boys in a high school and 27 percent of the girls sometimes drank beer, wine, or liquor; at ages 15 and 16, 28 percent were already drinking, and at ages 17 and 18, 47 percent; of those who drank liquor, it appeared that some 15 percent drank to escape from unsolved problems and were on their way to becoming adult alcoholics. There is need for more studies of high school populations before adequate material becomes available.

There is a similar lack of comprehensive material on drug addiction, although in this matter also there is certainty that the size and gravity of the problem are beyond the available statistics. Major efforts to reach the young addict through many channels are now being made. For example, in New York the first specialized clinic for treatment and study of the young drug addict has recently been opened. In 1961 Federal hospitals for the treatment of drug addicts admitted only 3939 patients,[27] but this number is more an indication of how few come to treatment than of how many addicts there are.

Many agencies come into contact with the young addict, for his problem pervasively, acutely, and immediately involves those around him, because the

---

[26] H. Whitman, "Our Drinking Habits," *Alcoholism Review and Treatment Digest* (Division of Alcoholic Rehabilitation, State of California, 1959), 38 pp., p. 28. See also, E. J. Bauer, "Drinking Patterns of Kansas High School Students," *Social Problems*, 5:317–326, 1958.

[27] *Annual Report, 1961* (Washington, D.C.: U.S. Department of Health, Education and Welfare, 1962), 418 pp., p. 188.

drug habit absorbs all aspects of his life. Therefore research on this problem is in progress in many fields. Such research is beginning to yield a variety of insights into the emotional nature of the youth prone to addiction. One recent study [28] finds the young addict to be deeply involved in conflicts around a father-figure, in problems of managing sexual drives and aggressive feelings, and in an unresolved oral conflict. He gets immediate pleasure and relief from the drug, and often he knows of no other way to escape the constant pressure of his problems. This study suggests the great importance of offering him situations in which he can have other rewarding experiences, to prevent him from depending exclusively on the brief, cruel pleasures of addiction. Another study [29] also emphasizes that the immediate, known reward of the drug experience as against the uncertainty of other rewards is an important factor in the return to addiction after the use had been temporarily halted by treatment. Certain other attitudes also contribute to the situation. The young addict is usually "geared for failure"; he is a peripheral observer of life, he is not related by close bonds to his normal social or peer group, and he finds the strain of therapy hard to bear because he is not able to deal with uncertainty.

Since the peddler of drugs is well aware that he has a fertile market at the high school level, it is the responsibility of all teachers to notify suitable medical authority in their schools if it seems to them that a pupil shows any signs of being under the influence of drugs. Many a high school "junkie" gets his supplies very close to the school, and he becomes, almost inevitably, an agent for the extension of the habit to other young people. Diagnosis and treatment should be left to doctors, but awareness of the problem is the concern of the entire staff.

▶ Prevention of Emotional Deviation

Anyone who seriously contemplates the dimensions of the problem involved in a program of mental health is likely to be overwhelmed by its mere size. It is clear that if significant gains are to be made in reducing the tragic intensity of individual suffering, prevention must be a primary concern. There are signs on the horizon of medical and social advances in the development of interdisciplinary teams, in group techniques, and in the concern of the entire community for better mental health. Indeed, prevention is an international concern, receiving world-wide emphasis through the facilities of the World Health Organization.[30]

The importance of the teacher in the program of mental health can

---

[28] T. L. Frazier, "Treating Young Drug Users: A Casework Approach," *Journal of the National Association of Social Workers,* 7:95–101, 1962.

[29] L. Gold, "Toward an Understanding of Adolescent Drug Addiction," *Federal Probation,* 22:42–48, 1957.

[30] "Mental Health Programs in Public Health Planning," *World Health Organization Chronicle,* 16:306–311, 1962.

hardly be overemphasized. She is in an excellent position to observe and to provide the helping atmosphere [31] which, after adequate evaluation, is essential in the treatment of emotional deviation. Recent studies indicate that the teacher of today is more sophisticated and more able to observe than her predecessors were. One study reported specifically that the classroom judgments of the well-qualified teacher were very like those of the psychiatric clinicians.[32] The teacher is probably indispensable in the process of bringing to professional attention those children and adolescents who are just beginning to show deviations in behavior and attitudes.

► **Summary**

There is at present a large segment of the adolescent population, sometimes estimated as high as 10 percent, which is in acute need of diagnosis and supportive care because of emotional deviations which can be crippling to the individual and to society. There are many types of behavior that represent deviations from normal adolescent reactions. A teacher needs to understand something of both causes and treatments, but she needs above all to be a good observer. In this capacity she can be invaluable. As a significant adult in the life of the adolescent, she can help to establish a supporting, helpful relationship with him in a class atmosphere which is conducive to creative development for all her students. Collaboration between the psychological adviser and the teacher will enable students to solve some of their problems themselves, may help others to seek the proper help at the proper time, and may prevent profound distress to the individual and inestimable loss to the society in which he lives.

References for Further Reading

BOOKS

Other Books and Monographs

Basowitz, H., *Anxiety and Stress* (New York: McGraw-Hill Book Company, 1955), 303 pp. (any two chapters).

Bender, L., *Aggressive Hostility and Anxiety in Children* (Springfield, Ill.: Charles C Thomas, Publisher, 1953), 184 pp. (Chap. 6 or 7).

Blos, P., *On Adolescence* (New York: Free Press, 1962), 269 pp. (pp. 215–244).

Greenblatt, M., *et al.*, *Mental Patients in Transition* (Springfield, Ill.: Charles C Thomas, Publisher, 1961), 480 pp. (pp. 163–175).

---

[31] C. Rogers, "The Characteristics of a Helping Relationship," in M. I. Stein, *loc. cit.*, pp. 95–112.

[32] E. M. Bower, "A Process for Early Identification of Emotionally Disturbed Children," *Bulletin of the California State Department of Education*, No. 73, 1958, 108 pp., p. 62.

Hutt, M., and R. G. Gibby, *Patterns of Abnormal Behavior* (Boston: Allyn and Bacon, Inc., 1957), 437 pp. (Chap. 7, 9, or 18).

Jahoda, M., *Current Concepts of Positive Mental Health* (New York: Basic Books, Inc., 1958), 136 pp. (Chap. 3).

Stevenson, G. S., *Mental Health Planning for Social Action* (New York: McGraw-Hill Book Company, 1956), 458 pp. (Chap. 19).

Weinberg, H., and A. W. Hire, *Case Book in Abnormal Psychology* (New York: Alfred A. Knopf, Inc., 1956), 320 pp. (any two chapters).

White, R. W., *The Abnormal Personality*, 2d ed. (New York: The Ronald Press Company, 1956), 625 pp. (Chap. 1, 2, 3, or 5).

ARTICLES

Barnes, M., *et al.*, "The Collaboration of Child Psychiatry Case Work and Group Work in Dealing with Mechanisms of Acting-Out," *American Journal of Orthopsychiatry*, 27:377–387, 1957.

Dunlop, K. W., "Some Observations on Acute Difficulties at the College Level," *Mental Hygiene*, 43:237–243, 1959.

Erwin, E. F., *et al.*, "Promoting Effective Relations between School and Child Guidance Clinic," *Mental Hygiene*, 41:542–546, 1957.

Garland, J. A., *et al.*, "Social Group Work as an Adjunctive Therapy for the Emotionally Disturbed Adolescent," *American Journal of Orthopsychiatry*, 32:691–705, 1962.

Lacy, J. I., "Differential Emphasis in Somatic Response to Stress," *Psychosomatic Medicine*, 14:71–81, 1952.

Landy, E., and E. Scanlan, "Relationship between School Guidance and Psychiatry for Adolescents," *American Journal of Orthopsychiatry*, 32:682–690, 1962.

Masterson, J. F., "Psychotherapy of the Adolescent: A Comparison with Psychotherapy of the Adult," *Journal of Nervous and Mental Diseases*, 127:511–517, 1958.

Maudler, G., and S. B. Sarason, "A Study of Anxiety and Learning," *Journal of Abnormal and Social Psychology*, 47:166–173, 1952.

Simmons, O. B., and J. A. Davis, "Interdisciplinary Research in Mental Illness," *American Journal of Sociology*, 58:297–308, 1957.

Suggestions for Research Problems [33]

1. Teachers are often frustrated by their inability to deal constructively with pupils who show emotional deviation. It would be helpful to devise a brief manual for their guidance, telling them what agencies within the school, the community, or the state can help them.

---

[33] See note, p. 11.

2. There are dozens of case histories of adolescents in the literature, but these life stories are not easily available to teachers. It is suggested that a collection of descriptions—some from the literature and some from actual cases in the local schools—should be prepared. Such a collection should be useful in helping teachers to recognize emotional deviation as it appears in the schoolroom, rather than in the mental clinic.

PART FOUR | Social
Development

Chapter 16 | Normal Social Growth

T_{HE} adolescent years are, pre-eminently, a period of social development and adjustment. During the preceding years of childhood there has been, to be sure, a beginning of socialization, through the acquisition of fundamental social skills. The elementary school child can learn how to get along with others of his own age and sex in such social situations as arise during his schoolwork or his play outside school. He can also develop a workable relationship between himself and his parents or teachers. It is quite necessary that these childish adjustments take place, since they serve as a basis for the more complete development of the adolescent years. The social development of children is, however, limited both by their immature mentality and by their inattention to many social stimuli.

With the oncoming of adolescence, the boy or girl becomes acutely aware of social relationships and pressures. For a few years, in fact, these relationships become of overwhelming importance. The period is a somewhat trying one for parents, because they recede into the background and no longer can exert much influence. It is, of course, best that this development should take place, since an adolescent has to become independent of his home, but the process is sometimes a strain.

The next two chapters form a unit, with the topics assigned to one or the other in a perhaps arbitrary manner. This present chapter will deal with measurement of normal social growth, acceptance or rejection by one's peers, self-evaluation, prestige or status, and the nature of adolescent spontaneous social life. Assigned to the following chapter are the topics of dating, leadership, and the selection of friends.

▶ Measurement of Social Behavior

In order to see the total picture and to develop a sense of what is and is not normal growth, it seems best to begin with consideration of such rating scales or other measuring instruments as will give a standard against which the behavior of a single individual or group of individuals may be checked. The measures are at least partially objective. Those that are based upon the impressions of the raters as to some pupil's personal characteristics are relatively unsatisfactory, partly because the impressions are too general and partly because the opinions are too subjective. Ratings that are based upon descriptions of actual behavior are better, because they are more objective. Short samples from a scale will be presented later. It is old but still good and has the advantage of running from birth to maturity. Three categories from this scale seem worth demonstrating as samples of what is meant by social maturity at different levels. It can be seen in Table 16–1 that there is progressive development in each category of behavior as babies become children and children become adolescents and the latter become adults. The norms show rapid increases in mastery of the basic social skills during childhood, and preadolescence but relatively small gains later on. Perhaps the scale does not contain enough items for the upper levels, perhaps the elementary skills are merely broadened and deepened, or possibly there are so many social demands during adolescence that boys and girls become confused and really do learn slowly.

Perhaps a word should be said about the concept of social age, a measurement parallel to that of mental or emotional age, which could be derived from the use of scales like the one presented in part below. Pupils show an infantile social age if they are noisy, if they get their materials into a mess and then walk off and leave them, if they grab what they want, if they are destructive, if their humor runs to slapstick, or if they have little perception of their own relation to their peers. Abject conformity and loyalty to one's friends represent a somewhat higher social age. A socially mature person is characterized by his awareness of his own role in his group, by his desire to keep the peace, by his sense of fair play, by his honest, considerate treatment of others, by his use of general principles in guiding his conduct, and by his customary conformity to the mores, which is, however, linked with a willingness to be a nonconformist if necessary when the mores run counter to his convictions. In the course of time it is probable that measurements of social age will be in as common use as those of mental maturity.

▶ The Adolescent Peer-Group

The unit of social life during adolescence is a small group that is often referred to by adolescents as "the crowd" but by psychologists as the "peer group." It is typically composed of an equal number of boys and girls. The core of it contains six to eight members, with perhaps another half-dozen adolescents around the fringes. Those who are steady members of the group customarily live within short driving distance of each other, attend the same school, and come from roughly the same socio-economic background.

The activities of the crowd vary somewhat from one season of the year to another, but at almost any season they include listening to the radio, watching TV, occasionally going to a movie, eating, dancing together at the home of some member, and listening to phonograph records. In the summer they

Table 16–1: THREE CATEGORIES OF SOCIAL MATURITY

Communication	Self-direction	Socialization
Imitates sounds (0–1) *		Reaches for familiar persons (0–1)
Follows simple directions (1–2)	Overcomes simple obstacles (1–2)	Plays with other children (1–2)
Relates experiences (2–3)	Initiates own play activities (2–3)	
		"Performs" for others (3–4)
	Goes about neighborhood unattended (4–5)	Plays vigorous games (4–5)
Prints simple words (5–6)	Goes to school unattended (5–6)	Plays simple table games (5–6)
Uses pencil for writing (6–7)	Goes to bed unassisted (6–7)	Participates freely in childish play (7–9)
	Reads on own initiative (8–9)	
Writes occasional short letters (10–11)	Goes about home town freely (9–10)	Talks to friends on the telephone (10–11)
Enjoys books, newspapers, magazines (11–12)	Is left to care for self or others (11–12)	
	Buys own clothing accessories (12–15)	Plays difficult, organized games (12–15)
Communicates freely by letter (15–18)	Goes to nearby places alone (15–18)	Engages in adolescent group activities (15–18)
Follows current events (15–18)	Goes out unsupervised, daytimes (15–18)	
	Looks after own health (18–20)	
	Goes out nights unrestricted (18–20)	
	Uses money providently (20–25)	Assumes responsibility beyond own needs (20–25)
	Purchases for others (25+)	Directs or manages affairs of others (25+)
	Creates own opportunities (25+)	Shares community responsibility (25+)

* Numbers in parentheses indicate age level.

SOURCE: E. A. Doll, *Vineland Social Maturity Scale* (Minneapolis, Minn.: Educational Test Bureau). Used with the permission of the publisher, Educational Test Bureau Division, American Guidance Service, Inc., Minneapolis.

go on picnics together, or they sit on someone's porch and talk—with at least one trip each evening to the neighborhood drive-in—or they go swimming, and so on. In the winter the group sits around in the home of a member, watches TV, and raids the icebox from time to time. None of this comes under the heading of adventure as seen through the eyes of late childhood, but it is apparently exciting to the adolescent. It is adventure, not into the world of things but into the world of social relationships. An adult listening to the conversation of such a crowd for an evening can hardly see that the chatter has been worthwhile. It does not seem to start anywhere, to go anywhere, or to be about anything. It is, however, satisfactory to the participants. It obviously gives them an opportunity to develop their conversational powers on other people whose abilities are no better than their own. Other values obtained from such a crowd include experiences in getting along with other people, practice in social skills, development of loyalty to a group, practice in judging people, assistance in the emancipation-from-home procedure, and experience in love-making under circumstances in which the participants are protected from serious consequences. Moreover, the group gives its members a feeling of social security, of "belonging."

The peer group plays such an important role in the lives of adolescents that a teacher should understand its nature and its values to the members. It should be remembered that adolescent boys and girls are very uncertain of themselves because they are changing so rapidly. One function of the peer group is to defend the adolescent from his own uncertainty through the security of his membership in a group. It also provides a chance for him to achieve status on his own merits—not those of his family—in terms of the values held by his age-mates. It gives him an opportunity for further developing his self-image, especially as regards the behavior that differentiates him or her from members of the opposite sex. And, as any group can do, the peer group helps the adolescent to develop the qualities that he will need in adult life. It is necessary for the school to work in terms of this spontaneous organization of youth and not try to work against it, since it has more authority over adolescent behavior than adults have.[1]

The "peer culture," the sum total of spontaneous social manifestations among age-mates, is most clearly defined and most influential during the middle years of adolescence. At this time adult values have less power to produce behavior than peer values.[2] That is, if "everyone" is wearing berets, it is almost impossible to persuade an adolescent to wear any other sort of headgear, no matter how formal the occasion or how inappropriate the beret; if "no one" is wearing berets, then an adolescent will not wear one even to keep the hair out of his eyes while he is sailing a boat. Apparently, one of the deep-

---

[1] R. L. Simpson and I. H. Simpson, "The School, the Peer Group, and Adolescent Development," *Journal of Educational Sociology,* 32:37–41, 1958.

[2] C. E. Bowerman and J. W. Kinch, "Changes in Family and Peer Orientation of Children between the Fourth and Tenth Grades," *Social Forces,* 37:206–211, 1959.

est of adolescent needs is the need to be supported and approved by his peers. Deviations of any sort from the mode of the group are painful. An adolescent cannot afford to risk the ridicule of his intimate friends because he is too dependent upon them for approval. A teacher should always keep in mind this dependence of adolescents upon their age-mates. She has to work with it, because she will certainly be unsuccessful if she tries to work against it. As the years pass, the values of the crowd gradually mature and approach the adult norm for their social group. Also, the crowd tends to disintegrate under the pressures of later adolescence and early maturity. But while it endures, it is the most formative influence in the life of the average boy or girl.

On the debit side, it is probable that the crowd encourages some degree of snobbery and that it has an undesirable effect upon those who belong to no crowd at all. Sometimes an intense rivalry springs up between two crowds and leads to extremely silly behavior and occasional outbreaks of violence in some communities under economic or social stress, but such situations do not usually last long. If some observant and tactful older person can bring about an attachment to an existing crowd for the isolates or can influence the growth of a new crowd among those who belong to none, and can manage to curb the occasional excesses of loyalty, this spontaneous social group could become even more valuable than it is naturally. Even as it is, the crowd probably does more to bring about normal social growth than teachers and parents combined.

The clique, the fraternity, and the sorority are less healthy manifestations at the secondary school level. Adolescents go to enough extremes in social adulation and social ostracism even at best, without the encouragement of group support. The clique, of whatever character, is too tight an organization for a member's own good, it is by nature intolerant, it is usually based upon either wealth or social class, and it demands a loyalty from its members that prevents many possible social contacts from taking place and reduces the effectiveness of those that do occur. A clique is really a caricature of a crowd, an out-of-proportion drawing with the least desirable traits overemphasized. Cliques are unhealthy both emotionally and socially, and they precipitate unhealthy reactions among both the outsiders and the members. The high school fraternity or sorority is no better than any other clique. It serves no useful function—in colleges these societies at least provide rooming space —it is mainly a mark of "caste," and it encourages its members to ignore other school groups.

The spontaneous groupings of the adolescent population can be, and have been, studied and classified in a number of ways. One set of groupings is based upon consideration of socio-economic status, preferred activities, and self-identification as to role.[3] Four groups to be found in almost any high school are the following:

---

[3] H. R. Phelps and J. E. Horrocks, "Factors Influencing Informal Groups of Adolescents," *Child Development,* 29:69–86, 1958.

1. A group, largely lower-class and of low ability, emancipated from home, and playing adult roles.

2. A higher socio-economic group of high moral code, moderate emancipation, and conforming to the demands of home and school but carrying on independent activities.

3. A group that is not emancipated from home and centers its activities around home, school, and community.

4. A group whose ways are those of people in the lowest socio-economic levels.

In this study there was a total of ten groups, each reflecting a way of life that was derived from common backgrounds, common interests and activities, and common concepts of role.

The pupil who does not belong to a crowd is miserable indeed. Youngsters are not self-reliant enough to stand alone. The sense of belonging is an indispensable ingredient for their happiness. Sometimes social isolation springs from deep-seated factors of personality but usually from relatively superficial matters of dress, manners, and attitudes. A teacher can often help such adolescents to become acceptable by persuading them to alter their appearance, to conform better to superficial social requirements, and to drop one or two annoying mannerisms. If the causes of isolation lie in a distortion of personality, a teacher can still provide sympathy and understanding, and she can try to bring the pupil into contact with those who can help him directly with his basic problems.

One way in which children and adolescents test each other and win respect from one another is by the giving and taking of "dares." This type of behavior is interesting in itself as a social phenomenon, and it is also a contributing cause to many accidents, as when a teenage boy dares a friend to drive at 90 miles an hour. A total of 720 rural pupils in grades 4 through 12, both boys and girls, were asked to answer a series of questions concerning what dares they had been asked to take and which they had taken. Actually, there was little difference between the two; the refusal to take a dare carried so much loss of face among one's peers that most of the dares were accepted. The things the pupils dared each other to do were of several types: dangerous physical acts, rejection of authority in home or school, social or physical aggression toward the same or the opposite sex. The percent of children who had received dares involving dangerous physical acts or resistance to home control are shown in Figure 16–1. The curve for the boys begins and remains fairly high until the ninth-grade level, at which time this type of dare apparently becomes "kid stuff" and loses its popularity. The girls show the same development, except that the drop begins sooner, with a steady decline from grade 6 on. In contrast, the girls at most ages received more dares involving a flouting of home authority, and the percents were still rising in grade 12. The boys' curve shows a somewhat similar situation, but suggests that conflicts

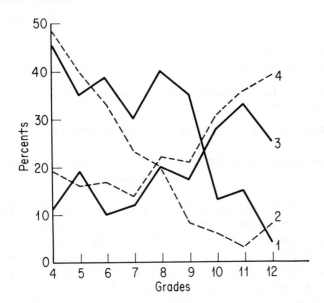

Fig. 16–1. The taking of "dares" 1. Dangerous physical acts, boys; 2. dangerous physical acts, girls; 3. challenge of home authority, boys; 4. challenge of home authority, girls

Based on S. L. Witryol and S. E. Calkins, "Marginal Social Values of Rural School Children," *Journal of Genetic Psychology,* 92:81–93, 1958. Adapted from Table 4, p. 89.

between mother (probably) and son were less frequent than those involving mother and daughter.

To an adult, the social behavior of boys and girls when they are left to themselves often seems silly, awkward, or merely wasteful of time that might well be used otherwise. It is true that adolescent social skills are undeveloped and awkward, but for that very reason boys and girls need precisely the kind of experiences they crave, in order that they may acquire poise and adjust themselves to the demands of society. The adult, whether teacher or parent, has a definite role in relation to the spontaneous social life of adolescence. The main thing is that the adult should remain not far away and available when wanted but should not interfere when not wanted, or make attempts at guidance that can be detected for what they are. Attempts to mingle with the group as if one were of the same generation are not only futile and ridiculous but are practically certain to alienate the adolescents. Any obvious effort at control has the same effect. It is one of the minor mysteries of life that some fine, educated, well-intentioned men and women are quite incapable of providing acceptable supervision, while certain quite ordinary, uneducated, only moderately interested adults do so admirably. One of the writers remembers one family from her own adolescent days in which the mother was unable to make any but the most distant contacts with the cronies of her adolescent daughter, whereas the Irish cook was perfect in the role of "teacher, philosopher, and friend." The mother greeted her daughter's guests courteously and pleasantly, but then retired to the second floor. The cook stayed in her kitchen, except when she was bringing food to the guests, but almost every boy and girl in the group went to her once or twice every evening with problems, great or small, and was given hardheaded advice. She never intruded, but she was available when wanted, and her mere presence not only prevented misbehavior, but spread a feeling of complete security.

▶ Social Acceptance and Rejection

Study of the traits which make an adolescent popular or unpopular has indicated that both acceptance and rejection of an individual by a group are complex phenomena. The commonest method of investigation has been to have each student in a class select from his schoolmates the one or two whom he most admires, most prefers to work with, likes best to play with, would choose as an intimate friend, would want for a class or club president, and the like. The students also list the names of those whom they dislike. In addition, the teachers may submit what evidence they have as to who is accepted and who is not. The popular students are those who are mentioned by the largest number of classmates as first or second choice in the largest number of situations, are not listed as being disliked, are considered by their teachers as being easy to find partners for in any group undertaking, are noticed by their teachers as being continually with others and often in the center of a group, and have a record of having been actually elected by their classmates to sundry positions of honor. The unpopular students are those who are never or almost never mentioned as admired or liked in any situation but are often listed as disliked, are avoided by others and rejected if they make advances, are difficult to find partners for in group undertakings, and are regularly the last ones to be chosen for team games on the playground.

One early study was based upon results from 665 college girls who named which girls of the group they regarded as best friends and which they disliked.[4] The total number of positive choices was 1860, or 2.8 per girl; for negative choices, or rejections, the total was 682, or 1.02 per girl. By assigning positive numerical values to first, second, or third position of choice on another girl's blank and negative values for first, second, or third position of rejection on another's blank, and then subtracting the negative from the positive, the investigator obtained "prestige status scores" which varied from the least popular girl at -76 to the most popular at $+607$. Of the 665 girls, 200 rejected no one. It will be noted that liking was commoner than disliking;

---

[4] C. Smucker, "Management of Group Tension through the Use of Negative Sociometric Data," *Sociometry,* 10:376–385, 1947.

acceptances exceeded rejections by a rate of 3 to 1. This reflection upon human nature should be a comforting thought.

The second investigator studied the interpersonal relations among 400 girls in a reform school.[5] The technique was much the same as that just described. There were 1045 choices, or 2.6 per person, and 587 rejections, 1.4 per girl. These figures agree well enough with those from the first study. The investigator next identified those girls who were conspicuously "overselected," that is, the 21 girls who were most popular; also, those who were conspicuously "underchosen," the 22 who were least popular. As a group, the unpopular tended to claim a disproportionate number of the most popular as their friends and to ignore each other, neither choosing nor rejecting. The popular girls tended to choose each other and to assign such rejections as they made to the most unpopular members of the group, often rejecting the very girls who had chosen them.

In addition to the selections by the girls, the investigator obtained ratings for each girl from the housemothers in the school. In evaluating these judgments, one has to remember that the girls were in a reform school, and the housemothers were probably influenced unduly by the amount of trouble each girl caused her. The unpopular girls were mainly of the aggressive, "chip-on-the-shoulder" type. Conspicuously missing are the girls who are withdrawn, shy, inactive, repressed, negative, and unsocial, presumably because they do not indulge in enough overt behavior of any kind ever to be put into a reform school. The popular girls, however, showed two constellations of traits: one type is friendly, placid, motherly, and reasonably dependable; the other is more dynamic, has many qualities of active leadership, but does get into trouble with the rules and regulations and shows certain basic antagonisms toward others that leaders of her type do not usually show.

The behavior and attitudes of individual girls were recorded both by diagrams and by case studies. The diagrams show the number of choices and rejections made by each girl, plus the choices and rejections expressed toward her by others. In Figure 16-2 there are eight diagrams. Jean and Jacqueline were among the most popular girls in the reform school; Beatrice and Sarah were also popular, but less so. Vera, Alice, Eva, and Amelia were all extremely unpopular. Vera was a complete isolate; she received no votes at all. The other three were near isolates, each being chosen once. The diagrams are constructed in the following manner: in the smallest circle is the girl's name; in the next larger is a record of her choices and rejections—the former shown by arrows with unbroken lines in the upper half of the diagram and the latter by arrows with broken lines in the lower half; the outside ring records the reactions of other girls toward the one whose name appears in the middle area. When the heads of two unbroken arrows, one from the outer and one from

---

[5] H. H. Jennings, *Leadership and Isolation: A Study of Personality in Interpersonal Relationships,* 2d ed. (New York: David McKay Company, Inc., 1950), 349 pp.

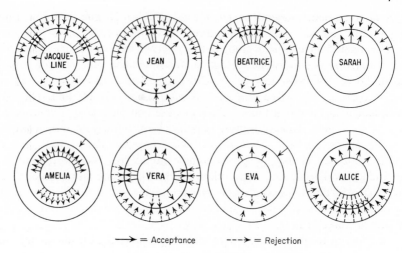

→ = Acceptance   ---→ = Rejection

Fig. 16–2. Popular and unpopular girls

From H. H. Jennings, *Leadership and Isolation* (New York: David McKay Company, Inc., 1950), pp. 105–111. Used with the permission of the publisher.

the middle circle meet, the liking between the two girls involved was mutual; when the heads of two broken arrows meet, the girls disliked each other; when the heads of an unbroken and a broken arrow meet, the first girl liked the other while the second rejected the first—or vice versa.

Jacqueline is the most outgoing and sociable of the popular girls. She made relatively many choices—ten. Of the ten she chose, all but one chose her. She was chosen also by another thirteen girls whom she had not selected as friends. She rejected five girls, but was not herself rejected by anyone. Jean made fewer choices (seven), of which five were mutual; nineteen other girls also chose her. Jean rejected four girls, one of whom rejected her. One other girl also disliked her. The picture is not quite as good as that for Jacqueline, but nevertheless shows a girl who is highly popular, even if she does arouse occasional friction. Beatrice's diagram shows five mutual choices, one unreciprocated choice on her part, and eleven additional choices directed toward her. She rejected three girls and was rejected by one. Sarah is near the lower limit of the twenty-one overchosen girls. She made one mutual choice, and three additional ones; eleven other girls liked her. She neither has nor arouses dislikes. Her own selections are remarkably few. Her acceptance seems to consist largely in being unobjectionable rather than in being truly popular. Eva has little emotional reaction toward others. She has established no mutual contacts either positive or negative with anyone. Two girls disliked her and one liked her, but perhaps without her knowing it. Amelia, equally isolated, although less actively disliked, does not share Eva's resignation to the indifference of others. She made fifteen positive choices and nine rejections, but got only one vote in return. She is emotionally active but seems unable to establish even enough contact with others to be disliked. Alice and Vera are of a different type altogether. Alice expressed a liking for five girls, one of whom liked her. She thus does have *one* friend. On the debit side, she was involved in seven mutual antagonisms and was disliked by an additional nine girls, toward whom she is neutral. Alice gives evidence of being a fighter who meets hate with hate. Vera shows a pathetic attempt to make contacts, which lead her into rejection. Of her nine choices, six disliked her. She rejected four girls, and was rejected by two of them, plus ten others, not counting the six already mentioned. No one voted for her. Unlike Alice, she has no friend to fall back on, and she has a positive genius for persuading people to dislike her.

The popular girls showed various constellations of such traits as good looks, vitality, intelligence, sympathy, quick insights, enjoyment of life, outgoing manner, high verbal ability, appreciation of others, generosity, tact, and lack of nervous mannerisms and habits. One was appealing mainly because she was young, full of energy, vivacious, and friendly; another, because she was understanding and tactful, and so on. The unpopular girls sometimes had the ingredients of good looks, but they did not make use of them. They were unsure of themselves or else they overcompensated for a fundamental unsureness by pestering others. Some were self-conscious, shy, and withdrawn; others had objectionable mannerisms; some seemed to be pale nonentities. As a group, they did not know how to make normal contacts with others, and they were markedly self-centered. One or two had developed compensatory mechanisms by trying to buy friendship in return for services. Inevitably, they were dejected and unhappy.

Traits Admired or Disliked The list of traits to be presented in Table 16–2 was derived from a number of sources. In some cases a trait that contributed to unpopularity is merely the reverse of one that is admired, but this contrast does not always appear.

According to this list, appearance and manner are often of great importance in determining social acceptance. An attractive face, a trim figure, a pleasant manner, a fluency in small talk, a stylish hairdo, and clothes prescribed by the fad of the moment are elements of attractiveness. Homeliness, dirtiness, excessive fatness or thinness, excessive perspiration, out-of-date or shabby clothes, hesitancy in speech, crudeness in manner or any real variation from the group norm are sources of unpopularity. Those girls who rate lowest in appearance are found to be negative, withdrawn, self-effacing, and not interested in people or events. Rejected by their age-mates, they have evidently stopped trying to maintain social contacts. An unpopular girl could

Table 16–2: LIST OF TRAITS

Liked	*Disliked*
A. *Appearance and manner*	A. *Appearance and manner*
1. Has good looks	1. Is unattractive
2. Is neat and clean	2. Has physical handicap
3. Wears appropriate clothes	3. Dresses inappropriately
4. Is natural	4. Is dirty
5. Is well mannered	
B. *Leadership type of popularity*	B. *Withdrawal behavior*
6. Makes many contacts	5. Is listless
7. Is active, energetic, enthusiastic	6. Is absorbed in self
8. Is already somewhat of a leader	7. Is too bookish
9. Is a good talker	8. Is too prissy, too "good"
10. Pursues many activities	9. Is timid, shy, embarrassed
11. Shows initiative	10. Is overdependent on others
12. Is usually good in athletics	11. Is poor in athletics
	12. Has no interest in activities
	13. Has inadequate social skills
C. *Social type of popularity*	C. *Retaliatory, attention-seeking, behavior*
13. Is kind and friendly	14. Is resentful, carries a grudge
14. Is cooperative	15. Is quarrelsome, often fights
15. Is unselfish	16. Is a bully
16. Is usually cheerful	17. Is rude and bad mannered
17. Is even tempered	18. Is noisy, obstreperous
18. Is quiet	19. Shows off, brags
19. Is sympathetic	20. Is stuck-up, snobbish
20. Is responsible	21. Interferes with others
21. Is loyal	22. Is domineering
22. Is truthful	23. Thinks he is picked on
23. Has high ideals	24. Is constantly making alibis
24. Has good sense of humor	25. Is effeminate
25. Has maturity	26. Is stubborn
26. Is good company	27. Is untruthful
27. Has adequate social skills	28. Is disloyal
	29. Is moody
D. *Miscellaneous*	D. *Miscellaneous*
28. Is intelligent	30. Is stupid
29. Gets good marks	31. Is immature

30. Has good reputation	32. Is "queer" or "silly"
31. Is a good sport	33. Is a poor sport
32. Has a good home	34. Is lazy

SOURCE: Based on the following references: A. Anastasi and S. Miller, "Adolescent Prestige Factors in Relation to Scholastic and Socioeconomic Variables," *Journal of Social Psychology*, 29:43–50, 1949; M. E. Bonney, R. E. Hoblit, and A. H. Dreyer, "A Study of Some Factors Related to Sociometric Status in a Men's Dormitory," *Sociometry*, 16:287–301, 1953; M. L. Northway, "Outsiders," *Sociometry*, 7:10–25, 1944; A. Schoepper, "Sex Differences in Adolescent Socialization," *Journal of Social Psychology*, 38:175–185, 1953; M. R. Feinberg, M. Smith, and R. Schmidt, "An Analysis of Expressions Used by Adolescents at Varying Economic Levels to Describe Accepted and Rejected Peers," *Journal of Genetic Psychology*, 93:133–148, 1958.

presumably improve her status by remedying her defects of appearance; indeed, this is precisely the path that unpopular girls of financially adequate families follow, often with success.

Study of popular and unpopular students usually reveals at least two types of the former and three of the latter. Some greatly admired individuals have a high degree of social aggressiveness; that is, they are expansive, talkative, daring, energetic, and enthusiastic; they make at least superficial contacts with almost everyone. Others who are equally popular have no dash or verve whatever and have achieved their acceptance through being friendly, kind, sympathetic, good natured, and happy. They are also more mature emotionally and socially than their friends. Individuals of this second type are not so much admired as loved. The first group of "outsiders" includes those maladjusted youngsters who are aggressive, noisy, rebellious, boastful, overtalkative, and selfish. These children are actively disliked by their age-mates. The second type includes those who are not interested in social life and are therefore immature in social skills, shy, easily embarrassed, passive, and quiet when in a group. The boy or girl who loves to study may sometimes belong in this last category; so also does the radio enthusiast or the eager young philatelist who pores over his stamp collection instead of going to football games and cheering for the team. This second type of unpopular pupil is the isolate whom no one mentions at all. He does not repel people; he merely fails to get their attention. The third type includes those pupils who are introverted, listless, under par physically, and withdrawn emotionally. The normal youngsters disregard such human oddities, label them as "queer," relegate them to social limbo, and forget them.

The Effect of Social Class upon Friendship Selection and Social Prestige As teachers have known for a good many years, pupils from the same socio-economic level tended to form more or less exclusive groups, which sometimes have a disruptive influence upon the social life of the school. One quite recent study of all the 16-year-old adolescents in a small city makes clear the pervasiveness of social class in the activities and attitudes of the pupils. As a first step, all the families that had 16-year-old children were grouped into five socio-economic classes, upon the basis of several types of evidence. The investigators then administered tests of various kinds, interviewed the adolescents, collected their opinions, and studied their social interrelations. The relation of the data on social class to the activities and attitudes of the pupils in the high school is of special interest because it demonstrates how social stratification, even in a democracy, can produce marked inequalities of many types. A few outstanding examples are shown in Figure 16–3. Since there were relatively few pupils in the two upper classes, they have been put together.

As one might expect, intelligence showed a rough relation to class. No pupil in Classes I and II had an IQ below 90. The bulk of the lowest IQs was found in Class V. It should be noted, however, that there were also some high IQs in the lowest class. Marks showed an even higher relationship to social class than intelligence did. Half the pupils in Classes I and II were doing good work, and no one was failing; in Class V, nearly a third were failing and less than a tenth were doing good work. Every pupil in Classes I and II wanted to continue in school, and everyone took some part in extracurricular activities. Almost 90 percent of the Class V pupils wanted to leave school at once, and only 25 percent of them participated in activities. Those from Classes III and IV occupied a position between the two extremes in almost every trait or measurement. The data on attendance at football games are particularly revealing. Ninety percent from Classes I and II and 65 percent from Class III attended all or almost all the games. Evidently they felt the team was "their" team and the school was "their" school. Pupils from Class V and over half of those in Class IV attended few if any games, thus giving indisputable evidence that they did not feel themselves bound to the school by emotional ties. The data on vocational plans followed the lines one might expect, in view of the home backgrounds from which the pupils came. Both boys and girls had from a half to two thirds of their dates with members of their own social class, although it is improbable that they made their selections with social standing in mind. In no instance was there any dating between the members of the highest and the lowest classes. In the particular high school under consideration the students attached "labels" to each other, thus expressing their spontaneous attitudes. The three labels in current usage were the "elite," the "good kids," and the "grubbies." The members of the first two groups were socially accepted, the difference being that the elite set the tone and furnished the leadership. The grubbies were rejected. No one in Class I or II was characterized as a grubby, and only 1 percent of those in Class III were so labeled. The percent increased to 20 in Class IV and burgeoned to 85 for the lowest social group, from which there was no contribution to the ranks of the elite.

In the above sample, the boys and girls who had dates with adolescents

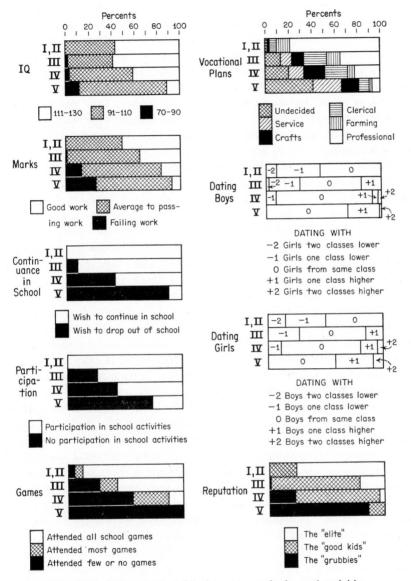

Fig. 16–3. Influence of social class upon attitudes and activities

Based on figures in A. B. Hollingshead, *Elmtown's Youth* (New York: John Wiley & Sons, Inc., 1949, 480 pp.), pp. 172–216.

one or two classes above their own, those from the lower groups who did well in school and participated in its activities, and those who were planning to enter the professions were all trying, by various routes, to improve their status. Some of them will succeed, and their children will start upon a higher rung of the social ladder than that originally occupied by their parents. At the other end, the small number of births in Classes I and II families leads to a constant shrinking of their proportional representation. Some of these families die out, some deteriorate, and some meet financial reverses; their places are then taken by families from Classes III and IV who have prospered financially and now function as social arbiters in the community. These processes go on all the time, and their effects are reflected in the attitudes of high school pupils toward each other. Probably the high school involved in this study should initiate measures to make school more attractive to boys and girls from Classes IV and V and to help them make themselves more attractive to other students. One trouble may be that prestige in different social groups rests upon different characteristics. Thus, members of a lower class tend to value self-assertion and aggressiveness, presumably because these are the traits which might lead one upward in the world and also because, in any case, they represent a protest against being considered "lower." Members of an upper class among adolescents usually tend to conform to adult standards and therefore resent the aggressiveness. Sometimes a joint undertaking in the school leads to a greater understanding on both sides, with resulting better adjustment. In the study just reported, the degree of exclusion and rejection seems somewhat higher than it needs to be. One has to remember, however, that differences in ability and achievement will continue to exist and will inevitably lead to differences in the attitudes of pupils toward each other.

It is possible to select socially gifted children, perhaps about as reliably as one can select those who are intellectually gifted. The procedure consists in applying measures of social maturity and attitudes and assembling opinions from both teachers and age-mates as to each pupil's personal qualities. The pupils who were ranked as highest in social skills in one such study showed a behavioral pattern in their reactions to the tests that did not appear in the reactions of those who were ranked as low in social skills by both teachers and other pupils.[6] This type of ability is in some ways as useful to society as any other kind, and it needs to be fostered and developed. And in some situations it is indispensable. One of the writers knows a middle-aged woman who has marked social gifts. Intellectually she is about average, and her academic interests are nil. But she can walk into an office in which there are 30 unhappy, disgruntled workers and have the place humming like a happy bee-

[6] R. K. Jarecky, "Identification of the Socially Gifted," *Exceptional Child,* 25:415–419, 1959.

hive in about two days. Or she can organize a group of women for some other special project, usually without even leaving her own house—just by telephone—and the whole thing moves forward without any serious setbacks, and everyone is working happily and well. It is precisely the type of skill of which the typical academic recluse has none. But in order to make maximum use of such abilities, the possessors have to be identified and encouraged to use their talents.

▶ **Summary**

Adolescents are tremendously sensitive to social stimuli; no other problem seems to them as important as the establishment of themselves in their own society. They react faster and more deeply to the influence of their age-mates than to that of adults. High school boys and girls tend to form small, shut-in cliques, the members of which are intensely loyal to each other and highly critical of outsiders. Degrees of popularity among students vary from those who are desired as "best friend" by a large proportion of their classmates to those who are rejected or ignored. The traits that are admired by adolescents are known, and the combinations most likely to lead to either acceptance or rejection can be recognized. Since students will educate each other quite sufficiently in uniformity, perhaps the teacher should concentrate upon educating her pupils in diversity! It is possible to measure with some accuracy the social adjustment of a student and to see in which phases of his life his adjustment is adequate or inadequate. In the course of time it is probable that social age, as a definite measurement, will take its place with intellectual and emotional age as an indication of maturity.

References for Further Reading

BOOKS

Other Texts

Ausubel, *Theory and Problems of Adolescent Development* (Chap. 12).

Baller and Charles, *The Psychology of Human Growth and Development* (Chap. 12).

Breckenridge and Vincent, *Child Development*, 4th ed. (Chap. 13).

Garrison, *Growth and Development*, 2d. ed. (pp. 239–267).

Horrocks, *Behavior and Development* (Chap. 4).

Hurlock, *Adolescent Development*, 2d. ed. (Chap. 5 or 6).

Jersild, *Psychology of Adolescence* (Chap. 11).

Jones, *Growth and Behavior in Adolescence* (Chap. 8 or 9).

Kuhlen, *Psychology of Adolescent Development* (Chap. 7).

Strang, R., *The Adolescent Views Himself: A Psychology of Adolescence* (New York: McGraw-Hill Book Company, 1957), 581 pp. (pp. 286–322).

Other Books and Monographs

Baller, *Readings in the Psychology of Human Growth and Development* (pp. 490–510).

Bottrell, H. R., and R. H. Broadhead, eds., *Educational Sociology* (Harrisburg, Pa.: The Stackpole Company, 1954), 473 pp. (Chaps. 5, 7).

Gesell, A., F. L. Ilg, and L. B. Ames, *Youth: The Years from Ten to Sixteen* (New York: Harper & Row, Publishers, 1956), 542 pp. (Chap. 15).

Gottsegen, M. G., "The Use of the Vineland Social Maturity Scale in the Planning of an Educational Program for Non-institutionalized Low-Grade, Mentally Deficient Children," *Genetic Psychology Monographs,* 55:85–137, 1957.

Seidman, *The Adolescent: A Book of Readings,* rev. ed. (No. 23).

Taba, H., *With Perspective on Human Relations* (Washington, D.C.: American Council on Education, 1955), 255 pp. (Chap. 3 or 4).

ARTICLES

Ausubel, D. P., *et al.,* "A Preliminary Study of Developmental Trends in Socio-empathy: Accuracy of Perception of Own and Others' Sociometric Status," *Child Development,* 23:111–128, 1952.

Bonney, M. E., *et al.,* "A Study of Some Factors Related to Sociometric Status in a Men's Dormitory," *Sociometry,* 16:276–301, 1953.

Bowerman, C. E., and J. W. Kinch, "Changes in Family and Peer Orientation of Children between the Fourth and Tenth Grades," *Social Forces,* 37:206–211, 1959.

Bretsch, H. S., "Social Skills and Activities of Socially Acceptable and Unacceptable Adolescents," *Journal of Educational Psychology,* 43:449–458, 1952.

Coleman, J. S., "The Adolescent Subculture and Academic Achievement," *American Journal of Sociology,* 65:337–347, 1960.

Feinberg, M. R., *et al.,* "An Analysis of Expressions Used by Adolescents at Varying Economic Levels to Describe Accepted and Rejected Peers," *Journal of Genetic Psychology,* 93:133–148, 1958.

Gronlund, N. E., "Relationship between the Sociometric Status of Pupils and Teachers' Preferences for or against Having Them in Class," *Sociometry,* 16:142–150, 1953.

Jarecky, R. K., "Identification of the Socially Gifted," *Exceptional Child,* 25:415–419, 1959.

Maisonneuve, J., "A Contribution to the Sociometry of Mutual Choice," *Sociometry,* 17:33–46, 1954.

Phelps, H. R., and J. E. Horrocks, "Factors Influencing Informal Groups of Adolescents," *Child Development,* 29:69–86, 1958.

Schoepper, A., "Sex Differences in Adolescent Socialization," *Journal of Social Psychology,* 38:175–185, 1953.

Simpson, R. L., and I. H. Simpson, "The School, the Peer Group and Adolescent Development," *Journal of Educational Sociology,* 32:37–41, 1958.

Suggested Research Problems [7]

1. Intensive, long-time study of social isolation, to determine its causes, to devise realistic means of identifying the isolate, and to suggest methods of treatment.

---

[7] See note, p. 11.

THE present chapter is really a continuation of the one just preceding. Both deal with basic points in the interpersonal relationships among adolescents. This chapter will summarize the available data about the selection of friends, the selection of "dates," and the selection of leaders. There is a formidable mountain of material on these topics, far more than could be discussed in a short chapter. The authors have therefore tried to select representative studies that demonstrate modern thinking on these matters.

▶ **Selection of Friends**

Adolescent boys and girls are most eager to have friends of both sexes and are inclined to measure their social status in terms of their ability to establish friendships with their peers. In recent decades there has been a good deal of research into the age-old problem of who will choose whom, and why. The matter is far from settled, but at least a few points have become clear.

Bases of Friendship The usual study of this type proceeds as follows: The investigator asks each of a group of adolescents to list the people whom he would choose as friends—or, perhaps, merely to list his friends—and often also those whom he would not choose. The investigator next gives a variety of tests to all members of the group, inquires into their standing among their peers, and finds out all he can about each individual concerned—especially such things as may reflect personality. He then tries to relate the various traits of each pair or group of friends, in an effort to find out why they appealed to each other. Sometimes there are such refinements as asking the adolescents to choose a companion for a specific purpose: as a roommate, a companion for a day's excursion, or a person to study with, and so on. It is at once clear that friendship choices vary somewhat from one activity to another, especially if any need for leadership is involved.

The greatest single reason for selecting an individual as a friend is neither dramatic nor psychologically revealing; it is mere propinquity. Obviously the environment limits the number of possible associates, but it does not force boys and girls to choose as best friends those who live in the same block or in the same dormitory or are in the same classes in school. Yet in all studies, the factor of propinquity emerges as of utmost importance.[1] Thus, college girls who were asked to name what three girls they would most want to keep in touch with after college chose over 50 percent from their own dormitories. The next most important basis was membership in the same college class; the 103 freshmen cast 74 percent of their votes for other freshmen; the sophomores, 60 percent for other sophomores; the juniors and seniors, 50 percent for their own classmates. A third and much less important basis was concentration in the same major subject, but one does not know how much of this result was again due to propinquity, since majors meet each other more often than they meet other classmates and with increasing frequency as they advance through college. Two other studies of similar character showed that college men tended to choose friends not only from the same dormitory, but even from the same floor.[2] More often than not girls choose girls as their "best" friends, and boys choose boys, in both high school and college.

One of the writers is reminded by the above statements of her own experiences in a college dormitory. There were twenty freshman girls in this particular building; the number remains in memory because there were just enough to fill two tables of ten each in the dining room. Of the subsequent history, the following facts can be given: In their senior year six of the twenty occupied a suite of rooms; four pairs were roommates; one had joined a group of girls from another dormitory who came either from her preparatory school or her home town, or both; three of the twenty lived together in a double room and immediately adjoining single; of the remaining two, one was too nervous to live with anyone, and the other was extremely unpopular. Since graduation most of these friendships have continued, insofar as is possible when all twenty are married and have families. In this instance, these twenty girls not only lived in the same dormitory, they sat at the same tables three times a day, attended many of the same classes—since most freshman subjects were required—and played on the same teams, so that the propinquity begun in the dormitory was reinforced by other experiences.

An individual's selection of friends depends also upon two factors that are not external—his perception of himself and the nature of his needs.[3] Everyone has some idea of what kind of person he is, but the average adolescent does not have either a clear or an accurate idea. In some cases there is

---

[1] B. Willerman and L. Swanson, "Ecological Determinants of Different Amounts of Sociometric Choices within College Dormitories," *Sociometry*, 15:326–329, 1952.

[2] M. E. Bonney, R. E. Hoblit, and A. H. Dreyer, "A Study of Some Factors Related to Sociometric Status in a Men's Dormitory," *Sociometry*, 16:287–301, 1953.

[3] D. P. Ausubel and H. M. Schiff, "Some Intrapersonal and Interpersonal Determinants of Individual Differences in Socioempathic Ability among Adolescents," *Journal of Social Psychology*, 41:39–56, 1955. See also W. R. Thompson and R. Nishimura, "Some Determinants of Friendship," *Journal of Personality*, 20:305–313, 1952.

little relationship between his concept of himself and other adolescents' perception of him. Overestimation or underestimation both contribute to the development of personality.[4] In general, the greater the agreement between the self-estimate and the objective description by others, the better adjustment one is able to achieve, because there is less need for defense.[5] For example, if a boy thinks he has artistic talent when everyone else thinks he has none, he is under constant strain to defend himself against revelation of his probable inadequacy. Or if a girl sees herself as popular and sought after when she is really shunned, she has to be constantly on the watch to defend what she believes is her status. Naturally, everyone makes some errors in self-concept, but adolescents make large ones.

This matter of self-estimate is of importance, since one's concept of one's self inevitably influences one's behavior and one's interpersonal relationships. It probably plays a part also in the selection of an occupation. Probably no one is completely objective about himself, but some people show far less serious errors of estimate than others. The self keeps on growing throughout life, and one's concept should also keep on growing as new experiences and incidents continue to shed light. Probably most people have also an ideal self, toward which they strive. In adolescence, boys and girls begin to wonder just what kind of persons they are and begin to evaluate themselves. The high school could contribute a good deal to this evaluation through the assignments given in various classes, especially in English.

Perhaps the most useful idea about the selection of friends is the notion that each individual chooses friends to meet his own emotional needs. The bond becomes firm if the chooser has the qualities that meet the needs of the chosen.[6] If not, the former hangs around the latter, who rejects him. As an explanation, the mutual meeting of inner needs seems as satisfactory as one is likely to find. This statement does not mean that only opposites attract each other; indeed, the members of a pair of friends often have much the same personality profile [7] and share the same background and interests, but generally in some one or two respects they complement each other.

Dates and Dating   Normally, boys and girls develop friendships with each other during the early and middle years of adolescence, with the girls leading the way. Sometimes the transfer from preadolescent friendships with members of one's own sex to the heterosexual interests of

---

[4] H. M. Schiff, "Judgmental Response Sets in the Perception of Sociometric Status," *Sociometry,* 17:207–227, 1954.

[5] B. Chodorkoff, "Perceptual Defense and Adjustment," *Journal of Abnormal and Social Psychology,* 49:508–512, 1954; and L. Festinger, J. Torrey, and B. Willerman, "Self-Evaluation as a Function of Attractiveness in a Group," *Human Relations,* 7:161–174, 1954.

[6] J. M. Luck, "A Study of Peer Relationships," *Group,* 17:13–20, 1955.

[7] J. Maisonneuve, "A Contribution to the Sociometry of Mutual Choice," *Sociometry,* 17:33–46, 1954.

adolescence takes place gradually and easily and sometimes it is sudden and bewildering. The wise parent not only refrains from comment or opposition, but is thankful that the transfer has occurred. Whether sudden or gradual, the boy-and-girl friendships of adolescence are essential to normal adjustment. Nothing that results from them could possibly be as serious as their failure to develop.

The "boy-crazy" and "girl-crazy" periods, which occur at about the ages of 13 to 14 and 16 to 17, respectively, are extremely trying to adults, but this stage and the many brief, intense episodes during it serve a practical purpose. They give experience in courtship and provide the basis for the subsequent selection of a mate. If a girl is "protected" from such youthful love affairs she is likely in later years to think herself in love with the first man who courts her. If a boy has already had a few attacks of puppy love he knows how to discount mere excitement. Far from being dangerous, the somewhat sentimental boy-and-girl attachments of adolescence are highly educative at the time and are essential for self-protection in the years after home supervision has been left behind.

Investigators have of late years been turning the light of scientific inquiry upon the path of true love. Most high school boys and girls report as normal a series of boy-and-girl affairs, courtships, engagements, quarrels, friendships, crushes, and broken engagements. Numerous difficulties are encountered, especially at first in meeting a sufficient variety of the opposite sex. If the advertisements in the "personal" columns of newspapers and the number of "clubs" of the matchmaking type are any criterion, this problem does not stop with the end of adolescence.

The typical age for beginning to date was judged to be 13 or 14 by nearly half the 2000 adolescents in one study [8] and 15 or 16 by almost the other half. The actual facts, however, would indicate that dating starts somewhat earlier, certainly for girls, since they are more mature than boys. In one study of girls,[9] 20 percent under 14 dated some, 70 percent over 14 said they dated regularly, as did 90 percent over 16. The adolescent relationship of "going steady" is popular. It has its advantages—mainly that a companion for social activities is automatically provided—but it also has the great disadvantage of restricting an adolescent's emotional interests to a single person at too early an age, before either member of the pair knows what he or she really wants. About a fourth of 2000 typical high school students were "going steady." [10] Most of these adolescent attachments will break up of their own accord, but a few will terminate in early marriage, of which some but not many will survive the test of time.

---

[8] Purdue Opinion Panel, "Youth's Attitudes toward Courtship and Marriage," *Report of Poll, No. 62, 1961*, 16 pp.

[9] M. M. Dixon, "Adolescent Girls Talk about Themselves," *Marriage and Family Living*, 20:400–401, 1958.

[10] Purdue Opinion Panel, No. 62, *loc. cit.* See also R. D. Herman, "The 'Going-Steady' Complex: A Re-examination," *Marriage and Family Living*, 17:36–40, 1955.

Marriages during high school are becoming more frequent, especially among girls. The ratio is 10 girls to one boy. In a study published in 1958, 2.4 percent of the sophomores in a number of schools were already married, as were 4.0 percent of the juniors and 5.7 percent of the seniors.[11] Fear of pregnancy or actual pregnancy was a factor in at least half the early marriages, but it was not the only factor.[12] Girls who marry in high school are, as a group, socially and sexually precocious. They begin to date earlier than most girls, they "go steady" at intervals with one boy or another, they consider themselves in love at an early age—usually more than once—and they have a plethora of boy friends. In short, they act as if they were five or more years older than they are and they show an early and compulsive obsession with marriage.[13] Whether early marriage is good or bad probably depends upon the individual boy and girl in each case and upon the attitudes of their parents.

Boys begin dating later,[14] partly because they mature later, partly because they do not feel secure enough to take the initiative of asking a girl for a date, and partly because they do not have enough money. Even at the end of high school there are still a few boys who have not yet summoned the courage to ask a girl for a date; but among the girls, those who still have not had dates are mostly "rejects," for one reason or another. A few are presumably not allowed to go out in the evening, a few are bookworms, a few are unattractive, and a few are still so immature as to have no interest in boys.

There are certain traits that definitely promote acceptance as a partner for dating. Results from two studies will be presented. The items listed most frequently by 8000 boys and girls in high school are as follows: [15] Girls want a date who is well mannered, who makes no undesired advances, who does not talk loudly, who treats them with respect and compliments them—presumably upon their clothes and appearance. After a girl has gone to a good deal of trouble to prepare for her date, she does not like it if her escort never comments verbally upon the results. Boys want a girl who does not look down upon them, who does not refuse absolutely all advances, who does not easily become hurt or annoyed, and who does not make too great demands upon their probably precarious financial condition.

Another study reports the traits desired in a future mate by high school

---

[11] H. T. Christensen, "Why All These Young Marriages?" *National Parent-Teacher,* 52:4, 1958.

[12] L. Burchinal, "Adolescent Role Deprivation and High School Marriage," *Marriage and Family Living,* 21:378–384, 1959.

[13] L. Burchinal, "Comparison of Factors Related to Adjustment in Pregnancy-Provoked and Non-Pregnancy-Provoked Youthful Marriages," *Midwest Sociologist,* 21:92–96, 1959.

[14] P. D. Bordis, "Attitudes towards Dating among the Students of a Michigan High School," *Sociology and Social Research,* 42:274–277, 1958.

[15] H. T. Christensen, "Dating Behavior as Evaluated by High School Students," *American Journal of Sociology,* 57:580–586, 1952.

boys and girls. The results are given in Table 17–1. The first group of traits does not differ materially from those desired in friends of either sex, whether or not marriage is being considered. They are the characteristics of the "nice" boy or the "nice" girl. The items in the second and third groups suggest that even adolescents realize there is more to marriage than just physical attraction. Both boys and girls—but especially girls—want to marry with family approval, they want a home and children, they want to avoid in-law problems, and they realize that similarity of interests and attitudes will help a marriage to survive. They are keenly aware that both partners must understand about the handling of money. The girl wants her prospective husband to have a job—only 7 percent of them think this point unimportant—and the boys want their prospective wives to know how to manage a household.

The 2000 young people involved in the study had some other sane ideas about marriage. Only a fourth of them believed that high school students

Table 17–1: PERCENTAGE OF BOYS AND GIRLS INDICATING A TRAIT
AS BEING VERY DESIRABLE FOR A FUTURE MATE

Traits	*Boys*	*Girls*
Is physically attractive and good looking	45	17
Is popular with others	46	42
Shows affection	84	85
Takes pride in personal appearances and manners	89	90
Mixes well in social situations	51	59
Is considerate of me and of others	84	95
Is dependable, can be trusted	92	96
Has a pleasant disposition	77	84
Acts his (her) age, is not childish	77	87
Is clean in speech and action	72	82
Does not pet or try to get too familiar	22	39
Does not use tobacco	42	29
Does not use liquor	49	49
Is approved by my parents	56	74
Desires normal family life with children	77	87
Is independent of his or her parents	45	64
Has interests similar to mine	49	48
Has ideals similar to mine	46	52
Is as intelligent as I am	27	42
Knows how to budget and manage money	62	75
Has a job	9	93
Is started on a professional career	8	42
Knows how to cook and keep house	79	15

SOURCE: Purdue Opinion Panel, "Youth's Attitudes toward Courtship and Marriage," *Report of Poll No. 62*, 1961.

were old enough to know when love was real and when it was just infatuation, less than 10 percent believed that teenage marriages were more likely to be successful than later marriages, and only 10 percent thought parents should contribute to the support of adolescents who married. They believed overwhelmingly that married couples were justified in limiting the size of their families and that sex instruction should be given in the high schools. Nearly half of them have either outgrown or never had the idea that each person in the world has a "one-and-only soul-mate" waiting somewhere. Boys were more liberal than girls in their sex standards; 45 percent of them thought sexual experience need not be delayed until after marriage, while only 11 percent of the girls subscribed to this idea.

In the beginning at least, and often throughout high school, dating is primarily a matter of social support and security. It makes a boy or girl feel accepted and may have little sexual significance. If no opposition is raised by parents it rarely leads to marriage. The first date is likely to be a good deal of a strain for both the boy and the girl because neither knows just what to do or even what is expected. Thereafter, the matter is somewhat easier, but dating contributes so much to adolescent social adjustment that it remains important. At first, boys and girls tend to date with those who are in the same school classes, but later on they branch out a bit. It is probable that the early dates have nothing much to do with preferences on the part of the individuals concerned. A boy selects a girl from his own social class, who may be presumed to have similar ideas and background, so as to ease the initial strain as much as he can; if the girl is reasonably presentable, it does not matter much to him which girl it is, although his own status is enhanced if she happens to be very popular. These tentative efforts at socal security usually proceed without serious incident, if the parents avoid an authoritarian approach to the matter. The time for authority has gone by. Perhaps the best approach is to persuade a boy or girl *always* to bring dates home, for at least part of the evening. Nothing convinces an adolescent so quickly that he or she has made an unwise choice as to see the date against his or her home background. Usually, the parents need say nothing at all.

Sometimes adolescents, especially boys, purposely seek dates with those from a lower social class.[16] These girls are less demanding than those at their own level. This phase is likely to be short and to do no harm, provided it does not meet with opposition. Girls tend rather to make dates with boys from an upper social class, probably because marriage is never too far from their minds. Since the average marriage age for girls is 20, they are wise to begin thinking about the matter while they are still in high school.

As adolescents grow older, the dating may involve some sexual experiences, which, however, usually stop short of actual intercourse. This phase also has its usefulness, even though it may lead to trouble. Since it cannot be

---

[16] W. W. Ehrmann, "Influence of Comparative Social Class of the Companion upon Premarital Heterosexual Behavior," *Marriage and Family Living,* 17:48–53, 1955.

prevented, it might as well be used as constructively as possible. One may regret the too early experiences of some boys and girls, but such episodes take place and are part of an adolescent's education for life.

The matter of premarital relations is agitating adults in other countries than the United States. The London *Times* recently published an article on the increase in promiscuity among adolescents, especially among girls under 16 years of age. In 1960–1961 a single home for the care of unmarried mothers dealt with 91 girls who were less than 16; by the end of October, in 1961–1962 it has dealt with 162. The social workers attributed the increase to several factors: lack of control by parents, boredom with the last year or two of required schooling, lack of adequate outlets for adolescent needs, lack of anything better to do with leisure time, the combination of sexual maturity with emotional immaturity, and the financial obstacles to early marriage. Most worrisome to the social workers was the complete absence of any sense of sin or shame on the part of the girls, who seemed to think intercourse outside of marriage was a normal part of modern adolescence. They felt they had merely been unlucky—not sinful.[17]

Comparative statistics on three Western societies are also available: from a group in the western part of the United States, from a Midwestern group, and from a group in Denmark (Fig. 17–1). The degree of allowed intimacy was tabulated in relation to the stages of courtship from the first date up to the marriage.[18] It should be added that before the recorded relationship, which terminated in marriage, some girls and some men had already had intercourse with previous partners. The percents for the women in the Western, Midwestern, and Danish groups were, respectively: 10, 20, and 60 percent. Corresponding figures for the men were 39, 51, and 64 percent. These earlier experiences doubtless influenced the progress of the particular relationship under consideration. There is a good deal of difference between the various samplings in the degree of intimacy permitted at different stages of courtship and in the general observance of traditional moral standards. It is hard to tell to what extent these figures represent changes from previous generations, since there are no figures from earlier times with which to compare them.

Dating behavior and success in courtship are related to family background and interrelationships. Whenever any circumstance had intervened to affect normal relationships between parents and children, the latter were less successful in having dates during high school and in progressing through the normal stages of courtship.[19] The most obvious of such background condi-

---

[17] London *Times,* Nov. 1, 1962, p. 5g.

[18] Since the lapse of time from the first date to marriage differed from one person to another, all cases have been expanded or reduced proportionately to fit a time lapse of 18 months, which was approximately the commonest period.

[19] See, for example, R. O. Andrews and H. T. Christensen, "Relationship of Absence of a Parent to Courtship Status: A Repeat Study," *American Sociological Review,* 16:541–543, 1951, and D. Wallin, "Marital Happiness of Parents and Their Children's Attitudes to Marriage," *American Sociological Review,* 19:20–23, 1954.

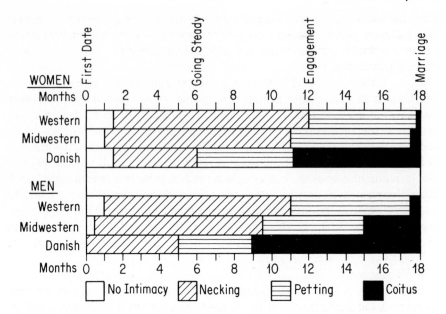

Fig. 17–1. Cultural differences in degrees of intimacy at successive stages from acquaintance to marriage

T. Christiansen and G. R. Carpenter, "Timing Patterns in the Development of Sexual Intimacy: An Attitudinal Report on Three Modern Western Societies," *Marriage and Family Living,* 24:30–34, 1962. Used with the permission of the publisher.

tions were the absence of one parent from the family group, the foreign nativity of the parents, open revolt of the children against parental authority, and serious tension of any kind. Senior high school students who did not date at all were found to have an appreciably less wholesome family background than other seniors. As shown in Table 17–2, boys who had no fathers and girls who had no mothers tended to be low in their ability both to make social contacts and to progress through the usual stages of courtship. Orphans were equally ineffective. The figures are clearer for the boys than for the girls. In

Table 17–2: EFFECT OF BROKEN HOMES UPON DATING

Courtship Status	Boys (Father missing) (%)	Boys and Girls (Both parents missing) (%)	Girls (Mother missing) (%)
High	18	35	43
Low	82	65	57

SOURCE: Based on R. F. Winch, "The Relation between the Loss of Parents and Progress in Courtship," *Journal of Social Psychology,* 29:51–56, 1949.

most instances, high school students who do not date at all present a picture of inadequate family relationships, unwholesome attitudes toward themselves, negative attitudes toward others, and poor adjustments in even the most casual of heterosexual contacts.

As in the selection of friends, mere propinquity plays a role in the selection of a mate. In a sample study, 54 percent of the engaged couples lived near each other.[20] In another, 91 percent of the couples belonged to the same religious group, 58 percent to the same race, and 83 percent to roughly the same social class.[21] These background factors are far more important in choosing a life partner than they are in choosing a friend. It is probable that the selection also rests upon the mutual needs of the two persons involved.[22] Such complementary needs would pair off the dominating character with the one who wants to be dominated; the humorist and talker with the listener; the erudite man with the dull but pleasant woman; the young man in need of a mother-substitute with an older woman; the shy girl with a man old enough to give her security; and so on.

Engagement is a stage of courtship that seems very necessary. Without it, the chances for marital happiness are definitely lowered. It is now the custom for an engagement to last not more than six months, if that long. In Grandmother's day it lasted longer.[23] Its usefulness is attested to by the number of people who have been engaged two or three times and have broken off such relationships because—during this period of concentration upon each other—the two people concerned found that they were not as congenial as they had thought. In one investigation of 1000 engaged couples,[24] it was found that 24 percent of the men and 30 percent of the women had been engaged at least once before.

▶ **Leadership**

Because of the social prominence of the leader and because of his strategic position, psychologists have been trying for years to find out what qualities result in leadership. Although the number of leaders is small, their influence is always large because of their position in their own society. The high school that can influence its student leaders to exercise their

---

[20] A. C. Clarke, "An Examination of the Operation of Residential Propinquity as a Factor in Mate Selection," *American Sociological Review,* 17:17–22, 1952.

[21] A. B. Hollingshead, "Cultural Factors in Mate Selection," *American Sociological Review,* 15:619–627, 1950.

[22] R. F. Winch, "The Theory of Complementary Needs in Mate Selection," *American Sociological Review,* 19:241–249, 1954.

[23] M. R. Koller, "Some Changes in Courtship Behavior in Three Generations of Ohio Women," *American Sociological Review,* 16:366–370, 1951.

[24] E. W. Burgess and M. Fishbein, *Successful Marriage* (New York: Doubleday & Company, Inc., 1955), 552 pp.

power along desirable lines is not likely to have serious difficulties with the student body as a whole.

Within the last two decades there has been an unusual interest in leadership, possibly as a reflection of how urgently the world needs wise leaders. The army and the navy have also been greatly interested in the problems of leadership, since in these days of mobile warfare there has to be a leader for even small units, with authority to make at least minor decisions. An understanding of leaders thus seems highly desirable.

Leadership seems to consist of a cluster of traits, a few inborn but most of them acquired or at least developed by contact with environment. It is also a permanent type of behavior; the leaders in elementary school usually become leaders in high school and in time become leaders in college.[25] As a general thing, leaders are superior in several respects: they are above average in physical equipment, intelligence, vitality, attractiveness, range of interests,[26] and scholarship. But they have other traits as well; it is not enough to be healthy, energetic, bright, and interested in schoolwork.

Most studies of student leaders have consisted in locating, either through observation or by the adolescents' own ratings of each other, the leaders in a school and then comparing the standing of these leaders in a number of traits with the standing of the other students of the same age in the school. A typical study of leaders is summarized in the next few paragraphs.

An investigator asked all the 223 students in a private junior college, between the ages of sixteen and twenty, to state their choices for the chairman of a certain project, and for a roommate. They were also asked to give the names of those they thought least likely to succeed as chairman or least acceptable as a roommate. The answers of the entire student body were then divided into four sections, as shown in Table 17–3. More students were rejected as leaders than as roommates, presumably because many amiable people who are nice to live with have no ability to lead. Study of the first and second groups showed three main differences between them. The leaders expressed the positive emotions—joy, pleasure, satisfaction, humor, happiness —while the rejected specialized in negative reactions—gloom, anxiety, and hurt feelings. The leaders had definite goals in their activities, while the rejected did not seem to be going anywhere in particular. The leaders gave others a sense of security, but the rejected merely made others feel uncomfortable. The neglected ones, who were simply forgotten, proved upon investigation to show little emotional reaction of any kind, to be formal and correct in their demeanor, to be easily distracted from any goal they might have, to be quite banal in their thinking, and to have few friends or even acquaintances. They were not noticed even enough to be rejected.

---

[25] H. M. Hodges, "Campus Leaders and Nonleaders," *Sociology and Social Research,* 37:251–255, 1953.

[26] J. C. Gowan, "The Interest Patterns of Student Leaders," *Educational Psychology Measurement,* 14:151–155, 1954.

Table 17–3: GROUPINGS ON THE BASIS OF POPULARITY

	Chairman of Committee (%)	Roommate (%)
1. Those who received more choices than rejections	17	40
2. Those who received more rejections than choices	50	23
3. Those who received the same number of each	18	34
4. Those who received neither rejection nor choice	15	3

SOURCE: Based on M. A. Price, "A Study of Motivational and Perceptual Factors Associated with Leadership Behavior of Young Women in a Private School," *Ohio State University Abstracts of Dissertations,* no. 58, 1950, pp. 59–64.

A psychologist cannot yet definitely say which child will become a leader, but the many specific investigations at least set the limits of personality within which to look for the leaders of the next generation. The necessary traits may be listed and classified as indicated in the following list:

1. *Capacities* (inborn or acquired early in life): Average or better intelligence, mental alertness, verbal facility, good health, efficiency, animal courage, cheerfulness, humor, maturity

2. *Attainments to date:* Average or better schoolwork, athletic accomplishments, former experience as leader, special knowledge needed by situation

3. *Appearance and manner:* Average or better attractiveness, appropriately clothed (as judged by standards of group to be led), good voice, features, body build, and poise

4. *Motility:* Unusual degree of participation in whatever is going on, greater than average activity, enthusiasm for undertakings

5. *Contacts with others:* (1) Aggressiveness, self-confidence, ambition, initiative, persistence; (2) dependability, integrity, responsibility; (3) sociableness, kindliness, approachability, cooperativeness, adaptability, capacity to mix with subordinates without making them feel subordinate, willingness to stay within conventional limits

6. *Special intellectual qualities:* Judgment, originality, insight into people and situations, impartiality (ability to see both sides), diplomacy

7. *Background factors:* Better than average social status, better than average income, membership in family that already has leaders in it [27]

It should be noted especially that under the fifth heading there is a subdivision of traits, some of which not only seem contradictory but are. They are all

---

[27] Adapted from B. M. Boss, C. R. Wurster, P. A. Doll, and D. J. Clair, "Situational and Personal Factors in Leadership among Sorority Women," *Psychological Monographs,* Vol. LXVII, no. 366, 23 pp., 1953; E. S. Dexter and B. Stein, "The Measurement of Leadership in White and Negro Students," *Journal of Abnormal and Social Psychology,* 51:219–221, 1955; F. E. Fuller, "Good Leadership: Nature or Nurture?" *Contact Pensacola,* 12:22–24, 1954; R. M. Hodges, "Campus Leaders and Nonleaders," *loc. cit.;* E. P. Hollander, "Study in Group Leadership among Naval Aviation Cadets," *Journal of Aviation Medicine,* 25:164–170, 1954; J. B. Marks, "Interests, Leadership, and Sociometric Status among Adolescents," Ph.D. Thesis, University of California, 1952; M. Roff, "A Study of Combat Leadership in the Air Force by Means of a Rating Scale," *Journal of Psychology,* 30:229–239, 1950.

needed, however, in order to maintain balance. A leader is aggressive, but his aggressiveness is controlled by his sociability and his willingness to conform to social standards. If these other traits were lacking, he might become a braggart or a delinquent, both of whom are also aggressive. A leader gets along well with others, but without his ambition and persistence he would be just another good mixer and pleasant companion. And even though an individual has great initiative and much social ability, he still will not lead for long unless he can be trusted. As one thinks of the various types of would-be leaders, one can see what they lack. Thus, the fanatic has great enthusiasm, self-confidence, and drive, but lacks judgment and can see only one side of a question at once. And the foreign agitator rarely openly succeeds as a leader because his appearance, features, build, voice, clothes, and manners are not those of the people he wants to lead, although he may exert influence if he can find a good "front," behind which he can hide.

In general, leaders tend to match their background and to direct their abilities toward whatever goals are of interest to those being led. More will be said presently about the characteristics of groups and the influence that the group-to-be-led exercises upon the nature of the leader whom it will accept. For the present it should suffice to point out that gang-leaders differ in their objectives and attitudes from student leaders in a boarding school, but their drive, their enthusiasm for what they are doing, their ability to attract followers, and many other traits remain fairly constant.

It may be noticed that the capacity to learn out of a book does not contribute much to leadership, perhaps because the student who reads many books learns about books instead of about people. Also, he has less time to be with people than he would otherwise have. He can therefore hunt down an elusive reference in a catalogue but not an elusive antagonism in a group. It is not surprising that the student who impresses his age-mates as undisguisedly intelligent or as having superior academic standing does not often become a leader. This is not the same thing, however, as saying that intelligence has no relation to leadership. Certain phases clearly have—judgment, versatility, organizing ability, originality, alertness, and insight, for instance. Even tests of "intelligence," which admittedly measure only one or two phases of mental ability and measure academic skills at the same time, show a medium amount of correlation with leadership, probably because they indubitably measure the alertness and quickness of one's mental machinery. If they tapped other mental abilities also, the correlation would probably be much higher.

The two students described below belong to quite common types of high school leaders. An experienced teacher can probably identify both among the boys and girls she has known.

Dot and Fritz are both leaders in a small high school. Both are seniors. In a recent sociometric study they were the two main "stars" of their class.

Dot is a rather small but extremely lively girl. She radiates good health and normalcy. She is not pretty, but she is attractive in both face and figure. Her intelligence is in the highest 25 percent of the class, but not in the highest 5 percent. She comes of a good family, and she is always well and appropriately dressed. Her classwork is above average but not so good as to arouse either envy or scorn among her peers. She does a reasonable amount of studying, but not too much. Her mind is nimble and of an inquiring nature, but she is satisfied with small bits of knowledge about many things and shows no desire for real mastery in any field. She is an excellent conversationalist. Dot has many interests; she is the drum majorette for the school's band, a cheerleader, a member of the school glee club, secretary of the senior class, president of two school clubs, and a member of the editorial board for the school yearbook. She never lacks invitations to dances and parties. Both boys and girls like Dot, and she has become an arbiter in social matters. She has a fair amount of tact and a moderate understanding of people, but she depends upon appearance, family background, and manner for her popularity rather than upon any remarkable ability to understand others. When one examines Dot's record and watches her behavior, one learns something more about her. She has never been in any disciplinary difficulty, she observes the conventions, and her behavior, while lively, is never indiscreet or indecorous. This strain of propriety in her make-up is of value to her because it commands respect from both boys and girls and prevents her name from being linked with scandals, unfavorable gossip, or revolts. Dot has abounding vitality, manifold interests, a quick mind, a pleasant appearance, a good background, irreproachable manners, a moderate degree of extroversion, and a fair understanding of people. Presumably, like everyone else, Dot has some small problems, but there are no serious conflicts or tensions in her life. Dot's chief charm lies in her normalcy.

Fritz is high-strung, handsome, intelligent, and very successful as an athlete. He is a member of all the school's major teams, but has been especially satisfactory as a quarterback. Fritz is a good student and would be an excellent one if he had more time for study. As it is, he will be on the school's honor list. His IQ has varied on different tests from 130 to 150. He intends to be a doctor, and will probably become a serious student as soon as he passes beyond the age for school and college athletics. Fritz tends to burn himself out by the intensity of his application to whatever catches his interest, and to be rather moody; his periods of exertion and excitement are often followed by periods of sloth and irritability. He is nervous, but he has remarkable control; and the greater the pressure, the cooler he gets. Fritz's good looks make him popular with the girls, and his athletic success makes him the idol of the boys. Fortunately, Fritz's real interests are in intellectual pursuits—although he keeps this fact carefully hidden—and his prowess at running and throwing and jumping strikes him as incidental, childish, and amusing. Athletic success has its values for him, and he uses it for all it is worth, but he has no illusions about it, and his ideals lie elsewhere. This boy's greatest defects of personality are the shortness of his temper, his impatience, and his sensitiveness. Leadership was made easy for him by his size and strength; at entrance to high school he was already postpubescent, he was taller and heavier than his classmates, and he had already passed through the period of poor muscular coordination. His social abilities are only average, but they are good enough to maintain his status. Fritz's interests are rather narrow. He belongs to only one club, in addition to athletic teams, and is the president of the school's athletic association. During his junior year he was one of the student judges, and was re-elected this year but resigned because the sessions conflicted with his chemistry laboratory, and he regarded the laboratory as the more important.

As may be seen, these two leaders are successful for different reasons. Fritz depends upon maturity, physical size, good looks, intelligence, athletic success, a controlled quickness, a high degree of concentration, and general good judgment. He was not a leader in childhood and is one of those who had to conquer himself before he could lead others. He has proceeded along the usual path to male adolescent leadership, via size and athletic prominence. Although Fritz is still quick-tempered and although he has moods and is a sensitive boy, he has no strain of the prima donna in him. He is modest about his success as a quarterback largely because he does not enjoy the furor and because he does not think football really important. Dot is of a quite different type. She shares Fritz's pleasant appearance, but she depends chiefly upon her healthiness, her vivacity, her drive, her quick interests, her alertness, her skill at repartee, her social prominence, her conformity, and her musical talents for her success. Moreover, she enjoys being a leader. She has been one ever since she can remember. She probably has more understanding of people on a rather superficial level than Fritz, but his grasp is deeper. She is also less mature, except in her willingness to conform to approved custom. In both cases, family status is an important background factor.

There have been a considerable number of efforts to classify leaders into types, but none of them has been especially successful or convincing. One sample study should suffice. The leaders were classified into a number of types, as has often been done, but with the added information about the reasons why they were able to lead—what the bond between them and their followers might be. A list of the types appears below:

Characterization of Leader	*Nature of Relation to Followers*
1. The patriarchal sovereign	The group wants to accept his values, although they may or may not resent him as a person
2. The natural leader	The members of the group simply like him
3. The tyrant	The group accepts his values, although they fear him

4. The seducer	The group follows him because he does a wrong thing first and thus encourages them to follow their own hitherto suppressed desires
5. The bad influence	This leader has no feelings of guilt and no conflict over his misdeeds; he can therefore carry the guilt feelings of others
6. The good influence	This leader has a strong superego (conscience) and reinforces the superego of his followers, so that the group moves toward socially accepted behavior

These types are recognizable, whether or not one agrees with the somewhat psychoanalytic explanations for their success.[28]

The task of following up a group of students after they leave school requires an enormous amount of work and a staff of fieldworkers who have a dash of both the bulldog and the bloodhound in them. The American family's well-known habit of constantly changing its abode and of losing contact with its younger members makes the tracing of experience subsequent to school days extremely difficult. There are, therefore, relatively few studies on this point. One, however, may well be quoted.[29] A follow-up of all the 485 living graduates of ten consecutive classes, 1927–1936, of a small high school to determine their degree of leadership in their community gave interesting results, which are summarized in Table 17–4. Adult success in leadership was judged on the basis of general reputation, positions of trust (school superintendents, bank managers, judges, superior officials), or superior positions in business or industry, ownership of business, and election to chairmanship of community undertakings. In their high school days the 186 male graduates had shown four degrees and kinds of leadership in school life: 64 were prominent athletes, 22 played dominant roles in nonathletic student affairs, 23 were outstanding in both these classifications, and 77 had no record of any leadership. Nearly two thirds of the second and third groups became leaders in adult life. The student who was prominent in athletics but nothing else did not fare so well in later years. Only a few nonleaders in high school became leaders as adults. Among the 299 women graduates, only 59 had occupied positions of

---

[28] A. W. Goulder, ed., *Studies in Leadership* (New York: Harper & Row, Publishers, 1950), 736 pp., based on pp. 42–44. See also V. Ballard, "Developing Leadership," *Personnel Guidance Journal,* 32:135–138, 1953 and D. C. Barnlund, "Experiments in Leadership Training for Decision-Making Discussion Groups," *Speech Monographs,* 22:1–14, 1955.

[29] J. J. Crowley, "High School Backgrounds of Successful Men and Women Graduates," *School Review,* 48:205–209, 1940.

Table 17–4: LEADERSHIP IN COLLEGE AND COMMUNITY

	Number of Men	*Number and Percent Who Became Leaders*
1. Leadership in athletics	64	10 (15%)
2. Leadership in student affairs	22	14 (65%)
3. Leadership in both	23	14 (60%)
4. Leadership in neither	77	11 (15%)
Total	186	

SOURCE: Based on J. J. Crowley, "High School Backgrounds of Successful Men and Women Graduates," *School Review*, 48:205–209, 1940.

leadership in school. Of these, 37 percent held such positions as adults. Only 2 percent of the 240 other women graduates, all nonleaders in high school, had had success as leaders in their communities.

It appears that to some extent leadership can be learned, provided one has the right kinds of ability in the first place. That is, training and experience can refine, polish, develop, and encourage what is there, but thus far there is no evidence that leaders can be created out of nonleaders. A class in which the problems of leadership are discussed may prove valuable in hastening the growth of the potential leader. Such a class can give help in the understanding of themselves, in the understanding of other people's motivations, and in the solving of interpersonal problems; and it can provide contact with and observation of leaders in the community.[30] Those with the proper potential develop faster with such treatment, probably because they are given in organized form what any leader learns sooner or later by experience; they just learn these things sooner than they otherwise would.

In recent years there has been a good deal of discussion as to the relative advantages of the "group-centered" and "leader-centered" types of leadership.[31] In the former type, the presumed leader stays in the background, elicits as much as he can from the group members, and merely guides them in their thinking. His main objective seems to be to work himself out of a job. He tries to get the group to lead itself. If a leader is of the second type, he will impose his ideas upon the group, insofar as he can, and leave the participants less able than they were before to think for themselves. So far as mental health is concerned, probably the first type is superior to the second.[32]

---

[30] R. N. Cassel and A. E. Shafer, "An Experiment in Leadership Training," *Journal of Psychology*, 5:299–305, 1961.

[31] R. H. Wischmeier, "Group-Centered and Leader-Centered Leaders: An Experimental Study," *Speech Monographs*, 22:43–48, 1955.

[32] G. Terrell and J. Shreffer, "A Developmental Study of Leadership," *Journal of Educational Research*, 52:69–72, 1958.

Since study of the leader as a person has not been productive of such useful results as had been hoped, attention has been turned to the group to be lead as a determining factor in the matter of who should lead. That is, a given group situation calls for, and gets, a leader. Hence, presumably, the many "types" of leaders, since different individuals are required to meet the varying needs of the same or different groups at different times and in different situations.[33] Thus, an Augustus, a Savonarola, a Metternich, a Robespierre, or a Garibaldi is called forth by the needs of the people, but these men became leaders because they possessed the particular cluster of traits that fitted them to meet the particular needs. Leadership is therefore a spontaneous sort of social interaction between individuals and groups. If the needs continue or if the behavior and personality of the leader arouse emotional reactions of an enjoyable sort, the leader maintains his position, but if the needs are satisfied or if the leader arouses antagonistic emotions, his position becomes precarious and he is able to continue only if in the period of his real leadership he has built up enough control and power to maintain himself, even though he has become unpopular. As time passes, both the members of a group and its leaders change, and yesterday's idol becomes today's forgotten man.

It is, however, not enough that a leader should be accepted by his followers, although his acceptance is basic to everything else because without it he cannot function. However, there are just as many well-loved and accepted people who never become leaders as there are who do, so the trait is not, in and of itself, productive of leadership. In fact, some leaders are accepted and followed, but not liked at all, because they have the essential qualities that are needed for the solution of a particular problem. One need think only of Adenauer in Germany and De Gaulle in France to realize that a man can lead as large a group as a nation without being particularly liked by more than his personal friends. Both countries needed men of iron; such men get the job done, but they are neither loved nor lovable. Thus, although a leader needs acceptance by his followers, the acceptance can rest on many other feelings than affection. It is, in fact, necessary that a leader should be able to detach himself emotionally from those whom he wishes to control.[34] Otherwise, he cannot see himself and them clearly, and he is vulnerable to his own feelings of affection—and shows his weak spot by appointing his friends to important

---

[33] For discussion of these points of view, see T. Gordon, "The Challenge of a New Concept of Leadership," *Pastoral Psychology,* 6:15–24, 1955, and "Leadership: Shall It Reside in the Leader or in the Group?" *American Journal of Nursing,* 54:1087–1088, 1954; G. A. Talland, "The Assessment of Group Opinion: Typical Leaders and Their Influence on Its Function," *Journal of Abnormal and Social Psychology,* 49:431–434, 1954; R. H. Wischmeier, "Group-Centered and Leader-Centered Leaders: An Experimental Study," *Speech Monographs,* 22:43–48, 1955.

[34] F. E. Fiedler, *Leader Attitudes and Group Effectiveness,* Final Report of ONR Project NR 170–106, N6-ori-o7135 (Urbana, Ill.: University of Illinois Press, 1958), 69 pp. and F. E. Fiedler, "A Note on Leadership Theory: The Effect of Social Barriers between Leaders and Followers," *Sociometry,* 20:87–94, 1957.

posts in the group without much respect to their appropriateness. Unless he maintains a degree of psychological distance from his key men, the group he is leading is likely to fall apart and not get the job done.

Groups have many characteristics, and no two are exactly alike. Some of the determining factors are quite obvious, but others are considerably less so. The results from two careful considerations of groups have been combined, since there was a good deal of overlapping between the two, although each contains one or two group characterizations lacking in the other. The most important determinants are listed below, with a pair of contrasting examples, taken from college life where possible, after each:

GROUPS VARY FROM ONE ANOTHER IN:

1. *Size*

    Lecture class in elementary chemistry (large)
    Seminar in metallurgy (small)

2. *Homogeneity*

    College preparatory Latin class in an expensive, exclusive private girls' school (homogeneous)
    Freshman English class in an average American high school (heterogeneous)

3. *Flexibility*

    College glee club (established, persisting mode of behavior)
    Departmental clubs (no established model, clubs come and go)

4. *Permeability*

    Small, self-contained, highly "social," snobbish fraternity, whose members mix little with others
    Good-fellowship club, to which anyone can belong and whose members mix with everyone

5. *Polarization*

    Campaign committee for electing the campus queen (a group with a single, clear goal)
    Executive committee of the student government (a group that deals with whatever needs to be done)

6. *Stability*

    Basketball team, honors society (these exist year after year)
    Chess club, fencing team (these depend on whether or not anyone is interested)

7. *Intimacy*

    Sorority (everyone knows everyone else)
    Political club (members are only acquaintances)

8. *Control*

    Training table (diet is controlled)
    Eating club (for pleasure and sociability; no control over diet)

9. *Potency*

    Phi Beta Kappa, fraternities, varsity teams (strong drives satisfied by membership)

Debating teams, dance committees, newcomers' club (relatively weaker drives satisfied by membership)

10. *Affective Tone*

Special sections for best students (agreeable feelings associated with membership)
Special sections for students on probation (unpleasant feeling tone)

11. *Participation of Members*

Discussion class ⎫
Lecture class   ⎭ of same size

12. *Dependence*

Cast of a play (dependent on director, without whom rehearsals usually do not even start)
Staff of college newspaper (not dependent upon the physical presence of the editor to get started)

13. *Autonomy: Independence of other groups*

Stamp collectors club
Committee on planning the junior prom

14. *Stratification: the extent to which a group arranges its members into a hierarchy*

Membership in a fraternity or the students at West Point or Annapolis
Group of students listening to records and drinking beer

15. *Viscidity: the extent to which the group functions as a unit, without dissension*

Glee Club or students' theater group when dominated by faculty representative
Members of tennis club playing tennis

SOURCE: Based on R. M. Stogdill, "Personal Factors Associated with Leadership: A Survey of the Literature," *Journal of Psychology,* 25:35–71, 1948; and J. K. Hemphill, "Situational Factors in Leadership," *Bureau of Educational Research Monographs* (Columbus, O.: Ohio State University, No. 32, 1949), 136 pp.; J. K. Hemphill and C. M. Westie, "The Measurement of Group Dimensions," *Journal of Psychology,* 29:324–343, 1950; A. P. Hare, "Interaction and Consensus in Different Sized Groups," *American Sociological Review,* 17:261–267, 1952.

As the groups that need leaders vary in their composition, so does the nature of the leader who best meets the requirements.

► Summary

It seems fairly clear that the simple factors of propinquity and common membership in various groups operate to delimit the choice of friends. But there are other elements. The two elements mentioned above merely furnish the framework. From the available supply each adolescent chooses those who best fit his own personal needs, either because they are like him or because they are not! Some friendships are based upon similarity of traits and interests; others show the leader-follower pattern. In addition to these are the friendships in which the respective weaknesses and strengths of the two friends complement each other. The problem of who will be attracted to whom and why is far from being solved.

Dating is an almost universal social enterprise among America's adolescents. In the early stages at least it seems to offer primarily social security. The relationship may develop into a love affair, but usually it does not. In the course of adolescence most boys and girls have a number of brief affairs, which furnish them with the experiences they need in order to know what kind of person they really wish to marry in later years. Such love affairs can be serious, but they can also be educative.

Certain traits seem to be associated with leadership, although few if any leaders show all of them. Indeed, there are so many kinds of leaders that some investigators have questioned the value of traits or trait constellations in the study of leadership. A common approach at present is through the nature of the group to be led, on the principle that, from among those with potential powers of leadership, the needs of the group will determine the selection. The traits of leaders may therefore be expected to vary widely. Whether or not leadership can be developed and perhaps even taught is a problem that remains for the future.

References for Further Reading

BOOKS

Other Texts

Ausubel, *Theory and Problems of Adolescent Development* (Chap. 13).

Garrison, *Growth and Development* (pp. 322–371).

Horrocks, *Behavior and Development* (any three: pp. 84–97; 194–206; 219–233, 240–246).

Hurlock, *Adolescent Development*, 2d. ed. (Chap. 13).

Jersild, *Psychology of Adolescence* (Chap. 12).

Jones, *Growth and Behavior in Adolescence* (Chap. 9).

Strang, *The Adolescent Views Himself* (pp. 324–355).

Other Books and Monographs

Fiedler, F. E., *Leader Attitudes and Group Effectiveness* (Urbana, Ill.: University of Illinois Press, 1958), 69 pp. (pp. 42–46 and any appendix A–I).

Hall, D. M., *Dynamics of Group Action* (Interstate, 1957), 240 pp. (pp. 10–29 or 100–125; any one appendix A–F).

Ehrmann, W., *Premarital Dating Behavior* (New York: Bantam Books, Inc., 1960), 396 pp. (any 25 pages from Chap. 2, 3, 4, or 5).

Lindzey, G., *Handbook of Social Psychology*, Vol. II (Reading, Mass.: Addison-Wesley Publishing Company, 1954), "The Perception of People," by J. S. Bruner and R. Tagiuri, pp. 634–654.

Merrill, F. E., *Courtship and Marriage*, rev. ed. (New York: Holt, Rinehart and Winston, Inc., 1959), 451 pp. (any 25 pages).

Pepinsky, P. M., *et al.*, *Leadership Acts: II. The Relation between Needs for

Achievement and Affiliation and Attempts to Lead under Conditions of Acceptance and Rejection (Columbus, O.: Ohio State University Press, 1955).

Ross, M. G., and C. E. Hendry, *New Understanding of Leadership* (New York: Association Press, 1957), 158 pp. (Chap. 2, 3, or 4).

Seidman, *The Adolescent: A Book of Readings,* rev. ed. (No. 28).

ARTICLES

Barbe, W. B., "Peer Relationships of Children of Different Intellectual Levels," *School and Society,* 80:60–62, 1954.

Davits, J., "Social Perception and Sociometric Choice of Children," *Journal of Abnormal and Social Psychology,* 50:173–176, 1955.

Dittes, J. E., "Attractiveness of Group as Function of Self-Esteem and Acceptance by Group," *Journal of Abnormal and Social Psychology,* 59:77–82, 1959.

Fey, W. F., "Acceptance by Others and Its Relation to Acceptance of Self and Others. A Revaluation," *Journal of Abnormal and Social Psychology,* 50:274–276, 1955.

Herman, R. D., "The 'Going-Steady' Complex: A Re-Examination," *Marriage and Family Living,* 17:36–40, 1955.

Keislar, E. R., "Peer Group Ratings of High School Pupils with High and Low Marks," *Journal of Experimental Education,* 23:375–378, 1955.

Keislar, E. R., "The Generalization of Prestige among Adolescent Boys," *California Educational Research,* 10:153–156, 1959.

Levine, G. N., and L. A. Sussmann, "Social Class and Sociability in Fraternity Pledging," *American Journal of Sociology,* 65:391–399, 1960.

Lundy, R. M., *et al.,* "Self-Acceptability and Description of Sociometric Choices," *Journal of Abnormal and Social Psychology,* 51:260–262, 1955.

Munro, B. C., "The Structure and Motivation of an Adolescent Peer Group," *Alberta Journal of Educational Research,* 3:149–161, 1957.

Phelps, H. R., and J. E. Horrocks, "Factors Influencing Informal Groups of Adolescents," *Child Development,* 29:69–86, 1958.

Bordis, P. D., "Attitudes toward Dating among the Students of a Michigan High School," *Sociology and Social Research,* 42:274–277, 1958.

Burchinal, "Adolescent Role-Deprivation and High School Marriage," *Marriage and Family Living,* 21:378–384, 1959.

Christensen, H. T., "Why All These Young Marriages?" *Parent-Teacher,* 52:4–7, 1958.

Crist, J. R., "High School Dating as a Behavior System," *Marriage and Family Living,* 15:3–28, 1953.

Dixon, M. M., "Adolescent Girls Tell about Themselves," *Marriage and Family Living,* 20:400–401, 1958.

Ehrmann, W. W., "Comparison of Comparative Social Class of the Companion upon Premarital Heterosexual Behavior," *Marriage and Family Living,* 17:48–53, 1955.

Katz, A. M., and R. Hill, "Residential Propinquity and Marital Selection," *Marriage and Family Living,* 20:27–35, 1958.

Cassel, R. N., and A. E. Shafer, "An Experiment in Leadership Training," *Journal of Psychology,* 51:299–305, 1961.

Cattell, R. B., and G. F. Stice, "Four Formulae for Selecting Leaders on the Basis of Personality," *Human Relations,* 7:493–507, 1954.

Fiedler, F. E., "A Note on Leadership Theory: The Effect of Social Barriers between Leaders and Followers," *Sociometry,* 20:87–94, 1957.

Hodges, H. M., "Campus Leaders and Nonleaders," *Sociology and Social Research,* 37:251–255, 1953.

Terrell, G., and J. Shreffler, "A Developmental Study of Leadership," *Journal of Educational Research,* 52:69–72, 1958.

Wischmeier, R. H., "Group-Centered and Leader-Centered Leadership," *Speech Monographs,* 22:43–48, 1955.

Suggested Research Problems [36]

1. A long-time follow-up study of 1000 "natural leaders" from the time they first showed their ability to lead until they are 50–60 years old.
2. Comparison of courtship patterns in different social classes, different countries, or different cultures.

---

[36] See note, p. 11.

Chapter 18 | Home and Family

TEACHERS have at least two good reasons for wanting to understand homes. The first is that homes have a profound effect upon the behavior and attitudes of pupils. Without some knowledge of their home conditions, a teacher cannot understand her students and cannot, therefore, adjust her work to their needs or help them in their personal development. The second reason is that her classroom is a kind of home, and she should know what the characteristics of a good home are so that she can introduce these into her classroom, thus making it a good environment for her students. This chapter will therefore present certain basic data about the trends in the modern development of the family, the structure of families, the patterns of parental behavior, the effects of the home upon its children, the special sources of difficulties during adolescence, the desirable characteristics of a home for adolescent boys or girls, and some of the undesirable outcomes if normal developments do not occur.

▶ The Modern Family

The American family has changed greatly during the last half century. In 1900 most families were still country families or else they had become urban so recently that the mores of the country were still being observed. In a rural setting the family has strong bonds of kinship, which furnish the basis for most activities, it depends upon propinquity for most of its social life, and it is an excellent transmitter of established tradition.[1] In contrast, the urban family attaches little value to mere kinship; its members tend to place personal interests above blood relationship, and the urge to carry on activities "as a family" is low. It does not need to rely upon propinquity for social intercourse because rapid transportation permits a member to have geographically distant friends. Members are concerned with cultural, social, and economic status—and they are often driven into the familiar pattern of living beyond their means in order to make a good showing in the community. The personal bonds are loose, the children have lives of their own, adolescents tend to drift away from home, grown sons and daughters

---

[1] See E. G. Erickson, *Urban Behavior* (New York: The Macmillan Company, 1954), 482 pp.

live at a distance and may become completely out of touch with relatives, and old people no longer expect to be supported by their grown children or to live with them. At the present time, the pattern of the urban family is almost universal, even among those who actually still live on the land, since modern transportation and communication make mere distance no longer a serious handicap. During a year, the small child in a rural family probably travels farther, going back and forth to school, than his grandfather traveled in a lifetime. As a result of this relatively new family pattern and of modern conditions, there have been many changes in such matters as the selection of mates, the number of children, the relative authority of mother and father, the relation of the parents to each other, the nature of home discipline, and the stability of the union. All these changes have affected the attitudes of the children toward family life and their relationship to their parents.

Modern marriage is often based on mutual sexual attraction, romantic interest, and glamour, with little consideration of suitability, financial arrangements, social contacts between the two families involved, future care of any children, or more thought of stability than the perennial conviction that love will last forever. The present theory seems to be that these practical problems will be worked out after the marriage, not before. Most young men are looking for a glamorous, exciting mistress with a pretty face rather than for a good housekeeper or a satisfactory mother for their children. A young woman is trying to attract a handsome, exciting, romantic lover, although she does have some thought of improving both her social and economic position. At the beginning, marriage is chiefly a man's diversion, but to a woman it is always a career, even if she has a profession or a job outside her home. If the partners become good friends the marriage has at least a chance. Since, however, the man was originally attracted by his wife's appearance, he is likely to find her first pregnancy a trial. Gone is the slender, alluring, eager, energetic girl he fell in love with, and in her place is an awkward, lethargic, unaesthetic young woman. If a man marries because he wants children, he may be as interested and excited about the pregnancy as his wife; but if what he wanted was a mistress, he is likely to react negatively to her condition. He also finds the next year or two after the child's birth very difficult. As the marriage continues, the woman's role becomes complicated, especially if there are children. She must remain glamorous, she must be motherly, she must be domestic, she must be an intelligent companion, she must maintain the family's social prestige, she must be the chief emotional prop of the household, and quite possibly she may want to pursue some line of work outside her home. The father's role, while onerous, is simpler: he has to earn money. He almost always spends the major part of the day away from his home and family. He is likely to find satisfaction and stability in his occupation, if it is at all suitable, but he often becomes a secondary figure in his home because his children see so little of him. The patriarchal father whose word is law has practically disappeared from the American scene, largely because social conditions have caused the foundations on which he stood to crumble. He no longer has any actual power over either his wife or his children. However, the modern father usually tries to be a friend to his children and is sometimes so successful that they look to him for their main emotional satisfactions.

The mother's relation to the children is complex. She is almost the only influence in a baby's life until it is about two and she is the main figure until the child enters school. Her position is so commanding that American families are more in danger of matriarchal than patriarchal domination. The mother's position as the most immediate love-object is, however, more or less offset by her position as the source of control. She does most of the reproving and punishing because she is on the scene, and in the case of her daughters she does practically all of it. The American mother serves, also, for her daughters as a figure with whom they can identify themselves—that is, she can be, and usually is, a model that her daughters imitate. As long as her sons are little boys, they too are likely to worship their mother, but as they grow older, they cannot identify themselves with her. They must leave her and prepare to enter the masculine world. The boy's typical revolt against the dominating feminism of both home and elementary school is to become tough, to excel in games, to be irresponsible, to pummel his companions and be pummeled by them, to play hooky, to be unpunctual, to neglect home chores, to admire "badness," to protest against going to church or Sunday school (unless his father also goes), and in general to react in a negative way to whatever seems to him to be feminine. This reaction is normal and healthy. Perhaps the members of those primitive groups who separated boys of nine or ten from their mothers and educated them together under exclusively masculine guidance were not such poor psychologists. In the modern family, the father should step in to become the guide and friend of, and model for his son.

A second source of difficulty arises from the modern theory that marriage is a relation between two people and not between two families. When any two people fall in love, there is no guarantee that their backgrounds are such that they can live together in harmony, no matter how much attraction they may feel toward each other. As long as families did the choosing, certain problems of adjustment did not arise. For instance, Catholic families did not choose Jewish ones, a native family did not choose a foreign one, and wealthy or high-status families did not choose their opposites. Consequently, the young people had much in common, and they were not likely to have trouble with their in-laws, since each had been approved by the other's relatives. The modern engagement is usually contracted between two young people who are unknown to each other's families. They may be of different creed, race, nationality, or social status. The marriage may or may not receive family approval. The older method of using marriage for furthering family alliances had its great disadvantages, but it avoided most of the clash that comes from antagonisms based upon divergent backgrounds.

Finally, a word should perhaps be said concerning the modern social forces that operate to pull the family apart. Each member has his own friends, his own interests, his own diversions. Modern uses of leisure are different for each age level, and most of them require a leaving of the home premises. It is not surprising that family life has a tendency to disintegrate. The family automobile ride, the family picnic, the family vacation, and now the family television are forces that still bind members together, but there are not as many integrative as disintegrative forces operating upon the average family group.

Modern psychologists and sociologists have been studying homes in great detail in recent years. The main results of their researches have been to demonstrate the extreme importance of a child's home upon his personality, attitudes, reactions, and behavior. The remainder of this chapter will deal with the results of outstanding investigations into such topics as the classification of homes into types, the emotional interrelationships among the members, discipline in the home, special problems of maintaining a good home for adolescents, and the effect upon all concerned by various factors: size of family, absence of one parent, socioeconomic status, and so on.

▶ Classification and Characteristics of Homes

When a stranger visits a home, he inevitably notices its characteristics more or less, depending upon his powers of observation, and, on the basis of what he has observed, draws his own conclusions as to familial affections and tensions. Use of a rating scale for homes requires primarily a series of such observations as any visitor might make, except that the trained adults who study homes are more systematic, careful, and thorough than a casual visitor is likely to be.

Within the past twenty years two especially important contributions to the understanding of family interrelationships have appeared. One contains a rating scale of thirty items, by means of which one may characterize homes. The other gives a classification of the patterns of authority and control within the home. The present section will be concerned primarily with the presentation of results from these two studies.

Patterns of Parental Behavior   Although each pair of parents has its own individuality, the behavior of parents in general toward their offspring may be classified roughly into eight types,[2] based upon differ-

---

[2] A. L. Baldwin, J. Kalhorn, and F. H. Breeze, "Patterns of Parental Behavior," *Psychological Monographs*, Vol. LVIII, no. 3, 1945, 75 pp.

ent combinations of three main variables. The first of these is the degree to which the parents accept the child. They may reject him, accept him, or be casual or indifferent toward him. The second variable concerns the extent of their indulgence and varies from subservience to his every whim to a nonchalant indifference to his needs. The third is the pattern of authority within the family, which may vary from an autocratic issuing of commands by the parents to a family democracy in which everyone's vote is of equal value. In theory there could be many possible combinations of these three variables, but actually there are only eight frequent configurations. These will be described briefly.

1. *Actively rejectant* parents are consistently hostile, unaffectionate, disapproving, critical, and distant. They seek actively to dominate the child by means of autocratic commands. Warm, social, trusting relations are missing. The home is full of tension and conflict, and there is a feeling of resentment on both sides. These parents dislike children, have no understanding of them, and rule them in a dictatorial manner. They are not intentionally cruel and they do not physically mistreat their offspring. They are cold, unsympathetic, and irritable toward those who are to them mainly a nuisance.

2. *Nonchalant, rejectant* parents have the same basic dislike for and indifference toward the child, but instead of continually nagging at him, they are merely indifferent to what he does, as long as he does not bother them. They ignore him as completely as possible and maintain only the slightest contact with him. When, however, the child does get in their way, they become autocratic and hostile, so as to get the point at issue settled quickly and with as little inconvenience to themselves as possible.

3. *Casually autocratic* parents neither accept the children with understanding nor reject them with resentment. Some are more consistently autocratic than others. All of them believe that a parent's authority is definitely above the desires of a child, but some of them are autocratic on principle, all day and every day, on matters large or small; whereas others try to maintain a friendly atmosphere, but resort to commands on important matters, merely from expediency. These autocratic-by-expedience parents have no theories about child training, so they react to each situation as it arises. They are likely to have no fixed policy about anything, and their home is usually on the chaotic side, with the children having a good deal of freedom and a moderate degree of affection, but meeting an autocratic handling if an issue is important enough.

4. *Casually indulgent* parents are mildly indulgent and in general tolerant, but rather haphazard. They maintain a fairly pleasant atmosphere in the home, and they often let the child do as he pleases, provided he does not bother them too much. They do not go out of their way to be indulgent, but they find that giving in is easier than resisting. They take their children easily, have no rigid standards for them, have no fixed policy about handling them, are often diverted from punishing them, and are inclined to baby them at times, although not consistently.

5. *Acceptant-indulgent* parents show a deep emotional attachment to the child, they are unduly anxious about him, they protect and baby him, they identify themselves so completely with him that they try to live their own lives over in his. They almost smother him with demonstrations of affection, and they put themselves to end-

less inconvenience in order to keep him happy. They do not, however, admit him as an equal who helps them make decisions. Their attachment to him is definitely neurotic and is so close that they cannot be objective about him or his problems. These parents have, however, definite standards for their child's behavior, although their method of procedure consists in leading him gently through their love for him rather than in coercing him.

6. *Acceptant-casual-indulgent* parents are sometimes just as indulgent as those in the above groups—although usually they are less extreme—but their indulgence is based on impulse, and they do not identify themselves with their child. They let junior have almost unrestrained freedom, and they submit to a good deal of disobedience and bad manners on his part. They admit their child's shortcomings, but they think freedom is the best way to let him develop his capacities, even though it may be trying at times. Because they are basically casual in their relationship, they do not smother their child with affection, or seek to overprotect him, or try to make him conform to an ideal. They just let him run wild most of the time and give in to him when conflict arises, because it seems to them easier than opposition.

7. *Acceptant-indulgent-democratic* parents are basically indulgent and believe in treating children as their own equals in a family democracy. The children are allowed to criticize their parents, to express their own views, and to make decisions on most minor and some major issues. They are treated on the surface as if they were adults, but they are also subject to a good deal of parental pressure that is applied indirectly via the close bond between parent and child. The parents use democratic practices as a means of making their child into the ideal companion they want him to be. The home is child-centered and rests upon a neurotic degree of contact between parent and child, and a neurotic identification of the former with the latter.

8. *Acceptant-democratic* parents are emotionally mature people who believe in the participation of children in family decisions and the independence of the child as an individual. Some parents of this type purposely repress expressions of affection and try to be objectively scientific in their treatment of their children. They are so afraid of influencing him too much that they often do not help him, even when he needs their aid to resolve a conflict. They make little or no effort to protect him from dangers of any kind. The more "scientific" parents do not act impulsively, but think matters over in view of basic educational principles and try to be rational. The child is respected as an individual, is encouraged to voice his opinions, is often consulted, and his decisions are allowed to stand without adult coercion. Children in such families often call their parents by their first names, an outward evidence of complete democracy. Parents and children meet on a companionable intellectual ground, but there is little overt affection between them. The child has his own place in the family council, and his desires are given whatever weight seems just in relation to the needs and wishes of the remaining members of the group.[3]

The chart in Figure 18–1 has been constructed to show the contrasts among these various home atmospheres. Since the figure would be more confusing than helpful if all types of parents were included, it has been limited

---

[3] Condensed from Baldwin, Kalhorn, and Breeze, *loc. cit.* Used by permission of *Psychological Monographs.*

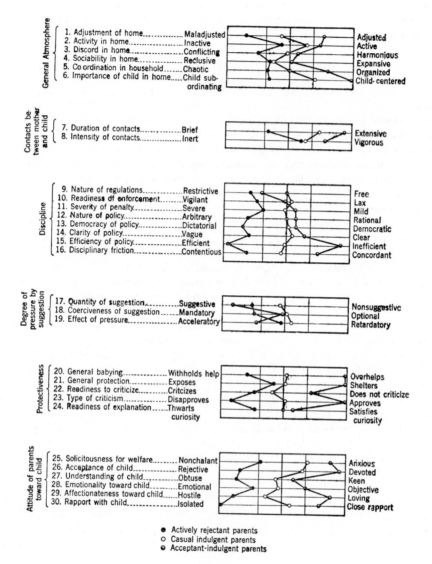

Fig. 18–1. Parental attitudes

Based on A. L. Baldwin, J. Kalhorn, and F. H. Breeze, "Patterns of Parental Behavior," *Psychological Monographs,* 58:19, 26, 43, 1945.

393

to only three: the actively rejectant, the casually indulgent, and the acceptant-indulgent. As may be seen at once, the first and third types of parent score at the two extremes, while the casually indulgent scores nearly in the middle of the figure on most traits.

Effects of Parental Attitudes upon Children   A careful and experienced observer can make a shrewd guess about a child's parents from noticing his behavior when he is away from them, because the child reflects to some extent at least the environment in which he has lived and the treatment he has received. It should be understood, however, that there are individual variations in the reaction of children and adolescents to their homes and that the following remarks apply only in general when one summarizes results from a large number of cases.

Thus the child who has been actively rejected by his parents is passive toward authority, docile, outwardly decorous—since only by such behavior can he escape their nagging and punishment—but he is also hostile, withdrawn, fearful, frustrated, insecure, stubborn, and passively resistant.[4] He is hostile in response to his parents' hostility, withdrawn because his contacts have been reduced to a minimum, fearful with good reason, but stubborn and resistive, since only thus can he achieve a small assertion of his ego, a slight retaliation of hostility, and an inactive expression of resentment. In one interesting study of twenty-six children who had dominating parents, fifteen of the children were passive, submissive, and dependent, six were rebellious and resentful, and five were passively resistant.[5]

The child of nonchalant, rejectant parents shows a different picture. He does not have to fight against hostility but against indifference. He is a type of neglected child. There is so little interaction between him and his parents that he can get their attention only by misbehaving. He has a moderate degree of independence, thrust upon him by parental refusal to help him. He makes desperate attempts to get attention, to arouse affection, and to achieve status. He soon discovers that he can obtain from age-mates the satisfactions that his parents deny him, and from then on he is likely to be in open conflict with his home.

Children whose parents maintain a neutral attitude but are at the same time autocratic in discipline are likely either to be nervous, timid, and compliant in their efforts to win recognition, or else to be aggressive and rebellious in order to assert their independence and individuality. If, in addition, the autocratic handling alternates with indifference—as is the case if treatment is based upon expediency and impulse—the children learn to be sly, to wriggle out of difficulties, to test the limits to which they can go, to bend temporarily before the storm, to delay requests until mother is in an amiable mood, and generally to circumvent a discipline that is of an uncertain and varying nature. If the casual parent is indulgent rather than autocratic, the less assertive child

---

[4] L. R. Wolberg, "The Character Structure of the Rejected Child," *Nervous Child,* 3:74–88, 1944; and D. D. Mueller, "Paternal Domination: Its Influence on Child Guidance Results," *Smith College Studies in Social Work,* 15:184–215, 1945.

[5] Mueller, "Paternal Domination: Its Influence on Child Guidance Results," *loc. cit.*

reacts by feeling insecure and anxious, by showing a tendency to be withdrawn when among other children, and by clinging silently to the fringe of groups without trying to take an active role. The aggressive child reacts to the same situation by running wild, by being destructive, and by thrusting himself into groups. Children of indifferent parents thus tend either to resign themselves to receiving little attention or else to become determined attention-getters.

The children of indulgent parents are likely to feel secure, protected, and comfortable. They soon learn to give an outer conformance to parental desires, at the same time getting their own way by being loving, cute, wheedling, disappointed, hurt, or amusing, as the occasion demands. Behind the façade of compliance and close attachment, however, they are domineering, self-centered, selfish, and determined to do as they please. Because they feel absolutely secure, they become smug, self-confident, somewhat self-righteous, and certain of their power over others. When they go to school, however, they discover that their age-mates are not so easily handled, and these overprotected children are usually unpopular. If they are smug enough to resist the shock, they become more aloof from others than before and more firmly entrenched in their own superiority. Success in meeting parental pressure intensifies the complacency of the accepted child into a precocity of mind, a maturity of outlook, a cocksureness of attitude, and an absolute belief in his own powers that makes him thoroughly obnoxious to everyone but his parents. Since, however, "democratic" parents tend to withhold open demonstrations of affection toward a child—lest they overprotect him— he is inevitably caught in a conflict: those who approve of him give him little warmth, and those from whom he might get affection either dislike or despise him. A vigorous child makes violent attempts to break out of his isolation. Since his democratic home treatment has taught him that he need fear no one, he is uninhibited, aggressive, and confident. As he grows older and develops understanding, his desire to be popular may lead him to try a more friendly means of approach. An extreme of democratic treatment may thus set up undesirable reactions.

Parents who are acceptant, moderately indulgent, democratic, and warmly affectionate have a home that is as near to satisfaction as can be expected, and their children are generally well balanced, secure, and happy. They may, however, be a little too comfortable within the family circle and reluctant to leave it, either actually or emotionally. They are sometimes too much exposed to pressure from siblings because their parents will not step in and protect them from aggression. Those who can come up to expectations, protect themselves, and adjust their desires to those of other people emerge as successes from this type of home.

In another investigation children of demanding parents were found to score high in intelligence, reading, and general achievement in school. Children of overanxious parents were equally high in intelligence, but their school achievements were far lower. Children of unconcerned and indifferent parents scored low on all tests. It would seem that even scores on objective tests taken in school may also reflect parental pressures—presumably through the amount of stimulation and orientation towards success in school.[6]

---

[6] N. Kent and D. Q. Davis, "Discipline in the Home and Intellectual Development," *British Journal of Medical Psychology*, 30:27–33, 1957.

Teachers in general tend to prefer as pupils those youngsters who come from homes in which the parents are dominant to those who come from homes in which the parents are submissive to their children's demands. Since teachers have twenty-five to forty children in a class, one can see the reason for this preference. The child with dominating parents is usually courteous, obedient, interested in school, modest, generous, responsible, docile, attentive, loyal, and careful. He accepts authority, keeps his desk in order, is careful of his clothes, has good manners, does not talk back when reproved, puts things back where he found them. Children from homes with submissive parents are rated by their teachers as being disobedient, irresponsible, disorderly, lazy, selfish, stubborn, sulky, aggressive, self-confident, talkative, independent, and antagonistic. They defy authority, are fussy about their food, lack interest in school, have bad manners, are often tardy, express themselves well and fluently, get on with their age-mates, and are general classroom nuisances. It should be noted that the two groups of children show both virtues and faults. One child is pleasant for a teacher to have around, but lacks initiative; he depends upon authority, he is hesitant in speech, and he has a better adjustment to older people than to his age-mates. The other child has the faults of irresponsibility, selfishness, and disobedience, but the virtues of independence, initiative, and fluent self-expression.

Patterns of Authority in the Family [7] Since there are two parents, there can be only three general patterns, although subdivisions within each are possible. Authority may be in the hands of the father or of the mother, or it may be equally divided between them. In the investigation here reported, based upon an intensive analysis of thirty-seven homes, five main types were recognized: the mother-controlled, the mother-led, the father-controlled, the father-led, and the equal-controlled, of which there were four subtypes. These groupings are listed in Table 18–1. Brief descriptions are given below.

The mother-controlled family contains the *passive* husband so frequently referred to in discussions of the (supposedly) increasing number of matriarchal families in America. Characteristically, this husband is indifferent to his wife; he looks upon child rearing as a woman's responsibility; and he prefers men's companionship and masculine activities to the company of his wife and children. His wife controls the home and family, first, because he apparently delegates that responsibility to her while he earns the living or not, as the case may be; and second, because she apparently feels some compulsion or need to assume the dominant role in family control.[8]

In the mother-led family the decisions regarding family policy are jointly made, but with the wife assuming the lead. She is apparently recognized as the stronger, more

---

[7] Based upon H. L. Ingersoll, "A Study of Transmission of Authority Patterns in the Family," *Genetic Psychology Monographs,* 38:225–302, 1948.

[8] The quotations are condensed from pp. 287–293 of Ingersoll, *loc. cit.*

Table 18–1: TYPES OF PARENTAL CONTROL

A. Mother-controlled, autocratic   4 ⎱
B. Mother-led, democratic   5 ⎰ 9

C. Balanced
  1. Equalitarian, democratic   7 ⎫
  2. Equalitarian, indulgent   2 ⎬ 13
  3. Equalitarian, neglectful   2 ⎪
  4. Equalitarian, inconsistent   2 ⎭

D. Father-led
  1. Autocratic   2 ⎫
  2. Democratic   7 ⎬ 15
E. Father-controlled, autocratic   3 ⎪
  1. Pseudo father-controlled   3 ⎭

SOURCE: H. L. Ingersoll, "A Study of Transmission of Authority Patterns in the Family," *Genetic Psychology Monographs,* 38:239, 1949.

capable person of the partnership, and her leadership appears to be accepted without resentment on the husband's part. There is warmth and affection in this family. The husband tends to be less secure emotionally, and thus to need more affection than his wife.

The partners in a democratic marriage have worked out a complex but unified system of authority based on a common philosophy of family life. This philosophy becomes so much a part of their thinking about the family that one partner often knows without asking what the other's reaction will be to a proposal. Therefore, authority over the various spheres of home and family life in the equalitarian family, for the most part, becomes a joint activity except in areas where one partner is felt more capable of judgment than the other.

In the father-led family the father is definitely the head of the family. Although family policy is apparently unified and arrived at through agreement of both husband and wife, the husband's leadership is more often followed in family planning and decision making than is his wife's, although she manages the home and family, including the rearing of the children, to conform with joint family policy and with his expectations. His authority supports her discipline consistently and firmly. Occasionally he may "lay down the law" or become autocratic in his control but for the most part he is the respected and loved democratic husband and father.

In the father-controlled family the husband expects to be absolute master of the home. He sets the family policy and makes the major plans and decisions. His unpredictable temper is his keenest and most feared weapon in maintaining control over his wife and children. He is likely to set standards of behavior for his children that are beyond their abilities to achieve. He expects his wife to see that his children are brought up to suit him. He criticizes her when they are not a credit to him. He takes the attitude that he is a superior being and his wife is inferior. He prefers men's company and masculine sports and activities. Wife and children are almost compelled to share his interests. Conflicts between him and his wife are often unresolved. There is little or no affection expressed toward each other by either of the partners.

The reaction of the children could be prophesied from the family situation. In the mother-controlled homes they are erratic in maturing, some showing parental "fixations," some rebelling against or withdrawing from parental authority, and others escaping from the family group as rapidly as possible. Generally speaking, these children show symptoms of disturbance in personality adjustment.

When the mother is a leader but not a despot the children appear to be more attached to her than to their father. They respect, admire, and love her, but like their father also. The children confide in their parents. The general family atmosphere is warm and acceptant. The husband and wife who are equalitarian in their relationship to each other tend to guide their children from early dependency to a place of responsibility and individuality in the family group. These children learn how to cooperate, how to share in family crises, how to contribute to family planning, and how to use so-called democratic techniques in group living. They are encouraged to become self-reliant and independent of parents as they approach adulthood.

Children in a father-led home often feel that their punishment is unfair and unnecessarily strict. The authoritarian father loses the confidence of his children, especially during adolescence. They may rebel, withdraw, or become overdependent. He may tie them to himself by his overprotection or force them to premature independence in order to escape his domination. Since the father in the father-controlled home is autocratic, erratic, and unpredictable, he is not loved. He sets up adult standards for his children that suit his ends and represses them into docile submission. He discourages adolescent independence, and is disapproving of his children's association with the opposite sex. He apparently hopes to run their lives as long as he can.

A quite recent investigation concerned patterns of authority in 93 families, who had been studied in a guidance clinic. The children in the families were asked to rate their parents as to authority, affection, and degree of involvement with themselves; these ratings were supplemented by records kept by the guidance center. Several patterns of relationship appear in the results, although two seemed commoner than the others. The results are summarized in Table 18–2. The "H" stands for "high" and the "L" for "low." The commonest ratings for mothers was H in authority, and L in affection and involvement, while the commonest one for the fathers was exactly the reverse: L in authority and H in the other two qualities. The second most common pattern of parental attitudes was a rating of H in all three qualities. In the next two most frequent ratings of mothers, the mother was L in either affection or relationship to the children; for the fathers, the next two showed a low rating in all three or a high rating only in authority. These four types made up a total of 76 of the mothers' ratings and 66 of the fathers'.

Factors Affecting the Impact of the Home upon the Child and Adolescent

The "normal" home contains two parents, their children, and no one else. If the home is broken by the absence of a parent, whether

Table 18–2: PATTERNS OCCURRING IN 93 HOMES

	Mothers								*Fathers*							
Authority	H	H	L	H	H	L	L	L	L	H	L	H	L	H	L	H
Affection	L	H	H	H	L	L	H	L	H	H	L	L	H	L	L	H
Involvement	L	H	H	L	H	L	L	H	H	H	L	L	L	H	H	L
Number	24	23	15	14	8	7	2	0	21	18	14	13	9	8	6	4

SOURCE: W. C. Bronson, E. S. Katten, and N. Livson, "Patterns of Authority and Affection in Two Generations," *Journal of Abnormal and Social Psychology*, 58:143–152, 1959. Used by permission of the American Psychological Association, Inc.

through death, divorce, or desertion, the home has a different character. If the number of children is unusually large or small, the family customs and relationships show differences. If there are conflict and tension in the group, such as arise when one child is jealous of another or when the parents quarrel frequently, the children are affected. The nature of the discipline in the home is of importance in a child's development. So also is the economic level of his home and its social status. The effects of variation from "normal" in these matters are of considerable importance in conditioning the behavior of adolescents, especially in influencing the nature and course of their emancipation from home control.

The broken home exists everywhere, even without divorce: one parent may have died, deserted his family, or been put into an institution. Among 4400 high school seniors in one state in 1953, 20 percent of the homes were broken—11 percent by the death of one parent, 7 percent by divorce, and 2 percent by separation.[9] The boys and girls from the broken homes had appreciably more problems than their classmates from complete homes. They were under more tensions, and their adjustment was poorer. High school students from broken homes do poorer schoolwork and rate lower on personality scales than do those who come from complete families. Even when one equates pairs of boys for intelligence, in each pair the adolescent from the broken home has more social and emotional problems than the other boy.[10] He is quicker to anger, more self-centered, less sensitive to social approval, less able to control himself, and more easily discouraged when things go wrong. However, the adjustment of a child may be just as good or better in a broken home as it is in an unbroken one that is unhappy and full of tension.[11]

[9] E. W. Burgess, "Economic, Cultural, and Social Factors in Family Breakdown," *American Journal of Orthopsychiatry*, 24:462–470, 1954; P. H. Landis, "The Broken Home in Teen-Age Adjustment," *Washington Agricultural Experiment Station Bulletin*, no. 542, 1953, 33 pp.

[10] R. Torrance, "The Influence of Broken Homes on Adolescent Adjustment," *Journal of Educational Sociology*, 18:359–364, 1945.

[11] F. I. Nye, "Child Adjustment in Broken and in Unhappy Unbroken Homes," *Marriage and Family Living*, 19:356–361, 1957.

The size of the family has an effect upon the adjustment of the children, but there seems to be some disagreement as to just what the effect is, especially in the case of the large family.[12] Some authorities report greater security in the large family, and some report less. It seems a priori reasonable to suppose that the members of large families would almost automatically acquire simple social skills, and perhaps this would be the case if one studied large and small families from the same social background. Often, however, the large family occurs at the lower end of the social scale and is therefore subject to privations that do not affect smaller families in the upper income brackets. One report characterizes adolescents from large families as receiving less than normal support in their problems, as being less able to continue with their education, as receiving less aid of any kind from their parents, as being less well adjusted, especially the girls, among whom there was a disproportionate number of adolescents with inadequate social life.[13] Another study characterizes the youngest child as feeling unable to compete with the others and the oldest as feeling neglected.[14] Perhaps the most defensible conclusion would be that the child in a large family has just as many problems as the child in a small one, but the problems are different.[15] It may still be that a large and economically stable family is a better social unit than a small family, especially as it is more likely to preserve family rituals and traditions—such as hanging up Christmas stockings, going to church together, walking in a park on Sunday, wishing on a wishbone, and so on—all of which customs lead to an integration of family life.[16] When a family begins to deteriorate it loses its traditions, which are often unimportant in themselves but serve as the cement that holds the members together.

At the other end of the distribution in respect to size of family is the only child. He is automatically deprived of constant contact with other children and he is continually subjected to adult presence, adult ways of life, and adult conversation. It is not necessary for an only child to be maladjusted, but it is easy for him to become so. For one thing, his mother has enough time to baby and spoil him, if she wants to. For another, he is not forced to overcome jealousy of his siblings and to content himself with his fair share of his mother's attention, and, if he is a boy, he comes into sharp and direct

---

[12] J. H. S. Bossard and E. S. Boll, "Security in the Large Family," *Mental Hygiene,* 38:529–544, 1954; P. H. Landis, "Teen-Age Adjustment in Large and Small Families," *Washington Agricultural Experiment Station Bulletin,* no. 549, 1954, 23 pp.; C. P. Loomis, W. B. Baker, and C. Proctor, "The Size of Family as Related to Social Success of Children," *Sociometry,* 12:313–320, 1949.

[13] Landis, "The Broken Home in Teen-Age Adjustment," *op. cit.*

[14] P. Schmidt, "Über die Stellung in der Geschwisterreihe," *Heilpädagogisches Werkbuch,* 23:149–156, 1954.

[15] G. R. Hawkes, L. Burchinal, and B. Gardner, "Size of Family and Adjustment of Children," *Marriage and Family Living,* 20:65–68, 1958.

[16] J. H. S. Bossard and E. S. Boll, "Ritual in Family Living," *American Sociological Review,* 14:463–469, 1949.

rivalry with his father for his mother's affection. If his parents quarrel, the only child has little if any protection from the resulting emotional atmosphere, even when the quarrel has nothing to do with him. On the other hand, an only child usually matures faster in social, emotional, and intellectual reactions than a member of a large family.

There is certainly a tendency for only children to be overprotected; that is, they receive too much maternal attention and companionship, they are abnormally protected from the ordinary hazards of childhood, they receive constant indulgence of their desires and such an outpouring of maternal love as to isolate them from other influences. The mother in these instances is usually not an abnormal person and shows no abnormal drives; she merely displays too much ordinary maternal behavior, too intensively and over too long a period. The danger of this development is greater if the child is a boy, if the father is ineffectual as a person, if the child is sick a great deal in infancy, if he is not merely the only child but the only possible one, or if he was born or adopted toward the end of the mother's years of possible childbearing.[17] The "only" child who is overprotected is sure to have difficulties in school, since neither his teacher nor his age-mates are going to give him the treatment he receives at home. If he rejects his peers and they reject him, he becomes more tightly tied than ever to his mother; if he tries to win status among them, he is soon in conflict with her. One of the relatively late evidences of overdependency is the chronic homesickness of a few college freshmen each year.[18] Some cannot survive the separation, and others do so only with difficulty. One hears more about homesick girls at the college level, probably because boys regard the attitude as unmanly and therefore repress the symptoms if they can or assign some other explanation to them, but in boarding schools both boys and girls are homesick and show it.

The Conflict between Generations There is no dearth of papers upon the matter of conflicts between parents and adolescents. Probably some amount of conflict within a family is inevitable, merely because two—and sometimes three—generations are living together. Four studies should suffice to point out the main areas of conflict. One report gives figures by age, as shown in Figure 18–2. The period of greatest conflict came when the children were between 13 and 16 years old; that is, during the years of beginning emancipation from parental control. These ages coincide also with the first years in high school. The main area of conflict was over friendships with members of the opposite sex; in addition, there was some difficulty

---

[17] Harry Bakwin, "Pure Maternal Overprotection," *Journal of Pediatrics,* 33:788–795, 1949.

[18] A. A. Rose, "The Homes of Homesick Girls," *Journal of Child Psychiatry,* 1:181–189, 1948, and "A Study of Homesickness in College Freshmen," *Journal of Social Psychology,* 26:185–203, 1945.

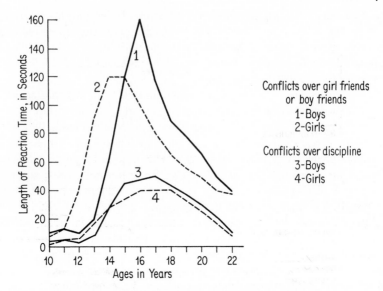

Fig. 18–2. Conflicts between parents and adolescents

Based on M. Powell, "Age and Sex Differences in the Degree of Conflict within Certain Areas of Personal Adjustment," *Psychological Monographs,* Vol. LXIX, No. 387, 1955.

over discipline. Conflicts began earlier for the girls than for the boys, presumably because the former develop heterosexual interests earlier than the latter. It is surprising that such difficulties should still continue into early adulthood.

A second investigation involving 2000 high school students included questions about the constant problem of the hour at which adolescents should return from an evening date. The results show, in general, for week nights, that about a third had to be home by ten and another fourth by eleven; the least supervised fourth came home when they wanted to. The girls had somewhat stricter rules than the boys. It is interesting that these same students do not show much difference between the requirements of their parents and their own desires, as stated when they were asked at what hour they *should* come home, although both boys and girls wanted to stay out later on weekend dates. The girls do not seem too dissatisfied, but the boys want fewer restrictions.

A third study not only shows the nature of the conflicts between parents and adolescents but also relates the number of conflicts to the type of home, of which 38 were democratic, 41 were intermediate between the two extremes, and 51 were authoritarian. On only a few items was there any real difference between boys and girls as regards the number of conflicts. In all types of home, there was less trouble between parents and daughters about schoolwork than between parents and sons; and in the authoritarian home the

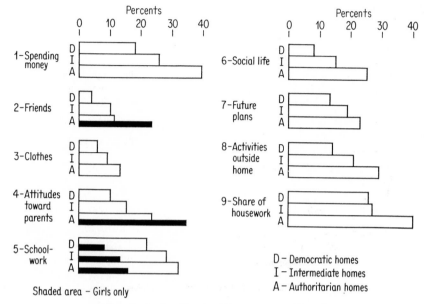

Fig. 18–3. Conflicts in different types of homes

Based on figures in P. H. Landis, "The Ordering and Forbidding Techniques and Teen-Age Adjustment," *School and Society,* 80:105–106, 1954.

daughters had more quarrels than did the sons over friends and attitudes toward parents. It can be seen at once that the number of conflicts is related directly to the type of home, but there were some in all types—as is probably inevitable when people of different generations live together. The results are summarized in Figure 18–3.

The fourth study gives some miscellaneous information about the conflicts between college students and their parents.[19] It involved one thousand students and was carried on by means of check lists and questionnaires, plus follow-up interviews with 20 percent of the cases. The areas of difficulty are reflected in the list presented in Table 18–3. The students' grievances seem to spread over a good deal of territory and suggest that these young people have not managed to achieve any real independence from their families. It is probable that at the college level most direct criticism from parents will be interpreted as interference, no matter how well meant.

One hears and reads less now about home discipline than formerly, since the present idea is to be as permissive as possible. However, some form of

[19] R. E. Lloyd, "Parent-Youth Conflicts of College Students," *Sociology and Social Research,* 38:227–230, 1952. See also R. Conner, T. B. Johannes, and J. Walters, "Parent-Adolescent Relationships: I. Parent-Adolescent Conflicts," *Journal of Home Economics,* 46:183–186, 1954.

Table 18–3: LIST OF CONFLICTS BETWEEN COLLEGE STUDENTS
AND THEIR PARENTS

Resenting parental interference with social life	22%
Resenting having no part in family planning	29
Resenting inadequate financial assistance	69
Resenting interference with academic work	20
Resenting familial criticism of school grades	35
Resenting slights and mistreatment (nature unspecified)	48
Resenting failure of parents to give them sex information	42
Resenting criticism of their friends	30

SOURCE: R. E. Lloyd, "Parent-Youth Conflicts of College Students," *Sociology and Social Research,* 38:227–230, 1954.

control of children and adolescents by parents is necessary. If it can be effected without the younger generation realizing that control is there, so much the better. Discipline may be positive or negative in character. If parents talk over an offense with their child until he understands why what he did was unacceptable and if they permit him to assign his own punishment to himself—in case they feel some punishment is still needed—the discipline is positive. In fact, any method may be so considered if it leads a child or adolescent to understand both himself and the problem better and allows a free expression of any hostility there may be on either side, without the otherwise almost inevitable suppression that in the end will do more harm than a brief outburst of hostility. Most punishment administered from above and without explanation or opportunity for the offender to state his point of view is negative in character. It may succeed in stopping a particular reaction, but it leads mainly to a permanent hostility as time goes on.

The situation has probably improved a good deal since the "good old days," but one still finds three types of home discipline that are basically dangerous to good mental health: the control by domination, the lack of any discipline beyond that which arises from temporary annoyance, and an unpredictable—to the children—variation between extreme severity and extreme leniency. The first type produces either shy, insecure children or overbold, insecure ones—depending upon how much vitality they have to fight back with—and is certain to precipitate severe storms during adolescence. The second type produces either a child who can manage himself or one that can manage his parents. In the former case, he has acquired independence at the cost of considerable strain. Adolescence in a permissive home is likely to be relatively free of disciplinary difficulties (although there may be other kinds), but in a child-dominated home the emancipation is far from simple, because the adolescent who has dominated his parents practically ever since his birth has never learned much about self-control. The third case, that of alternating control and neglect, combines the disadvantages of both and has the advantages of neither. The adolescent has not been able to develop either security or self-confidence, and his childhood uncertainties pursue him into adolescence, if not longer.

In spite of all the criticisms that have been leveled against the home, the writers feel quite sure that most homes furnish a background in which a boy or girl may develop normally. That there will be occasional friction is to be expected, but if the feeling of security is present, both parents and adolescents can weather a few differences of opinion. One of the writers watched with interest some years ago the working out of a family conflict between a strong-minded small girl who would not eat enough and her parents. After two or three years of "trying everything" in order to get enough food into the child, the parents finally lit upon the following plan: the child was to tell her father exactly what to serve her at each meal, and he was to put upon her plate only what she told him to put there; but, having made her selection, she must then eat everything on her plate, without comment and without protest. This arrangement resulted in the child's eating less than her parents thought she should but appreciably more than she had ever eaten before—and there was peace at the dinner table. This kind of cooperative mixture of parental discipline and self-discipline is coming more and more into style in American homes, with resulting benefits to everyone in the family.

▶ **Good Homes for Adolescents**

For adolescents the first trait of the good home is that it is willing to release gradually the control by the parents, but this release cannot be carried out without disaster unless children have been prepared for it in the preadolescent years. Emancipation has to take place and will take place, either peacefully or otherwise. The parental share of this operation is an acceptance of the basic fact.

There are numerous ways in which an adolescent may gradually achieve the necessary freedom from parental attachments. For instance, there is the matter of handling money. As children approach adolescence it is highly desirable that their allowance be increased so that they may buy independently a large proportion of what they need. A large but typical investigation [20] reported the actual extent and amount of weekly allowances as running from none to ten dollars or more. It is rather shocking that over half of the 2000 boys and girls included in the study had no allowance at all. They were therefore missing the resultant training in the handling of money. Naturally, adolescents usually buy some things inappropriate for their age, they use up their allowance before the week is over, and they buy things they do not really want. However, they will never learn to spend money wisely and appropriately

---

[20] Purdue Report of Poll No. 60, *loc. cit.,* p. 15a.

by any other method than by actually spending it. If parents do not make some arrangement as that suggested above, they encourage their adolescent sons and daughters to ask or tease for money, exactly as if these near-adults were children. Such a situation not only prolongs childishness but may eventually bring on revolt, and in any case is likely to result in a carelessness with money that persists into adult life.

Dan, a young man of 27, is the despair of his parents because he seems unable to realize the value of money. Dan's family is quite wealthy. His mother has been a semi-invalid ever since his birth—he is the youngest of four children—and she has left his care to nursemaids, governesses, teachers in day schools, counselors in summer camps, and to housemasters and teachers in boarding school and college. During his childhood and early adolescence, whatever he wanted was procured for him. He constantly saw his parents charging things, and as he grew older he simply used their accounts in various stores. At the boarding school he attended, the boys were supposed to be given only two dollars a week for spending money, but Dan's parents usually sent him five dollars or ten dollars, although the headmaster asked them several times to observe the limit more conscientiously. When Dan was 16, his father opened a cash account for him. There followed four or five years of constant difficulty because Dan overdrew his account almost every month. He did not intend to write bad checks, but he was unwilling to keep track of what he spent. When Dan was 19, he went into the Army, where he remained for two years as a private. He was constantly in monetary difficulties of one sort or another, and on a few occasions spent time in the guardhouse because he had failed to pay the bills he owed to the local merchants. Dan was kept in the United States as a clerk because he seemed too irresponsible for active service. When he developed fallen arches the Army was quite willing to let him go back into civilian life. At 25 he came into an inheritance from his grandfather. Dan's habits are not in the least wicked but they are expensive, and he has each year spent a good deal more than his income. His capital is therefore decreasing at an alarming rate. The endowment is enough to last, with moderate care, for his entire lifetime, but at the present rate it will be used up by the time he is forty. His parents worry constantly, partly because they do not like to see Dan remain so childish and partly because they feel some concern over leaving him a fourth of their own wealth. The older brother and the two sisters have shown no tendency to irresponsibility. The parents have about decided to put Dan's portion into a trust fund, of which he will be allowed to spend only the income.

In contrast, one of the writers is reminded of her own training in the proper handling of money. One of her earliest memories is of the Sunday morning ceremony of being given three new, shiny pennies for each week's allowance. One she put at once into the bank, one she put upon the collection plate in church, and the third was hers to spend as she liked. In the course of time, the amount was raised to five cents, then ten, twenty-five, and fifty cents, and eventually to one dollar and two dollars. With each advance, however, the contributions to bank and church were raised correspondingly. Also, as the amount of the allowance increased so did the number of things it was supposed to cover. There were three rigid rules about this allowance: first, no more money was forthcoming when it was gone; on many a cold winter's morning she tramped two miles to school through the snow because she had spent her allowance and had nothing left for carfare. The only way of adding to the amount was to earn small sums by doing whatever errands or other work could be found in the neighborhood. Second, there was no adult interference in the spending of the "free" portion of the allowance, nor were the more silly and childish uses of it belittled or commented upon. Third, items that were supposed to come out of the allowance were not forthcoming from any other source. If she did not buy toilet soap for herself, she did not borrow someone else's or raid the family supply; she washed with Fels-Naphtha from the kitchen. Such systematic and eminently fair training results in the establishment of habits that last a lifetime.

Insofar as it is possible, a good home allows an adolescent boy or girl to get himself out of his own difficulties. Thus if a boy gets into a row with one of his teachers, he should not be allowed to run away from the situation while his parents see the teacher and patch up the trouble. If a girl buys a dress and then suddenly decides it is not suitable, she should return the dress to the store and do the necessary explaining herself; if the store will not take the dress back, then she should not be given money to buy another. If a girl has offended some acquaintance she may, of course, be given advice about what to do, but she should certainly carry out the advice independently. If a boy insists upon taking an extra course in school, he should not be allowed to drop out of it as soon as he thinks himself overworked. If a boy wants to ask a girl to a dance he should ask her himself—not get some member of the family to do it for him. The first impulse of an adolescent who gets into difficulty is to follow a childish pattern of behavior and run at once to a sympathetic adult who, he hopes, will straighten out matters for him. Many adolescents are not resourceful and therefore need advice, but they should never be allowed to dodge the outcome of their own bad judgment. The sooner they learn that the tail goes with the hide, the better. Parents and teachers both need to learn how to stand aside and let adolescents make mistakes, and then see to it that the youngsters profit by their errors. Protection from experience does not educate; it only prolongs childishness.

A good home for adolescents permits them to choose more and more of their own friends until the matter is entirely in their hands. Naturally, guidance is needed at first, and if it is unobtrusive, the adolescent will welcome it. It is inevitable that a boy or girl will make some unwise choices of friends, but no serious harm is likely to be done if the parents accept the friend, ask him or her to the house, and do not get into a panic. The danger arises when parents become uncompromising and drive their adolescent son or daughter out of the house, to meet the undesirable friend in some unprotected place. Successful parents use unwise friendships as education for their child in the judgment of character.

It might be mentioned in passing that one of the commonest sources of difficulty between parents and their adolescent sons is the temporary infatuation of the lad for some girl from an unsatisfactory and even vulgar background. Such an episode is part of almost every adolescent boy's experience. He selects such a girl largely because he is socially too immature for those in his own social group, and she does not hold him to standards that are so high they make him uncomfortable. Such a relationship usually does no harm, and if the boy comes from a good home, he will soon be repelled by the girl's lack of refinement—provided the parents do not make an issue of the matter.

As a final step in encouraging emancipation, the parents in a good home leave their boy or girl free to find a mate. If, since the beginning of adolescence, there has been opportunity for adequate social relations with numerous members of the opposite sex, the adolescent has probably already gone through a series of temporary attachments and has educated himself sufficiently to know what he wants. Even though the final attachment leading to marriage may not find favor with the parents, the latter are likely to produce only revolt and estrangement by opposition. Parents can prevent many tragedies if, in their children's early years of adolescence, they arrange for an abundance of social contacts for their children. When permanent attachments are made, the time for parental control has already gone by.

The degree of emancipation typical at the present time is well reflected by answers to questions in Table 18–4. The parents still exerted some control over the hour for return from a date, especially for girls, and they contributed to such joint undertakings as planning a summer vacation or college attendance, matters in which they were directly involved. The degree of emancipation is all one could ask, but there are still areas of conflict as indicated by the unusually large percent of students who did not reply. These are perhaps those who are in the process of emancipation and do not know at the moment who does make the decisions.

Parental Adjustment to Society In a good home the parents do not pass their own maladjustments on to their children. Presumably no parents intend to, but some of them do. The difficulty may be seen in its simplest form in the immigrant home, in which the parents are trying to maintain their native customs in the face of American social forces. Such parents, because they do not accept American standards, pass on their own maladjustment to the next generation. Parents who insist upon a fundamental-

Table 18–4: DEGREE OF EMANCIPATION FROM HOME

Who makes the decisions about each of the following?	Percent	
	Boys	*Girls*
How late you stay out on a date?		
My parents	48	70
I do	42	20
No answer	10	10
What time you go to bed at night?		
My parents	20	17
I do	72	78
No answer	8	5
How you spend most of your money?		
My parents	8	5
I do	79	86
No answer	13	9
What you will do this summer?		
My parents	14	12
I do	72	72
No answer	14	16
Whether or not you go steady?		
My parents	10	20
I do	80	69
No answer	10	11
Whether or not you will go to college?		
My parents	15	17
I do	67	66
No answer	18	17
What your future occupation will be?		
My parents	3	2
I do	85	89
No answer	12	9

SOURCE: Purdue Opinion Panel, "Youth Looks at Politics, College Education, Jobs, and Family," *Report of Poll No. 60* (Lafayette, Ind.: Division of Educational Reference, Purdue University, 1960), 22 pp., pp. 19a and 21a.

ist view of religion force their children into conflict between schoolwork and home beliefs. Parents who will not tolerate smoking, use of cosmetics, or social dancing are almost sure to have maladjusted adolescent children. If boys and girls from such homes insist upon maintaining their parents' standards, they will become ostracized by their own social group; if they secretly abandon parental ideas, they develop a chronic habit of deceit; if they show the pro-scribed behavior openly, they are forced into revolt against their homes. Many parents who have not formulated a consistent point of view on modern life force their adolescent children to make decisions on exactly the same prob-lems for which they themselves can find no comfortable solution.

Mrs. M. and her three children came to America in about the year 1900. She had been carefully brought up in the old country and had absorbed her native customs and manners so thoroughly that they seemed to her the only acceptable mode of life. Mrs. M. liked the material comforts of America, but she never made head or tail of American social life. She guarded her children as if she expected them to be kidnaped at any moment. The two oldest ones, both boys, were eager to become "real Americans" as soon as possible. Gradually they rejected their home and parents and escaped from maternal control.

Helene, the daughter, however, lived at home and docilely absorbed what her mother told her. Since she heard no English in her home and since she spent more time there than elsewhere, her English is still hesitant and accented, al-though she was only two years old when she arrived in America. Little Helene was not exactly unpopular in school, but she was rejected on account of her queer-ness—broken speech, foreign clothes, foreign manners, and so on. Her mother had managed so to imbue Helene with her own love of the old country that Helene gladly wore clothes markedly different from those of other people and willingly submitted herself to the regime considered proper by her mother. There was never any revolt of consequence, even when her high school classmates laughed at her gaucheness. In her youth Helene might have attracted masculine attention, since she was a rather good-looking girl, but her appearance was foreign and her ideas about the conduct of escorts were rigid. American boys would not be squeezed into the desired mold, American girls liked the process no better, and most second-generation foreigners were trying to escape similar parental molds and had no intention of handicapping themselves with an un-American wife or friend. Helene lived at home, worked in a nearby library, and never questioned her mother's judgment. Three years ago the mother died suddenly. Helene now finds herself in a difficult position. She has tried living with several different acquaintances, but her ways of doing things and her modes of thought are so alien that no one can be comfortable with her. A year ago she became desperately unhappy because of her extreme isolation and loneliness, and she finally initiated attempts to be-come Americanized. She now finds that her mother has passed on to her the same problems of Americanization that she herself found insoluble in 1900.

Identification in the Home   A good home furnishes its children with models. In the early years of childhood the parents are the people with whom children identify themselves, and sometimes this process continues for many years. That most homes are good in this respect is shown by a study of college men, whose ages were above twenty.[21] Seventy percent reported that they regarded their fathers as models. In fact, their fathers seem to have been their chief sources of identification. This is as it should be. From parents and from parental attitudes toward each other, adolescents derive most of their ideas about home life and marriage. Adolescents are already beginning to think about a home of their own. They can have no greater help in developing healthy attitudes than a good model of happy marriage in their own home.

Duncan Smith is a high school sophomore. He has a sister who is just through college and a foster brother in the eighth grade. His mother is dead. The three adults in his home are his father, his father's younger sister—who has lived with the family since Duncan's birth—and a faithful Negro servant of more than middle age. This somewhat heterogeneous group has been welded into a real family by the efforts of the aunt, nicknamed "Dodo" by the children. She is still a young-looking woman of whose appearance Duncan is very proud. The father is a lawyer by profession and an educated gentleman by preference.

Duncan's sister, Marie, graduated from college last year and is now at home. She has a boy friend whom she hopes some day to marry; in the meantime she is learning how to run a house, cook, plan meals, and make simple repairs. She and Dodo have a session every morning while they divide the day's work between them. Marie admires her aunt's gay disposition, her good looks, and her efficiency. The girl's ambition at the moment is to become as capable as her aunt, to have her fiancé develop into as nice a man as her father, and to have a home in which her children can have as much fun as she has always had in hers. She threatens to take white-haired Nannie, the maid, with her. In short, she wants her home of the future to duplicate her home of the past.

Duncan studies at home most evenings, going to his father whenever he needs help. During the past summer he and his father visited about a dozen colleges, staying at each two or three days, so that he might be better able to decide which he prefers to attend. He and his father play tennis together in the father-and-son doubles in the summer and bowl together in the winter. He goes out with various girls, but says he won't fall in love till he finds a girl who is as pretty as Dodo and can cook as well.

The family have many joint enterprises and amusements. On a stormy eve-

---

[21] D. H. Funkstein, S. H. King, and M. E. Drolette, "Perception of Parents and Social Attitudes," pp. 98–119, in P. H. Hoch and J. Zubin, *Experimental Psychopathology* (New York: Grune & Stratton, Inc., 1957), 275 pp.

ning Mr. Smith reads aloud, Dodo darns socks, Marie hems dish towels for her hope chest, Duncan whittles wooden buttons and brooches that he will later use for Christmas presents, and Nannie goes to sleep in a corner. On Sunday mornings there is a great stir all over the house; Nannie makes popovers for breakfast, Marie and Duncan pull the linen off the beds and make them up fresh, and at ten thirty the family is ready to set out en masse for church, where Duncan and Mr. Smith both sing in the choir.

One day last summer, when Marie had had an argument with her boy friend, Dodo told her about her own most serious love affair that had gone on the rocks after a quarrel. The two talked more as if they were older and younger sister than niece and aunt. With similar frankness and companionship Mr. Smith has recently talked over some of his cases with Duncan.

At the beginning of every month the family makes a joint budget. Mr. Smith announces what funds are available, Dodo presents the house accounts of the previous month, everyone puts in bids for the things he or she needs or wants, there is much discussion, and eventually a budget emerges. One small sum is always set aside for joint expenditures, such as a family visit to the movies. The money is given in turn to each child, who keeps an account on what Dodo calls the "swindle sheet" and reports his expenditures at the beginning of the next month.

As a result of all these activities, Duncan and Marie are reaching maturity with a deep love for all three of the adults in their home and a sincere admiration for each. To be sure, Duncan refers to his father merely as a "good egg." Marie says her aunt is "crazy but O.K.," and all the children call Nannie "Gold Dust" when she is not around, but the careless speech does not fool anyone but themselves. All three are modeling themselves upon the adults they know best, with whom their relation is now more nearly that of one friend toward another than that of a child toward a parent.

Interest in the Home   A good home is interesting, exciting, and stimulating. As a result, adolescents feel a desire to stay there during a portion of their leisure time. If hours spent at home mean only an endless round of chores and the ever-present likelihood of being scolded or criticized, adolescent boys and girls will remain there only long enough to eat, bathe, dress, and sleep. As places given wholly to entertainment, homes cannot compete with such commercialized offerings as the movies or the amusement parks, but they can furnish the adolescent with interesting things to do or think about, and with a background for an abundant social life. A radio or record player, a clearable space for dancing, simple equipment such as a ping-pong table, access to the larder, privacy, and a relaxed atmosphere will do much to make home an interesting and exciting place in which adolescents want to stay because they enjoy themselves. Parents may have to help their sons and daughters with suggestions, but they should rarely try to take part in the activities.

The Jones family lives in a large, one-story, rambling house. There are four children—two boys, ages 16 and 15, one daughter, age 13, and an adopted daughter, age 14. All four children are just entering adolescence. Up until a year ago each child had his or her own room, but as they approached adolescence and began to go out to movies and parties, the parents suggested that the two girls should share a bedroom and the two boys another, while each pair fitted up one room for social purposes. A small fund was made available to them, and while the parents made some suggestions, the expenditure was determined mainly by the children. The boys first bought a secondhand pool table, the girls a ping-pong table and a small radio. Later on, the boys bought a number of small items—cards, an ancient slot machine, a basketball, and a hoop which they affixed to the wall. The girls took out subscriptions to two magazines, acquired a number of puzzles, and got some paints. Both boys and girls made some of the furniture for their rooms. They are also responsible for keeping the rooms in order. All four of them are permitted to play anything that is quiet even on weekday evenings, if they feel they do not need the time for study. The rooms are usually occupied by a number of youngsters Friday evenings, Saturday, and Sunday afternoons. There is a fireplace in the girls' room, where they cook wieners and toast marshmallows. The ping-pong table folds up when not in use, and the youngsters have a space for dancing. In the course of the past two years they have accumulated a number of books and magazines, and it often happens that they and their friends spent hours together reading, sometimes aloud. They make Christmas presents, May baskets, Easter gifts, and so on, in these rooms, and they have a number of collections—stamps, rocks, miniature animals, and the like. They have recently acquired a record player and some records, to which they listen avidly. Since these two rooms have been available for their use, the children have made their home the center of their social activities, simply because they can have more fun there than they are likely to have in any other place. They still go to the movies sometimes, to school dances, or to parties at their friends' houses, but home is the most interesting place they know.

A desirable home for adolescent boys and girls has thus four main characteristics: first, it allows its children to grow up; second, it does not pass on its own maladjustments; third, it serves as a model; and fourth, it is a stimulating and interesting place.

Application of Principles to the Classroom A teacher who wishes to maintain a classroom in which adolescents will feel comfortable can do no better than to imitate the characteristics of a good home. She can encourage her pupils to be just as independent of her as possible. She can keep her own troubles and problems to herself. She can keep on good terms with her pupils and be available for help in time of stress. She can develop her own maturity so that she will appear to adolescent boys and girls as a model to be admired. And she can make her work so interesting and exciting that the pupils want to stay in her classes as long as they can. The good home and the good classroom are thus similar in their fundamental psychological characteristics.

▶ **Summary**

There are many types of parental relationship to both children and adolescents, and the type of home in which a child grows up is a main factor in shaping his personality and attitudes.

As a child becomes an adolescent certain features of the home become increasingly important. In the best type of home, an adolescent is allowed to grow up and take responsibility for himself as soon as he is able to do so. His parents do not pass on to him their own unsolved problems. The boy or girl should be proud of his home and should feel secure in its harmony. Such problems as still require some degree of parental control should be settled jointly by the parents and the adolescents on a rational and not emotional basis. By the end of adolescence the parents in a good home have become the friends, rather than the controllers, of their children. If homes are inadequate in these respects, an adolescent either fails to grow out of his emotional and social childhood, or else he is driven into open revolt. Neither situation is desirable, but the latter is healthier than the former.

References for Further Reading

BOOKS

Other Tests

Ausubel, *Theory and Problems of Adolescent Development* (Chap. 8).
Baller and Charles, *The Psychology of Human Growth and Development* (pp. 336–350, 357–360).
Garrison, *Growth and Development,* 2d. ed. (pp. 295–320).
Horrocks, *Behavior and Development* (pp. 49–74).
Hurlock, *Adolescent Development,* 2d. ed. (Chap. 14).
Jersild, *Psychology of Adolescence* (Chap. 13).
Jones, *Growth and Behavior in Adolescence* (Chap. 14).
Kuhlen, *Psychology of Adolescent Development* (Chap. 12).
Wattenberg, *The Adolescent Years* (Chap. 8, 9, 10, or 22).

Other Books and Monographs

Baller, *Readings in the Psychology of Human Growth and Development* (pp. 556–582).

Pearson, G. H., *Adolescence and the Conflict of Generations: An Introduction to Some of the Psychoanalytic Contributions to the Understanding of Adolescence* (New York: W. W. Norton & Company, Inc., 1958), 186 pp. (Chap. 7).

Seidman, *The Adolescent: A Book of Readings,* rev. ed. (Nos. 7, 31, 32, and 56).

Strang, *The Adolescent Views Himself* (pp. 356–400).

Winch, R. F., *The Modern Family* (New York: Holt, Rinehart, and Winston, Inc., 1952), 522 pp. (pp. 182–258).

ARTICLES

Bossard, J. H., and E. S. Boll, "Security in the Large Family," *Mental Hygiene,* 38:529–544, 1954.

Bronson, W. C., *et al.*, "Patterns of Authority and Affection in Two Generations," *Journal of Abnormal and Social Psychology,* 58:143–152, 1959.

Butler, R. N., "Mothers' Attitudes toward Social Development of Adolescents," *Social Casework,* 34:219–225, 280–287, 1956.

Connor, R., *et al.*, "Parent-Adolescent Relationships: Parent-Adolescent Conflicts," *Journal of Home Economics,* 46:183–186, 1954.

Hawkes, G. R., *et al.*, "Size of Family and Adjustment of Children," *Marriage and Family Living,* 20:65–68, 1958.

Kent, N., and D. R. Davis, "Discipline in the Home and Intellectual Development," *British Journal of Medical Psychology,* 30:27–33, 1957.

Landis, P. H., "The Ordering and Forbidding Techniques and Teen-Age Adjustments," *School and Society,* 80:105–106, 1954.

Lloyd, R. E., "Parent-Youth Conflicts of College Students," *Sociology and Social Research,* 36:227–230, 1952.

Nye, F. I., "Child Adjustment in Broken and in Unhappy Unbroken Homes," *Marriage and Family Living,* 19:356–361, 1957.

Scheerer, E. T., "Family Life Counseling with High School Students," *Marriage and Family Living,* 20:290–293, 1958.

Suggested Research Problems [22]

1. Research study of home discipline: types, effects on parent-child relationships, long-time results, influence upon personality and adjustment, possible differences of values at different age levels—with recommendations to parents.

---

[22] See note on p. 11.

Chapter 19 | Delinquency

ATTITUDES toward the causes of delinquency and crime have shown an interesting development. When efforts were first made to understand the criminal, the basic assumption was that his abnormality was basically physical. That is, he was a "type." Measurement of several hundred criminals soon exploded this idea, as far as the scientist was concerned, because as a group wrongdoers showed a normal human variability in physical structure—and nothing more. The general public, however, seems still wedded to the idea that a criminal looks like Neanderthal man. The next viewpoint of scientists was that criminals and delinquents were mental defectives. This idea also did not hold up long under careful investigation. Use of intelligence tests soon proved that inferior intelligence is at most only a contributory cause in perhaps a quarter of the cases. Attention then turned from the man to his surroundings, and the environmental theory of delinquency found favor. This theory seemed the more likely since it had long been known that some areas of any city produced more delinquents than others. Under the sway of the environmental theory, investigators analyzed the families, homes, friends, schools, neighborhoods, and districts from which delinquents came. They found a great deal that was amiss, and for two or three decades social scientists thought they had the answer to the age-old problem of wickedness: if there were no congested, filthy slums, there would be no crime. However, the environmental theory alone could never explain why one of two brothers who grew up in the same family, in the same tenement, in the same dirty street became a criminal while the other did not. Nor did it account for the delinquent who emerged from an excellent home situated in a good neighborhood. The fact that delinquents come in larger numbers from some areas than from others suggests that the environmental theory contains some elements of truth.

In recent decades there has arisen a theory that all delinquents are emotionally disturbed and that it is their maladjustment which has led them into unacceptable modes of expression. This theory seems to be in need of amendment. Children and adolescents can be deeply disturbed without being delinquent at all, and they can be delinquent without any sign of emotional maladjustment. As has already been pointed out, delinquents may come from all levels of society, although the greater proportion comes from the lowest economic level. The extent to which emotional maladjustment is a factor in misbehavior depends apparently upon the offender's social background, as indicated in Table 19–1. Only 15 percent of the delinquents in the group studied came from the upper class, but 10 percent of this total were emotionally dis-

Table 19–1: DISTRIBUTION OF DELINQUENT INDIVIDUALS AND
EMOTIONAL DISTURBANCE
(In Percents)

Class Status	Demonstrable Emotional Disturbance	Little or No Serious Emotional Disturbance	Total Percents
Middle and Upper Classes	10	5	15
Lower Class	15	70	85

SOURCE: W. C. Kvaraceus, *et al., Delinquent Behavior* (Washington, D.C.: National Education Association, 1959), 147 pp., p. 54.

turbed. That is, if a delinquent comes from an upper class home, he is twice as likely to be emotionally disturbed as he is to be normal in his emotional reactions. The "good" home furnishes a basic standard of conduct that most of the children follow willingly and such a home protects its youth from some of the more damaging ideas that are current in poorer homes. Therefore, if a boy misbehaves, he is presumably led into trouble by his maladjustments, not by external circumstances. For the delinquents from the lowest class—who made up 85 percent of the total—70 percent showed no emotional maladjustment as compared to only 15 percent who did. This relation is at a rate of about eight adolescents with no serious maladjustment to every one with such a condition. In fact, the delinquency itself may come primarily from an adolescent's excellent adjustment to the worst elements in his lower-class culture rather than from a lack of adjustment to it.

Everyone has his or her own idea of what delinquency is, but many of these concepts are inadequate for a study of the problem. Delinquency is basically a legal definition of behavior. According to law it consists of "behavior by nonadults which violates specific legal norms or the norms of a particular societal institution with sufficient frequency and/or seriousness so as to provide a firm basis for legal action against the behaving individual or group." [1] For purposes of the present discussion juvenile delinquency may perhaps better be defined as norm-violating behavior. That is, the act—whatever its nature—has violated some rule or regulation of society. But it is at once evident that different segments of society have different norms and that behavior which would be accepted by one group would be considered norm-

---

[1] Kvaraceus, *loc. cit.,* p. 54.

violating by another. Thus, profanity is not only heard but expected in lower-class homes and neighborhoods, where it passes without comment as normal, whereas it is punished severely in upper-class groups. At just what point the behavior of an individual child becomes "delinquent" is hard to define. The form of his norm-violating behavior, the seriousness of it, and its frequency determine the answer.

In reporting the recent trends in the study of delinquency, the writers have encountered some difficulty in achieving a proper synthesis, because the reports from research workers have put the emphasis upon different inter-pretations of causality. Some emphasize the personality of the delinquent boy or girl; others emphasize interfamilial relationships; still others vote for the importance of environmental influences. The writers wish to give a fair picture of the matter and have therefore included a great variety of reports, some of which have a tendency to contradict others. It has seemed to them that many investigators had become so involved in their own view of delinquency that they had lost sight of what others were doing. It is the writers' belief that all lines of investigation have value and that all should be faithfully reported, even though there may be some confusion in the mind of the reader.

There is some reconciliation of the divergent points of view as to basic causes in the following classification of delinquents. One writer has grouped delinquents into four types.[2] Like all such groupings, it tends to become rigid and to omit from its framework anything that does not easily fit into it, but on the other hand it does contribute something to the understanding of delin-quency. The first group is made up of (1) the open delinquents. These are adolescents who have been rejected by their families, expelled from school, and often have served a term in a corrective school. Their crimes are of a violent nature: armed robbery, burglary, rape, vandalism, assault, gang vio-lence. Society rejects this group completely. And in return, they reject the world, they take pride in their delinquencies, they scorn conformity as weak-ness, and they turn to other delinquents for approval. The second group is made up of (2) the extreme nonconformists who waiver between acceptance of moral values and rejection of them, who are confused in all respects, in-cluding their concept of themselves. Their main crimes are petty larceny and promiscuity, with an occasional loss of control that ends in a manslaughter charge. They have met with much disapproval from home and school, but they are not completely rejected. They have received police warnings, suspensions from school, and they may have been referred to agencies for treatment. They remain emotionally and socially on the fence, sometimes conforming and sometimes not. The third group contains those adolescents who might be called (3) the minor nonconformists. They have not broken with school,

---

[2] R. S. Cavan, *Juvenile Delinquency* (Philadelphia: J. B. Lippincott Company, 1962), 366 pp., pp. 20–21.

church, or family, and they do not regard themselves as being really delinquent. Their misconduct consists of pilfering, borrowing cars without permission, smoking marijuana, vandalism, and general rowdiness. They are tolerated but not approved. They are disciplined by parents and school, and in general they accept the conventional moral values. As a result they constantly feel more or less guilty. The last group is made up of (4) the misbehaving nondelinquents who have kept their contacts with family, church, and school and accept authority in general. Their friends are among the conformers, whereas in the three first groups most of the adolescent's friends were themselves delinquents. These adolescents in the last classification are weighted down with feelings of guilt. Their depredations are extremely minor—such as cheating on a school test or swiping oranges off a fruit stand. Most of their behavior is acceptable. It should be noted that as one reads through these descriptions two general principles emerge: first, the open delinquent is a more adequately organized individual than the nonconformist or the misbehaving nondelinquent. His attitudes are consistent, and he is well adjusted to his immediate environment, even though the bases upon which his organization rest are inacceptable to the majority of citizens. Second, the load of guilt is usually inversely proportional to the seriousness of the delinquencies. It is the boy who is basically "good" who carries the heaviest emotional load and the highest degree of confusion and maladjustment, because he cannot reconcile his misdeeds to his principles. It seems likely that some of the difficulty in describing "the delinquent" arises not only from the many individual differences to be found in any group of people but also from which kind of a delinquent one is talking about.

► **The Number of Delinquents**

It is extremely difficult to find out how many delinquents there are at any given time because the various states use different methods of recording offenses, and even the same state changes its methods from time to time, so that data from different years are not comparable. It takes an expert to compile an intelligible record from various sources. Figure 19–1 presents such a record for the entire country over two decades, 1940 through 1960. The solid line shows the number of delinquents; from 1954 on, the line splits in two, depending upon whether or not one includes traffic violations. The column of numbers to the left is to be used in reading this curve; for example, for the year 1946 there were almost exactly 300,000 juvenile delinquents. The broken line indicates the number of individuals between the ages of 10 and 17 in the total population. This curve is to be read from the numbers at the right; thus, in 1954 there were approximately 20,-000,000 inhabitants of these ages. It can be seen at once that the number of adolescents is growing, but that the rate of delinquency is growing much

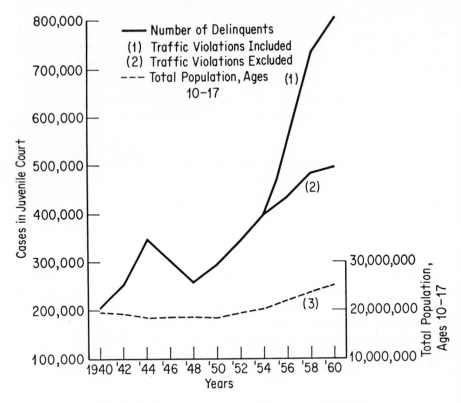

Fig. 19–1. Increase in juvenile delinquency, 1940–1960

From R. S. Cavan, *Juvenile Delinquency* (Philadelphia: J. P. Lippincott Company, 1962), p. 30. Used with the permission of the publisher.

faster. The first peak in the curve, in 1944, was attributed to the general disorganization of family life during the war. After the war ended, the rate declined for about five years, but then it began to shoot up at accelerated pace—and is still climbing.

During the last few years a total of 400,000 boys and girls have made their first appearance each year in juvenile court on charges aside from traffic violations.[3] These figures represent 1.7 percent of the general population between the ages of 10 and 17. If traffic violations are included, the proportion rises to 2.3 percent. It is probable that nearly 20 percent of adolescents come at one time or another to the attention of the court—although not all of them are counted in the statistics in all states. Juvenile crime is, therefore, a common phenomenon of the middle decades of this century.

Many people do not realize the extent of unpublicized delinquency—that

---

[3] Cavan, *Juvenile Delinquency, loc. cit.,* p. 27.

is, the number of misdeeds that are handled by family and school and never come to the attention of the police. To investigate this matter high school boys with no record of delinquency were compared with known delinquents (Table 19–2). Having a fist fight with another boy, driving without a license, stealing things of small value, skipping school, driving a car recklessly, and doing de-

Table 19–2: COMPARISON OF HIGH SCHOOL STUDENTS AND DELINQUENTS AS TO MINOR DELINQUENCIES

	Frequency of Occurrence			
	Once or Twice		More Than Twice	
Offense	*High School*	*Delinquents*	*High School*	*Delinquents*
Taken car for ride	15	75	4	53
Driven too fast or recklessly	46	76	19	52
Driven car without license	75	91	49	73
Been expelled or placed on probation by school	11	68	3	31
Skipped school	53	65	23	86
Had fist fight with one person	81	95	32	75
Beat up kids who'd done nothing	14	49	3	26
Hurt someone on purpose	16	33	3	18
Taken part in gang fight	23	67	5	47
Run away from home	13	68	2	38
Defied parents' authority	33	52	6	24
Stolen things:				
Worth less than $2	61	92	13	65
Worth $2 to $50	16	91	4	61
Worth over $50	5	91	2	48
Used force to get money	6	68	2	36
Damaged property deliberately	45	84	8	50
Had normal sexual relations	40	88	20	74

SOURCE: J. F. Short and F. I. Nye, "Extent of Unrecorded Juvenile Delinquency," *Journal of Criminal Law, Criminology and Police Science,* 49:296–302, 1958, p. 297.

liberate property damage were all indulged in by 40 to 81 percent of the high school boys at least once. But such behavior was rarely persistent. Driving a car without a license, missing school, and fighting are the only offenses committed by a third to a half of the boys. However, one is almost forced to believe that a little delinquency here and there is normal for the young American male!

The first marked upswing of the crime rate came during and just after World War II, but the change was not so much in the ranks of the returning soldiers as in those who were children or preadolescents at the beginning of that war. It is understandable that upon this generation the stories and movies about the war and the general upsetting effect of frequent moving about, less supervision, and general restlessness might have had an unsettling effect. The crime rates slowed down some in the late 1940s and early 1950s but then began again to rise, especially for crimes of violence. This is not an exclusively American phenomenon. In the postwar decades, delinquency has been on the rise over the entire world—at least over those portions of it with which communication is unobstructed. A 1960 report to the United Nations showed only four countries in which there had been no increase in the juvenile crime rates—Switzerland, Italy, Belgium and Canada.[4] Not only were the general increases about the same everywhere, even the crimes were identical. In all other member countries adolescents, mostly boys, stole cars for temporary use, committed acts of vandalism, rioted, and formed gangs for purposes of forcibly collecting money from individuals. Similar also have been the efforts to curb the rising tide: judges have meted out severe punishments and have fined the parents for damage done by their children; cities have passed and enforced curfew laws and have devoted themselves to slum clearance and to the construction of various facilities for recreation in the areas that most lacked them. It has by now become clear that punitive treatments are worse than useless and that measures to improve the environment will not automatically have any influence at all upon the number of delinquents—although such measures may prove extremely useful if accompanied by adequate guidance. However, some communities have been able to reduce the rate materially by methods that will be discussed in a later section.

One other development seems worthy of comment: the change in the proportion of female to male delinquents. Thirty years ago there was only 1 girl to every 18 boy delinquents. In 1940, the ratio was 1 to 15; by 1946, 1 to 10. In 1950 the proportion for the entire country had changed to 1 in 5; in 1956 the figure was 1 in 4.[5] This particular expression of the female's right to enter any male activity is perhaps not wholly admirable! Boys and girls show quite different patterns of offenses in their delinquent behavior. Nearly two-thirds of the boys came before the court for some form of stealing or for vandalism, whereas 63 percent of the girls were charged either with being unmanageable or with sex offenses.[6]

In presenting results from the specific studies of delinquency it seems a good idea to discuss the confusing material under four heads: (1) characteristics of the delinquent adolescent, (2) characteristics of the "delinquent" home, (3) characteristics of the "delinquent" school, and (4) characteristics of the "delinquent" neighborhood. In this way, the contributing causes of the basic human maladjustment known as delinquency may become clear and all points of view may be presented.

---

[4] Cavan, *loc. cit.,* p. 12.

[5] Cavan, *op. cit.*

[6] "Juvenile Court Statistics," *Children's Bureau Statistical Series,* No. 52, 1959, p. 6. (Includes results from 15 states.)

▶ Characteristics of the Delinquent Adolescent

An already oldish but excellent study [7] gives a detailed comparison of five hundred delinquent and five hundred nondelinquent boys who were carefully paired for age, residence in the same area of the same city, intelligence and racial origin. The delinquents were first selected, and then public school boys who matched the delinquents were located. The five hundred boys of the control group had no record of delinquency. Searching inquiry failed to reveal more than an occasional, ordinary, childish misdeed, such as swiping a neighbor's fruit from his tree or jumping onto the backs of trucks, and 75 percent of the nondelinquents did not show even such minor misbehavior. The five hundred delinquents were all chronic offenders. Over 80 percent of both groups lived in tenement or business areas. Their ages were between 11 and 17, two thirds of them being over 14. The entire thousand were given a medical examination, a test of intelligence, achievement tests in reading and arithmetic, a Rorschach test, and a psychiatric interview. This study will be referred to at various points in this chapter as the Glueck study.

The distribution of IQs from the Glueck study appears in Figure 19–2. The range is from below 60 to above 120 with a median at 82. Fifty-three percent would be classed as normal, 5 percent as bright, 32 percent as low normal, and 10 percent as defective. These results are typical of many other studies.[8] On the basis of such results one can hardly regard low intelligence as the only cause of delinquency. Moreover, for every delinquent adolescent with a low IQ, there are many socially normal adolescents of no higher intellectual level.

There is little evidence to suggest that delinquents are in poorer physical condition than others from the same economic levels. The delinquent boys in the Glueck study were very slightly stronger than the nondelinquents, and the latter were in slightly poorer general health. The only real difference between the two groups was in a skin condition that is known to be largely if not wholly of neurotic origin, in the degree and persistence of enuresis, and in general restlessness. All three symptoms come presumably from the greater incidence —as will presently be shown—of neurotic conditions among delinquents. So far as general health, freedom from physical defect, and resistance to disease are concerned, the small differences are all in favor of the delinquent group. The delinquents grew a little more slowly up to the age of fourteen, when they overtook and surpassed the other group. In body build, the delinquents tended to the mesomorphic type; almost none of them were conspicuously ectomor-

---

[7] S. S. Glueck and E. T. Glueck, *Unraveling Juvenile Delinquency* (Cambridge, Mass.: Harvard University Press for The Commonwealth Fund, 1950), 399 pp.

[8] See, for example, U. Shanker, "Juvenile Crime and Intelligence," *Education,* 10:143–148, 1956.

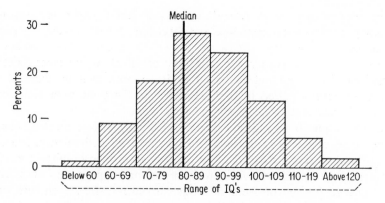

Fig. 19–2. Distribution of IQ's for a delinquent group

Based on S. S. Glueck and E. T. Glueck, *Unraveling Juvenile Delinquency* (The Commonwealth Fund, 1950), p. 356.

phic. They usually had clearly masculine proportions and relatively heavy muscles.[9] It does not, therefore, seem that physical defects are outstanding causes of delinquency.

An outstanding trait of delinquents as a group is their educational retardation, which is usually more than can be explained by their slight intellectual inferiority. They generally average about a year's retardation mentally, but nearly three years educationally. In the Glueck study 84 percent of the delinquent boys had repeated grades in school; 69 percent were retarded from two to five years. Twice as many of the nondelinquents as delinquents had always been promoted. The reading and arithmetic quotients of the control groups averaged five or six points higher than those of the delinquents, although both groups had the same range and both made relatively poor showings. The delinquents loathed school (62 percent), wanted to leave school (43 percent), were chronic truants (63 percent), misbehaved persistently (96 percent) and from an early age (73 percent).

Delinquents are generally inadequate where verbal symbols are concerned. Reading is difficult for them, and many never read well enough to derive satisfaction from books. As they pass through the grades, they find the work less and less suited to their needs because of the ever-increasing need to read easily. These boys and girls come from backgrounds in which little value is placed upon verbal abilities, and they usually belong to a peer group that definitely devaluates any kind of academic success. There may be an actual deficiency of a specific kind, but perhaps the explanation is to be found in the attitude of the boys rather than in their learning ability. They may not learn

[9] W. H. Sheldon, *Varieties of Delinquent Youth* (New York: Harper & Row, Publishers, Inc., 1949), 899 pp.

merely because they see no reason for doing so and a good many reasons for not doing so. The delinquent who states baldly, "I hate reading" is possibly making his own diagnosis.[10] It should be noted also that delinquents and pre-delinquents are restless creatures; they are not given to sitting still. One can hardly read under any other condition, and it may well be that the mere physical restraint involved in reading is more than they can tolerate, especially as their tolerance level in this respect is very low.

There seems to be little if anything the matter with the native social capacities of delinquents. They are unpopular enough with their teachers and other school officials, but once they are on the playground or in the gymnasium they participate freely and naturally in whatever is going on. They usually show a capacity to get on with their age-mates that others would do well to imitate. Some delinquents even show distinct qualities of leadership. Although the forms of expression are usually unacceptable, the underlying social competency of delinquents seems at least average. If it were not, these adolescents would not be as successful as they are in forming and maintaining gangs with adequate leadership. The gang has a culture of its own. It offers its members an intimate group association with their peers, a more or less permanent leadership, the satisfaction of belonging and a chance to work off resentments and frustrations in the company of others who have the same problems.[11] In short, the gang does not differ in what it offers its members from any socially approved adolescent group. And it is often the only group open to the boy from a lower-class family. One has to distinguish, in this connection, between the underlying capacity for social adjustment and the often undesirable forms through which it finds expression. Delinquents are rarely isolated, introverted characters. They are "sociable" and make contacts with others quite easily.

It is in the field of emotional development that one finds the important differences between delinquents and normally behaved children or adolescents. Many investigators have found the delinquent to be emotionally immature. His emotional age is below both his mental and his chronological ages. One study of 276 delinquent and 151 nondelinquent adolescent girls between the ages of 13 and 17 gave especially interesting results. The median score of the normal adolescents was 10 points. Ninety-one percent of the delinquents scored as less mature. Over a third of them scored above the ninetieth percentile for the normals.[12] On this test the lower the score, the higher is the maturity.

---

[10] H. J. Greenblatt, "I Hate School." *National Probation and Parole Association Journal,* 1:8–14, 1955. See also, M. Roman, J. B. Margolin, and C. Harrari, "Reading Retardation and Delinquency," *National Probation and Parole Association Journal,* 1:1–7, 1955.

[11] F. M. Thrasher, "The Gang as a Symptom of Community Disintegration," *Journal of Corrective Work,* 4:54–56, 1957.

[12] M. A. Durea and A. L. Assum, "The Relation of Personality Traits as Differentiating Delinquent and Non-Delinquent Girls," *Journal of Genetic Psychology,* 72:307–311, 1948.

Delinquents are sometimes, although not always, emotionally unstable individuals, and they are abnormally sensitive to emotional tensions in their families or neighborhoods. Unlike the neurotic, who may experience similar feelings, they do not allow themselves to be beaten by the world. They fight back. As a result they become aggressive, hostile, suspicious, jealous, and quarrelsome. They blame others for their own shortcomings. This tendency for projection appeared in results obtained from 250 delinquents, 10 to 13 years of age. Of the entire group, 189, or 76 percent, gave responses that projected blame onto others, as compared with only 36 percent among normal children and adolescents.[13]

The typical "delinquent" personality already begins to emerge from these studies of individual traits. Two studies take the characterization a little further. In one case, 382 boys and 140 girls who had police records were compared with 200 boys and 200 girls with absolutely no record of misbehavior.[14] All were from the ninth grade. The test of personality types used revealed the delinquents to have profiles of the psychopathic, paranoiac, or hypermanic types, as compared with the essentially normal outlines of the control groups. That is, the delinquents were of the irresponsible, defiant, suspicious, destructive, overactive, extroverted type—not depressed, introverted, withdrawn, or underactive. The investigator in the second study gave the Thematic Apperception Test[15] to 34 delinquent girls and 834 delinquent boys. There were some minor differences between the sexes, but because these do not seem important, results will be given for the group as a whole. The themes of the stories told reflect an unhappy personality that is fighting back. If the various kinds of aggression were not reported separately, this trait would be very close to the top of the list.

The stories told centered about parents and children. Such incidents as the following appeared: the parents are hurt, ill, dead, absent from home, in poverty, working hard; the parents are angry at the child, punish him, refuse his wishes, require work from him, lock him in a closet or out of the house; the child disobeys the parents, runs away from home. On the positive side, there are also some items: the parents hunt for the child, advise him, are proud of him, give him a gift, love the child, play with him, help him, forgive him, take care of him; the child also helps the parents. The negative incidents involved the father with an average of 22 percent, and the mother with an average of 18 percent. The positive incidents involving either parent amounted

---

[13] F. T. Gatling, "Frustration Reactions of Delinquents, Using Rosenzweig's Classification System," *Journal of Abnormal and Social Psychology*, 45:749–752, 1950. See also R. L. Jenkins, "Motivation and Frustration in Delinquency," *American Journal of Orthopsychiatry*, 27:528–537, 1957.

[14] S. R. Hathaway and E. D. Monachesi, "The MMPI in the Study of Juvenile Delinquents," *American Sociological Review*, 17:704–710, 1952.

[15] See pp. 295ff.

Table 19–3: TAT THEMES OF JUVENILE DELINQUENTS

Attributes	*Percent*
Desire for love or praise	100.0
Overt sex interest	95.6
Dejection	82.4
Desire for achievement	79.4
Acquisition (of material things)	75.0
Aggression, verbal	64.7
Failure	52.9
Conflict	44.1
Aggression, physical, antisocial	41.2
Running away from home	38.2
Rejection	33.8
Domination	32.4
Aggression, physical, social	25.0
Abasement	20.6
Destructiveness	17.7
Passivity	11.8

SOURCE: Based on F. M. Young, "Responses of Juvenile Delinquents to TAT," *Journal of Genetic Psychology*, 88:251–259, 1956.

to 14.6 percent. In view of the types of home from which delinquents come one can assume that most of the positive stories are expressions of wish-fulfillment. Some of the attitudes shown by the test are listed in Table 19–3.

The recreational life of the two groups in the Glueck study also shows marked differences and is revealing of personality. The delinquents favored adventurous activities and shunned competition; they were heavy patrons of the movies; their idea of fun consisted in stealing rides on streetcars or trucks, in staying away from home, in destroying property, in smoking, and in gambling. They played in the streets, and they roamed afar. Their companions were more often than not members of a gang. The nondelinquents show contrasts in almost all respects, although they also attended movies frequently and played on street corners, presumably for lack of any better place. However, they used playgrounds wherever these were available. What the delinquent does when he is merely amusing himself shows clearly what kind of person he is. One can easily understand that he would be in constant conflict with others and in constant disciplinary difficulties.

The vital differences between the normal and the delinquent child are to be found, then, not in intelligence, health, or basic social competency, but in the latter's infantilism, his deep sense of dependency, his inability to obtain satisfaction from realistic gratifications, his permanent frustration, his inadequate control over his instinctual drives, and his deep hostility to all the world.

▶ Characteristics of a "Delinquent" Environment

Three elements in the total social situation seem to be of utmost importance in influencing the behavior of delinquents—the home, the neighborhood, and the school. Because of their outstanding importance they will be dealt with in some detail.

The Delinquent Home   The homes of the delinquent and nondelinquent boys in the Glueck study were of much the same external type—overcrowded tenements with poor sanitation and poor furnishings—but those of the nondelinquents were cleaner, and fewer of the families were on relief. The family stock of the two groups was definitely poorer for the delinquents. Among both the immediate ancestors and the living relatives there are appreciably more defectives, emotionally disturbed people, drunkards, and criminals. The parents and siblings of the delinquents also show an excess of these same traits. The differences between the two groups run from 6 to 39 percent; and in all categories the delinquents show the higher percentage.

The broken home also plays its part, although its role is not as significant as was once thought. In general, the earlier the break, the more extensive is the effect on the children. One important long-time effect upon the boys in the family is their deprivation of the customary father image, which usually acts as a model for their own development. If a boy has only a mother or only mother and sisters he has to live in a feminine atmosphere, which may nudge him into delinquencies in his revolt against too many women and his desire to be a "man." [16]

Of late, the emotional currents and tensions within the homes of delinquents have been analyzed and studied. Many investigators feel the fundamental causes of delinquency are to be found in the treatment accorded a child by his parents, especially during his preschool years. The basic theme is one of rejection, for various reasons, on the part of the parents.[17] The emotional interrelationships of the families in the Glueck study are typical. These are summarized in Figure 19–3. The parents of the normal boys expressed warm affection for them and received affection from them. The discipline was usually firm and kindly and included other types of punishment than merely physical. Between the delinquent boys and their mothers, affectional relationships were fairly good, but between the boys and their fathers there was too little warmth and too much hostility. Discipline by both parents was lax, erratic, or overstrict, and both depended mainly upon physical punishment as a means of

---

[16] T. P. Monahan, "Broken Homes by Age of Delinquent Children," *Journal of Social Psychology*, 51:387–397, 1960.

[17] See, for example, H. M. Shulman, "The Family and Juvenile Delinquency," *Annals of the American Academy of Political and Social Science*, 261:21–31, 1949.

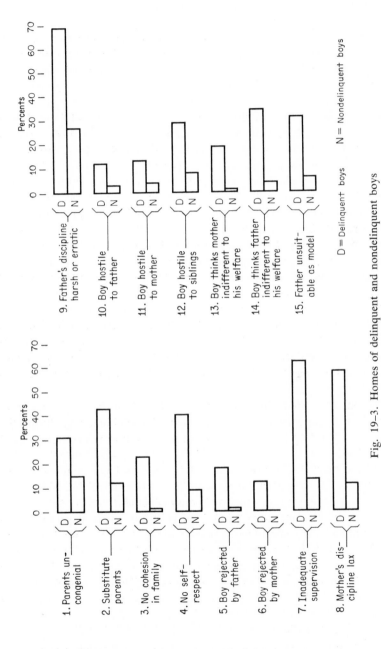

Fig. 19-3. Homes of delinquent and nondelinquent boys

Based on figures in S. S. Glueck and E. T. Glueck, *Unraveling Juvenile Delinquency* (The Commonwealth Fund, 1950), pp. 108–112 and 125–132.

control. Although the two groups of boys came from the same social milieu and although the external features of their homes were similar, the affectional interrelationships show marked differences. The nondelinquent has the affection, interest, and support of his parents; the delinquent does not. Furthermore, the families of the normal boys were characterized by careful planning, self-respect, good relations between the parents, adequate supervision of children, and marked cohesiveness of the group. The families of delinquents lived in a haphazard sort of way and had poor standards of conduct; the parents did not get along together, the children were not supervised, and joint family recreations were virtually absent. Nearly twice as many delinquents as nondelinquents came from broken homes, and nearly four times as many were living with people who were substituting for their parents.

When one talks with delinquents and with their parents one is struck with the lack of normal friendliness between them, with the attitude of each toward the other, and with the inability of the parents to establish control without arousing resentment. For instance, among the parents of 1465 delinquent boys, only 8 percent played with their children or went on excursions or picnics with them; an even smaller proportion was found among 672 boys who were "repeaters"; and the smallest proportion of all was found for parents of boys who were before the court on serious charges.[18] Such facts suggest considerable estrangement between the generations. Finally, there are some parents who use their child either to satisfy their own suppressed desires or to serve as a scapegoat for these desires. They derive satisfaction through their child's delinquencies. They maintain their own emotional equilibrium at the expense of the child's development. If the parents would like to be quarrelsome and get into fights but repress this desire, their child is likely to fight; if they have repressed impulses to steal, he is likely to steal. This process works just as efficiently when it is unconscious as when it is not. The child's response to the situation is usually a deep hostility toward the person who has so overburdened and misused him.

One of the most obvious difficulties with a wholly environmental theory of delinquency has always been the presence in any deteriorated neighborhood of a large number of nondelinquents, who are presumably subject to the same influences that are assumed to "cause" misbehavior in their peers. These "good" boys attend the same schools, play in the same streets, read the same newspapers, hear the same profanity and obscenity, see the same number of drunks and perverts and criminals—but they do not follow the delinquent pattern. In 1956 and again in 1960 investigators studied 103 adolescent boys from a deteriorated neighborhood who were nominated by their sixth-grade teachers as being least likely to become delinquent. Of the 103 pupils, who were sixth graders in 1956, 93 were still in school in 1960 at an average age of 16, a proportion far above the average for the neighborhood. The main

---

[18] W. W. Wattenberg, "Family Recreation and Delinquency," *Focus*, 29:6–9, 1950.

elements in their immunity to the delinquency they saw around them were found to be: a stable and cohesive family, parents who took an interest in their sons and supervised them, a favorable self-image on the part of the boys themselves—which influenced them to avoid association with their delinquent peers, to seek trustful associations with adults, and to desire an education. Since the same boys four years later showed much the same patterns, the investigators concluded that once a favorable self-image was developed by a preadolescent, in respect to friends, parents, school, church, and the law, this self-image will be a protection from harmful environmental influences and will be just as hard to alter as the delinquent self-image has already proved itself to be.[19]

In almost all American homes the mother is the outstanding personality as far as the children are concerned. She probably contributes more to the development of her sons or daughters than the father does. One investigator compared the mothers who had one delinquent son with those who had one nondelinquent son, in an effort to highlight the differences in attitude and treatment that might be causes for the wide differences in conduct shown by the adolescent boys. The results appear in Table 19–4. These categories are listed in order of their production of nondelinquent sons. If a mother shows normal affection, there are three chances in four that her son will avoid de-

Table 19–4: MATERNAL ATTITUDES AND DELINQUENCY

Types of Mother	Percent (with a Criminal Son)	Percent (with a Nondelinquent Son)
Loving, considerate, normal	27	73
Loving but overanxious	34	66
Overprotective	37	63
Loving but neurotic in attachment	43	57
Cruel	45	55
Absent from the home much of the time	50	50
Passive and noninterfering	57	43
Neglectful of children's welfare	72	28

SOURCE: W. McCord and J. McCord, *Origin of Crime* (New York: Columbia University Press, 1959), p. 99.

linquency, but if she is in any way abnormal in her affection for him, the chances become about two in three. It is interesting that neither cruelty nor absence from home are as productive of delinquency as indifference and

[19] P. R. Scarpitti, E. Murray, S. Dinitz, and W. C. Reckless, "The 'Good' Boy in a High Delinquency Area: Four Years Later," *American Sociological Review*, 125:555–558, 1960. See also, W. C. Reckless, S. Dinitz, and B. Kad, "The Self-Component in Potential Delinquency and Potential Non-Delinquency," *American Sociological Review*, 22:566–570, 1959.

neglect. In the last category the chances are almost the reverse of those in the first.[20]

The Delinquent Neighborhood   During the last forty years many studies have been made in various places to show the occurrence of delinquency in different areas of a city. The approach has been entirely pragmatic. Investigators have first taken a detailed map of the city or area under investigation and have tabulated upon it the location of those homes from which delinquents came. In all cases these homes centered in a few districts, sometimes in not more than two or three. Having located the critical neighborhoods in this way, the investigators next made a careful survey of these localities to determine the characteristics which differentiated them from other districts. Most of this work was done under the influence of the environmental theory of delinquency. It remains valuable and makes contributions to an understanding of delinquency.

The map presented in Figure 19–4 of Cambridge, Massachusetts, shows a number of "delinquent" areas. The largest is a rundown district of poor housing that stretches eastward from the outer edges of Harvard College toward Boston. And even within this general area there are two centers of concentration, one just northwest of the Massachusetts Institute of Technology and one along the line between North Cambridge and Somerville. The other cases are sprinkled about, here and there. The North Cambridge area is commercial and industrial, whereas the sections west of Harvard College are almost wholly residential. The effect of both universities has been to clear the space immediately around them of delinquencies. This concentration of delinquency in one or two areas and its infrequency in the remaining sections of a city is typical of every community thus far studied.

Another characteristic of high-delinquency neighborhoods has recently been emphasized, namely the acceptance by one neighborhood of much behavior that would be regarded in other parts of a city as unacceptable. The difference appears to rest upon a difference in the basic philosophy of life between middle-class or upper-class and lower-class groups. These classifications are not based wholly upon income but include attitudes and behavior. The "poor" district is likely to contain various elements that are obviously harmful to normal growth, such as extreme poverty with its resulting deprivations. But perhaps more harm is done ultimately by the standards of behavior that such a neighborhood accepts as normal. The following complex of ideas is basic to life in the lower levels of society:

1. One must always avoid "trouble."
2. One must be tough and hard.

---

[20] From W. McCord and J. McCord, *Origin of Crime* (New York: Columbia University Press, 1959), 219 pp., pp. 95–103

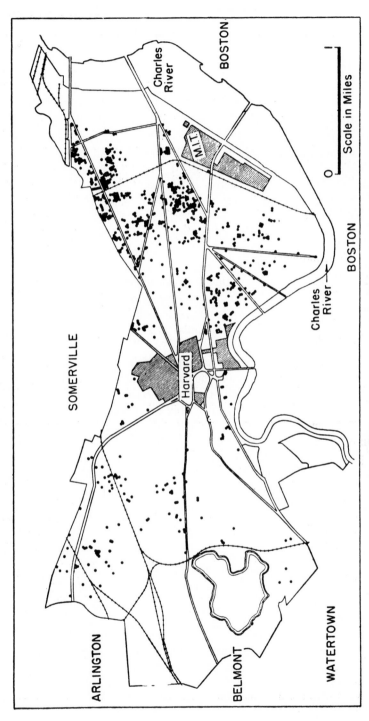

Fig. 19–4. Delinquent spot map of Cambridge, Massachusetts

From E. Powers and H. Witmer, *An Experiment in the Prevention of Delinquency: The Cambridge-Somerville Study* (New York: Columbia University Press, 1951), p. 20. Used with the permission of the publisher.

3. One must be smart.
4. One must be completely independent.
5. One must expect life to be dull and must therefore seize upon any possible form of excitement to offset the dullness.
6. One must expect life to be dominated by sheer luck—good or bad.

The above principles of behavior accepted by most lower-class homes and neighborhoods are at variance to the norms of the dominant middle class. These parents want their children to be well-mannered and kind rather than tough and hard, to be good rather than smart, to think of others rather than of themselves, to find work and a mode of life that is interesting and satisfying, to make their way by merit and achievement rather than by luck. These differences between the dominant middle-class and the "submerged" lower class are related only indirectly if at all to differences in economic background. They are differences in the philosophy of life, and the more completely a child accepts them, the more likely he is to be, first a juvenile delinquent, and then an adult criminal. The children are therefore not in conflict with parental and neighborhood values and have no reason for being maladjusted—unless they are striving to escape from these values and gain others, as is sometimes true. In short, an entire district can be delinquent in its norms of acceptable behavior.[21]

The greater world outside his immediate neighborhood also exerts an effect upon the young offender through the various means of communication— the newspapers, the comics, the radio, the movies, and television. Newspapers that glorify crime in lurid pictures and morbid detail have their greatest sale in the most delinquent neighborhoods of a city. Such publicity not only focuses the attention of the children on crime but furnishes them with rationalizations for any later misconduct. From newspapers the children learn also of the inconsistent moral values of adults, of sexual misconduct, of business dishonesty, of fraudulent tax returns, of bribery, of abortions, of fee splitting, of bootlegging, of black markets, and of political corruption. From this type of reading children derive the ideas that any crime is all right if one can get away with it and that adult obedience to law is only selective at best, not at all the cast-iron system of right and wrong about which they have been told. Since the sensational press wastes no space on the ordinary citizen who behaves himself, it is not surprising that children get extremely warped ideas about adult morality from their newspaper reading. This conflict of attitudes is very unsettling, especially to adolescents.

The neighborhood furnishes the setting in which a child is educated either for an acceptance of conventional attitudes or for an acceptance of rebellion

---

[21] Kvaraceus, *Delinquent Behavior, loc. cit.*, pp. 63–68. See also W. B. Miller, "Lower Class Culture as a Generating Milieu of Gang Delinquency," *Journal of Social Issues,* 14:5–19, 1958.

toward such attitudes. It furnishes him with his models. It limits the forms in which he may express his instinctive drives. It provides him with standards— from the conventional mores to those of organized crime. Perhaps the most confusing neighborhoods are those in which several standards thrive alongside each other. Delinquency is learned behavior; it therefore requires association with and instruction by other delinquents, who are provided by the neighborhood—and sometimes by the immediate family. In such cases, the children learn their delinquency through the perfectly normal process of identification, either with their parents or with outstanding adults in their environment. The neighborhood also makes its pressure felt after a child's first misdeeds. It may label him as a delinquent, deprive him of participation in normal childhood groups, and eventually banish him to those areas that will sanction his aggressiveness; or it may take him to its bosom—if it is already well populated with adult criminals—and give him the first real approval and acceptance he has ever known.

The relation of the deteriorated neighborhood to delinquency is made clear by a number of solid facts about the slums of large cities. In a slum section of over 125,000 people, mostly Negro, 70 percent of the boys and girls between 16 and 21 were both out of school and unemployed. The resources of the district are so limited that almost no legitimate activities are possible. There was a very high mobility of the families involved, but almost invariably within the district; that is, the families moved frequently from one dirty tenement to another. For at least a third of the children, one parent was in prison, on parole, or had a criminal record. A third of the boys had no father figure of any kind as a model—no father in the home or even in jail, no minister or priest, no male teachers, no scout leader, no one. The schools were old and understaffed. A bare 10 percent of the parents graduated from high school, and 32 percent from grammar school; the remaining 58 percent had less than a grammar school education or were illiterate. Less than 10 percent of the families had a private doctor, and the children examined in the free clinics were in poor physical condition. The really alarming point about this situation is that there is no end in sight. It used to be that incoming foreigners occupied such areas, but within a generation most of them moved out and up. Because of the steadily diminishing demand for uneducated hands and minds these adolescents cannot find work even if they want it, and as they grow older their chances will become less and less because automation is steadily decreasing the demand. These people, mostly native Americans, are caught in a net of continued poverty and support by welfare agencies, without hope for anything but a miracle to rescue them. It is not strange that delinquency rates are high. A slum is not merely an aesthetically unpleasant place; it is an area loaded with dynamite for the entire community.[22]

---

[22] J. B. Conant, "Social Dynamite in Our Large Cities," *Crime and Delinquency,* 18:102–115, 1962.

The Delinquent School   The public school in general is a contributor to mental health rather than to delinquency, but there are still a few characteristics of the average school that may produce abnormal behavior. The chief adverse element is the nature of the curriculum. Delinquents are typically nonbookish, nonintellectual, nonacademic, nonverbal individuals who do poorly in the traditional school subjects. It is probable that young delinquents experience a good deal of frustration in the course of their school life. By now it is certainly evident that they soon revolt against the traditional school and leave it at the earliest possible age, usually after periods of truancy and long records of aggressive misconduct. When they leave school they abandon one of the potentially constructive influences in their lives.

It is highly probable that some teachers also contribute to the creation of the delinquent child. They influence him, as they do all other children, through the emotional atmosphere of their classrooms. If they are demanding, harsh, domineering, and authoritarian, they arouse the aggressive hostility of the already rejected child, who now finds himself rejected once more. If, as sometimes happens, such a child has a different teacher every semester in elementary school and another eight teachers during junior high school, he may have gone through the painful period of rejection as many as twenty times. One can hardly blame him for hating school, for playing truant, or for leaving as soon as possible. Perhaps the worst teacher for the delinquent-in-the-making is the one who not only cannot accept him but also takes his reactions to her rejection as a personal insult. Such a teacher regards misbehavior as a reflection upon her competence, she becomes so involved personally that she loses her self-control—sometimes descending to the child's own level of bad manners—and she is quite unable to make an objective study of the pupil and his problems, largely because she is a good deal sorrier for herself than she is for him. School discipline is sometimes so administered as to be thoroughly unacceptable even to well-balanced, normal children and adolescents. The effect upon delinquents is disastrous and stimulates them to even greater hostility toward their school.

The delinquent adolescent makes his presence soon felt in school. Indeed, he is impossible to overlook. He gets into overt emotional battles with all constituted authority—including his teachers—he has no interest in school, he plays truant often and leaves school altogether as soon as he can, he does not take part in extracurricular activities, he may actually do average work but he considers himself a failure in school—just as he is a failure in all areas of life—and he makes aggressive responses in meeting the problems of daily living. It is suggested that the truancy is a sort of "emotional recess" from the constant frustration of school and, while against the rules, may be more helpful than harmful.[23]

---

[23] W. C. Kvaraceus, "The Delinquent Pupil," *New York State Education,* 46:193–194, 234, 1958. Also M. T. Easton, L. A. D'Amico, and B. N. Phillips, "Problem Behavior in School," *Journal of Educational Psychology,* 47:50–57, 1956.

In school, adolescents who are tending toward delinquency often try to test their teachers and all school authority by misbehavior of various kinds. Such activity may spring from an unadmitted desire to be cared for and to be controlled. Many predelinquents would like to have someone upon whom they can depend not only for sympathy but for control and guidance—although they do not admit the need and even deny it by most of their overt behavior.[24] The testing out of teacher and school often ends in a rejection of all education, but on the grounds that both have failed because they are not strict enough to offer any real help. Understanding is necessary, but so is strictness and adherence to accepted norms. It is always difficult for the average teacher to deal with predelinquents and delinquents. The teacher is usually a middle-class product, with ideals of doing good in the world. For dealing with delinquents a teacher needs to have a genuine liking for all children and a genuine attractiveness to all children. She needs to know how to reject undesirable behavior without rejecting the child. She has to have sufficient strength herself to absorb some direct hostility and defiance without arousal of her own emotions, and she must know herself well enough to avoid working out her own problems of adjustment through the child. She should be able to sense emotional disturbance, although she need not put a name to it—and it is probably better if she does not. Such a teacher can do a good deal to alter the philosophy of a pupil who has already started down the road to delinquency.[25]

A "delinquent" environment consists, then, of three main elements: a home in which parents are unsuccessful economically, are of not more than average native ability, are of undesirable personal habits, and are of questionable morality, who are ineffective in discipline, unable to furnish emotional security, and inclined to reject their delinquent child both before and after his misdeeds; a neighborhood that is devised for adults, quite without safeguards for children, largely without safe outlets for emotional and social life, and full of unsatisfactory models and conflicting standards; and a school that tries to make scholars out of nonacademic material and sometimes furnishes teachers who are too rejective in their attitudes. When all three elements are affecting the same unstable child at the same time, a delinquent is likely to be produced.

▶ **Factors Contributing to Delinquency and Theories about Them**

It is not difficult to list the factors that have been shown by various investigators to be related to delinquency. Some of those in the list appearing in Table 19–5 are doubtless of more importance than others.

Because of the somewhat conflicting current ideas as to the causes, de-

---

[24] See A. Bandura and J. R. H. Walters, "Dependency Conflicts in Aggressive Adolescents," *Journal of Social Forces,* 14:52–65, 1958.

[25] Adapted from Kvaraceus, *Delinquent Behavior, loc. cit.,* pp. 110–111.

velopment, and treatment of delinquents, it seems wise to review briefly the possible causes and to present two somewhat opposed, but not mutually exclusive, interpretations. Delinquency is a highly complex phenomenon, for it is a way of life that a child develops during his first ten or fifteen years of

Table 19-5: FACTORS CONTRIBUTING TO DELINQUENCY

Heredity	1. Bad family stock—incidence of feeblemindedness, insanity, epilepsy higher than in families of nondelinquents.
	2. Defective mentality—average IQ of delinquent groups is 85 to 90 instead of 100. (However, about two thirds of all delinquents are of normal or above-normal mentality.)
	3. Specific inability to handle verbal symbols, resulting in slow progress in school.
	4. Unusual vitality, drive, and energy, resulting in restlessness, overactivity, and aggressiveness.
Home	5. Poverty and crowding in home.
	6. Delinquency and crime among parents or older siblings.
	7. Home broken by death, separation, divorce, desertion, or prison term.
	8. Lack of emotional security, high degree of tension in home; lack of emotional stability in parents.
	9. Lack of proper or uniform discipline.
	10. Rejection of child by parents, neglect of child, lack of interest in his activities.
School	11. Poor work in school; one or more retardations.
	12. Dislike of school.
	13. More or less truancy.
	14. Rejection by some of the teachers.
Neighborhood	15. Existence of many criminal models in the neighborhood.
	16. Lack of adequate supervision and protection.
	17. Lack of adequate outlets.
	18. Exposure to low or conflicting adult morals.
	19. Exposure to minority conflicts.
Resulting Personality Traits	20. Feelings of inferiority, insecurity, and rejection.
	21. Constant frustration and development of deep hostility.
	22. Emotional immaturity.
	23. Aggressive drives turned toward parents, school, and society.
	24. Identification with criminal models.
	25. Emotional satisfaction found in antisocial groups.
	26. Strong impulses, uninhibited by conscience.

existence. If there are two explanations, each emphasizing different phases supplementing each other, it seems worth while to consider both, and then to attempt a synthesis.

According to one outstanding authority, delinquency is an impulsive reaction made in order to find direct or indirect satisfaction for instinctive urges. The young delinquent does not find in his home and neighborhood enough love or attention or admiration to satisfy his needs, nor does he find many suitable outlets for his drives toward activity or play. His social urges find their readiest expression in the gangs that already exist. Such groups are made up of others like himself. The members are rejected by their homes and are in acute conflict with the community. They rebel openly with direct acts of aggression. Such behavior is well calculated to awaken a desire to imitate in the bosom of the child who has a similarly acute, but as yet only indirectly expressed, conflict of his own. His hostile urges are of the same sort as theirs, and by joining forces with them he can not only express himself more directly, but can even obtain in return admiration and absolution from a lurking sense of guilt that might otherwise mar his content. One can see that from the delinquent's point of view there is not much to be gained by a reform in his behavior. Moreover, a delinquent act, such as stealing, often becomes an outlet for tension. The connection between the act and the release may be quite accidental in the beginning, but soon the child discovers this new outlet for his insecurity and unhappiness. When tensions pile up inside him, he can discharge them by stealing something, an act which makes him feel much more comfortable. It is also probable that the delinquent act gives him pleasure. Thus, the tearing up of a small grocery by pulling things off the shelves and spilling them on the floor may serve not only to "get even" with a grocer against whom he has a grudge but also to give him a feeling of omnipotence, with accompanying release from his usual fears and inferiorities. He may therefore indulge in periodic destruction, perpetrated against entirely unknown owners of property, because these episodes contribute to his sense of success and well-being more than any resulting detection or punishment is likely to offset. The outstanding point in this explanation is the constant interchange between childish needs and environmental rewards and pressures.

The psychoanalytic school has presented an explanation that rests primarily upon a faulty personality structure [26] that has already developed before the child is old enough to leave his home. During the first two or three years all children are "delinquent"—that is, they take what they want immediately, directly, and without inhibition, and they derive pleasure from their unsocial reactions. By the time they are three years old, however, they should have learned to wait a little while for satisfaction and to accept substitutes for gratifications that are denied them. That is, they can derive enough pleasure from the approval of their mother that they can keep themselves from tossing books on the floor, for instance. They should be able to bear a little tension in order to reach a goal. When there is a conflict between immediate instinctual gratification and their affective relationship to their parents, they

---

[26] E. P. Bernabeu, "Underlying Ego Mechanism in Delinquency," *Psychoanalytic Quarterly*, 27:383–396, 1958.

should be able to inhibit the former in order to improve the latter. If, however, the child has not advanced to this level, he cannot bear the tensions that an increasingly active life puts upon him, so he regresses to his earlier direct, uninhibited behavior of letting his drives have full and immediate expression and deriving great satisfaction and pleasure from their fulfillment. Since the youthful predelinquent is already a rejected child, his natural attachments to his mother have become weak. His failure to gain what he deeply wants turns his love into hostility, and he expresses his feelings by aggression toward her. If development has been normal, between the ages of three and six a child should have developed a superego, or conscience, and a strong enough ego to control many of his impulses and to meet some of the demands of the superego; at least, he knows what he should do, and in general he tries to do it, even though his control is not always strong enough. Because the delinquent has already begun his regression, he makes little progress in the development of a superego. He is probably more comfortable if he fails completely, since then there is no inner conflict; but often he does develop just enough conscience to stir up feelings of guilt in himself and yet not enough to be of much guidance to him. Once in a while one finds a delinquent with a very severe superego that is strong enough to make him indulge in antisocial acts in order to punish himself. More often, however, any urge to self-punishment is transmuted into blame against the environment, a far more comfortable attitude, especially as the child can now discharge some of his hostile feelings against the straw man he has just set up.

As life becomes more complex and makes more demands upon him, the child gets into more and more open revolt. He continues to carry out his primary desires and to ignore environmental pressures. His attachments to people are never strong enough to act as inhibitions upon his drives. His parents usually meet his behavior either by excessive severity or by excessive indulgence, and sometimes by an oscillation between the two extremes. While the neurotic is greatly influenced by the attitudes of others toward him, the delinquent is affected very little by them. He continues to act on the pleasure principle. The delinquent is, then, an individual in whom instinctive drives are strong, conscience is weak, and the ego is bent upon immediate pleasure without respect to the generally accepted norms of behavior. This combination of traits keeps him in conflict with everyone and leads him to attack reality before it gets a chance to overwhelm him. Delinquency gives him, therefore, his most satisfactory defense against a world that frightens and annoys him without giving him any adequate compensatory pleasure.

These two views are not in contradiction, although they emphasize different aspects of the total problem. The most important difference between them is the emphasis put by the Freudians upon the first two or three years of life and the tracing of delinquency to a faulty structure of personality, without much apparent regard for other possible elements. Both views have much to offer to the student of human behavior.

When reading through the three short case histories below, the student is advised to refer to the list of contributing causes given on page 438. It might be well to list which causes seem to have been operative in which cases, so as to see how the various forces merge together and reinforce each other in the production of delinquency.

George Banks belongs to a gang of adolescent boys, most of whom have been expelled from school. The half-dozen members of the gang have looked in a desultory fashion for work, but with only about ninth-grade education and bad records for behavior, they have not found any. Most of the time they hang around a street-corner, making objectionable remarks to passers-by. If occasion offers, they snatch a purse or converge en masse upon some boy and knock him down, apparently just for fun. Of late the group has been indulging in vandalism of a mild sort and in calling people selected at random from the telephone book, shouting lewd remarks or making threats. All the boys live in a deteriorated district and have the kind of home in which no one would stay unless he had to. There are no facilities for normal amusement, and the boys have no money to seek legitimate diversion elsewhere. The police have been watching them, but thus far they have not been able to catch them in the carrying-out of any misdeeds. There is a settlement house not far away, but the boys will not go to it because they think all the activities there are too "sissy." These boys are typical of today's delinquents. They are not employable, and they have literally nothing to do. They receive no support from their homes or from the society in which they live. At present, a street worker is trying to rescue them from their *Slough of Despond*, but he has to proceed slowly, and it is quite possible that they will be arrested before he has enough time to effect any changes in their attitudes or activities.

Elaine was a child with a normal personality and a normal degree of intelligence. She was somewhat precocious, to be sure, but there was no sign of conflict or abnormal emotional preoccupation in her early years. Her progress in school was normal, and she was popular with both her age-mates and her teachers. She had no record of trouble until her thirteenth year, when she began to have sexual relations with boys and men.

Elaine's father had died when she was about four years old, and her mother had supported herself and her daughter by being the hostess in the dining room of a large hotel. She and Elaine lived in a back room of the hotel. She tried hard to provide a normal life for her daughter and to shield her from the seamier sides of hotel life. Elaine had her lunch at school, and since her mother was free during the last part of the afternoon, they usually went to a park or out on errands together after school hours. Elaine was put to bed about six-thirty, just before her mother went on duty in the dining room. The mother sometimes augmented her income by visiting the rooms of men guests after the dining room closed. Although she was very discreet, Elaine nevertheless learned about these episodes and assumed them to be normal. She does not seem to have been upset in the least, but she did develop a precocity and an indifference to conventional morality as a result. During her twelfth year she began to have relations with the bellboys and some of the waiters. It does not appear that she sought them out or that she was impelled by any strong inner urge. She seemed to think such behavior was expected of her and submitted to advances without much interest. Her mother was genuinely horrified when she was told of this development and much more deeply distressed over Elaine's misdeeds than Elaine was. At the suggestion of the school psychologist, she gave up her hotel job and took a place as companion to an elderly woman in the country. So far as could be determined, the mother lived a strictly moral life from that time on. Elaine went to a consolidated school, finished the twelfth grade, and soon afterward married a boy who lived on a neighboring farm. She is now a happy farm wife, with three small children. There has never been the slightest sign of further delinquencies. Elaine would appear to have been a normal child who lived under abnormal circumstances and wandered into delinquency mainly because she had developed at the age of 13 the precocity and hardness that are likely to characterize adults who live in hotels.

Walter first came to official notice in the seventh grade, to which a liberal promotion policy had carried him, although his mastery of schoolwork would have placed him not above the fifth, and his reading more nearly in the fourth. No teacher had ever been able to awaken a spark of interest in the boy. Twice he had been detected slapping and knocking down smaller boys on the playground, but he had been able to convince authorities that he had had no wrong intentions—had merely given a rather too husky boyish love pat. Walter's teachers had always characterized him as flighty, superficial, easily led, impatient, suggestible, irresponsible, and sly, but his small size had kept his aggressions within bounds. With the beginning of adolescence he grew rapidly. Moreover, he became more and more disorganized as a personality. One evening he and three other boys a little older than he were roaming around a residential district, looking for something loose that they could appropriate, but after an hour's fruitless search, they became weary of this pastime. One of the older boys suggested that they "jump" some passerby and take his money. Presently, a rather small, middle-aged man came past. The boys surrounded him, knocked him down, searched his pockets and found only eighteen cents. Infuriated by their small haul, they began to kick the man, now lying unconscious on the ground and to beat him with a pop bottle one of them had picked up. The boys ran away and were not caught for this offense, although they later admitted it. A few nights later the same group went into a park and pulled up several plants, broke windows in the conservatory, and threw rocks out onto the roadway. The following week they broke into an elementary school and tore one room almost to pieces before a watchman's approach caused them to flee. Then, one evening after dark they went out in pairs on bicycles to try a trick they had devised. Two of them rode with arms interlocked so that their two headlights looked like those of a car. When a motorist approached them, they suddenly broke apart, one going on each side of the approaching car. Before the state police managed to catch them they had put four startled motorists into the ditch and had caused one serious accident, besides scaring an unknown number of drivers. Walter was one of the two apprehended. After an hour with the police his general disorganization finally did society some good, for he "broke" and told all about what he and the others had been doing to amuse themselves. As he talked, it became all too evident that this disorganized, aggressive, heedless, adventurous life exactly reflected his personality. Walter is now in a reform school, but the chances of a reform are very slight. He and delinquency have too much in common.

▶ The Prevention of Delinquency

Delinquency is extremely hard to "cure." Thus, in one sample study begun many years ago, 1000 delinquent boys were followed for fifteen years.[27] The total number of known arrests during the three successive five-year periods was 2551, 2194, and 1819; in all three periods the arrests per person whose whereabouts were known was 2.5. Other reports, usually on a much smaller number of cases, sometimes give slightly better figures, but the percentage of "cures" is never high. If there has been little or no treatment, the percentage of recidivism is very high indeed.

It is hard to reform a delinquent because his mode of life is to him extremely satisfactory. It provides what he wants with the least possible delay, it brings him prestige among his fellows, it satisfies his urges, it permits him to punish those who have neglected and rejected him, and it "matches" his personality. There is for him *no other life* that is so rewarding. The typical delinquent does not, therefore, want to be reformed; he wants only not to get caught. He can rarely be reclaimed through love, because he is no longer capable of giving or receiving affection. His deep hatred of schools and teachers prevents a rescue through education. And it is of little use to talk about "congenial work," because no work could be as congenial to him as delinquency. What the would-be reformer often overlooks is that the delinquent *likes* to steal from adults, because the act pays back in small measure the multiple rejections he has received from the adult world. He *likes* to "gang up" on a "good" boy, because the attack will do something to cancel the hurt of rejection by other "good" children. He *likes* random vandalism, because it gives him a chance to work off a bit of his long score against society. He *likes*

---

[27] S. Glueck and E. T. Glueck, *Juvenile Delinquents Grown Up* (Commonwealth Foundation, 1940), 330 pp., p. 309.

to feel callous toward people, because this attitude prevents him from getting hurt. Moreover, success in such activities as those just mentioned brings him prestige among other delinquents. Their approval he wants; that of the world he can do without.

Since cures are hard to bring about, one has to rely upon prevention. And the first question that arises concerns the possibility of identifying the delinquency-prone child far enough ahead of his overt reactions to allow time for remedial treatment. The investigators of the Glueck study went over their data to study the possibility of using scores on tests of personality or items from case histories as bases of prediction, and worked out three prediction tables based on different groups of items. The records of 424 boys (205 delinquent and 219 nondelinquent) were next examined to find out to what extent each table correctly classified the boys. The results are summarized in Table 19–6. Almost half of the boys were correctly identified as being delin-

Table 19–6: PREDICTION OF DELINQUENCY

	Percent	
1. Boy correctly classified on all three prediction tables	49	87%
2. Boy correctly classified by two but wrongly by one	38	successes
3. Boy incorrectly classified on two and correctly on one	11	13%
4. Boy wrongly classified on all three	2	failures

SOURCE: S. Glueck and E. T. Glueck, *Unraveling Juvenile Delinquency* (Cambridge, Mass.: Harvard University Press, 1950), p. 268. Copyright 1950 by The Commonwealth Fund.

quent or nondelinquent on all three predictions, and more than another third on two of the three, giving a total of 87 percent. It would seem that an early identification of the delinquent is already feasible.[28]

The age of first observed delinquent behavior among the boys of the Glueck study was as follows: before 8, 29 percent; before 10, 73 percent; before 12, 90 percent; before 15, 100 percent. These figures refer only to overt behavior. Presumably, if one investigated the first appearance of characteristic traits of behavior, the percentages would be even higher at the early ages. It is the writers' guess that typical traits had appeared in well over half the cases by the time the children entered school, although for girls the attitudes develop rather later than for boys.

There is one psychological danger that is inherent in prediction. Once a youngster has been classified as a predelinquent, he is likely to be regarded as different from and dangerous to other children. He therefore meets with discrimination from those who could help him most. But he is still acceptable to already-delinquent groups, so he turns to them. He might never have done

---

[28] See E. Herzog, *Identifying Potential Delinquents* (Washington, D.C.: U.S. Department of Health, Education, and Welfare), 1960, 6 pp.

so had he not been "labeled." That is, the classifying itself may be an element in producing the delinquency that it foretold. The "prediction tables" have all been worked out after the boy or girl was already a delinquent. As far as the writers know, no one has yet made a prediction of pupils in, say, the fifth grade of school, put the results into a safe, and then waited for 15–20 years to see how good the prediction was.

Delinquency is an end result of a long process that continues for many years. It could be said that all babies are delinquents, in the sense that they want what they want when they want it and they do not care how many other people are inconvenienced. A baby is completely egocentric and a born nonconformist. By the time a normal child is four, he has begun to learn that conformity pays off in terms of affection and the successful pursuit of happiness, whereas nonconformity brings rejection and failure. For one reason or another the predelinquent does not learn this valuable lesson. He continues to be completely absorbed in himself, but soon he becomes frustrated because in this world no one can have his own way all the time. As a child he is impulsive and thoughtless, he indulges in much nonconformist behavior, but he is usually not identified as predelinquent because his misdeeds are—like himself—so childish. As long as a small boy's "delinquent act" consists of shoving a child away from the jungle-gym and usurping his place in line, he will probably escape with nothing more than a mild reproof and an explanation that this sort of thing is not done. But his purposes and attitudes are just as delinquent as are those of an older boy who knocks another lad down and takes the money out of his pocket by force. What is added during adolescence is the deliberate intent to do something the individual knows to be wrong. Therefore it often appears that delinquency does not arise until the adolescent years, when actually so far as basic attitudes are concerned, it has been there ever since the child's birth. Because the adolescent is better able to plan and execute his crimes and because most of them take place outside the protecting circle of his family, it often appears that he has changed overnight from a "good" boy to a "bad" one. It is more probable that, like all children, he was born without moral standards and has not found enough satisfaction in being "good" to modify his infantile egocentricity.

In previous decades most of the recommendations for the prevention of delinquency have centered around the alteration of environment. Such enterprises as the clearance of slums, the opening of playgrounds or swimming pools, and so on, come under this head. These changes are certainly needed, but it is doubtful if they will prevent delinquency all by themselves. One has to add to them procedures for changing the emotional atmosphere within homes and schools. Such suggestions as those outlined below are beginning to appear in the literature.

It has been found helpful if parents and children have one night together every week, if the evening is spent at home, and if the entire family engages as a group in some kind of communal, constructive, and pleasurable activity. No listening to radio, watching television, or going to a movie or a hockey game was to be considered as a proper activity for "family night," because these, while all right for other evenings, did not involve group effort. Many simple amusements of former generations had to be gotten out and relearned: taffy pulls, making a birthday cake, charades, simple card games, pinning the tail on the donkey, bobbing for apples, putting on a family show, reading aloud, singing together, developing a family orchestra, designing and making Christmas cards or Easter baskets together, or joint construction of new furniture. The only rule was that everyone in the family should take an active part in reaching some group objective, however trivial either the part or the objective. At first these efforts at man-made enjoyment in a machine-made age were not too successful, but gradually parents and children learned to like and trust each other, and the basic hostility vanished. For the parents there should be several frank talks and discussions, at first with leaders from either school or community and later among the parents by themselves. They have a common problem, and they are more likely to solve it together than separately. Some parents resist outside interference, some project all the blame for their child and his misdeeds onto his playmates, some recognize their problem but are too secretive and ashamed to ask for help, while others beg for aid from any and all agencies. The first meetings of parents with such different outlooks are likely to be stormy, but gradually a better understanding develops, and the children begin to receive a different treatment in their homes, usually with a marked reduction of tension.

Most of the recommended procedures [29] for the prevention of delinquency—or for its treatment during its early stages—are aimed at providing activities in which the child or adolescent can be successful, experiences that make him feel accepted, and outlets that are socially approved for his emotional drives. The attack upon the problem is indirect and consists essentially in substituting acceptance for rejection by means of activities that are within the established social norm but are *more satisfying to the adolescent than his delinquency.* A series of suggestions to teachers by one writer on the subject are listed below:

1. Provide children with a variety of experiences—crafts, art, music, athletics—covering a wide range of difficulty and interests, so that every child engages in some activity in which he can win outstanding success.

2. Understand each child's capacities and help him to recognize and develop his abilities—social, emotional, and artistic as well as intellectual—and accept his irremediable limitations.

3. Help him to gain skills and knowledge without unnecessary failure. Be on guard against occasions and incidents which might cause him to feel inadequate.

---

[29] See, for example, M. B. Novick, *Community Programs and Projects for the Prevention of Juvenile Delinquency* (Washington, D.C.: U.S. Department of Health, Education, and Welfare, 1960), 12 pp.

4. Guide the experiences of the class so that each pupil will gain satisfaction and moderate success in human relationships when he is acting along socially constructive lines.

5. Provide opportunities for normal emotional responses and accept minor instances of bad manners without comment.

6. When an outburst of delinquent behavior occurs in the classroom, do not be disturbed; handle it with objectivity and understanding; try to get into the delinquent's world and see things from his point of view.

7. Do what you can to change conditions in the home, school, or community that seem to be giving rise to types of behavior that are "expensive" to the individual and to society.[30]

None of these recommendations is either revolutionary or dramatic, but taken together they are likely to be effective. The writers would add one more precept to the list: Try to *like* the delinquent, even when he is being most objectionable. Children are exceedingly quick to sense rejection, no matter how well it is camouflaged, and will see through a pretense. Since the delinquent adolescent has probably not been loved since he was a baby, a small amount of genuine affection will often do more to help a boy rehabilitate himself than all other "treatments" combined.

All but one of the American cities with a population of 500,000 or more have had within the period from 1955 to 1960 one or more projects specifically designed to prevent delinquency. These are, however, of too recent origin for an estimate of results. For this purpose, one has to go back to an earlier study.

The methods used may be classified roughly as being of three types: the better coordination of services that already exist, the alteration of depressed areas so as to make them better environments for children, and the detached-worker service.[31] The first two are good as far as they go, but they do not get to the heart of the problem. The "detached-worker" is a relatively new phenomenon. He goes into an area, seeks out groups of adolescents who are in the process of becoming openly delinquent, makes friends with them, and tries to guide them into using legitimate outlets for their normal desires for activity and adventure. The worker becomes a guide, philosopher, and friend upon whom a group or gang can count. The basic problem is to persuade such a group to accept the guide. However, some men and women have proved to be equal to this difficult task, and their work gives hope that with enough such adults it will be possible to prevent much delinquency, especially if the worker can get to the group soon enough. Very few of the groups are completely oriented toward delinquency. They have many interests of a socially approved nature. The work has to be done in the open—not in an office,

[30] Condensed from R. Strang, "First Steps to Progress in the Prevention of Delinquency," *Forty-Seventh Yearbook of the National Society for the Study of Education,* 1948, Pt. I, pp. 267–269.

[31] Z. A. Aarons, "Some Problems of Delinquency and Their Treatment by a Casework Agency," *Social Casework,* 40:254–262, 1959, and K. E. Marshall, "Working with a Street Gang," *Autonomous Group Bulletin,* 11:9–10, 1955–1956.

clinic, or settlement house, because the members of the group will enter none of these places. Such work is dangerous—but rewarding.

▶ Summary

Although there are some exceptions, delinquent adolescents tend to share certain distinctive traits. They often show an average or slightly below-average intelligence, they are markedly overactive, they are retarded educationally far beyond the degree one might expect from their slight mental retardation, they dislike the traditional school, and they are not content with modes of emotional expression that are accepted as norms by their age-mates. They often show a high degree of hostility, aggressiveness, and suspicion. Their typical escape from their frustrations consists in making an attack upon their environment. Their homes may be undesirable places in which to raise children, usually for reasons having little to do with economic impoverishment. The homes most commonly fail to give the delinquent or predelinquent child the needed support, even though other siblings find the homes supportive enough for their needs. In some cases the neighborhood may accept and even encourage delinquent behavior as a means of achieving status for both juveniles and adults. The varied frustrations that find expression in antisocial reactions may come from the general social background, the familial structure, internal pressures within the individual, or from any combination of these factors. Overindulgence, undercontrol, or sheer indifference on the part of the parents may contribute to the individual's delinquency. It is probable that the emergence of full-scale delinquency depends upon the way in which the potentially predetermining factors come together in a particular case and the reactions of family, friends, school, and neighborhood to the first manifestations of maladjustment or delinquency.

References for Further Reading

BOOKS

Other Texts

Ausubel, *Theory and Problems of Adolescent Development* (Chap. 16).
Garrison, *Growth and Development,* 2d ed. (pp. 441–470).
Horrocks, *Behavior and Development* (Chap. 8 or 9).
Jones, *Growth and Behavior in Adolescence* (Chap. 10).
Kuhlen, *Psychology of Adolescent Development* (pp. 359–394).

Other Books and Monographs

Bandura, A., and R. H. Walters, *Adolescent Aggression* (New York: The Ronald Press Company, 1959), 475 pp. (Chap. 7, one of the two case studies).
Blake, M. E., *Youth Groups in Conflict* (Washington, D.C.: U.S. Department of

Health, Education, and Welfare, Children's Bureau, 1958), 52 pp. (pp. 10–17 and 30–37).

Cavan, R. S., *Juvenile Delinquency* (Philadelphia: J. B. Lippincott Company, 1962), 366 pp. (any two of Chaps. 1, 4, 5, 7, 9, 11 or 17).

Glueck, S. S., and E. T. Glueck, *Unraveling Juvenile Delinquency* (Cambridge, Mass.: Harvard University Press, 1950), 399 pp. (any two of Chaps. 4, 10, 11, 12, 18 or 19).

Herzog, E., *Identifying Potential Delinquents* (Washington, D.C.: U.S. Department of Health, Education, and Welfare, Children's Bureau, 1960), 6 pp.

Kvaraceus, W. C., *et al.*, *Delinquent Behavior; Culture and the Individual* (Washington, D.C.: National Education Association, 1959), 147 pp. (any three of Chaps. 5, 9, 10 or 13).

McCord, W., and J. McCord, *Origins of Crime* (New York: Columbia University Press, 1959), 219 pp. (Chap. 5 or 8).

Novick, M. B., *Community Programs and Projects for the Prevention of Juvenile Delinquency* (Washington, D.C.: U.S. Department of Health, Education, and Welfare, Children's Bureau, 1960), 12 pp.

Seidman, *The Adolescent: A Book of Readings*, rev. ed. (Nos. 42 and 43).

Strang, *The Adolescent Views Himself* (pp. 440–484).

ARTICLES

Aarons, Z. A., "Some Problems of Delinquency and Their Treatment by a Casework Agency," *Social Casework*, 40:254–262, 1959.

Bakwin, H., "Causes of Juvenile Delinquency," *American Journal of Diseases of Children*, 89:368–373, 1955.

Ball, J. C., "Delinquent and Non-delinquent Attitudes toward the Prevalence of Stealing," *Journal of Criminal Law, Criminology, and Police Science*, 48:259–274, 1957.

Bernabeu, E. P., "Underlying Ego Mechanisms in Delinquency," *Psychoanalytic Quarterly*, 27:383–396, 1958.

Conant, J. B., "Social Dynamite in Our Large Cities," *Crime and Delinquency*, 8:102–115, 1962.

Eaton, M. T., *et al.*, "Problem Behavior in School," *Journal of Educational Psychology*, 47:350–357, 1956.

Glueck, E. T., "Efforts to Identify the Delinquent," *Probation*, 24:49–56, 1960.

Grygier, T., "Leisure Pursuits of Juvenile Delinquents," *British Journal of Juvenile Delinquency*, 5:210–228, 1955.

Herskovitz, H. H., *et al.*, "Antisocial Behavior of Adolescents from Higher Socio-Economic Groups," *Journal of Nervous and Mental Diseases*, 129:467–476, 1959.

Jenkins, R. L., "Motivation and Frustration in Delinquency," *American Journal of Orthopsychiatry*, 27:528–537, 1957.

Miller, W. B., "Lower Class Culture as a Generating Milieu of Gang Delinquency," *Journal of Social Issues,* 14:5–19, 1958.

Nakamura, G. Y., "The Relation between Children's Expressions of Hostility and Methods of Discipline Exercised by Dominant, Overprotective Parents," *Child Development,* 30:109–117, 1959.

Roman, M. J., *et al.,* "Reading Retardation and Delinquency," *National Probation and Parole Association Journal,* 1:1–7, 1955.

Scarpitti, F. R., *et al.,* "The 'Good' Boy in a High Delinquent Area: 4 Years Later," *American Sociological Review,* 125:555–558, 1960.

Shanker, U., "Juvenile Crime and Intelligence," *Education,* 10:143–148, 1956.

Thrasher, F. M., "The Gang as a Symptom of Community Disintegration," *Journal of Corrective Work,* 4:54–56, 1957.

Wattenberg, W. W., and F. Saunders, "Sex Differences among Juvenile Offenders," *Sociology and Social Research,* 39:24–31, 1954.

Suggested Research Problems [32]

1. Comparative study of delinquent and nondelinquent girls of equal intelligence and similar social background.
2. Refinement of prediction techniques and of treatments appropriate for delinquency-prone children.
3. Evaluation of community efforts to prevent delinquency.

---

[32] See note on p. 11.

PART FIVE | Moral Development

Chapter 20 | Growth in Attitudes

THE present chapter contains a number of sections, each of which contributes something to an understanding of growth in attitudes, habits, personal traits, and ideals that, taken together, constitute development in morality. Investigators have measured all kinds of attitudes with more or less success. The writers have limited the discussion to a relatively few topics upon which research has been especially fruitful and interesting, and have selected only two or three illustrative studies for inclusion in each section. The first section deals with conservatism and liberalism at different ages and with changes over periods of time; the second section contains discussions of the usual developments in the establishment of prejudice, of the extent of prejudice toward various minority groups, of their reaction toward the restrictions placed upon them, and of attitudes toward foreign nations and peoples; the third deals with the changes in the type of person most admired at different ages. The next chapter will discuss problems of religious attitudes, the extent of church affiliation among adolescents, the growth of generalized ideas of right and wrong, and the adolescent beginnings of a philosophy of life. Together, these two chapters should present a picture of the moral attitudes and ideas of youth.

▶ Typical Liberal or Conservative Attitudes

It is generally believed that young people tend to be more liberal—if not actually radical—than older people, and that those who were once liberal tend to develop a conservative attitude as they grow older, but actual investigations suggest that forces other than mere age are of importance in conditioning points of view.

In general, adolescents tend to follow the pattern of attitudes held by their parents, even to favoring the same political parties. In one study 74 percent of the boys belonged or intended to belong to the same party as their fathers, and 76 percent of the girls to the same party as their mothers.[1] In the relatively few cases of divergence from the parents' political views, the cause seemed to be not so much a difference of opinion as an expression of

---

[1] E. E. Macoby, R. S. Matthews, and A. S. Morton, "Youth and Political Change," *Public Opinion Quarterly*, 18:23–39, 1954.

rebellion and hostility toward parental authority. Apparently, some adolescents feel that becoming a Democrat is a revolt against two Republican parents! Or vice versa.

One investigator in 1950 followed up over nine hundred adults who were college students in one of sixteen colleges in 1936 and administered again to them a test of attitudes that they had taken as students.[2] In the intervening fourteen years changes had taken place, but not in the expected direction. There was no shift in 18 percent of the cases, a change to greater conservatism in 31 percent, and a shift toward radicalism in the remaining 51 percent. These figures seem to contradict the usual assumption that people become more conservative with age, but these retested students were still under forty. Perhaps the conservatism will set in later. Students or adults from the South were more conservative than those from the North.

The degree of conservatism or radicalism is related directly to occupational, economic, and social status, as revealed by Figure 20–1, which gives results from groups of adults. The heads of large businesses tended strongly to be conservative, and over half of them were ultraconservative. Skilled laborers evidently were not sure which side they should be on. The semiskilled were inclined to be radical, as were the unskilled, if they had an opinion. This figure reflects the usual attitudes of the "haves" and the "have-nots." Those whose income and prestige depend upon a perpetuation of the *status quo* are opposed to change. The tendency toward radicalism begins with the laboring groups, who might profit by change; but many of them do not seem to be at all sure that a change would do them any good. In general, America is too economically comfortable a country for the growth of ultraradicalism.

▶ **Prejudice: Its Nature, Causes, and Expression**

There is a great deal of material about attitudes toward minorities, presumably because this problem is such an important one in present-day American culture. In order that a teacher may see her role and that of the school in the prevention of intolerance, it seems best to begin the discussion by giving a brief explanation of its bases, its growth, its nature, and its causes.

There seem at present to be two schools of thought concerning the development of prejudice. The older one assumes, at least tacitly, that the prejudice arises from a combination of personality traits and external circumstances, and, if allowed to grow without restriction or control, will eventually lead to aggressive and hostile activity toward the person or group upon which the prejudice has already centered. The second theory reverses the sequence

---

[2] E. N. P. Nelson, "Persistence of Attitudes of College Students," *Psychological Monographs,* Vol. LXVIII, no. 373, 1954, 12 pp.

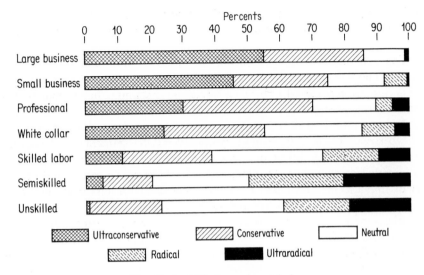

Fig. 20–1. Attitudes and social class

Based on R. Centers, *The Psychology of Social Class* (Princeton, N.J.: Princeton University Press, 1949), 244 pp., p. 57.

and assumes that a person develops a prejudice because he has already made a series of discriminatory responses, not necessarily violent in character. Thus, if a child grows up in a city in which the Negroes go to different schools from those attended by white children, if he always sits in the "white" end of a bus and in the "white" waiting room at the station, if he refrains from playing with Negro children, if he goes to a "white" church, if he is waited on by Negro servants and gives them orders, he has already had a long experience of discriminatory behavior. As he grows older, he develops a prejudice against Negroes, because he has already discriminated against them. He has, of course, only followed the pattern of behavior he saw around him, and he has probably discriminated without knowing what he was doing, but the behavior will produce the prejudice just as quickly as if it were intentional. One is reminded of William James' theory of emotions: that the man who saw a bear and ran away became frightened, while the one who stood his ground and shot the bear was not frightened at all. That is, the behavior aroused the emotion—not vice versa. The main outcome of holding one theory or the other lies in the field of treatment. If the prejudice comes first, one would try to reduce the feeling and thus eventually diminish the number of hostile acts; but if the behavior comes first, then one can bypass the emotion by altering the behavior. For instance, it is probable that a white child born in 1962 will, by the time he is old enough to observe the social mores about him, find that white and Negro children go to the same school, ride on the same busses, use the same waiting rooms, swim in the same pools, eat in the same restaurants, and so on. He will not, therefore, himself commit discriminatory acts every day of his life—and will not develop prejudice. If this theory is correct, the thing that will cure the deep-seated prejudices in this country is time, plus an initial boost from law enforcement and groups of people with democratic ideals. But the attack is to be made upon the discriminatory practices, not upon the prejudice.

It may be noticed that the writers tend to waver between the two points of view, largely because they feel they should report significant articles without respect to the philosophy underlying the articles. In fact, the writers' own attitudes do not enter into the picture at all, except sometimes in the discussion of implications. They are reporting what is in the literature, not what they think, and since the men and women who did the research and wrote the articles were of various opinions, and since they used terms that best expressed their meaning, it may seem to the reader that the point of view often changes. It does. Both sides are presented in proportion to their contribution to the subject of prejudice.

Social Background of Intolerance   America is often and fondly referred to as the "melting pot." To it have come members of all races, nationalities, political faiths, and religious beliefs. Up to a point there has been the kind of assimilation that was expected, but it has now become obvious that some of the ingredients that went into the pot show little inclination to melt. If fusion is to take place there has to be a desire on the immigrant's side to become Americanized and on the American side to absorb the newcomer. Sometimes the immigrant wishes to remain apart. The orthodox Jew, for instance, vehemently resists absorption and mourns as he sees his children, his grandchildren, and his great-grandchildren depart ever more and more from ancestral customs. Sometimes the aversion is mutual. Thus the small groups of Portuguese fishermen who settled nearly a century ago here and there along the coast of Maine wanted no truck with the native Yankees, who, in turn, regraded the Portuguese as a low order of humanity. Often, but not always, the prejudice is on the American side, as in the earlier rejection in the West of the Japanese, who wanted desperately to be Americans. In the course of centuries, the problem of interracial adjustment is likely to solve itself through biological assimilation, and the discordant elements will disappear into the general population through intermarriage, just as the Indians of many former tribes have been absorbed, or as the Roman Empire absorbed the surrounding barbarians. This long view, however, does not offer much that is practical in the easing of present-day tensions.

The elements of the population that are proving most difficult to assimilate—in all parts of the country—are the Negroes, the Orientals, and the Jews. In limited areas, the Mexicans, French Canadians, Irish, Germans, Italians, Portuguese, and Poles are also proving resistive to absorption. Certain religious groups fight against assimilation—the Dunkards and the Mormons, for instance—as do a few political groups, of which the Communists may serve as an example. The Negroes, Japanese, Chinese, Filipinos, and Indians present racial variations that are of a fundamental nature. The biological differences remain even after the descendants of the original immigrants have become as Americanized as the Bostonian of purest Anglo-Saxon ancestry, and these differences mark off the individual and make him "feel different," a basic attitude that easily leads to submission in a timid soul and to violence in an aggressive one. Further differences between national groups are social, political, ethnological, religious, or economic, all of which are acquired by the respective groups through social tradition. They become almost as ineradicable as inborn differences between races, however, and are actually just as potent in causing prejudices as are inherited traits, although aversion may be centered upon the latter, as was demonstrated by one investigator [3] who showed a large number of adults a series of 10 photographs of Negroes, all of whom were of mixed blood and showed varying degrees of white inheritance. If the adults identified the subject of a photograph as a Negro, he attributed to the individual the usual traits of the Negro stereotype, but if the features were strongly Caucasian, the characterization showed far less prejudice, even though the judger stated verbally that he suspected the pictured man was really a Negro. That is, the cues which set off the prejudice were superficial. This investigation points out the essential difference between absorbing Negroes into the population and absorbing most foreigners. Within a generation the latter look like any other Caucasian, whereas the Negroes do not.

It is a curious thing that the further off people are from the target of their hostility and the less contact they have with members of the "hated" group, the deeper is their prejudice. Thus, in one investigation, those who lived at the greatest distance from Negroes had the most prejudice against them, while those who lived in the same apartment houses with them had appreciably less. And the ones with no prejudice at all were those who not only lived in the same public housing but treated their Negro neighbors in a neighborly fashion. Presumably the members of this last group were rather more accepting in their attitudes than the average to begin with; but whatever prejudice they had felt earlier vanished when they adopted neighborly attitudes toward the Negro families in the same building.[4]

Intolerance and Religion   Many studies during the last two decades have presented results that indicated a positive relationship between religion and prejudice. Since an acceptance of the Christian—or any

---

[3] P. F. Secord, "Stereotyping and Favorableness in the Perception of Negro Faces," *Journal of Abnormal and Social Psychology,* 59:309–314, 1959.

[4] D. M. Wilner, *et al.,* "Residential Proximity and Intergroup Relations in Public Housing Projects," *Journal of Social Issues,* 8:45–69, 1952.

other—religion involves a feeling of brotherhood toward all men, it is hard to reconcile such finding with common sense. There are at least two sources of error in this argument. In the first place, belonging to a church may have nothing to do with religion. A person may belong because his parents did and he has never cared enough to make a break, or because being a member of a particular church gives him social status, or because he can often get help on nonreligious problems. For example, one of the writers knows a young man who "belongs" to no less than eight student religious groups, but only for the free meals that, with eight groups involved, cut down his living expenses! Actually, he is a renegade, violently anticlerical Catholic who has not been to his own church for over a decade and has no use whatever for religion except as a source of free meals. Yet, in any research study, he would be classified as a church member. If church membership alone is used as a criterion, one certainly will include a large number of people whose religious convictions are mainly absent and whose presence in the congregation springs from nonreligious motives. A second and less obvious difficulty comes from the type of person who feels the need for a church connection in order to bolster his ego. He is uncertain of himself, confused, unsuccessful in many phases of life, and already hostile toward a world that he thinks has treated him badly. Probably he has been using projection for many years as a means of escape from his own insufficiency. And he doubtless brings to the church a degree of rigidity that cannot be modified by religious experiences. He seeks the help of religion because he has an inadequate personality structure, and those with inadequate personalities are the ones who also easily become fanatics. Both his prejudice and his "religion" are projections, by means of which he tries to escape from himself. With two such obvious difficulties it is not surprising that many studies have found the church member to be more prejudiced than the free thinker who has no great need for projection or for religion either. For centuries the religious person has been noted for his rigidity, whether he were a member of the Spanish Inquisition or an English Puritan. But perhaps history has put the cart in front of the horse. It can just as well be that people who are already rigid flock to religion because there their rigidity meets with less opposition than elsewhere.

Two studies,[5] both in 1960, have reported much the same findings as in earlier investigations. In one, college students with no affiliation showed less anti-Semitism than students who belonged to a church. In the other, ten sizable groups from many Christian denominations and of widely varied composition, involving over 2000 adults, also showed an undue amount of anti-Semitism. In both cases, there was prejudice in every denominational group

---

[5] B. S. Blum and J. H. Mann, "The Effect of Religious Membership on Religious Prejudice," *Journal of Social Psychology*, 52:97–101, 1960, and W. C. Wilson, "Extrinsic Religious Values and Prejudice," *Journal of Abnormal and Social Psychology*, 55:286–288, 1960.

against practically every other denominational faith. This attitude—that God is in "our" church and not in other people's—has been the curse of religion for generations. The emergence of many community churches that do not hew to any denominational line suggests that there has been, here and there, a breakthrough to a more moderate attitude.

One further study seems worth quoting because it calls attention to one fact that is all too often overlooked.[6] The investigator first determined the degree of participation in religious activities among 200 Jewish college students, all of whom had been brought up in the traditional faith, classifying them as high, middle, or low in present observance, or else entirely without participation. He then administered attitude tests to all the students. Those classified as "middle" were the most tolerant, and the "low" group was moderately so; but *both* extremes were equally rigid. One hears much about the rigidity of the extremely religious person, but almost nothing about the equal rigidity of the godless.

Development of Prejudice in Individuals   A fanatic intolerance, being a form of projection, is one means of escape from emotional difficulties. The growth of a prejudice runs about as follows. (1) An individual is frustrated in his efforts to satisfy his basic needs, is rejected and neglected; (2) he feels insecure and defenseless, he wants at least enough power to defend himself and, by preference, enough to compensate for his past and present low status; (3) he feels hostile toward almost everyone, but he cannot express his hostility toward those who are more powerful than he is, in any more active way than wishing them ill or grumbling about them. What he needs is a victim who is accessible and in no position to fight back. (4) The individual then displaces his hostility from its natural objects to his victim. (5) The prejudiced person is now ready to commit an act of aggression, and will do so when outside stimuli prompt him. By this series of reactions the fanatic has rid himself of his emotional burden. He no longer feels helpless, because he has someone to attack; and he is no longer isolated, because he can ally himself with others of the same opinions and attitudes. (6) As a final stage, the fanatic adds reasons and justifications for his intolerance. This step is necessary in proportion to the fanatic's intelligence. If he has an otherwise logical and able mind, it soon tells him that he has no sensible reason for hating the people he does. Since this notion, if listened to, would reduce his prejudice and bring back his former state of insecurity, he makes haste to bolster his emotional attitude with "good" reasons. This step is always possible because no group is perfect; as long as one likes the members, or most of them, one overlooks the shortcomings, but as soon as one begins to hate the members, the faults are not hard to find. When a fanatic is queried

---

[6] L. Appleby, "The Relationship between Rigidity and Religious Participation," *Journal of Pastoral Care,* 11:73–83, 1957.

about his prejudice, he justifies it with his "reasons," which actually came at the end of the process, not at the beginning, as he probably thinks. He is usually not aware that the early steps were parts of the development. It should be noted that the basic causes of prejudice are emotional and have no necessarily integral connection with whatever group the prejudice is directed against. It is this lack of connection, plus the fictitious logic of the superimposed justification, that makes intolerance so hard to "cure." The deep-rooted prejudice that is based primarily upon fear of some sort is often impossible to eradicate, because the fear prevents its possessor from seeing any new fact clearly and produces so much distortion of new data that little if any progress can be made. To the true fanatic prejudice is a way of life, to which he clings because he feels his safety and success are too involved for him to change. New facts are therefore only threats, and he will have none of them. Such a person is described below:

Mr. R. is a man of 55 who expresses a violent anti-Semitic attitude. He asserts that Jews are exploiters of others, Christ-killers, and fakers, that they are dishonest, that they sell second-rate goods at high prices, that they are too successful, too rich, and too powerful. Mr. R. will not work for a Jewish employer or for a firm that employs Jews. He criticizes President Roosevelt for having been too friendly with Jews and he praises Hitler's anti-Semitism and regrets that a few European Jews escaped death.

Mr. R. is the son of a Presbyterian minister who ruled his numerous children with an iron hand. The atmosphere of the home was intensely and narrowly religious, permeated with the gloomiest of Calvinism. The father threatened his sons and daughters with hell fire for minor transgressions and thrashed them for major deviations from what he considered proper conduct. The other three boys eventually escaped from their father by running away from home, and the girls all married at an early age, two of them eloping with suitors who had been sent away by the father in a dictatorial manner. Mr. R. was always terrified of his father, but at the same time he admired him for his strength and power. On the whole he conformed better to requirements than any other member of the family and never revolted openly against authority.

In the Jews Mr. R. has found a convenient target for the hatred he has for his father. They, like his father, are strong, successful, and powerful. Moreover, he can hate them without danger to himself, whereas he never dared to express openly his hostility toward his father. They are only substitutes, but they permit him to escape from the inferiority that he would otherwise feel because he lacks the courage to flee from parental domination. His hatred is great because his need is great.

The above account outlines the stages in the development of prejudice in a person who received little or no help from others. Actually, most people short-circuit the process by imitating attitudes that they observe in people whom they admire or love. Thus, the attitudes of pupils and their teachers agree more than they would by chance, and children's attitudes resemble closely those of their parents.[7] Adolescents, especially, imitate the opinions of their age-mates. In addition to family, teachers, and friends, the movies, the radio, books, and television are constantly presenting them with possible fixations. Society thus furnishes the models, which do not seriously affect those who have no need of them but are accepted uncritically by those who, for their own emotional comfort, need someone to project their frustrations upon.

The typically prejudiced person comes most frequently from a family background such as described below. The parents put great emphasis upon outward forms, conventional standards, and social status, but do not show much affection toward the child. Their discipline is fair but strict and rigid. They are more concerned with mores than with morals and tend to feel superior about whatever is "theirs"—their church, their home, their social set, their school, their clubs, and so on. The child identifies himself early with his parents and eventually idealizes them, taking over from them their glorification of whatever group they belong to, their devotion to appearances, their rigidity of thought, their lack of emotion, and their absence of moral convictions.[8] By the time such a child has reached adolescence, he has acquired a good enough adjustment on the surface. He is polite, self-confident, optimistic, conventionally moral, and kind, when kindness is no particular trouble. He is markedly conservative, mentally rigid, and fanatically loyal to his own group. He admires power, is a social or political climber, and believes in harsh punishment for misdeeds. He has an unusually deep need to feel superior to others. He solves his daily problems by projecting the blame for his difficulties onto someone or something else. He is markedly lacking in ability to love but is well equipped with suspicions, incipient hatreds and callousness toward those outside his own narrow group. He is usually a member of "the best church in town" and may give generously to its support—partly because it is "his" church and partly because he likes the increased status that follows the gifts—but he misses the spiritual values of religion. He has many

---

[7] M. Weltman and H. H. Remmers, "Pupils', Parents', and Teachers' Attitude: Similarities and Differences," *Purdue University Studies in Higher Education*, No. 50, 1946.

[8] See, for example, R. Gordon, "Personal Dynamics and the Tendency toward Stereotypy," *International Social Science Bulletin*, 6:571–576, 1954. See also N. W. Ackerman and M. Jahoda, *Anti-Semitism and Emotional Disorders* (New York: Harper & Row, Publishers, Inc., 1950), 135 pp.; W. Adorno, *et al., The Authoritarian Personality* (New York: Harper & Row, Publishers, Inc., 1950), 982 pp.; F. H. Corder, "A Factorial Approach to Anti-Democratic Activities," *Purdue Studies in Higher Education*, 1954, no. 82, 42 pp.; S. Crown, "Some Personal Correlates of War-Mindedness and Anti-Semitism," *Journal of Social Psychology*, 31:131–143, 1950; E. Frenkel-Brunswik and R. N. Sanford, *The Anti-Semitic Personality* (New York: Harper & Row, Publishers, 1950), pp. 26–124; R. Stagner, "Attitudes toward Authoritarianism: An Exploratory Study," *Journal of Social Psychology*, 40:197–210, 1954.

unsolved conflicts; his stereotype is a defense against the anxieties that arise from his maladjustment to society. Since he is already rigid, righteous, and unfeeling, he is ready for violence, sadism, or hostility, the extreme to which he will go being governed mainly by his deep regard for his status. If he can become anonymous behind the sheets of the Ku Klux Klan, his aggressive cruelty may slip the leash completely. Since the typical fanatic has been slowly becoming one ever since he left the cradle, it is not surprising that he is hard to "cure." Like the delinquent his disease is his way of life. Not only does he have great difficulty in changing his attitudes, he does not even want to change them.

Stereotypes and Scapegoats [9]   Many people develop stereotypes for the nationalities or races with which they come into contact. They generally assign to the groups they like the traits of which they approve and to the groups they dislike the traits of which they disapprove. Also, they tend to reject their own least acceptable traits when they think they recognize them in others. A stereotype usually has or has had some slight basis in fact, but the fact may or may not have been relevant. For example, one of the writers remembers one sentence from a childhood geography which gave the following stereotype: "The French are a gay people, addicted to light wines and dancing." This entire concept is presumably based upon the kind of entertainment furnished by enterprising Parisians to American tourists, upon the assumption that gaiety was a desideratum. At the time the geography was written the French were certainly "addicted to light wines" because their water was not safe to drink. Certain facts thus served as a basis for the stereotype, but they were irrelevant.

The American stereotype of the Negro describes him on the negative side as being uneducated, lazy, stupid, ignorant, immoral, overassertive, unstable, and dirty, and ascribes to him on the positive side a genuine interest in religion, a cheerful disposition, a pleasant singing voice, a superior sense of rhythm, and a good deal of dancing ability. This concept also has or has had some basis in fact. As long as Negroes were slaves, they were kept ignorant on purpose, and they were often lazy because slaves have little motive to be anything else. They were uneducated, because the schools and teachers provided for them were inadequate; but wherever the same educational facilities are open to them, they have reached the same levels as white Americans. They appear to have the same range of intelligence as any other racial group. Surely a race that stepped out of slavery only a hundred years ago and in that short period has reached its present level can hardly be regarded as being inherently stupid. It is, of course, true that individual Negroes may have one or more of these negative traits, but so also do individual white people. It

---

[9] See G. W. Allport, *ABC's of Scapegoating*, rev. ed. (Anti-Defamation League of B'nai B'rith, 1948), 56 pp.

is not surprising that Negroes are usually religious, for religion is the refuge of those who need it and serves the black man as an emotional outlet for his many frustrations. Another outlet is supremacy in athletics, one line of endeavor in which the Negro meets with much less discrimination than in other fields.

There does not appear to be any necessary connection between the degree of hostility toward a group and the overt actions of those who hold the prejudice. Thus, the owner of a Southern department store may hold and express great prejudice toward Negroes, but his feelings do not prevent him from hiring Negro girls as clerks. Women customers who are known to have deep-seated prejudice against Negroes or Orientals do not object at all to being waited on by clerks of the supposedly hated group. If a woman goes into a store to buy her husband a shirt, she does not walk out without it just because the saleslady was Jewish, Japanese, Negro, or foreign. Conversely, parents who have literally no racial prejudices may bitterly oppose the marriage of their daughter to a member of some other race than their own for reasons that have nothing to do with racial attitudes. Thus, behavior and prejudice are not necessarily linked.[10]

Stereotypes of Jews differ from those of Negroes. The Jews have formed an "out group" in almost all cultures, largely because their religion has always led them to resist absorption. The feelings of inferiority aroused by intolerance are usually revealed only through the Jew's frequent overcompensation. According to the stereotype, he pushes himself forward—lest he be overlooked —fawns upon those who can help him to be accepted socially, and puts his trust in money as a source of power. He is also considered to be clever, deceitful, overambitious, and sly. Because Jews are commonly successful in material matters, they arouse envy, which Negroes do not. The prejudice against them is therefore strengthened by their success.[11]

It is a curious fact that in Europe, where there are few Negroes and these meet with almost no discrimination, the stereotype of the Jew is almost exactly that of the American Negro in America. Since the two stereotypes of the Jew, as they exist in America and Europe, almost completely contradict each other, it is clear that the source of both lies in the prejudiced person, not in the object of his intolerance.

Reaction to Prejudice   The reaction of the out group to its exclusion may take several forms. Its members may docilely comply with the restrictions set upon them and resign themselves to being unwanted.

---

[10] B. Kutner, et al., "Verbal Attitudes and Overt Behavior Involving Racial Prejudice," *Journal of Abnormal and Social Psychology*, 47:649–652, 1952.
[11] B. Bettelheim and M. Janowitz, *Dynamics of Prejudice: A Psychological and Social Study* (New York: Harper & Row, Publishers, Inc., 1950), 227 pp. See also L. Berkowitz, "Anti-Semitism and Displacement of Aggression," *Journal of Abnormal and Social Psychology*, 59:182–187, 1959.

One sees this attitude among many of the Untouchables of India. Or they may seek protection from the worst of their wrongs by allying themselves with prominent individuals of the in-group. Thus, during the prewar and early war years in Germany, many Jews escaped persecution through individual alliance with powerful non-Jewish figures. A third and very common reaction is to close their ranks and live among themselves, ignoring others as they are ignored. One sees this in the Chinatowns, the Harlems, and the ghettos. Fourth, they may fight back. The most conspicuous modern example of this reaction is furnished by the Israelis. After centuries of trying to solve their problems by not attracting attention to themselves, they seem to have decided to stand and fight. Finally, they may show various forms of compensatory behavior, which show a certain amount of defiance but are not important enough to arouse more than passing resentment. Thus, lower-class Negroes may buy Cadillacs as soon as they can afford them, because these cars are symbols of a higher social status—and they are available without racial restrictions. To a few Negroes they are perhaps also compensatory; that is, the car makes up for some of their earlier deprivations.[12]

Negro children and adolescents have often reported their feelings, which consist of resentment, inferiority, shame, hurt feelings, embarrassment, and fear. Very few can remain indifferent. Their first impulse is usually either to accept the discrimination stoically or to fight, either actually or verbally. Their permanent solution is often a voluntary and complete withdrawal from white children, in order that future situations which might make them uncomfortable should not arise.

Jewish as well as Negro children also usually experience prejudice before the end of their elementary school days. The Gentile children strongly tend to select their best friends from among their own group, thus rejecting their Jewish age-mates except as casual acquaintances. Jewish children and adolescents react to this situation by establishing friendships with other boys of the same faith, although Jewish girls sometimes try to escape from prejudice by seeking social acceptance among Gentile boys and girls. Foreign groups have similar experiences. A study of two thousand 11- to 15-year old children of Italian-born parents shows that rejection by the majority group occurred and had definite effects upon personality. These children manifested feelings of inferiority, awareness of their rejection, poor social adjustment, and emotional instability.[13] If the feeling of frustration becomes sufficiently deep and permanent, serious maladjustment may result.

---

[12] R. I. Yoshino, "The Stereotype of the Negro and His 'High-Priced Car!'" *Sociology and Social Research*, 44:112–118, 1959.

[13] J. W. Tait, "Race Prejudice and Personality," *School*, 34:795–798, 1946; and R. L. Cooper, "The Frustrations of Being a Member of a Minority Group: What Does It Do to the Individual and to His Relationships with Other People?" *Mental Hygiene*, 29:189–195, 1945.

Desegregation   The South has admittedly a great deal to contend with in the matter of desegregation, and changes are sure to come slowly. Thus, in one case, college students—who are presented with all kinds of ideas in their classwork—showed no change as a group between 1955 and 1958. Although the women students had become slightly more tolerant, the males had become equally more intolerant.[14] In Little Rock, Arkansas—the scene of violent riots a few years ago—the white adolescents were still in the main against desegregation, although the Negro pupils still wanted it, but even some of them have their doubts as to its desirability. Both white and Negro students perceived the adult whites of the community as being strongly opposed. It is interesting that those white children who favor desegregation had a more favorable stereotype than did the majority.[15] All the pupils were acutely aware of the general social situation, and all showed intense resistances, mostly of a nature that would make desegregation difficult but not impossible, with time. Not all southerners are, however, equally prejudiced.[16] Those who are young, college educated, and belong to professional occupations tend to be more accepting. It also helps if the individual is well informed concerning the nature of legal sanctions and has a general respect for law. It sometimes seems as if no progress were made in the matter of decreasing prejudice, but actually much has been made, especially in the last decade—enough to be measurable.[17]

Desegregation is not a problem that is restricted to the southern states, although it appears there in acute form. In many cities of the North there is a *de facto* segregation which arises from housing restrictions. If the Negro families live in a given section, the elementary school in that neighborhood is going to be primarily a Negro school. In the area surrounding San Francisco Bay, there are a number of schools in which the enrollment is between 60 and 80 percent Negro, although the division does not rest upon law. Federal, state, and municipal governments are trying to use Negroes all they can in such positions as postmen, firemen, policemen, officials in tax offices, or inspectors for determining who may drive a motor vehicle. This lead has been followed by some of the larger private companies. The outlook is good, but as elsewhere in the United States, the progress is slow, though in the right direction.

It is highly desirable to reduce prejudice for a number of reasons. First,

---

[14] R. K. Young, W. M. Benson, and W. H. Holtzman, "Changes in Attitudes toward the Negro in a Southern University," *Journal of Abnormal and Social Psychology*, 60:131–133, 1960.

[15] M. M. Grossack, "Attitudes Towards Desegregation of Southern White and Negro Children," *Journal of Social Psychology*, 46:299–306, 1957.

[16] L. M. Killiam and J. L. Haer, "Variables Related to Attitudes Regarding School Segregation among White Southerners," *Sociometry*, 21:159–164, 1958.

[17] E. S. Bogardus, "Racial Distance Changes in the United States during the Past Thirty Years," *Sociology and Social Research*, 43:127–134, 1958.

it is a constant threat to the American way of life. Americans cannot go on indefinitely believing that all men are created equal and acting as if 10 percent of them were not. Second, any conflicts that arise between races at once tears a community to pieces, slows down productive work, and interferes with normal social life. Third, prejudice creates an atmosphere in which the greatest bigot can become the leader—as witness, Adolf Hitler. And fourth, as happened in Germany, if the basic rights of man are withheld from one group of citizens, they are soon lost to all. Either everyone's rights are safe, or no one's are. The very people who helped Hitler to deprive the Jews of their right to a trial found themselves not only without rights but even without courts. It is because of the serious situations resulting from discriminatory behavior that the elimination of prejudice in this country has become one of the major problems of the day.[18]

Typical Degrees of Prejudice Shown by Children and Adolescents   What might be called the "normal" growth of attitudes toward two minority groups, the Negroes and the Jews, is shown by a study that extended from the early grades through high school or college. In this investigation, pupils from grades 5 through 12 wrote compositions on "What Is an American?" "What Is a Jew?" and "What Is a Negro?" [19] The topics were given as a routine assignment, without special preparation or reading. It is interesting, incidentally, that criticism of the United States made a spontaneous appearance in these productions, increasing from 6 percent in grade 5 to 21 percent in grade 12. More pupils actively opposed discrimination than actively supported it. Some percent between 2 and 13 volunteered the information that they liked either Jews or Negroes and a similar range volunteered a dislike; in high school a few students (1 to 5 percent) stated that they "hated" Negroes and from 3 to 6 percent that they "hated" Jews. Those who read the compositions classified the characteristics imputed to each group as favorable, inferior, bad, or unique. The percentages in each grade appear in Table 20–1. These particular pupils regarded Negroes mainly as inferior and different rather than bad, and Jews as bad but not inferior. The percentage of favorable comments decreased with age. Some children and adolescents expressed a favorable attitude toward both groups; others had a prejudice against only one, and some expressed intolerance toward both. The percents appear in Table 20–2. Prejudice increases, and those who feel it toward one group tend to feel it toward the other also.[20]

---

[18] E. Raab and S. M. Lipset, *Prejudice and Society* (Anti-Defamation League of B'nai B'rith), 1959, 48 pp.

[19] M. Radke and J. Sutherland, "Children's Concepts and Attitudes about Minority and Majority American Groups," *Journal of Educational Psychology*, 40:449–468, 1949.

[20] See also E. T. Prothro, "Ethnocentrism and Anti-Negro Attitudes in the Deep South," *Journal of Abnormal and Social Psychology*, 47:105–108, 1952.

Table 20–1: CHARACTERISTICS IMPUTED TO NEGROES AND JEWS
(*The figures are percentages*)

	Negroes Grades				Jews Grades			
Characteristics	5–6	7–8	9–10	11–12	5–6	7–8	9–10	11–12
Favorable	34	36	27	21	20	13	13	16
Inferior	26	41	39	67	4	4	3	8
Bad	0	18	23	27	50	45	69	80
Unique	22	10	12	25	22	21	7	5

SOURCE: Based on M. Radke and J. Sutherland, "Children's Concepts and Attitudes about Minority and Majority American Groups," *Journal of Educational Psychology,* 40:449–468, 1949.

Reduction of Prejudice Various people have attempted to reduce the amount of already measured prejudice in a given group. The logical assumption was that an intolerant person will lose his negative attitudes once he is given adequate information about, and adequate contact with, those whom he dislikes. The matter is, however, not so simple, because prejudice rests upon emotional rather than intellectual grounds. There seems to be practically no relationship between knowledge of and feeling toward a group, and an already established prejudice is reduced only a little if at all by supplying facts to counterbalance it. Nor does more education have much effect. Increased education can give information about Negroes, their problems, and the condition under which they live but can still fail to dent basic attitudes.

Table 20–2: CHANGES IN TOLERANCE TOWARD NEGROES AND JEWS
(*The figures are percentages*)

	Grades			
	5–6	7–8	9–10	11–12
Favorable to both Negroes and Jews	54	47	32	32
Favorable to one group but not the other	29	20	20	8
Negative to both groups	17	33	48	60

SOURCE: Based on M. Radke and J. Sutherland, "Children's Concepts and Attitudes about Minority and Majority American Groups," *Journal of Educational Psychology,* 40:449–468, 1949.

Another favorite suggestion for the reduction of intolerance between races has been the establishment of personal contacts between individual members of two cultures. This idea is just a variation on the theme that prejudice is due to ignorance and will disappear if one becomes acquainted with members of a disliked group. Simple contact does not, however, prove effective, and it sometimes increases rather than decreases prejudice. In one actual experiment of having Negro and white boys in the same summer camp, the boys of both races who were already frustrated, inclined to aggression, and defiant of authority, became more intolerant than before.[21] There was, at the same time, a decrease in prejudice among those who already had many friends, were well adjusted, and showed few signs of aggressive needs. The contact in this instance acted selectively, having its greatest influence where it was least needed. Obviously, if contact alone were enough, some of the most deep-seated cases of intolerance would never have arisen. There is more daily contact between whites and Negroes in the South than in the North, but the intolerance is higher. What does seem to have some effect is acquaintance-ship with *superior* members of another group.[22] Thus a concert by Marian Anderson or a commencement address by Ralph Bunche may modify anti-Negro prejudice more quickly than daily contact with the Negro men who collect the trash.

Perhaps the most effective method of reducing prejudice is to reduce the discrimination first and let the prejudice decrease itself from lack of nourish-ment. To use this method, however, one must have some form of authority at the outset. Both organized baseball and the armed forces have been able to use this technique.

Community practice in the 1920 to 1930 decade was opposed to the hiring of Negro baseball players. At that time, although there was no law against hiring a Negro, the community attitude was in favor of restricting the game to white men. However, no one knows better than a baseball scout that talent is where you find it. The existing clubs needed new talent to keep the game alive, and the Negroes represented the greatest reservoir of untapped talent in the country. Once the color line was crossed, Negroes poured into the game. The youngster who now goes to a ball game sees for himself that from a third to a half of the players are Negroes, he hears the wild applause for many of them, and his baseball hero may well be a Negro. He probably does not think of it, but it can hardly fail to influence him that the Negro's batting average is calculated just like a white man's, that his participation in the game is exactly the same, that an inferior white player is not substituted for a superior Negro player, and so on. As a result, the present generation of small boys should grow up with less prejudice, because they see and indulge in less discriminatory behavior than did the small boy of 1920. This approach to the problem of reducing prejudice is likely to prove more fruitful than endless arguments.

---

[21] P. H. Mussen, "Some Personal and Social Factors Related to Changes in Chil-dren's Attitudes toward Negroes," *Journal of Abnormal and Social Psychology*, 45:423–441, 1950.

[22] B. K. MacKenzie, "The Importance of Contact in Determining Attitudes toward Negroes," *Journal of Abnormal and Social Psychology*, 43:417–441, 1948.

Another example comes from the military. In 1948 President Truman ordered that the armed forces be thoroughly and effectively integrated. By 1953, only five years after the original directive, Negroes and whites not only trained together, they slept in the same barracks, ate at the same tables, and went to church or movies together. The officers' clubs were thrown open to Negro officers—and there were some—and to Negro aviators. There have been no incidents of any moment between recruits of different races. The *de facto* situation has been accepted even by the boys from the Deep South. By acting in a nondiscriminatory way, the amount of prejudice has been visibly reduced.

Perhaps solution-by-fiat is the best single answer, but in dealing with the general population it is difficult to find a voice that can speak with enough authority to be obeyed without the use of force.

▶ Identifications

The world is full of heroes and hero worshippers of all ages and conditions. Identification of oneself with a hero and conscious imitation of him are presumably as old as humanity. The process is extremely useful at all ages and is especially so in adolescence, when ideals are in process of formation.

Identification begins early, with the small child's intense love of his parents and his efforts to be like them. Most children develop a similar attitude toward at least one elementary school teacher or a Sunday school teacher, a Boy Scout or Camp Fire Girls leader, a movie hero, a camp counselor, or other adult who is the embodiment of perfection at the moment. That the hero has a great effect upon the young worshipper cannot be doubted. One has only to count Spaceman shirts—or whatever other kind may be in vogue by the time this book appears—worn by the neighborhood small fry to find evidence of hero worship. Some youngsters prefer a fictional character or one taken from popular cartoons. During preadolescence and adolescence, most girls find the personification of their ideals in movie, television, or stage actresses, or occasionally in men singers, and sometimes in their teachers. Adolescent boys tend to choose either athletic heroes or men who play glamorous but highly adventurous roles in the movies or on television; they reject the "great lovers," who appeal mainly to girls in their late adolescence and to maladjusted women. As children grow older and learn about historical or present-day public figures, some of them substitute characters they read about for people they know.

Three investigations of ideals at different ages will be summarized briefly. The first concerns the identification of school pupils at three age levels—7 to 8, 11 to 12, and 15 to 16. The main results appear in Table 20–3. There is a decrease in the proportion of school pupils who identify themselves with any

Table 20–3: IDENTIFICATIONS AT DIFFERENT AGES
(*The figures are percentages*)

	Age Groups		
	7–8	11–12	15–16
With members of the family	52	20	13
With adults in family	38	17	10
With well-known persons	12	28	44
With movie or radio stars	8	30	31
With age-mates	7	5	21

SOURCE: Based on J. B. Winker, "Age Trends and Sex Differences in the Wishes, Identifications, Activities, and Fears of Children," *Child Development,* 20:191–200, 1949.

member of their own family but especially in the identification with adult members. Hero worship of well-known characters increases. At later stages of adolescence the percentages would probably be even higher. Identification with age-mates begins to be important in the early adolescent years and continues to increase throughout the period.

Reports from other countries suggest that the development outlined above may well prove to be universal. Thus, when Australian adolescents were asked to write on the subject, "The Person I Would Like to Be," they showed a similar development with age.[23] The older the pupils were, the fewer parental figures they wished to resemble, and the more they tended either to imaginary ideals or to a combined image of two or more real people, usually people in the public eye. A group of 537 Javanese adolescents showed the same trend. As their model, 35 percent of them chose a person from their own family, school, or friends, while 65 percent selected someone from public life.[24]

In 1956 a total of 1251 German children and adolescents were asked to write two brief compositions, one on the person whom they would most want to be like and why, and a second on the person they would least want to resemble and why.[25] In each case they were also asked to state whether the person were still alive, dead, or purely imaginary. The answers were rather easily classified into the usual groups—persons from the immediate environment, outstanding individuals of the past or present—some, like Sir Galahad of fictional source—and persons who were not and never had been real, but were sometimes combinations of two or more actual people. The younger

[23] D. K. Wheeler, "Development of the Ideal Self in Western Australian Youth," *Journal of Educational Research,* 54:163–167, 1961.

[24] K. Danziger, "Choice of Models among Javanese Adolescents," *Psychological Reports,* 6:346, 1960.

[25] H. Glöckel, "Eine Vergleichsuntersuchung zur Frage jugendlichen Idealerlebens," *Psychologische Rundschau,* 11:1–20, 1960.

members of the group, at ages 10 through 12, saw people as either good or bad, without much in the way of shading or understanding of personality. Those from 12 through 16 were less dogmatic, they often modified their judgments, and they were concerned with traits of character. However, they put more stress than either the younger or the older groups upon external appearance. The members of the oldest group, ages 17–20, were more concerned than either of the others with intrinsic worth; they seemed also to be searching for a personification to provide unity and sense in a chaotic world.

A few samples of childish and adolescent levels might be of interest. The first series contains explanations given as to the person that one would most want to resemble; the second series concerns those that one would least wish to be like. The former are taken from known and living persons, the second from historical or more or less literary characters.

A. Most want to be like: (Girls)

1. My mother because she loves me and takes such good care of me.
2. My mother because she can get along so well with other people. I value her very highly because she shows tact and understanding for the silly things I do and calls my attention in a friendly way to the outbreaks in my behavior. I emphasize that I do not regard her wholly as an ideal but rather I see her as a person who possesses the traits that I should like to make my own. Above everything she possesses intelligence and a keen understanding.
3. I would like to be like my mother. We live in straitened circumstances. But we always managed somehow, thanks to my mother. She is never demanding, and she has taken all the sorrows without ever saying a word. She never complains. May I also be able to carry sorrows and burdens and worries and pain as well as she did!

B. Least wish to be like: (Boys)

1. Tarzan because he is the greatest liar and because he never dies. There is no one so strong that he is equal to twenty or thirty gorillas.
2. Hitler because he condemned to death so many Jews and many other people and butchered them so horribly.
3. Hannibal, not because he showed any bad personal characteristics but far more because of his sad fate. He found no gratitude of any kind from his own city, and he had to die by poison and had moreover a most unpleasant life.

C. Refusal of Ideal:

1. I don't want to be like anyone, because I want to be a unique personality.
2. I have no ideal person, and I wouldn't want to have one. I'll do what I consider good and not rely upon other people.[26]

---

[26] H. Glöckel, "Eine Vergleichsuntersuchung zur Frage jugendlichen Idealerlebens," *Psychologische Rundschau,* 11:1–20, 1960, pp. 6, 8, 11.

The first two series show a quite clear development from a childish attitude to a late adolescent level. The last group proves only that Germany still has young people with their own ideas!

▶ **Summary**

Research into attitudes and beliefs shows that young people reflect faithfully the attitudes of their elders, but also that they tend to modify these points of view as they grow older and are influenced by various individuals and agencies outside the home. Their attitudes toward the members of various nationalities, races, and ethnic groups are compounded of those of their parents and teachers, plus those which grow out of current events. Certain traits of personality and certain background conditions tend to produce intolerance and prejudice, while contrasting influences tend to produce tolerance. Information, as usually given at least, does not seem to be an important factor in the development of attitude. Most prejudices are of emotional origin and may be merely projections by means of which an individual rids himself of emotional tension.

Children tend to identify themselves with some older person from their immediate neighborhood—a parent, family friend, teacher, Scout leader, and so on. In preadolescence and early adolescence many boys and girls select either a more or less public character or a successful young adult or a historical character as an ideal. This phase is relatively short and seems to be based upon glamour or financial success. The commonest ideal in the later adolescent years is an imaginary person who has the positive characteristics of former identifications and acts as an "ideal" self.

References for Further Reading

BOOKS

Other Texts

Ausubel, *Theory and Problems of Adolescent Development* (Chap. 9).
Breckenridge and Vincent, *Child Development* (Chap. 14).
Garrison, *Growth and Development* (pp. 160–188).
Horrocks, *Behavior and Development* (pp. 597–601 and 611–619).
Jones, *Growth and Behavior in Adolescence* (pp. 215–232).
Kuhlen, *Psychology of Adolescent Development* (pp. 399–438).
McCandless, *Children and Adolescents* (Chap. 11 or 12).
Wattenberg, *The Adolescent Years* (Chap. 16).

Other Books and Monographs

Buchanan, W., and H. Cantril, *How Nations See Each Other* (Urbana, Ill.: University of Illinois Press, 1953), 220 pp. (any 25 pages).

Clark, K. B., *Prejudice and Your Child* (Boston: The Beacon Press, 1955), 151 pp. (any two chapters).

Corder, F. R., "A Factorial Approach to Anti-Democratic Attitudes," *Purdue University Studies in Higher Education,* No. 82, 1954, 42 pp.

Hirsh, S. G., *The Fears Men Live By* (New York: Harper & Row, Publishers, Inc., 1955), 164 pp. (Chap. 1, 2, 3, or 5).

Raab, E., and S. M. Lipset, *Prejudice and Society* (Anti-Defamation League), 1959, 48 pp.

Seidman, *The Adolescent: A Book of Readings,* rev. ed. (Nos. 56 and 57).

ARTICLES

Albright, L. E., *et al.,* "A Longitudinal Comparison of Student Attitudes Toward Minorities," *Journal of Educational Psychology,* 47:372–379, 1956.

Berkowitz, L., "Anti-Semitism and the Displacement of Aggression," *Journal of Abnormal and Social Psychology,* 59:182–187, 1959.

Bogardus, E. S., "Racial Distance Changes in the United States during the Past Thirty Years," *Sociology and Social Research,* 43:127–134, 1958.

Fitt, A. B., "A Study of Racial Attitudes during and after the War, by the Thurstone Technique," *British Journal of Psychology,* 46:306–309, 1955.

Gordon, R., "Personal Dynamics and the Tendency toward Stereotypy," *International Social Science Journal,* 6:571–576, 1954.

Kelly, J. C., *et al.,* "The Measurement of Attitudes toward Negroes in the South," *Journal of Social Psychology,* 48:305–317, 1959.

Killian, L. M., and J. L. Haer, "Variables Related to Attitudes regarding School Segregation among White Southerners," *Sociometry,* 21:159–164, 1958.

Kohn, J. D., and E. T. Prothro, "National Preferences of University Students from 23 Nations," *Journal of Psychology,* 42:283–294, 1956.

Lambert, W. E., and O. Klinsberg, "A Pilot Study of the Origin and Development of National Stereotypes," *International Social Science Journal,* 11:221–238, 1959.

Lief, H. I., and I. P. Stevenson, "Psychological Aspects of Prejudice with Special Reference to Desegregation," *American Journal of Psychiatry,* 114:816–823, 1958.

Nelson, E. N. P., "Persistence of Attitudes of College Students Fourteen Years Later," *Psychological Monographs,* Vol. 68, No. 373, 1954.

Smythe, H. H., and M. Seidman, "Name-Calling: A Significant Factor in Human Relations," *Human Relations,* 6:71–77, 1957.

Tumin, M., *et al.,* "Education, Prejudice, and Discrimination: A Study in Readiness for Desegregation," *American Sociological Review,* 23:41–49, 1958.

Wheeler, D. K., "Development of the Ideal Self in Western Australian Youth," *Journal of Educational Research,* 54:163–167, 1961.

Winkler, J. B., "Age Trends and Sex Differences in the Wishes, Identifications, Activities, and Fears of Children," *Child Development,* 20:191–200, 1949.

Suggested Research Problems [27]

1. Study of adolescent ideals and philosophy of life by means of case histories, with inclusion of *all* standards, whether or not socially approved.

---

[27] See note on p. 11.

Chapter 21 | Religious Beliefs and Moral Behavior

THE material of the present chapter is concerned with three main topics: the typical religious beliefs and attitudes of adolescents, the growth of ideas about morals and moral behavior, and the development of a philosophy of life. Whenever possible, the writers have selected articles that show developments with age, but such articles are not to be found on every topic. All the material taken together gives a fair picture of the religious attitudes and experiences of adolescents.

▶ Religious Attitudes and Interests

Ideas on religious questions, interest in religion, degrees of conviction, and attitudes toward religious matters all vary with age and develop by a fairly orderly series of changes that continue into adult life.

Small children often show a free, unconventional, and vigorous imagination in their thinking about religion. For instance, one little boy drew three lines that swept across a page as if he were trying to represent a windstorm and said that he had drawn a picture of God. Another drew the back of a man's head and said that one could not draw God's face because it shone so brightly one never saw it. Many children show a tendency to deify their parents, as their first concept of God. One writer has postulated three stages of religious development among children: [1] the fairy-tale stage, during which children have all manner of fanciful beliefs; the realistic stage, during which they reject earlier imaginings and give explanations in terms of natural phenomena; and the individualistic stage, during which they begin to select from religion the elements that satisfy their own needs and drives. In general, children tend to accept such formal religious concepts as their elders choose to offer them, without doubt as to their correctness but not without many questions as to their nature. As children approach adolescence and begin to question authority of all kinds, they may revolt from church as well as from both home and school domination. A considerable number of adolescents investigate religion anew as a possible source of both emotional and intellectual stimulation and satisfaction. At each age beyond 15, more and more boys and

---

[1] E. Harms, "The Development of Religious Experience in Children," *American Journal of Sociology*, 50:112–122, 1944.

girls become critical of religion. After becoming adults, many of them settle down to a rather indifferent, though tolerant, attitude. Religion would seem to have some value to children, although probably none of the usual adult values, since children do not have the mental ability to understand the basic ideas and ideals. Perhaps they derive a measure of security from their belief in a God who watches over them and a relief from their feelings of guilt if they have trust in God's forgiveness. Adolescents want to find something in religion, but many of them fail to do so, and their reactions to failure often take

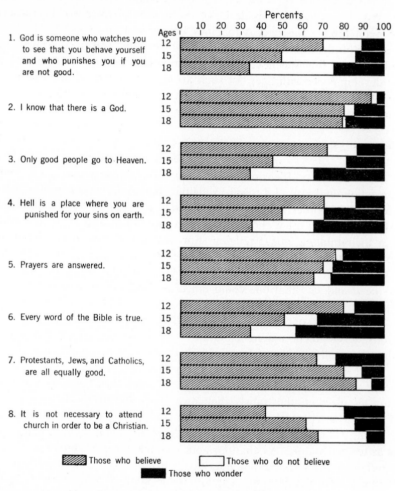

Fig. 21–1. Changes in religious beliefs with age

Based on R. G. Kuhlen and M. Arnold, "Age Differences in Religious Beliefs and Problems during Adolescence," *Pedagogical Seminary and Journal of Genetic Psychology,* 65:291–300, 1944.

the form of intolerance, cynicism, and withdrawal from contact with church activities. The hostility eventually dies out, however, and adults again find values, although not necessarily religious ones, in religion.

In an old but still informative study, the investigator traced the growth of attitudes on eighteen religious problems between the ages of 12 and 18. Results for a few typical items appear in Figure 21–1. At the right are three shaded lines indicating the percentage of pupils at ages 12, 15, and 18 who believed, did not believe, or wondered about each proposition. In some cases the decrease in belief is due to an increase of pupils who rejected the proposition (No. 1); in some cases the decrease is due primarily to an increase in those who merely wondered about its correctness (No. 4).

In spite of more or less talk to the contrary, presumably by a highly vocal minority, there is still a good deal of interest in religion on the part of adolescents. One of the more impressive reports comes from an analysis of 3676 essays written anonymously by high school seniors in Los Angeles. Of this number, 36 percent attended church regularly, 52 percent irregularly, and 12 percent never or almost never. Their urge for going came from a desire to honor or learn more about God (41 percent), from pressure by their parents (28 percent), from pressure by their own consciences (23 percent), or from a desire for fellowship (8 percent). Of the 436 who never went to church, only 18 (4 percent) stayed away from lack of belief; almost 90 percent of the nonattenders said they believed in religion, but were prevented from attendance by work or lack of transportation. A total of 3317 seniors also wrote on prayer, but only 520 of the papers were sufficiently articulate to be worth analyzing. The reasons given for praying are listed in Table 21–1.

Table 21–1: REASONS FOR PRAYER

Reasons	Percent
1. To ask for personal benefits	22
2. To express thanks	19
3. To talk to God	15
4. To ask for guidance	11
5. To comply with habit	10
6. To seek comfort	8
7. To ask help for others	5
8. To ask for forgiveness	5

SOURCE: Based on E. Pixley and E. Beekman, "The Faith of Youth as Shown in the Public Schools of Los Angeles," *Religious Education*, 44:338, 1949.

The impression one gets from this study is that these adolescents, at least, were far from godless. A few brief quotations from their papers on prayer are reproduced below:

Of course many people need prayer as a spiritual cleansing. Even as you sometimes feel you would like to talk to someone heart to heart, I can understand how others would get things off their chest and stabilize their perhaps tottering beliefs through prayer.

I, like many teen-agers, am very close to God in my feelings, yet often do not show this openly. Many young people have more faith than adults believe. I can talk to God when I can talk to nobody else. He is a friend who will always be with me in the darkness of my room. I often say prayers that are memorized but I get more satisfaction from making up my own—I feel that I am talking to God and that he is listening.

Like all humans, I only call upon God's help when everything else seems to fail. It is not right to do this; I think there should be time for prayer in every day. But to be truthful, I only give prayer when I need help, when a situation arises which is too large for me to untangle.

I, for one, do not pray often, and I know of few people who do, except when they want something. Whether it was the same situation in past generations, I do not know, but I imagine it was different. Why the change is in our generation I do not know. But I do know that one who is brave enough to admit that he prays is laughed at by most high school students of today. This is not because of the training we have had, but the lack of it.

I don't believe in prayers. When I was ten years old I wanted a bicycle very much, so prayed in order to get it, I would pray every morning, and at night before I would go to bed; sometimes when I had time during the day I prayed too. I didn't get the bike, so I could never again see any sense in praying. Since that time on I never prayed again.[2]

This series of reactions represents a wide range of opinions and feelings, such as might probably be obtained from any other large group.

There have been a number of good studies concerning the degree of religious interest typical among high school or college students. In one case,[3] the majority of high school students held favorable attitudes toward religion, and more than half went to church every Sunday and prayed every day. Among a group of college students, 80 percent said they had faith in Christ,[4] but only a third read the Bible or prayed regularly. However, those who scored highest in religious beliefs were less worried, less introverted, and had better adjustment to their families than the nonbelievers. Among Catholic students, the figures for church attendance were somewhat higher. Of the 1668 questioned, over 90 percent went to Easter confession and a similar number attended Mass every Sunday.[5]

---

[2] E. Pixley and E. Beekman, "The Faith of Youth as Shown in the Public Schools of Los Angeles," *Religious Education*, 44:338–340, 1949.

[3] M. S. Myers, "The Role of Certain Religious Values for High School Youth," *Studies in Higher Education*, Purdue University, 79:79–85, 1951.

[4] D. G. Brown and W. L. Lowe, "Religious Belief and Personality Characteristics of College Students," *Journal of Social Psychology*, 33:103–129, 1951.

[5] J. H. Fichter, "The Profile of Catholic Religious Life," *American Journal of Sociology*, 58:145–150, 1952.

A 1961 English study, involving nearly 4000 adolescents in eight secondary schools, tested attitudes toward religious training by means of an attitude scale. The highest possible score was 11 and the lowest 0; the lower the score the more favorable the attitude. The 1950 girls were slightly more favorable (average, 3.66) than the 2088 boys (average, 4.40) but the entire group average was low, at 4.04, showing in general an acceptance of values in religious education and training. The first-year pupils scored lowest—most favorable—and there was a steady rise to a slightly less favorable attitude by the fourth-year boys and girls.[6]

In 1950 a total of 8000 high school students were asked to mark such items as "I believe that religious faith is better than logic for solving life's important problems," or, "I believe that God knows our every thought and movement."[7] On the basis of the results, the investigator calculated an "orthodoxy" score, with the distribution shown in Figure 21–2. These students varied from those who were completely unorthodox to those who were completely orthodox in their beliefs. Moreover, the four largest groups are all at the orthodox end of the scale. These studies suggest that the youth of today retain rather faithfully the religious attitudes of their elders.

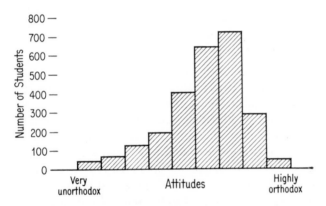

Fig. 21–2. Orthodoxy scores

Based on M. S. Myers, "Latent Role of Religious Orientation," *Studies in Higher Education,* Purdue University, 78:61–94, 1951.

In 1952 a Swedish investigator asked school pupils of various ages to complete a story or episode that began with the words: "One time I thought of God . . . ." The pupils were to finish the story in any way they saw fit. Some of the writers were children, and some were adolescents. The greatest

[6] F. D. Garrity, "A Study of the Attitude of Some Secondary Modern School Pupils towards Religious Education," *Religious Education,* 56:141–143, 1961.

[7] M. S. Myers, "Latent Role of Religious Orientation," *Studies in Higher Education,* Purdue University, 78:61–94, 1951.

single reason for thinking about God was in an emergency of some kind; 44 percent of the boys' statements and 26 percent of the girls' concerned some difficulty in which the thought of God came to them. Sometimes a moral question was involved, and sometimes not. Others were stimulated to think of God during church services or when they were in a particularly beautiful environment. Two typical reports are presented here:

> Child, age 10: One time I was alone in a room. There were 20 kroner [coins] lying on the table. I was greatly tempted to take them. In fact, I had already stuffed 10 kroner into my pocket when something inside me said, "Put them back! Put them back!" I think that it was God who talked with me. I laid the 10 kroner back on the table. At the time I knew surely that God had spoken to me.

> Adolescent: When we read about astronomy in school I immediately became greatly fascinated by how ingeniously the universe was constructed. Then the thought came to me: "Who has created all this?" God, naturally. God cannot help wanting to look after what He has created. Yes, He is, as everyone says, all-powerful. Never before had I really thought what it meant that God was almighty. But it became clear to me in that hour.[8]

One investigator has studied the nature of religious controls and the benefits that arise from them.[9] The notion that ethical behavior is a central religious requirement was strong in ancient Judaism and has remained strong in all derived religions, probably because of its great value to society in contributing to social stability. The church has also always provided leaders with whom the young could identify themselves. In general, the religions have not tried to eliminate basic instinctual drives but only to control and redirect them. Religions have also always tried to control aggressive behavior—and have often succeeded. By providing surrender and expiation, a religion makes it possible for a wrongdoer to cast off the burden of guilt and start anew. All of these elements have value for modern society. Although religious matters give rise to a good deal of dispute and emotional upheaval, it may well be that the church will turn out to be one of the great stabilizing forces of the world.

Before making any assessment of the value of religion and of its relationship to other factors, such as prejudice, personal maladjustment, or normalcy, one should consider that there are two fundamental patterns in religion, and the conclusions will depend upon what pattern is meant. There is a type of religion that is destructive because it fosters dependency, unreality, and rigidity; the second type fosters the growth of inner resources and a better adjustment to other people.[10] It is this dichotomy in what religion means to different people that leads to much contradictory evidence.

The outstanding emotional values of religion to adolescents, and prob-

---

[8] G. Klingberg, *Studier Barnens Religiösa Liv*, Diakonistrylses Bokforlag, 1953, pp. 103 and 116.

[9] M. Ostow, "The Nature of Religious Controls," *American Psychologist*, 131:571–574, 1958.

[10] W. Oates, *Religious Factors in Mental Illness* (Association Press, 1955), 239 pp.

ably to adults also, are three in number. There is first the catharsis of guilt feelings through prayer, the confessional, or talks with ministers. The resulting feeling of being cleansed of sin, of being given another chance, and of reduced tension is of great value in adjustment. A second value is the increase of security, sometimes relatively superficial and sometimes profound, that may result from religious belief. A trust in God prevents the panic of despair, a belief in personal immortality with its promise of an everlasting perpetuation of the ego prevents the fear of death, the membership in a group gives a sense of belonging, and the chance to work with and help others leads to helpful identifications and attitudes. These values are not all of a religious nature, but they are of assistance in the search for happiness and adjustment. Religion may, therefore, be an important contributing factor to mental health.[11] Finally, religion can become the basis for a sound philosophy of life, even though it does not always do so.

▶ Moral Attitudes and Behavior

The studies to be reported are of three types. First comes a brief summary of an old but extremely good study into the behavior of school children and adolescents. The pupils were given chances to cheat without their knowing it, and a record was kept as to whether or not they availed themselves of the opportunity. Honesty was studied in both school and play activities. The second type of investigation is concerned with ideas of honesty and moral behavior. A third section deals with the development of ideas as to what is right and what is wrong.

The extent of dishonest behavior, as measured in the first study mentioned above, correlated directly or inversely with a number of factors, some of which are shown in Figure 21–3. The first set of bars shows the percentage of cheating on school examinations by children at different levels of intelligence; the brighter the children were, the less they cheated. The second part of the figure gives the percentage of dishonesty shown by children from homes of different cultural and economic levels; the better the home, the less the dishonesty. The third set of bars illustrates the relation between suggestibility and dishonest behavior. The more suggestible children were, the more they cheated. The last section of the figure shows dishonesty to be related positively to retardation in school and negatively to acceleration. If a child is bright, accelerated, resistant to suggestion, and a member of a good family, there is little likelihood that he will be dishonest; if he is dull, retarded, suggestible, and a member of an uncultured family he is almost certain to be.

Three studies present the opinions of children and adolescents, in one

[11] L. G. Fein, "Religious Observance and Mental Health," *Journal of Pastoral Care,* 12:99–101, 1958. See also R. F. Gayle, "Conflict and Co-operation between Psychiatry and Religion," *Pastoral Psychology,* 7:29–36, 1956 and *Report of the Academy of Mental Health and Religion,* 1957, 107 pp.

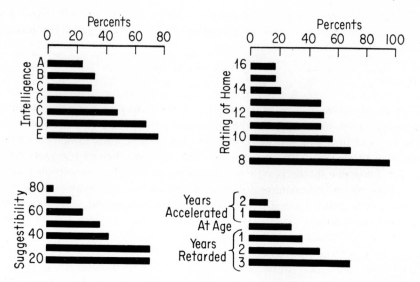

Fig. 21-3. Factors correlated with dishonesty (Bars indicate percent of cheating.)

From H. Hartshorne and M. May, *Studies in Character* (New York: The Macmillan Company, 1928), I, 183, 261, 215, and 279. Used with the permission of the publisher.

case about stealing, in another about various mild forms of deception, and in a third about lying under different circumstances. Among 184 pupils who answered a series of questions about various forms of stealing, only 12 percent maintained an absolute standard of honesty in their answers and insisted that stealing was wrong, no matter what it was called, or what was stolen, or who had previously owned the stolen object, or what circumstances prevailed at the time.[12] Just two thirds of the pupils showed a sliding scale of morality by condoning stealing under at least one and often several such circumstances as these:

1. Stealing from a corporation, not an individual.
2. Stealing from either corporation or individual who would never notice the loss.
3. Stealing whatever careless people had left lying around.
4. Stealing from people who are strangers or members of a despised racial or social group.
5. Stealing things of low intrinsic value.
6. Stealing from members of the family.
7. Stealing that is never detected.
8. Stealing from a person whom you dislike or who has been disagreeable to you.

The remaining 22 percent marked the statement that they would refrain from stealing only if they were fairly sure of being punished.

[12] C. B. Stendler, "A Study of Some Socio-Moral Judgments of Junior High School Children," *Child Development,* 20:15-28, 1949.

In the second study, 328 normal boys of 9, 12, and 15 years of age were presented with a series of described situations, such as the following:

A boy got on to a bus. The crowd pushed him into the bus and got between him and the conductor, so that he could not drop his fare into the box. The boy thought that it was not his fault that he did not pay, so he got off the bus without doing so.[13]

The pupils answered two questions about each story: "If this had happened to you, would you have done what he did?" and "Would it be right for you to do what he did?" Between the ages of 9 and 15 the anticipated behavior became steadily less moral. That is, more 15-year-olds than 9-year-olds admitted they would indulge in minor dishonesties. But their awareness that such behavior was wrong increased steadily with age. Only 37 percent at age 9 condemned the dishonesties, but by age 12, 84 percent did so, and by age 15, 92 percent. This study suggests strongly that knowledge of right and wrong is by no means sufficient to produce moral behavior.

This last point is further emphasized by another study that shows no relation between moral knowledge and moral behavior.[14] Indeed, the two traits seem to have different rates of growth and to be produced by different conditions. Moral knowledge alone is not adequate for the production of moral behavior, although it undoubtedly is one of the contributing factors.

It does not take an adolescent long to find out that there is a difference between what he is told in generalized terms to do and what is demanded specifically by a given situation. Granted that one must never tell a lie, and that lying is wrong, but what does one do when the truth would hurt a dozen people? It is "wrong" to deceive and "wrong" to resist authority, but it is also "wrong" to tell on one's friends. These clashes between generalized truths and specific situations are constantly arising. Most adolescents compromise by paying lip-service to whatever they think is expected of them and then solving the problems of daily life on other terms.[15] This dichotomy can be distressing, and its end results can be very bad indeed. It explains perhaps why the man who attends church and really believes all the doctrines but pays no real attention to them in his daily life is precisely the one who can become a fanatic, because his daily behavior easily leads him into discriminatory practices which are in contradiction to everything he believes. But it has probably always been so since his adolescent days; there has been one set of rules that he subscribed to and another that he followed.

The need of preadolescents to form groups for mutual support and the value of these groups in helping develop moral attitudes is clearly shown in a study of juvenile cliques in Australia and England by means of an inquiry into

---

[13] E. K. Beller, "Two Attitude Components in Younger Boys," *Journal of Social Psychology*, 29:137–151, 1949.

[14] D. McRae, "A Test of Piaget's Theories of Moral Development," *Journal of Abnormal and Social Psychology*, 49:14–18, 1954.

[15] J. F. Morris, "II. The Development of Adolescent Value Judgments," *British Journal of Educational Psychology*, 28:1–14, 1958.

the history of prospective teachers in training during the years 1948–1955.[16] Of the young men, 90 percent had been members of preadolescent groups that were noncriminal and nonviolent, although sometimes mildly antisocial. Only 40 percent of the girls had belonged to such a clique. A total of 326 "gangs" was reported by the men and only 54 by the women. In all cases the groups dispersed of their own accord as the members reached adolescence. The boys indulged in a number of slightly predatory acts such as raiding orchards or teasing girls, in socially disapproved acts such as smoking or swearing, in socially approved acts such as collecting money for charities, in sports, and in a limited amount of exploratory sex activity. These small groups seem to have served a real function in transferring a boy's or girl's main allegiance from home to peers, and thus preparing the way for eventual emancipation. They also served to help the boys and girls in an establishment of modified, workable values and in the submission of the individual to the desires of the group. On the whole, they were probably more helpful than harmful.

What adolescent intellectual development can add to the notions of honesty held by children is an ideal of honesty. A child typically lacks ideals, because he does not have the intellectual capacity to understand them. His behavior is therefore based mainly upon the specific habits in which he has been trained. He regards as "right" those actions he has been allowed to do, or rewarded for doing; he regards as "wrong" both those actions of his own that have met with punishment and whatever other behavior he has heard condemned verbally by elders in whom he has confidence. Since concepts grow out of experiences, the child with socially acceptable habits usually grows up into the adolescent with socially acceptable ideals. Hence the vital importance of training children in desirable habits. The small boy who "swipes" other pupils' erasers, buys candy with money given him to put on the collection plate, and cheats in games is laying the basis from which he will develop the ideal that dishonest conduct is wrong only when it is detected. No other general principle could reasonably be deduced from his early experiences. To be sure, the period of adolescence may bring new experiences, and these will, in turn, lead to modifications. However, the essential connection between childhood experiences and adolescent ideals should not be forgotten.

The adolescent can identify the common element in his many previous experiences with honesty and can therefore obtain a generalized meaning of the term. He can also apply his concept to new situations. When this stage is reached, the adolescent has achieved an ideal, which becomes his "guide to conduct" in situations that are unfamiliar. Every normal adolescent has ideals, although they are not necessarily acceptable. The boy who sees in many diverse situations the ability of the strong to coerce the weak may develop the ideal that "might makes right." He then uses it to guide his own conduct and

---

[16] R. A. Crane, "The Development of Moral Values in Children: II. Preadolescent Gangs," *British Journal of Educational Psychology,* 28:201–208, 1958.

as a basis for judging new situations. His generalization is just as truly an "ideal" as a conviction that the strong should protect the weak.

A few examples of how a guiding principle may grow out of specific experiences may be of interest. In some cases, the ideals were translated into vocational ambitions.

Marjorie and Ellen were classmates in a fashionable day school. Marjorie was the daughter of the local tycoon. Ellen's father was a minister, and she was at the school on a scholarship. However, the two girls were friends. One rainy day Marjorie found that she had left her purse at home and asked Ellen for the necessary dime for carfare—this happened in the days before automobiles. Ellen had only a dime, but she gave it willingly to Marjorie, not telling her that it was all she had. Marjorie went off on the streetcar, and Ellen walked home in a downpour of rain. The next two days Ellen was absent, and on the third Marjorie stopped off at Ellen's house to find out what was wrong. She was met by Ellen's father who told her that Ellen was just paying for her own carelessness; she had had a dime for carfare, but she had lost it and had had to walk home in the rain. Consequently, she had caught a bad head cold. Suddenly it crashed through to Marjorie that the supposedly lost dime was the one which Ellen had given her, so that she should not get wet. She explained to Ellen's father and wanted to see her friend and thank her. But the minister refused. He told Marjorie, "If Ellen had wanted you to know she would have told you at the time. She doesn't want to be thanked for doing what she thought was right." This was a point of view that Marjorie had never met before in her wealthy home. She was aware that her father gave money to charities of various kinds, but a simple act of anonymous kindness was new to her. She thought about it for some time, carefully refrained from telling Ellen that she had found her out, watched Ellen unobtrusively doing similar small acts of kindness for many other girls, and decided that here was a way of life about which she wanted to know more. At the end of her secondary school course Marjorie was supposed to become a debutante, but instead she shocked her family by announcing that she was going into the local hospital and become a nurse. What is more, she did—and has not regretted it. This girl whose normal future would have been that of the social butterfly was influenced to become something more useful to humanity through a small incident that made a great impression upon her.

When I was 15 years of age my daddy was out of work, as he is now. I liked to look through the catalogue of children's clothes and then tell mother how I would like to have a little girl and boy and buy them anything on that page that they wanted. I often said that I would like to have a big car piled full of packages and then go in some poor sections and give food, clothing, and toys to poor families. I joined the Girl Scouts when I was 10 and from them derived an ambition to become a leader. Then I have done a lot of welfare work in our community and I am greatly interested in it. My mother also had some influence over me in that matter because she said she always had the same desire.

My mother and I had been to the theater and decided to follow Tremont Street and see where it led. It led to no pot of gold. I had never seen such absolute filth and laziness before, not even in New York (although I have never been to the poorest sections of New York). I never want to see it again.

It was not so much that these people are throwing their lives away but for the future generations that I care. No children should live like that. They should live in the country and bring up their children there. . . . I have seen the babies in the tenement houses with swollen heads because of lack of milk. The hot, sweaty odor that comes from unsanitary conditions. The mothers fainting, while trying to keep their young alive. The husbands drunk, beating their wives and children. The low, petty thief who never had a chance to better himself.

It sounds rather farfetched for me, a girl, to attempt to better these conditions, but in newspaper work, if you ever acquire much of a following, you can do most anything and I plan to make people see just what a little money and kindness can do for these people.[17]

Hans was a German boy of 16 at the end of the last war. At the beginning he had been a child of 10. His family lived not far from the Polish border. Toward the end of the war it became necessary to flee to the West. Up until the middle years of the conflict he had been a normally warm-hearted, kind, considerate child, and he seemed destined to grow up into the same type of person as his parents—socially-oriented, sympathetic, responsible. In the course of his long trek by foot he saw old people, cripples, and little children lying exhausted by the roadside, where they had been left because they could not keep up with the hurrying refugees. He saw people fight for a crust of bread. He saw men trample women and children to reach shelter when a bomber flew over the road. For three years he lived from hand to mouth, stuffing himself with food on the rare occasions when he could and going without food for days when he could not. He stole if he had to. After the war was over and he had completed his education and was living a normal life, he was not at all the adult that would have been predicted from the child he had been. He is inconsiderate, indifferent to the needs of others, ruthless in gaining his ends, and unmoved by the sight of suffering. He clings to his own possessions, belongs to no organizations, makes no effort to help his parents financially—although he earns more than his father does—refuses to marry, and stockpiles food in his own rooms. His parents never ask for help, but they do reprove him for his utter indifference toward mankind. His only responses are: "In this world it is every man for himself. The strong live,

[17] H. H. Moore, "Autobiographical Sketches of High School Students Revealing Their Social Impulses," *Social Studies*, 26:436–439, 1935. This excerpt is used by permission of *Social Studies*.

and the weak die. I look after myself; let other people do the same." This young man has a "guide to conduct" which influences practically everything he does, and his "ideal" is based upon his own experiences.

▶ **Philosophy of Life**

The modern adolescent wants to find a meaning to life, a synthesis of its discordant values. Certain elements in modern life make this effort of his especially difficult. First, he has from infancy been brought up on an objective, unemotional presentation of scientific facts. He usually knows just enough science to block his acceptance of traditional religion but not enough to make a synthesis of science with religious and moral beliefs. Second, he has moved about a good deal in a radius—large or small—around the center of his home and community; he is acquainted with many people, many customs, and many points of view; he often no longer has any roots in the place of his birth and early childhood. Consequently, he does not inherit a ready-made point of view from his surroundings. Third, he is met on all sides with the most divergent adult opinions. He sees no single, accepted mode of life, and he does not know what will satisfy his notions of right and wrong. Indeed, because of changes in adult opinions he may not know what *is* right and wrong—and the adults of his acquaintance may not be sure, either. They have no clear-cut principles to hand down to him. Finally, he and his friends have extraordinary freedom from adult control. Many hours are his to do with as he pleases. It is not surprising that the world seems chaotic and meaningless. Some adolescents find consolation in organized religion, but more of them have to work out their own salvation.

As one boy of 15 recently said to his father, "You had it easy. When a man killed his wife, everyone said he was bad and had done something evil; now, the newspapers say he was driven by an uncontrollable impulse and his act was not his fault. If a man was unfaithful to his wife, he was condemned by the women and looked down upon by the men, even if they may have envied him secretly. But even my counselor at school does not wholly disapprove of premarital intimacy, or even of infidelity, so far as I can make out. You were brought up to think that a shoplifter should be punished; I'm brought up to think that she should be understood. I'm quite sure you believed in God, but my professor in genetics believes in genes. What am I supposed to think?" Up to a point this boy was right. While there was plenty of evildoing in previous generations, there was a solid disapproval of it. To the oncoming generations the general public tried to present a unified front, and even though every boy and girl sooner or later found out that there was something behind the front, the early conditioning was likely to provide a basis for the development of attitudes. Today, adults go openly in all directions and frankly admit a large variety of attitudes on moral questions. It is not surprising that adolescents find the world confusing and that they are unable to establish moral concepts upon a firm foundation.

Further accounts of both religious and moral striving appear in the diaries and letters written by adolescents. These young people are more verbal than the average boy or girl, but one can assume that their feelings are not unusual.

Age 22: I busied myself yesterday evening for a rather long time with the question of religion, after there had been a discussion of religion as superstition in school. And I came to an entirely negative conclusion, namely, that according to my convictions there is no God and no soul. . . . My principles are entirely atheistic and yet I regard myself as a religious man in that I believe it is better to be a respectable man and behave myself than to earn money; that is the contrast between Idealism and Materialism.[18]

Age 16: What is this incomparable greatness, the one who stands over all the happenings of our time; is it God or fate? It is ridiculous that aside from my friends and myself no one sees an ultimate purpose, or, better said, feels one. I could not imagine my life without the striving, without the belief. There must be some final purpose for which we strive; what would life be otherwise? . . . I saw the goal, the great end purpose again beckoning me. It is not only truth, not only right, but love that brings us to things of the spirit—love of beauty, worth, and goodness. There must be a final goal that all recognize, toward which all strive. . . . Otherwise why should we bring up children and educate them to be respectable?

Most adolescents want an understandable set of morals, a meaning to life, some guiding principles to help them see the discordant details as a sensible whole. Adolescents have always needed such help, but never more than now. For most high school pupils the lack of traditional morality among their elders is a source of confusion. Because they cannot get consistent guidance from older people, they turn to the various youth groups, many of which are intentionally quite independent of and antagonistic to whatever they regard as characteristically adult opinion. These youth organizations tend to set up their own standards—some good, some bad, some radical, some conservative. Although they help boys and girls to become independent, they do not always add materially to the clarity with which their members view the world. However, one cannot blame the youth of today for trying in any way open to them to set up their own standards.

Young people want chiefly two things from their philosophy—a feeling of security that a rapidly-changing society does not give them and an emotional satisfaction that is not always supplied by the world of facts and statistics. They want to participate in a meaningful way in a philosophy of life

---

[18] These two sketches are from W. Abegg, *Aus Tagebuchern und Briefen junger Menschen* (Basel: Ernst Reinhart, 1954), pp. 124, 127.

that gives perspective and understanding. For many students the excitement of the emerging worlds that scientific exploration is unfolding is stimulus enough for the imagination and challenge enough for the mind, but the integration of these concepts into the life of the individual remains a major task of adolescence, even for those to whom the scientific approach is most rewarding. For some, religious traditions provide a starting-point for a coherent philosophy. Still others develop a synthesis of socioscientific and religious values into an ethic and a philosophy that is satisfactory to them. A few adolescents feel no need as yet for a comprehensive personal outlook on life, but most of them emerge from their adolescent years with a fairly coherent interpretation of the complex world about them and a reasonably accurate evaluation of their place in it. Their philosophy may or may not conform to the traditional values which are the formal basis of their society, but they will certainly reflect those aspects of that society which observation and emotional impact have made meaningful to them.

► Summary

An interest in or a revolt against religion is an integral part of adolescence. In spite of a small minority of highly verbal cynics, religion continues to play a part in human existence and is of special value during the adolescent years in formulating ideals and standards of conduct. During the high school years the majority of students attend some church, at least at intervals, and not far from half of them attend regularly. The lowering of the attendance average during college comes perhaps more from the competition of other activities than from any actual loss of interest.

The results of almost any investigation of honesty leave one with a sense of disappointment. It is clear that by adolescence boys and girls have learned to adapt their standards to the social pressures of the moment. Cheating in school is frequent, especially among those for whom the curriculum is either too hard or irrelevant. As long as schools give marks, someone is going to be at the bottom, and adolescents will make every effort to prevent themselves from appearing in such an unfavorable light. Teachers should expect dishonesty from certain of their pupils, and should take what measures they can to prevent it, so that the honest ones may not be subjected to unfair competition.

Young people need and want a philosophy of life, from one source or another. Even if they are not yet able to formulate a coherent philosophy, they should make a beginning. The need for such an integration becomes more apparent with every decade, because modern life is so full of conflicting attitudes that neither parents nor children are able to find their way through the discordant elements. The recent development of mass media of communication has rather added to the confusion, since everyone's ideas are made available through these media to everyone else, but the integration is usually left to the consumer.

Most young people want to find a satisfactory philosophy of life. In the course of their efforts they often subscribe to a number of more or less extreme points of view, most of which are transitory and experimental. Adolescence is the time par excellence of "isms." The desire to reform the world and to do some good during life is strong, partly because such ideas are new and partly because experience with the ways of the world has not yet had time to dent youthful idealism. The church and other religious forces do not contribute as much as they could to the formation of a philosophy of life.

References for Further Reading

B O O K S

Other Texts

Ausubel, *Theory and Problems of Adolescent Development* (Chap. 9).
Garrison, *Growth and Development,* 2d ed. (pp. 190–214).
Horrocks, *Behavior and Development* (pp. 619–624).
Hurlock, *Adolescent Development,* 2d ed. (Chap. 10 or 11).
Kuhlen, *Psychology of Adolescence* (pp. 439–456).
Jersild, *Psychology of Adolescence* (Chap. 16).
Wattenberg, *The Adolescent Years* (Chap. 26).

Other Books and Monographs

Clark, W. H., *The Psychology of Religion* (New York: The Macmillan Company, 1958), 485 pp. (Chap. 6, 9, or 14).
Seeley, J. R., *et al., Crestwood Heights: A Study of the Culture of Suburban Life* (New York: Basic Books, Inc., 1956), 499 pp. (Chap. 11 or 12).
Seidman, *The Adolescent: A Book of Readings,* rev. ed. (Nos. 49, 50, 52, 54).
Strunk, O., ed., *Readings in the Psychology of Religion* (Nashville, Tenn.: Abingdon Press, 1959), 288 pp. (No. 6 and No. 46).
Yinger, J. M., *Religion, Society, and the Individual: An Introduction to the Sociology of Religion* (New York: The Macmillan Company, 1957), 655 pp. (Chap. 4 or 10).

A R T I C L E S

Bender, I. E., "Changes in Religious Interests: A Re-test after 15 Years," *Journal of Abnormal and Social Psychology,* 57:41–46, 1958.
Blum, B. S., and J. H. Mann, "The Effect of Religious Membership on Religious Prejudice," *Journal of Social Psychology,* 52:97–101, 1960.

Dreger, R. M., "Some Personality Correlates of Religious Attitudes as Determined by Projective Techniques," *Psychological Monographs*, Vol. 66, No. 3, 1952.

Fein, L. G., "Religious Observance and Mental Health," *Journal of Pastoral Care*, 12:99–101, 1958.

Garrity, F. D., "A Study of the Attitude of Some Secondary Modern Pupils toward Religious Education," *Religious Education*, 56:141–143, 1961.

Lowe, W. L., "Religious Beliefs and Religious Delusions," *American Journal of Psychotherapy*, 9:54–61, 1955.

Morris, J. F., ed., "II. The Development of Adolescent Value Judgments," *British Journal of Educational Psychology*, 28:1–14, 1958.

O'Reilly, C. T., and E. J. O'Reilly, "Religious Beliefs of Catholic Students and Attitudes toward Minorities," *Journal of Abnormal and Social Psychology*, 49:378–380, 1954.

Ostow, M., "The Nature of Religious Controls," *American Psychologist*, 13:571–574, 1958.

Rettig, S., and B. Pasamanick, "Changes in Moral Values over Three Decades, 1929–1958," *Social Problems*, 6:320–328, 1958.

Suggested Research Problems [19]

1. Study of the numerous "odd" religions to determine what need they satisfy and what constellation of traits leads people to these religions.

2. Modern study of the degree to which parables and other materials from the Bible are (a) understood by adolescents, and (b) used by them in daily living.

3. Investigation of the concepts of God from early childhood to senescence, perhaps by means of pictures.

---

[19] See note on p. 11.

Chapter 22 | Community Influences

E<small>VEN</small> before he is born, every individual is influenced by the standards and customs of the community into which he is about to emerge: his mother's diet and his prenatal care, his family's pattern of organization, and even the chances of his survival when he is delivered are all part of the society of which he will become an influenced and influencing member. From his first howl—be it in a fetid hut or an irradiated air-conditioned hospital—he reflects, participates in, and acts upon the community.[1] Only in relatively static societies does the child necessarily remain in the community where he was born, and even in such societies he usually becomes a member of a subcommunity at adolescence by a definite change in his peer group, in his work role, and often even in his residence. These "rites of passage" help the adolescent to identify clearly the role he is to play in the society in which he lives, to establish immediately the proper modes of conduct for him, and to achieve an integration of himself. By contrast, adolescents in contemporary America exist in a world in which the patterns are themselves in a process of unprecedented fluidity and regrouping.[2]

The adolescent of the middle decades of the twentieth century is influenced by communities which are local, national, and international. And the nature of these "communities" is in a constant state of flux. It is no longer possible to speak and think of change in terms of generations. A decade is long enough to produce environmental changes which alter everyone's daily life and have a profound effect upon the whole viewpoint and program of the secondary schools, which are already feeling directly the pressures of a world in which "reaching for the moon" becomes daily less an expression of fantasy and more a statement of fact. If schools are to fulfill their obligation to educate toward greater command of self and environment, they must help the developing citizen toward perceiving his possibilities of active participation in the elective and positive aspects of his developing world. Speaking on a radio broadcast soon after the launching of the first earth satellite, a prominent edu-

---

[1] For contrasting views on the degree and manner in which culture and personal development are interwoven, see A. R. Lindsmith and A. L. Strauss, "Critique of Culture-Personality Writings," *American Sociological Review*, 15:587–600, 1950.

[2] E. O. Moe, "Consulting with a Community System," *Journal of Social Issues,* 15:29–35, 1960.

cator thus defined some of the problems and potentials of education [3] in an expanding world: the early identification and scientific education of potentially gifted scientists, the reinforcement of the available mass-communication stimuli in science education (such as television, motion-picture, and radio programs) by concrete, disciplined science courses in the schools, and the provision of gifted and adequately paid teachers for adolescent secondary school and college students, who are expected to be over twice as numerous by 1970 as they are in the already crowded secondary schools of 1963. These young people will be coming from a greater range of subcultural backgrounds than have any large college population in the past. They will bring with them a greater amount of experience in living with people of many cultural, racial, and economic backgrounds than their predecessors have had. However, it remains essential for the school to provide historical and cultural frames of reference for integrating and expanding this knowledge at the same time that they give the training in human relationships necessary to understand and develop ever-widening contacts with the world. The adolescent of the mid-century must learn to function within a wide range of responsibility and to grasp the great challenge of living in a world in which another youngster at a distance of 10,000 miles—10–12 hours away by jet transport, seconds away by radio on many of the 145 million sets in the United States—may both influence, and be influenced by, his own daily living pattern.

The community is a strong pressure factor in the development of the educational pattern for its young people, and is itself influenced in its decisions by various groups that try to influence the school program so that it will conform to their special viewpoints. During periods of crisis or of accelerated change, these pressures are at a maximum. The present difficulties over desegregation of the public high schools throughout the country bring into clear focus the nature and extent of the forces bearing on educational patterns within a community, because they involve fundamental attitudes already fixed among the adult population. It is because of the profound interaction between the adolescent and the community that this chapter has been written.

▶ **Living Patterns in Transition**

1. Changes in the Labor Force   Objective evidence concerning the changing patterns of American life is presented in Figure 22–1, which shows the proportions of the working force engaged in different types of occupation at three points in time—1900, 1930, and 1960. In 1900, farmers and farm workers made up 36 percent of the working population and day laborers another 14 percent; these three groups included exactly half the total

---

[3] R. Allen, "Sputnik and the Student," *University Explorer Broadcast 3705, U.E. 1,591,* 1958.

working force. In 1960, farmers and farm workers totaled only 6 percent and day laborers 5 percent, or 11 percent in all. The heavy line in each bar divides the producers of goods from those who render services. In 1900 it took almost three-fourths of the laborers to produce the necessary goods; today far more goods can be produced by less than half the labor force. Over the last six years the proportion of professional men and men with a high degree of technical training has increased from 5 to 12 percent, and the managers and proprietors from 5 to 8 percent. The clerical force has mushroomed from 4 to

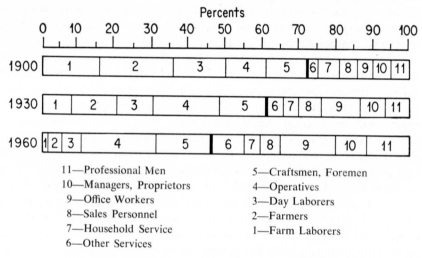

Fig. 22–1. Occupations of the labor force, 1900, 1930, 1960

Based on P. M. Hauser, "More from the Census of 1960," *Scientific American,* 207:35–37, 1962.

15 percent of the entire working force. The proportion of those who render services has steadily increased as machines have taken over the work once done by gangs of laborers. With the further development of automation, there will be more and more technicians at various levels and more and more clerical workers to prepare the materials that are fed into the computers.

These changes in prospective jobs have profound effects upon the curriculum of the schools, and especially of the high schools. They also lend weight to the present efforts to keep adolescents in school, because there will be no jobs—or at most only a few—for the uneducated. In previous generations there was a great demand for the labor of the untrained adolescent. Modern technical developments demand a longer educational preparation for the young, potential member of the working force. The changes just discussed are also related to the steady urbanization which has characterized American life during the last few decades.

2. Urbanization   In the year 1900, 42 percent of the population was urban, and 58 percent rural. For 1960 the corresponding percents were 70 and 30. This migration from farm to city has not only produced huge metropolitan centers but has also transformed the pattern of life for millions of people. Urbanization has some undoubted advantages, such as wider vocational opportunities, better equipped schools, more ready access to medical care, greater variety in entertainment—provided one has money enough—greater cultural opportunities, and more kinds of stimulation. It also has glaring disadvantages: overcrowding at almost all levels, lack of accessible or adequate recreational facilities, areas of urban decay and slums, too much pressure, lack of leisure or privacy, overfatigue, and the difficulties of merely transporting oneself from place to place.

For children and adolescents city life is difficult under the best of circumstances. Cities may be fine places for adults, but without a good deal of modification they are not suitable for children and adolescents. On the one hand, they do not offer any variety of safe, healthy outlets for childish and youthful energy, and, on the other, they offer too much adult stimulation and too soon. The net result is often a surface sophistication that arises from too much and too advanced contact with adult thought and attitudes and too little healthy nourishment of young emotions. In the depressed areas life can be almost unbearable. It weighs especially upon the newcomers. If they are able to enter higher education or special training, the city offers a faster advance up the white-collar ladder than would have been possible in the more rigidly structured small towns. However, unskilled workers [4] flowing into the city are usually forced to take jobs and housing at the lowest levels and obtain little advantage occupationally unless they come for a specific job. The native workers advance, usually, at the expense of unskilled newcomers.

Teachers who come from other environments into the deprived areas in which high schools are under the maximum strain in handling adolescents who are almost entirely consumed by their efforts to make an existence in this inimical atmosphere are sometimes prone to jump to conclusions about the meaning of the behavior they see in class. Either they are prepared to battle a blackboard jungle, with every pupil's hand against them, or they see the belligerence and the apathy as deliberate misbehavior of the individual. The plain facts are that often the pupil's reactions are triggered by events which have little meaning to the teacher with middle-class values and viewpoints. For example, one observant author [5] speaks of seeing adolescents in the slum areas either openly asleep at their desks, or so flattened with fatigue

---

[4] S. M. Lipset and R. Bendix, *Social Mobility in Industrial Society* (Berkeley, Cailf.: University of California Press, 1960), 309 pp., p. 207.
[5] J. B. Conant, *Slums and Suburbs* (New York: McGraw-Hill, 1961), 147 pp., pp. 20–21.

that they are virtually unreachable, and points out that this condition is in many cases neither the result of real apathy nor of gay living, but rather of the home conditions which subject the children of the household to the exhausting pressures of family fights in confined quarters, chronic malnutrition, filth, emotional upheavals through the night, or even the outright lack of a bed to sleep in. By the time these young people reach their teens, they have become so deadened that the school cannot act as a substitute for the homes from which they are often completely alienated.[6]

One recent intensive study pointed out that the social and economic pressures in large cities were the intensified, not the atypical, problems of the total culture. Interpersonal stresses are common to all levels of society, but in a city, long periods of economic hardship and physical inadequacy in the environment often lead to such exhaustion that families and individuals have little reserve strength for meeting these stresses or for controlling crises. Practically every city has depressed areas and most cities have slums. The continual efforts at clearance are not always successful. When a six-block area, for example, is cleared, the residents have to find temporary lodgings elsewhere, and since their incomes are extremely low they usually flow into other substandard districts, which then become more overcrowded than usual. The immediate effects upon adolescent boys and girls who have already been exposed to years of life in a depressed area are likely to be acute and often explosive.[7] An eventual readjustment may take place, and it may not. That there is no easy answer to slum clearance or to the migration of families into new housing, in which they find infinitely improved physical surroundings but often greatly decreased supportive relationships, does not invalidate the efforts to substitute good homes for bad ones. It does mean that communities need to mobilize their resources to solve the problems more effectively.[8]

The housing project has become an almost universal technique for building new homes, whether to replace old and outworn buildings or to provide for increases in population. In the larger cities the project takes the form of 20-floor-high apartment houses around which there is more or less space for playgrounds and for parklike areas where older people can walk or sit. On the outer edges of large cities and almost anywhere except in the business center of smaller cities, there are new developments of homes for those with low to average incomes. Two contrasting plans appear in Figure 22–2. The "Linear" community, shown in the upper two panels, is the older of the two. The "Cluster" community is relatively new. One might think that the linear

[6] For some further considerations of the possible effects of urbanization on the personality, see M. B. Sussman, ed., *Community Structure and Analysis* (New York: Thomas Y. Crowell Company, 1959), 454 pp., pp. 433–444.

[7] L. Eisenberg, "The Sins of the Fathers: Urban Decay and Social Pathology," *American Journal of Orthopsychiatry*, 32:5–17, 1962, p. 14.

[8] A. Dunham, "Urban Renewal and Redevelopment: the Community's Stake," *Social Service Review*, 36:306–315, 1962, p. 308.

The Linear Community

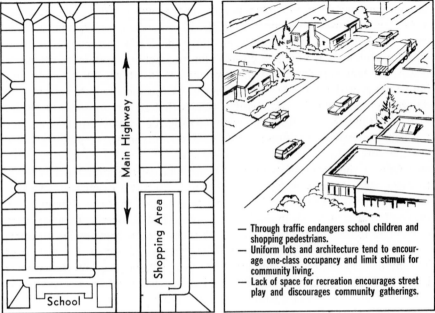

— Through traffic endangers school children and shopping pedestrians.
— Uniform lots and architecture tend to encourage one-class occupancy and limit stimuli for community living.
— Lack of space for recreation encourages street play and discourages community gatherings.

The Cluster Community

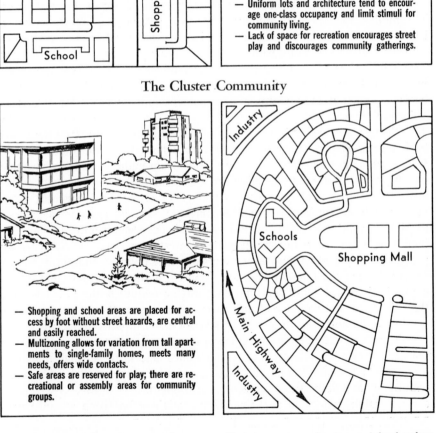

— Shopping and school areas are placed for access by foot without street hazards, are central and easily reached.
— Multizoning allows for variation from tall apartments to single-family homes, meets many needs, offers wide contacts.
— Safe areas are reserved for play; there are recreational or assembly areas for community groups.

Fig. 22–2. The "cluster" community as an effort to conserve human and land values

arrangement would house more people, but actually it does not. It uses a higher proportion of the land for streets, it contains fewer housing units because the homes are mostly only one story high, and it has little space left over for recreational use. The cluster plan not only escapes from the deadly uniformity that characterizes the more conventional type, but also conserves both human and land values. Moreover, it is much more flexible, since the different clusters may be composed of homes that are appropriate for families in a wide range of incomes. The routing of through traffic around instead of through the housing addition should decrease the number of traffic accidents considerably.

One of the accusations brought against urban life is that it has tended to disrupt the basic structure of the family. To some extent this charge is probably true. The family, which is a primary group [9] in social structure, often fails to function as a unit in modern life. The different members tend to attach themselves to secondary groups—clubs in school and out, athletic associations, scouts, campfire girls, YMCA or YWCA, groups of age-mates, and so on. The mother may become interested in civic activities, in bridge clubs, in Little Theaters, or in the neighborhood kaffeeklatch, while the father joins a men's club, plays cards with other men, plays golf at the golf club, and spends little time at home. Although some families have preserved mores and interfamilial relationships from previous generations, the family of today tends to function as a group of independent individuals rather than as a solidly knit unit.

There are elements in modern life that are operating to draw the family back together again. Technological advances have freed the modern father from long, exhausting labor and the mother from endless drudgery at home. Opportunities for family recreation are increasing and there is enough money in most families for at least a small budget for recreational purposes. Community facilities for family recreation increase steadily, and the magnificent municipal, state, and national park systems encourage family outings. The family car takes the entire group to the nearest open space on Sundays and provides transportation for longer excursions over holidays and during the vacations. Within the family circle, television is offering something that all can enjoy. Perhaps the most vital and encouraging feature is the new leisure of the parents to become friends with their children, something that was hardly possible when both were in a chronic state of exhaustion from overwork.

Moreover, although a city is large, it rarely functions as a single social unit. Every city is made up of subcommunities, and in these small units children and adolescents develop much as they would in any small neighborhood, with family and home ties of considerable strength. It is so easy to see certain surface disintegrations in an urban area that there has been a tendency to

---

[9] For a more complete definition of the primary and secondary groups, see M. S. Olmsted, *The Small Group* (New York: Random House, Inc., 1959), 158 pp., pp. 17–19.

lump an entire city population under the categories that are applicable to the least favorable aspects. However, some recent studies [10] have indicated that family cohesion and social interrelationships in urban situations have retained their important supportive functions in many relatively small neighborhood units of which any large city is composed. A study in San Francisco,[11] surveying over 700 adults in four quite different neighborhoods, found reason to question just how much actual impersonality does exist in urban life. It was found that the community did in fact offer sources of satisfaction in many types of social organization, and that families were quite as cohesive in kinship as their status would have permitted in many nonurban situations. It is very easy to overlook the fact that the stereotypes many people hold for the "good old days" of neighborhood and family closeness were never true for the lower economic levels in cities. Nor was it true in, for example, villages in the coal mining areas, which were quite as real a form of "village life" as any other; these grimy communities offered less chance of family contact, shared leisure, and cultural participation than most city dwellers now have.

3. Suburbia Since World War II, the flow of urban, and some rural, families into the suburbs, and the development of the huge housing tracts where veterans (and some others) are able to own their own homes, have led to a profound repatterning of life for many American adolescents. People from every geographical area of the country, and from a huge range of economic and occupational levels, have come together as neighbors. Most of the parents have been roaming over the United States, practically all of the fathers have been overseas and have become aware to some extent of other nationalities and ways of life; their experiences have brought an increasing knowledge of many other lands and customs to the group experience available in the newly formed suburban units.

For example, one of the writers lived, with her young son, in such a community for three years. There was seldom a class in geography or social studies to which some neighborhood youngster could not bring a relevant personal or parental souvenir from a foreign country or another state. The occupations of the breadwinners on just one block ran, from house to house, as follows: auto mechanic, social worker, airline pilot, garageman, airplane technician, maintenance worker in schools, teacher, garage hand, and refrigeration engineer. They came from the Tennessee hills, the Midwest, Brooklyn, and there were wives from Mexico, Japan, Germany, and North Carolina! The children wore sandals from India and skirts from Mexico, carried bags made in Italy, and ate

---

[10] M. Axelrod, "Urban Structure and Social Participation," *American Sociological Review*, 21:73–78, 1956.

[11] W. Bell and M. D. Boat, "Urban Neighborhoods and Social Relations," *American Journal of Sociology*, 62:391–398, 1957.

an international menu over their backyard barbecue pits, which collected from three to fifteen kids in a backyard on every balmy evening. The parents were active in PTA, boys' clubs, and community projects. It is true that few fathers had enough time for much supervision of adolescent activities. But more fathers and mothers spent long weekends working on their homes or taking the family to the beach than would have been possible a generation ago. Every effort was made to individualize the mass-produced houses, and a year after the tract opened they were far more the expression of the family within than were the city or rural dwellings of the middle classes before them.

While such developments certainly have some drawbacks in terms of initial uniformity, group pressures toward credit, and so on, the over-all influence on young people of an increasing stake in their community through the possession of stable housing and the international flavor of their daily casual way of life probably can be considered as offering more opportunity for real community ties to more adolescents than before, as the trend away from the rigidly rural or urban patterns continues. Naturally, concern with the inner problems of living is scarcely lessened by these circumstances, but in communities that are increasingly aware of the need for meeting these problems, the techniques and conditions for dealing effectively with human problems are more available to more people of modest position than they have ever been before.[12]

On the other hand, there are numerous problems arising from this way of life, some of which were not foreseen by the enthusiasts for suburbia. As the expansion of the suburbs forces greater and greater commuting distances on the working parent, the much-sought chances for "togetherness" have been reduced, by the mile, so to speak. And the oversentimentalization of the drive for togetherness, which was itself a response to the disrupting influences of urban life, has by now led to a "counter-revolt" toward emphasis on the needs for privacy and diversity. These elements must be kept and respected if a society is to avoid stagnation. Those who find suburbia an easy target for criticism forget that its vices are mainly extensions of the tendency toward bleakness which typifies any city slum, toward conformity which characterizes almost any small town, and toward mobility which is a fixed feature of current American culture.

4. Social Mobility   At any particular moment the inhabitants of a given community may be grouped into fairly distinct social classes, but some families are moving up the scale, and some are moving down. There is nothing fixed or stable about the grouping of the moment. The next generation will arrange itself more or less differently. One of the writers had

---

[12] See also B. D. Paul, ed., *Health, Culture, and Community* (Russell Sage Foundation, 1955), 493 pp., p. 295.

a demonstration of this kind of mobility not long ago. During a visit to her home town, she developed an earache and was sent by her friends to a highly recommended specialist, a Harvard Medical School graduate who had studied in Vienna for two years on a special scholarship. Dr. C. was a local leader not only in medicine but in many civic projects. His wife came from an old and distinguished local family. It was a little surprising to the writer to recognize Dr. C. as the Shanty-Irish boy with whom she had not been allowed to play in her childhood! Such social mobility is an American commonplace.

The parents in middle-class homes are especially likely to push their preadolescent and the adolescent offspring into social groups which reflect too much the ambitions and fears of the parents and too little a genuine creative interest on the part of the youngsters. Not infrequently these groups are over-organized to such a point that the child is pushed into adult competitive forms, as in the less-well-supervised baseball teams which are rather surrogates for the fathers than normal activities for their sons. Sometimes they exert too much pressure on the social abilities of their children, who at 12 are seldom ready for the formal dances and dating which are becoming popular in the more socially ambitious sets. In some cases the young boy or girl who would just like to sit and smell a flower is rushed into a round of "activities" which would tax a sturdy and experienced clubwoman or businessman. The trend is at present limited by economic requirements to a middle-class group in which the mother is available for transportation, time, and money to meet the demanding schedules. However, with the increased leisure and income of the lower-middle classes, and even the group classically thought of as "lower" or "working" classes, the upward mobility strivings of many more parents may move their children into these status-symbol rat races unless a careful re-evaluation of these activities takes place at the level which sets the standards.

Americans have always been noted for their emphasis upon the importance of drive, speed, and achievement. In a social group that is trying to move upward there is great pressure upon children and especially upon adolescents to conform to this pattern. Wholly aside from the emotional overload upon a sensitive adolescent, the pressure forces him into frustration because society provides him with little or no realistic chance of attaining through extra drive the presumably attractive goals toward which he is working.[13] In a society in which upward mobility is held almost essential by the middle classes, however, much of the apathy of which young people are rather dubiously accused may spring from a realistic evaluation of these questionable chances by those from the lower classes who can at most (with some

---

[13] M. Lerner, *America as a Civilization: Volume II, Culture and Personality* (Essandess Press, 1961), 1010 pp. See also pp. 954–972 for a superior annotated bibliography of titles dealing with related problems.

rare exceptions) expect to attain a few well-advertised material status symbols, without much improvement in the day-to-day conditions of their lives.[14]

Contemporary sociological thinking has developed a concept expressed by the word, "anomie," literally a state of being without identity. The word is often used, with some variation in shades of meaning by different writers in the field,[15] to indicate a sense of being disconnected, anonymous, and lost, such as arises when an individual cannot establish a stable image of himself or of his proper function in his group. This feeling of being nobody arises often among those who themselves move about or live in a society that is changing rapidly. In a temporary form it occurs among travelers in a foreign country. If they have a sufficiently strong drive to see the world that they constantly run from one objective to another, they may escape this occupational disease of tourists; but if they stay for a while in one place, they begin to wonder if they really exist at all. Life flows by around them, but they have no place in it, no identity, and no future. Their troubles are soon over, but those of the adolescent who has just moved into new surroundings have just begun. The resulting emotional bleakness has many manifestations, such as withdrawal, apathy, or anxiety. If the social and educational conditions produce a cultural emptiness, then the feeling may erupt in violence and noise, as a protest against the void of not belonging to anyone, anywhere. The feeling of anomie may be produced by any situation that leads to a break in normal social contacts. It has far-reaching effects and leads to the kind of frustration with which the adolescent finds it peculiarly difficult to cope; it defeats his faith in the adequacy of his education, in the probability of economic adjustment, and in his development of a constructive viewpoint for meeting the changes around him. The sense of being somehow lost is not uncommon among the young people of groups which are particularly highly mobile and for boys and young men in the suburbs;[16] frequently it is a concomitant of having few male figures available during much of the day to which they can tie some stable concept of proper and suitable conduct in the community in which they currently find themselves. The young people who are subjected to constant shifts of social background are usually quite sensitive in picking up cues regarding expectations of a relatively stable community, but where most of the prominent members are more or less in transit themselves, there is a lack of firm role-delineations for the incoming adolescent. Unless he has had sufficient firmness of relationships with the primary group prior to the dis-

[14] J. K. Coster, "Some Characteristics of High School Pupils from Three Income Groups," *Journal of Educational Psychology,* 50:55–62, 1959.

[15] R. May, E. Angel, and H. F. Ellenberger, *Existence—A New Dimension in Psychotherapy and Psychology,* 2d. ed. (New York: Basic Books, Inc., 1958), 445 pp., pp. 57–58, and R. M. Williams, Jr., *American Society: A Sociological Interpretation* (New York: Alfred A. Knopf, Inc., 1960), 575 pp., pp. 507–508.

[16] R. E. Gordon and K. K. Gordon, "Emotional Disorders of Children in a Rapidly Growing Suburb," *International Journal of Social Psychiatry,* 4:85–97, 1958.

rupting social contacts, he may become uncertain and "lost." It should be noted, however, that there is still much uncertainty about the relationship between the social and personal balance of togetherness and loneliness,[17] because both are real parts of the organic whole of life. It seems unreasonable to attack the social structure that leads to "too much conformity" or the social structure that leads to "too much alienation" unless it is pointed out that the balance of these factors has to be developed ultimately within the individual, in accordance with his capacity or incapacity to make the necessary integration.

5. Physical Mobility Although social mobility is more significant, geographical mobility in America is also remarkable and continues to increase from year to year. In 1961, about 33 million families moved; at least half moved to another city, and about one-sixth to another state, taking with them problems of readjusting to the resources, mores, environment, and relative social isolation of the initial phases of relocations for themselves and their children. Since by 1970 it is estimated that there will be almost 50 percent more in the 10–17 age group than there are now, and since there is no reason to believe that families will move less, there will be an enormous number of mobile adolescents in the next decade.

In 1961 there was one private car for every 2.5 persons in the United States. This figure is eloquent of a physical mobility far beyond man's most nomadic dreams of a century ago. The car allows the adolescent to share in the great mobility of the period. Within an hour's time he can get so far away from home that no one is likely to know him. He thus escapes easily from the indirect supervision that adults in his own community automatically exercise by merely being there. Many adolescents have not yet developed sufficient internal control to dispense altogether with this direct form of protection. Of course, adolescents have always been able to escape more or less, even if they had only their own feet as a means of transportation; the car merely allows them to escape to a greater distance in a briefer time. An automobile is not in and of itself a moral corrosive. If a boy or girl belongs to a peer group of similar standards, all members may be sufficiently self-censoring to give themselves protection, especially if one element in their thinking is their desire to maintain their reputation with their friends, their parents, and their community. The physical mobility of youth at the present time only intensifies an age-old problem.

Geographical mobility, upon either a large or a small scale, is neither good nor bad. It is merely different, and it leads to new problems which existed only in miniscule proportions in previous generations. A few families have always moved, usually over short distances, and there have been periods

---

[17] C. E. Moustakas, *Loneliness* (Englewood Cliffs, N.J.: Prentice-Hall, Inc., 1957), 107 pp., pp. 24–53 and p. 103.

of expansion that precipitated large-scale but self-limiting migrations. However, the mass movements of the present time are something new. And thus far most communities have not been able to adjust themselves adequately. The teacher should be especially sensitive to the immediate needs of the newly-arrived child or adolescent, and both school and community need greater awareness of the dangers to the individual and through him to society in the increasing numbers of the anonymous. Many of the problems in adjusting to new community settings depend on the amount of support available within the family at the time of the movement, and on the degree to which there is an ongoing internal consistency in the goals presented. The two brief cases below illustrate parallel instances of mobility, with very different outcomes for the adolescents involved.

As is common in the suburban development of a rapidly growing area, two families moved simultaneously into the new, middle-income housing tract of College Heights in a large, primarily agricultural county. Both were from out of the state, and each family had among its children an adolescent son.

Paul Meeks entered the 11th grade of his new neighborhood with eager anticipation. His father, who had come to the area to accept a minor administrative position with the new local hospital, had told him about the good reputation of the high school he was entering, something about the area from which the pupils were drawn, and quite a bit about the activities which would be available to him in contrast with the limited program of the economically distressed school district from which he had moved. The family regarded this move to the father's new location as a fine, rewarding, and adventurous event, and the mother conveyed to each child a sense of how proud they could be in the father's achievement in gaining such a responsible position after his long siege of hard study which had kept them in a meager city apartment while he completed some courses at the University. They had never had much money in the past, for the father started out as a bottle-washer in the laboratory of a huge general hospital in a crowded metropolis. He married a very intelligent nurse who happily settled into raising a family for whom she had great ambitions tempered with the realism which is almost certain to develop after five years of nursing life and death in a metropolitan hospital. Paul found the new school impressive, but not overwhelming. He looked on everyone he met as an exciting new friend, and he could hardly contain his eagerness to explore the sudden wealth of clubs, laboratories, gardens, and other minor marvels which he suddenly found he had access to for the first time in his school life. He met with some rebuffs, but talked them over at home to sympathetic parental attention. Although he missed seeing his father very often —minor administrators on the move upward being favorite targets for all the extra work in a hospital—he settled for the greater freedom the whole family had to reach the nearby beaches for family picnics on Sunday, and for the glow of accomplishment with which his family was suffused by this change in status. He found himself with some additional problems in the way of higher academic standards, too, but again moved toward their solution, by seeking help from his teachers, to whom it was natural for him (trusting adults and respecting learning) to turn in a pinch. Within a year, he was an integral part of his community, active in it, contributing to it, and rather offhand about the whole thing, as becomes a traveled man.

Nick, on the other hand, was resentful, fearful, and ready to fight at the drop of an eyebrow as he walked into his senior class at the same high school. His father had moved to the community to get the high wages available at the electronic plant nearby, but the whole family had bitterly resented having to leave the small southern industrial city where they thought they had "settled down" after a long period of constantly moving to follow the job market. The father had become a very skilled craftsman, and was both needed and well-rewarded financially in the booming electronics industries of the area, so the family left their associations with the corner grocer, the coffee-klatches the mother cherished with her neighbor down the hall, the uproarious concrete playground the children were used to, albeit the play sometimes included some pretty bloody fights. Nick was especially resentful, because he was going to have been a "big shot" senior in the high school at home that year, a position won by many a battle and considerable athletic ability. He was not an unintelligent boy, but he had absolutely no preparation for the free-wheeling, nonsegregated, school life in which he suddenly found himself. He was horrified to find that he was neither as physically impressive nor as athletically competent as he had felt himself to be, in comparison with this new group of adolescents raised on a lifetime of outdoor activity and optimum nourishment. He was scornful and scared, bitter and worried, and it is hardly remarkable that his attitude radiated something less than warm friendliness—which was, of course, reciprocated by the in-group of the seniors, many of whom had forgotten how recently they themselves had become "in." At home, where he finally had a place to study in a room of his own, this gain was largely made empty by the fact that his family was so preoccupied with their own struggles to meet the alien pattern of the community that they had little time for him, and he would have liked only too well to have had a closer association with them. Privacy he had never had and could do without. What he missed was the close, if sometimes uncomfortable, association with his old street buddies. Difficulties arose at school because he failed to adjust from the rigid regimentation needed for controlling the obstreperous young of the industrial area to the relaxed democratic methods used by his teachers with a group of essentially school-oriented pupils of the middle classes, and mistook their permissiveness for license to misbehave outrageously. Bewildered by the resulting wrath of the school authorities, he lost interest in classes and attended with little profit to anyone. Before the semester was over, Nick felt he was unwanted, cheated, and lost in a new world which gave him more of almost everything he ever desired, except a sense of belonging anywhere in it.

▶ The Community and the Adolescent

1. Positive Contributions by the Community   Almost any reasonably stable community has a number of cultural and social resources, by means of which an adolescent can develop his interests and abilities. The most outstanding among these are the schools, the churches, the libraries, the art museums, and the theaters. The contributions of the school and church are discussed elsewhere in this text and may therefore be mentioned here only in passing. Nobody denies the influence of the other agencies just listed, but its extent has not been fully measured.

Efforts are continually being made to use more adequately the opportunities offered youth for instruction and development in art and music. Every year more children and adolescents visit museums and art galleries, and more go to concerts and to operas whenever these are presented. The average museum constantly tries to present displays which will be of such vital interest as to compete successfully with other types of diversion. Moreover, the museum staffs send circulating exhibits from school to school and from place to place, and teachers take or send entire classes to museums from time to time.

Education in music for the general public received its first great impetus with the invention of the phonograph. Progress has since been enormously accelerated by the radio. Knowledge of music and musical appreciation have both been directly affected. In spite of some worthless musical programs heard over television and radio, the average adolescent is hearing more good music and is receiving a better education in musical appreciation than any previous generation of adolescents has ever had. A generation ago, perhaps ten thousand people a year heard any one great orchestra; during the past year probably fifty million people heard the same group of artists. It is not uncommon for a small boy to walk along his paper route whistling arias from grand opera. Such universal musical education is something new. Adolescents often have large collections of records, many of excellent quality, to which they listen for hours at a time. Even more significantly, the participation in small groups for instrumental or singing enjoyment is encouraged by schools and by leisure groups as a way of creative and personal development in contrast to mere "spectator" attitudes.

In the entire country there are over eight thousand libraries with some thirty million registered users. Most children and adolescents who live in communities of ten thousand or more have access to some kind of a library, although young people in rural areas may be dependent mainly upon the library truck that makes its round through the countryside. A study from a decade ago explored the extent to which people of different ages and degrees of education use the libraries. The facts are probably about the same at the present time as they were in 1950. The first point to note is that their use is very unevenly distributed. Ninety-eight percent of all the books taken out in a single year were taken out by the 10 percent of the population that individually read the most library books. Eighty percent of the adult population did not use the library at all. Throughout the school years children and adolescents take out books with fair regularity, but use of the library drops off sharply after pupils leave school. The amount of schooling also has an effect upon reading habits. In the general population, 27 percent of the adults never finished grammar school; they furnish only 5 percent of the regular users of the library. The high school and college graduates make up only 38 percent of the population but furnish 75 percent of the library's steady customers. Either the amount of education has an effect in habituating pupils to the frequent use of books, or, what is more likely, those who already used and liked books were the ones who extended their education beyond the minimum requirements. Of the entire adult population, only 18 percent had been in the public library during the year before the investigation; 44 percent had used it in previous years, and 38 percent had never used it. These figures suggest that the library is of great service to the community, but that it could be of greater service if use of its offerings could be spread a little more evenly.

There is no question that reading is still a major activity at all ages, in spite of the intrusion of radio and television. Every year, for example, the New York Public Library checks out about four million books, and the American Book Publishers' Council reports steady increases of books published each year. In the year 1960, the total number of new book titles was 15,013 in the United States alone.[18] For further evidence of the popularity of reading, one need only glance at the array of paperback books and magazines in the corner drugstore or tobacco shop. To be sure, some are worthless, but many are reprints of classics and new editions of worthwhile books. They would not be on the shelves, if there were not a strong demand for them. Incidentally, these outlets for books in inexpensive editions are increasing the spread of available literature.

It remains to point out one other way in which the community is contributing more and more to adolescent development. Schools and teachers are using community resources as never before. They are trying hard to relate education in school to life outside the school. One of the best techniques thus far developed is to use the community as an original source. Thus if pupils are to be taught about trade unions, they go to members of local unions for interviews instead of merely reading a chapter in a textbook. The study of history is often vivified by visits to historical sites in the locality. An understanding of different countries may be heightened by having foreign

---

[18] *Statistical Yearbook, 1961* (United Nations Publishing Service, 1962), 679 pp., p. 632.

residents come into the classroom and tell about their homeland. Vocational counselors often send pupils to visit local industries and to interview local businessmen. Pupils may learn mathematics by following construction work that is being done in the neighborhood. Excursions to police stations, courts, garbage disposal plants, or license bureaus throw light upon civic problems. In some towns the high school students take over the city government for a day, after going through all the processes of electing their officials. Such activities appeal to pupils as being "real" rather than just practice. Moreover, they help to integrate life in and out of the schoolroom.

Community surveys are now used as a basis for curricular developments. Teachers and students study the industries and the needs of their community and its environs. Committees on the course of study compare the results with the curricular offerings to find out if these are adequate to prepare pupils for the life of their locality. Such contacts between school and community are most helpful in adjusting education to life's needs.

During the college years of one of the writers contacts between the college and community were relatively few; and when they occurred at all, their existence was due either to accident or to voluntary effort on the part of an individual student. The life of the college went on by itself, and the townspeople pursued whatever interests appealed to them; the only points of contact were the local churches (attended by a few of the students), the families and friends of students who lived in the community, and the various residents who worked in noninstructional positions at the college. In general, however, the college was a self-sufficient world that was tolerated by the community because of the business it brought. For the most part the two groups simply ignored each other, but if there was any feeling, it was usually one of distrust, based largely upon ignorance of each other's activities and interests.

Recently the same writer had occasion to observe the college scene again. In the intervening forty years the community had become the laboratory of the college, and the college had become a means of self-expression for the community and a source of help in time of need. Students in the statistics classes obtain their material from the records of the city offices; students of political economy and economics make surveys of the city or county; psychology students test the school children; and youthful dietitians get their first practical training in the city hospitals. Little children from the community come to the college's nursery school; older ones come to Saturday morning classes in dancing, swimming, or other sports taught by college students, and high school pupils use the college library. Every few days a bus brings youngsters coming to look at the collections in the art museum. The community often asks members of the faculty to give lectures on their specialties, to serve on the school board, to assist the park commissioner, and to man the voting booths on election days. The college play that was currently being rehearsed had this cast: four students from the college, some girl's boy friend who drove over from a nearby technical school every week end for rehearsals, a druggist, a housewife, and a retired doctor from the community, plus one of the college gardeners and the college postmaster. The play, when given, would be open to the public. When a community committee was appointed by the mayor at the request of the local court to look into the causes of juvenile delinquency and to suggest possible preventive measures, the mayor selected five citizens and asked the college to select for him two students and two members of the faculty to join the townsmen. The college paper carries a column about what goes on in the city, and the city papers carry a column about affairs at the college.

In short, the college has learned to serve the community and at the same time to use it as a source of raw data for study. In one very popular class the students each year first meet with representatives from the community to plan a survey. They then make a house-to-house canvass, tabulate the results, and write a report to the original committee. At the end, the entire group meets two or three times to plan definite action on the basis of the report. As practical training for the students, nothing could be better. Incidentally, both the community and the college have been surprised and pleased to discover how much intelligence and skill the other possesses.

Another kind of interrelation between school and community is the "community college," the two-year or junior-college pattern of post-high school education which is aimed at the needs of the adolescent who cannot devote four more years to schooling, or does not care to do so. The adults of the community who wish to continue their education and personal or professional development also derive help from the community college. This type of education tends in turn to contribute to the enrichment of the total community through its cultural resources and by formulating and stimulating higher goals for community development.

At all educational levels, the relationship between school and community becomes steadily closer as the years roll on. It is one of the movements that is making both high school and college work less academic and better adapted to the requirements of the average pupil, who is not a scholar and who needs to have education made real and of practical significance for his daily living.

2. Negative Influences in the Community The typical American community does not exercise steady, widely accepted controls over its adolescents. Adults of different economic and social levels more or less supervise their young people, according to varying standards of "proper" conduct, but there are wide differences in the desired, as well as in the effective, controls. If too much is expected of an adolescent in conformity and aspiration, his chances of failure are increased; if too little is demanded by the community, his potentials will lie undeveloped through dispersion of his resources in unproductive or even harmful activities. An adolescent who moves from one community to another may be caught in a conflict of community standards of behavior. Some investigators point out that even the dominant value patterns spoken of as "American" may be contradictory—acquisitiveness and democracy, a monotheistic religion and scientific inquiry, monogamous marriage and personal freedom—and that both the conception of and the means of attaining these goals are interpreted variously in the different subcommunities in which American adolescents move. When the goals are accurate reflections of the standards held by the majority of the adults, controls can be effective. The worst difficulties arise when the adults have one standard for themselves, but expect the adolescents to conform to controls that run contrary to easily observed adult behavior.

Cities often fail to offer a sufficient variety of safe, healthy outlets for childish and youthful energy or for harmless kinds of thrills and excitement. Even when the offerings are adequate, they are often not available to the young people who need them most, either because boys and girls do not have the money for transportation or because they are not aware that the facilities exist. The out-of-school adolescents who are living in depressed areas feel the deprivation most keenly. The attitudes of such subcommunities may be inimical to such participation, and unless an adolescent has a source of strength and a drive beyond the ordinary, he may find it difficult to reach even those things in the community which he himself sees as desirable. In a society which tends to establish activities in terms of middle-class values, the large number of adolescents who come from other groups may be not only rejected, but repelled. The efforts now made to "rescue" the idle adolescent need to take forms which he can respond to, otherwise, the resource might as well not be there.

Most communities lack adequate safeguards for adolescents. For example, an adolescent is usually able, by one means or another, to buy tobacco, alcohol, or drugs; indeed, in some parts of the country adolescent use of drugs has become a serious problem and a menace to normal development and health. There are laws against the sale of liquor or tobacco within a certain distance of a high school, but in these days of easy transportation, such laws have little effect. It does not take a high school boy long to learn that some of the young women he meets in the neighborhood of the school are prostitutes; he also finds out at an early age about homosexual men. Only doctors and juvenile courts are constantly aware of the tragedies that overtake those youngsters who cannot resist temptation. The blame lies fundamentally with the indifferent community in which these adolescents live. It does not matter how large or how small the community may be, opportunities for early indulgence will offer themselves. If it wants to badly enough, an alert and enlightened community can prevent many of the tragedies.

A community may also regulate its places of amusement. Some effort in this direction is usually made, but the laws are by no means rigidly enforced. In fact, the owners of places of amusement depend primarily upon the young people for support. Naturally, the character of such places varies with the ownership; many proprietors attempt to give reasonable protection to those who frequent their place of business. There are some public dance halls, night clubs, and roadhouses where reasonable standards are enforced, but no owner can afford to be too scrupulous if he wishes to keep his customers. Most such places offer practically no protection to the adolescent using them, and some make a direct appeal to the baser motive of boys and girls. Dancing is, in and of itself, a wonderful outlet for youthful energy and exuberance when the setting is suitable, where it can also help to satisfy the need for developing social skills and making friends. However, if healthy surroundings are not available, adolescents may have to seek unsuitable environments and find their energies diverted into less desirable channels. The community that permits dance halls with low stands of morality, unsupervised night clubs and roadhouses, salacious burlesque shows, and the like, can expect a harvest of adolescent moral collapse that is largely its own fault.

Finally, there are the various places maintained by organized vice. Houses of prostitution, gambling rooms, poolrooms, and the like, damage thousands of adolescents every year. The dangers connected with the house of prostitution are too obvious to need comment. Adolescents lose money on gambling machines, horse racing, dog racing, roulette wheels, crap shooting, and card games. Gambling is often carried on openly if illegally, with the authorities looking the other way most of the time and contenting themselves with sporadic raids. The community in which the laws are "liberal" can expect some of its adolescents every year to be forced into stealing in order to meet debts incurred through gambling. Some of them commit suicide. Boys and girls of high school age do not have the judgment, the knowledge, or the financial resources to gamble with safety. There is nothing inherently wicked in shooting pool or playing billiards; the trouble comes from the nature of the adults who hang around the average poolroom. In its indifferent attitude toward organized vice many a community sows the wind and reaps the whirlwind.

One of the gravest evil influences on young people is the tendency of adults to use the adolescent as a scapegoat [19] and to act as if the young victim of society were the cause of the evils he reflects! It is hardly the fault of the young person that his substandard slum school receives not the special tax investment needed to provide optimal services for his greater needs, but rather is given minimal tax support because of the reluctance of his elders to endow the best on the "worst" and poorest communities. Little is done in deprived areas to make the school the vital youth center it might become—and when youngsters lack expected vitality and ambition, the disapproval falls in

---

[19] E. C. Kelley, *In Defense of Youth* (Englewood Cliffs, N.J.: Prentice-Hall, Inc., 1962), 145 pp., pp. 4 and 62–93.

all too many cases on them rather than on their conditions of development. Relatively, they do quite well under hazard.

▶ **Summary**

The community influences the adolescent in many ways. It sets his standards of conduct, it gives him his physical environment and his schools, it provides more or less for his leisure and general enjoyment of life. It influences and to some extent controls his behavior. His life is conditioned by the increasing degree of urbanization, by the types of housing developments, by the social mobility open to him, and often by the geographical mobility of his family. These factors present him with special problems, of which the chance of getting "lost" is of major importance. There are many resources—probably not enough but still an appreciable number—although he may not know about them and they may not be suitable for his needs. His community also presents him with an assortment of pitfalls. Communities are more and more contributing indirectly to adolescent happiness and security by their cooperation with schools in providing adolescents with a type of education best fitted to adapt them to community needs. In view of the great technological developments of the last two decades, it seems reasonable to suppose that the wider community of the world will impinge more and more upon the little world of the adolescent and that he will have to learn how to live in many new interpersonal relationships.

References for Further Reading

BOOKS

Other Texts

Ausubel, *Theory and Problems of Adolescent Development* (Chap. 7 or 11).
Breckenridge and Vincent, *Child Development*, 4th ed. (Chap. 5).
Garrison, *Growth and Development* (pp. 353–371).
Horrocks, *Behavior and Development* (pp. 97–102).
Jones, *Growth and Behavior in Adolescence* (pp. 83–102).
Kuhlen, *Psychology of Adolescent Development* (pp. 146–187).
Wattenberg, *The Adolescent Years* (Chap. 27).

Other Books and Monographs

Bannis, W. G., *et al.*, eds. *The Planning of Change, Readings in the Applied Behavioral Sciences* (New York: Holt, Rinehart, and Winston, Inc., 1961), 781 pp. (pp. 18–42).
Havighurst, R. J., and B. L. Neugarten, *Society and Education*, rev. ed. (Boston: Allyn and Bacon, Inc., 1962), 585 pp. (pp. 322–348).

Kelley, E. C., *In Defense of Youth* (Englewood Cliffs, N.J.: Prentice Hall, Inc., 1962), 145 pp. (pp. 62–93).

Lerner, M., *America as a Civilization, Vol. II: Culture and Personality* (Essandess Press, 1961), (pp. 541–582 or 954–972).

Lipset, S. M., and R. Bendix, *Social Mobility in Industrial Society* (Berkeley, Calif.: University of California Press, 1960), 309 pp. (pp. 205–226 or 76–113).

Pressey, Robinson, and Horrocks, *Psychology in Education* (Chap. 6).

Sanderson, R., *The Church Serves the Changing City* (New York: Harper & Row, Publishers, 1955), 252 pp. (Chap. 9).

Seeley, J. R., *et al., Crestwood Heights: A Study of the Culture of Suburban Life* (New York: Basic Books, Inc., 1956), 499 pp. (Chap. 1, 2, or 3).

Srole, L., *et al., Mental Health in the Metropolis* (New York: McGraw-Hill Book Company, 1962), 428 pp. (pp. 104–126).

Sussman, M. B., ed., *Community Structure and Analysis* (New York: Thomas Y. Crowell Company, 1959), 454 pp. (pp. 433–444 or 388–412).

Williams, R. M., *American Society: A Sociological Interpretation*, 2d. ed. (Alfred A. Knopf, Inc., 1960), 575 pp. (pp. 561–575 and 507–508 or 415–468).

ARTICLES

Axelrod, M., "Urban Structure and Social Participation," *American Sociological Review*, 21:73–78, 1956.

Bell, W., and M. D. Boat, "Urban Neighborhoods and Social Relations," *American Journal of Sociology*, 62:391–398, 1957.

Cloward, R. A., "Illegitimate Means, Anomie, and Deviant Behavior," *American Sociological Review*, 24:164–176, 1959.

Udry, R. J., "The Importance of Social Class in a Suburban School," *Journal of Educational Sociology*, 33:307–310, 1960.

White, M. S., "Social Class, Child Rearing, and Behavior," *American Sociological Review*, 22:704–712, 1957.

Suggested Research Problems [20]

1. Study of the social adjustments and educational achievements of 12th grade pupils whose families have been so mobile as to change residence (enough for the children to attend another school) at least four times since the beginning of grade 7. The results might well be compared with similar figures for a group of pupils having the same scores on tests of intelligence whose families were stable in residence throughout the period.

[20] See note on p. 11.

PART SIX | Educational
Applications

Chapter 21 The High School and College Population

PART SIX

Educational Applications

Chapter 23

The High School and College Population

THE American high school is a unique institution. It does not correspond to any of the secondary schools of Europe, although it is their lineal descendant and was influenced by them in its early years, especially by the secondary schools of England. It started in the same tradition of an intellectual aristocracy, but it has changed its nature. American colleges and universities were also originally imitations of such institutions in Europe, especially those in Germany, but they too have broken away from their ancestral type. Although the high school is a fairly venerable institution as far as mere age goes, its characteristic modern development dates from after World War I. Almost exactly 70 years ago the husband of one of the writers was unable to attend high school in the borough of Manhattan in New York City because there was no high school there. At present, the same district has over 25 high schools enrolling 250,000 pupils. This same mushroom growth has taken place all over the country. In fact, the high schools and the colleges have grown so rapidly that their aims and courses have had to be altered from one decade to the next in order to meet the needs of the students. In both instances, the main precipitating factor has been the enormously increased enrollments. An education that was appropriate for the seven adolescents in each hundred between the ages of 14 and 18 who attended high school in 1869 is not in the least suitable for the eighty to ninety in a hundred who will enter high school in 1963. Similar changes in enrollment and in the nature of the student population have occurred at the college level, but the increases came about a decade later. The first point to consider in this chapter is the record of enrollments at different periods and of the relation of these enrollments to the total increases of adolescent population.

▶ Size of High Schools and Colleges

Until 1889 the high schools were small and few. A gradual growth took place during the two decades from 1889 to 1909, but it was not until 1919 that the first spectacular increase occurred. This sudden growth was followed by further accretions until the beginning of World War II. After 1941, enlistments in the armed forces and employment in war industries cut down the enrollments in the high schools and colleges. The totals in 1943 were almost a million below those of 1939. This decrease was, however, only temporary. By 1950 the high schools had recovered their losses and had again started to grow. Because of the high birth rate during and since the war, the enrollment in 1960 was already over twelve million.

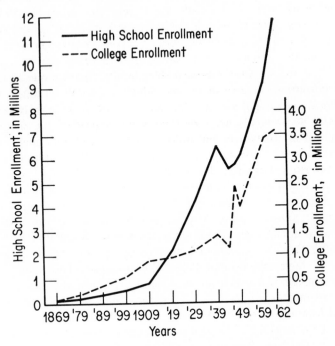

Fig. 23–1. High school and college enrollments (1869–1962)

Based on figures from the United States Census Reports in *The World Almanac,* 1962.

The colleges began their record according to the census in 1879, when there was an enrollment of barely 100,000. The growth was slow until after World War I, reaching about 890,000 by 1919. In the next two decades the colleges almost doubled their population. During World War II, most men of college age were in the armed forces, but on their return, and thanks to the allowances made under the GI Bill for their continued education, the numbers rose to 2,225,000. This high point was followed by another decline to a normal proportion of the adolescent population. The "war babies" are already in college, and the total for 1960 was over 3,500,000. The changes in enrollments for both high school and college are shown in Figure 23–1. No other country in the world has such a record of educational holding power. The American high school has achieved its size partly as a result of extending the compulsory school age to 14, 16, or 18, but it has also made great changes in its offerings, so that pupils remain in school, even after they have passed the age at which they could legally leave.

Colleges and universities give bachelor's degrees, and the latter give master's and doctor's degrees. The A.B. comes at the completion of the normal four years of college, the M.A. at the end of a fifth year, and the Ph.D. at least two years later—and usually five to ten years later. In 1890, a total of 15,539 seniors received an A.B. or its equivalent; in 1950, 394,889. During the same interval the number of master's degrees conferred rose from 1009 to 74,499, and the recipients of doctor's degrees developed from a mere 126 to 9829. These figures show that education on the higher levels has also had the same mushrooming growth as that which occurred earlier in the high schools. Figure 23–2 gives a graphic picture of the development within a single state. This university is, at the time of publication of this book, already over 25,000. With increasing demands for higher education, the enrollment in 1965 is expected to be well over 26,000. The relative estimates for this one state hold equally for the rest of the country.

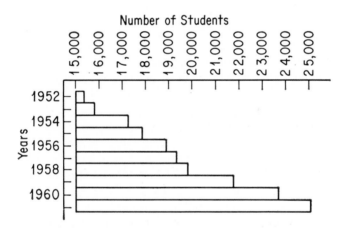

Fig. 23–2. Increase in the number of students in one university in one decade

From *Progress at Berkeley* (Berkeley, Calif., University of California Press, 1962), 27 pp., p. 18.

One method of demonstrating the extent to which schools are holding their pupils is to compare the number of adolescents in the total population with the number in high school. The more pupils there are between 14 and 18 in high school, the greater is the holding power. In 1889, only 7 adolescents out of each 100 were in school. Ten and twenty years later, the figures were 12 and 15, respectively. By 1939, the number had risen to 73. In 1949, it was 82, and in 1952 it was 89. In short, the high schools are approaching a perfect record. Naturally, the proportion of those between 18 and 22 who are in college is much lower, but here also there has been a marked increase. As late as 1929 only 10 persons in each 100 in the appropriate age range were in colleges or universities. The proportion has shown great increases since 1949 and has now reached the imposing figure of 43 in every 100. This holding power is a typically American phenomenon. England and Canada come the closest to the American level, but most other, equally civilized countries have no intention of holding everyone in school after the end of the first eight years.

▶ Range of Abilities in High School

Almost any entering class of freshmen at the high school level may be expected to show a wide range of intellectual capacities. The mental ages range from that of an average fourth-grade child to that of an upperclassman in college. A teacher of the present teaches a cross section of the population with almost as great a variability as that found in the lower grades.

The question of what effect the increases in enrollments have had upon the average and the distribution of intellectual abilities was once assumed to have been settled, but upon logical rather than empirical grounds. The argument ran as follows: The pupils in private academies and such high schools as existed in 1890 were highly selected and highly intelligent; they were the children of people above the average in wealth, and since intelligence is related positively to income, they were presumed to be above average in intelligence; inasmuch as the secondary schools already enrolled pupils from the upper intellectual strata of society, any addition must have come from the lower levels, with a presumed lower general ability; the average for the enlarged secondary school group would therefore be reduced. This argument seems to have been fallacious, so far as one can judge from available evidence.

Quite possibly the small enrollment in earlier days represented certain social classes containing children of all degrees of mental capacity rather than certain intellectual levels drawn from several social and occupational groups. Since the development of tests it has been demonstrated conclusively that while intelligence does show a rough correlation with family income, the total distribution of abilities from all income groups is almost the same, and that the overlapping from one such group to another is so great as to make the slight difference at the average of little significance. It was also shown many years ago that nearly half the children in a very large number of those with IQs above 120 came from families in lower occupational groups.[1] It is therefore probable that in the decades from 1890 to 1920, the differences in intellectual level between in-school and out-of-school adolescents were greatly

---

[1] S. M. Stoke and H. C. Lehman, "Intelligence Test Scores of Social and Occupational Groups," *School and Society,* 31:372–377, 1930.

exaggerated. During these decades boys and girls could get good jobs if they left a school in which the curriculum was too narrow to be interesting for most adolescents. The proportion in each generation that can and will complete four years of Latin and three each of Greek and mathematics is very small and by no means coincides with the highest 10 percent in the distribution of intelligence. Such a curriculum selects those of genuine scholarly tastes to whom such a curriculum is exciting, plus those to whom the prestige of a diploma is worth the hours of boredom necessary to obtain it. The group in 1890 was certainly "selected," but quite possibly upon social and economic rather than intellectual grounds. Indeed, in view of the curriculum, perhaps the brightest of the nonacademically minded pupils were the ones who left! One cannot produce objective evidence on this matter of selection before 1915 at the earliest, and arguments without data are notoriously fallacious. All one can say is that decreases in intelligence do not seem to have occurred since 1920, although the population of the high school has risen from $2\frac{1}{2}$ to 12 million.

▶ Withdrawal from School

Many who enter high school fail to graduate, especially in states in which the compulsory age limit is 14 or 16. Withdrawal may be for involuntary reasons: departure of the family for another state, or entrance of the adolescent into a private school, a reform school, a sanitarium, or a mental hospital, or his death. In a study covering withdrawals from the high schools of ten typical cities of 200,000 or over, the total percentages for withdrawals for voluntary reasons was found to be, for four successive years, 4.7, 9.7, 11.4, and 8.0.[2] These pupils withdrew because, for some reason, they wished to do so or felt they must.

In 1960 there were 2,500,000 adolescents who were 18 years of age. One-third of them had stated their intention to attend college, one-third of them were working, and one-third had already dropped out of school but were unemployed.[3] It is estimated that between 1960 and 1970 there will be $7\frac{1}{2}$ million drop-outs from the high schools.[4] The usual rate of elimination in high school is one in three. In general two boys leave school for each girl. While girls as a group show a higher verbal ability than boys, the writers are inclined to prefer other explanations. It may be that the preponderance of women teachers creates an atmosphere that is too feminine for adolescent boys who are deeply concerned with developing an adequate degree of mas-

---

[2] D. Segel and O. J. Schwarm, *Retention in the High Schools in Large Cities* (Washington, D.C.: U.S. Office of Education), Bulletin 1957, no. 15, p. 5.

[3] *National Education Research Bulletin*, "High School Dropouts," 1960, Vol. 38, no. 1, pp. 1–14.

[4] *Ibid.*

culinity. Their revolt against school may be only one phase of their revolt against female domination. A girl often feels that she can make a better marriage and can become more successful socially if she finishes high school, and so she tries harder than her brother and is far less willing than he to leave school, even though the classwork may bore her just as much. This motive is especially strong among girls from low socioeconomic backgrounds who hope to advance socially through marriage. Moreover, as long as a girl remains in school she has at least casual contact with dozens of boys; but if she leaves and goes to work, her main business contacts will be with other girls or with married men. Neither of these reasons has any immediate relevance to education, but probably both contribute to the greater elimination of boys and the greater continuance of girls in high school.

A study covering withdrawals in an entire state gives typical results.[5] The ages of 1296 withdrawals during a single year varied from 13 to 18; only 16 percent withdrew before 16, 46 percent at 16, and 38 percent after 16. The entire group had IQs ranging from below 85 to over 115, with an average at 92. This figure suggests that one reason for leaving school is sheer lack of ability, since the average is twelve points lower than the 105 that is customary for those who graduate from high school. Over a third of the students who withdrew had repeated at least one grade and a few had repeated as many as three. About one-fourth of these students were doing A or B work in high school, about half of them were doing C work, and the remaining fourth either D or failing work. These last two items indicate a difficulty in mastering school material. But failure is clearly no more than a contributing cause, since three-fourths of the pupils who withdrew were making at least satisfactory grades, and some were doing very well indeed. In general, the reasons for leaving school are personal and may best be thought of as reactions to social or emotional maladjustments of various kinds. Students who leave school are, as a group, unacceptable to their peers, more or less isolated from adolescent social life, and unable to solve their personal problems.[6] Such reasons probably outweigh the difference in intellectual ability between those who stay and those who leave.

An excellent study of underachievers who were still in school but probably on their way out gives an idea of what kind of situations, habits, and traits contribute to producing the drop-out. These various points are sum-

[5] S. E. Hecker, "Early School Leavers in Kentucky," *Bulletin of the Bureau of Service* (Lexington, Ky.: College of Education, University of Kentucky, 1953), Vol. XXV, no. 4, 1953, 78 pp.

[6] R. G. Kuhlen and E. G. Collister, "Sociometric Status of Sixth and Ninth Graders Who Fail to Finish High School," *Educational and Psychological Measurement,* 12:632–637, 1952. See also, R. E. Iffert and R. Axen, "Drop outs: Their Nature and Causes; Effects on Student, Family, and Society," in the *National Conference on Higher Education,* 1956, pp. 94–103; and E. S. Cook, "Analysis of Factors Related to Withdrawal from High School Prior to Graduation," *Journal of Educational Research,* 50:191–196, 1956.

marized in Table 23–1 under the headings of home conditions, attitudes toward school, study habits, and traits of personality. The typical about-to-dropout student emerges from these data. He is not on good terms with his family, he finds nothing in school to stimulate him, he has already developed makeshift and inadequate methods of work, he is a nonbookish person, he

Table 23–1: TRAITS OF UNDERACHIEVERS IN HIGH SCHOOL

	Percent
1. Home Conditions	
Rejected by parents	66
Oldest child in family	49
High economic status	60
2. Attitudes toward School	
No interest in schoolwork	75
Dislike of teachers	28
Work considered extremely dull	40
Work had no practical value	50
Unwillingness to seek teachers' help in personal difficulties	91
3. Study Habits	
Took verbatim notes in class	66
Had no idea how to prepare for exams	50
Could not express self in writing	50
Could not concentrate in class	60
Could not study unless material was interesting	57
4. Traits of Personality (no percents given)	
Isolated from peers of both sexes	
Self-rejective	
Indecisive	
High rating in masculinity	
More interest in action than in reflection	
Unrealistic vocational goals	

SOURCE: Based on D. S. Chabasson, "Correlates of Academic Underachievers in Male Adolescents," *Alberta Journal of Educational Research,* 5:130–146, 1959. See also E. W. Bragg, "A Study of Student Withdrawals at W.U.," *Journal of Educational Psychology,* 47:199–202, 1956.

has unsatisfactory relations with his peers as well as with both his parents and teachers, he lacks self-confidence, he rejects himself as being worthless, he is unrealistic about his vocational ambitions; and although 91 percent knew they were underachievers, they had no idea what they could do about it. It is a question how one can best hold such a student in school, or if he should be held at all. The objection to letting him go is that he will lose his last chance to become more successful in life than he is otherwise likely to be. And in the labor market of the future his position will always be precarious.

Dropping out of school has always been more or less undesirable, even for those who had no academic interests, because the adolescents lost the supportive influence of their classmates and teachers and they were separated from a schedule of activities that had acted as the supporting framework of their lives ever since they could remember. In previous generations, however, the 16-year-old drop-out could find work, and he soon developed a new frame of reference. The adolescent who leaves school today is not so fortunate, because what he has to offer—youth and strength—are no longer widely needed. He may get some trifling job, such as opening packing cases, in the store of a family friend, but usually he does not find even that. At an age when he should be up and doing, he is idle. The scene in Figure 23–3 shows the kind of aimless activity in which he is likely to engage, not perhaps because he wants to but because he can thus kill some time, of which he has an over-abundance. Many types of diversion are closed to him because he has no money, and those that are available often verge upon the illegal. It is because the present situation is so dangerous to unemployed and unemployable youth, that schools should make every effort to keep adolescents in school and to offer them guidance in case they leave.

Elimination continues throughout the college years. Of 25,334 entering freshmen, an average of 40 percent graduated in four years, and another 11 percent were still in college. An average of 12 percent has transferred to another school, and several of these will graduate sometime. The differences

Table 23–2: STUDENT RECORDS OF GRADUATION, TRANSFER, AND DROP-OUT, BY TYPES OF FOUR-YEAR INSTITUTIONS

| | Percent by Type of Institution | | | | |
Student Record	University	Technological Institutions	Liberal Arts College	Teachers' College	Total
Graduated in 4 years from institution of first registration	39.0	42.8	41.3	36.0	39.5
Not graduated but still attending after 4 years	13.1	13.3	9.3	8.6	11.6
Transferred to another institution	10.7	11.2	15.4	8.6	12.0
Dropped out, no record of transfer	42.7	35.3	39.7	44.1	41.5
Total Number of Students	5775	783	4197	1912	12,667

SOURCE: R. E. Iffert, *Retention and Withdrawal of College Students* (Washington, D.C.: U.S. Department of Health, Education, and Welfare, 1958), Bulletin No. 1, 177 pp., p. 18.

Fig. 23–3. Adolescent drop-outs from school

between types of school are small but consistent; the technological institutions have the best record and the teachers' colleges the poorest. The voluntary withdrawals for all types together was 41.5 percent. It is probably a fair guess that 50 to 55 percent of an entering freshman class will graduate somewhere, sometime and that 45 to 50 percent will not.

The figures above are about groups of students, and they leave out of account the reasons for withdrawal. The studies given below are included to illustrate problems of social and emotional maladjustment that operate in individual cases. One is from the high school level and the other from college.

Justine entered high school at the age of 16, with a record of two retardations in elementary school. During the primary grades her work had been fair, but from the fourth grade on she had received poorer and poorer marks. The comments made by her successive teachers showed a progressive deterioration of personality, presumably the result of her chronic frustration. Her fourth-, fifth-, and sixth-grade teachers thought her a bit uncooperative, but believed that she did really make an effort to learn her lessons. Outside class, they found her pleasant and willing to help by doing little chores about the school. Her seventh- and eighth-grade teachers were almost unanimous in labeling her sullen and lazy. In all grades, however, Justine had been fairly popular with the other children, although she was not a leader. At the end of the first semester in high school Justine failed every course she was taking. She was therefore sent to a counselor for an interview. At first, the girl was sullen and uncommunicative, but presently she began to tell about her difficulties, once she discovered that she had a sympathetic listener. She did not hate school, but she was most unhappy in class. She liked the teachers well enough and the other pupils very much. She enjoyed games and various cocurricular activities. Her vocational ambition was to become a cook. Justine did not seem to understand why she could not do the schoolwork that other pupils enjoyed—in fact, she appeared rather preoccupied with this problem. The counselor therefore gave the girl two tests of intelligence and let her score them herself. Then the counselor and Justine went over the results and compared them with the norms. One might have thought the girl would be discouraged by the findings, but actually she was greatly relieved. She exclaimed at once, "Then I'm *not* lazy!" She was reassured on this point and advised to elect a light program of courses that would lead directly to her vocational objective. Justine was cooperative and willing to be guided. She took only two courses—both in foods—plus classes in physical education, how to study, and remedial reading. She continued with her membership in three or four clubs. At the end of the year Justine passed her small amount of classwork, although by no great margin. At the beginning of her sophomore year the counselor found Justine a half-time position as assistant to the cook in a nearby bakery. Nothing was said about Justine's dropping out of school, but as the year progressed and she became more and more interested in her work at the bakery, she gradually stopped coming to class. As a means of keeping her social contacts, she continued to belong to one or two clubs and to play games with her former classmates. Instead of penalizing her for her nonattendance, the counselor let her drop the courses she did not finish. Justine's high school career petered out completely in the middle of what would have been her junior year if she had taken a normal schedule. By this time she had worked up to a responsible position in the bakery, she had many friends whom she had met through her work, and she had no more need for the high school. Justine has no sense of failure; she says that she went to high school as long as she wanted to do so and then left of her own accord. Her case was handled so wisely that she no longer feels frustrated or unhappy.

A rather good-looking but sulky girl came to her supervisor in a small college with the complaint that she simply did not like college and was unhappy there. It was evident after a few minutes of conversation that she had no interest in any of her courses. The counselor at first assumed that she wanted advice about further work in college, so he went through the catalogue, asking her if she would like to take this or that course that was open to freshmen. Nothing aroused the faintest spark. Indeed, as the possibilities for study were revealed to her, the girl grew more and more glum. Eventually, the counselor asked her what she intended to do after she was through college and received the surprising reply that she wanted to be a hostess in a night club. The counselor explained that college was no place to acquire whatever skills she might need, nor did he even know what the skills were, having always supposed that such positions were obtained mainly through being a friend of the owner of the club. He was also somewhat puzzled as to what helpful advice he could give. He told her he thought that she should withdraw from college, since the work offered had no bearing on her vocational objective, but this solution was not acceptable. The girl had got it into her head that at least a year or two of college was necessary for general social acceptance. She left the office still unhappy and even sulkier than before. A few weeks later she flunked out of college. At a final interview with her counselor she blamed her failure upon her teachers and complained bitterly about the unfairness of the marking system. The counselor tried to argue her into a better frame of mind but without much success. The next day she presumably left for home. The counselor was therefore not a little surprised to meet her on the street about three months later. She was wearing an air hostess's uniform and looked both pretty and happy. She voluntarily hailed the counselor and told him that she had been ashamed to go home, so she had registered at a training school for air hostesses. She was now working and was thrilled with her job.

This girl is an extreme case of a common type of dropout. She had no interest in anything offered by higher education. She was not stupid, but her intellectual abilities were of too low an order for success in college without a great deal of application. She disliked studying, reading, or even thinking. She neither understood nor wanted to understand what her teachers were talking about. She had been swept along by the general exodus from her high school into college and had merely gone with her friends. Graduation from college had become for her a symbol of social success—an odd concept of the life academic. Many voluntary withdrawals are of this type. Such students do not belong in college, but it is often hard to convince them of this fact.

It is probable that there will always be withdrawals from schools and colleges. Sometimes the grounds are purely financial, sometimes the students are too dull to profit by further work, and sometimes they have no interests that could be served by the school. What is needed is a better "exit" service so that those who leave can do so without the feelings of disgrace and failure that often accompany the process. The counselor in many high schools tries to give this type of help, and in some places all pupils who want to withdraw have a series of talks with a counselor first. Some of them can—and should—be readjusted to school life, but others are definitely better off outside the school, provided the separation can be brought about without emotional trauma.

▶ The Intention to Attend College

Some present-day high-school students have intended from childhood to go on into college, but for many the decision must be made as the senior year of high school comes to an end. There are two fundamental problems: How many high school seniors intend to go further with their education? And, which ones? Of the two, perhaps the second is the more important for society.

The first question is the easier to answer. Out of a total of 2000 high school seniors in 1959, 39 percent intended to enter college and 15 percent to continue their education in special schools of some kind.[7] These figures are typical of many other similar investigations. In the fall of 1957 and spring of 1958 an investigator [8] gave the same 8500 high school students a questionnaire about their future plans. In order to be considered as a college prospect, a student had to state either that he intended to go to college or that he was still undecided on *both* questionnaires. At all four years of high school more and more boys stated a desire for college, while fewer and fewer girls did. Of the 1029 seniors, 50 percent were considered in the prospect group. The investigator checked the students in 1959 and found that only a third of them were actually attending college. A more extensive study of 35,000 high school seniors

---

[7] Purdue Opinion Panel, "Youth Looks at Education," *Report of Poll No. 54* (Lafayette, Ind.: Division of Educational Reference, Purdue University, 1959), 26 pp., p. 19a.

[8] P. Cutright, "Students' Decision to Attend College," *Journal of Social Education,* 33:292–299. 1960.

gave similar results but added some new points.[9] The percentage of students in any given community planning to attend college is related to a number of factors, such as: ability level of the individual student, professional status and education of his father, ability of the family to provide a major share of the expenses (especially important for girls), level of marks in high school, number of friends with college plans, availability in the high school of guidance and counseling, socioeconomic background of the family, number of younger siblings in the family. A follow-up study a year later indicated that of the entire 35,000 seniors 36 percent of the boys and 27 percent of the girls were in college. Obviously, by no means everyone who had planned succeeded in arriving and remaining; only 65 percent of the planners were actually there, plus an additional 7 percent who had had no college plans as high school seniors but just got in the car and went anyway. Of the "best" prospects— those of high general intelligence, high standing on tests of academic aptitude, and high record in schoolwork—78 percent were in attendance, with a resultant loss in academic training for 22 percent of the country's best minds. A third study upon a much more modest scale concerned the college-going plans of country youth. Residence in the country and attendance at small country schools had a negative influence upon plans for further education beyond high school, and for those who had hopes of college attendance the majority seemed to regard college more as a means of escape from the farm than as a training for the future.[10]

Everyone is interested in the continuation into college of the academically gifted student. This group makes up about 15 percent of all high school students. While more of them come from the upper economic groups, there are members from even the lowest slums. For this group a college education is essential; if families cannot provide the necessary funds, then governments or private foundations will have to do so, since society cannot afford to leave any of its best minds untrained. However, not all the good students enter college, and of those who enter not all remain long enough to graduate.

The freshmen who entered the University of Wisconsin in 1953 were followed up four years later to find out what their academic history had been. In 1957, 37 percent of the entering freshmen had graduated, 14 percent were still in college and would presumably graduate, 6 percent had transferred to other colleges. This gives a total of 60 percent either graduated or about to do so at Wisconsin, plus another 6 percent whose present status is unknown but of whom at least some have probably graduated or will do so. Even at best, however, the loss was 34 percent. This loss was not, unfortunately,

---

[9] G. Stice, W. G. Mollenkopf, and W. S. Torgerson, "Background Factors Relating to College Plans and College Enrollment among Public School Students" (Princeton, N.J.: Educational Testing Service, 1956), 117 pp.

[10] E. G. Youmans, "Background of Rural Youth Planning to Enter College," *Journal of Educational Sociology,* 32:152–156, 1958.

evenly distributed among the students of different academic levels at entrance. To be sure, the poorer the previous preparation had been, in terms of marks and test scores, the greater the percent that was eliminated, but since students with varying academic records in secondary school do not attend college in equal proportions, the actual loss in number of students was greatest in the highest group. For example, out of every 100 entering freshmen, 65 are from the highest third of their high school class, 25 are from the middle third, and 10 from the lowest third. The elimination percents for these three groups are, respectively: 39, 57 and 78 percent. But the numbers work out as follows:

		Elimination Rate	Number of Students Lost
Highest third	65 students	39 percent	25
Middle third	25 students	57 percent	14
Lowest third	10 students	78 percent	8

In short, there is more actual loss in numbers from the top third than from the two lower groups combined. This situation is serious. Even though this upper third furnished half the graduate students five years later and five out of six honor students as undergraduates, it lost over a third of its initial number; seven (11 percent) were dismissed for failing academic work.[11]

▶ **Summary**

The basic fact about the high school population is that there is a great deal of it. The spectacular growth in all education above the elementary school level has, within the last 50 years, precipitated many problems—aside from such obvious ones as the mere providing of enough buildings and equipment. In 1909 a total of 20,000 college professors was enough; now 150,000 are needed, with a resulting increase in the number of those who must get a Ph.D.—hence an enlargement of the graduate school, hence a need for more professors! The arrival of nearly 90 out of every 100 adolescents upon the high school doorstep has precipitated profound revisions in the philosophy of secondary education and in the nature of the curriculum. The statistics given in this chapter are, therefore, not just numbers in a vacuum. They summarize the basic, inescapable facts of life as far as secondary education is concerned.

Some who enter high school do not remain to graduate, and at least 40 percent of the entering class in college will fail to obtain a degree. Pupils leave school for a variety of reasons, some academic, some personal. The

---

[11] J. K. Little, "The Persistence of Academically Talented Youth in University Studies," *Educational Record*, 40:237–241, 1959.

high school drop-out is likely to be in a precarious position, both immediately and in the future. He will probably remain idle for some time, and he will be ill-fitted for the types of work for which there will be the greatest demands. Every year boys and girls of well above average ability drop out of school. The loss of good minds is a tragedy for the community.

References for Further Reading

BOOKS

Other Texts

Kuhlen, *Psychology of Adolescent Development* (pp. 469–480).

Other Books and Monographs

Hand, H. C., *Principles of Public Secondary Education* (New York: Harcourt, Brace & World, Inc., 1958), 369 pp. (Chap. 5).

Iffert, R. E., "Retention and Withdrawal of College Students," *United States Department of Health, Education, and Welfare,* Bulletin No. 1, 1958, 177 pp. (Chaps. 3 and 4 or 9 and 10).

Iffert, R. E., and R. Axen, "Dropouts: Their Nature and Causes; Effects on Student, Family, and Society," *National Conference on Higher Education,* 1956, pp. 94–103.

Nason, L. J., "Academic Achievement of Gifted High School Students," *Southern California Educational Monograph,* No. 17, 1958, 92 pp.

"High School Drop-Outs," *National Education Association Research Bulletin,* Vol. 38, No. 1, 1960 (pp. 11–14).

Seidman, *The Adolescent: A Book of Readings,* rev. ed. (No. 6).

Stice, G., *et al., Background Factors and College-Going Plans among High-Aptitude Public High School Seniors* (Princeton, N.J.: Educational Testing Service, 1956), 117 pp. (pp. 45–73).

ARTICLES

Bragg, E. W., "A Study of Student Withdrawal at W. U.," *Journal of Educational Psychology,* 47:199–202, 1956.

Chabassol, D. J., "Correlates of Academic Achievement in Male Adolescence," *Alberta Journal of Educational Research,* 5:130–146, 1959.

Cook, E. A., "Analysis of Factors Related to Withdrawal from High School Prior to Graduation," *Journal of Educational Research,* 50:191–196, 1956.

Cutright, P., "Students' Decision to Attend College," *Journal of Educational Sociology,* 33:292–299, 1960.

Davie, J. S., "Social Class Factors and School Attendance," *Harvard Educational Review,* 23:175–185, 1953.

Little, J. K., "The Persistence of Academically Talented Youth in University Studies," *Educational Record*, 40:237–241, 1959.

Magnifico, L. X., "Social Promotion and Special Education," *School and Society*, 86:216–218, 1958.

Moore, P. L., "Factors Involved in Student Elimination from High School," *Journal of Negro Education*, 23:117–122, 1954.

Nesbit, E., "Finding the Causes of Non-attendance," *Social Work*, 2:81–86, 1957.

Thomas, R. J., "An Empirical Study of High School Drop-Outs in Regard to Ten Possible Related Factors," *Journal of Educational Sociology*, 28:11–18, 1954.

Youmans, E. G., "Background of Rural Youth Planning to Enter College," *Journal of Educational Sociology*, 32:152–156, 1958.

Suggested Research Problems [12]

1. Methods of preventing drop-outs or methods of rehabilitating drop-outs.
2. A study of students who transfer once, twice, or more between grade 7 and grade 12, (a) to determine what happens to their social and emotional development and (b) to suggest ways in which the sometimes traumatic effects may be avoided.

---

[12] See note on p. 11.

Chapter 24 | Emotional Problems in the Schoolroom

THE present chapter will deal with four main topics: the common problems of high school pupils, mental hygiene in the classroom, the recognition of maladjustment, and the control of the class. All these topics involve emotional reactions. Even though some of the problems are themselves of physical or academic origin, the reactions that pupils make to them are emotional.

▶ **The Problems of Boys and Girls**

It seems a good idea to start with a list of the problems that trouble adolescents. Many of these are at least partially solved, one way or another, during the high school years. Some of them are so troublesome that pupils cannot make much academic progress, even when they very much wish to do so. The list that will be presented in the next few pages is based upon a large number of studies that reported results from some 10,000 students in high school or the freshman year of college. The list of problems is detailed. It has been made so purposely in order that one may see the problems in as concrete a form as possible. The main divisions and the subgroupings are intended to give the list some degree of organization and to make it easier to grasp. The figures in Table 24–1 are percentages and are taken from several different sources. Some items were mentioned in only one study, in which case the figure comes from that one. Other items appeared in two or more reports; in such instances, the percentages from all of them have been averaged. These figures are only approximations of frequency and are included because they provide a rough estimate of how common a difficulty is among adolescents. An average student in high school will have at least a dozen of these problems; many will have twenty or thirty, of which, however, only two or three are basic, the rest being pyramided on top of the fundamental ones. The list includes problems mentioned by more than 15 percent of the adolescents.

One study that reports changes over a period of several years gives a good introduction to the subject of what problems agitate high school pupils. An investigation made in 1935 was repeated in 1957—after a lapse of 22 years. The results appear in Figure 24–1. In 1935 the first problem for boys

533

Table 24–1: PROBLEMS OF HIGH SCHOOL STUDENTS
(Figures are percentages)

I. Problems of Health and Growth

Not getting enough sleep	42	Eating the wrong foods	24
Getting too tired	19	Suffering from nausea	64
Being unable to relax	27		
		Being too big or too small	28
Having bad posture	39	Being under- or overweight	52
Having poor figure	25		
Having bad complexion	31	Being nervous or tense	30
Being awkward	22	Biting nails	26
Sexual development	61		

II. Problems of Personality

Feeling inferior	41	Worrying about little things	31
Feeling bashful	19	Being blue frequently	18
Disliking responsibility	22	Getting discouraged easily	24
Lacking self-confidence	30	Taking things too seriously	37
Feeling self-conscious	28		
Feeling pushed around	25	Daydreaming too much	32
Feeling not wanted	21	Feeling guilty about things one	
Feeling unsure of oneself	24	has or has not done	26
Fearing humiliation	26	Feeling lonesome	20
Feeling stupid	33	Feeling unhappy	16
		Being too easily hurt	31
Having outbursts of temper	33		
Being too restless	24	Being too intolerant	18
Being too excitable	23	Being tactless	19
Being too careless	26	Hurting the feelings of others	21
Losing head in emergencies	23	Arguing too much	15
Feeling misunderstood	19	Fearing criticism	20

III. Problems of Home and Family

Having no place to study	31	Quarreling with siblings	18
Having no room to oneself	18	Talking back to parents	26
Having no privacy	26	Constant bickering over	
		money in home	15
Feeling too distant from		Having parents who quarrel	
parents in interests	19	with each other	16
Being unable to discuss personal			
things with parents	29	Being treated as a child	34
Being unable to discuss sex		Being denied use of family car	29
problems with parents	30	Having too little freedom	29

III. Problems of Home and Family (*cont'd*)

Being afraid to tell parents when one has done wrong	19	Not being allowed to go out on school nights	39
Being unable to think of parents as friends	28	Being made to get home at a certain hour	31
Feeling parents expect too much	28	Being regarded as irresponsible	21
Interference of parents in choice of friends	27	Not having enough spending money	26

IV. Problems of Social Status

Being awkward at social affairs	27	Not knowing how to get rid of a person one does not like	20
Fear of making social errors	43	Not having good table manners	17
Fear of meeting people	28	Not knowing how to order in a restaurant	16
Feeling unable to converse	35		
Feeling awkward in daily relations with one's age-mates	17		
Wanting to be in a "crowd"	18	Having too few friends	38
		Wanting to be more popular	54
Worrying over what to wear	16	Being left out of things	26
Worrying over correct manners	34	Wanting to join more clubs	15
Wanting to learn to dance	34	Having too few activities	18
Not knowing how to act at social affairs	28	Having no one for a chum	38
Not knowing how to introduce people	29	Having no one to discuss personal problems with	26
Not knowing how to plan a party	16	Wanting to make new friends but not knowing how	42
Not knowing how to select the right clothes	15	Being unpopular	20
		Wanting to be more of a leader	23
		Wanting to be elected	17

V. Problems of Sex and Heterosexual Relationships

Not having a boy (or girl) friend	35	Worrying over marrying the right person	19
Wanting more dates	45	Wondering about marriage	21
Falling in and out of love	23	Wanting to marry now	27
Not knowing how to ask a girl for a date	19		
Wondering how to get a boy to ask one for a date	15	Wanting to be more attractive	38
Not knowing what to do on a date	24	Wanting to be more interesting to boys (or girls)	30
Not knowing what is proper on a date	17	Being embarrassed by dirty jokes	21
Not knowing how to refuse a date politely	26	Not knowing if petting is right or necessary for popularity	21
		Thinking too much about sex	18
Not knowing if one should go on blind dates	22	Needing correct information about sex	35

V. Problems of Sex and Heterosexual Relationships (*cont'd*)

Not knowing if one should "go steady"	26	Worrying about masturbation	29
		Worrying because organs show through clothes	31

VI. Problems of Religion and Morals

Needing advice on religious matters	28	Wondering what life is all about	18
Wondering about life after death	24	Trying to break a bad habit	21
Fear of death	34		
Being confused about beliefs	17	Worrying over the next war	31
Knowing one is not living up to one's own ideals	19	Worrying over racial prejudice	25
		Worrying over social inequalities	16
		Worrying over problems of government	15
Not knowing what is right or wrong	28	Worrying over intolerance	22
Not knowing what the standards are for right and wrong	23	Worrying over reforming	29
		Worrying over atomic warfare	49

VII. Problems of School and Study

Being unable to concentrate	47	Worrying over examinations	51
Having poor methods of study	36	Worrying about low marks	28
Being unable to plan time	34	Not knowing how to prepare for examinations	26
Being inattentive in class	39		
Being unable to use library	21	Not knowing how well one is doing	40
Being too slow	26	Getting too low marks	29
Daydreaming while studying	51	Disliking school	22
Wasting time	35		
Being unable to take notes	27	Being afraid to talk in class	36
Having trouble in outlining	17	Being unable to speak before a group	53
Being unable to express oneself in speech or writing	41		
Having too small a vocabulary	26	Wondering if one has enough ability to do work	59
Being unable to read well enough or fast enough	35	Doubting ability to do schoolwork	40
Having teachers who are unfair	15	Doubting ability to go to college	42
Having teachers who are sarcastic	17	Fearing failure in college	27
Having teachers who give too little encouragement	15	Needing help in selecting courses	26
Having teachers who have favorites	22	Needing help in selecting college	38
		Having too many activities that interfere with study	32
Doubting the value of what is taught	21	Watching TV or listening to radio too much	27

VIII. Problems of Choosing a Vocation

Needing help in choosing vocation	43	Having no interest in any line of work	17
Needing help in selecting necessary courses	42		
Needing experience in different kinds of work	49	Needing to earn money now	27
Needing help in discovering one's abilities	43	Needing to earn money to go to college	21
Needing help in learning about openings in different fields	28	Needing to learn how to budget money	28
Not knowing where to look for a job	35	Not knowing how to write a letter of application	18
Not knowing what work is suitable for one's abilities	56	Not knowing how to act during an interview [1]	24

SOURCE: [1] Based mainly upon the following references: D. P. Ausubel, "Problems of Adolescent Adjustment," *Bulletin of the National Association of School Principals,* 34:1–84, 1950; J. A. Bond, "Analysis of Factors Affecting Scholarship of High School Pupils," *Journal of Educational Research,* 46:1–16, 1952; J. V. Hanna and A. Crossman, "The Problems of College Freshmen Entering Washington Square College," *Counseling,* 12:2–3, 1954; R. A. Hunter and D. H. Morgan, "Problems of College Students," *Journal of Educational Psychology,* 40:79–92, 1949; B. P. Monks and C. W. Heath, "A Classification of Academic, Social, and Personal Problems for Use in a College Student Health Department," *Student Medicine,* 2:44–62, 1954; H. H. Remmers, A. J. Drucker, and B. Shimberg, *Examiner's Manual for the SRA Youth Inventory* (Chicago, Ill.: Science Research Associates, 1950), 12 pp.; M. T. Tate and V. A. Musick, "Adjustment Problems of College Students," *Social Forces,* 33:182–185, 1954; E. W. Waters, "Problems of Rural Negro High School Seniors on the Eastern Shore of Maryland," *Journal of Negro Education,* 22:115–125, 1953; G. G. Wertheril, *Human Relations Education* (American Social Hygiene Association, 1951), pp. 10–11; A. Lent, "A Survey of Adolescent High School Girls 14–18 Years of Age," *Alberta Journal of Educational Research,* 3:127–138, 1957.

was money and the first one for girls was personal attractiveness; in 1957 the main problem for both sexes was study. Money became slightly less important for boys but slightly more so for girls. Personal problems were judged to be one step more important for boys and one step less so for girls. Health as a center for concern dropped out of the boys' first five choices, and reappears for the girls only as mental health. Perhaps, as the goal of universal medical care is being approached, this particular worry will recede still further. The girls failed to list manners in their first five choices in 1957, but the boys added it, at the bottom, in that year. The outstanding change, however, is in the realization of both boys and girls that they have to study and that study involves a number of problems which they have not yet solved.[2]

As can be appreciated from the nature and number of the problems listed

[2] D. B. Harris, "Sex Differences in the Life Problems and Interests of Adolescents," *Child Development,* 30:453–459, 1959.

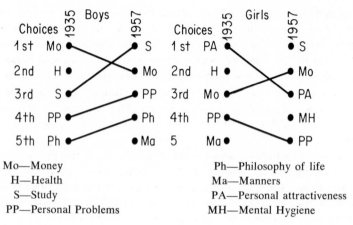

Fig. 24-1. First five worries of high school boys and girls, 1935 and 1957

Based on D. B. Harris, "Sex Differences in the Life Problems and Interests of Adolescents, 1935 and 1957" *Child Development* 30:453–459, 1959.

in Table 24–1, adolescence is a period of great insecurity and instability. If a teacher keeps these problems in mind, she can contribute to their solution through her procedures and assignments. The main force, however, that cures an adolescent of his difficulties is more growth and more living. Often a pupil does not realize that his difficulties are not permanent. He sees no end to them nor does he sense their relation to his stage of development. A teacher can often relieve a good deal of strain merely by telling a pupil that his troubles will soon pass. She does not need to add that the present problems will be replaced by others!

▶ Mental Health in the Schoolroom

The secondary school teacher of today is responsible for teaching subject matter, just as teachers have always been, but in addition she is responsible for improving her pupils' mental health. Consequently she needs to avoid practices that will produce problems of mental health and to substitute those that will promote normal emotional development. This section contains suggestions for the maintenance of a serene emotional atmosphere in the classroom.

Fears Caused by Schoolwork   Three fears are so common that they sometimes seem natural and unavoidable accompaniments of schoolwork: fear of teachers, fear of examinations, and fear of talking before the class. None of these is necessary, all are destructive to either progress in school or normal personal development, and all are learned from experiences in school.

Teachers of whom pupils are afraid may have any of several unpleasant characteristics, but perhaps sarcasm and ridicule are the most common negative traits. Sarcasm is an unfair weapon that the sophisticated adult in a position of authority uses against pupils whose respect she cannot obtain. It usually precipitates even worse manners on the part of the student involved, and it is always emotionally disrupting. The shy students are hurt, the verbally quick students, "talk back," and the ill-mannered and the hostile ones make scenes. In the resulting emotional storm no one in the room gets much learning done.

Fear of examinations arises when teachers stress the police functions of examinations instead of their educational functions. It may also come from too great a pressure for marks by either parents or teachers. This fear is quite real; indeed, its physical effects can be measured. Most pupils, however, recover from their apprehension as soon as they start working on a test. If the fear of examinations to come is sufficiently intense, it prevents the learning of the subject matter, although the student conscientiously makes what should have been an adequate preparation, and it sometimes produces an actual distortion of the material, in case the student reads only to prepare for examination questions. Perhaps some degree of anxiety is unavoidable, but at least teachers should do what they can to alter this attitude on the part of those pupils who show it.

Fear of talking in class is common among adolescents, especially among boys, perhaps because their voices are changing. If pupils are required to stand when talking, they may be embarrassed by their own awkwardness. Except for the occasional student who is pathologically shy, a good teacher should be able to eliminate this fear by making classwork informal and by giving special help to those who are apprehensive.

Control of the Class Class control should be constructive. That is, it should lead the pupils to control themselves. Its objective is not quietness but the creation of an environment in which pupils can grow in both achievement and personality. The modern theories of control condemn the use of fear or intimidation in any form, and not only on humanitarian grounds. Fear leads to rigidity, not relaxation, it introduces a destructive emotion into what ought to be a constructive relationship, it prevents learning, it does not lead to a healthy attitude of mind, it favors the growth of all manner of escape mechanisms. In short, except for producing quiet, it is useless. Instead of fear, today's teacher is supposed to base her control upon the interests of the pupils and upon their friendly feelings toward her and toward each other. She is supposed to develop such good group morale that the pupils will control each other for the most part. The latest way of describing the best form of control is to call it "permissive," "accepting," and "nondirective." A teacher is "permissive" if she has few rules and if she does not demand routinized schoolroom manners from her pupils. She is "accepting" if she lets the pupils act naturally and if she remains unruffled in the face of whatever conduct the "natural" behavior produces. She is "nondirective" if she does not tell her pupils what to do but sets before them a problem and then lets them tell her. The good modern classroom is not especially quiet; it is a hive of industry in which most of the pupils are engaged in doing something useful and in minding their own business.

The nondirective teacher controls her class by many methods: absence of rules, great flexibility of her plans, adjustment of work to the individual capacities of her pupils, absence of any considerable amount of tension plus the discharge of what little there is, transfer of the responsibility for discipline for any acts of aggression from herself to the pupils, her own efforts to give each child the stimuli he needs for healthy growth, encouragement to participation for the already-withdrawn, affection for the neglected, self-confidence for the insecure, diversion of expression for the attention seeker, and so on. As will be noted, such a teacher's efforts are directed toward avoiding situations that demand discipline. By so doing she prevents the arousal of the destructive emotions that ruin the relation between her and her pupils and make learning difficult. The strict, authoritarian, domineering teacher piles up emotional problems for herself and for her students. They become hostile toward her and perhaps, by displacement, toward all teachers and all schools.

In theory, discipline should never be necessary. The need for punishment is evidence of someone's failure—not necessarily the teacher's. However, even after a teacher has prevented all the friction she can, has made her classwork as interesting as she knows how to make it, has created a relaxed and permissive atmosphere in her room, has reduced the rules and formalities to the smallest possible number, and has led her pupils to a reasonably high level of self-control, she still finds herself faced with an occasional situation that requires punishment. For the discouragement of mere restlessness or unintentional lack of manners, nothing more than a word of restraint or reproof is generally needed when the relationship between the class and the teacher is good, but as all teachers know, in any class there are a few who are at times recalcitrant and a few who are so impertinently aggressive that their bad manners cannot be overlooked. Teachers are therefore forced into using punitive measures from time to time.

Good discipline for adolescents has certain outstanding characteristics. It is, first, the natural result of the misbehavior. For instance, if a boy loses his temper and throws a paste jar at the wall, the natural punishment is to make him clean up the mess, not to require him to solve six extra problems in algebra after school. Second, punishment must be certain; if a mathematics teacher sometimes laughs at a smart-aleck comment and sometimes punishes it, the offender is actually encouraged to continue his antics because the possible satisfaction derived from making the teacher laugh more than offsets the possibility of disapproval. Third, punishment should be just; the English teacher who gives a failing mark to a boy because, on the final examination, he split one infinitive is being so unjust as to defeat her own ends. Fourth, punishment must be impersonal; the history teacher who gets annoyed at a pupil's general inattention and assigns a penalty that springs primarily from her own exasperation will never succeed with adolescents. They know that the penalty is only an outlet for the teacher's emotions, and they blame her rather than themselves. Fifth, punishment should always be constructive and conducive to better self-control. Letting pupils suggest and carry out their own punishment is more likely to develop self-control than the assignment of penalties from above. Sixth, punishment should be withheld until the teacher is sure that she understands the student's motives and that she is seeing through the symptoms to the causes. Perhaps when her grasp of the situation is adequate, she will find little or nothing to punish. Seventh, punishment must avoid the arousal of fear, partly because fear is disorganizing and partly because it is useless. A frightened pupil will agree to anything, but after he has recovered, his behavior may be worse instead of better. Finally, punishment should never involve the assignment of extra schoolwork. Adolescents should have only pleasant associations with study and learning. In spite of one's best efforts they will acquire some unpleasant associations with certain elements of their schooling, but the teacher who requires a boy to translate twenty-five extra lines of French because he shouted ill-mannered remarks in class is doing her best to kill any interest he may ever have had in the subject. One cannot use schoolwork as a big stick on Monday and expect pupils to find it interesting and stimulating on Tuesday.

Teachers may well follow the advice given to parents: to realize that most aggressive behavior stems basically from a need to be loved and to feel secure, and is preceded by a period during which the aggressor feels hurt, angry, or scared. The constructive approach is to give the offending pupil a normal amount of affection and security and to determine what hurt, angered, or frightened him. If possible, he should take an active part in the study of his motives. In the end, some punishment may yet seem desirable, but it can then be given on the basis of understanding and with the offender's cooperation.

Over thirty years ago an extremely important investigation was made into the attitudes of teachers and clinical psychologists toward common types of misbehavior, including whispering, inattention, careless work, impertinence, defiance, temper, daydreaming, overactivity, cheating, laziness, and rudeness. The total comes to 51 different forms of offense or kinds of personal traits that interfere with peace and order in the classroom. The average boy showed 10 of these reactions or characteristics; the average girl, 6. The most maladjusted children averaged 17, the chronic liars and thieves averaged 19, and the aggressive delinquents, 21. The investigator asked several teachers as well as a group of mental hygienists to rate the seriousness of each offense. The two sets of ratings almost contradicted each other, as indicated in Table 24–2. The correlation between the two ratings was —0.05.[3] It was suggested that

Table 24–2: MISDEMEANORS IN SCHOOL

	Teachers' Ratings	Mental Hygienists' Ratings
Most serious	Immorality	Shyness
	Dishonesty	Lack of participation
	Impertinence	Oversensitiveness
	Defiance	Suspicion
	Temper	Daydreaming
	Rudeness	Imaginative lying
Least serious	Shyness	Impertinence
	Lack of participation	Defiance
	Oversensitiveness	Temper
	Suspicion	Rudeness
	Daydreaming	Whispering
	Imaginative lying	Restlessness

SOURCE: Based on E. K. Wickman, *Children's Behavior and Teachers' Attitudes* (Cambridge, Mass.: The Commonwealth Fund, 1929), 249 pp.

the teachers were rating as most serious the traits and reactions that were annoying to *them* rather than those that were worst for the pupils' development. The hygienists felt that there was always hope for the youngster who fought back, but not nearly as much for those who had already withdrawn from life. The investigation, with some minor variations, has been repeated at least three times: in 1936, with a resulting correlation of 0.49 between teachers and hygienists; [4] in 1942, with a correlation of 0.70; [5] and in 1951, with 0.56.[6] These figures show that teachers are acquiring an attitude toward symptoms of maladjustment that reflects some understanding of mental hygiene.[7] Presumably the ratings of hygienists and teachers should not correlate perfectly since they are estimating the importance of a given reaction by different criteria and each has something to add to the other's evaluation. The

[3] It should be stated that the teachers and hygienists did not have exactly the same directions in this first investigation.

[4] D. B. Ellis and L. W. Miller, "Teachers' Attitudes and Behavior Problems," *Journal of Educational Psychology,* 27:501–511, 1936.

[5] J. A. Mitchell, "A Study of Teachers and Mental Hygienists' Ratings of Certain Behavior Problems of Children," *Journal of Educational Research,* 36:292–307, 1942.

[6] M. H. Schrupp and C. M. Gyerde, "Teacher Growth in Attitudes toward Behavior Problems in Children," *Journal of Educational Psychology,* 44:203–214, 1951.

[7] For a summary of these studies see: E. C. Hunter, "Changes in Teachers' Attitudes towards Children's Behavior," *Mental Hygiene,* 41:3–11, 1957.

teachers have probably become less interested in maintaining order and more interested in developing normal personalities among their pupils.

Application of Mental Hygiene   Although the actual instruction in mental hygiene is the responsibility of one or two teachers who are especially equipped for giving it, every teacher needs to make what contributions she can to the solution of typical problems and to the maintenance of mental health. For example, if a history teacher has in her class a boy who thinks the present world is going to the dogs and that no one can save it, she might assign him a few paragraphs of reading in Seneca, who was as gloomy as anyone could be and complained unceasingly that the world of the first century A.D. was so bad that it could not survive. A pessimistic outlook about the future does nothing to improve learning, and it is an unnecessary emotional load for a lad to be carrying around with him. One of the writers was once in a class in calculus when she decided that the whole subject was impractical and useless, but it was too late to withdraw without the teacher's permission. Upon being requested to sign a withdrawal slip, the teacher talked over the matter a bit and then said she would consider what solution was best. The solution was an excellent one—but not what could be expected. The instructor looked around and found in the nearby city a factory in which a certain cutting machine had to be reset at intervals of about two weeks and assigned the writer to go and reset it—and the job required calculus. This assignment ended the "higher-mathematics-is-useless" complaint, and there was no withdrawal. Some teachers are in a position to make assignments that will throw light upon such perennial problems as the antagonism between generations or the intense youthful love affair. Many novels present these problems, with or without solution, in readable and interesting form. If a social studies teacher finds a good deal of prejudice and misunderstanding in her class, she can organize any of a half-dozen projects that are aimed at the decreasing of ignorance—which is a considerable element in the creation of unfavorable attitudes. If Mary Jane makes a flat statement that in her opinion the French amount to nothing, let her read about Denis Papin (1649–1710) who invented the steam engine—and chugged up a river in Germany about a hundred years before Fulton made his historic trip on the Hudson. He also invented the pressure cooker and was chased out of his home town of Blois for being in league with the devil, because he could cook carrots in three minutes.

The teacher of English is in a particularly good position to provide emotional outlets and emotional stimulation through her assignments, both in writing and in reading. Creative writing gives great satisfaction to its author and often serves as an outlet for emotional problems. The form is a minor consideration, and a teacher who fusses unduly about spelling and punctuation is almost sure to diminish the therapeutic values of writing. Naturally, one has to correct errors, but the time for correction is after a pupil has expressed his interests and drives and feels that his manner of writing could be improved. One might consider the following excerpts, which are quoted as originally composed:

1. Last truthday a friend of min were have a ras. We were still ras antilt we come to a car and my frend ran me of road and hit the car the biskly trind a somer saw and I flow through the air.

2. I think I'm coming out this summer only I'm not staying on the desert. With rattle snakes crawling around my neck, and cactuses in my pants, with a black widow crawling up my leg and a teranchla biting my tow and a scorpion stinging my back. A hawk pecking my head. I hope to go to the mountain.

3. I am in the fourth grade now. I sit in the fourth row in the sixth seat from the front. On my report card I got three A and three B four S. I weigh 61 pounds. I am 52 inches tall.

4. Yesterday my dad and I went riding on our horses. We went down to the field to hunt for fish in the ponds the river had left when it flooded. Once my dad looked around and I was in a mud puddle and the poney was on its side. My dad thought I was mud turtle with a cowboy hat and boots.[8]

These compositions leave much to be desired in the matter of form, but they are spontaneous and vivid. The writers of 1 and 4 had experiences that, if suppressed, might have become traumas; 3 is showing something of an obsession about his schoolwork; 2 is expressing his overdeveloped anxiety about things that crawl and bite. Such creative writing is good for children because it provides both a satisfaction of and an outlet for emotional drives.

Each teacher should apply the principles of mental hygiene to her own instruction and should use her assignments, when possible, to aid in the normal development of her pupils and in the solution of their problems.

Provisions for Emotional Outlets   Another important contribution of the school to emotional stability is the provision of adequate outlets for the easily aroused emotions of adolescents. It is better for all concerned if, by providing frequent outlets, the school allows emotions to be expressed as they are generated so that a feeling which must in the interest of others be temporarily suppressed will soon be worked off. Such outlets are of various types.

Fortunately for mental hygiene, man is a talkative creature and finds it possible to work off much of his tension by merely talking. Modern school methods provide adolescents with abundant opportunities for conversation. Much work is done by committees of students, who plan their assignment, talk over what each has to contribute, and work out a joint report. These informal groupings produce relatively little tension and provide an excellent

---

[8] E. J. Swenson and C. G. Caldwell, "The Content of Children's Letters," *Elementary School Journal*, 49:149–159, 1948. © 1948 by The University of Chicago.

means for the draining off of destructive emotion and the expression of integrative feelings.

Since emotions generate muscular tension, practically anything that requires exertion acts as a relief. Games of all sorts give excellent opportunity to work off pent-up feelings generated either in or out of class. If every pupil in a high school has some agreeable form of exercise during his last period in school, or after school, he is automatically provided with an outlet of a socially accepted sort. Kicking a football is just as good as kicking a chair and much better than kicking the cat. Sheer physical exertion uses up the extra supply of blood sugar with which the muscles are already well provided and allows them to relax again. Games may also act as compensatory activities for those pupils whose academic work is poor but whose athletic skills are superior.

Any kind of extracurricular activity may also function in the same way, even though little or no physical exertion is involved. Such developments distract the pupil's mind from his worries, provided the activities are interesting to him and he does not find them too competitive or too difficult. Then, too, they offer such opportunities for emotional expression as singing, acting, or pursuing an emotionally satisfying hobby. If a boy has a lively interest in electronics, for instance, he may be able to work off, during the time he spends with the electronics club, the feelings of inferiority and discouragement he has developed earlier in the day because his English composition was unsatisfactory. Or a girl may be able to express her drives for domination and prestige by making a stunning poster to support an appeal for funds on behalf of some charity. Extracurricular activities do not always function automatically as outlets for emotional stress, but they may be made to do so if they are correctly guided.

Finally, the school should provide plenty of opportunity for social intercourse in the form of purely social meetings, dances, picnics, chances for groups to lunch together, and so on. One has to remember, however, that school dances and parties can sometimes precipitate more emotional stress than they relieve if discrimination becomes involved. The high school needs no new techniques or equipment in order to provide for the working off of tensions. It needs merely to use what it has and use it wisely.

Recognition of Maladjustment   In general, people seem to be somewhat inattentive to the signs of emotional disturbance, but most normal people can learn to recognize the major symptoms of maladjustment once they know what to look for. A list of those deviations which have appeared with the greatest frequency in the extensive research done in recent decades will guide teachers in the recognition of abnormal behavior, the first step in the prevention of abnormal personalities. Children regularly showing more than one or two such behavior traits as those listed below are showing clear symptoms of emotional or nervous difficulty. These are the danger signals. The teacher's task is to make sure that they are not flown in vain.

Physical Symptoms Frequent headaches, attacks of nausea, dizziness, loss of weight, loss of appetite, habitual twitching of muscles, grimacing, nail biting, stammering, lack of coordination, sudden blushing or paling, frequent complaints of aches and pains, obesity, mannerisms, rigidity, constant restlessness, chronic fatigue, nervousness, affectations or posturings, jumping at sudden noises, inability to stop talking.

Symptoms of Emotional Immaturity Dependence on teacher, frequent requests for help, efforts to attract teacher's attention, crushes on teachers, efforts to curry favor with teacher, staying persistently after class to talk with teacher, behavior too young for age, irresponsible behavior, impulsive behavior, mischievousness, frequent interruptions in class, inability to work alone, frequent requests for special attentions and favors, unwillingness to state an opinion, preoccupation with marks.

Symptoms of Social Inadequacy Excessive shyness, lack of self-confidence, preference for remaining alone, overt rejection by other pupils, lack of friends of either sex, avoidance of members of opposite sex, absence from school parties or other events, homesickness, chronic attitude of insecurity or anxiety, unwillingness to recite, refusal to take part in games, tendency to stay alone at recess or to go home alone from school, refusal of recognitions or rewards, expectation of special privilege as a right, snobbishness, efforts to join groups where not wanted.

Symptoms of Abnormal Emotionalism Frequent absorption in daydreaming, irrelevant answers to questions, failure to hear when spoken to, tendency to worry unduly, lack of voluntary participation in class, absent-mindedness, withdrawal from work that looks new or difficult, chronic attitude of apprehension, moodiness, overexcitability, melancholy or apathy, indifference to stimuli that excite other pupils, unusual sensitivity to annoyances, frequent laughing at nothing or failing to laugh when others do, uncontrolled laughing or giggling, high distractibility, tendency to have feelings hurt, marked fears or anxieties or obsessions, shrieking when excited, sudden attachments to people (usually older), extravagant expression of any emotion, undue and prolonged anxiety over mistakes, marked distress over failures, meticulous interest in details, frequent bad dreams, hangdog attitude of guilt or hopeless acceptance of frustration or rejection.

Symptoms of Exhibitionism Teasing other pupils, pushing or shoving them (especially in corridors between classes), trying to act tough, trying to be funny, wanting to be conspicuous on public occasions, effusiveness, exaggerated courtesy, marked agreement with everything the teacher says, constant bragging about exploits or places seen or people met, frequent attempts to dominate younger or smaller pupils, inability to accept criticism, constant efforts to justify self, frequent blaming of failures on accidents, on false causes, or on other individuals, refusal to admit any personal lack of knowledge or inability, frequent bluffing, attempting either far too little or far too much work, showing off.

Symptoms of Intellectual Involvement   Marked pressure of ideas that crowd forward so fast that one sentence is left unfinished as another is begun, marked slowness of answers to questions, frequent breaking off of speech in the middle of a sentence, apparent blocking of ideas, fixity of ideas, explosive tone in argument, unwillingness to change opinions in the face of evidence, seeming inability to grasp the basic ideas of a course, tendency to repeat gestures or words several times, false interpretations of other people's behavior, false accusations of others, complaints that teachers or parents "pick on" or "have it in for" one or that other pupils are antagonistic, constant negative criticism of others, frequent complaints of unfair treatment, rationalization and projection of failures, "chip-on-the-shoulder" attitude, marked suspiciousness of other people's motives, interest in schoolwork to the exclusion of everything else.

Symptoms of Antisocial Tendencies   General attitude of aggressiveness in all relations, insolence, frequent loss of temper when corrected, destructiveness of school property, defacing of books, bullying, abusive or obscene language, undue interest in sex, telling of dirty stories, writing obscenities on walls, showing pornographic pictures, fierce resentment of authority, unwillingness to conform to regulations, bad reaction to discipline, "hoodlum" behavior whenever unsupervised, irresponsibility, frequent minor delinquencies—lying, cheating, swiping things—profound dislike for school work, inability to profit from experience, delight in nonintellectual competition.

▶ Summary

Adolescents as a group have a great many problems, and even individual boys and girls have more than a few. The school should certainly help them in solving those that are most pressing. As time goes on, teachers are becoming more and more concerned with the needs of their pupils and with the importance of the emotional atmosphere within their classrooms. They are developing a mental hygiene point of view that should contribute a good deal to the normal growth of their pupils. Whenever possible, the regular assignments should be selected to help students in either expressing or solving their difficulties.

References for Further Reading

BOOKS

Other Texts

Horrocks, *Behavior and Development* (pp. 486–496 and 503–518).
Kuhlen, *Psychology of Adolescent Development* (pp. 461–468).
Wattenberg, *The Adolescent Years* (Chap. 23 or any two of Chaps. 14–20).

Other Books and Monographs

Alexander, W. M., and P. N. Halverson, *Effective Teaching in Secondary School* (New York: Holt, Rinehart and Winston, Inc., 1956), 564 pp. (Chap. 6).
Hansen, K. H., *High School Training* (Englewood Cliffs, N.J.: Prentice-Hall, Inc., 1957), 420 pp. (Chap. 13).
Hardee, M. D., *Counseling and Guidance in General Education* (New York: Harcourt, Brace & World, Inc., 1955), 444 pp. (Chap. 2).
Pearson, *Adolescence and the Conflict of Generations* (Chap. 1 or 2).
Seidman, *The Adolescent: A Book of Readings,* rev. ed. (Nos. 34 and 35).
Strang, *The Adolescent Views Himself* (pp. 485–522).

ARTICLES

Hanna, J. V., and A. Crossman, "The Problems of College Freshmen Entering Washington Square College," *Counseling,* 12:2–3, 1954.
Harris, D. B., "Sex Differences in the Life Problems and Interests of Adolescents, 1935–1957," *Child Development,* 30:453–459, 1959.
Leonard, C., "Tension Areas in the Adolescent," *Counseling,* 6:1–4, 1954.
Lucas, C. M., and J. E. Horrocks, "An Experimental Approach to the Analysis of Adolescent Needs," *Child Development,* 31:479–487, 1960.
Monks, J. P., and C. W. Heath, "A Classification of Academic, Social, and Personal Problems for Use in a College Student Health Department," *Student Medicine,* 2:44–62, 1954.

Suggested Research Problems [9]

1. A study of school examinations: their nature, the stated goals of the teachers, the reaction of the pupils, the systems of grading, the functions of the examination, its contribution to a pupil's grade in a course, its educational values, together with suggestions for more constructive use than is commonly made.

---

[9] See note on p. 11.

Chapter **25** | **The Social Life of the School**

THE social life of the school has three major manifestations—the voluntary groupings among the students, the relationships developed in the classroom, and the cocurricular activities of the school. The first
of these manifestations has been discussed in an earlier chapter. The present
chapter will therefore be devoted to two main topics: the social anatomy of
the classroom and the cocurricular interests of high school pupils.

▶ **Social Life of the Class**

Social Anatomy of the Classroom A class is, or soon becomes, a social unit,
not just a random assortment of isolated individuals.
Even if the pupils are strangers at the beginning of the year, they will not remain that way for long. During the elementary school years the social life of the
classroom is extremely important to a child because he spends about half his
waking time in it and, perhaps, another quarter in playing with the children
he works with there. In secondary school, students have several classes and
several teachers. Each class has a structure of its own, since the individuals
composing it are different. But no single class is likely to be as important in
the adolescent's social development as the elementary school class is to the
child's. However, it is desirable for a teacher in secondary school to know
how to investigate social relationships by making a sociogram and to know
how to use the results.

The first step consists in asking the students—usually just before the
class is to be divided into small groups for some joint undertaking—to write
down the names of the one, two, or three classmates with whom they would
prefer to work, and also the names of the one, two, or three with whom they
would prefer not to work. These acceptances and rejections are then made
into a diagram of a type that will be discussed shortly.

Before considering results for an entire class, however, it seems best to
demonstrate the nature and interpretation of the symbols to be used in the next
few diagrams. A solid line is used to indicate preference and a broken one
to show rejection. The arrows indicate the direction of the feeling. In Figure
25–1 the first two children, John and May, appear to be isolates. John received no choices at all, expressed none, was rejected by five classmates, and

rejected three. May made two choices and rejected no one, but she received no mention at all. Henry and Paul form a mutual pair—in this case, an exclusive one, since neither boy expressed a liking for anyone else. Ann and Bea are not quite so close, because Ann made one other selection. Dan, Ted, and Tom, or Dot, Pat, and Sue form triangles of attraction—in the case of the boys, a closed triangle. That of the girls is less exclusive since there is only one mutual attraction instead of three; moreover, Dot has attachments outside the triangle. The boys' chain, in which Joe likes Lee who likes Ed who likes Ben, is an open one, because there is no relation between Ben and Joe, while that of the girls is closed. The boys' chain is interrupted by one rejection. Bill and Edna are "stars," one positive and one negative. Bill was selected by twelve other boys, two of whom he selected in return. Edna was rejected by

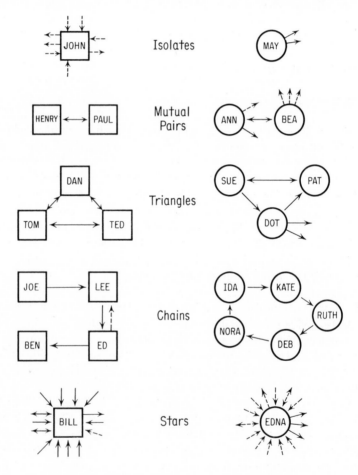

Fig. 25–1. Typical results from sociometric studies

eleven others, of whom she rejected two; in addition, she rejected one other girl and expressed preference for three more.

To make a sociogram one records all the choices and rejections in either a single chart or in two charts—one for positive and one for negative reactions. The separation is merely in the interests of clarity. The only guiding principle in arranging the names on the chart is to avoid as many crossing lines as possible. Boys are represented by squares or triangles, and girls by circles. The name of each child in the group appears inside one of these symbols. The maker of the diagram next draws an unbroken line, terminating in an arrowhead, from the square or circle to that of each of the child's choices. For aversions, one uses a broken line. If either feeling is mutual, there is an arrowhead on both ends of the line. When the diagram is completed, one is almost sure to find certain arrangements and groupings.

Use of Sociograms As examples of the uses to which sociograms may be put, the results of two investigations will be reported. The first illustrates the interrelations, positive and negative, in a small class; the second demonstrates the practical value of a sociogram in arranging committees.

The sociogram in Figure 25–2 shows the attractions and repulsions among the seventeen boys and fifteen girls in a high school English class. Each pupil was asked to indicate the two other pupils with whom he would prefer to work on the preparation of a joint report and the two with whom he would least like to work. For purposes of simplification, the attractions are recorded on the left half of the diagram and the rejections on the right.

Among these seventeen boys and fifteen girls there was one small clique, composed of five boys (Numbers 4, 6, 10, 11, and 12), plus the suggestion of another among girls (Numbers 7, 8, 9, 10, 11, and 12). There are also four pairs of mutual friends among the boys, three pairs among the girls, and one pair composed of a boy and a girl. Pair 14–15 among the girls has no voluntary contacts with other members of the class. The pair composed of Boys 1–2 is nearly as isolated. The other pairs have some contacts beyond each other. There are also two chains (Boys 8, 9 and Girls 5, 1; Girls 1, 8, 9, 10, 12, 7, and 5). The stars are Girl 7 and Boy 10. There are five isolates (Boys 5, 7, 13, and Girls 2 and 13); they made choices, but no one chose them. Boy 1 chose only his chum, while Boy 10 was unable to choose two from his three intimates and so selected all of them. There are eight choices of girls by boys and five of boys by girls. Boys 9 and 17 chose only girls. Boy 5, an isolate, is trying to attach himself to both a mutual pair and a chain. Boy 7 chose the most popular boy, and Girl 13 chose the most popular girl. This selection of central figures by rank outsiders is a common phenomenon.

One boy, Number 17, and two girls, Numbers 2 and 6, are the main centers of admitted hostility. In five instances a choice in one direction is met with repulsion in the other (Boys 1–5; Boys 8–5; Girls 8–9; Girls 8–6, and Boy 8–Girl 5). There were eight mutual rejections (Boys 4–5; Boys 4–7; Boys 4–17; Girls 2–4; Girls 5–14; Girls 5–15; Boy 17–Girl 2; Boy 9–Girl 6). The chums, Girls 14, 15, selected only each other, ignored boys, rejected the same two girls, were rejected jointly by two girls, and were jointly ignored by everyone else. Eight boys rejected girls, and four girls rejected boys. Boys 2 and 11 rejected no one; if they could not work with their chums or with the most popular boy they did not care with whom they worked. Girl 13 also rejected no one. Boys 5, 16, and

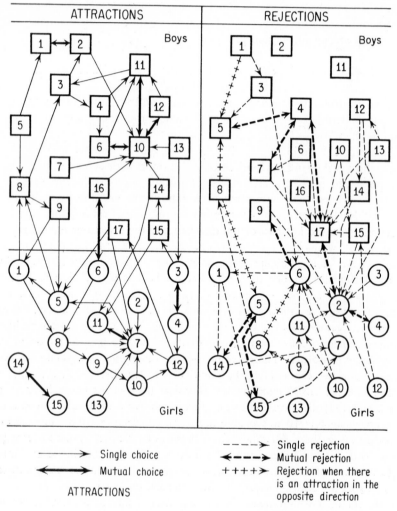

Fig. 25–2. Attractions and repulsions in a high school English class

Girls 3, 4, 7 made only one rejection each, while Boy 4 made three. Boys 1, 2, 6, 10, 11, 13, and 16 and Girls 3, 9, 10, 12, and 13 received no rejections.

In order to try out the effect of these various interrelationships upon the work of small groups, one of the writers persuaded the teacher of this class to divide it into (A_1) one good group, (B_1) one that was composed of small cliques, (C_1) one that contained many antagonisms, and (D_1) one in which the members had relatively few contacts with each other. The interrelationships are shown in Figure 25–3. The groups were given a list of a dozen topics, any one of which they might choose to work on, their first task being to

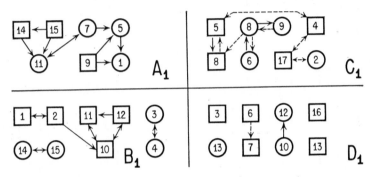

Fig. 25–3. First arrangement of class into committees

select their subject. So far as the academic result was concerned Groups A_1 and B_1 turned in good reports; that from Group C_1 was poor, while Group D_1 never finished any joint report, although most of the members put in individual ones of varying merit. Girl 11 became the leader of Group A_1 from the start. For a few days, Boy 10 tried through his general popularity to whip the cliques in Group B_1 into line, but not without a good deal of resistance. Whenever he stopped prodding, the group fell to pieces. In the end, he broke the work up into units and assigned one unit to each clique—thus showing that his popularity rested upon the foundation of an insight into social behavior. Group C_1 was full of discord and argument, as might have been expected, since there were three mutual rejections and three cases in which a liking in one direction was met by a dislike in the other. There was no leader, and twice the teacher had to intervene to keep the peace. If anything, the antagonisms among the members were deeper at the end of their joint effort than at the beginning. Group D_1 discussed the selection of a topic in a listless and desultory way for nearly two weeks but never came to an agreement. In the end the group simply disintegrated; a few members wrote individual reports.

For the next assignment, the teacher rearranged the students to the best possible advantage, as shown in Figure 25–4. She put one student with some qualities of leadership into each group, broke up most of the cliques, and distributed the isolated and disliked pupils so that there were no more than two in each group. They were soon drawn into at least a slight degree of activity by their more socialized mates and by their leader. Aside from the isolates, positive bonds held the members of each committee together. All four groups worked through several projects in harmony and with excellent results academically. It should be noted that in this second series of committees there is not a single expressed antagonism to interfere with the progress of the work in hand.

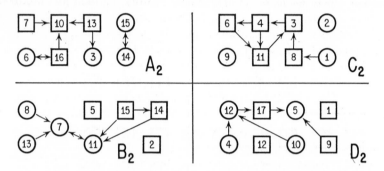

Fig. 25–4. Second arrangement of class into committees

It is to everyone's advantage that the social interrelations within a class be used as much as possible, if only for purposes of getting the work done better, since harmony produces better results than strife. Moreover, if the rejected pupils lose some of the antagonism directed against them, they have less need for hostile, aggressive defense reactions. The isolates and neglected ones begin to establish contact with the world. Even if they learned no more, and they often do, such results in character development would make the procedures worthwhile. The intelligent use of a sociogram thus permits a teacher to work with adolescent society instead of against it, as she is likely to do if she ignores the social behavior of her students.

▶ Relation of Teacher to Class

Some of the relatively recent studies of the relation of teachers to their classes have consisted of obtaining a verbatim report of what went on in class during a given unit of time on several occasions, and of then analyzing this record. In many cases, however, the observation of experts was the main method of investigation. Sometimes the teachers knew they were being observed, and sometimes they did not. Naturally, no two records of a teacher's behavior, either by different observers on the same day or by analysis of verbatim records on different days, show perfect agreement. Wholly aside from any variability in the observers, the teacher does not proceed in exactly the same manner every day, because of differences in subject matter, if for no other reason. Since she is influenced by human stresses and strains, she herself changes more or less. The earlier reports of reliability of either verbatim recordings or expert judgment gave correlations from 0.74 to 0.93 between raters or observers. Probably these coefficients were high because only well-trained judges attempted to make the estimates. More recent reports have been much less encouraging.[1] The first such effort at judgment is said to be worthless—although why anyone should expect it to be anything else is a mystery. In the day when the elder writer learned to give the Binet Examination, the rule was to give 50 Binets for practice and throw them all away before even expecting that the results one obtained would be worth keeping. Not only is a first observation of no value; the writers would guess that at least twenty should be made under guidance and another eight or ten independently before one should expect his results to have a reasonable reliability. If the judges are experienced, their reports should be of sufficient reliability to merit attention.

The figures in Table 25–1 summarize results from the first study to be reported. The six teachers involved differed widely from each other in the intent behind their contributions to class guidance or discussion. One teacher (C) spent only 42 percent of her time in making constructive suggestions. She used up 20 percent of her time in making announcements, in giving directions, or in merely repeating what a pupil had said, presumably while she communed with herself as to what might next be done. She used the remaining 38 percent of her time in dominative or destructive contacts with the pupils. Teacher F, on three separate occasions, used 85, 87, and 86 percent of her time constructively. Her need for neutral comments varied greatly, probably according to the subject matter and the practical needs of the moment. For example, such an occurrence as a special assembly, a bank day, a prospective fire drill, or an excursion will require more than the customary number of merely informative remarks. Her need to reprove members of the class was infrequent, and during two observation periods she neither gave orders nor spent time justifying herself.

Teachers represent a continuum from the very authoritative to the very permissive teacher, and classrooms form a parallel continuum from the teacher-centered to the pupil-centered. In all comparisons between the two extremes, the permissive, pupil-centered treatment has been found to be usu-

---

[1] E. Wandt and L. Ostreicher, "Validity of Samples of Classroom Behavior for Measurement of Social-Emotional Climate," *Psychological Monographs,* Vol. LXVIII, no. 376, 1954, 12 pp.

Table 25–1: CLASSIFICATION OF THE SPOKEN COMMENTS OF TEACHERS [a]

	A	B	C	D	E	Three Ratings of Teacher F		
	Teachers					1	2	3
1. Statements reassuring or commending pupil	18	20	8	2	2	0	8	0
2. Statements conveying to the pupil the feeling that he was understood and to help him elucidate his ideas	5	8	3	0	5	69	58	64
3. Statements or questions proffering information or raising queries about the problem in an objective manner, with the intent of facilitating the solving of the problem	29	40	31	53	70	16	21	22
Constructive comments	*52*	*68*	*42*	*55*	*77*	*85*	*87*	*86*
4. Remarks consisting of polite forms, names of pupils, conveyance of brief administrative items, verbatim repetition of something already said								
Neutral comments	*10*	*22*	*20*	*21*	*9*	*15*	*11*	*0*[b]
5. Statements exhorting or directing the pupil to follow a recommended course of action	15	7	24	14	6	0	0	2
6. Statements reproving the pupil for undesirable action or deterring him from inacceptable future behavior	9	2	9	7	0	0	2	6
7. Statements justifying teacher's own position or course of action	14	1	5	3	8	0	0	6
Destructive comments	*38*	*10*	*38*	*24*	*14*	*0*	*2*	*14*

[a] Figures express percentage of time spent by teachers in various types of contact with their pupils.

[b] This result seems most unlikely, though it is possible that a teacher might not call any pupil by name or say "Thank you" or "Would you please continue" during a period of observation. Since the figures are combined to the nearest whole number, a teacher may have used some percent less than 0.5 in neutral remarks.

SOURCE: J. Whithall, "The Development of a Technique for the Measurement of Social-Emotional Climate in the Classroom," *Journal of Experimental Education*, 17:347–361, 1949. Used by permission of the publisher.

ally superior and never inferior, whether one is considering academic achievement, personal adjustment, or the behavior of the pupils.[2] The objective of the modern teacher is to create a permissive atmosphere in her classroom, arrange a series of problems that are interesting to the pupils, put the materials for solving the problems within reach, and then keep out of the way while the pupils work. She gives help as needed but no orders. This concept of teaching is still fairly new, but it continues to prove its worth as the decades roll by.

The authoritarian type of teacher is no longer admired. Her domineering procedures break up or repress natural groupings among the students and result in frequent conflict between herself and them. The students often develop similar attitudes toward each other, and they become overdependent upon authority. Since adolescents are going to work together anyway, they will form a resistive unit to the domineering teacher. Such a teacher may achieve good academic results but at the cost of injury, temporary or permanent, to the development of those in her charge and of no little injury to herself, because of the heavy strain under which she works. The acceptable teacher of today has very different objectives, although she also is interested in the mastery of subject matter. She tries, first of all, to know the children and to provide for individual differences among them. She wants to induce as much natural growth—physical, social, and emotional—as she can. She gives information, arranges the work so that the pupils can inform themselves, and she expects to do a good deal of counseling. She studies the relationships within her class, and she tries to weld the members together into a working, living unit. Finally, she is a vital cog in the machinery of putting pupils who need expert attention of any kind in touch with the person who can best help them. In the eyes of her pupils she is a friend, not a despot. Naturally, not all teachers can attain this ideal, but at least the modern teacher tries to do so.

▶ The Cocurricular Program

The social activities sponsored by the high school take the form of the "extracurricular" or, to use a more appropriate name, the "cocurricular" program. Although the activities should always be based upon the spontaneous interests of adolescent boys and girls, they are nevertheless to some extent organized and supervised by the school. Because of the intense social interests of most adolescents, these cocurricular activities constitute an important part of school life.

---

[2] O. E. Thompson and F. K. T. Tom, "Comparison of the Effectiveness of a Pupil-Centered versus Teacher-Centered Pattern for Teaching Vocational Agriculture," *Journal of Educational Research,* 50:567–678, 1956; M. L. Cogan, "The Behavior of Teachers and the Productivity of Their Pupils," *Journal of Experimental Education,* 27:107–124, 1958; C. G. N. Hill, "Teacher Trainees and Authoritarian Attitudes," *Australian Journal of Psychology,* 11:171–181, 1959.

Nature and Types of Activity   Theoretically, the cocurricular program should
                                   include opportunities for students to develop their in-
terest and skill along any line, whether or not it is already adequately provided for in the program of classes. Actually, however, the expansion of activities is always conditioned by the size and facilities of any particular school.
Unless it owns a printing press, a school cannot, for example, have a club in
which pupils actually print their own stories. There is a limit also to the
number of clubs a member of the faculty can supervise and the number to
which a pupil can profitably belong.

In order to illustrate the number and type of cocurricular activities that
a teacher can expect to find in a school, the list below is presented. This list
came from a high school in a California city with a population of about
75,000. In large city high schools the variety of organizations is much wider
and may run as high as 50 or 60 different clubs that are fostered and to some
extent supervised by the school.

A. Clubs Associated with a Specific Department of Instruction
    1. Applied Arts Club
    2. Art Federation
    3. Drama Club
    4. French Club
    5. Girls' Athletic Association
    6. Junior Engineering Technical Society
    7. Quill and Scroll Club
    8. Science Club
    9. Mathematics Club
B. Clubs Developed to Meet Student Interests
    10. Amateur Radio Club
    11. Argonauts' Club
    12. Camera Club
    13. Forum
    14. Library Club
    15. Latin American Club
    16. Forensic Club
    17. Pan-American Club
    18. Girl-Cheerleaders Club
    19. Stamp Club
C. Clubs Based on Vocational Interests
    20. Future Business Leaders of America
    21. Future Nurses' Club
D. Clubs Based upon Some Kind of Special Ability
    22. Scholarship Federation
    23. Leadership Group
    24. High Potential Group
    25. Junior Honor Society
    26. Leaders of Tomorrow's America
    27. Lettermen (Athletics)

E. Clubs Based on Community Service
   28. Junior Red Cross

In addition to the specific clubs there were four permanent committees that were maintained by the students: The Rally Committee, the School Pride Committee, the Service Committee—an organization of girls who serve as hostesses for school affairs—and the Student Safety Committee. This particular list does not include the various groups involved in student government, such as the Student Council or the Student Court. Missing also are the music clubs—school chorus, glee club, orchestra, or band—and such national organizations as the Junior YMCA or YWCA, the Boy or Girl Scouts, or the Camp Fire Girls, all of which are likely to have chapters in the high school. The list is, however, typical of what one may expect to find in a small high school.

Many high schools have student government which operates through the student council and the student court. Through these activities the pupils practice techniques of government and participate in the conduct of school affairs. They learn how voting is done, how laws are formulated and passed, how a court functions, how rules are enforced. These activities give practical training in citizenship. The more the students take part in their own government the better, but there are obvious limitations to their participation. In the first place, there are several matters that are not at all their business; for example, the repair of buildings, the employment of teachers, and—in considerable measure—the curriculum. The main objective of student government is the education of pupils through the control of behavior in the school, the punishment of those who violate the students' own regulations, and the management of small units of government—such as the homeroom or any of the clubs developed by the school. These responsibilities usually appeal to adolescents because they feel themselves old enough to determine rules for their own behavior. While these functions do need supervision, because the pupils are too young and inexperienced for completely independent action, the values are quickly lost if the control is too obvious or if it is so extreme as to stifle initiative.[3] The student council and the student court will both make mistakes. It is not the function of the supervisor to prevent the mistakes but to make sure that the students profit by them, that they live with their errors of judgment until they see them as errors and that they are encouraged to admit and correct their mistakes.

Distribution of Cocurricular Activities   If adolescents are left to themselves, the activities will almost certainly be dominated by the best adjusted students in the school. The pupil who tends to participate volun-

---

[3] For a good discussion, see, W. Held and W. Bear, "What are the Aims, Objectives, and Purposes of the Student Council?" *Bulletin of the National Society of High School Principals,* 42:88–93, 1958.

tarily and successfully is usually a little more intelligent and more mature than the nonparticipant, he comes more frequently from the upper socio-economical levels, his personality is better organized, and he has wider interests than the average. These statements are based upon a study of 115 adolescents who were mentioned in their school newspapers as compared with those whose names never appeared.[4] They are the "natural" leaders, and they tend to overparticipate, probably because they have the necessary traits and social position and because they derive satisfaction of their social drives by such activities. By contrast, the shy, self-conscious, or repressed pupils who most need cocurricular activities for their own best development are likely to have the least opportunity for the participation that would give them the experience they need in order to gain social poise and social skills.

It is not necessary for pupils who do not spontaneously participate in activities to remain aloof throughout their adolescent years. Those who are shy, easily embarrassed, and withdrawn can be helped to a better adjustment and eventually to some degree of participation in the social life of the school. Counseling that is directed specifically toward helping students appreciate the value of cocurricular activities yields results. It is not a matter of requiring participation but of encouraging isolated pupils so that they have a desire to join in the activities going on about them.

In many schools the administration has tried to regulate participation by a point system or other method. This technique, if used alone, has been rather ineffective for two reasons. In the first place, the number of points, indicating the number of positions a pupil may hold simultaneously, is generally too high. Second, those pupils who love to expand their egos by participation in nonacademic activities often resort to the following trick: they use up their own points and then get their friends elected to other positions that they covet, whereupon they shelve the obliging friends and do the work themselves. Some better method than those usually employed is needed for distributing participation in terms of needs as well as in terms of interest.

There are very few studies that relate the participation in extracurricular activities to the needs of the students. What evidence there is suggests that those who most need the socializing experience of these activities have the least chance to take part in them, and that those who need them least get the lion's share.

As an example of development in extracurricular activities within a single school, some statistics will be presented from a private school that has a complete set of yearbooks running back for nearly 100 years. The earlier ones sometimes mentioned the various clubs and sometimes gave the names of the officers—but not the names of the members of each club—and sometimes they reported nothing about extracurricular activities. The earliest year-

---

[4] M. C. Jones and H. E. Jones, "Factors Associated with Prominence in Extra-Curricular Activities at the High School Level," *American Psychologist*, 4:251, 1949.

book to include all the facts needed for the present investigation was published in 1881. In this year there were 73 girls in the school and sixteen clubs, with a total membership of 189. The sixteen clubs were titled as follows: orchestra, choir, singing (for any girl who liked to sing without test of her ability to do so), drawing, painting, athletics, gymnasium, canoeing, literature, French, Latin, Greek, Christian Association, Bible, cooking, and drama. Each club had four officers, giving a total of sixteen presidencies and forty-eight other offices. The record of the nine girls with the greatest degree of participation is listed below.

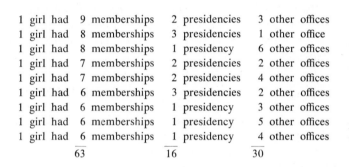

1 girl had	9 memberships	2 presidencies	3 other offices
1 girl had	8 memberships	3 presidencies	1 other office
1 girl had	8 memberships	1 presidency	6 other offices
1 girl had	7 memberships	2 presidencies	2 other offices
1 girl had	7 memberships	2 presidencies	4 other offices
1 girl had	6 memberships	3 presidencies	2 other offices
1 girl had	6 memberships	1 presidency	3 other offices
1 girl had	6 memberships	1 presidency	5 other offices
1 girl had	6 memberships	1 presidency	4 other offices
	63	16	30

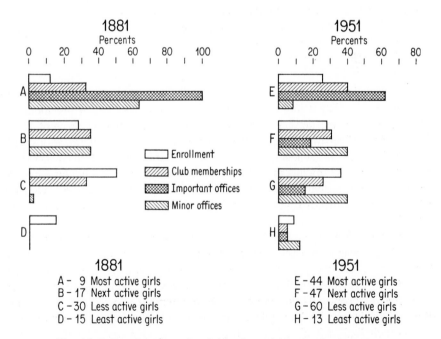

Fig. 25–5. Development of activities in a girls' school, 1881–1951

At this time the clubs were relatively unsupervised, and each girl joined as many as she wished. It will be noted at once that these 9 girls averaged 7 clubs each, held all the presidencies and 63 percent of the other offices. Of the 73 girls in the school, 46 (63 percent) had no office of any kind, and 15 percent belonged to no club. The situation is pictured in the upper bars of Figure 25–5.

In 1951 the same school enrolled 164 girls. All of them belonged to Student Government, all but 4 to the Christian Association, all but 7 to the Dramatic Association, and all but 3 to the Athletic Association. The 14 non-memberships in this school group represented only 9 girls, of whom 5 abstained from two organizations. In addition, there were 42 clubs, a student court with 5 judges, a yearbook committee (with 1 chairman and 7 members), and 3 dormitory committees, totaling 3 chairmen and 6 other members. The 42 clubs were as follows:

> Orchestra, choir, singing, glee, opera, radio, and record clubs
> sketching, art appreciation, painting, and architecture clubs
> leather working, woodcarving, and jewelry clubs
> gymnasium, games, swimming, skating, and rowing and canoeing clubs
> literature, French, German, Italian and Spanish, and classical clubs
> ancient history, European history, and current events clubs
> Bible and philosophy clubs
> biology, physics and chemistry, and mathematics clubs
> child care, home economics, and family living clubs
> drama production and puppet clubs
> social dancing and folk dancing clubs
> writing and newspaper clubs

There were 42 presidencies of clubs, 4 presidencies of the four large school organizations, 5 student judges, 4 chairmen of committees, and 4 presidencies of the school classes, making up a total of 59 major offices. The clubs each had one other officer (42 secretary-treasurers), the four large organizations had each 3 other officers (4 vice-presidents, 4 secretaries, and 4 treasurers), the committees had 13 members besides the chairmen, and each class had a secretary-treasurer, giving a total of 71 minor offices. The student government had passed rules several years earlier limiting membership to 4 clubs or committees in addition to the 4 large organizations to which practically everyone in the school belonged, and requiring membership by each student in at least 1 club. There was also a recognized principle that every student should hold at least one office every year, and the secretary of student government was charged with the responsibility of keeping a list of the students, rejecting the names for any proposed offices in excess of the number allowed and suggesting names of students who had held no office as substitutes for those who had reached their limit. Membership on the various school athletic teams was also counted on a student's record. There were therefore enough offices of some sort to go around for all, and the few girls who were inclined to be overactive were prevented from having more positions than they should.

In 1951 the important positions were still held by the more active girls, but this situation is to be expected, since shy isolates are not likely to be elected to a major office—and would probably go into a panic from fright if they were. However, there has been an enormous gain since 1881. Essentially everyone belongs to four groups, and the memberships in clubs are much better distributed. One cannot hope for a completely even distribution because all students do not show the same degree of interest, ability, or social skill. All one can do is to persuade the students themselves to limit participation for several reasons: to prevent overfatigue and a too great distraction from classwork among their extremely active members, to give the isolates the experiences they need for developing greater security in their social milieu, and to provide training in leadership for the few who have the necessary qualifications.

The effect of participation in cocurricular activities upon scholarship is almost always favorable. The pupil who has an integral part in the social life of the school does better academic work than the pupil of equal ability who does not. Teachers who feel that cocurricular activities absorb too much time would do well to remember this point. Moreover, the majority of 9000 students in the high schools of one state rated their noncurricular activities as equal in educational value to their academic work.[5]

Most students have at one time or another belonged to clubs or other student groups from which they have, or have not, derived considerable value. It is suggested that each student might find it useful to write a summary such as that given below of his or her own secondary school experiences with activities:

Extracurricular activities in the secondary schools are usually patterned by, and in turn evoke, the interests of the developing adolescent, as evidenced by the four-year trend of one girl going to a large suburban public high school. In the ninth grade she avidly joined the Spanish Club, the Drama Circle, the Tennis Club, the Art Appreciation Club, the Graphic Arts Club, the Choir, and was an active member of the Scholarship and School Honors societies. In the next year her interests were becoming focused in the areas of art and literature, and she moved to an older social group composed largely of senior (12th grade) students, so her memberships shifted rather radically to the Writers Club, the Graphic Arts Club, the Modern Dance Group, the Stagecrew Society; she dropped the other clubs. She remained with the last four activities throughout high school, adding participation in student government in her senior year through her honorary membership in the Girls' Honors society and through appointment

---

[5] H. Brinegak, "Pupil Attitudes toward Extra-class Activities," *School Review,* 63:432–437, 1955.

as art representative on the Student Council. In college she continued to participate in Little Theater and Dance groups, but incorporated her art and writing
activities into her private avocations except when they became useful in the pursuit of her organized activities, adding the University Chorus to her activities in
her junior year in a resurgence of the interest found in her early Choir membership. This constellation of activities is fairly representative in pattern, although
specialized in the field of interest.

The Nonacademic Program   Cocurricular activities among high school students presumably date back to the first high school,
since adolescence is a period of social interest. In most schools a variety of
clubs and societies grew up in a decidedly hit-or-miss fashion. Thus, for a
few years a literary society would be very attractive and then almost die out
for a decade, only to be resuscitated by some strong personality or by popular
interest. From the first there were school parties, school plays, and school
ceremonies of various kinds. Within the past forty years these somewhat incidental activities have become more numerous and better organized. Many
schools have supervisors who devote their full time to the routine necessary
for keeping the entire program moving forward. Although many of the societies and other forms of organization are old, an integrated program—functioning as a complement to the curriculum—is new. Consequently, one finds
in only a few places a program of activities that approaches what it could become.

Some school officials and teachers do not understand the basic function
of the program. They fail to see in the activities any values beyond enjoyment
and relaxation. Some teachers regard the cocurricular program as a competitor
with their own work—an unfair competitor with lower standards. The greatest
values of these activities cannot be obtained if teachers have not learned to
use them as supplementary methods for the education of adolescents.

Many clubs are outgrowths of the work in some department of the school;
therefore the teachers in that department are the individuals best equipped to
supervise these activities. Naturally, the boys and girls should exercise as
much control as they can, but they are neither inventive enough nor mature
enough to keep a club as interesting or as soundly managed as it will be if it
has the assistance of a sympathetic teacher. It is not the idea at all that a
teacher should dominate the activities of the students, but rather that she
should help them to make the activities more interesting and valuable to themselves. Most teachers have fundamentally no objection to such participation
in the nonacademic program of the school. Difficulty arises, however, when
a teacher who has already taught six or seven classes in a day is asked to
remain after school to assist with a club. Adequate supervision cannot be
given casually because it imposes a real burden upon a teacher's time, vitality,

and ingenuity. If a school wants its teachers to develop the cocurricular program as well as the course of study, it must make time in the teacher's schedule for work of this sort. One of the writers knows one school that requires its teachers to return one evening a week for club meetings; some of them are back at the school two or three evenings a week. No teacher can carry such a load of nonacademic work and still be able to give her pupils something worthwhile during class. The two school programs will have to find some way of cooperating, instead of competing, with each other. One method already tried is to lengthen the school day, two or three times a week at least, and to include the activities during the last hour or two as part of the school's regular program. If some such arrangement can be made, most teachers will enjoy working with groups of adolescents who have come into a club because of spontaneous interest. Even so, a teacher's class load needs to be reduced before she is in a position to render her best service to the cocurricular program.

A good deal of criticism has been directed of late against the cocurricular program as it is actually administered in the schools, and the criticism has stimulated a reappraisal of values in this area of activity.[6] One complaint is that the program is dominated by teachers, who are appointed by the administration, not chosen by the students. In one study [7] over 80 percent of the faculty sponsors were so appointed. A second complaint is that the activities do not arise naturally from adolescent interest but are the result of adult pressures from the community, sometimes expressed through the parents and sometimes not. A third complaint centers around the bases for voting by the students upon issues or officers; in many places only those with "student-body cards" may vote, and since these cards often cost money—even though only a small sum—there are many disenfranchised students. And a fourth complaint again emphasizes the uneven distribution of activities and especially the lack of participation on the part of two groups: the students from low economic status and those who are underactive in all fields because of their withdrawn personalities.

These and other criticisms have precipitated efforts to set up new goals for the cocurricular program, or to re-establish earlier goals. It is recommended: (1) that there be concerted effort to relate the class and nonclass activities in both values and objectives, (2) that both over and underparticipation be studied to determine more precisely the underlying causes, (3) that both the participation in and responsibility for activities should be controlled by the student government rather than by either the administration or the teaching staff, (4) that provision be made in the teacher's day for allowing her

---

[6] Much of this discussion is based on M. J. Eash, "The School Program: Non-Class Activities," *Review of Educational Research,* 30:57–66, 1960.

[7] R. S. Erickson, "Student Decision-making in Secondary School Extracurricular Activities," *Dissertation Abstracts,* Vol. 19, No. 2824, 1959.

to guide activities as part of her regular teaching load, and (5) that better relations with the community should be established so that adults will understand better the nature of the cocurricular program.[8]

The program of activities in a given school can be evaluated in more objective ways than merely by the opinion of teachers or supervisors. One can measure changes in attitudes and interests from the time that a program is instituted until after it has been going on for a couple of years. One can keep anecdotal and other records as to participation and its effect in individual cases. One can administer sociograms. One can ask the students to write, presumably in their English composition class, on what significance the activities have had for them, either in general or in specific instances. In general, the opinion of those most closely concerned is that the extracurricular activities of the school make a real contribution; what is not so clear is just how or just how much.[9]

▶ Summary

A class is a social unit, the members of which are related by bonds of attraction or repulsion. These social pressures are very powerful, and in general a teacher should try to work with them, although small, tight cliques and closely bound mutual pairs are sometimes better off if the members do not work together. A sociogram is a most useful device in revealing to a teacher the social and emotional forces that are operating in her schoolroom.

The position of the teacher in the group is steadily changing from the traditional authoritarianism to a constructive, nondirective, permissive type of leadership. A teacher is well advised if she develops a habit of checking her own classroom techniques to determine what proportion of them could be classified as constructive.

The cocurricular life of the school can be of great value to the students and should therefore be encouraged by teachers. It is, however, necessary that all pupils should have some part in it and that no pupil should carry too heavy a load. Perhaps the three basic difficulties in developing an adequate program are the lack of relationship between the academic and nonacademic activities of the school, the lack of clearly realized objectives, and the overabundance of faculty control. Adolescent social life tends to "just grow." It is often purposeless and inchoate. Pupils should, of course, enjoy their activities, but

---

[8] D. Rennicke and A. C. Hearn, "Some Basic Trends in School Activities," *School Activities,* 26:147–148, 1955 and "Symposium: Reassessment of the Extra-Curriculum," *California Journal of Secondary Education,* 34:283–312, 1959.

[9] R. Crum, "Evaluation of An Activities Program," *School Activities,* 26:243–247, 1955.

they should also grow into better poised and more mature individuals because of them. Merely having a good time is not enough. The academic and nonacademic work of a school should be so correlated that each reinforces the other and they become two related means by which pupils may best realize their possibilities, develop their talents, expand their horizons, pursue their interests, and obtain practice in democratic procedures. These objectives cannot, however, be reached if students are prevented from learning democratic responsibility by overcontrol from above.

References for Further Reading

B O O K S

Other Texts

Ausubel, *Theory and Problems of Adolescent Development* (Chap. 15).
Garrison, *Growth and Development*, 2d. ed. (pp. 378–403).
Jersild, *Psychology of Adolescence* (Chap. 14).

Other Books and Monographs

Alexander and Halverson, *Effective Teaching in Secondary School* (Chap. 7 or 8).
Hand, *Principles of Public Secondary Education* (Chap. 8).
Hansen, *High School Teaching* (Chap. 12).
Jennings, H. H., *Sociometry in Group Relations,* rev. ed. (American Council on Education, 1959), 105 pp. (Chap. 2, 3, or 4).
Kettlecamp, G. C., *Teaching Adolescents* (Boston: D. C. Heath and Company, 1954), 550 pp. (Chap. 7).
Seeley, *et al., Crestwood Heights* (Chap. 8).
Seidman, *The Adolescent: A Book of Readings,* rev. ed. (No. 37).
Wandt, E., and L. Ostreicher, "Validity of Samples of Classroom Behavior for Measurement of Social-Emotional Climates," *Psychological Monographs,* Vol. 68, No. 376, 1954, 12 pp.

A R T I C L E S

Crum, L. R., "Evaluation of an Activities Program," *School Activities,* 26:243–247, 1955.
Eash, M. J., "The School Program: Non-Class Experiences," *Review of Educational Research,* 30:57–66, 1960.
Held, W., and W. Bear, "What are the Aims, Objectives, and Purposes of the Student Council?" *Bulletin of the National Association of Secondary School Principals,* 42:88–93, 1958.

Recktenwald, L. N., "Effective Interpersonal Relationships in the Classroom," *Education*, 75:13–17, 1954.

Suggested Research Problems [10]

1. Comprehensive survey of cocurricular activities in 25–50 representative high schools in a single state—based on actual visits and not on results from questionnaires. Such subtopics as the methods of choosing teacher counselors for activities, the expenses if any of the groups, the equipment needed, the degree of participation, the reaction of pupils, and so on should be included.
2. Evenness or unevenness of student participation, with the development of techniques for insuring 100 percent participation.

---

[10] See note on p. 11.

Chapter 26 | The High School Teacher

In recent decades a good many investigations of teaching efficiency at the high school level have been made. One can now say quite definitely what is and what is not good teaching for adolescents. The present chapter will be concerned with a brief summary of such facts as seem reasonably well established. There will also be consideration of the typical problems that teachers have to solve and the difficulties inherent in their work.

Next to a child's parents, his teachers are the most important formative influence in his life. He is with them five or six hours a day, five days a week, for at least eight years and probably longer. The first teachers a child has are extremely influential in conditioning him. By adolescence, some of their authority has worn off, but the boy or girl has developed a new and friendly relation with teachers, on a more mature level. A teacher continues to exert influence through personal contacts, through the atmosphere she creates in the classroom, through her instructional methods, and through her observation of her pupils. In the promotion of mental health and normal personalities she is undoubtedly the key person in the educational world.[1]

▶ The Teacher's Personality

In all investigations certain traits of personality have been shown to be especially significant for acceptance of a teacher by adolescents and certain others for rejection. The usual method of investigation has been to determine by vote of the students themselves which teachers in a high school are particularly successful and which are thoroughly disliked. The students then rate whichever of these teachers they have had in class for at least a semester. There is always some criticism of such student ratings, on the grounds that they are unreliable. So far as ratings of instructional competence are concerned, they may very well be, but the students are the consumers, and they know what they can consume and what they cannot, even if they are sometimes foggy as to the reasons. They also know whether or not they like or dislike a given teacher, and they can often tell why. In any case,

---

[1] E. B. Cason, H. V. Funk, R. Harris, R. Johnson, F. L. Newbold, and H. H. Willis, "School Practices in Promoting Mental Health," *American Council on Education Studies*, Series I, No. 40, 14:121–136, 1950.

they are the *only* people who know what goes on in a classroom day after day. If one asks them questions that are specific enough, they can give reliable answers.

Table 26–1: CHARACTERISTICS OF GOOD AND POOR TEACHERS

The Good Teacher	*The Poor Teacher*
A. Traits of Character	A. Traits of Character
1. Has a genuine love for young people and enjoys being with them	1. Dislikes young people and does not enjoy being with them
2. Finds great emotional satisfaction from teaching	2. Regards teaching as a form of drudgery
3. Is vigorous and healthy	3. Is not vigorous and is sometimes sickly
4. Has enthusiasm and drive	4. Is bored and apathetic
5. Is attractive and neat	5. Is slovenly in appearance
6. Is emotionally mature	6. Is emotionally childish
7. Is emotionally stable	7. Is emotionally unstable
8. Feels personally secure	8. Has feelings of insecurity
9. Is reasonably free from fears and anxieties	9. Is ridden by fears and anxieties
10. Is generous in approval	10. Is generous with criticism
11. Gets along well with others	11. Has feuds and quarrels
12. Is well integrated	12. Is disorganized
13. Is tolerant	13. Is intolerant
14. Is fair and impartial	14. Has favorites and scapegoats
15. Has a good sense of humor	15. Has little humor
16. Is patient and even tempered	16. Is impatient and irritable
B. Social Adjustment	B. Social Adjustment
17. Has so satisfying a life outside school that she does not need to work off her emotions in school	17. Has so unsatisfactory a life outside school that she uses pupils to work off her emotions
18. Can accept pupils as they are, even the dull and the hostile	18. Rejects pupils, especially those who are hostile
19. Does not use pupils to meet her own needs	19. Uses pupils to work out her own problems
20. Identifies herself with pupils	20. Cannot identify herself with pupils
21. Treats pupils as individuals	21. Rarely treats pupils as individuals
22. Understands adolescents	22. Does not understand adolescents
23. Adjusts to pupils by being friends with them	23. Adjusts to pupils by domineering over them
C. Instructional Methods	C. Instructional Methods
24. Plans work carefully	24. Rarely makes plans
25. Realizes that learning stems from creative effort of each pupil	25. Had rather "tell" pupils than let them learn for themselves

C. Instructional Methods (*cont'd*)

26. States facts but does not judge

27. Understands and uses principles of learning

28. Emphasizes understanding

29. Is prompt and systematic

30. Helps individual students

31. Utilizes student opinion

32. Relates work to student life and interests

33. Has ingenuity; varies work

34. Wants pupils to express opinions

35. Prevents most disciplinary situations from arising

36. Uses, when necessary, discipline that is constructive to pupil's growth

37. Has strong interests in reading

38. Participates in social groups

39. Has superior verbal intelligence

40. Uses community as source material in assignments

41. Makes constant use of films, or other visual aids

C. Instructional Methods (*cont'd*)

26. Colors facts with her own conclusions

27. Pays little attention to psychological principles

28. Emphasizes memorizing

29. Is casual and unsystematic

30. Teaches students as a group

31. Presents her own opinions

32. Is not interested in students or in their ideas

33. Is rigid; work is monotonous

34. Imposes her opinions on pupils

35. Rarely heads off disciplinary crises and may enjoy them

36. Uses frequent and destructive discipline

37. Reads little and unwillingly

38. Participates little and without enthusiasm

39. Has average or lower verbal intelligence

40. Ignores community as much as possible

41. Never or almost never bothers about films.

SOURCE: Based on the following articles: M. Amatora, "Self-Appraisal in Teacher Personality," *Journal of Educational Psychology*, 46:94–100, 1955; P. R. Grimm and C. J. Hoyt, "Excerpts from Two Instruments for Appraising Teaching Competency," *Journal of Educational Research*, 46:706–710, 1953; E. R. Guthrie, "The Evaluation of Teaching," *American Journal of Nursing*, 53:220–222, 1953; C. H. Leeds, "Teacher Behavior Liked and Disliked by Pupils," *Education*, 75:29–37, 1954; D. G. Ryans, "The Investigation of Teacher Characteristics," *Educational Record*, 34:371–396, 1953; P. M. Symonds, "Characteristics of the Effective Teacher, Based on Pupil Evaluation," *Journal of Experimental Education*, 23:289–310, 1955; C. A. Weber, "Some Characteristics of College Teachers," *Journal of Educational Research*, 46:685–692, 1953; N. Cantor, *The Teaching-Learning Process* (New York: Holt, Rinehart and Winston, Inc., 1953, 350 pp., pp. 269–283; D. G. Ryans, "Some Correlates of Teacher Behavior," *Educational and Psychological Measurement*, 19:3–12, 1959.

In reading through the descriptions given in Table 26–1 a prospective teacher would do well to try a little soul searching to make sure that he or she is fitted for teaching, or can develop the essential traits. Many fine individuals of irreproachable character do not make good teachers because, fundamentally, they are not interested in people. They make excellent research chemists, catalogers in libraries, or commercial artists. Other, and most admirable, people belong in social work or in some form of religious endeavor rather than in teaching. It is no disgrace to be a type of person who makes a poor teacher; what is disgraceful is to persist in teaching when one has no talent for it. By examining herself with this list and with the tests of personality now available, a prospective teacher can find out whether or not she has a suitable or sufficiently modifiable personality structure for teaching, before she spends time, money, and effort in preparing herself for this type of work. If she lacks several of the more important traits, interests, and abilities, she would be well advised to consider some other occupation.

Teachers have their own problems just as other human beings do. They need security, affection, recognition, acceptance, and self-respect. In addition they need freedom and independence in their work and a sense of accomplishment.[2] Everyone expects teachers to be "dedicated," but dedication cannot survive without a sense of accomplishment or in the midst of chronic frustration. Problems, great and small, are unavoidable, because they are a part of any life, but certain mental and emotional hazards which affect the average teacher's work are not inherent in the task of instruction but in various restructions and situations that do not need to exist. If a teacher could be sure of progressing upon the basis of her merit, if she could participate in the determination of the policies under which she must live and in the development of the curriculum that she must teach, if she could be paid a salary commensurate with her social usefulness, if she could enjoy a secure status of respect, and if she could be asked to handle only a third to a half as many children as are generally assigned to her, many of her worst difficulties would never arise.

An excellent study of the problems encountered by teachers lists twenty-five as being most frequent. The percentages that appear in Table 26–2 are for those who reported each problem as being serious and pressing. Over twice as many found these problems frequent and sometimes disturbing but were able to handle them with only minor difficulty. Teaching is complex, responsible work, and it is not surprising that teachers have many problems, both personal and professional. When a teacher's morale gets low, as it does if she has unsolved problems, the achievement of her pupils also becomes low. Moreover she is likely to warp her own personality and to have a disorganizing effect upon the pupils.[3]

A teacher has two problems that are peculiar to her profession. First, she is the natural "target" for the displacement of any hostility that her pupils may feel toward their homes, parents, or communities. Moreover, her pupils may develop a complete misapprehension of her, based upon their stereotype of a teacher, which derives from what they have heard, read, and seen. Some pupils are hostile because they oppose all figures of authority and have been

---

[2] O. E. Byrd, "Teacher Health: Factors in Mental Health," *National Education Association Journal,* 49:77–78, 1960.

[3] L. W. Anderson, "Teacher Morale and Student Achievement," *Journal of Educational Research,* 46:693–698, 1953.

Table 26–2: PERSONAL PROBLEMS ENCOUNTERED BY TEACHERS
(*Figures are percentages*)

	Men	Women			Men	Women
1. Inadequate salaries	50	29	18. Lack of preparation		22	7
2. Arranging interviews with parents	50	31	19. Teaching gifted pupils		18	18
3. Teaching dull pupils	42	37	20. Problems of discipline		18	10
4. Finding living space	42	16	21. Problem parents		16	8
5. Grading and marking	40	34	22. Grade level expectations		18	21
6. Promotion or retention	38	35	23. Course of study requirements		18	16
7. Teaching load	38	29	24. Social life		10	15
8. Individual differences	36	34	25. New educational ideas		10	10
9. Too large classes	36	41	26. Need to reconcile ideals with realities			
10. Domestic obligations	30	12	27.* Problems of managing emotional transference ("crushes" or hostility)			
11. Handling maladjusted pupils	30	35				
12. Aiding pupils after absence	30	35				
13. Teaching pupils who dislike school	28	12				
14. Community demands and pressures	26	14				
15. Range of maturity among pupils	26	17	28.* Need for accepted means for expressing her own emotions			
16. Outdated school plant	24	13				
17. Teaching handicapped pupils	22	15				

* Added by the writers.
SOURCE: Based on Q. B. Mills and D. Rogers, "Personal and Professional Problems of Elementary School Teachers," *Journal of Educational Research,* 48:279–288, 1954; and J. C. Solomon, "Neuroses of School Teachers: A Colloquy," *Mental Hygiene,* 44:79–90, 1960.

thus conditioned long before they ever saw a particular teacher. She is a natural target because she cannot strike back, not if she wants to keep her job, at least. A second problem arises from a teacher's need to be above suspicion. No other profession is so exposed to the public.[4] A teacher is really never off duty, and she can be criticized for such a minor offense—if it is one—as sipping a cocktail in public. A good deal of the external pressure comes from the need to live a life of rectitude both in and out of school.

The teacher is thus a person with a "public image," and she does not have complete control over the image, either, because it derives some of its elements from the social milieu in which the pupils live. One interesting ex-

---

[4] J. C. Solomon, "Neuroses of School Teachers: A Colloquy," *Mental Hygiene,* 44:79–90, 1960.

periment concerns the public image of the teacher among 3178 seventh-grade pupils in Germany, England, Mexico, and the United States.[5] Results from the two more democratic countries—England and the United States—contrast with those of the more authoritarian countries—Germany and Mexico. All the students completed in their own language the story of a fellow-pupil who was already late in handing in a piece of homework, and had lost her completed, important composition on the way to school. The pupils wrote what they thought would be the conversation between pupil and teacher under these circumstances, and told what if any consequences took place. In the authoritarian countries the students were inclined to picture the pupil as lying, the teacher as not believing the story, and the outcome as some kind of punishment. In the democratic countries the pupils were inclined to picture the child as truthful, the teacher as believing, and the outcome as adjustment without punishment. The percent of students who perceived the teacher as a punishing figure was 70 in Mexico City, 61 in Hamburg, and 32 in Knoxville, Tenn.—to select a few examples. The niche occupied by the teacher is thus different in different cultures.

Communities do not seem to learn very rapidly that good teaching has to be paid for just as much as good dentistry, or good carpentry, or good plumbing. As long as teachers are underpaid and overworked, many of them are going to develop warped personalities unnecessarily. There are, to be sure, some elements of tension that are more or less inherent in the teaching situation. Teachers as a group suffer from an inability to relax, from overstrain, from a sense of futility—especially when their best efforts do not seem to be producing a reasonable amount of learning in their pupils—from fatigue, from too-restricted social contacts, from boredom with routine, from too much verbalism, from too much administrative and supervisory pressure, and —unless married—from sex starvation. Like other human beings, when they have personal maladjustments, they are likely to project their troubles upon those nearest, in this case their pupils, and to use their teaching as an outlet for their own frustrations. The stories below describe two teachers, both of whom were unsatisfactory:

Mr. T was a limp, unhealthy-looking man with a low voice and a monotonous manner of speaking. He taught English composition. The work of his class was of a uniform dullness and drab monotony. Literally nothing ever happened. For an hour a day he droned on about something—I do not know what, because after the first week I rarely listened. Each day he read and discussed somebody's paper. Each punctuation mark, each phrase, each detail was considered. I remember one day when he spent fifteen minutes in teaching the whole class

[5] H. H. Anderson, G. L. Anderson, I. H. Cohen, and F. D. Nutt, "Image of the Teacher by Adolescents in Four Countries—Germany, England, Mexico, and the United States," *Journal of Social Psychology*, 50:47–55, 1959.

to spell the word "daguerreotype" because one student had used and misspelled it. From time to time he gave us drill exercises in punctuation. These were undoubtedly the most interesting part of the course! They would have been more valuable if he had not been so careless in preparing them that they contained many errors. Mr. T gave his assignments each day with meticulous care and long-winded precision. No detail was too small for him to waste time over. We were told how wide a margin we should have on our papers, at what slant we should write, and how many words long each theme was to be. Most of the topics he assigned for writing were of little interest to me at least, and he permitted no deviations. Early in the course he asked us to read an English translation of either the Iliad or the Odyssey and write a summary of the story. I already knew the story of both; so I asked him for permission to read the Nibelungenlied in German and write a resume of it instead. As I explained to him, I could get practice in two subjects at once if he would allow this substitution. He refused, but I nevertheless read the German epic and wrote a reasonably good summary. I was given a failing grade on this assignment because I had not followed instructions. After this experience, when he wanted a thousand words, I gave him a thousand; when he wanted five hundred, I gave him five hundred. Mr. T was a poor teacher because he was utterly rigid in his thinking and hopelessly dull, both in class and out.[6]

Mrs. B. had a fine reputation in the high school where she had taught for five or six years. She was a cheerful, extroverted, energetic person, who was the administrator's delight, because she always got reports in on time, completely made out, and without urging. With the other teachers she was moderately popular, although some of the more perceptive among her colleagues had often wondered about her. The dean of girls and the dean of boys also had some questions in their minds about her, as did some of the counselors. There were not many actual complaints about Mrs. B. on the part of the students, but altogether, too many girls and boys arrived at the class following hers in an emotionally upset condition.

In the course of Mrs. B.'s fourth year in the school, her oldest daughter had a "nervous breakdown," and her son, a boy of 12, became a delinquent. The daughter, a girl of 14, remained at home under a doctor's care for about three months. After an attempt at suicide she was put into a "home" for further observation and treatment, although Mrs. B. was most reluctant to let her go. The first definite evidence against Mrs. B. came by the grapevine route from the doctor who was treating the daughter; he told the school doctor that the girl was terrified of her mother. The school doctor then had a talk with the delinquent son and found much the same reaction in him; his thefts had been for the purpose of getting together enough money to run away from home and to hide himself thor-

---

[6] L. Cole, *The Background for College Teaching* (New York: Holt, Rinehart and Winston, Inc., 1940, 616 pp.), pp. 585–586.

oughly from his mother. Then the school doctor began to ask questions of Mrs. B.'s students, and from them he got similar but less definite evidence. When he had accumulated enough ammunition, he talked with the principal of the high school, who simply did not believe that Mrs. B. could be an unsatisfactory teacher. He had always found her cheerful, chatty, rather witty, and full of energy. He did, however, make a few inquiries of his own among some of the older members of his staff, and what he heard, while not definite, did not please him.

At the beginning of the next semester, there were an unusual number of voluntary withdrawals from school. With an idea of finding some reason for the increase, he had his secretary list the courses each dropout had just completed. To his surprise, all but two had been in one of Mrs. B.'s classes. He already had begun to suspect that underneath her cheerful exterior this woman was domineering, narrow-minded, petty, and mean whenever she could show these traits without being caught. In a subsequent interview with Mrs. B. he could not penetrate her façade. None of the voluntary withdrawals had failed a course with her, and most of them had received fairly good marks. He then went to three or four homes of these dropouts and talked with the adolescents, but he came away only with the conviction that something was very wrong. Some of the parents were sure their son or daughter was "scared to death" of Mrs. B., but the youngsters themselves were too cowed to talk. Matters finally came to a head when a sensitive and sickly girl rushed out of Mrs. B.'s classroom and tried to throw herself out of a window, being prevented only by the janitor who happened to be passing. The principal discharged Mrs. B. that day, telling her that she could sue the school for breach of contract if she wanted to. The next day he met her classes. When the pupils learned that the woman was gone, they talked. After that, he had too much evidence rather than not enough. She had maintained her position by a combination of surface amiability with those in authority and such mean, sadistic persecutions in class that pupils literally did not dare to complain about her. Mrs. B. is an example of probably the most dangerous type of unsatisfactory teacher—a person with deep, unsolved emotional problems who has achieved a deceptively good superficial adjustment.

▶ Teaching Adolescents

This is not a book on teaching methods but a text on the psychology of adolescence. No attempt will therefore be made to comment upon general principles of teaching or upon teaching techniques in any particular subject. The following paragraphs are not intended to discuss methodology in high school, but rather to focus attention upon a few outstanding characteristics of adolescents, to whom the teaching must be adjusted.

Boys and girls of high school age are rather impatient of drill or monotony. They went an ever-shifting variety and excitement in their lives. The teacher who day after day simply assigns the next ten pages in the textbook allows the preparation of lessons to become unbearably monotonous. These statements do not mean that no drill subjects should be taught. Work involving drill should, however, always be directed toward some purpose the adolescent wishes to achieve. Thus the boy who has become interested in attending a foreign university willingly spends countless hours in mastering the necessary language. The girl with ambitions to become a private secretary will spend similar amounts of time in monotonous drill on stenography and typing. The student who wishes to enter a private college for which severe entrance examinations must be passed is no longer resistive to drill. The point to remember is the difference in motivation between children and adolescents. Children will memorize addition combinations either to please the teacher or to have a gold star placed after their name on the blackboard. During adolescence, the students must be stimulated to drill themselves because they can see, through the drill and monotony, a goal they are eager to reach.

The work in high school must be interesting. This statement is not made in defense of a painless education. Classroom work must compete with all the other things a boy or girl likes to do. The adolescent will spend time in studying only if the work is as interesting as the other things to which the same time might be put. If classwork is not interesting it will be neglected in favor of athletics, extracurricular activities, individual schemes of various sorts, money-making tasks, reading of light fiction, dances, or other such diversions. The adolescent can no longer be controlled, as the child can be, by mere authority, and he is not yet old enough to be controlled by economic pressure. In the intervening years he will therefore follow his interests. It is part of the teacher's business to capitalize on them.

Dissatisfaction is not restricted to a feeling of resentment, which is bad enough, but spreads quickly to school work and to social relationships. Satisfied students of a given level of intelligence do better in school, learn faster, are more desirable as students, have more friends, and show more tendency to lead than do dissatisfied pupils of the same level.[7] In terms of both achievement and adjustment, it is best to teach in such a way as to produce satisfaction.

Classroom work must furnish adolescents with an opportunity to exercise their minds. Naturally, the assignments appropriate for the more capable are too difficult for the dull, but for pupils of all levels of ability there must be a real opportunity for mental effort. Boys and girls of this age spontaneously spend hours in solving all kinds of puzzles or in playing games that demand quick thinking and cleverness in outwitting one's opponent. Assignments therefore need to present puzzles that will intrigue the adolescent into thinking.

Whenever possible, subject matter should be approached through the

---

[7] P. W. Jackson, and P. W. Getzel, "Psychological Health and Classroom Functioning: A Study in Dissatisfaction with School during Adolescence," *Journal of Educational Psychology*, 50:295–300, 1959.

emotions and imagination rather than through impersonal logic. Adolescents are stimulated by anything in which there is a bit of romance. They show this inclination clearly in their choice of movies or reading matter and in their hero worship of some idealized historic or fictional character. The chemistry teacher might bring about more learning of chemistry if he would start his course with the reading of *Crucibles;* the biologist would be well advised to begin his elementary classes with the reading of *The Microbe Hunters.* Such reading is stimulating to the imagination and ideals of youth and serves to maintain adolescent effort through the hours of drill necessary in the first year of any science. Perhaps, a profound arousal of the emotions is undesirable, but too little stimulation is equally fatal to schoolwork.

One of the adolescent's favorite illusions is his conviction that he is now an adult. He therefore insists upon his ability to manage his own affairs and resents having his work arranged for him. Instead of regarding detailed directions for preparing an assignment as a help, he is likely to regard them as an unwarranted intrusion upon his sense of independence. Pupils in high school should be allowed, within reasonable limits, to plan their own work and the means of getting it done. Some guidance must, of course, be given—but primarily when asked for. Arranging his own work not only gives an adolescent a feeling of independence but arouses responsibility for getting the work done. If he has planned a particular task, he is working for himself, not the teacher. Decisions made in relatively unimportant matters often bring about a quite disproportionate conviction of self-direction. Thus if an English teacher wants pupils to read part or whole of an epic, she may either assign a particular epic or she may tell the pupil to find out what epics there are and then to select for himself which one he will read. The second type of assignment is decidedly preferable.

Whenever possible a pupil should be allowed to tell his classmates what he has found out about a given topic and to discuss it with them. The traditional recitation, during which the student talks to the teacher, is not a desirable method for socialization—aside from being a poor method for other reasons. The strong drives for social approval and prestige make socialization especially desirable.

The material that goes into a course has to be selected upon one basis or another from the total data available in a given field. It is best to select those items that have the greatest immediate practical usefulness to the adolescent, in school or out. Pupils have many problems of their own, to the solving of which schoolwork should contribute. Whenever teachers see a chance, they should make such applications and give such examples as will be of greatest service to the pupils in their daily living.

Finally, teaching should emphasize, insofar as the particular group being taught can appreciate, the general implications, conclusions, and theories inherent in the facts under consideration. For the first time in his life, the high school pupil is able to regard a general principle as something more than a series of words to be memorized. When he discovers that theories give him an explanation of otherwise puzzling facts, he is eager to have more of them and thus achieve further enlightenment. Most adolescents want explanations of *why* things happen. In contrast, the child is content to know *what* happens. As will be pointed out in the last chapter, an adolescent has not become an adult until he has achieved some integrated attitude toward himself and the world about him. Although too much theory leads to bewilderment, too little leads to failure in achieving an adult point of view.

Teaching in high school should, then, have the following eight characteristics if it is to motivate the learner into getting his work done: it must relate drill to some desired purpose and must eliminate sheer monotony as much as possible; it must be interesting; it must give the adolescent mental exercise; it must stir his imagination; it must allow him to feel and develop his independence; it must socialize him; it must give him insight into his daily life; and it must provide him with as many explanations as he can understand. Work that lacks these characteristics simply does not get done because learning cannot be brought about without the earnest cooperation of the learner.

The extent of the changes in the objectives and methods of the secondary school is well reflected in an excellent analysis of the modern teacher's duties.[8] She is to study her pupils as individuals and as members of groups; to study group processes to determine what leads to acceptance, rejection, leadership, values, participation; to create an environment in which the emotional atmosphere, the feeling of belonging, and the security will lead to learning; to establish the best possible personal relationship with her class; to organize classroom situations so that learning will take place, largely by using the interests of the pupils; to observe the needs, interests, and frustrations; to help pupils organize themselves in groups for carrying on the activities of the classroom; to aid pupils in the selection of the most worthwhile experiences; to apply such therapy as may be needed to remove fear, insecurity, prejudice, and so forth; to record the progress of each pupil in health and in social and emotional adjustment; and to help the pupil to interpret the facts relative to his own growth and adjustment. Conspicuously absent from this long list is any direct mention of subject matter, of "teaching" in the conventional sense, or of discipline. The fundamental theory is that all children will learn spontaneously and will behave themselves acceptably if their surroundings furnish them with security and if their personal frustrations can be eliminated. The teacher therefore concentrates upon the pupil and the social situation and lets the learning look after itself. Perhaps this procedure is better

---

[8] Based on C. B. Mendenhall and K. J. Arisman, *Secondary Education* (New York: Holt, Rinehart and Winston, Inc., 1951), 424 pp., pp. 76–81.

adapted to the present generation of high school students than are the traditional methods, but one sometimes wonders if the modern emphasis upon socialization and integration is not so extreme as to precipitate a partial return to earlier instructional procedures, with an eventual blending of what is best in both.

▶ **Summary**

There are thousands of excellent teachers in the secondary schools. They do a great deal to help adolescents develop normally, and they find for themselves great emotional satisfaction in their work. It is perhaps unfortunate that in the literature one finds more about the unsatisfactory teacher than one does about those who are outstandingly good. The good teacher is aware of social currents in her classroom, she treats her pupils as individuals, she tries to set the scene for spontaneous learning and for normal development, she sets problems and gives only such guidance as may be needed, insofar as possible she prevents disciplinary situations from ever arising. She maintains a permissive atmosphere, in which the students are comfortable and relaxed, in order that they may develop their abilities and may learn as much as they can.

Teachers, like everyone else, can become maladjusted if their lives contain unsolved problems or if for any reason they are unhappy in their work. Among the commonest symptoms of maladjustment among teachers may be listed the following: the presence in the class of favorite pupils and "goats"; the use of status or size to overawe or menace pupils; an abnormal classroom quietness that comes from repression, alternating with outbursts of noise, quickly repressed and punished; general physical inactivity of the children, plus much minor, unofficial, secretive activity; punishment or criticism of pupils for things they cannot help—such as scolding a near-sighted child for getting out of his seat to see what is on the chalkboard, or punishing a hysterical child for vomiting, or ridiculing a fast-growing adolescent for being lazy; use of many dogmatic statements and absence of discussion; frequent displays of emotion, whether appeals to the pupils to perform certain tasks out of loyalty to the teacher or threatening attitudes toward childish wrongdoers, or habits of caressing the pupils, or frequent outbursts of rage against the whole class; reluctance of the pupils to talk in class; use of frequent punishments or constant nagging; use of sarcasm or ridicule or any attempt to shame a given pupil, especially in public. To these observable symptoms may be added the less objective characteristics of an inability to get on with one's colleagues and supervisors and a bad reputation among one's students. Teachers showing such traits are a menace to the mental health of their students, and they are further damaging themselves by a continuance in work that does not satisfy their needs.

References for Further Reading

B O O K S

Other Texts

Baller and Charles, *The Psychology of Human Growth and Development* (Chap. 15).

Jones, *Growth and Behavior in Adolescence* (Chap. 12).

Kuhlen, *Psychology of Adolescent Development* (pp. 481–488).

Wattenberg, *The Adolescent Years* (Chap. 23).

Other Books and Monographs

Alexander and Halverson, *Effective Teaching in Secondary School* (Chap. 16).

Bush, R. N., *The Teacher-Pupil Relationship* (Englewood Cliffs, N.J.: Prentice-Hall, Inc., 1954), 252 pp. (Chap. 2, 5, or 6).

Cantor, N., *The Teaching-Learning Process* (New York: Holt, Rinehart and Winston, Inc., 1953), 350 pp. (pp. 269–283).

Fleming, C. M., *Teaching: A Psychological Analysis* (London: Methuen & Company, Ltd., 1958), 291 pp. (pp. 19–44).

Hansen, *High School Teaching* (Chap. 14).

Jersild, A. T., *When Teachers Face Themselves* (New York: Bureau of Publications, Teachers College, Columbia University, 1957), 169 pp. (Chap. 2, 3, 4, 5, or 7).

Kettlecamp, *Teaching Adolescents* (Chap. 6).

Lane, H., and M. Beauchamp, *Human Relations in Teaching* (Englewood Cliffs, N.J.: Prentice-Hall, Inc., 1955), 353 pp. (Chap. 2 or 19).

Phillips, E. L., D. N. Wiener, and N. G. Haring, *Discipline, Achievement, and Mental Health* (Englewood Cliffs, N.J.: Prentice-Hall, Inc., 1963) (any 25–30 pages).

Pressey, Robinson, and Horrocks, *Psychology in Education* (Chap. 14 or 17).

A R T I C L E S

Anderson, H. H., *et al.*, "Image of the Teacher by Adolescents in Four Countries: Germany, England, Mexico, United States," *Journal of Social Psychology*, 50:47–55, 1959.

Byrd, O. E., "Teacher Health: Factors in Mental Health," *National Education Association Journal*, 49:77–78, 1960.

Cogan, M. L., "The Behavior of Teachers and the Productivity of Their Pupils," *Journal of Experimental Education*, Part I, 27:89–105 or Part II, 27:107–124, 1958.

Eaton, M., *et al.*, "Some Reactions of Classroom Teachers to Problem Behavior in School," *Educational Administration and Supervision*, 43:129–131, 1957.

Jackson, P. W., and P. W. Getzelo, "Psychological Health and Classroom Functioning—A Study in Dissatisfaction with School among Adolescents," *Journal of Educational Psychology,* 50:295–300, 1959.

Novak, J. D., "An Experimental Comparison of a Conventional and a Project-centered Method of Teaching a College General Botany Course," *Journal of Experimental Education,* 26:217–230, 1958.

Ryans, D. G., "Some Correlates of Teacher Behavior," *Educational and Psychological Measurement,* 19:3–12, 1959.

Solomon, J. C., "Neuroses of School Teachers: A Colloquy," *Mental Hygiene,* 44:79–90, 1960.

Symonds, P. M., "Characteristics of the Effective Teacher, Based on Pupil Evaluation," *Journal of Experimental Education,* 23:289–310, 1955.

Thompson, O. E., and F. K. T. Tom, "Comparison of the Effectiveness of a Pupil-Centered versus a Teacher-Centered Pattern for Teaching Vocational Agriculture," *Journal of Educational Research,* 50:667–678, 1956.

Weber, C. A., "Some Characteristics of College Teachers," *Journal of Educational Research,* 46:685–692, 1953.

Suggested Research Problems [9]

1. A collection of at least 100 careful, accurate descriptions of high school teachers, based upon prolonged observation of each teacher and several discussions with her about her work and problems.

2. A study of teachers' attitudes toward discipline and the nature of disciplinary problems that arise in their classes. Presumably the teachers would first be asked to arrange in order of agreement several statements about the nature of discipline. Then a record would be kept of what pupils were sent to the principal for discipline or to the student court. The purpose of the study would be to show to what extent a teacher's own ideas about classroom control contributed to her ability or inability to handle specific types of problem.

---

[9] See note on p. 11.

Chapter 27 | Personnel Work in the High School

M ANY people have stated the goals of personnel work. These statements differ more or less in detail but all of them reveal an intense concern for the development of the student as a whole person. They also agree that personnel work should help a student to express, to work through, and to deal productively with his problems. The freeing of the creative capacities of each adolescent is presumably the ultimate goal of counseling at the secondary school level.

In general, the word "guidance" refers to the more specifically vocational aspects of personnel work and the word "counseling" to the interpersonal and emotional phases. There is much overlapping of meaning, practice, and philosophy between guidance and counseling, especially since the same adolescent more often than not presents problems in both fields. One also finds in the literature a good many comparisons between "directive" and "nondirective" counseling. In directive counseling the main emphasis is upon the giving of advice. Nondirective counseling consists mainly in permitting the student to talk about whatever is puzzling him, to explain his attitudes to a sympathetic listener who will take time to hear him out, and to solve—or at least adjust—his own problems largely by his own efforts; if he talks he usually finds the solution for himself. Of the two types of counseling the nondirective is much the better, but it certainly takes more time, because it is far easier to tell a student what to do than to let him arrive at an answer by himself.[1]

Most students come willingly and voluntarily to talk with the counselors,[2] but there are a few who resist counseling, although they are aware that they have problems which they cannot solve alone. The main source of resistance—except in the occasional instance of a personal dislike for a particular counselor—is the fear of revealing oneself to others, and especially to an older

---

[1] W. E. Dugan, *Counseling Points of View* (Minneapolis, Minn.: University of Minnesota Press, 1959), 48 pp.; K. W. Dunlap, "Some Observation on Acute Difficulties at the College Level," *Mental Hygiene,* 43:237–243, 1959; D. C. Stratton, "Interpretation of the Findings of the National Study of Adolescent Girls," *Journal of the National Association of Women Deans and Counselors,* 21:18–20, 1957; and C. A. Gilgash, "Identification of Possible Adjustment Areas Confronting Adolescents upon Entering Junior High School," *Journal of Psychological Studies,* 11:108–109, 1960.

[2] M. Holman, "Adolescent Attitudes towards Seeking Help with Personal Problems," *Smith College Studies in Social Work,* No. 3, 25:1–31, 1955.

person, who may have a different point of view and a different standard of conduct from those of the student. A few students also show the same resistance with which a psychoanalyst is all too familiar—a fear of finding out about themselves. Quite frequently a student who needs counseling but is resistive toward it arrives at the counselor's office by the indirect route of a medical referral, which he is perfectly willing to accept. In the course of the medical examination the school doctor lets the student talk about himself and encourages him to accept an appointment with the counselor. There are other students who need counseling but do not in the least perceive their own need. Teachers often refer such pupils to the counselor for some simple objective reason, such as advice on courses; they then tell the counselor privately about the student's unrecognized problem and leave the counselor to guide the student from discussion of his schedule to other matters of probably greater concern. It is quite likely that students who go to their counselors voluntarily are less in need of the service than those who have to be led into the counselor's office by indirect means.

Table 27–1: COUNSELING PROBLEMS PRESENTED BY HIGH SCHOOL STUDENTS

Main Subject of Interview	Number of Interviews with Pupils				
	Requested by Pupil	Requested by Counselor	Referred by Teachers or Classmate	Total Interviews	Percent of Total
1. Selection of course, involving choice of vocation	1412	3546	445	5403	28
2. Request for, or interpretation of, standardized tests	1580	737	434	2751	14
3. Choice of career or other vocational planning	1384	412	430	2226	12
4. Changes of course, schedule, or possibility of failures	1067	128	259	1454	8
5. Selection of or admission to program of higher education	1284	68	56	1408	7
6. Selection of courses, without discussion of vocation	546	418	54	1018	5
7. Problems of personal adjustment, social acceptance, popularity	659	137	56	852	4
8. Requests for help in finding part-time job	515	22	47	584	3

	Number of Interviews with Pupils				
Main Subject of Interview	Requested by Pupil	Requested by Counselor	Referred by Teachers or Classmate	Total Interviews	Percent of Total
9. Conflicts in inter-personal relation-ships	389	79	68	536	3
10. Requests for infor-mation concerning military service	434	18	37	489	2.5
11. Inquiries about extra-curricular activities	245	174	33	452	2
12. Requests for help in getting job after leav-ing school	331	36	62	429	2
13. Breaking of school reg-ulations, absences, and so forth	229	82	57	368	2
14. Discussion of drop-out possibilities	164	115	70	349	2
15. Transference to another school	167	6	65	238	1
16. Problems of marriage, courtship, etc.	85	4	2	91	0.5
17. Miscellaneous	415	172	61	648	4
Total Number	10,906	6154	2236	19,296	100

SOURCE: W. Garner, "Problems Discussed during the Counseling Interview," *Vocational Guidance Quarterly*, 6:69–72, 1958, p. 71. Used with the permission of the publisher.

▶ Counseling in the High School

The high school counselor has to deal with many different problems. In a recent series of studies, based primarily upon lists submitted each month by six counselors in six high schools, a master check list was evolved, which is shown in Table 27–1. It will be noted that some interviews were requested by the students themselves, some were requested by the counselor, and some were the result of referrals by teachers or classmates. The number of interviews arising from each of these three classes varied according to the nature of the problem involved. For example, if the selection of courses involved indirectly the choice of vocation the counselor initiated over twice as many interviews as the student. However, when the immediate problem was the direct choice of a vocation, the pupils initiated three times as many interviews as the counselor. It would be interesting to know at what point a student begins to realize that his selection of courses and his vocational aims have an intimate relation to each other. Most of the interviews in regard to purely personal matters were initiated far more frequently by the pupils themselves than by anybody else, although both teachers and classmates occasionally took a hand in bringing a student to the counselor. The interviews dealing directly or indirectly with vocational choices come to 40 percent of the total. Discussion of admission to college or general selection of courses occupied another 13 percent. The remaining 47 percent of the interviews were concerned with personal problems, aside from a few routine matters such as absence from class or transfer to another school.

One of the serious handicaps in all personnel work is the scarcity of counselors. A typical situation was shown by the state-wide survey of a midwest state in 1959.[3] The counselors reported that about 35 percent of their counseling time was devoted to educational planning for students, 24 percent to occupational planning, 16 percent to the discussion of personal needs, and the remaining 25 percent to various administrative or teaching duties. Because of the small number of counselors and the large number of students the assignment to each counselor for each hour that was available for appointments worked out to the impossible total of 120 students per hour! This condition generally holds true in other areas also. In self defense counselors have developed techniques to be used with groups of students. The "talking-out" procedure has a number of positive values to those adolescents who can make use of it and is a useful addition to personal interviews, partly because it gives students a chance to stimulate each other into thinking.

Because there are not enough trained counselors, teachers are sometimes asked to put in part of their time in this work. This arrangement has a good many disadvantages, especially if the pupil has been in the teacher's classes. Moreover, it is an uncomfortable arrangement for the teacher, who is asked to play two roles which are more or less opposed to each other. Some people are flexible enough to be a teacher in the morning and a counselor in the afternoon, but even they find the roles themselves to be incompatible.[4] For example, if a boy has broken a school rule and the results are so worrying to him that he wants to talk the situation over with a counselor in order to get the matter straight in his own mind, he probably will not talk freely with a teacher, because he has an idea that she might feel in duty bound to report him to the school authorities.

Since the classroom teacher is sometimes asked to assist in the counseling of students, she needs to understand what those engaged in counseling and guidance are trying to do and of what the program consists. She should have

---

[3] D. H. Davis, "Counseling and Vocational Education," *Vocational Guidance Quarterly,* 9:37–43, 1960.

[4] J. W. Loughary, "Some Considerations Regarding Full-time Counselors Versus Teacher-Counselor Assignments," *Educational Administration and Supervision,* 45:199–205, 1959, and D. S. Arbuckle, *Guidance and Counseling in the Classroom* (Boston: Allyn and Bacon, Inc., 1957), 397 pp., pp. 54–118.

a sympathetic understanding of the entire guidance movement, plus some comprehension of the specific techniques in use. The details do not concern her, unless she wishes to enter this type of work, or unless she has sufficient interest to inform herself about them.

One caution might well be given: a teacher should be careful not to give off-hand advice about either educational or vocational planning. She does not have access to all the facts about her students, nor does she have the requisite specific information about either the requirements of a given course of study or possible occupations. Advice given under such circumstances may easily contradict the conclusions that emerge from a series of interviews between counselor and student.

A teacher should, then, understand what the counselors are doing, she should encourage students to seek help when they need it, she should co-operate with the counselors when the occasion arises, but she should leave the counseling and guidance to those who are trained for the work.

▶ Vocational Guidance

An adult's chief business is to work, and many of his chief joys come from his successes in the world of practical accomplishment—whether his achievement consists in selling real estate, composing operas, laying sewers, or designing hats. Because success on the job is so important in adult life, it is a terrible blow to fail—either actually or in relation to one's expectations. In addition, an individual who has failed—now handicapped by an exhausting emotional experience—must start all over in some new line of work, which must obviously be no better than a second choice. Not all debacles can be foreseen, but much travail of spirit and loss of self-confidence may be avoided if high school pupils can be guided into types of work for which they are fitted.

The making of a vocational choice is an outstanding problem of adolescence. The ambitions of children have too little relationship to reality to be used as a basis in selecting a career, and after the days of adolescence are over there is no time left. The typical development of vocational interest is from active, exciting occupations of low prestige value—being a cowboy—to emotionalized ambitions having great prestige—being a famous trial lawyer—and finally to some occupation that represents a compromise between what a person would like to do and what he thinks he can do.

The Need for Guidance Nothing is easier to demonstrate than the need of an adolescent group for help in making sensible vocational choices. One sample study should suffice, although it could be duplicated many times over without much searching of the literature. In 1954, 800 boys and 772 girls in several high schools were asked to state their vocational choice. The nature of these choices is shown in Figure 27-1. In the same figure appear the percentages in the general population that are employed in each line of work chosen by the high school students. It is at once obvious that the selections are impractical. Over two fifths of these boys and girls wanted to enter professional fields, but less than 9 percent of adults are so employed. Unless there is a great increase in the demand, there would be no room for most of these adolescents. Society can use only a given number of doctors, lawyers, ministers, nurses, teachers, and so on. Although the needed number varies somewhat from one generation to another, it is a safe guess that too many of these particular adolescents are trying to enter fields in which there will be no room, with resulting intense competition. On the other hand, there are a number of areas in which the supply would be woefully inadequate if all these adolescents were to enter the occupations of their choice. Not enough boys show an interest in trade and manufacturing; the deficit in skilled and semiskilled labor is even greater. The girls are concentrated in two fields—professional and clerical work—with a few who plan to go into business. In all other lines there is a conspicuous lack of women workers. Although it does not appear in the chart as a separate item, far too few of these adolescents were planning to go into any kind of personal service. The world could use five times as many workers in this field as it can now find. Finally, about 15 percent of the boys and 5 percent of the girls had made no choice. Unless the distribution of intelligence in this entire group of boys and girls was most unusual, at least a third and possibly more have selected an occupation that demands a higher degree of native ability than they possess. The situation shown above is typical of all such investigations, although the lack of relation between desire and opportunity is sometimes higher and sometimes lower than shown here.

Certainly there can be little question of the urgent need for vocational planning in a rapidly changing society. For the well-trained young person the outlook is good, but for those of moderate or little special training, the prospect is bleak—and is likely to become more so. At a conference in 1962 it was pointed out that 6 percent of the labor force was already unemployed and that the numbers of young people in the unemployed group was disproportionately large.[5] The million youths without jobs in 1962 was expected to reach 2.5 million by 1965 and 3.0 million by 1970. If young people have nothing to offer except their youth and strength, they are not likely to obtain jobs in the present highly technical work required by today's and tomorrow's needs.

The extent to which automation has already affected employment is well illustrated by the following examples, taken at random from innumerable similar reports: (1) the glass plant that produces 90 percent of all the electric light bulbs used in the country does so with a staff of only 14 workers;

[5] E. E. Cohen, "The Employment Needs of Urban Youth," *Vocational Guidance Quarterly*, 10:85–94, 1962.

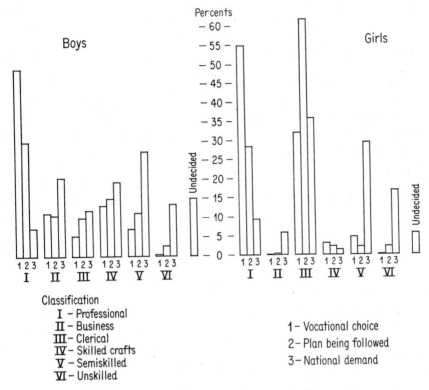

Fig. 27–1. Vocational choice versus vocational opportunities

Based on R. M. Stevenson, "Occupational Aspirations and Plans of 443 Ninth Graders," *Journal of Educational Research,* 49:27–35, 1955.

(2) in Detroit the number of "entry" jobs is being reduced by about 2000 a year. The kind of job formerly held by an adolescent just starting work at the end of high school, or perhaps without graduating, is gradually being eliminated. It is true that automation brings with it many new types of employment, but they are all of a highly technical character and present no openings for untrained adolescents. The problems of guidance are therefore likely to become more rather than less serious.

There is considerable evidence that the patterns of vocational concepts undergo significant changes between the beginning of junior high and the end of senior high school.[6] It therefore seems well to provide early guidance

---

[6] R. P. O'Hara, "Acceptance of Vocational Interest Areas by High School Students," *Vocational Guidance Quarterly,* 10:101–108, 1952. See also R. A. Dolan, "What Constitutes an Adequate Guidance and Counseling Program for the Junior High School?" *National Association of Secondary School Principals Bulletin,* 44:40–44, 1960 and "Educational and Vocational Guidance: Theory and Practice," *National Association of Women Deans and Counselors,* 24:90–94, 1961.

for adolescents and to continue it throughout the secondary school—and perhaps on into college. At the junior high school level the individual differences among the pupils is especially clear. These early adolescents vary from the 12-year-old who is already sure that he wants to be a doctor and is well organized toward his objective to the late-maturing youngster who is still absorbed in sports or social activities and can offer no more of a plan than the guess that he might like to become an electronics technician. A continuing plan for counseling, both personal and vocational, is needed if each generation of school children is to be adequately guided into normal development and useful adult activities.

The Traditional Bases for Selection of an Occupation   There are three traditional bases for the selection of a lifework: following one's father, following familial ambitions, and following interest. The first two are sometimes the same and sometimes not. It is probably rash for parents to destine a child from birth to any one type of work, because they cannot know his potentialities, but by the time he is 16 his parents may know him better than anyone else and can often therefore suggest a suitable line of work. Parents are not always wrong!

Investigators have studied the relation of boys' choices to the occupation of their fathers.[7] The work done by the 8000 fathers was first classed into ten groups. In five of the ten groups the sons tended strongly to follow in the same general type of work as that done by their fathers. Thus 71 percent of boys whose fathers were skilled workmen planned to engage in some kind of skilled work, and 63 percent of boys whose fathers were nonmanual workers were planning to enter nonmanual occupations. When the son intended to become something radically different from the father he tended to move upward in the occupational scale. Sons follow their fathers most consistently in professional, managerial, and official jobs, and in the crafts.

The use of interest as a main basis for the selection of an occupation is a matter that has received much attention. The first point to consider is the permanence of vocational interests. If they are continually changing they are obviously unsuitable as bases for guidance. The evidence is almost overwhelmingly in favor of the continuity of interests from adolescence to adulthood. For example, a survey made of an entire freshman class after nineteen years showed that 50 percent of them did not change their main interest at all and that another 30 percent were engaged in work that was closely allied to their interest nineteen years earlier.[8] In only 20 percent of the cases was

---

[7] P. G. Jenson and W. K. Kirchner, "A National Answer to the Question: 'Do Sons Follow Their Fathers' Occupations?'" *Journal of Applied Psychology*, 39:419–421, 1955.

[8] E. K. Strong, "Validity of Occupational Choice," *Educational and Psychological Measurement*, 13:110–121, 1953.

the present work unrelated. In another study the relation was very high between what senior high school boys preferred, what they intended to do, and what they actually did.[9] Choices expressed by over 1000 students in 1933 as freshmen and in 1937 by the same students as seniors were the same in 64 percent of the cases; four years later, in 1941, 62 percent still made the same choices they had made twice earlier.[10] These various results indicate an adequate stability after about the middle of high school.[11]

The second and crucial question about interests is whether or not they are trustworthy bases for guidance, even after they have become stable. That is, does a burning desire to be a doctor, for example, have a fixed relation to general intelligence, special abilities, personality, or adequate preparation? The argument of those who accept interest as a main basis for selecting an occupation runs in this wise: If a boy wants to be a doctor, he will read everything about medicine that he can get his hands on, ask questions, find out what courses to take, and be so stimulated by his interest that he will do well in his work. Also, he will have the appropriate personality for a doctor, or he would not have been attracted by the profession in the first place. The results of many investigations have not supported this theory. Indeed, quite the reverse. There is either a low relation or none at all between interest and intelligence, interest and success, or interest and special skills.[12] On the other hand, there is an appreciable relation between intelligence and success. In some instances, the coefficient of correlation between a measure of intelligence and marks in college courses has been somewhat raised by adding a measure of interest to that of intelligence, but the difference in prediction was not spectacular. There is also some relation between personality and interest, although this may be due to the fact that measures of interest are often used as subtests in measures of personality, on the assumption that a boy who wants to be a lens grinder has a different set of personal traits from the lad who wants to sell automobiles. Some degree of special ability is also often associ-

---

[9] J. R. Porter, "Predicting Vocational Plans of High School Senior Boys," *Personnel Guidance*, 33:215–218, 1954.

[10] M. I. Wightwick, "Vocational Interest Patterns," *Teachers College Record*, 46:460–461, 1945.

[11] For further studies, see P. R. Lebine, and R. Wallen, "Adolescent Vocational Interests and Later Occupations," *Journal of Applied Psychology*, 38:428–431, 1954; C. McArthur, "Long-Term Validity of the Strong Interest Test on Two Subcultures," *Journal of Applied Psychology*, 38:346–353, 1954; C. McArthur and L. B. Stevens, "The Validity of Expressed Interests as Compared with Inventoried Interests: A Fourteen-Year Follow-Up," *Journal of Applied Psychology*, 39:184–189, 1955; E. K. Strong, "Permanence of Interests over Twenty-Two Years," *Journal of Applied Psychology*, 35:87–91, 1951.

[12] R. G. Anderson, "Do Aptitudes Support Interests?" *Personnel Guidance*, 32:14–17, 1953; L. Long and J. D. Perry, "Academic Achievement in Engineering as Related to Selection Procedures and Interests," *Journal of Applied Psychology*, 37:468–471, 1953; L. G. Schmidt and J. W. M. Rothney, "Relationship of Primary Ability Scores and Occupational Choices," *Journal of Educational Research*, 47:637–640, 1954.

ated with interest. For example, a boy who is interested in music probably has some kind of special ability, which may or may not have been developed, but the amount is not necessarily sufficient for his ambitions. One of the writers knew a young man of above average musical talents who wanted to enter the field of musicology, but he lacked absolute pitch, which is considered essential for the type of work that he had planned.

No matter what outside forces are involved in the choice of an occupation, the ultimate decision rests upon the young person himself. Quite probably he can best be helped to his decision by the encouragement of the ability to evaluate with some accuracy both the socioeconomic realities of life and the realities of his own inner capacities. There have been a number of studies which have indicated that adolescents may be quite aware of the directions in which their over-all temperaments [13] tend to find satisfactory vocational goals. In the long run, few careers stand or fall on the basis of the reactions of anyone but the worker himself. Naturally, it cannot be expected that a mature self-evaluation will develop in the adolescent years. However, the counseling program should certainly encourage the gradual awareness, the acute insights, and the over-all soundness of self-concept, which will not only contribute to the making of a sound vocational choice but will help the adolescent in his total adjustment to his environment.

Some students of vocational guidance have assumed that there is a general orientation of each individual's total personality toward a particular type of activity, because of the special abilities he has either inherited or developed before reaching maturity. For example, a person may have abilities and interests that are motor, intellectual, supportive, conforming, persuasive, aesthetic, manipulative, verbal, and so on. The proponents of these theories also assume that the vocational choice of each individual should rest upon the general orientation of his inherited and acquired traits.[14] Although this theory appears reasonable in general, it does present difficulties in individual cases. For example, one adolescent may have a desire to work with people because he finds satisfaction in supportive, helping relationships, such as are involved in social service, ministry, medicine, nursing, or teaching; another adolescent may also have a desire to work with people because he finds satisfaction in the power he can exert upon them by such means as salesmanship or exploitive advertising. That is, the basic orientation is the same, but the motives are different. The extent to which occupations can be matched to the fundamental characteristics of people remains to be seen, although when they can be matched it would appear that the chances for success are greater.

---

[13] For example, S. M. Chown, "Personality Factors in the Formation of Occupational Choice," *British Journal of Educational Psychology,* 29:23–33, 1959.

[14] J. L. Holland, "A Theory of Vocational Choice," *Journal of Counseling Psychology,* 6:35–44, 1959; see also R. M. Stephenson, "Realism of Vocational Choice," *Personnel and Guidance Journal,* 35:482–488, 1957.

The Giving of Vocational Information   Probably most high school students need some kind of over-all look at the vocational scene. An adolescent knows what work is done by his father, by various family friends, by neighbors, and by the fathers of his chums; but he may know little beyond the name of even these occupations, and certainly he has no conception of the vast array of existing vocations. The appropriate time for him to acquire this information is before he has crystallized his interests.

Table 27–2 shows a grouping of occupations which, while not perfect, at least brings in two dimensions that are useful. The fundamental grouping is in terms of interests: interest in physical activity, in service, in modern technology, in creative art, and so on. The occupations are thus grouped according to their appeal. Second, the specific jobs are listed according to level of responsibility. This arrangement, aside from its dependency upon personal traits, shows a young person who has to go to work early for financial reasons what kind of work may lead him upward in the scale of responsibility in a chosen area. It also suggests that there is far more need for supportive workers, and for those dealing with application or transmission than for inventive geniuses—that is, insofar as mere number is concerned. A young lad who has dreams of being a nuclear physicist and riding a space ship to the moon, but most certainly has not the ability to complete the necessary preparation, may be more willing to compromise on being an airplane mechanic if he sees that this work may eventually get him off the ground and into the air if not to the moon. The listing of occupations by the level of responsibility should also prove useful for those who do not feel themselves capable of leadership but wish to enter a given vocational field at some less responsible level. Thus, the girl who idealizes social work may find an outlet for her urge to help humanity in becoming a practical nurse or a deaconess. Any presentation that can make a possible second choice seem related to an impossible first one ought to help a counselor in guiding youth.

In one study [15] students were asked to group some fifty occupations according to their own idea of which jobs had common characteristics. The results are presented not merely because they are of some interest in themselves, but mainly because they suggest a method of approach that might prove useful to others. Nine general clusters emerged from the students' work. They put together sundry professions as requiring ability, education, social skills, but not physical strength, and as being highly paid. As needing the same qualities but in lesser degree the students grouped businessmen and businesswomen. Under verbal skill as the main requirement they put secretaries, stenographers, bank clerks, and the like. Their fourth group, for which manual skill and strength were the main needs, included most of the crafts. The fifth and sixth

---

[15] W. F. Grunes, "On Perception of Occupations," *Personnel Guidance Journal*, 34: 276–279, 1956. See also, R. Remstad and J. W. M. Rothney, "Occupational Classification and Research Results," *Personnel and Guidance Journal*, 36:465–472, 1958.

Table 27–2: TWO-WAY
CLASSIFICATION OF OCCUPATIONS

	Group		
	I	*II*	*III*
Level	*Service*	*Business Contact*	*Organization*
1. Professional and Managerial: Independent Responsibility	Personal therapists Social work super- visors Counselors	Promoters	United States Presi- dent and Cabinet officers Industrial tycoons International bankers
2. Professional and Managerial, 2	Social workers Occupational thera- pists Probation, truant officers (with training)	Promoters Public relations counselors	Certified public ac- countants Business and govern- ment executives Union officials Brokers, average
3. Semiprofessional and Small Business	YMCA officials Detectives, police sergeants Welfare workers City inspectors	Salesmen: auto, bond, insurance, etc. Dealers, retail and wholesale Confidence men	Accountants, aver- age Employment man- agers Owners, catering, dry-cleaning, etc.
4. Skilled	Barbers Chefs Practical nurses Policemen	Auctioneers Buyers (DOT I) House canvassers Interviewers, poll	Cashiers Clerks, credit, ex- press, etc. Foremen, warehouse Salesclerks
5. Semiskilled	Taxi drivers General house- workers Waiters City firemen	Peddlers	Clerks, file, stock, etc. Notaries Runners Typists
6. Unskilled	Chambermaids Hospital attendants Elevator operators Watchmen		Messenger boys

		Group		
IV *Technology*	*V* *Outdoor*	*VI* *Science*	*VII* *General* *Cultural*	*VIII* *Arts and* *Entertainment*
Inventive geniuses Consulting or chief engineers Ships' com- manders	Consulting specialists	Research scientists University, college faculties Medical specialists Museum curators	Supreme Court Justices University, col- lege faculties Prophets Scholars	Creative artists Performers, great Teachers, univer- sity equivalent Museum curators
Applied scientists Factory man- agers Ships' officers Engineers	Applied scientists Landowners and operators, large Landscape archi- tects	Scientists, semi- independent Nurses Pharmacists Veterinarians	Editors Teachers, high school and elementary	Athletes Art critics Designers Music arrangers
Aviators Contractors Foremen (DOT I) Radio operators	County agents Farm owners Forest rangers Fish, game wardens	Technicians, medical, X-ray, museum Weather observers Chiropractors	Justices of the Peace Radio announcers Reporters Librarians	Ad writers Designers Interior dec- orators Showmen
Blacksmiths Electricians Foremen (DOT II) Mechanics, average	Laboratory testers, dairy products, etc. Miners Oil well drillers	Technical assist- ants	Law clerks	Advertising artists Decorators, window, etc. Photographers Racing car drivers
Bulldozer operators Deliverymen Smelter workers Truck drivers	Gardeners Farm tenants Teamsters, cow- punchers Miner's helpers	Veterinary hospital attendants		Illustrators, greeting cards Showcard writers Stagehands
Helpers Laborers Wrappers Yardmen	Dairy hands Farm laborers Lumberjacks	Nontechnical helpers in scientific organization		

SOURCE: Reprinted with permission from Anne Roe, *Psychology of Occupations* (New York: John Wiley & Sons, Inc., 1956), 340 pp., p. 151.

groups were similar but these the students felt were on a lower level—one included farmers, truck drivers, and so on, and the other ditch diggers and other day laborers. The seventh group was based upon social skills mainly—salesmen, for example. The eighth overlaps the sixth to some extent but involves less physical strength; it included unskilled labor, dish washing, cleaning, and so on. The last group was the "glamour" cluster of actors, models, airline stewardesses, firemen, and the like. These students did not do at all badly; they paid more attention than some of their adult advisers do to the appeal of different kinds of work.

▶ The Value of Vocational Guidance

It is difficult to estimate how valuable a guidance program has been. A mere counting of how many "guided" graduates from high school have found jobs and remained on them for a given period of time, as compared with a similar group of "unguided" graduates, is not very revealing, although it is perhaps a start in the right direction. Only one typical study will be reported, as a sample of the results obtained when one tries to estimate the value of guidance. The study was made by asking college graduates about two years after their graduation to answer a number of questions concerning the value to them of the help they had received at the university's guidance center. The results are given in Table 27–3. Only 10 percent of these students answered that they were dissatisfied in their work; the remaining 88 percent were either very well or reasonably well satisfied. In addition to giving a general rating to show the degree of satisfaction, the graduates were asked to state what specific values they had received from the guidance. The testimony on the four more frequent comments is summarized in the lower part of the table. The degree of satisfaction with the guidance is high enough, although one cannot know to what extent each counselee has incorporated the information and insight from his guidance into his own attitudes and behavior.

Perhaps the most convincing proof of the value of guidance is still the success of the individual case. The following case histories illustrate two aspects of productive vocational guidance:

Edna was a high school junior who came voluntarily to the counselor to ask for advice about possible vocations. She felt that her mother's ambitions for her were hardly appropriate, but she didn't like to go against her mother's wishes. It then developed that Edna had some artistic talent. She had taken art courses, in which she had done well enough, but her teachers rated her as having good technique and an unusually rapid rate of work but as being utterly without imagination or perception or appreciation. Her pictures, in their estimation, were nearly as accurate as colored photographs, but they "said" nothing.

Table 27–3: A STUDENT EVALUATION OF COUNSELING

	Very *Satisfied*	*Satisfied*	*Dis-* *satisfied*	*Very Dis-* *satisfied*	*No* *Answer*
Percent of Students Expressing Various Degrees of Satisfaction with Program:	47	41	7	3	2
Comments on Specific Values	*Number of Students (Total = 118)*				
1. Better understanding of interests and abilities	38	28	0	0	
2. Help in changing vocational or educational goal	20	14	0	0	
3. Assistance in changing curriculum with resulting greater satisfaction	10	7	0	0	
4. Increased understanding of self	23	21	1	0	

SOURCE: S. H. Glaser, "Counselee Attitudes Toward Counseling," *Vocational Guidance Quarterly*, 8:235–238, 1960, pp. 236, 237.

Edna herself was a modest, somewhat withdrawn adolescent, whose social contacts were few. Her intelligence was good, but in all her work she lacked initiative or inventiveness. She merely reproduced what she had heard or read, without additions or opinions. Her mother had evidently assumed that the girl's artistic ability was of the highest order, because she could draw so accurately. The mother was a widow who supported herself and her daughter by practical nursing. For her daughter she wanted "something better." Edna herself dimly realized that her work lacked something, but she was not clear as to just what, and she was wondering if she should not follow in her mother's steps and go into nursing, perhaps taking a degree and entering the profession at a higher level. Upon questioning, it appeared that she had already made contacts with a hospital through the services of an old friend of her father's, a successful surgeon, who had arranged for her to watch several operations. She had been enchanted, but she did not know how the news could be broken to her mother. It happened that the counselor knew of a surgeon who was looking far and near for an illustrator to draw diagrams and illustrations for a book he was writing. Some of the work would have to be done on the spot, with the artist peering over the surgeon's shoulder—and trying to keep out of the way of essential personnel. For this work Edna seemed ideal. She drew fast, she drew accurately, she added nothing, she changed nothing. In the course of the next five years Edna finished high school by taking evening courses, for she was much too busy making illustrations, copying slides, and peering through microscopes to attend school in the daytime. She has found precisely the job for which she is fitted, and she rejoices in every accurately colored cross section of cancer tissue, and in every detailed drawing of an incision. Her visit to the counselor has paid off a hundredfold.

When Duncan R. entered the counselor's office of an urban junior high school, he was preceded by a reputation for apathy, a medical report of a recent suicide attempt, and a belligerent father, who strode through the door so fast that the return swing almost knocked Duncan off his feet. Before the counselor could get a word in concerning Duncan, the father had cited his own credentials by stating his position as production head of a local chemical plant, by mentioning his "obviously" intelligent family of whom Duncan would not be allowed to become the black sheep, and by referring to his valuable time, now at the very brief disposal of the rather numbed counselor. During this tidal approach, Duncan sat quietly in a corner kicking the leg of the chair and resenting bitterly that his father had been called into the matter by the counselor when actually it was his own business if he wanted to die. Certainly living seemed an unrewarding activity at that point. The counselor was unable to see the fruitfulness of this particular three-way conference, especially since it was clearly becoming one-way, so he insisted firmly that he have a separate conference with the father in the near future and discuss today with Duncan the arrangements for his re-entry to school. The father insisted that the suicide attempt was "just an attention-getter," that naturally his son would be re-admitted since he was a taxpayer, and that he possibly could give the counselor a few moments next week. He swept out of the office, nodding briefly to Duncan as he passed. When the dust settled, the counselor invited the boy to move closer to the desk and relax.

Duncan could not have cared less. At 14 he was in the ninth grade, but only in body, as his interest in school had lapsed years before. Because he had been slow in reading and had made poor grades in most of his subjects, he had been recommended for a prevocational program on entering junior high, and was stumbling through even that. His tests were low-normal in almost all aspects, but there was an occasional unexpected answer showing the kind of insight which is usually associated with exceptional capability. Such answers made the counselor wonder if Duncan were as dull a boy as his record would suggest. For the first session, however, he concentrated on helping Duncan to develop enough confidence in himself and in the counselor to volunteer for weekly discussions of the problem. That Duncan did so was a tribute to the skill of the counselor, for not often did this boy make good contacts with anybody, peer or adult.

A few counseling sessions and consultation with a psychiatrist established the fact that Duncan was deeply disturbed but probably not psychotic. An attempt was then made to give Duncan tests to determine more exactly both his general intellectual level and his special abilities. At first he refused to take them, but on the strength of reassurance by the counselor that the tests would be of real aid in planning his school program, he consented. The results were not staggering in absolute IQ level but did indicate that Duncan R. had truly exceptional ability to perceive relationships, and organize material in new, creative ways. On the strength of these indications, Duncan was asked if he would like to transfer the next semester to the academic program. His first response was enthusiastic. The next day he returned in a furiously sulky mood, and refused to go on with further counseling. From the boy's comments, it appeared that he had serious conflicts in his home, to which he was making extreme responses. The counselor therefore called the psychiatric consultant to arrange for some sessions for Duncan, as the counselor felt that the personal problems of the family situation were too intense for the boy to manage without expert assistance.

It was a very long semester for everyone concerned, but by the end of it, the staff conference on Duncan yielded a consensus that he should be transferred to a more challenging program in the coming semester, if he would consent to try it. He did. There were many rough times, and the sessions with the counselor sometimes became stormy as Duncan tried to work through his poor relationship with his father by projecting his problems onto the counselor, but gradually the lad became strong enough to manage his new school work and to take the first vital move toward self-confidence—in this case a request to try the qualifying test for an advanced mathematics course. He took it, did remarkably well, and was on his way toward what eventually became an outstanding career in the theoretical aspects of biochemistry. It was not a smooth course, but once Duncan had gone away from home to college, he found security in his academic ability and in his new social contacts. Gradually he emerged as a whole person in his own right—troubled at times, given to occasional periods of despair, but with the fundamental strength to pull out of a depression and move forward in his chosen work.

▶ Summary

Personnel work in the high schools has become a permanent part of the services rendered to students. Each year more schools introduce counseling, and the many that already have it expand the activities of the counselors. Recent years have seen a decided trend toward the student-centered type of counseling, which merely guides the student's own thinking and helps him to find a solution to his problems after he has identified them. The main problems center around the selection of courses, the selection of a vocation, and the attainment of a good social adjustment, but many others appear from time to time.

The selection of a vocation is a matter of vital importance to the adolescent because of the influence it will have upon his future. Adolescents often concentrate upon a comparatively few occupations, without much respect to either the demands of the work or their own abilities to meet the requirements. They need therefore to be guided, not so much by advice as by information.

Boys and girls should, of course, take their interests into consideration as one element in the situation, but they need to see that interest is not the only factor. At entrance to high school many young adolescents still have no realistic information about the work they want to do, and they need help in developing an informed and mature evaluation of their own capacities and prospects. Many adolescents come to the counselor's office voluntarily to obtain an appraisal of themselves so that they may know what their strong and weak points are. This development is highly desirable, since the students come in a frame of mind that permits the most valuable types of guidance.[16]

References for Further Reading

BOOKS

Other Texts

Ausubel, *The Theory and Problems of Adolescent Development* (Chap. 14).
Garrison, *Growth and Development,* 2d. ed. (pp. 404–440).
Horrocks, *Behavior and Development* (pp. 631–644, or 647–654 and 662–668).
Jersild, *Psychology of Adolescence* (Chap. 15).
Jones, *Growth and Behavior in Adolescence* (Chap. 13).
Kuhlen, *Psychology of Adolescent Development* (Chap. 11).
Wattenberg, *The Adolescent Years* (Chap. 19).

Other Books or Monographs

Arbuckle, D. S., *Guidance and Counseling in the Classroom* (Boston: Allyn and Bacon, Inc., 1957), 397 pp. (Chap. 7).
Cottingham, H. F., and W. E. Hopke, *Guidance in the Junior High School* (Bloomington, Ill.: McKnight and McKnight Publishing Company, 1961), 390 pp. (pp. 241–276).
Kettlecamp, *Teaching Adolescents* (Chap. 9).
Krugman, M., "Appraisal and Treatment of Personality Problems in a Guidance Program," in *Education in a Free World* (American Council on Education, 1954) (pp. 114–121).
Polansy, N. A., *Social Work Research* (Chicago: University of Chicago Press, 1960), 307 pp. (pp. 24–47).

---

[16] Students who are interested in counseling might find it useful to look into the material presented in the journals listed below; almost every issue includes at least one article that bears upon problems of counseling and guidance in secondary school: *Vocational Guidance Quarterly, Personnel and Guidance Journal, National Association of Women Deans and Counselors Journal, Journal of Counseling Psychology.* See also M. E. Hilton and E. P. Fairchild, eds., *Guide to Guidance* (Syracuse, N.Y.: Syracuse University Press, published yearly); 1962 is Volume 24. Also the numerous monographs and bulletins published by the United States Department of Health, Education, and Welfare. A full list may be obtained from the Department. Especially recommended is D. Segel, F. E. Wellman, and A. T. Hamilton, *An Approach to Individual Analysis in Educational and Vocational Guidance,* 1959, 39 pp.

Review of Educational Research, 30:96–179, 1960 (pp. 97–104, 131–140, 148–157, or 168–175).

Rothney, J. W. M., *Guidance Practices and Results* (New York: Harper & Row, Publishers, Inc., 1958), 542 pp. (pp. 1–34).

Seidman, *The Adolescent: A Book of Readings*, rev. ed. (Nos. 38–41, 70).

Strang, *The Adolescent Views Himself* (pp. 637–736).

Super, D. E., *The Psychology of Careers* (New York: Harper & Row, Publishers, 1957), 362 pp. (Chap. 14, 15, 17, 18, or 19).

Traxler, A. E., *Techniques of Guidance* (New York: Harper & Row, Publishers, 1957), 373 pp. (Chap. 4, 5, 6, 7, or 16).

ARTICLES

Anderson, R. G., "Do Aptitudes Support Interests?" *Personnel Guidance Journal*, 32:14–17, 1953.

Congdon, R. G., and F. M. Jervis, "A Different Approach to Interest Profiles," *Journal of Counseling Psychology*, 5:50–57, 1958.

Gilgash, C. A., "Identification of Possible Adjustment Areas Confronting Adolescents upon Entering Junior High School," *Journal of Psychology*, 11:108–109, 1960.

Levine, P. R., and R. Wallen, "Adolescent Vocational Interests and Later Occupations," *Journal of Applied Psychology*, 38:428–431, 1954.

McArthur, C., and L. B. Stevens, "The Validity of Expressed Interests as Compared with Inventoried Interests: A Fourteen Year Follow-up," *Journal of Applied Psychology*, 39:184–189, 1955.

Meadow, L., "Toward a Theory of Vocational Choice," *Journal of Counseling Psychology*, 2:108–112, 1955.

Montague, J. B., and B. Pustilnik, "Prestige Rankings of Occupations," *British Journal of Sociology*, 5:154–160, 1954.

Schmidt, L. G., and J. W. M. Rothney, "Relationship of Primary Ability Scores and Occupational Choices," *Journal of Educational Research*, 47:637–640, 1954.

Singer, S. I., and B. Stefflre, "Sex Differences in Job Values and Desires," *Personnel Guidance Journal*, 32:483–484, 1954.

Stainbrook, E., "Health and Disease in the Changing Social and Cultural Environment of Man," *American Journal of Public Health*, 51:1005–1012, 1961.

Strong, E. K., "Permanence of Interests Twenty-Two Years Later," *Journal of Applied Psychology*, 35:89–91, 1951.

Strong, E. K., "Validity of Vocational Choice," *Educational and Psychological Measurements*, 13:110–121, 1953.

Thorne, F. C., "Critique of Recent Developments in Personnel-Counseling Theory," *Journal of Clinical Psychology*, 13:233–244, 1957.

Suggested Research Problems [17]

1. A study of several hundred high school graduates who did not go to college but did have adequate guidance in the secondary school, to determine the extent to which the counseling helped them (a) in their evaluation of themselves, (b) in obtaining their first job, (c) in achieving satisfaction from their employment, (d) in interpersonal relationships, and so on. What is suggested is a thorough evaluation of high school counseling involving enough cases and covering a wide enough field to make the findings definitive.

---

[17] See note on p. 11.

Chapter 28 | The High School Curriculum

SINCE the high school is a public institution, it should serve the needs of all the adolescents who attend it. It must concern itself with social adjustment, growth of personality, development of moral attitudes, vocational choice, and physical development, as well as with mastery of academic subjects. Some of these points have been discussed in other chapters, but there remain a few topics that require further consideration.

The secondary school curriculum in the United States has a fairly long history, dating from the early eighteenth century. Certain of the elements still contained in it and certain of the attitudes toward it are survivals of an earlier day. It therefore seems desirable to begin the present chapter with a brief summary of developments in the American secondary school. Various investigators have stressed the need for a general reorganization of the high school curriculum. The curricular offerings—both required and elective—of the high school will therefore be discussed in a second section. If a high school is to serve the needs of youth, it must offer an appropriate course of study and teach it by methods that stimulate growth and mastery.

▶ A Backward Glance at the High School Curriculum

It is not the intention to write a history of the curriculum in the schools of the United States. The writers do not have the competency for such a history, nor is one needed in a book on the psychology of adolescence. However, some slight historical background is needed if the prospective teacher is to see today's curriculum with understanding. The writers have therefore decided to restrict the discussion to what one or the other of them can remember as taking place in her own lifetime. The story begins, then, in about 1900. At that time, the classical program was still basic to secondary education, although both scientific and prevocational courses were beginning to make serious demands for more room in the curriculum. As a starting point, the older of the writers presents her own class schedule in grades 9 through 12. It was in no way different from that of almost all adolescents who were preparing for college, although there were modifications for students who intended to call a halt at the end of secondary school, if not before. The writer's schedule called for four years of Latin, three of mathe-

Table 28–1: DAILY SCHEDULE OF COLLEGE PREPARATORY STUDENT
(1908–1912)

Periods				Credits
1	*Mathematics*	1st year: Algebra	3d year: Trigonometry	
		2d year: Geometry	4th year: Review	15
2	*Languages*			
	Latin:	1st year: Grammar	3d year: Cicero	
		2d year: Caesar	4th year: Virgil	20
3	French:	1st year: Grammar	3d year: Literature	
		2d year: Literature	4th year: Composition	20
	German:		4th year: Grammar 5th period	5
	English			
4	Composition:	Every school day for four years		20
5	Literature:	1st year: American		
		2d year: English		10
	Science			
	MWF		3d year: General Science	
	TTh		3d year: Laboratory	
			(also 6th period)	5
	History			
6	MWF	1st year: Ancient	3d year: European	
		2d year: American	4th year: Review	9
	Bible			
	TTh	1st year: Old Testament		
		2d year: New Testament		4
	Fine Arts			
7	MWF	1st year: Line Drawing	3d year: (Water Colors)	
		2d year: (Charcoal)	4th year: (Oil Paints)	0
	TTh		4th year: History of Art	
			Practicum: 6th period	2
	Physical Education			
	TTh	1st year: Gymnasium		
		2d year: Gymnasium		0
8	*Games*			
		1st year: Tennis	3d year: Bowling	
		2d year: Hockey	4th year: Archery	0

Total Credit Hours: 110 (Review courses carried no credit)
Total Free Hours: 2
Total Elective Hours: 9 (Indicated by being in parentheses)

matics (with a year of review), five years of modern languages, four years of English composition, two of literature, two of Bible study, one of history of art, and one lone year of general science. Drawing was required during the freshman year, but was thereafter an elective. It should be noted that all 35 class hours every week were used for classes; there were no free periods for study, although there could have been three without the drawing. There were 5 to 7 preparations to make every evening.

An outstanding characteristic of this schedule is that virtually everything was required. Naturally, a student did not have to take the college preparatory course, but once this sequence was elected, there were very few choices. One might reverse the number of hours for French and German, but otherwise everything was required. Since the schedule left only 3 free hours a week— and in the first year, no free hours—only one elective was possible; and if a student took an elective, there was no study time during the day. There is heavy concentration on the classics, ancient history, and languages—including English, and especially English composition. This schedule shows also the last lingering trace of religious education and an early offering of work in the arts. The amount of science was about equal to that now given in the seventh or eighth grade.

The second schedule to be presented is that of the younger writer, who was in high school between 1930–1934. This schedule differs from the first in a number of ways. The load of strictly academic subjects is less, the electives are more numerous, and there is some free time during the day for study. The amount of work in the social sciences was much greater in the second schedule, but there was far less concentration upon languages—20 hours as compared to 45. History as such does not appear in the 1930–1934 schedule, although the classes in social science doubtless included some historical material. And everything having to do with antiquity had vanished.

The third schedule combines features of the first two. It has more required hours and fewer electives than appear in the 1930 schedule, but fewer requirements and more electives than in the 1908 schedule. There is more mathematics and much more science than in the earlier plans. The classes in the social sciences are less diversified than in 1930 but more varied than in 1908. The modern language requirements are highest in the earliest schedule, which is the only one in which the classics figure at all. Both of the last two are superior in the field of fine arts. This most recent curriculum represents a return to requirements, a substitution of science for the classics, and a continuing emphasis upon art, music, and drama, with a resulting decrease of time spent in English and foreign language.

There were, as there still are, other programs of study than that which leads to college entrance. Commercial, secretarial, and mechanical courses were established in high schools by about the beginning of the present century —and in some places, earlier. Even before the big increases in enrollment began, it was clear that a great many high school students did not have the academic interests which would fit them for college work. Since for the majority the high school marked the end of formal education, there was need for vocational training. In the school attended by the older writer there were approximately 125 girls, of whom only 12 were in the college preparatory course. This ratio was about average for the period, 1908–1912. Over half the students were following a liberal arts curriculum, while the others were pursuing special courses in music, painting, or prevocational subjects. In 1930–1934 about a third of the students were college-bound, and in 1960 about a half.

The processes of differentiation and liberalization of the high school curriculum had already begun by 1900, and many new courses were intro-

Table 28–2: DAILY SCHEDULE OF COLLEGE PREPARATORY STUDENT
(1930–1934)

Periods				Credits
1	*Mathematics*	1st year: Algebra	3d year: Free	
		2d year: Geometry	4th year: (See below)	10
	Languages			
2	Spanish:	1st year: Grammar	3d year: Literature	
	French:	2d year: Grammar	4th year: Literature	20
	English			
3	Composition:	1st year: Writing	3d year: English	
	Literature:	2d year: American	4th year: World	20
4	*Physical Education*	1st year: Dancing	3d year: Dancing	
		2d year: Dancing	4th year: Dancing	20
5	*Social Sciences*	1st year: U.S. Government	3d year: Civics	
		2d year: (Sociology)	4th year: (Economics)	20
6	*Science*	1st year: Free	3d year: General Science	
		2d year: Free	4th year: Chemistry	10
	Fine Arts			
	Drama		4th year: (1st period)	5
7	Art	1st year: (Appreciation)	3d year: (History of Art)	
		2d year: (History of Art)	4th year: (Painting)	20

Total Credit Hours: 125
Total Free Hours: 15
Total Elective Hours: 35 (Indicated by parentheses)

Table 28–3: DAILY SCHEDULE OF COLLEGE PREPARATORY STUDENT
(1960–1964) *

Periods				Credits
1	*Mathematics*	1st year: Algebra	3d year: Advanced Algebra	
		2d year: Geometry	4th year: (Trigonometry)	20
2	*Languages* French:	1st year: Conversational	3d year: Literature	
		2d year: Grammar	4th year: Free	15
3	*English* Composition:	1st year: General	3d year: (Creative Writing)	
		2d year: General	4th year: (Journalism)	20
4	Literature:	1st year: World	3d year: Free	
		2d year: World	4th year: Free	10
5	*Social Science*	1st year: Social Studies	3d year: American History	
		2d year: World History	4th year: U.S. Government	20
6	*Physical Education*	1st year: Games		
		2d year: Games		4
	Science MWF TTh MWF TTh		3d year: Chemistry Laboratory (also 7th period) 4th year: (Physics) Laboratory (also 7th period)	10
7	*Fine Arts* MWF		3d year: (Drama) 4th year: (Drama)	6
	Applied Arts TTh	1st year: (Mechanical Drawing) 2d year: (Shopwork)		4

Total Credit Hours: 109
Total Free Hours: 21
Total Elective Hours: 30
  * The last two years show what this student expects to take.

duced, often as electives. In 1906 a group of typical schools offered an average of 24 subjects and a total of 53 different courses; in 1930, the average in the same schools had risen to 48 and the total to 306.[1] The most frequent

  [1] J. P. Leonard, *Developing the Secondary School Curriculum*, rev. ed. (New York: Holt, Rinehart and Winston, Inc., 1953), p. 36.

arrangement was for all courses of study to have a small, common core—usually English, history, or science, in different years—plus a few units of required work each semester for those in each course, with the remaining hours to be chosen from an array of electives. The new classes that were introduced during the period from 1900 to 1920 were of five types: further subdivisions or extensions of traditional subject matter, new material drawn from the growing social sciences, additions of a vocational and utilitarian nature, classes in the appreciation of music and art, and expanded work in physical education. As will shortly appear, these sundry additions represent variant points of view as to what is desirable in a high school curriculum.

As a result of the onslaught of students just after and since World War I, the high school curriculum sprang new leaks that were plugged up as well as seemed possible with a variety of temporary corks, but it was soon clear that the curriculum needed a thorough re-evaluation in terms of modern objectives, a complete overhauling of courses, and the establishment of a much closer relationship between what was taught and the characteristics of both the learner and the environment in which he lived. The overhauling is still in progress, and shows no sign of stopping, since the basis of the modern curriculum is its relation to life—and life refuses to stand still.

Indeed, the events of the last two decades have posed new problems for the makers of the high school curriculum. The bomb that fell on Hiroshima is still echoing down the halls of learning; 1945, like 1914, began a new period of history. The education that was appropriate before the atomic age is already not entirely suitable for today's adolescents. In recent years, the appearance of Sputnik and its many followers underlined the need for certain curricular changes. In a less dramatic way, the beginnings of automation have also delivered a warning. Two trends have already become observable: a need for greater emphasis upon science and the necessity for a thorough mastery of the "old-fashioned" high school subjects, because education in scientific fields has to have a firm foundation. Lads who would have avoided algebra a decade ago are now taking it, for example. This trend to better mastery of subject matter has already collided with the inescapable fact that a considerable percentage of the high school population cannot achieve mastery of such subject matter. What the solution will be remains for the future. It is, however, already plain that the curriculum of today and tomorrow is going to be highly social in its aims and highly psychological in its methods. It will try to bring about an adaptation of each pupil to the increasingly demanding society in which he must live, and it will draw some of its materials from the daily life of the world. For those who do not plan to go beyond high school there is already available a large assortment of vocational courses. For those who contemplate a college course the choice is rather limited. There are only a few general electives, and a basic required curriculum has again come into favor.

The Various Theoretical Bases of the Curriculum   Any high school offers courses that are reflections of numerous attitudes on the part of past administrators as well as of circumstances. The most obvious of these are the size and the financial support of the school. A high school with no more than fifty pupils can offer only one main course of study because its teaching staff of perhaps four or five teachers will be inadequate for anything more. Such a school does not have the funds with which to install equipment for certain types of vocational training or for laboratory work. These limitations are mainly responsible for the appearance of consolidated or union high schools, each serving a district that previously would have supported a half-dozen smaller schools. The need for such consolidation is well demonstrated by one writer [2] in his demand for rather large, well-equipped, comprehensive high schools that are capable of giving the training that the youth of today requires in order to live in his world.

In addition to these practical considerations, certain well-established points of view have exerted great influence upon the growth of the curriculum. First in historical sequence comes the theory that high school courses should prepare students for college. For those who go on to college this preparatory function is still vital. The concepts and skills learned in algebra, geometry, English composition, and elementary work in languages, history, and science are the tools of scholarship: without them one can be a respectable, useful, God-fearing, honest citizen and workman, but one *cannot* be a scholar. Objections arise therefore only when the preparatory function is applied to the wrong pupils. Not more than 50 percent of high school graduates enter college, of whom considerably less than half will graduate. For half of the students the years in secondary school mark the end of formal schooling, and for them the traditional subjects are irrelevant, since they lead the learner into paths that at least two thirds of the freshmen in grade 9 have neither desire nor ability to enter.

A second theory instrumental in forming and sustaining the traditional curriculum was the concept of mental discipline—the idea of training the mind by means of proper mental exercises just as one trains the body. In the words of a modern exponent of this point of view, "An intellect properly disciplined, an intellect properly habituated is an intellect able to operate well in any field. An education that consists of the cultivation of intellectual virtues therefore is the most useful education, whether the student is destined for a life of contemplation or a life of action." [3]

For many decades, Latin and geometry were thought of as subjects that would teach the pupil to memorize quickly, to reason accurately, and to think

---

[2] J. B. Conant, *The American High School Today* (New York: McGraw-Hill Book Company, 1959), 140 pp.

[3] R. M. Hutchins, *The Higher Learning in America* (New Haven, Conn.: Yale University Press, 1936), 119 pp., p. 64.

closely, thus producing mental powers that could be directed against any new problem. If this assumption were only true, education could be greatly simplified! One would need only to determine which courses gave the greatest mental discipline and then require all pupils to take them. The content, since it would be merely for purposes of exercise, would not need to be relevant to anything. Unfortunately, no such short cut exists. Modern experimentation has shown that those who study geometry surpass others of equal intelligence who do not study the subject *only* in their ability to reason in geometry, but not in their capacity to think out problems involving data drawn from chemistry, politics, literature, aesthetics, or any other field of thought that impinges little upon geometry. The students of any given subject do learn how to reason within their subject, and they do acquire skills and ideas which can be transferred to other subjects. What they do not get is an ability to think that transcends the data by means of which it has been nourished. Courses cannot therefore be included in a curriculum merely as sources of mental discipline, because all courses give a certain amount of discipline so far as the data studied are concerned, all provide facts and skills that can be transferred to other schoolwork and to life outside school, all provide more or less training in habits of study or techniques of thought and procedure, and all give the learner a basic vocabulary by means of which he can think, but no course is better than any other, except as there may be variations in difficulty, which in turn produce variations in effort on the part of the learner. A course must, therefore, stand or fall upon the value of its content for some other end than mental discipline.

As soon as high schools began to grow rapidly and to enroll students of widely varying interests, it became evident that what many pupils needed was vocational education. There have been enthusiasts who wanted to turn practically all higher education into vocational training. The vocational motif certainly has its place in the total plan of secondary education, but it would not appear to be adequate as a sole basis for the selection of courses.

Up until the last four decades the curriculum rested mainly upon its preparatory, its disciplinary, or its vocational justification. During the recent period, several groups of individuals have made determined assaults upon the existing curriculum. One group wanted to do away with traditional, scholarly training, another wanted to do away with specialization, a third wanted to base high school courses exclusively upon the present needs of pupils, and a fourth wanted to prepare students for their daily lives as future American citizens. In actual practice, the last two groups often joined forces. There have been, then, in recent decades, three main kinds of rebels: the antitraditionists, the antispecializationists, and the education-related-to-life progressivists. The curriculum of today is a direct result of these attacks.

In the days when only 5 to 8 percent of adolescents continued their education into secondary school, the curriculum was quite rightly devoted to the producing of scholars, since that proportion is needed in each generation. Preparation for scholarship is just as specialized as preparation for carpentry, only there is more of it and therefore it takes longer. The scholar serves an eight-year apprenticeship—roughly from the ninth grade through college; then he enters a six-to-ten-year advanced training period parallel to that of a journeyman—from the beginning of graduate work to the achievement of permanent tenure as an associate professor—at which time he becomes a "master" of his trade, is authorized to vote in his guild, and may participate in the training of successive generations of journeymen. An academic education is certainly irrelevant to the needs of the youthful army now enrolled in high school, nor could society absorb such a large number of scholars even if they could be trained. Presumably every high school graduate should know something about scholarly pursuits, just as he should know something about plumbing or salesmanship or modern art. The revolt against the traditional curriculum which began about 1910, gathered momentum and in some places almost eliminated from the curriculum many of the traditional elements, except as these may be desired as electives or as necessary parts of a preparation of some pupils for college. Insofar as those who end their education in or before grade 12, this elimination is a good thing, provided that what takes its place is better.

Along with the revolt against tradition has gone an equally violent rebellion against specialization of all sorts, not only against the dividing off of subject matter into a hundred sharply differentiated compartments but also against highly concentrated vocational training, which was just as narrow as any other restricted type of education. The object of these particular rebels was to break down the artificial barriers between fields of learning, to integrate allied fields on the lower levels at least, and to present learning as a single picture instead of as a mosaic. One outcome of this movement has been the substitution of survey courses for the required work of previous decades. Thus, instead of taking five hours of modern history, three of ancient history, and three of civics, every student took one five-hour survey course in the social studies, in which he was given an integrated presentation of whatever material from these allied subjects seemed most vital for the future citizen. It should be noted that the basis of selection was general usefulness to the student who was *not* going to take further work in the social sciences rather than general usefulness in building a firm foundation for the student who was.

Members of the modern, progressive school of thought wanted to base the curriculum upon either the present or the future needs and interests of the pupils. The resulting program is supposed to provide for the acquisition of such information, skills, understandings, ideals, attitudes, and interests as are demanded by the different areas of living in which all people must make some adjustment—notably home life, vocational life, civic life, leisure life, and healthy survival, both mental and physical. Some of the investigators who wished to remake the curriculum along these lines began by studying the average day of many thousands of adults, to determine what was needed that had not already been supplied by the years below secondary school, while other investigators began to study the here-and-now needs of high school students, often by asking them to list questions to which they needed answers. The resulting lists are long and heterogeneous. Any such accumulation of questions runs the entire gamut from an inquiry by some child who wants to know if she is old enough to use lipstick to a mature question as to whether or not a good citizen is bound to obey a law he knows is unjust and, if he does obey it, how he can register his disapproval. If one follows this approach to its logical conclusion, one establishes courses in acceptable social usages, in effective methods of study, in courtship and marriage, in the concepts of morals and religion, in modern social problems, in mental hygiene, and so on, because such subject matter contains whatever answers may be given to the questions that are most commonly asked. That is, the curriculum is "adolescent-centered."

It is not difficult to find objections to any of these theories of curriculum construction. The preparation-for-college approach by itself produces a course of study quite inappropriate for most people because it stresses the technical preparation needed by a scholar, and most people will not become scholars. The mental-discipline theory has been shown to be false in its main contentions. The sociological approach, if used alone, would produce a curriculum that crystallizes things-as-they-are rather than things-as-they-should-be and would, if adhered to strictly, eliminate some of the courses that adolescents like best. A purely vocational basis is no better than any of the others, since it produces a course of study that is extremely narrow and does not prepare a pupil for the American custom of changing jobs at frequent intervals, nor for the wise use of leisure, nor for the business of being a good citizen and an intelligent voter. The basing of the curriculum exclusively upon the needs and drives of youth produces a curious and unbalanced course of study. It is, of course, not necessary that the student-centered curriculum should be superficial or trivial, but it sometimes turns out to be. Yet all of these bases contribute something to the determination of what the curriculum should contain. A high school has to prepare some pupils for college, it has to furnish as much transfer of training as possible, it has to help students to live in the world of today and tomorrow, it has to meet at least some of the students' more pressing needs and help them solve some of their more pressing problems, and it has to prepare for earning their living those who will go no further. In an effort to meet all these demands, many high schools present a curriculum without unity or coherence, and leave it to each student to find his way through the numerous offerings to whatever goal he seeks.

One can see that the underlying philosophy of secondary and higher education has changed markedly. Whether for better or for worse depends upon one's point of view, but in any event the changes are here to stay. The clock runs in only one direction.

The curriculum is never settled; it goes on and on, developing, modifying, and changing—or at least it should. In the last decade the research has continued with what is known as the "core curriculum" and with the increased use of college level courses for the most academically advanced students in high school, wherever there is a college or university near enough for the purpose. Both these movements began in previous decades. There has been renewed interest in the development of special programs for the talented, the delinquent, and the dull adolescent, probably because the new demands of American life and of the American college are so pressing that some sort of classification and special treatment has become the only realistic way of meeting the emergency. The high schools have also found it necessary once again to increase the number of course offerings, in order to meet student interest in the sciences and in such applied fields as electronics and automation. Naturally, criticisms of the high school have been numerous, as they always are in a period of rapid social and economic change. The same phenomenon appeared after World War I, when the first and largest wave of new students descended upon the high schools and soon forced those in authority to the conclusions that the old, classic education would have to be greatly modified to produce a curriculum that was tailored to the needs of the many. In the process, many of the values of the "old" education were lost, and now the colleges are again raising standards, in order to compel a mastery of the tools of learning, so that entering students will be able to do work of college caliber.[4]

It would be hard to overestimate the importance of the curriculum. It furnishes pupils with many of the basic ideas and skills that they are going to use throughout their lives. It influences and often determines their future vocational level. It keeps them in school or drives them out of it. And, unfortunately, it is sometimes a potent source of irritations and frustrations. If the curriculum loses touch with reality, the students will devote their energies to extracurricular activities or else leave school. Because of society's pressing need for trained personnel, the curriculum has assumed a new importance in the lives of adolescents—or perhaps it would be more accurate to say that subject matter has resumed its once central position in secondary education. It takes the combined efforts of philosophers, sociologists, psychologists, research experts, school administrators, teachers, and pupils to keep the curriculum up-to-date, vital, and healthy. Curricular research should always be in progress, especially during periods of rapid social change. Any curriculum that is "finished" and "settled" will almost certainly be outmoded in a few

---

[4] C. B. Mendenhall, H. Laughlin, and E. W. Hammer, "The School Program: Curricular Content and Organization," *Review of Educational Research,* 30:34–48, 1960.

years. With adequate cooperation among all those who have something to contribute, a school's academic offerings can give adolescents precisely the intellectual food they need for their maximum personal development.

▶ Summary

The curriculum of the high school is a heritage from former days, both remote and recent, and at the same time it is a preview of things to come. It represents many trends and many points of view. It is not as well adapted to the needs of adolescents as it could be. The writers are still old-fashioned enough to believe that the center of school life ought to be its classwork and that a school is no better than its curriculum. Many people would not agree with either notion. The details of curricular development are, however, not as important as the conviction that what is taught in class really matters. The methods of presentation also matter. Both content and method should be adapted to the nature of adolescent needs, adolescent abilities, and adolescent attitudes. Classwork ought to be about something that boys and girls want to learn because it is important to them, either immediately or in their plans for the future. And classes ought to be fun. When these two conditions are met, the curriculum has a chance to be a vital force in adolescent life.

Almost no one is ever satisfied with any curriculum, mainly because a course of study is likely to be outmoded about as soon as it can be adopted and implemented. It is an erroneous idea to suppose that a curriculum is ever settled or finished. It requires constant remodeling. As long as the curriculum remains in an unsettled state and as long as it is the object of criticism, it is in a fine and healthy condition!

References for Further Reading

BOOKS

Other Texts

Ausubel, *The Theory and Problems of Adolescent Development* (Chap. 15).
Garrison, *Growth and Development*, 2d. ed. (pp. 378–403).
Jersild, *Psychology of Adolescence* (Chap. 14).
Wattenberg, *The Adolescent Years* (Chap. 12).

Other Books and Monographs

Adler, M. S., and M. Mayer, *The Revolution in Education* (Chicago: University of Chicago Press), 1958, 221 pp. (pp. 151–183).
Bloom, B. S., *et al., Taxonomy of Educational Objectives* (New York: David McKay Company, Inc., 1956), 207 pp. (Chap. 2).

Conant, J. B., *The American High School Today* (New York: McGraw-Hill Book Company, 1959), 140 pp. (Section II or III).

Faunce, R. C., and N. L. Bossing, *Developing the Core Curriculum*, 2d. ed. (Englewood Cliffs, N.J.: Prentice-Hall, Inc., 1958), 386 pp. (pp. 101–127).

Hand, *Principles of Public Secondary Education* (Chap. 4 or 10).

Herrick, V. E., and R. W. Tyler, "Toward Improved Curriculum Theory," *Supplementary Educational Monographs*, No. 71 (Chicago: University of Chicago Press), 1950, 124 pp. (any chapter).

Lane and Beauchamp, *Human Relations in Teaching* (Chap. 8).

Lurry, L., and E. J. Alberty, *Development of a High School Core Curriculum* (New York: The Macmillan Company, 1957), 297 pp. (Chap. 2 or 3).

Pritzkau, P. T., *Dynamics of Curriculum Improvement* (Englewood Cliffs, N.J.: Prentice-Hall, 1959), 450 pp. (pp. 323–336).

ARTICLES

Eiserer, P. E., and S. M. Corey, "Adapting the Secondary School Program to the Needs of Youth," *The Fifty-Second Yearbook of the National Society for the Study of Education, Part I* (Chicago: University of Chicago Press, 1955) (pp. 48–58).

Mendenhall, C. B., *et al.*, "The School Program: Curricular Content and Organization," *Review of Educational Research*, 30:34–48, 1960.

Newsom, N. W., "Curriculum Building Practices on the College Level," *Peabody Journal of Education*, 35:160–171, 1957.

Schoobs, N. E., "The Curriculum as a Means of Personality Adjustment," *Psychological Bulletin*, 9:70–85, 1952.

Wright, G. S., "Ten Years of Research on the Core Program," *School Review*, 64:397–401, 1956.

Suggestions for Further Research [5]

1. The curriculum of any high school is constantly in need of change, because time does not stand still. The commonest fault with any given plan of study is its failure (1) to adapt itself to local needs and (2) to furnish those who will not go beyond high school or will drop out before finishing the 12th grade with the materials they most require. An analysis of a single curriculum, showing how it could be adapted more adequately to the community and to the less academically-minded pupils, would be helpful.

---

[5] See note on p. 11.

CONCLUSION

Chapter **29** | **The End of Adolescence**

ADOLESCENCE is an interesting period to the teacher and an exciting period to the individual who is in the midst of it, but eventually it must end and make way for the emergence of adulthood. It seems, therefore, useful to consider of what maturity consists, as reported by several people competent to judge. Although these excerpts do not say all there is to be said on the matter, they contain food for thought.

1. A person is emotionally mature to the extent that he is able to use and enjoy his emotional resources; able to get satisfaction from enjoyable things; able to love and laugh; able to experience anger when faced with thwartings that would arouse the temper of any reasonable person; able to accept and to realize the meaning of the fear that arises in him when he faces frightening things, without needing to put on a false mask of courage; able to reach out and seek what life might offer, even though to do so means to face the possibility of gain and of loss, of enjoyment and of grief.[1]

2. An adult is a person who is successful (a) in functioning as an independent unit with gratification of his desires in terms of the culture in which he lives; (b) in establishing satisfactory and acceptable biologic and social interaction with other people; and (c) in finding self-expression, self-extension, and self-objectivation in his social milieu.[2]

3. An adult is one who (a) has an integrated personality; (b) has sublimated or socialized his basic impulses and drives; (c) can accept reality, tolerate frustration, inhibit his impulses, accept his own inadequacies and unavoidable pains, humiliations, and losses, and is free from excessive anxieties, worries, or fears; (d) can solve the common problems of living; (e) is happy in his work; (f) accepts responsibility for his own actions; (g) can establish and maintain satisfactory and lasting relationships with other people; and (h) is able to feel strong emotions but also able to control their expression.[3]

---

[1] A. T. Jersild, *The Psychology of Adolescence* (New York: The Macmillan Company, 1957), 438 pp., pp. 192–193.

[2] J. Ruesch, "The Infantile Personality," *Psychosomatic Medicine,* 10:134–144, 1948.

[3] P. M. Symonds, *The Dynamics of Personal Adjustment* (New York: Appleton-Century-Crofts, Inc., 1946), 666 pp. Essentially the same traits are given by R. G. Kuhlen, *Psychology of Adolescent Development* (New York: Harper & Row, Publishers, Inc., 1952), 675 pp., p. 573.

Another author has listed the goals of mental health, which may also be regarded as goals of maturity:

(1) accuracy in the perception of reality, (2) absence of hostility and anxiety in their chronic forms, (3) capacity for friendly and co-operative relationships with other people, (4) spontaneity and warmth toward others, and (5) social responsibility.[4]

A simple nontechnical definition from a nontechnical source follows:

This is maturity: to be able to stick with a job until it is finished; to be able to bear injustice without wanting to get even; to be able to carry money without spending it; and to do one's duty without being supervised.[5]

These authors are referring primarily to emotional and social maturity. An adult faces reality, estimates it objectively, and adjusts himself to it. To be sure, the standards above are set so high that most people will not reach all of them. The child that each individual once was remains within him, and from that child he never quite escapes.

Some of the criteria by which one may know that adolescence has come to an end are more definite and more easily recognizable than others. The measures of maturity to be discussed in the following section have been derived partly from analysis of adults who failed to grow out of childish or adolescent points of view, partly from experimental results in the longitudinal studies already referred to at various times, and partly from a consideration of the essential problems of adolescence—as summarized from many sources in the first chapter of this book.

► Adult Levels

Physical Maturity   For physical adolescence, the end of the period may be seen most objectively. A high school pupil is physically an adult when he has reached his final height, when his body has assumed adult proportions, when his heart and other organs are of adult size, when his bones have reached their final size and density, when his sexual functions have become established, and when all secondary sexual characteristics are in evidence. Skeletal growth and establishment of primary and secondary sexual functions are usually complete by the age of 18. Some people hold that all gains in weight after the age of 25 are abnormal and consist of unnecessary deposits of fat; others think that small increases of weight should take place until the later years of adult life.

Physical adulthood is almost certain to arrive; indeed, it can be prevented only by extreme deprivation or deficiency. It is one type of maturity

---

[4] F. Barron, *Personal Soundness in University Graduate Students* (Berkeley, Calif.: University of California Press, 1954), 31 pp.

[5] "Dear Abby" in the *San Francisco Chronicle*. May 1962. Used by permission of Abigail Van Buren.

that is not appreciably affected even by the greatest coddling or the most ardent wishes to remain a child.

Emotional Maturity This type of maturity is more difficult to estimate. As long as people become angry over superficial social situations, are dependent upon older people or members of their own sex for happiness, are inclined to take things personally, or continue to run away from reality, they are not yet adults emotionally. It is at once clear that some people never grow up and that others do not become mature until long after they have passed beyond the age of legal responsibility.

The homosexual adult, the promiscuous adult, and the person who falls in love with much older people are showing behavior appropriate to an earlier period and inappropriate to mature life. The true adult has selected what he or she believes to be a permanent mate, has left experimentation behind, and has settled down to normal sexual restrictions. Not all people—especially not all women—marry. The unmarried adult has special problems of maturity. He, or more likely she, learns to substitute other drives and interests for those that are sexual. Most unmarried people have at one time or another intended to marry and have gone through the preparatory emotional stages of increasing heterosexual interests and concentration upon one person. They were therefore adults at one time. The chief danger for them is that, having failed in their first major emotional venture, they will retrogress to the earlier levels of dependency upon older people or upon homosexual attachments for emotional satisfaction. Such a regression not only is undesirable in itself but may prevent a second marital venture. The hectic rushing about, the sowing of wild oats, the search for a thrill belong to the years of adolescence. The adult who still shows these symptoms has not completely grown up.

Adolescents tend to take everything personally, to get their feelings hurt if they are criticized, and to be quite unwilling to face unpleasant situations— especially of their own making. As long as these reactions persist, an adult is still an emotional adolescent, no matter if he is the head of a corporation or the president of a bank. The businessman who tells his secretary to get him out of an appointment he does not want to keep—although he may have made it himself—so that he can keep some other engagement that appeals to him more is showing no more mature behavior than the adolescent who, on the ground that he now likes some other girl better, wants his mother to get him out of going to a party with the girl he has already asked. Facing reality is admittedly a tough job, but it has to be done if one is to grow up.

The child knows he has limitations, but generally he does not care a great deal, and the adolescent likes to hide his shortcomings even from himself. The adult, however, has to admit to himself at least that there are things he cannot do and that he is not the genius he may once have believed himself to be. If he evaluates himself objectively and plans his life to suit his capacities, he has entered emotional adulthood. Thus, for instance, the drug-store proprietor in a small town who says, "I'd be a failure in a big city, but I'm doing fine here; I've a nice home and family, and I'm happy," has made his compromise with life and is now a true adult.

The small child inhibits his emotions hardly at all; whatever he feels is translated into action. If he does not like a new acquaintance, he pushes him away. An adolescent has somewhat more self-control and can inhibit his ex-pression well enough to observe common courtesies toward those whom he does not like, although he soon regresses to childish levels if he is forced to work with or to be frequently with a disliked person. It takes an adult with well-developed powers of inhibition to work day after day in moderately close contact with someone he dislikes and neither wear out under the strain nor precipitate scenes.

The typical causes of emotional behavior among adolescents and the reactions commonly made to these stimuli have already been discussed in an earlier chapter. As long as these stimuli produce these results, an individual is emotionally adolescent—not emotionally mature. Naturally adults have emotions that can be just as violent as those produced at any earlier age. The exhausting ones are, however, not as easily aroused, and when aroused they are better controlled and more readily diverted into relatively harmless chan-nels. Experience with sundry forms of escape has provided means for resolv-ing minor conflicts. Even the pleasant emotions are not as easily aroused as they once were, nor are they quite as enjoyable.

In order to illustrate the points made concerning each type of maturity, a few case histories are presented from time to time. These persons were all within the limits of normality, and in many respects they were delightful in-dividuals, but each showed more or less serious and pervasive forms of im-maturity.

Mr. B. is at present a man of 62, by profession an account-ant. In his youth he went to work for an old friend of his family, a man whom he greatly admired. The older man was a rather domineering person who derived much satisfaction from "helping" others through what he conceived to be his own unique abilities. Although he "ran" his office and everyone in it, he was fair, effi-cient, and generally good natured—traits which served to prevent the development of active antagonism toward him on the part of his employees. Mr. B. became a sort of protégé and was, indeed completely willing to be one. He wanted to be told exactly what to do and exactly how to do it, and he wanted encouragement along the way. He remained with the firm for 35 years, at which point his friend and employer died and the business was closed. Mr. B. found another job, but he held it only briefly because he was unable to take responsibility, although his work was good enough if he were constantly supervised. Since then, there has been a procession of jobs, in none of which he did well. He cannot get on with people, he expects special privileges, he asks questions interminably, he will not accept criticism. Although his manner is usually docile and childish, he has an occasional period of overcompensation during which he becomes officious and assumes responsibilities that are none of his business. He is hopelessly prejudiced and dogmatic in his statements on almost any matter. He insists upon doing everything his own way, probably because he lacks the security and self-confidence to try something new. He is constantly in difficulties with both his superiors and his coworkers. None of his experiences seem to teach him anything about himself. He wants desperately to find a place where he can remain until the age of retirement. Recently he came to one of the writers to ask for advice. It was obvious at once that any fundamental change in Mr. B. was unlikely. It was too late to re-educate this childish, self-centered, opinionated, overly-dependent man; therefore, the only thing to do was to find a job that he could hold without more than the most superficial alterations in his reactions. A nearby library needed someone to stay in its maproom during the six hours a day that it was open. The maps were filed and had to be brought out to the user by someone familiar with the filing system, and, in addition, some of the maps were valuable and needed to be guarded. Mr. B. mastered the filing system in about an hour, and has since been content with his job. There are days on which no one comes near him and many on which only three or four map users appear. Mr. B. feels himself to be the boss, although of just what is not clear. He is happy, he is useful, and the library has solved one of its own chronic problems of personnel. However, he remains the kind of person who in the normal labor market is unemployable because he never grew up.

Millie is a woman, now in her seventies, with most of her life behind her. She is an odd creature in many ways, most of which are attributable to her extreme emotional childishness.

As an only child, Millie was the center of her parents' devotion. They had little money, but whatever they could save they spent on Millie, who always had more hair ribbons, prettier clothes, and more playthings than her friends. Her mother waited on her, dressed her, washed her, and guarded her. A princess could hardly have had a more devoted slave. Millie was not very happy with other children because she did not know how to adjust herself to them; in fact, it probably never occurred to her that there was any adjusting for her to do. She always wanted the leading role in every game, but since she was timid, hesitant in speech, deliberate in thought, and pathologically afraid of being hurt or of soiling her lovely clothes, she was not exactly equipped by nature for being a leader. Actually she trailed along with the other girls in the neighborhood, never popular, but overlooked rather than disliked. In school, Millie was docile and applied herself with moderate success to her lessons. Throughout her childhood she continued her dependence upon her parents and her avoidance of anything that was dirty, noisy, dangerous, or unfamiliar. She disliked all small boys on principle. With small girls she was not especially happy either, but she developed very early a habit of daydreaming about her daily experiences, assigning to herself a dominating role. As a result, the childhood that she now recalls was a golden age. Most of what she recalls either never happened at all or is so distorted as to be barely recognizable.

After she graduated from high school Millie remained at home. She read a good many books and magazines, spent hours in selecting materials for her dresses, and even more time in idle daydreaming. She changed all her clothes twice every day; she stepped out of whatever she was wearing, leaving everything on the floor while her mother prepared a bath and then redressed her in clean clothes and combed her hair. Millie never washed or ironed her own clothes or prepared a meal or washed a dish or sewed on a button. Once in a while she helped her father in his store by playing cashier for a few hours. She was willing also to take orders over the telephone, and she quite enjoyed adding up the monthly accounts and making out the bills.

When Millie was about 25, her father died, and she inherited his small grocery store. Millie left most of the waiting on customers to an elderly clerk who had worked in the store for years, and applied herself to the ordering of supplies and the handling of finances. She was quite successful at both. In the course of time she even helped somewhat in the store by waiting on such customers as she had known as a child, since she could in this way maintain a semblance of social life. Millie continued to live with her mother. She often complained because her acquaintances married and moved away, whereas she had to stay in one place and never had a chance to meet any eligible men. This latter statement was not true, for Millie had as many "chances" as any other girl in her group, but she regarded men and boys as ogres and would have nothing to do with them. She has never been to a party or a dance or to the movies with a boy or man in her entire life.

When Millie was about forty-five, her mother died, chiefly from overwork. This death left Millie not only alone but quite helpless in regard to the daily routine of eating, bathing, dressing, and so on. For instance, Millie had never combed her own hair or drawn the water for a bath or boiled the eggs for her breakfast. For some weeks her life was chaotic, as she slowly learned to meet her own personal requirements. Her mother's death was the one really bad shock of Millie's life. She reacted to it in two ways: by wailing hopelessly like a three-year-old and by becoming infuriated in the manner of small children who are too young to understand why anything they want should be denied them.

Gradually, Millie made sufficient adjustment for continued survival, chiefly through the hiring of a colored woman to whom she turned over all household matters. Millie then devoted her full time to the store, of which she has made a modest success. She was never lacking in intelligence, and after reading many books on how to manage a store, she developed enough confidence in herself to earn her own living.

Millie has now retired from active participation, although she is still a partner in the store and derives an income from it. She can hardly be said to have retired from social life also, because one cannot retire from what one has never entered. Millie sometimes sees an old acquaintance, but otherwise she talks only with her housekeeper. She could presumably talk intelligently about the management of a small store, but actually her only topics are her mother (whom she still calls "Mamma"), her childhood memories, and her resentment against the world because she has no parents, no husband, and practically no friends. Her only regular human contact, except with the housekeeper, occurs at noon when she goes to a nearby, small cafeteria for her dinner—a habit she developed in the period after her mother's death. There her performance is always the same: she cannot decide what she wants, so she takes a helping of everything she sees that appeals to her; as a result she arrives at the checker's desk with two kinds of soup, four different rolls, both tea and coffee, three salads, and four desserts. An assistant then carries her tray or trays to a table, gently but firmly removes two thirds to three fourths of the servings, collects the money for the balance, and settles Millie at her favorite table. This procedure has been going on for two decades. Millie prefers young men to young women, falls in love with each successive one (occasionally making so bold as to bring him a bag of candy), and talks endlessly about him to her housekeeper. The managers of the cafeteria rather foster these innocent attachments, since Millie's pleasure in her few "intimate" moments with her latest young man is sufficient stimulus to keep her from blocking the line, as will otherwise certainly happen.

Millie is not insane, merely extremely childish in all personal matters. She has never had an intimate friend, and it is improbable that she ever will. Whatever value she had for her community has already been contributed. From now on she will have to be looked after by hired guardians—and no matter how much attention she gets from them, it will never be enough.

Social Maturity The socially adequate adult is also difficult to describe, although the experienced clinician can recognize both social maturity and social immaturity without too much trouble. Blind loyalty to one's friends and blind prejudice against anyone who is different are adolescent characteristics; a person of adult years who shows them is still socially an adolescent. The true adult is able to get along in casual business relationships with practically any other normal adult. One naturally cannot be expected to like everyone in the world, or to approve of everyone, but the grown man who can work only under a friend's direction is on a social par with the adolescent who can do laboratory work only if paired with his chum.

Complete emancipation from home must take place, or adolescence is not yet over. No matter how old individuals are, they remain children emotionally if they must run continually to their parents for understanding or assistance. One should not suppose, however, that callous indifference to parents is a sign of maturity. Quite the opposite! Revolt and indifference are normal in adolescence because they are often necessary in order to break familial ties, but they are indicative of immaturity thereafter. The need for revolt should be over. If it nevertheless continues, or if the scars of previous antagonisms have culminated in either indifference or hatred, childhood and adolescence linger on. The true adult loves his parents and is willing to take their desires into consideration, but he makes his own decisions and lives his own life.

The adolescent is typically a person who feels insecure because he does not know what to do or how to act in various social relationships. Of course, an older person who finds himself in a quite new social situation—in a foreign country, for instance—may be as lost as an adolescent, but an adult is characteristically able to adjust himself easily and naturally to ordinary and recurrent social situations. The grown person who is still embarrassed and distressed by the customary daily contacts with people has not yet reached the end of his adolescence.

The adolescent is abnormally dependent upon his own small group of friends. He must have precisely the same clothes that they have, must enjoy the same things, must use the same catchwords, must hold the same opinions. Otherwise he will be considered "different"—a sad fate. A person is not an adult until he is free from such slavish imitation. Those of mature years who expend time, energy, and money in "keeping up with the Joneses" are showing a typically adolescent trait that has persisted after its period of usefulness.

The two individuals described in the following histories had not yet reached an adult level of social competence. The first was still a child and the second had prolonged her adolescent enthusiasms and attitudes into her mature years.

A few summers ago in one of the national parks, one of the writers met a man of about 40 and his mother. Young Mr. A called his mother, "Sweetheart," fetched and carried for her, made arrangements for her to go wherever she wished, remained in attendance at her side, consulted her on what food she wanted to order, accompanied her when she bought Christmas presents for the family, and deferred to her on all questions. Both mother and son seemed to be completely happy with this state of affairs. They talked willingly with other guests, but if there were a young woman in the group, the conversation did not last long. On one occasion when the mother was tired and had her dinner sent to her room, the son came down to dinner alone and sat with the writer and her husband. He talked well and freely on a number of subjects, but came back often to what his mother thought, how his mother felt, and so on. He did not appear to have a mind of his own, although he was basically intelligent. So far as could be seen this young man was perfectly content with his life and had no wish except to travel about—usually within a small geographical range—with his mother and to give her the kind of attention that most men of his age give to their wives. The mother was somewhat protective toward her son, but she was by no means a domineering type of woman, nor was she outwardly demanding. Her son waited on her apparently because he wanted to. Certainly he was making no slightest effort to escape from her and showed no sign of strain or discomfort. It is probable that he simply never left home because he was comfortable and protected there. In fact, it is doubtful if he ever wanted to leave.

Mrs. M. lives a crowded, hectic life that is chiefly her own fault, but it is having severe repercussions upon her husband and children, wholly aside from its exhausting effect upon her. She simply cannot restrict her activities to the number that she can manage and could integrate with her role as the home-maker. Mrs. M. is an efficient person of remarkable administrative ability. In her high school days she managed about half of the student groups within her school, played on school athletic teams, took part in dramatics, and took lessons outside of school in everything from horseback riding to oil painting. She has always done well almost anything she attempted. She married soon after graduation from high school, but even the birth and care of three children did not prevent her from carrying on a sideline of selling articles by telephone, although there was no financial reason for this activity. As soon as all the children were in school she plunged back into meetings, conferences, seminars, and lessons just where she had left off at the end of high school. The sheer weight of her special interests mounts up to more of a burden than one person can carry. She runs from one group to another, is chronically overfatigued, ignores her husband and his affairs, pays little attention to her children beyond merely feeding them, rushes off after dinner to meetings or rehearsals, and finally totters into bed exhausted at some hour after midnight. This kind of behavior one expects from adolescents, who characteristically undertake more than they can accomplish, but Mrs. M. shows no sign of limiting her activities to a reasonable number. She must still do everything. Her husband's eye is wandering from home, her children are unsupervised, and her home is falling to pieces. Ability to say "no" is an adult achievement; the effort to pursue every interest is adolescent.

Moral Maturity The end of moral adolescence is extremely difficult to define. It consists probably in the development of a relatively stable and relatively satisfying attitude toward life and the establishment of ideals by which one's own conduct is guided. A typical adult does not accept unthinkingly the existing code of morals or current social situations, but he does regard such matters as facts which exist and to which one must make some reasonable adjustment. The adult who is still in a state of flaming revolt against the world has not outgrown his moral adolescence. The desire to reform the world before tomorrow is an attitude of youth, not of maturity. Deep-set racial prejudices, bigoted religious beliefs, and uncompromising ethical standards are all typical of the adolescent period. The tendency from the days of childhood into the adult years is from conservatism and rigid belief toward liberalism and tolerance. The change is so gradual that the exact moment when the adolescent becomes an adult is impossible to determine, but a grown person who still carries the burden of uncompromising intolerance around with him has not yet reached his moral and ethical maturity.

One of the writers first knew Miss N. during their common childhood and has seen her at intervals ever since. Even as a child Miss N. was a rather timorous creature who clung to older people and wanted someone else to tell her what she ought to do in each small emergency. Just what gave Miss N. the idea that she could be successful in social service is not known, but after she had completed high school and a year in a teachers college, she entered a school for social work, eventually graduating from it. For a few years she worked for various charitable organizations, but never held a position for long. When she was nearly 30, she took on a quite routine job in the psychiatric ward of a large hospital taking brief case histories of the patients at their entrance into the hospital. Much of the information she obtained from whoever accompanied the patient at the time of entrance; she sent for any other person who might add data, and had to leave the hospital only if an informant whom she needed to question could not come to her. The histories she took went to the medical staff and eventually into the records. Miss N. usually never saw the patient. Once she had written something in every space on the blank used for recording the admission history, her work was done. She was conscientious and meticulous about filling every space on every blank. As a form of social work Miss N.'s job was deadly dull, but it suited her excellently, and she has held it for over thirty years. Her only complaint has been that from time to time the upper echelon of authority in the hospital saw fit to modify the blank, thus forcing her to omit a few questions she had been asking and add a few new ones.

In her life outside the hospital Miss N. always leaned on someone who would make decisions for her. Until she was nearly forty, her mother told her what was right or wrong. After her mother's death, Miss N. tried to attach herself to various people whom she admired, but without success. After some five years of failure in personal relations she became a devout Catholic, agreeing willingly with whatever doctrines she was told were true. Moreover, she began to live with a domineering, elderly woman, who told her what she should do and think. With her problems thus settled, Miss N. was completely content with her life. Not long ago she explained to the writer her method of attack upon a new problem. She said she asked herself two questions: Would my mother want me to do this? Would the Church want me to do this? If both answers were affirmative, or both were negative, she acted accordingly; if there were a tie score, she asked her housemate for an opinion, thus having someone else cast the deciding vote. Miss N. seems to have no concepts of right and wrong for her guidance. She leans on others for their opinions just as she leans on an unfilled case-study blank for guidance in asking questions.

Miss J. is a woman of about 50. She is an efficient worker and has held the same position for many years. By her own lights she is a moral person of blameless behavior. She belongs to what she at least regards as the "right" church, the "right" groups in the community, and the "right" charitable organizations, to which she devotes quite a bit of time and money. Her surface manners are impeccable, and her initial social contacts are uniformly good. She is supremely satisfied with herself and will accept no criticism. In fact, she promptly loses any friend she makes because, at the first adverse comment, she completely "blows up" and becomes so abusive that the friendship comes to an abrupt end. Her religious views are fixed and rigid. She condemns every point of view that does not coincide with her own. She is completely intolerant toward any group with which she has not had personal contact, and since she has spent her life in the upper social circles, her aversions include the major portion of humanity. She is anti-Semitic, anti-Negro, anti-Catholic, anti-Democratic, and anti-anyone who does not kowtow to her. She hates the police bitterly, apparently because they had the effrontery to arrest *her,* and she fights every traffic tag as if it were a personal insult. If she is called into the local tax office to explain some item that is not clear on her tax return, she arrives in a burst of fury, scolds the entire office, and becomes a general nuisance. She has been heard to say that what this country needs is a dictator who has the power "to make these fools obey him." She is especially rabid on the subject of crime and declares that all criminals should be executed at once without trial. This opinion is especially interesting because she herself has most of the basic traits of a criminal—the egocentricity, the utter disregard of others, and the resistance to restraint. As far as known she has never done anything criminal, but not because she would not like to; she is prevented by her fear of the damage that would be done to her social status if she were caught. But she has the lawbreaker's typical outlook upon life. In short, she expects and demands every right and every privilege for herself but is not willing to allow other people any rights at all—or even to admit that others are entitled to such things. From a moral point of view she has a developmental age of perhaps 5. She is most assuredly not an adult.

Intellectual Maturity Mature thinking is indicated by a number of more or less related developments. Unless an individual is a defective or a lunatic, he will achieve at least the minimum level of adult intelligence—that is, in objective figures, he will eventually have a mental age of at least 13. Mental, like physical, development takes place with age, and is prevented only by extreme deprivation. From present data one can reasonably assume that an adult mental level is reached at some time between the ages of 16 and 25. In the course of time it may be possible to tell when an individual has reached a mature level in judgment, reasoning, imagination, or other intellectual qualities, although such measurements are not as yet adequate for purposes of establishing the level of maturity. Nor have tests succeeded in tracing the growth of intellectual independence, or the ability to substitute the independent evaluation of evidence for dependence upon authority.

At the same time that a person's mental capacities are growing, his interests are changing. The man who continues to play strenuous team games and the woman who dotes on parties are both showing adolescent traits. So also is the adult for whom the sentimental love story and movie still have a fascination, or the one who hangs over the radio or television set by the hour. The true adult may have a keen spectator interest in games, but sports are not meat and drink to him—unless they are a legitimate part of his business. He occasionally listens for a few minutes to some catchy dance tune on the radio and is amused by the cowboy on the television screen, but he soon turns to something else. He goes to parties now and then, but they are no longer the high points in his life. He reads current-events magazines, a few short stories, and more or less technical material concerning his work. When he has become fully mature he discovers that the typical interests of adolescence not only fail to thrill him but actually bore him. He retains the intellectual vigor and at least some of the enthusiasm that characterized his adolescence, although he attaches these feelings and reactions to other stimuli. He should also become more creative, more perceptive, and more appreciative of other people's creative work in all fields of human activity. Not all people, however, succeed in developing mature intellectual interests and attitudes, even though their basic ability has reached an adult level.

Finally, a fully grown-up person has found work that he likes and can do satisfactorily. The selection of an occupation, the preliminary training, the search for a job, and the early adaptations to the conditions of employment are all problems of middle and late adolescence. A person is not economically adult until he is progressing normally and happily in his chosen field. The vocationally childish people are those who hate either all work or their particular work, those who change jobs constantly, those who have no interest in what they are doing, and those who are never satisfied with their working conditions, hours, or salaries. The adolescent frequently considers steady employment as an imposition—once the thrill has worn off. When he gets bored with some chore he is supposed to do, no one is surprised if he simply quits. Until boys and girls find their places in the world, one can expect unrest, boredom, and revolt. They become adults when they settle down to a job that appeals to them and exchange adolescent rebellion for adult dependability and interest in their work.

Miss T is a teacher of high school mathematics. She is a relatively popular teacher, both among the students and among her colleagues. It is admitted that she is not an especially exciting person, and students tend to speak of her pleasantness and sympathy rather than of her instruction. She is the teacher to whom pupils go when they are in trouble. On Sunday afternoons she has an "open house" where one can find a good share of the pupils in her current classes, as well as many who have been in her classes at some earlier time. Socially she is unusually well adjusted and seems thoroughly content with her life and work. Other teachers like her so well that there does not appear to be jealousy of her popularity with the pupils. Of late years, however, the boys and girls have begun to speak rather slightingly of her teaching; they call her a "nice old thing," pay attention courteously in class, but are inclined to regard the time they spend there as largely wasted. When Miss T began to teach, the high school required that each student take a year of algebra. Miss T was really in her element in explaining the mathematically obvious to dull pupils. At the present time, the requirement is no longer in force, and only pupils who like mathematics elect algebra. For these students Miss T is not a good teacher, and it is they who criticize her. An examination of her methodology reveals the reasons for their attitude. She uses the same textbook that she herself studied in her high school days, although the school has changed texts several times and she is supposed to be using a much more modern book. She knows the problems by heart. She plods through the book each semester, point by point, varying her performance from year to year not at all. Her manner in class is charming, but she gives the superior pupils she now has very little in the way of intellectual stimulation. The trouble with Miss T does not seem to be a deficiency in native ability but rather a childish dependence upon authority. She clearly does not feel secure with any text except the one she has practically memorized. When pupils ask questions that are outside the scope of her one book, she answers pleasantly enough but in effect brushes the queries aside and goes on as before. In faculty meetings Miss T speaks as though she were in favor of modern methods; and she is indeed a progressive teacher as far as her personal relations with her students are concerned, but she resists innovations that would force her into intellectual independence. She is socially an adult, but her mental life is still on the childish level of dependence upon authority.

Tim had always been a very handsome boy and had become a remarkably handsome young man. He lived a normal and happy life and was a popular member of the high school community. His school work was good enough although never brilliant. In the athletic line he went in only for swimming and diving, for which he developed considerable skill—and he certainly executed his dives with outstanding style and grace. In his junior year in high school Tim took a class in drama and succeeded in winning a tiny part in a school play. He was rather unhappy that he had not been given the leading male role, but he was comforted by his parents and friends with the idea that everyone has to begin in a small way and that would surely be so successful that he would soon move up to more important parts. However, on the stage, Tim's natural charm deserted him completely, and he was awkward and stiff. The dramatic coach gave Tim one small part after another and tried to help him become more relaxed, but Tim continued to be a fine-looking tailor's dummy. Soon he began to blame the coach for his own lack of success and arranged for private lessons, which did not help him in the least. If anything, he got worse. In the year after he left high school Tim had a job of sorts in the packing shed of a local company. The job was without a future, but he did not care because it enabled him to support himself and still left him time enough to join the Little Theatre group in his home town. Within a couple of years, however, he had worn out his welcome and had been told gently by the manager that he really had no talent and had better develop an enthusiasm for something other than acting. Tim again projected the blame, pulled up stakes, and went to New York where he got a casual job and spent most of his money on more lessons. He has been there for five years but has never had anything more than a walk-on part. For the last two years he has worked as a night watchman, so as to have part of his day free for study and practice. It has been a hard life, and at 26 he is already losing his one asset—his looks. It is probable that his hopes will continue to fade for another few years and that he will then become a hanger-on, working at ill-paid jobs in order to remain in some touch with the theater. Thus far Tim has shown no ability to accept himself as he is or to pursue any of the many lines of work in which his natural talents would soon bring him the respect and admiration that he craves.

Miss Addie, as she is generally called to distinguish her from her three maiden sisters, is a busy little person who may be seen almost any day tripping from her house to the library, where she is the curse of the library staff. Ever since she was 13 or 14 years old Miss Addie has been experimenting with religions. She was, as a child, well content with the Congregational church, to which her family belonged, but in her early adolescence, the church hired a new pastor, with whom she fell violently in love. The feeling was far from being reciprocated, and the girl decided that Congregationalism was the wrong denomination for her. She presently began to attend services at an Episcopal church nearby, but some episode there made her equally discontented. She next tried Catholicism, and for some time talked of becoming a nun. These ventures rather exhausted the local possibilities, and Miss Addie began to haunt the library, withdrawing books on all sorts of religions and religious movements. Her conversation centered around her readings, of which her comprehension was far from accurate. In the course of the following thirty years she joined everything from the Oxford Movement to Yoga, and was prevented from going to India to sit at Gandhi's feet only by lack of sufficient funds. She is now nearing 60 and is still passionately searching for a philosophy of life that she can accept. At one time she joined a "group" in the country, lived there for a few months, and was terribly upset when the "leader" was arrested for treating physical disabilities without a medical license—or medical training, either. Miss Addie lost about half her savings through this venture, but she still looks upon her days at "The Retreat" as the high point of her life, although what she seems to have enjoyed was the communal social existence rather than the religious or moral stimulation. She will soon reach the point at which she will run out of religions! This search is quite typical of adolescence, but at 60, it is an anachronism. In all probability what Miss Addie has been searching for is not religion at all, but some kind of human companionship that satisfies her; nevertheless, to herself she is an earnest seeker after a philosophy of life.

▶ **Summary**

A true adult is, then, a person of adequate physical and mental development, controlled emotional reactions, and tolerant attitudes; he has the ability to treat others objectively; he is independent of parental control, reasonably satisfied with his point of view toward life, and reasonably happy in his job; he is economically independent; he is not dominated by the opinions of those about him, nor is he in revolt against social conventions; he can get along in ordinary social situations without attracting unfavorable attention; and, above all, he has learned to accept the truth about himself and to face reality instead of either running away from it or making believe it is not there.

▶ **The Adult World**

The world is conducted primarily by and for adults. Recent emphasis upon childhood and adolescence has made many people forget that about 65 per cent of the population is over twenty and only 35 per cent under. Modern concentration upon infancy, childhood, and adolescence as interesting and important levels of development has sometimes distracted attention from the function of these stages in preparing an individual to live a normal adult life. The increasing need for such preparation may be demonstrated by consideration of the proportional age distribution of the general population, past and present.

Census figures have now been collected for approximately a century, although the early results contain data on only a few points. One can, however, trace changes in the proportional distribution of the population by ages. This distribution has been influenced by three main factors: the rate of immigration, the birth rate, and the death rate. Since middle-aged and elderly people leave their homes only in cases of catastrophe, most of the immigrants to America have been young people, often bringing with them babies and young children. During the decades since 1920 immigration has been restricted to a mere trickle. The birth rate had been falling for the last fifty years, with the exception of a five-year period during and just after each of the World Wars, but the recent "population explosion" has reversed the earlier trend. Over the same period the death rate was also falling because of better medical care, better nutrition, better living conditions, and better education. Figure 29–1 shows the proportion of the population in each in several major age groups in 1840, 1880, 1920, 1940, and 1960. In 1840 the average age of the entire

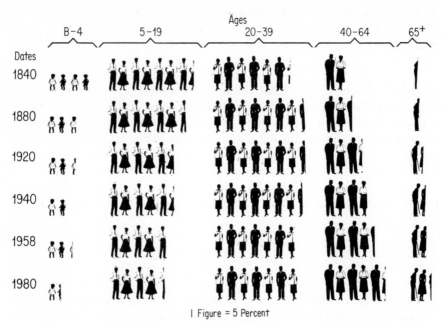

| Figure = 5 Percent

Fig. 29–1. Age distribution of population in the United States 1840–1960

Based on U.S. Census Reports.

population was 16; in 1880 it was 20; in 1940 it was 27; 1960 it was 30. In 1840 the country was decidedly a young man's country. Only twenty-eight people in a hundred were over 30 years old and not over three in a hundred were over 65. In 1960 fifty people in a hundred were over 30, and 20 were over 65. In 1840 there was less than one adult for every child or adolescent. Now there are about two for each child or adolescent. In 1960 there were nearly as many people over 65 years old than there were children under 5. With every passing decade, therefore, the need for a good adjustment to the adult world becomes more necessary. Adolescence is an interesting and, for most people, an exciting period of existence, but it has to end, even if the college graduates who return for reunions rarely believe this simple truth. As Robert Browning wrote: "Grow old along with me! The best is yet to be, the last of life for which the first was made."

References for Further Reading
BOOKS

Other Texts

Breckenridge and Vincent, *Child Development,* 4th ed. (Chap. 15).
Garrison, *Growth and Development,* 2d ed. (pp. 47–502).
Hurlock, *Adolescent Development,* 2d ed. (Chap. 15).

Other Books and Monographs

Seidman, *The Adolescent: A Book of Readings* (Chap. 22).
Symonds, P. M., *From Adolescent to Adult* (New York: Columbia University Press, 1961), 413 pp. (Chap. 11).

ARTICLES

Blos, P., "Prolonged Adolescence," *American Journal of Orthopsychiatry,* 24:733–742, 1954.
Ruesch, J., "The Infantile Personality," *Psychosomatic Medicine,* 10:134–144, 1948.

Suggested Research Problems [6]

1. Establishment by research among adults of goals for maturity. Perhaps there should be at least two levels: (a) a set of goals that can be reached by the "average" person and (b) a set that might be regarded as "ideals" but are still reached by many adults, at least in part. Most of the present goals are of this latter type and are probably too advanced and complex for the average. There may also turn out to be differences in goals for men and women.

---

[6] See note on p. 11.

Appendix A | List of Books

NOVELS

THE following references have been included because, even though most of the stories are pure fiction, they describe phases of development. The list by no means exhausts the full range of creative literature on the subject. Because they give a more detailed and more lifelike interpretation than the impersonal presentation of a text, novels are useful in connection with the study of adolescence. The instructor is urged to assign as many novels as the students can be expected to read. It is best to ask students to relate what they find in the novels to topics in the course—not to ask them to write a book review. Many students who have little interest in an abstract presentation learn the same principles when these are illustrated, vitalized, and simplified in an interesting narrative. Improperly used, fiction and biography may be misleading, but with reasonable safeguards, they form a valuable adjunct to a systematic text.

The list here presented is long and contains novels of many types. No effort has been made to classify the titles. A few of the books deal directly and almost exclusively with the adolescent period. Others trace the growth of a personality from childhood into the adult years, and still others deal with a single problem which is relevant to some portion of the textbook. From all of these varieties of presentation, a student should be able to find a reasonable number which will make vivid to him some of the more complex aspects of adolescence.

Book List of Fiction and Biography

Algren, Nelson, *The Man with the Golden Arm* (New York: Doubleday & Company, Inc., 1949).

Anderson, M., *My Lord, What a Morning* (New York: The Viking Press, Inc., 1956).

Anderson, R., *Tea and Sympathy* (New York: Random House, Inc., 1954).

Asch, S., *East River* (New York: G. P. Putnam & Sons, 1946).

Baldwin, J., *The Fire Next Time* (New York: The Dial Press, Inc., 1962).

Bellamann, H., *Kings Row* (New York: Simon and Schuster, Inc., 1940).

Bjarnhof, K., *The Stars Grow Pale* (New York: Alfred A. Knopf, Inc., 1958).

Bottome, Phyllis, *Jane* (New York: Vanguard Press, Inc., 1956).

Bowen, Elizabeth, *World of Love* (New York: Alfred A. Knopf, Inc., 1955).

Bristol, L. H., *Seed for a Song* (Boston: Little, Brown & Company, 1958).

Bromfield, Louis, *The Bromfield Galaxy* (New York: Harper & Row, Publishers, Inc., 1957, 3 vols.).

Burdick, Eugene, *The Ninth Wave* (Boston: Houghton Mifflin Company, 1956).

Canfield, D., *The Bent Twig* (New York: Grosset & Dunlap, Inc., 1934).

Capote, Truman, *The Grass Harp* (New York: Random House, Inc., 1951).

Carlson, E. R., *Born That Way* (New York: The John Day Company, Inc., 1941).

Cavann, B., *A Time for Tenderness* (New York: William Morrow & Company, Inc., 1962).

Caulfield, G., *The Kingdom Within* (New York: Harper & Row, Publishers, 1960).

Cather, Willa, *Lucy Grayheart* (New York: Alfred A. Knopf, Inc., 1935).

Coleman, P., *The Different One* (New York: Dodd, Mead & Company, Inc., 1955).

Cozzens, James, *By Love Possessed* (New York: Harcourt, Brace & World, Inc., 1957).

Cronin, A. T., *The Green Years* (Boston: Little, Brown & Company, 1944).

Davenport, M., *The Valley of Decision* (New York: Charles Scribner's Sons, 1942).

De Mille, A., *Dance to the Piper* (Boston: Little, Brown & Company, 1952).

Dostoevski, F., *The Brothers Karamazov,* translated by C. Garnett (New York: Modern Library, 1929).

Dreiser, T., *An American Tragedy* (New York: Simon and Schuster, Inc., 1929).

Farrell, J. T., *Studs Lonigan Trilogy* (New York: Vanguard Press, 1932).

Faulkner, W., *Intruder in the Dust* (New York: Random House, Inc., 1948).

Galsworthy, J., *Dark Flower* (New York: Charles Scribner's Sons, 1913).

Gibson, W., *The Cobweb* (New York: Alfred A. Knopf, Inc., 1954).

Gibson, W., *The Miracle Worker* (New York: Alfred A. Knopf, Inc., 1957).

Godden, Rumer, *The River* (Boston: Little, Brown & Company, 1946).

Goldman, Emma, *Living My Life* (New York: Alfred A. Knopf, Inc., 1934).

Goodrich, F., and A. Hackett, *The Diary of Anne Frank* (New York: Random House, Inc., 1956).

Hall, R., *The Well of Loneliness* (New York: Covici, Friede, Inc., 1932).

Harnnum, A., *Paint the Wind* (New York: The Viking Press, Inc., 1958).

Hesse, H., *Siddhartha* (New York: New Directions, 1957).

Hulme, K., *The Nun's Story* (Boston: Little, Brown & Company, Inc., 1956).

Hunter, Evan, *The Blackboard Jungle* (New York: Simon and Schuster, Inc., 1954).

Hutchinson, A., *If Winter Comes* (London: Hodder & Stoughton, Ltd., 1933).

Hutchinson, R. C., *The Stepmother* (New York: Holt, Rinehart and Winston, Inc., 1955).

Huxley, A., *The Genius and the Goddess* (New York: Harper & Row, Publishers, 1955).

James, Henry, *The Ambassadors* (New York: Harper & Row, Publishers, 1902).

Joyce, James, *A Portrait of the Artist as a Young Man* (New York: Modern Library, 1928).

Kazan, E., *America, America* (New York: Stein and Day, 1962).

Kern, J., *Yesterday's Child* (Philadelphia: J. B. Lippincott Company, 1961).

Lampedusa, C., *The Leopard* (New York: Pantheon Books, Inc., 1961).

Lawrence, D. H., *Sons and Lovers* (New York: The Viking Press, Inc., 1913).

Lehmann, R., *The Ballad and the Source* (New York: Reynal & Company, Inc., 1945).

Levin, Meyer, *Compulsion* (New York: Simon and Schuster, Inc., 1956).

Lee, H., *To Kill a Mocking Bird* (New York: J. B. Lippincott Company, 1960).

Lewis, O., *Children of Sanchez* (New York: Random House, Inc., 1962).

Lowe, F., *Somebody Else's Shoes* (New York: Holt, Rinehart and Winston, Inc., 1948).

McCarthy, Mary, *Groves of Academe* (New York: Harcourt, Brace & World, Inc., 1952).

McPartland, J., *No Down Payment* (New York: Simon and Schuster, Inc., 1957).

Mailer, Norman, *The Naked and the Dead* (New York: Holt, Rinehart and Winston, Inc., 1948).

Mann, Thomas, *Stories of Three Decades* (New York: Alfred A. Knopf, Inc., 1936).

Mansfield, K., *The Short Stories of Katherine Mansfield* (New York: Alfred A. Knopf, Inc., 1937).

Marquand, J. P., *B. F.'s Daughter* (Boston: Little, Brown & Company, 1946).

Marsh, E., *Dull the Sharp Edge* (New York: E. P. Dutton & Co., Inc., 1947).

Matthiessen, F. O., *The James Family* (New York: Alfred A. Knopf, Inc., 1947).

Maxwell, W., *The Folded Leaf* (New York: Harper & Row, Publishers, 1945).

Michener, James, *Fires of Spring* (New York: Random House, Inc., 1949), and *Sayonara* (New York: Random House, Inc., 1954).

Miller, Arthur, *Death of a Salesman* (New York: The Viking Press, Inc., 1949).

Miller, H., *A Man Ten Feet Tall* (Indianapolis: The Bobbs-Merrill Company, Inc., 1957).

Moll, E., *Seidman and Son* (New York: G. P. Putnam's Sons, 1958).

Mishima, Yukio, *Sound of Waves* (New York: Alfred A. Knopf, Inc., 1956).

Moore, George, *Confessions of a Young Man* (London: William Heinemann, Ltd., 1933).

Moore, Pamela, *Chocolates for Breakfast* (New York: Holt, Rinehart & Winston, Inc., 1956).

Moravia, A., *Two Adolescents* (New York: Farrar, Straus & Cudahy, Inc., 1950).

Motley, W., *Knock on Any Door* (New York: Appleton-Century-Crofts, Inc., 1947).

Mumford, Lewis, *Green Memories* (New York: Harcourt, Brace & World, Inc., 1947).

O'Neill, E., *Long Day's Journey Into Night* (New Haven, Conn.: Yale University Press, 1956).

Powys, J. C., *Wolf Solent* (London: Jonathan Cape, Ltd., 1933).

Proust, M., *Remembrance of Things Past* (New York: Random House, Inc., 1934).

Rolland, Romain, *Jean-Christophe* (New York: Holt, Rinehart and Winston, Inc., 1911).

Salinger, J., *The Catcher in the Rye* (Boston: Little, Brown & Company, 1951).

Santayana, G., *The Last Puritan* (New York: Charles Scribner's Sons, 1936).

Saroyan, W., *Tracy's Tiger* (New York: Doubleday & Company, Inc., 1951).

Schweitzer, Albert, *Out of My Life and Thought* (New York: Holt, Rinehart and Winston, Inc., 1949).

Shaw, Irwin, *Lucy Crown* (New York: Random House, Inc., 1956).

Shedd, M., *Run* (New York: Doubleday & Company, Inc., 1956).

Shulman, Irving, *Children of the Dark* (New York: Holt, Rinehart and Winston, Inc., 1956).

Sinclair, Jo, *The Changelings* (New York: McGraw-Hill Book Company, Inc., 1955).

Smithdas, P., *Life at My Fingertips* (New York: Doubleday & Company, Inc., 1958).

Steinbeck, J., *East of Eden* (New York: The Viking Press, Inc., 1952).

Stern, G. B., *The Reasonable Shores* (New York: The Macmillan Company, 1946).

Stone, Irving, *The Agony and the Ecstasy* (New York: Doubleday & Company, Inc., 1961).

Styron, W., *Lie Down in Darkness* (Indianapolis: The Bobbs-Merrill Company, Inc., 1951).

Szabo, T., *Boy on a Rooftop* (Boston: Little, Brown & Company, 1958).

Taylor, Kamala, *Nectar in a Sieve* (New York: The John Day Company, Inc., 1955).

Thompson, Morton, *Not as a Stranger* (New York: Charles Scribner's Sons, 1955).

Tolstoi, L., *Anna Karenina* (New York: Heritage Press, 1957).

Uris, L., *Exodus* (Philadelphia: J. B. Lippincott Company, 1958).

Undset, Sigrid, *Kristin Lavransdatter* (New York: Alfred A. Knopf, Inc., 1935).

Vidal, G., *The City and the Pillar* (New York: E. P. Dutton & Company, Inc., 1948).

Ward, M. J., *The Snake Pit* (New York: Random House, Inc., 1946).

Waugh, E., *The Loved One* (Boston: Little Brown & Company, 1948).

West, Anthony, *Heritage* (New York: Random House, Inc., 1955).

West, Jessamyn, *Cress Delahanty* (New York: Harcourt, Brace & World, Inc., 1954).

West, Rebecca, *The Judge* (New York: Hutchinson, 1933).

Wharton, Edith, *The Old Maid* (New York: Appleton-Century-Crofts, 1924).

Williams, J., *The Morning and the Evening* (New York: Atheneum, 1961).

Williams, T., *The Glass Menagerie* (New York: Random House, Inc., 1945).

Willingham, Calder, *End as a Man* (New York: Vanguard Press, 1947).

Wolfe, Thomas, *Of Time and the River* (New York: Charles Scribner's Sons, 1935).

Woolf, Virginia, *Orlando* (New York: Harcourt, Brace & World, Inc., 1928).

Appendix B | List of Films

WHEN the content of a course is chiefly concerned with the relationships of people, and the problems of individuals, one of the most satisfactory methods of making it vivid to the student is the use of motion picture films in which the problems and relationships are given extra reality by application to specific situations. Therefore, the list below has been prepared to suggest films which demonstrate many different aspects of adolescence and its related problems.

Since many new films appear each year, and since there is considerable variation in local resources, Section I lists the sources through which the instructor may get up-to-date listings and from which films may be obtained. Several hundred institutions produce films of interest in connection with adolescent psychology, and quite complete lists of them may be obtained through state and government publications. Films listed in Section II are available at the time of the publication of this text, and are suitable for use in connection with the various chapters which discuss similar problems. The list is selective, rather than comprehensive, and the teacher will find in both educational and commercial film libraries many other stimulating films for enriching the comprehension of her students.

SECTION I. *Sources of Information and Films*

Association Films (YMCA Motion Picture Bureau)
351 Turk Street, San Francisco 2

British Information Service
2516 Pacific Avenue, San Francisco

Educational Film Guide
950 University Avenue, New York 52

Educational Film Library Association
Suite 1000, 1600 Broadway, New York 19

International Film Bureau
57 E. Jackson Boulevard, Chicago 4

Local city, county, and state public health departments.

McGraw-Hill Text Films Series
330 W. 32nd Street, New York 36

Metropolitan Life Insurance Company, 1 Madison Avenue, New York 10
National Association for Mental Health, Film Board
13 E. 37th Street, New York 16

National Film Board of Canada
630 5th Avenue, New York 20
National Societies for:

  Crippled Children
  Heart Associations
  Infantile Paralysis
  Mental Hygiene,
  and many others, which may be reached through their local offices.

Psychological Cinema Register, Pennsylvania State University, University Park, Penn.

United Nations Film Division
32nd Street & 1st Avenue, New York 17

United States Department of Health, Education, and Welfare, *The 16 MM Film Library Guide,* published each year. Government Printing Office, Washington, 25, D.C.

United World Free Film Services
350 Battery Street, San Francisco

University extension services: almost all universities, and many local and private colleges, have film libraries which are excellent sources for films and for other visual material.

World Health Organization Films
See UN Film Division.

SECTION II. *Suggested Films for Use with This Text*

Full identification and addresses of most of these sources may be found in Section D.

Title	Comment	Minutes	Date	Source
Age of Turmoil	Early adolescence, with emphasis on emotional problems.	20	1957	McGraw-Hill
Angry Boy	Treatment of boy who steals because upset.	33	1951	International Film Bureau
A Respectable Neighborhood	V(enereal) D(isease) problems in a middle-class neighborhood.	25	1962	Los Angeles County Health Department

As Boys Grow	Physical development of adolescent boys.	17	1957	Medical Arts Productions
Borderline	Teen-age girl with behavior disturbance. Emergency interview.	28	1957	McGraw-Hill
Boy with a Knife	Group work with young gangs.	19	1957	International Film Bureau
Children's Emotions	Early development, and later growth of emotional patterns.	22	1951	McGraw-Hill
Challenge of the Gifted	Community participation in program for the gifted.	11	1957	McGraw-Hill
Child's Guide to a Parent's Mind	Teen-agers and parent understanding.	12	1955	National Association of Mental Health
Community Mental Health	Development of an effective program.	31	1960	International Film Bureau
Conflict	High school and college youths in various typical conflicts.	18	1956	McGraw-Hill
Depression	Development of anti-social personality.	30	1960	International Film Bureau
Development of Individual Difference	Heredity and environment, in two families.	13	1957	McGraw-Hill
Early Marriage	Adolescent marriage—Success and stresses.	24	1960	Churchill Films
Emotional Health	Emphasis on explaining upsets to young people.	21	1947	California Public Health
Face of Youth	Preventive mental health.	30	1951	Wisconsin State Board of Health
Facing Reality	Techniques for helping high school students.	12	1954	McGraw-Hill
Feeling of Depression	Jealousy between young boy and older brother.	28	1950	National Film Board of Canada
Feeling of Rejection	Problems of independent action for girl feeling rejected.	23	1947	National Film Board of Canada
Help before Headlines	Community-supported counseling in action.	11	1955	Community Welfare Council, Milwaukee
High Wall	Adolescent boy in problem of prejudice.	30	1952	McGraw-Hill
It Takes All Kinds	Teen-agers forming pattern for marriage.	20	1950	McGraw-Hill
Meaning of Adolescence	Difficulties of normal family adjustment, boy and girl.	16	1953	McGraw-Hill
Meeting the Needs of Adolescence	Girl 17, boy 14, in physical, mental, emotional growth.	19	1953	McGraw-Hill

Outsider	Young girls meeting rejection in school.	10	1951	Psychological Register
Parents Are People	Problem of authority and teen-age need for independence.	15	1955	McGraw-Hill
(The) Quiet One	Classic on minority youth.	67	1950	National Association for Mental Health
Report on Donald	Student with speech problem, and use of therapy.	20	1948	University of Minnesota
Role Playing in Guidance	Focused for teachers working with school behavior.	14	1952	Educ. Film Guide
Search	Boy shown as normal but as physically handicapped.	26	1951	Nat. Soc. Crippled Children and Adults
Snob	Social adjustments of high school girl.	13	1958	McGraw-Hill
Social-Sex Attitudes in Adolescence	Young couple facing marriage, and their developmental background.	22	1953	McGraw-Hill
Social Class in America	Development of three boys from three social levels.	16	1957	McGraw-Hill
(The) Son	Rural boy and the land as factor in his development.	28	1951	National Film Board of Canada
(The) Teens	Normal behavior, three teen-agers.	26	1957	National Film Board of Canada
Tomorrow Is a Wonderful Day	Rehabilitation of boy from concentration camp.	22	1952	National Film Board of Canada
Toward Emotional Maturity	Girl, 18, making decision, and background affecting it.	11	1955	McGraw-Hill
Your Body During Adolescence	Nature of change as puberty.	10	1955	McGraw-Hill

A rewarding project to be undertaken by the class in psychology of adolescents is to make an actual film of a few scenes, or write a script depicting the important problems of a particular aspect of adolescence. Simple cameras and good class cooperation can produce some very interesting results. Such a project will encourage independent organization of student thinking about the material the class has been studying.

Index